Game Theory Evolving

Game Theory Evolving:

A Problem-Centered Introduction to Modeling
Strategic Behavior

Herbert Gintis

Princeton University Press
Princeton, New Jersey

Published by Princeton University Press, 41 William Street, Princeton, New Jersey 08540
In the United Kingdom: Princeton University Press, 3 Market Place, Woodstock, Oxfordshire
OX20 1SY
Library of Congress Cataloging-in-Publication Data
Gintis, Herbert
  Game theory evolving: a problem-centered introduction to modeling strategic interaction/
  Herbert Gintis
    p. cm.
  Includes bibliographical references and index.
  ISBN 0-691-00942-2 (cloth: alk. paper)—ISBN 0-691-00943-0 (pbk.: alk. paper)
    1. Game theory. 2. Economics, Mathematical. I. Title.

  HB144.G562000
  330'.01'5193–dc21   99-054923

This book has been composed in Times and Mathtime by the author

The paper used in this publication meets the minimum requirements of ANSI/NISO Z39.48-1992
(R1997) (*Permanence of Paper*)

www.pup.princeton.edu

Printed in the United States of America

10 9 8 7 6 5 4 3 2 1

10 9 8 7 6 5 4 3
(pbk.)

Whilst this planet has gone cycling on according to the fixed laws of gravity ... endless forms most beautiful and most wonderful have been, and are being, evolved.

Charles Darwin

This book is dedicated to my wife Marci, my son Dan, my friend Sam, and the Creator who gave us consciousness, filled the world with love and joy, and made it understandable in terms of mathematical models.

Contents

Preface   xxi

Suggestions for Instructors   xxx

I Concepts and Problems

1 Game Theory: A Lexicon for Strategic Interaction   3

1.1	Introduction	3
1.2	Big Monkey and Little Monkey	3
1.3	The Extensive Form Game	10
1.4	The Normal Form Game	12
1.5	Nash Equilibrium	12
1.6	Reviewing the Terminology	14

2 Leading from Strength: Eliminating Dominated Strategies   15

2.1	Introduction	15
2.2	Dominant and Dominated Strategies	15
2.3	Backward Induction: Pruning the Game Tree	16
2.4	Eliminating Dominated Strategies	18
2.5	Concepts and Definitions	18
2.6	The Prisoner's Dilemma	19
2.7	An Armaments Game	20
2.8	Second-Price Auction	20
2.9	The Landlord and the Eviction Notice	21
2.10	Hagar's Battles	21
2.11	An Increasing-Bid Auction	21
2.12	The Debtor and His Creditors	22
2.13	Football Strategy	22
2.14	A Military Strategy Game	22
2.15	Strategic Voting	23

2.16   Eliminating Dominated Strategies *ad Absurdum*   23
2.17   Poker with Bluffing   24
2.18   The Centipede Game   25

3   Playing It Straight: Pure Strategy Nash Equilibria   27
3.1   Introduction   27
3.2   Pure Coordination Games   28
3.3   Competition on Main Street   28
3.4   A Pure Coordination Game   29
3.5   Twin Sisters   29
3.6   Variations on Duopoly   30
3.7   The Tobacco Market   31
3.8   Price-Matching as Tacit Collusion   31
3.9   The Klingons and the Snarks   32
3.10   Chess—The Trivial Pastime   33
3.11   The Samaritan's Dilemma   33
3.12   The Rotten Kid Theorem   34
3.13   The Illogic of Conflict Escalation   35
3.14   How to Value Lotteries   36
3.15   Payoffs in Games Where Nature Moves   37
3.16   Nature in Action: No-Draw, High-Low Poker   38
3.17   The Expected Utility Principle   41
3.18   Buying Fire Insurance   42
3.19   Neoclassical Economics and Game Theory   43
3.20   Markets as Disciplining Devices: Allied Widgets   46
3.21   The Truth Game   51
3.22   The Shopper and the Fish Merchant   52
3.23   Fathers and Sons   53
3.24   The Women of Sevitan   53

4   Catching 'em Off Guard: Mixed Strategy Nash Equilibria   54
4.1   Introduction   54
4.2   Mixed Strategies: Basic Definitions   55
4.3   The Fundamental Theorem   56
4.4   Solving for Mixed Strategy Nash Equilibria   57
4.5   Reviewing the Terminology   58
4.6   Big Monkey and Little Monkey Revisited   59
4.7   Dominance Revisited   59

4.8	Competition on Main Street Revisited	59
4.9	Battle of the Sexes	60
4.10	Throwing Fingers	60
4.11	One-Card Two-Round Poker with Bluffing	60
4.12	Trust in Networks	62
4.13	Behavioral Strategies in Extensive Form Games	63
4.14	Lions and Antelope	65
4.15	The Santa Fé Bar	66
4.16	Orange-Throat, Blue-Throat, and Yellow-Striped Lizards	67
4.17	Sex Ratios as Nash Equilibria	68
4.18	Tennis Strategy	69
4.19	A Mating Game	70
4.20	Preservation of Ecology Game	71
4.21	Hard Love	71
4.22	Coordination Failure	72
4.23	Advertising Game	72
4.24	Colonel Blotto Game	72
4.25	Number Guessing Game	73
4.26	Target Selection	73
4.27	A Reconnaissance Game	74
4.28	Attack on Hidden Object	74
4.29	Two-Person Zero-Sum Games	75
4.30	An Introduction to Forward Induction	76
4.31	Mutual Monitoring in a Partnership	77
4.32	Mutual Monitoring in Teams	78
4.33	Altruism(?) in Bird Flocks	79
4.34	Robin Hood and Little John	80
4.35	The Motorist's Dilemma	80
4.36	Family Politics	81
4.37	Frankie and Johnny	81
4.38	A Card Game	82
4.39	Cheater-Inspector	82
4.40	The Groucho Marx Game	82
4.41	Real Men Don't Eat Quiche	84
4.42	The Vindication of the Hawk	84
4.43	Correlated Equilibria	85
4.44	Poker with Bluffing Revisited	87

4.45   Equivalence of Behavioral and Mixed
      Strategies   87

5   Moving through the Game Tree: Subgames,
Incredible Threats, and Trembling Hands   90

5.1   Introduction   90
5.2   Subgame Perfection   92
5.3   Stackelberg Leadership   95
5.4   The Subway Entry Deterrence Game   96
5.5   The Dr. Strangelove Game   96
5.6   The Rubinstein Bargaining Model   97
5.7   Huey, Dewey, and Louie Split a Dollar   99
5.8   The Little Miss Muffet Game   99
5.9   Nuisance Suits   100
5.10 Cooperation in an Overlapping-Generations
      Economy   102
5.11 The Finitely Repeated Prisoner's Dilemma   103
5.12 The Finitely Repeated Prisoner's Dilemma II   109
5.13 Fuzzy Subgame Perfection   110
5.14 Perfect Behavioral Nash Equilibria   112
5.15 Selten's Horse   114
5.16 Trembling Hand Perfection   115
5.17 Nature Abhors Low Probability Events   117

6   Repeated Games, Trigger Strategies, and Tacit Collusion   118

6.1   Introduction   118
6.2   Big Fish and Little Fish   119
6.3   Tacit Collusion   121
6.4   The Folk Theorem: An Embarras de richesses   126
6.5   Variations on the Folk Theorem   127
6.6   The One-Stage Deviation Principle   129
6.7   A Trembling Hand, Cooperative Equilibrium   130
6.8   Death and Discount Rates in Repeated Games   131
6.9   The Strategy of an Oil Cartel   132
6.10 Manny and Moe   132
6.11 Tit-for-Tat   132
6.12 A Public Goods Experiment   133
6.13 Reputational Equilibrium   134

6.14	Contingent Renewal Contracts	134
6.15	Contingent Renewal Labor Markets	140
6.16	I'd Rather Switch than Fight	145

7 Biology Meets Economics: Evolutionary Stability and the Birth of Dynamic Game Theory — 148

7.1	The Birth of Evolutionary Stability	148
7.2	Properties of Evolutionarily Stable Strategies	149
7.3	Are Evolutionarily Stable Strategies Unbeatable?	152
7.4	Trust in Networks II	152
7.5	Cooperative Fishing	152
7.6	Nash Equilibrium That Is Not Evolutionarily Stable	153
7.7	Rock, Paper, and Scissors Is Not Evolutionarily Stable	153
7.8	Sex Ratios as Evolutionarily Stable Strategies	153
7.9	Invasion of the Pure Strategy Mutants	154
7.10	Multiple Evolutionarily Stable Strategies	154
7.11	The Logic of Animal Conflict	155
7.12	Hawks, Doves, and Bourgeois	157
7.13	Trogs and Farfel	158
7.14	Evolutionary Stability in Finite Populations	159
7.15	Evolutionary Stability in Asymmetric Games	161

8 Dynamical Systems and Differential Equations — 164

8.1	Introduction	164
8.2	Dynamical Systems	165
8.3	Population Growth	166
8.4	Population Growth with Limited Carrying Capacity	166
8.5	The Lotka-Volterra Predator-Prey Model	168
8.6	Dynamical Systems Theory	172
8.7	Dynamical Systems in One Dimension	175
8.8	Dynamical Systems in Two Dimensions	178
8.9	Exercises in Two-Dimensional Linear Systems	181
8.10	Cultural Dynamics	182
8.11	Lotka-Volterra with Limited Carrying Capacity	183
8.12	Take No Prisoners	183

8.13   The Hartman-Grobman Theorem   184
8.14   Special Features of Two-Dimensional Dynamical
         Systems   185
8.15   A Non-Hyperbolic Dynamical System   185
8.16   Liapunov's Theorem   186

9   Evolutionary Dynamics   188

9.1   Introduction   188
9.2   The Origins of Evolutionary Dynamics   189
9.3   Properties of the Replicator System   197
9.4   Characterizing the Two-Variable Replicator
        Dynamic   198
9.5   Do Dominated Strategies Survive under a
        Replicator Dynamic?   199
9.6   Equilibrium and Stability with a Replicator Dynamic   201
9.7   Evolutionary Stability and Evolutionary Equilibrium   202
9.8   Trust in Networks III   203
9.9   Bayesian Perfection and Stable Sets   203
9.10   Invasion of the Pure Strategy Mutants, II   204
9.11   A Generalization of Rock, Paper, and Scissors   205
9.12   *Uta stansburia* in Motion   206
9.13   The Dynamics of Rock-Paper-Scissors and
        Related Games   207
9.14   Lotka-Volterra Model and Biodiversity   208
9.15   Asymmetric Evolutionary Games   210
9.16   Asymmetric Evolutionary Games: Reviewing
        the Troops   214
9.17   The Evolution of Trust and Honesty   214
9.18   The Loraxes and Thoraxes   216
9.19   Cultural Transmission and Social Imitation   217

10   Markov Economies and Stochastic Dynamical Systems 220

10.1   Introduction   220
10.2   The Emergence of Money in a Markov Economy   221
10.3   Good Vibrations   228
10.4   Adaptive Learning   229
10.5   Adaptive Learning When Not All Conventions
        are Equal   233

10.6   Adaptive Learning with Errors   234
10.7   Stochastic Stability   235

**11 *Homo reciprocans*, *Homo egualis*, and Other Contributors
   to the Human Behavioral Repertoire   237**
   11.1   Introduction   237
   11.2   Modeling the Human Actor   239
   11.3   Behavioral Economics: Games against Nature
           and against Ourselves   244
   11.4   Experimental Game Theory: The Laboratory
           Meets Strategic Interaction   251
   11.5   *Homo egualis*   258
   11.6   *Homo reciprocans:* Modeling Strong Reciprocity   261
   11.7   Altruism and Assortative Interactions   266
   11.8   The Evolution of Strong Reciprocity   271
   11.9   *Homo parochius:* Modeling Insiders and Outsiders   278

**12 Learning Who Your Friends Are: Bayes' Rule
   and Private Information   284**
   12.1   Private Information   284
   12.2   The Role of Beliefs in Games with Private
           Information   289
   12.3   Haggling at the Bazaar   291
   12.4   Adverse Selection   294
   12.5   A Market for Lemons   295
   12.6   Choosing an Exorcist   296
   12.7   A First-Price Sealed-Bid Auction   299
   12.8   A Common Value Auction: The Winner's Curse   300
   12.9   A Common Value Auction: Quantum Spin
           Decoders   300
   12.10   Predatory Pricing: Pooling and Separating
           Equilibria   302
   12.11   Limit Pricing   304
   12.12   A Simple Limit-Pricing Model   305

**13 When It Pays to Be Truthful: Signaling in Games with
   Friends, Adversaries, and Kin   307**
   13.1   Signaling as a Coevolutionary Process   307

13.2   A Generic Signaling Game   308
13.3   Introductory Offers   310
13.4   Web Sites (for Spiders)   310
13.5   Sex and Piety: The Darwin-Fisher Model
        of Sexual Selection   312
13.6   Biological Signals as Handicaps   317
13.7   The Shepherds Who Never Cry Wolf   319
13.8   My Brother's Keeper   321
13.9   Honest Signaling among Partial Altruists   323
13.10   Educational Signaling I   325
13.11   Education as a Screening Device   328
13.12   Capital as a Signaling Device   329

**14 Bosses and Workers, Landlords and Peasants, and
Other Principal-Agent Models**   332

14.1   Introduction to the Principal-Agent Model   332
14.2   Labor Discipline with Monitoring   333
14.3   Labor as Gift Exchange   335
14.4   Labor Discipline with Profit Signaling   336
14.5   Peasants and Landlords   340
14.6   Mr. Smith's Car Insurance   341
14.7   A Generic One-Shot Principal-Agent Game   342

15 Bargaining   345

15.1   Introduction   345
15.2   The Nash Bargaining Model   346
15.3   Risk Aversion and the Nash Bargaining Solution   349
15.4   Rubinstein Bargaining with Outside Options   350
15.5   Bargaining with Two-Sided Outside Options   352
15.6   Rubinstein Bargaining and Nash Bargaining   353
15.7   Zeuthen Lotteries and the Nash Bargaining
        Solution   354
15.8   Bargaining with Fixed Costs   355
15.9   Bargaining with Incomplete Information   355

16 Probability and Decision Theory   357

16.1   Probability Spaces   357
16.2   DeMorgan's Laws   357

16.3   Interocitors   358
16.4   The Direct Evaluation of Probabilities   358
16.5   Probability as Frequency   358
16.6   Sampling   360
16.7   Self-presentation   360
16.8   Social Isolation   361
16.9   Aces Up   361
16.10   Mechanical Defection   361
16.11   Double Orders   361
16.12   Combinations and Sampling   361
16.13   Mass Defection   362
16.14   An Unlucky Streak   362
16.15   House Rules   362
16.16   The Powerball Lottery   362
16.17   The Addition Rule for Probabilities   362
16.18   Die, Die!   363
16.19   Les Cinq Tiroirs   363
16.20   A Guessing Game   363
16.21   Conditional Probability   363
16.22   Bayes' Rule   364
16.23   Drug Testing   365
16.24   A Bolt Factory   365
16.25   Color Blindness   365
16.26   Urns   365
16.27   The Monty Hall Game   365
16.28   The Logic of Murder and Abuse   367
16.29   Ah, Those Kids   369
16.30   The Greens and the Blacks   369
16.31   Laplace's Law of Succession   369
16.32   The Brain and Kidney Problem   370
16.33   Sexual Harassment on the Job   370
16.34   The Value of Eyewitness Testimony   370
16.35   The End of the World   371
16.36   Bill and Harry   371
16.37   When Weakness Is Strength   371
16.38   Markov Chains   372
16.39   Preferences and Expected Utility   381
16.40   Exceptions to the Expected Utility Principle   385

16.41   Risk Behavior and the Shape of the Utility
        Function   387

II   Answers and Hints

2   Leading from Strength: Eliminating Dominated Strategies   395

2.8   Second-Price Auction   395
2.10   Hagar's Battles   395
2.14   A Military Strategy Game   396
2.15   Strategic Voting   397

3   Playing It Straight: Pure Strategy Nash Equilibria   399

3.7   The Tobacco Market   399
3.9   The Klingons and the Snarks   400
3.10   Chess—The Trivial Pastime   401
3.11   The Samaritan's Dilemma   401
3.12   The Rotten Kid Theorem   403
3.13   The Illogic of Conflict Escalation   404
3.14   How to Value Lotteries   404
3.21   The Truth Game   405
3.22   The Shopper and the Fish Merchant   407
3.24   The Women of Sevitan   408

4   Catching 'em Off Guard: Mixed Strategy Nash Equilibria   410

4.9   Battle of the Sexes   410
4.11   One-Card Two-Round Poker with Bluffing   412
4.15   The Santa Fé Bar   413
4.17   Sex Ratios as Nash Equilibria   414
4.19   A Mating Game   416
4.20   Preservation of Ecology Game   416
4.22   Coordination Failure   417
4.23   Advertising Game   417
4.24   Colonel Blotto Game   419
4.25   Number Guessing Game   420
4.26   Target Selection   420
4.27   A Reconnaissance Game   421
4.28   Attack on Hidden Object   422

4.34   Robin Hood and Little John   422

4.35   The Motorist's Dilemma   423

4.37   Frankie and Johnny   424

4.38   A Card Game   425

4.39   Cheater-Inspector   427

4.40   The Groucho Marx Game   428

4.41   Real Men Don't Eat Quiche   431

4.45   Equivalence of Behavioral and Mixed
       Strategies   432

**5   Moving through the Game Tree: Subgames,
Incredible Threats, and Trembling Hands**   436

5.4   The Subway Entry Deterrence Game   436

5.5   The Dr. Strangelove Game   436

5.7   Huey, Dewey, and Louie Split a Dollar   437

5.10   Cooperation in an Overlapping-Generations
       Economy   438

5.12   The Finitely Repeated Prisoner's Dilemma II   439

5.15   Selten's Horse   440

5.16   Trembling Hand Perfection   441

6   Repeated Games, Trigger Strategies, and Tacit Collusion   442

6.13   Reputational Equilibrium   442

**7   Biology Meets Economics: Evolutionary Stability
and the Birth of Dynamic Game Theory**   443

7.2   Properties of Evolutionarily Stable Strategies   443

7.5   Cooperative Fishing   446

7.12   Hawks, Doves, and Bourgeois   447

7.13   Trogs and Farfel   448

7.14   Evolutionary Stability in Finite Populations   449

9   Evolutionary Dynamics   451

9.3   Properties of the Replicator System   451

9.13   The Dynamics of Rock-Paper-Scissors and
       Related Games   451

9.14   Lotka-Volterra Model and Biodiversity   454

9.18   The Loraxes and Thoraxes   455

**12 Learning Who Your Friends Are: Bayes' Rule
and Private Information**   457

    12.3   Haggling at the Bazaar   457
    12.8   A Common Value Auction: The Winner's Curse   458
    12.9   A Common Value Auction: Quantum Spin
           Decoders   458
    12.10 Predatory Pricing: Pooling and Separating
           Equilibria   460
    12.11 Limit Pricing   461
    12.12 A Simple Limit-Pricing Model   464

**13 When It Pays to Be Truthful: Signaling in Games with
Friends, Adversaries, and Kin**   466

    13.3   Introductory Offers   466
    13.4   Web Sites (for Spiders)   466
    13.7   The Shepherds Who Never Cry Wolf   468
    13.9   Honest Signaling among Partial Altruists   469
    13.11 Education as a Screening Device   470
    13.12 Capital as a Signaling Device   471

**14 Bosses and Workers, Landlords and Peasants, and
Other Principal-Agent Models**   473

    14.3   Labor as Gift Exchange   473
    14.4   Labor Discipline with Profit Signaling   474
    14.5   Peasants and Landlords   475
    14.6   Mr. Smith's Car Insurance   478
    14.7   A Generic One-Shot Principal-Agent Game   480

15 Bargaining   483

    15.2   The Nash Bargaining Model   483
    15.3   Risk Aversion and the Nash Bargaining Solution   484
    15.4   Rubinstein Bargaining with Outside Options   485
    15.6   Rubinstein Bargaining and Nash Bargaining   486
    15.7   Zeuthen Lotteries and the Nash Bargaining
           Solution   487
    15.8   Bargaining with Fixed Costs   487
    15.9   Bargaining with Incomplete Information   488

16   Probability and Decision Theory   489

     16.5   Probability as Frequency   489
     16.6   Sampling   489
     16.8   Social Isolation   489
     16.9   Aces Up   489
     16.10   Mechanical Defection   490
     16.11   Double Orders   490
     16.13   Mass Defection   490
     16.14   An Unlucky Streak   490
     16.15   House Rules   491
     16.16   The Powerball Lottery   491
     16.18   Die, Die!   492
     16.20   A Guessing Game   492
     16.23   Drug Testing   494
     16.30   The Greens and the Blacks   494
     16.31   Laplace's Law of Succession   495
     16.32   The Brain and Kidney Problem   496
     16.33   Sexual Harassment on the Job   497
     16.34   The Value of Eyewitness Testimony   497
     16.36   Bill and Harry   497
     16.37   When Weakness Is Strength   497

Sources for Problems   500

References   501

Index   521

Preface

Was sich sagen läßt, läßt sich klar sagen, und wovon man nicht sprechen kann, darüber muß man schweigen. [Translation on p. xxviii]

Ludwig Wittgenstein

The human brain is the most complex object we are aware of in the universe, and not the least of its many remarkable achievements is the partial elucidation of its own working.

Ian Glynn

This book is a *problem-centered* introduction to *evolutionary* game theory. For most topics, I provide just enough in the way of definitions, concepts, theorems, and examples to begin solving problems. Learning and insight come from grappling with and solving problems. The expositional material and many problems are appropriate for an undergraduate course, but some problems, especially those situated toward the end of a chapter, are better suited for a graduate course. I also provide extensive and complete answers to some problems, sketchy and suggestive answers to others, and no answers to some. In general, I have provided answers to the more ambitious problems in the text. The problems without answers are thus usually quite straightforward (unless marked with a star*) and should be assigned as homework, along with a selection of the more demanding problems for which answers are partially or fully supplied.

I am confident that students and instructors alike will welcome the *problem orientation* of this book. Students will doubtless appreciate the *evolutionary* orientation as well, both because that is where the future of game theory lies and because, in addition to money, it allows us to talk about sex (in the guise of fitness and mating) and violence (a.k.a. conflict). Instructors will be more wary, having learned and taught the older tradition of classical game theory. I can assure the reticent instructor that the benefits far outweigh the costs, and I have taken pains to go more slowly and completely through the evolutionary material.

Who should read this book? People study game theory for the darndest reasons. I am reminded of the story of the English professor at a midwestern university who asked a clearly quite bored and distracted young coed why she decided to go to college, and she replied "I come to get went with, but

I ain't yet."[1] Well, if you've come to get went with, we might be able to help—lots of the stories told in these pages make the sort of cocktail party conversation that attracts people seeking brainy yet creative mates.

But I think the main candidate for this book is the instructor and/or student who (a) wants to understand the stunning interplay of cooperation and conflict that accounts for the strengths (and weaknesses) of the market economy and our strengths (and weaknesses) as a species; (b) is open to the idea that to understand human sociality we have much to learn from primates, birds, termites, and even dung beetles and pond scum; (c) is willing to follow a mathematically sophisticated argument if it aids our understanding of strategic interaction; and (d) likes economics and biology.[2]

A word on mathematical prerequisites. Game theory is very demanding in terms of reasoning ability, but on a practical level, it requires surprisingly few mathematical techniques. Algebra, calculus, and basic probability theory suffice. I have found that economics students have poor grounding in differential equations, so the text develops what is needed to do evolutionary dynamics. I have also found that students need exercises in conditional probability and Bayes' Rule and have never seen Markov chains. Therefore, I have included a chapter at the end of the book covering these topics. This chapter is chock-full of gems. The instructor will probably want to introduce topics as needed, but must avoid the temptation of spending too much time on them—problems such as The Monty Hall Game (§16.27), Drug Testing (§16.23), The Value of Eye-witness Testimony (§16.34), The End of the World (§16.35) and The Logic of Murder and Abuse (§16.28).

However, game theory is what might be termed *notationally challenged*: it frequently requires a lot of huffing and puffing and a flurry of notational strutting and fretting to say intuitively simple things with adequate clarity. I have tried to minimize such notational flurries, but they cannot be avoided, since often the ideas are intuitively simple only *after* the student has seen their precise formulation. This material should *not* be treated lightly—it is not harder than the rest of the book, it just cannot be read as fast.[3]

---

[1]Translation: "I enrolled in college to meet a suitable marriage partner, an as yet unattained objective."

[2]I know some instructors will be offended by my harsh treatment of neoclassical economics, classical game theory, and other traditional topics. My defense is that this stance counters the more common bias of professors, which is to hold received wisdom in excessively high regard, doubtless recalling the pain and suffering they incurred in acquiring it and the misgivings they were obliged to swallow before believing it.

[3]A classic Woody Allen joke applies here (the words are approximate—from memory):

A few simple ideas unify this book. First, *learning game theory means learning how to solve a variety of sophisticated problems*. For most users, game theory is not a set of theorems but a box of tools. Using game theory means not so much knowing what theorems apply to a particular problem, but rather which of the tools in the toolbox may be fruitfully deployed in modeling particular behavioral phenomena. There is no way to become a skillful model builder in game theory without solving problems—not just toy problems that get you through the basics or display your mathematical prowess, but sophisticated problems that push the limits of game-theoretic reasoning and illuminate strategic situations from multiple perspectives.

Second, *game theory is a universal language for the unification of the behavioral sciences*. Games are about life and are increasingly recognized as basic to biology, anthropology, sociology, political science, psychology, economics, and the other behavioral sciences. Moreover, successful game theoretic models in one of the traditional disciplines often provide insights into the others. This idea is embodied in the choice of problems in this book. The majority of problems have economic content, but since I think there is much to be gained by a unification of biological and economic theory, a sizable number of problems deal with issues in biology and behavioral ecology.

Of course, in its original formulation, game theory applied to the restricted domain of "rational actors" with unlimited information processing capacity. A crucial turning point occurred, however, with John Maynard Smith and G. R. Price's (1973) application of game-theoretic concepts to animal behavior (§7.11), Maynard Smith's highly influential *Evolution and the Theory of Games* (1982), and Robert Axelrod and William D. Hamilton's (1981) notable collaboration in analyzing cooperative behavior (§6.11).

The marriage of economics and biology brought forth a most important offspring: evolutionary game theory, according to which the Darwinian processes of replication, mutation, and differential fitness are applied to behaviors themselves, rendering the concept of "rationality" unnecessary in analyzing strategic behavior (Boyd and Richerson 1985, Cavalli-Sforza and Feldman 1981). Of course, game theory is now widely applied not only in biology and economics, but in anthropology (Boyd and Richerson 1990, 1992), political science (G. Hardin 1968, R. Hardin 1982, Taylor

"I completed a speed reading course a while back," Woody remarks. "Wonderful training! Just last I night I read *War and Peace* in twenty minutes!" Allen stops and reflects sagely for a few moments, and then opines: "It's about Russia."

1987, Ostrom 1990), sociology (Coleman 1988, Kollock 1994), and social psychology (Dawes, Van de Kragt, and Orbell 1988) as well.

Third, *game theory is a tool for investigating the world.* By allowing us to specify rigorously the conditions of social interaction (player characteristics, rules, informational assumptions, payoffs), its predictions can be *tested*, and the results can be replicated in different laboratory settings. For this reason, *experimental game theory* has become increasingly influential in affecting research priorities (Tversky and Kahneman 1981a, Kahneman, Knetch, and Thaler 1991, Smith and Williams 1992, Davis and Holt 1993, Kagel and Roth 1995). I have thus included references to tests of the descriptive accuracy of particular models throughout the book. Ironically, game theory is often hoisted on its own pétard: many of its most fundamental predictions—predictions that would have been too vague to test with any confidence in the pre-game-theoretic era—are *decisively and repeatedly disconfirmed*, in laboratory settings, with substantial agreement among experimenters, regardless of their theoretical priors.

Chapter 11 reviews this material at some length, concluding that these predictive failures are due to game theory's adopting *Homo economicus* from neoclassical economics. *Homo economicus* is great when people are faced with anonymous marketlike conditions, but not when engaged in strategic interaction. Laboratory techniques have a lot to teach us about choice and strategic interaction, and it's up to us to develop rigorous, testable models of real human behavior. Want a Nobel Prize? You might try rooting around in this fertile research area.

Fourth, *game theory is about how people cooperate as much as how they compete.* We did not get where we are as a species because we are especially great *competitors*, but because we are especially great *cooperators*. One of the silliest (albeit tragic) debates in political philosophy is whether human nature is selfish or altruistic, whether nature is brutal or nurturing, and whether love and sympathy or hate and spite rule human behavior. In all cases the answer is: both—in complex and still to be fully revealed inter-action. Economists are fond of using the Folk Theorem of repeated games (§6.4) and the Tit-for-Tat simulations (§6.11) to argue that human coopera-tion can be understood in terms of long-run, enlightened self-interest, but we will argue in chapter 11 that this view is *profoundly incorrect.* There are two major problems with the idea that cooperation can be understood in terms of long-run self-interest (charitably interpreted to include regard for kin). The first is that self-interest results in cooperation only when agents are sufficiently future-oriented (i.e., the discount rate is very low); but in situations where a social system is threatened and likely to be destroyed, cooperation is most central to survival and agents are likely to be very present-oriented, since the probability of future interactions is low. Therefore, societies in which cooperation is based on long-run self-interest will invariably collapse when seriously threatened (§11.8). The second problem is that there is sizable evidence that we are considerably more prosocial than is predicted by the long-run self-interest models (§11.4).

Except in the context of anonymous market interactions, the idea that human beings are self-interested is particularly implausible. Indeed, some of the major predictive failures of game theory stem from not recognizing the positive and negative aspects of preference and welfare interdependence. *Homo economicus* might be reasonably described as a sociopath if he were to be set loose in society. Think about Hannibal Lecter (*Silence of the Lambs*)—he just happens to like to eat people, and their reaction to being eaten is of no more concern to him than is the lamb's fear of being eaten of concern to the lion—whence the title of the film. Note that the other sociopath in the film likes to skin women and tan their hides—all perfectly acceptable human behavior when applied to animals, but hideous when applied to humans. Clearly *Silence of the Lambs* is a vegetarian and animal rights manifesto, but from our perspective, it provides a window into the ludicrous assumptions behind *Homo economicus* when applied outside an anonymous market setting.

Fifth, *game theory is about the emergence, transformation, diffusion, and stabilization of forms of behavior*. Traditionally, game theory has been seen as a theory of how "rational agents" *do* behave, and/or how the rest of us *should* behave. Ironically, game theory, which for so long was predicated upon agent rationality, has shown us, by example, the shakiness of the concept. For one thing, the centipede game and others like it show that there is nothing substantively "rational" about even so simple a thing as eliminating dominated strategies (§2.18). Moreover, the solution to some games (even when unique) is often so sophisticated that it is implausible that ordinary people would be willing to spend the resources to discover it. This supports the evolutionary notion that good strategies diffuse across populations of players rather than being learned by "rational optimizers." Finally, experimental studies of dictator, ultimatum, and public goods games indicate that if people are "rational," it must be in a sense far more sophisticated than the simple, self-interested, maximization of expected utility.

It is better to drop the term "rational" altogether, which is what we do in this book (a word search shows that the term does appear a couple of times without surrounding quotation marks—consistency is surely not my hobgoblin!).[4] Similar remarks apply to the concept of "beliefs." In classical game theory, beliefs are characteristics of individuals that explain behavior. In evolutionary game theory beliefs are either shorthand ways of describing evolved behavior ("the bird believes the brightly colored butterfly is inedible") or are simply suppressed.[5]

In the same vein, we do not follow classical game theory in asking how agents "learn" to play optimal strategies, because the cognitive processes involved in "learning" are probably, under most conditions, much less important than the forms of imitation underlying the replicator dynamic (§9.2) and cultural transmission (§9.19). In short, evolutionary game theory replaces the idea that games have "solutions" that agents "learn," with the idea that games are embedded in natural and social processes that produce agents who play effectively.

Dispensing with the rationality postulate does not imply that people are *irrational* (whatever that means). The point is that the concept of "rationality" does not help us understand the world. What does this mean for the content of this book? We certainly assume agents solve sophisticated problems and we maintain the solutions are relevant for social life. We also routinely assume that agents choose best responses, eliminate strictly dominated strategies, and otherwise behave as good citizens of game theory society. But they may be pigs, dung beetles, birds, spiders, or even wild things like Trogs and Klingons. How do they accomplish these feats with their small minds and alien mentalities? By being displaced by the *strategy* as the active and dynamic game-theoretic unit.

This displacement is supported in three ways. First, we show that many static optimization models are stable equilibria of dynamic systems in which

---

[4]I still find some economists saying something to the effect that "all we mean by rationality is that people choose the best means toward achieving given ends." However (a) the same economists *in practice* routinely equate rationality with "self-interest," and (b) in strategic interaction, "choosing the best means" leads to a logical infinite descent, since how agent A chooses the best means depends on how he models how agent B chooses the best means, which depends in turn on how agent B models how agent A models how agent B chooses the best means, and so on, and conversely.

[5]The knowledgeable reader will note that this book dispenses with 'beliefs' even in dealing with Bayesian games, where they normally run rampant. This treatment is carefully prepared theoretically (§5.13, §5.14, §5.17, §12.1).

agents do not optimize, and we reject models that do not have attractive stability properties. To this end, after a short treatment of evolutionary stability, we develop dynamical systems theory (chapter 8) in sufficient depth to allow students to solve dynamic games with replicator dynamics (chapter 9). Second we provide animal as well as human models. Third, we provide agent-based artificial life computer simulations of games, showing that really stupid critters can evolve toward the solution of games previously thought to require "rationality" and high-level information processing capacity.

Sixth, *game theory is adventure and fantasy.* Of course we do game theory to understand life, but a lot of things in life are adventurous and fantastic. If there are boring and quirky ways to formulate a game, I prefer the quirky. Developing a model is an intellectual adventure requiring a lot more ingenuity than the uninitiated might think. Critics of model building are fond of saying "you can build a model to prove anything." Well, I can't. Turning a vague idea that is convincing at a cocktail party or on the financial page of the *Wall Street Journal* into an analytical model may sound easy, but it is not. It is an adventure because we create the characters and the setting, but then the characters take on a life of their own. This is the fantasy side of game theory!

I use problems in two ways in my game theory courses. First, I transfer selected problems to transparencies, and they provide the basis for all but one or two class meetings of the course (students are urged to take notes right on their personal copies of the book). Second, I assign the problems for homework. I find it takes two or three class sessions per chapter, so I do eleven chapters in a semester, and I assign one set of problems per three or four classes.[6] Generally I assign problems for which solutions are not provided in the book, but occasionally I consider a problem is important enough that I ask students to know the solution even if it appears in the book.

I have been shameless in appropriating the problems of others, citing sources where I can remember them, mostly in the Sources for Problems section at the back of the book. However, I tend to put my own twist on a problem, and rarely have I used others' solutions (*caveat emptor!*). In ad-

---

[6]As outlined in the Suggestions for Instructors many problems from later chapters in the book can be introduced earlier if the instructor so desires, so students can have a familiarity with signaling games, principal-agent problems, and bargaining models, for instance, without waiting until the corresponding chapter in the book is reached.

dition, many of the problems in this book have come from the professional literature, often streamlined to bring out central issues rather than curious details. Not a few of them are my own, or come from my long-term collaboration with Samuel Bowles. I want to thank the many students who have used my problem sets over the past several years for rooting out many errors and ambiguities. I will maintain a list of comments and corrections on my web site at http://www-unix.oit.umass.edu/~gintis, and readers can email me with corrections and other comments (including great new problems!) at hgintis@mediaone.net.

The Wittgenstein quote at the head of the Preface means "What can be said, can be said clearly, and what you can't say, you should shut up about." This adage is beautifully reflected in the methodology of game theory, which gives us a language and a set of analytical tools for *modeling an aspect of social reality with perfect clarity*. Prior to game theory we had no means of speaking clearly about social reality, so the great men and women who created the behavioral sciences from the dawn of the Enlightenment to the mid-twentieth century must be excused for the raging ideological battles that inevitably accompanied their attempt to talk about what could not be said clearly. If we take Wittgenstein seriously, it may be that those days are beyond us.

A generous research grant from the MacArthur Foundation afforded me the time to write this book. *Game Theory Evolving* was composed on Venus, a word processor that I wrote in Borland Pascal, and most of the figures and tables were produced by Econcad, which I also wrote in Borland Pascal. I wrote the simulations in Borland Pascal, Delphi, and Visual Basic and the results are displayed graphically using PsiPlot, Adobe Illustrator, and Mathematica. I used Mathematica regularly to check my algebra and solve equations, and I used NormalSolver, which I wrote in Delphi, to solve complex normal form games and check the solutions to easy ones. The camera-ready copy for *Game Theory Evolving* was produced by Leslie Lamport's LATEX, a beautiful and flexible program, provided you are willing to hack the code a bit in Donald Knuth's bizzare and arcane programming language TEX.

I would like to thank Robert Axtell, Larry Blume, Samuel Bowles, Robert Boyd, Songlin Cai, Colin Camerer, Graciela Chichilnisky, Catherine Eckel, Armin Falk, Ernst Fehr, Alex Field, Urs Fischbacher, Daniel Gintis, David Laibson, Michael Magill, Michael Mandler, Martine Quinzii, Larry Samuelson, Rajiv Sethi, and Lones Smith for helping me with particular points; Manuel Ferreira for comments on several chapters; numerous students who corrected errors in problems and answers; and Jeff Carpenter and Arjun Jayedev for going through the book systematically for errors and infelicities. Thanks go especially to Peter Dougherty, my editor at Princeton University Press, who encouraged me through a long writing process and chose manuscript reviewers who substantively helped improve the quality of the book, and Alice Calaprice, who helped me through the arduous but satisfying process of producing camara-ready copy of this book.

Suggestions for Instructors

> We are all familiar with [putting] off children who question a received orthodoxy by claiming that all will be made clear later. But when the same question is asked in a more advanced course, it is dismissed as childish.
>
> *Binmore (1998)*

> Open package. Eat Contents. Discard package. Caution: contains nuts.
>
> *Label on a bag of peanuts*

Each chapter begins with a set of guidelines for presenting and learning the material contained therein. I try to make the guidelines useful for both instructors and students, though it is impossible not to use terms prior to the point at which they are formally defined and developed in the text. The same applies to this section, which discusses the interrelations among the chapters. I also suggest how an evolutionary approach to game theory affects the way the basic game-theoretic concepts are introduced and motivated. For this reason alone, *do not skip this section*!

Chapter 1, "Game Theory: A Lexicon for Strategic Interaction," begins with an extended example (Big Monkey and Little Monkey, §1.2) that gives the reader a feel for where we will be going in the next four chapters.[1] The rest of the chapter is devoted to defining extensive and normal form games and explaining the Nash equilibrium concept, using (§1.2) as a concrete reference. Some instructors like to start with normal form games, which are easier to define, and introduce the extended form later. You can do this if you want (start with §1.4, then do the normal form parts of chapters 2 and 3—they're quite easy to pick out—then go back to the beginning and do the extensive form parts you skipped over). But from the point of view of evolutionary game theory, this is a questionable practice. The extensive form substantively precedes the normal form in all cases. It is a topographical

---

[1]Why do we use monkeys when what we really care about (in this book) is humans? We practice what might be called the "Occam's razor of evolutionary game theory": if you can explain a behavior just as well with dung beetles as with Ph.D.'s in philosophical logic, use the beetles.

map that depicts the setting for a strategic interaction, while the normal form is merely an analytical tool.[2]

As an example of confusion on this point, there is an experimental literature examining how people "learn to play" normal form games. This is interesting only as an exercise in cognitive psychology, since people *never play anything remotely like normal form games in real life*. The mistake is akin to developing a set of partial differential equations to model the spread of a disease and then test the model by seeing how people learn partial differential equations. If you start with monkeys, you are unlikely to make this mistake, since monkeys will *never* learn to play the normal form game (trust me on this one).[3]

If you were trained in classical game theory, you will find the justification of the Nash equilibrium concept in §1.5 unusual, but hopefully welcome. The classical notions of "common knowledge" and "rational actors," are replaced by the ideas that when we place games in their proper evolutionary setting (a concept not developed fully until chapter 9), Nash equilibria are always stationary states, and all asymptotically or neutrally stable steady states are Nash equilibria.

Chapter 2, "Leading from Strength: Eliminating Dominated Strategies," and chapter 3, "Playing It Straight: Pure Strategy Nash Equilibria" are independent, except for a stray reference to "dominant strategies" in chapter 3. However, §3.22 requires that the student know how to eliminate strictly dominated strategies.

Chapter 4, "Catching 'em Off Guard: Mixed Strategy Nash Equilibria," uses the three preceding chapters extensively. The major problem in teaching the concept of a mixed strategy equilibrium is the simple fact that in a true one-shot game, there is absolutely no reason to randomize. It is easy to explain why one would prefer that one's opponent not know which action we will take, and it is possible to work this up into a full-fledged justification of randomizing (Harsanyi 1973) but in a true one-shot, your opponent knows nothing about you, so even if you choose a pure strategy, you do no worse than by randomizing. Instructors usually try to slip one by the student by

---

[2]Similarly, *behavioral strategies* should be defined before *mixed strategies*, and the concept of a mixed strategy should not be applied to the extensive form at all. But here I bow to tradition in chapter 4.

[3]But, you might reply, the extensive form game is an even more complex analytical object than the normal form, so why bother studying how people play extensive form games? This is a very good question, for which we provide an answer in §11.2.1.

suggesting that the game is "really" a repeated game—as, for instance, in Throwing Fingers (§4.10)—but this is completely bogus, because when we get to repeated games (chapter 6), we learn from the Folk Theorem and other considerations that randomizing is unnecessary! The evolutionary justification is that in a large population of agents meeting randomly and playing the game in each period, in equilibrium a fraction of the population will play each of the pure strategies in proportion to that strategy's weight in the mixed strategy Nash equilibrium. We preview this in §4.11, where we provide an agent-based evolutionary simulation of the mixed strategy equilibrium of a sophisticated card game.[4]

Chapter 4 also presents some fairly sophisticated material on the relationship between behavioral and mixed strategies, and on the concordance between normal and extensive form games. This material is not mathematically deep, but it involves lots of notation. Students often do not like lots of notation (I think it's because they're used to reading three hundred words per minute, and this material slows them down to three hundred words per hour), so you may want to skip this material.

Chapter 5, "Moving through the Game Tree: Subgames, Incredible Threats, and Trembling Hands" depends on the material in all the previous chapters. The material is quite standard until section §5.11, where we use agent-based simulations and evolutionary considerations as a complement to classical arguments that explain why backward induction fails in the finitely repeated Prisoner's Dilemma. Starting with Fuzzy Subgame Perfection (§5.13), we introduce some nonclassical themes that are important in laying the foundation for a reasonable interpretation of experimental economics (see the relationship among §5.16, §5.17, and §11.2.1), and for our later development of the concept of Bayesian games without the concept of *beliefs*. In evolutionary game theory, beliefs have no explanatory value. Either beliefs do not exist (do dung beetles have beliefs?), or they are the products of strategic interactions. Beliefs are brought into classical game theory by asserting that agents' beliefs determine behavior "off the equilibrium path" (i.e., at nodes that are reached with zero probability). This is a conceptual mistake. What the game theorist really wants to do is require that all moves in a game be in some sense "local best responses," a concept that does not presuppose a concept of agent "beliefs" (or, rather,

---

[4]Actually, the situation is more complicated than that. In an asymmetric evolutionary game (§9.15) with a mixed strategy Nash equilibrium, population composition oscillates around the equilibrium level rather than moving toward it.

requires that beliefs be inferred from local best response behavior, not vice versa). This notion, whose importance for evolutionary game theory cannot be overstated, is developed in §5.13, §5.14, and §12.1. You may want your students to skip this material, but definitely read it yourself, since it is central to understanding methodological differences between evolutionary and classical game theory.[5]

The remaining chapters of the book depend on chapters 1–5, except for chapter 16, "Probability and Decision Theory," which is a resource chapter for the rest of the book. However, they do not depend on one another, unless explicitly mentioned in my remarks below.

Chapter 6, "Repeated Games, Trigger Strategies, and Tacit Collusion," is completely standard (whew!).

Chapter 7, "Biology Meets Economics: Evolutionary Stability and the Birth of Dynamic Game Theory," is of course not part of classical game theory at all, and it includes considerably more biology than previous chapters. Like most researchers in evolutionary game theory, I think biological intuitions are very important for economists, since economic behaviors diffuse, stabilize, mutate, and disappear rather than being rational expectations equilibria in the grand neoclassical fashion. This chapter also stresses the fact, discovered by Selten (1980), that evolutionarily stable strategies in asymmetric evolutionary games are always strict Nash equilibria.

Chapter 8, "Dynamical Systems and Differential Equations," is a self-contained treatment of differential equations, and makes virtually no reference to the rest of the book. However, it is carefully crafted to give the student exactly what is needed to deal with replicator dynamics, Lotka-Volterra models, and the other dynamic systems dealt with in the rest of the book. This chapter can be covered in about the same amount of time as any of the other chapters and presumes only trigonometry and undergraduate calculus. This chapter is required reading only for chapter 9 and parts of chapter 11.

Chapter 9, "Evolutionary Dynamics," depends on all of chapter 8. It should not be skipped, since it provides the justification for the whole methodology of evolutionary game theory. However, if you want students to understand the results but do not care if they can actually solve the problems (shame on you!), you can have them read simply the definition sections in chapter 8

---

[5]If you wish to delve further into these methodological issues, you might start with Myerson 1991, which is to my mind light years ahead of other texts (and most of the journal literature) in developing classical game theory systematically. Then read Binmore 1993 and the references therein.

(§8.2 and §8.6), and then do the theory sections in chapter 9 (§9.2, §9.5, §9.6, §9.7, §9.15, and §9.19). I would especially stress the result in §9.15 that *strictly mixed strategy Nash equilibria of asymmetric evolutionary games are not evolutionary equilibria under the replicator dynamic*. This is a stunningly important principle, completely absent in classical game theory, that illuminates why species/agent-types that occupy one niche in an ecological/economic environment are usually unique to that environment.

Chapter 10, "Markov Economies and Stochastic Dynamical Systems," is not used in other chapters. It represents an important trend in game theory, however, and if you choose not to present it in class, you might make it a paper project for interested students. The theory of Markov chains is presented in §16.38 and is a prerequisite for most of the chapter.

Chapter 11, "Homo reciprocans, Homo egualis, and Other Contributors to the Human Behavioral Repertoire," can be done any time after chapter 6, and indeed any time after chapter 5, except for a couple of allusions to the Folk Theorem, which is easy enough to explain informally, and a few remarks about the stability of equilibria. I would be less than candid if I did not mention that the material in this chapter is terrific, and even though it is nonstandard in the year 2000, developments from it will probably be standard in the year 2010.

Chapter 12, "Learning Who Your Friends Are: Bayes' Rule and Private Information," begins with some general remarks on the nature of games with asymmetric information, and continues the argument developed earlier that Bayesian games work just fine without a concept of beliefs (what is called "Bayesian updating" is required for a Nash equilibrium at information sets that are reached with positive probability, and cannot be done otherwise). But the problems in the chapter can be introduced anywhere after chapter 4. The only caveat is that the instructor should go over Bayes' Rule (§16.22) and the problems that use Bayes' Rule, including §16.23, §16.26, §16.27 (the famous Monty Hall problem), as well as §16.28. Haggling at the Bazaar is a particularly elegant game that can be presented as an application of mixed strategy equilibria in chapter 4, A Market for Lemons can be done at the same time, and may be too important a model to leave for the tail end of the course.

Chapter 13, "When It Pays to Be Truthful: Signaling in Games with Friends, Adversaries, and Kin," like the previous chapter, gathers together a number of problems that do not involve special solution techniques or theory, but are organized around a single topic—in this case, the nature of communication. There is a large economics literature on this topic, but I don't think it has gotten very far, so I mostly present the biological literature, which is rich and deeply insightful. This includes the runaway selection (§13.5) and handicap principle (§13.6) to explain sexual ornamentation (beauty) in sexually reproducing species, and a nice model of threatening signals (§13.4). I try to present these models in a way that makes them equally applicable to biology and economics; since most game-theoretic models in biology operate at the phenotypic level anyway, it turns out not to be hard to do. There are, however, plenty of traditional economic models of pooling and separating equilibria (§13.3, §13.10), as well as screening (§13.11) and signaling (§13.12) models.

Chapter 14, "Bosses and Workers, Landlords and Peasants, and Other Principal-Agent Models," and chapter 15, "Bargaining," can also be covered at any time after chapter 5, and their various problems can be assigned at earlier points in the course.

Chapter 16, "Probability and Decision Theory," is meant to fill gaps in students' knowledge of probability and decision theory. I review conditional probability (§16.21) and Bayes' Rule (§16.22), and give problems (the problems in this chapter are dynamite). Also, the axiomatic foundations of the expected utility principle are presented in §16.39 using Savage's approach, which is well suited for evolutionary game theory. Finally, since a number of problems touch on notions of risk aversion, §16.41 develops the requisite material.

I

Concepts and Problems

1

Game Theory: A Lexicon for Strategic Interaction

> High-rationality solution concepts in game theory can emerge in a world populated by low-rationality agents.
>
> *Young (1998)*

1.1 Introduction

This chapter defines and illustrates the fundamental tools of game theory: extensive form games, normal form games, and Nash equilibria. The reader is asked to take the importance of the Nash equilibrium concept on faith for the time being, since its justification requires the development of conceptual tools—evolutionary stability and dynamics—that appear only several chapters down the road. The chapter begins, however, with a carefully developed example—Big Monkey and Little Monkey—that showcases a major contribution of game theory to understanding social interactions: insisting on absolute clarity concerning the rules of the game and its informational assumptions. In the process, we touch on such engaging issues as credible and incredible threats and the value of precommitment, thus setting the tone for the next several chapters.

I have found that class time is best used by presenting the example in detail and the formal definitions relatively sketchily, relying on the problem set (§1.6) to drive home the subtleties of the formalities.

1.2 Big Monkey and Little Monkey

Big Monkey and Little Monkey normally eat fruit and berries from small ground-level bushes. But an important part of their diet is warifruit, which dangle from the extreme tip of a lofty branch of the waritree. A waritree only occasionally produces fruit, and then only one fruit per tree. To get the warifruit, at least one of the monkeys must climb the tree, creep part

3

way out the branch on which the fruit is growing, and shake vigorously until the fruit comes loose and falls to the ground. Careful energy measurements show that a warifruit is worth 10 Kc (kilocalories) of energy, the cost of running up the tree, shaking the fruit loose, and running back down to the ground costs 2 Kc for Big Monkey, but is negligible for Little Monkey, who is much smaller. Moreover, if both monkeys climb the tree, shake the fruit loose, then climb down the tree and eat the fruit, Big Monkey gets 7 Kc and Little Monkey gets only 3 Kc, since Big Monkey hogs most of it; if only Big Monkey climbs the tree, while Little Monkey waits on the ground for the fruit to fall, Big Monkey gets 6 Kc and Little Monkey gets 4 Kc (Little Monkey eats some before Big Monkey gets back down from the tree); if only Little Monkey climbs the tree, Big Monkey gets 9 Kc and Little Monkey gets 1 Kc (most of the food is gone by the time Little Monkey gets there).

What will Big Monkey and Little Monkey do if each wants to maximize net energy gain? We may safely put aside for the moment some of bigger questions, such as: (a) How do we know monkeys maximize anything? (b) How do monkeys come to know the costs and the benefits of the various actions? (c) Are monkeys smart enough to find an optimal solution? (d) Who cares about monkeys, anyway? We will come back to these larger issues later. We simply assume that monkeys do maximize, they do know the costs and benefits, they can find the optimal solution, they cannot enforce cooperative agreements, and, finally, that we will learn something interesting by solving this problem.

There is one more matter that must be resolved: Who decides first what to do, Big Monkey or Little Monkey? There are three possibilities: (a) Big Monkey decides first; (b) Little Monkey decides first; (c) both monkeys decide simultaneously. We will go through the three cases in turn.

Assuming Big Monkey decides first, we get the situation depicted in Fig. 1.1. We call a figure like this a *game tree*, and we call the game it defines an extensive form game. At the top of the game tree is the *root node* (the little dot labeled "Big Monkey") with two *branches*, labeled w (wait) and c (climb). This means Big Monkey gets to choose and can go either left (w) or right (c). This brings us to the two nodes labeled "Little Monkey," in each of which Little Monkey can wait (w) or climb (c).

Note that while Big Monkey has only two strategies, Little Monkey actually has four:

a. Climb no matter what Big Monkey does (cc).
b. Wait no matter what Big Monkey does (ww).

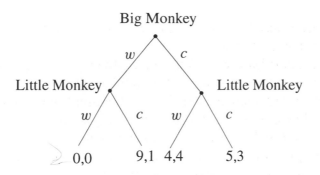

Figure 1.1. Big Monkey and Little Monkey: Big Monkey chooses first.

c. Do the same thing Big Monkey does (*wc*).
d. Do the opposite of what Big Monkey does (*cw*).

We call a move taken by a player (one of the monkeys) at a node an *action*, and we call a series of actions that fully define the behavior of a player a *strategy*—actually a *pure strategy*, in contrast to "mixed" and "behavioral" strategies, which we will discuss later, that involve randomizing. Thus, Big Monkey has two strategies, each of which is simply an action, while Little Monkey has four strategies, each of which is two actions—one to be used when Little Monkey is on the left, and one when Little Monkey is on the right.

At the bottom of the game tree are four nodes, which we variously call *leaf* or *terminal nodes*. At each terminal node is the payoff to the two players, Big Monkey (player 1) first and Little Monkey (player 2) second, if they choose the strategies that take them to that particular leaf. You should check that the payoffs correspond to our description above. For instance, at the leftmost leaf when both wait, with neither Monkey expending or ingesting energy, the payoff is (0,0). At the rightmost leaf both climb the tree, costing Big Monkey 2 Kc, after which Big Monkey gets 7 Kc and Little Monkey gets 3 Kc. Their net payoffs are thus (5,3). And similarly for the other two leaves.

How should Big Monkey decide what to do? Well, Big Monkey should figure out how Little Monkey will react to each of Big Monkey's two choices, *w* and *c*. If Big Monkey chooses *w*, then Little Monkey will choose *c*, since this pays 1 Kc as opposed to 0 Kc. Thus, Big Monkey gets 9 Kc by moving left. If Big Monkey chooses *c*, Little Monkey will choose *w*, since this pays 4 Kc as opposed to 3 Kc for choosing *c*. Thus Big Monkey gets 4 Kc for choosing c, as opposed to 9 Kc for choosing w. We now have answered Big Monkey's problem: choose w.

What about Little Monkey? Well, Little Monkey must certainly choose c on the left node, but what should Little Monkey choose on the right node? Of course it doesn't really matter, since Little Monkey will never *be* at the right node. However, we must specify not only what a player does "along the path of play" (in this case the left branch of the tree), but at *all possible nodes on the game tree*. This is because we can only say for sure that Big Monkey is choosing a best response to Little Monkey if we know what Little Monkey does, and conversely. If Little Monkey makes a wrong choice at the right node, in some games (though not this one) Big Monkey would do better by playing c. In short, Little Monkey must choose one of the four strategies listed above. Clearly, Little Monkey should choose cw (do the opposite of Big Monkey), since this maximizes Little Monkey's payoff no matter what Big Monkey does.

Conclusion: the only reasonable solution to this game is for Big Monkey to wait on the ground, and Little Monkey to do the opposite of what Big Monkey does. Their payoffs are (9,1). We call this a Nash equilibrium (named after John Nash, who invented the concept in about 1950). A Nash equilibrium in a two-player game is a pair of strategies, each of which is a *best response* to the other; i.e., each gives the player using it the highest possible payoff, given the other player's strategy.

There is another way to depict this game, called its *strategic form* or *normal form*. It is common to use both representations and to switch back and forth between them, according to convenience. The normal form corresponding to Fig. 1.1 is in Fig. 1.2. In this example we array strategies of player 1 (Big Monkey) in rows, and the strategies of player 2 (Little Monkey) in columns. Each entry in the resulting matrix represents the payoffs to the two players if they choose the corresponding strategies.

		Little Monkey			
		cc	cw	wc	ww
Big	w	9,1	9,1	0,0	0,0
Monkey	c	5,3	4,4	5,3	4,4

Figure 1.2. Normal form of Big Monkey and Little Monkey when Big Monkey moves first.

We solve the normal form of the game by trying to pick out a row and a column such that the payoff to their intersection is the highest possible for player 1 down the column, and the highest possible for player 2 across the row (there may be more than one such pair). Note that (w, cw) is indeed a Nash equilibrium of the normal form game, because 9 is better than 4 for Big Monkey down the cw column, and 1 is the best Little Monkey can do across the w row.

Can we find any other Nash equilibria to this game? Clearly (w, cc) is also a Nash equilibrium, since w is a best reply to cc and conversely. But the (w, cc) equilibrium has the drawback that if Big Monkey should happen to make a mistake and play c, Little Monkey gets only 3, whereas with cw, Little Monkey gets 4. We say cc is *weakly dominated* by cw.

But what if Little Monkey plays ww? Then Big Monkey should play c, and it is clear that ww is a best response to c. So this gives us another Nash equilibrium, (c, ww), in which Little Monkey does much better, getting 4 instead of 1, and Big Monkey does much worse, getting 4 instead of 9. Why did we not see this Nash equilibrium in our analysis of the extensive form game? The reason is that (c, ww) involves Little Monkey making an *incredible threat*. "I don't care what you do, says Little Monkey—I'm waiting here on the ground—no matter what." The threat is "incredible" because Big Monkey knows that if he plays w, then when it is Little Monkey's turn to carry out the threat to play w, Little Monkey will not in fact do so, simply because 1 is better than 0.[1] We say a Nash equilibrium of an extensive form game is *subgame perfect* if, at any point in the game tree, the play dictated by the Nash equilibrium *remains* a Nash equilibrium of the subgame (we give formal definitions and more examples in chapter 5). The strategy (c, ww) is not subgame perfect because in the subgame beginning with Little Monkey's choice of w on the left of Fig. 1.1 is not a best response. Nice try, anyway, Little Monkey!

But what if Little Monkey gets to choose first? Perhaps now Little Monkey can force a better split than getting 1 compared to Big Monkey's 9. This is the extensive form game (Fig. 1.3). We now call Little Monkey player 1 and Big Monkey player 2. Now Big Monkey has four strategies (the strategies that belonged to Little Monkey in the previous version of the game) and Little Monkey only has two (the ones that belonged to Big Monkey before). Little Monkey notices that Big Monkey's best response to w is c, and Big

---

[1] This argument fails if the monkeys can condition their behavior in one day on their behavior in previous days (see chapter 6). We assume the monkeys cannot do this.

Monkey's best response to c is w. Since Little Monkey gets 4 in the first case and only 1 in the second, Little Monkey chooses w. Big Monkey's best choice is then cw, and the payoffs are (4,4). Note that *by going first, Little Monkey is able to precommit to a strategy that is an incredible threat when going second.*

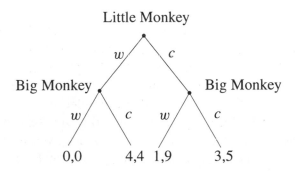

Figure 1.3. Big Monkey and Little Monkey: Little Monkey chooses first.

The normal form for the case when Little Monkey goes first is illustrated in Fig. 1.4. Again we find the two Nash equilibria (w, cc) and (w, cw), and again we find another Nash equilibrium not evident at first glance from the game tree: now it is Big Monkey who has an incredible threat, by playing ww, to which Little Monkey's best response is c.

		Big Monkey			
		cc	cw	wc	ww
Little	w	4,4	4,4	0,0	0,0
Monkey	c	3,5	1,9	3,5	1,9

Figure 1.4. Normal form of Big Monkey and Little Monkey game when Little Monkey moves first.

The final possibility is that the monkeys choose simultaneously or, equivalently, each monkey chooses an action without seeing what the other monkey chooses. In this case, each monkey has two options: climb the tree (c), or wait on the ground (w). We then get the situation in Fig. 1.5. Notice the new element in the game tree: the dotted line connecting the two places where Little Monkey chooses. This is called an *information set*. Roughly speaking, an information set is a set of nodes at which (a) the same player chooses, and (b) the player choosing does not know which particular node represents the actual choice node. Note also that we could just as well interchange Big Monkey and Little Monkey in the diagram, reversing their payoffs at the terminal nodes, of course. This illustrates an important point: there may be more than one extensive form game representing the same real strategic situation.

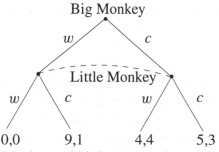

Figure 1.5. Big Monkey and Little Monkey choose simultaneously.

Even though there are fewer strategies in this game, it is hard to see what an equilibrium might be by looking at the game tree. This is because what Little Monkey does cannot depend on which choice Big Monkey makes, since Little Monkey does not see Big Monkey's choice. So let's look at the normal form game, in Fig. 1.6. From this figure, it is easy to see that both (w, c) and (c, w) are Nash equilibria, the first obviously favoring Big Monkey and the second favoring Little Monkey. In fact, there is a third Nash equilibrium that is more difficult to pick out. In this equilibrium Big Monkey randomizes by choosing c and w with probability $1/2$, and Little Monkey does the same. This is called a *mixed strategy Nash equilibrium*; you will learn how to find and analyze it in chapter 4. In this equilibrium Big Monkey has payoff 4.5 and Little Monkey has payoff 2. The reason for this meager total payoff is that with probability $1/4$, both wait and get zero reward, and sometimes both climb the tree!

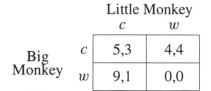

Figure 1.6. Big Monkey and Little Monkey: normal form in the simultaneous move case.

1.3 The Extensive Form Game

Now that you have seen an example of one, actually defining a game should not be daunting. The formal definition of an extensive form game is *notationally challenged* it requires much mathematic notation to express something that is conceptually simple. We will forego some of this in favor of a verbal description; but where the notation cannot be avoided without causing confusion, we will not hesitate to use it. An *extensive form game* G consists of a number of *players*, a *game tree*, and a set of *payoffs*. A game tree consists of a number of *nodes* connected by *branches*. Each branch connects a *head node* to a distinct *tail node* If b is a branch of the game tree, we denote the head node of b by b^h, and the tail node of b by b^t.

A *path* from node a to node a' in the game tree is a sequence of moves starting at a and ending at a'.[2] If there is a path from node a to a', we say a is an *ancestor* of a', and a' is a *successor* to a. We call k the *length* of the path. If a path from a to a' has length one, we call a the *parent* of a', and a' is a *child* of a. We require that the game tree have one node r, called the *root node*, that has no parent, and a set T of nodes called *terminal nodes* or *leaf nodes*, that have no children. We associate with each terminal node $t \in T$, and each player i, a *payoff* $\pi_i(t) \in \mathbf{R}$ ($\mathbf{R}$ is the set of real numbers). We say the game is *finite* if it has a finite number of nodes. We assume all games are finite, unless otherwise stated.

We also require that the graph of G have the following *tree property*. There must be *exactly one path* from the root node to any given terminal node in the game tree. One obvious but important implication of this property is that *every node except the root node has exactly one parent*.

Players relate to the game tree as follows. Each nonterminal node is assigned to a player who moves at that node. Each branch from a node represents a particular *action* that the player assigned to that node can take there, and hence determines either a terminal node or the next point of play in the game—the particular child node to be visited next.[3]

If a stochastic event occurs at a node a (for instance, the weather is Good or Bad, or your partner is Nice or Nasty), we assign the fictitious player

---

[2]Technically, a path is a sequence $b_1, \ldots, b_k$ of branches such that $b_1^h = a$, $b_i^t = b_{i+1}^h$ for $i = 1, \ldots k - 1$, and $b_k^t = a'$; i.e., the path starts at a, the tail of each branch is the head of the next branch, and the path ends at a'.

[3]Thus if $\mathbf{p} = (b_1, \ldots, b_k)$ is a path from a to a', then starting from a, if the actions associated with the b_j are taken by the various players, the game moves to a'.

"Nature" to that node, the actions Nature takes representing the possible outcomes of the stochastic event, and we attach a *probability* to each branch of which *a* is the head node, representing the probability that Nature chooses that branch (we assume all such probabilities are strictly positive).

The tree property thus means that there is a *unique* sequence of moves by the players (including Nature) leading from the root node to any specific node of the game tree, and for any two nodes, there is *at most one* sequence of player moves leading from the first to the second.

A player may know the exact node in the game tree when it is his turn to move (e.g., the first two cases in Big Monkey and Little Monkey, above), but he may know only that he is at one of several possible nodes. This is the situation Little Monkey faces in the simultaneous choice case (Fig. 1.6). We call such a collection of nodes an *information set*. For a set of nodes to form an information set, the same player must be assigned to move at each of the nodes in the set and have the same array of possible actions at each node.

For some purposes we also require that if two nodes *a* and *a'* are in the same information set for a player, the moves that player made up to *a* and *a'* must be the same. This criterion is called *perfect recall*, because if a player never forgets his moves, he cannot make two different choices that subsequently land him in the same information set.[4] We will assume perfect recall unless otherwise stated in this book, but whenever a result depends upon perfect recall, we will mention the fact.

Suppose each player $i = 1, \ldots, n$ chooses strategy s_i. We call $s = (s_1, \ldots, s_n)$ a *strategy profile* for the game, and we define the *payoff* to player i, given strategy profile s, as follows. If there are no moves by Nature, then s determines a unique path through the game tree, and hence a unique terminal node $t \in T$. The payoff $\pi_i(s)$ to player i under strategy profile s is then defined to be simply $\pi_i(t)$. We postpone the case where Nature moves to §11.2.1, since the definition depends on the so-called *expected utility principle*.

---

[4]Another way to describe perfect recall is to note that the information sets $\mathcal{N}_i$ for player i are the nodes of a graph in which the children of an information set $v \in \mathcal{N}_i$ are the $v' \in \mathcal{N}_i$ that can be reached by one move of player i, plus some combination of moves of the other players and Nature. Perfect recall means that this graph has the tree property.

1.4 The Normal Form Game

The *strategic form* or *normal form* game consists of a number of players, a set of strategies for each of the players, and a payoff function that associates a payoff to each player with a choice of strategies by each player. More formally, the *n*-player normal form game consists of

a. A set of *players* $i = 1, \ldots, n$.
b. A set S_i of *strategies* for player $i = 1, \ldots, n$. We call $s = (s_1, \ldots, s_n)$, where $s_i \in S_i$ for $i = 1, \ldots, n$, a *strategy profile* for the game.[5]
c. A function $\pi_i : S \to \mathbf{R}$ for player $i = 1, \ldots, n$, where S is the set of strategy profiles, so $\pi_i(s)$ is player i's payoff when strategy profile s is chosen.

Two extensive form games are said to be *equivalent* if they correspond to the same normal form game, except perhaps for the labeling of the actions and the naming of the players. But given an extensive form game, how exactly do we form the corresponding normal form game? First, the players in the normal form are the same as the players in the extensive form. Second, for each player i, let S_i be the set of strategies of that player, each strategy consisting of a choice of an action at each information set where i moves. Finally, the payoff functions are given by equation (3.2). If there are only two players and a finite number of strategies, we can write the payoff function in the form of a matrix, as in Fig. 1.2.

1.5 Nash Equilibrium

The concept of a Nash equilibrium of a game is formulated most easily in terms of the normal form. Suppose the game has n players, with strategy sets S_i and payoff functions $\pi_i : S \to \mathbf{R}$, for $i = 1, \ldots, n$ where S is the set of strategy profiles. We use the following very useful notation. If $s \in S$ and $t_i \in S_i$, we write

$$(s_{-i}, t_i) = (t_i, s_{-i}) = \begin{cases} (t_1, s_2, \ldots, s_n) & \text{if } i = 1 \\ (s_1, \ldots, s_{i-1}, t_i, s_{i+1}, \ldots, s_n) & \text{if } 1 < i < n \ . \\ (s_1, \ldots, s_{n-1}, t_n) & \text{if } i = n \end{cases}$$

In other words, (s_{-i}, t_i) is the strategy profile obtained by replacing s_i with t_i for player i.

[5]Technically, these are *pure strategies*, because later we will consider *mixed strategies* that are probabilistic combinations of pure strategies.

We say a strategy profile $s^* = (s_1^*, \ldots, s_n^*) \in S$ is a *Nash equilibrium* if, for every player $i = 1, \ldots, n$, and every $s_i \in S_i$, we have $\pi_i(s^*) \geq \pi_i(s_{-i}^*, s_i)$; i.e., choosing s_i^* is at least as good for player i as choosing any other s_i given that the other players choose s_{-i}^*. Note that in a Nash equilibrium, the strategy of each player is a *best response* to the strategies chosen by all the other players. Finally, notice that a player could have responses that are *equally good* as the one chosen in the Nash equilibrium—there just cannot be a strategy that is strictly better.

The Nash equilibrium concept is important because in many cases we can accurately (or reasonably accurately) predict how people will play a game by assuming they will choose strategies that implement a Nash equilibrium. It will also turn out that, in dynamic games that model an evolutionary process whereby successful strategies drive out unsuccessful ones over time, stationary states are, with some obvious and uninteresting exceptions, Nash equilibria. Moreover, dynamic evolutionary systems often either converge to a Nash equilibrium (we then say it is *asymptotically stable*) or follow closed orbits around a Nash equilibrium (we then say it is *neutrally stable*). We will also see that many Nash equilibria that seem implausible intuitively are actually *unstable* equilibria of an evolutionary process, so we would not expect to see them in the real world. Where people appear to deviate systematically from implementing Nash equilibria and in no sense appear ignorant or "irrational" for doing so, we will usually find that we have misspecified the game they are playing or the payoffs we attribute to them.

By contrast with our "evolutionary" approach, the older tradition of classical game theory justifies the Nash equilibrium concept by reference to the concept of *common knowledge*. We say that a fact p is "common knowledge" if all players know p, all players know that all players know p, all players know that all players know that all players know p, and so on ad infinitum. One can then show that if it is common knowledge that all players are rational (i.e., choose best responses), then under appropriate conditions they will choose a Nash equilibrium (see Tan and da Costa Werlang 1988 and the references therein). In his famous entry in *The New Palgrave*, for instance, Aumann (1987b) reflects the received wisdom in asserting, "The common knowledge assumption underlies all of game theory [otherwise] the analysis is incoherent."[6]

---

[6]Actually, more recent research shows that even within classical game theory this assumption can often be considerably weakened (Aumann and Brandenburger 1995).

However often repeated, such assertions are simply false. Common knowledge is a *sufficient* but not a *necessary* condition for agents to choose strategies forming a Nash equilibrium (and then only under quite restrictive conditions). Moreover, it is a ridiculously implausible assumption even for humans. Finally, the successful application of game theory to biology (see, for instance, §4.16 and §4.17), and the successful agent-based simulation of games (§4.11, §5.11, §7.15 and §13.8), show that such strong assumptions are unnecessary. Hence, unless otherwise stated (as for instance in §3.23), in this book we will use the term "common knowledge" to mean that all players know the fact in question, with no additional levels of recursion implied.

1.6   Reviewing the Terminology

The following exercises require that you understand fully and completely the concepts developed above.

a. Define an extensive form game. Be sure to include the definition of the following terms: game tree, path, successor, ancestor, parent, child, root node, terminal node, information set, action.
b. Define a normal form game.
c. Any extensive form game can be translated into a normal form game in a natural manner. Use the Big Monkey and Little Monkey example to describe how this is done.
d. What is a *best response* in a normal form game? What is a Nash Equilibrium?
e. Write out the conditions for a pair of strategies to form a Nash equilibrium of a two-player normal form game.

2

Leading from Strength: Eliminating Dominated Strategies

It is, perhaps, one of the astonishing features of intellectual life in our century that cross-disciplinary consistency should be treated as a radical claim in need of defense.

Cosmides, Tooby, and Barkow (1992)

2.1 Introduction

This chapter shows clearly that elementary game theory is extremely insightful in analyzing real-world problems. The challenge for the student in dealing with the material in this chapter is that of *thinking systematically and logically*—handwaving should not be tolerated. Even highly sophisticated students can fail to understand the logic of eliminating dominated strategies in the Prisoner's Dilemma (§2.6), the Second-Price Auction (§2.8), and the Centipede Game (§2.18), although the reasoning is completely elementary. I present these models in class, with answers and extensive discussion, as well as Hagar's Battles (§2.10) because it illustrates clear thinking, and I present Strategic Voting (§2.15) because it is a nice example from political theory. The problems are mostly straightforward, but Poker with Bluffing (§2.17) should be extra credit for computer hackers.

2.2 Dominant and Dominated Strategies

A powerful way of finding Nash equilibria of games is to eliminate what are called *dominated strategies*. Suppose s_i and s_i' are two strategies for player i in a normal form game. We say s_i' is *strictly dominated* by s_i if, for every choice of strategies of the other players, i's payoff from choosing s_i is *strictly greater* than i's payoff from choosing s_i'. We say s_i' is *weakly dominated* by s_i if, for every choice of strategies of the other players, i's payoff from choosing s_i is *at least as great* as i's payoff from choosing s_i'.

15

It is clear that a strictly dominated strategy s_i is never part of a Nash equilibrium, since the player i could do better by switching to a strategy that dominates s_i. We can therefore eliminate such strategies without losing any Nash equilibria. We call this process the *elimination of strictly dominated strategies*.

After we have eliminated strictly dominated strategies of one player, we may find that there are now strictly dominated strategies for another player, which we can eliminate as well. We can continue this until there are no strictly dominated strategies left. We call this the *iterated elimination of strictly dominated strategies*. If a unique strategy remains for the player, we call this the player's dominant strategy. If a unique strategy remains for all players, we call this a dominant strategy equilibrium.

What about eliminating weakly dominated strategies? If the iterated elimination of weakly dominated strategies leaves exactly one strategy for each player, the resulting strategy profile is a Nash equilibrium (§2.5). However, some Nash equilibria can be discarded this way. In particular, a player may use a weakly dominated strategy in a Nash equilibrium if, in the extensive form of the game, the resulting equilibrium does not reach those parts of the game tree where the strategy is worse than some alternative (§2.5). On the other hand, a Nash equilibrium that uses weakly dominated strategies has very poor dynamic properties: it cannot be evolutionarily stable (§7.2), it disappears when even an infinitesimal probability of player error is assumed (§5.16), and it is not stable under replicator and related dynamics (§9.2). Moreover, there always exists a Nash equilibrium in a finite game that does *not* use weakly dominated strategies.[1] For these reasons, we will always feel free to eliminate weakly dominated strategies unless there is a reason for not doing so. The interested reader can refer to the discussions in van Damme (1991) and Weibull (1995) for more ample treatments of this issue.

2.3   Backward Induction: Pruning the Game Tree

We can also eliminate dominated strategies in extensive form games with *complete information* (i.e., where each information set is a single node). Choose any terminal node $t \in T$ and find the parent node of this terminal node, say node a. Suppose player i chooses at a, and suppose i's highest payoff at a is attained at node $t' \in T$. Erase all the branches from a so a

---

[1]You can easily prove this, but you must use the fact that every finite game has a Nash equilibrium (§4.3).

becomes a terminal node, and attach the payoffs from t' to the new terminal node a. Also record i's move at a, so you can specify i's equilibrium strategy when you have finished the analysis. Repeat this procedure for all terminal nodes of the original game. When you are done, you will have an extensive form game that is one level less deep than the original game. Now repeat the process as many times as is necessary, until the game tree has just one node (except for Nature's moves, if any). When you reassemble the moves you have recorded for each player, you will have a Nash equilibrium.

We call this formally *backward induction*, because we start at the end of the game and move backward. We also call it more informally *pruning the game tree* because we successively lop off branches of the game tree, much as a gardener prunes a real tree. Note that backward induction eliminates weakly dominated strategies but cannot easily distinguish between strongly and weakly dominated strategies, since it never looks at the whole game tree. Therefore, backward induction can eliminate Nash equilibria that use weakly dominated strategies.

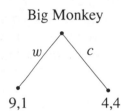

For an example of pruning the game tree, consider Fig. 1.1, the Big Monkey and Little Monkey game where Big Monkey goes first. We start with the terminal node labeled (0,0), and follow it back to the Little Monkey node on the left. At this node, w is strictly dominated by c since $1 > 0$, so we write down that Little Monkey chooses c there, erase the two branches, and label the new terminal node (9,1). We locate the next terminal node in the original game tree, (4,4), and follow back to the Little Monkey node on the right. At this node, c is strictly dominated by w, so we write down that Little Monkey chooses w there, erase the two branches, and label the new terminal node (4,4). This gives the little diagram depicted above.

Now we prune this smaller game tree—this time of course it's trivial. We find the first terminal node, (9,1), which leads back to Big Monkey. Here c is strictly dominated, so we erase the two branches, record that Big Monkey chooses w, and write (9,1) under the one remaining node. We now have our solution: Big Monkey chooses w, Little Monkey chooses cw, and the payoffs are (9,1).

2.4   Eliminating Dominated Strategies

Test your knowledge on the following questions.

a.   Solve the normal form game in of Fig. 2.1 by eliminating dominated strategies. Verify that the resulting solution is a Nash equilibrium of the game.

	N	C	J
N	73,25	57,42	66,32
C	80,26	35,12	32,54
J	28,27	63,31	54,29

Figure 2.1. Eliminating dominated strategies in a 3 × 3 normal form game.

b.   Can a Nash equilibrium to the game in Fig. 2.2 be found by the iterated elimination of dominated strategies? If so, describe exactly in what order you delete strategies.

	a	b	c	d	e
A	63, −1	28, −1	−2, 0	−2, 45	−3, 19
B	32, 1	2, 2	2, 5	33, 0	2, 3
C	54, 1	95, −1	0, 2	4, −1	0, 4
D	1, −33	−3, 43	−1, 39	1, −12	−1, 17
E	−22, 0	1, −13	−1, 88	−2, −57	−3, 72

Figure 2.2. Eliminating dominated strategies in a 5 × 5 normal form game.

2.5   Concepts and Definitions

Carefully answer the following questions.

a.   Describe *backward induction* in an extensive form game.
b.   Define the notion of a strategy being *strictly dominated* in a normal or extensive form game. Explain in words why a strictly dominated strategy can never be used by a player in a Nash equilibrium.

c. Describe the *iterated elimination of strictly dominated strategies* and explain why a strategy eliminated in this manner cannot be used by a player in a Nash equilibrium.

d. Explain why, if the iterated elimination of weakly dominated strategies leaves exactly one strategy for each player, the resulting strategy profile is a Nash equilibrium.

e. Unlike the case of strongly dominated strategies, when you eliminate weakly dominated strategies, you can throw away Nash equilibria. Show this by finding two Nash equilibria in the diagram below.

	c1	c2	c3
r1	~~1,0~~	~~2, 1~~	0,1
r2	1, 2	~~5, 1~~	~~0,0~~

f. Suppose strategy s_i is weakly dominated by s_i' for player i in an extensive form game, and suppose $s = (s_1, \ldots, s_n)$ is a Nash equilibrium for the game. Let a be a node where i chooses and s_i' gives i a higher payoff than s_i for some strategy profile of the other players. Explain why no path through the game tree compatible with s passes through node a. HINT: Remember our assumption that branches representing Nature's moves all have strictly positive probability, and refer to equation (3.2).

2.6 The Prisoner's Dilemma

Two partners in a law firm are accused of double billing their clients. The independent counsel has enough evidence to send them to jail for one year each. However, if one of the law partners confesses and provides incriminating evidence about the other, he will go free and his partner will go to jail for ten years. If both confess, however, they will each get eight years in jail—ten years for the crime minus two years for confessing.

a. Draw a game tree for the problem, labeling the nodes appropriately. You may assume the partners move simultaneously.

b. Show that there is a unique Nash equilibrium, obtained by eliminating dominated strategies.

c. Draw the normal form game for the problem, and use it to come to the same conclusion.

d. Suppose one law partner goes first and the other sees the move. Draw the normal form game now and find the unique Nash equilibrium by eliminating dominated strategies.

2.7   An Armaments Game

A fighter command has four strategies, and its opponent bomber command has three counterstrategies. The diagram below shows the probability that the fighter destroys the bomber. Use the elimination of dominated strategies to determine a solution to this game.

Bomber Command

Fighter Command	Full Fire, Low Speed	Partial Fire, Medium Speed	No Fire, High Speed
Guns	0.30	0.25	0.15
Rockets	0.18	0.14	0.16
Toss-bombs	0.35	0.22	0.17
Ramming	0.21	0.16	0.10

2.8   Second-Price Auction

A single object is to be sold at auction. There are $n > 1$ bidders, each submitting a single bid, in secret, to the seller. The value of the object to bidder i is v_i. The winner of the object is the highest bidder, but i pays only the next highest bid.

a. Show that "truth-telling" (i.e., each player i bids v_i) is a dominant strategy for each player. To simplify the argument, you can assume, where convenient, that there are no ties.

b. Does your analysis depend on whether or not others tell the truth?

c. What are some reasons that real second-price auctions might not conform to the assumptions of this model?

2.9   The Landlord and the Eviction Notice

A landlord has three tenants, Mr. A, Ms. B, and Msgr. C, in a rent-controlled apartment building in New York City. A new law says that the landlord has the right to evict one tenant per building. The landlord calculates that the value of a vacant apartment is $15,000, both to the tenant and to her. She sends the following letter to each of the tenants: "Tomorrow I will be visiting your building. I will offer Mr. A $1,000 if he agrees to vacate his apartment voluntarily; otherwise, I will evict him. If Mr. A agrees to vacate voluntarily, I will then offer Ms. B $1,000, and if she refuses, I will evict her. If she accepts, I will evict Msgr. C."

a. Write a game tree for this situation, and find the dominant strategy equilibrium.
b. What if there were ten tenants instead of three?
c. What if the landlord offered only $10 to a tenant who leaves voluntarily?

2.10   Hagar's Battles

There are ten battlefields with military values $a_1 < \ldots < a_{10}$. Each player is endowed with $n_i < 10$ soldiers ($i = 1, 2$). A player's strategy is a decision to send his soldiers to these various battlefields. A player can send at most one soldier to a given battlefield. When the fighting begins, each player wins a_j for each battlefield where he has a soldier but his opponent does not. The winner of the war is the army whose occupied territory has the highest total military value. Show that this game has a unique dominant strategy equilibrium.

2.11   An Increasing-Bid Auction

A Ming vase is to be sold at auction. There are n bidders, and the value of the vase to bidder i is $v_i > 0$, $i = 1, \ldots, n$. The auctioneer begins the bidding at zero, and raises the price at the rate of $1 per second. All bidders who are willing to buy the vase at the stated price put their hands up simultaneously. This continues until there is only one arm raised. This last and highest bidder is the winner of the auction and must buy the vase for the stated price. Show that this auction has the same optimal strategies and the same outcome as the Second-Price Auction. HINT: First show that the only undominated pure strategies for bidder i take the form of choosing a price

p_i and keeping a hand up until the auctioneer's price goes higher than this. Then find the optimal p_i.

2.12   The Debtor and His Creditors

A debtor owes $15,000 to each of two creditors, but he only has $25,000. If he defaults on the debt, he will lose the whole amount, and the legal costs of filing for bankruptcy and litigating the liquidation of his assets will be $15,000, so each of the debtors will collect $5,000. The debtor has his lawyer draw up the following letter, which he sends to each of the creditors: "I hereby offer you $5,001 if both you and my other creditor agree to cancel my debt. If either or both of you decline this offer, I will be legally in default."

Write a game tree for this situation, and show that it is a dominant strategy for each creditor to accept the offer, allowing the debtor to eradicate the debt and retain the amount $14,998 for himself. What does this tell you about bankruptcy law?

2.13   Football Strategy

In a football game, the offense has two strategies, Run or Pass. The defense has three strategies, Counter Run, Counter Pass, or Blitz the quarterback. After studying many games, the statisticians came up with the following table, giving the expected number of yards gained when the various strategies in the figure are followed. Use the elimination of dominated strategies to find a solution to this game.

		Defense	
Offense	Counter Run	Counter Pass	Blitz
Run	3, −3	7, −7	15, −15
Pass	9, −9	8, −8	10, −10

2.14   A Military Strategy Game

Country A and country I are at war. The two countries are separated by a series of rivers, illustrated in the figure below.

Country I sends a naval fleet with just enough sup-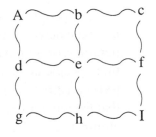
plies to reach A. The fleet must stop for the night at
intersections (e.g., if the fleet takes the path IhebA,
it must stop the first night at h, the second at e, and
the third at b). If unhindered, on the fourth day the
fleet will reach A and destroy Country A. Country
A can send a fleet to prevent this. Country A's fleet
has enough supplies to visit three contiguous inter-
sections, starting from A (e.g., Abcf). If it catches Country I's fleet (i.e., if
both countries stop for the night at the same intersection), it destroys the
fleet and wins the war. List the strategies of the two countries, and make a
payoff matrix for these strategies, assuming the winner gets 1 and the loser
−1. Eliminate dominated strategies to find the set of undominated strategies
for the two countries.

2.15 Strategic Voting

Three legislators are voting on whether to give themselves a pay raise. The
raise is worth b, but each legislator who votes for the raise incurs a cost of
voter resentment equal to $c < b$. The outcome is decided by majority rule.

a. Draw a game tree for the problem, assuming the legislators vote sequen-
    tially and publicly (i.e., the second voter sees the first's vote, and the
    third see the votes of the other two).
b. Find a Nash equilibrium for this game by using backward induction.
    Show that it is best to go first.
c. Show that there is a Nash equilibrium in which the third legislator votes
    no, whatever the other players do, and this equilibrium favors the third
    legislator. Why can't this equilibrium be found by backward induction?
    Is there something strange about this Nash equilibrium?

2.16 Eliminating Dominated Strategies *ad Absurdum*

Consider an n-player game in which each player announces simultaneously
an integer between 1 and 1000. The winner is the player whose announce-
ment is closest to 1/2 of the average of all the announcements. In the case
of a tie, the prize is given by a random draw among the winners.

a. Show that if players iterate the elimination of dominated strategies, the
    only remaining strategy is to announce 1.

b. To most people, this does not sound like what would actually happen if *n* people played this game, probably because people do, at most, a few iterations of dominated strategies. How many levels of iteration do you think people actually engage in?

c. Extra credit: Stage the game with some friends, with the payoff such that the winner receives $10.00. Can you estimate how many stages of elimination of dominated strategies people will go through?

2.17   Poker with Bluffing

Ollie and Stan decide to play the following game of poker. Each has a deck consisting of three cards, labeled H (high), M (medium), and L (low). Each puts $1 in the pot, chooses a card randomly from his deck, and does not show the card to his friend. Ollie (player 1) either stays, leaving the pot unchanged, or raises, adding $1 to the pot. Stan simultaneously makes the same decision. If both raise or both stay, the player with the higher card wins the pot (which contains $2 if they stayed and $4 if they raised), and if they tie, they just take their money back. If Ollie raises and Stan stays, then Ollie gets the $3 pot. However, if Stan raised and Ollie stayed, Ollie gets another chance. He can either drop, in which case Stan wins the $3 pot (only $1 of which is Ollie's), or he can call, adding $1 to the pot. Then, as before, the player with the higher card wins the pot, and with the same card, they take their money back. A game tree for Poker with Bluffing is depicted in Fig. 2.3 (the "?" in the figure means that the payoff depends on who has the higher card).

a. Show that Ollie has 64 pure strategies and Stan has eight pure strategies.
b. * Find the normal form game. Note that while Poker with Bluffing is a lot simpler than real poker, the normal form is nevertheless a 64 × 8 matrix! If you know computer programming solving this is not a hard task, however. (Recall that starred questions are more challenging and/or more time-consuming than others).
c. * Show that when you eliminate dominated strategies, there are only nine pure strategies left for Ollie and seven for Stan.
d. * Show that Ollie always raises with H or M on the second round, and drops with L.
e. * Suppose Stan sees Ollie's first move before deciding to stay or raise (i.e., the two nodes where Stan moves are separate information sets).

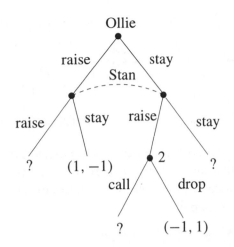

Figure 2.3. Poker with bluffing.

Now find the normal form game. Note that this matrix is 64×64, so calculating this by hand is quite prohibitive.

f. * Eliminate dominated strategies, and show that Ollie has only ten strategies left, while Stan has twelve.

g. * Show that Ollie always calls with a high card on the second round and Stan always raises with a high card.

2.18 The Centipede Game

Use backward induction to find a Nash equilibrium of the following game, which is called "Rosenthal's Centipede Game." The players, Mutt and Jeff, start out with $2 in each, and they alternate rounds. On the first round, Mutt can defect (D) by stealing $2 from Jeff, and the game is over. Otherwise, Mutt cooperates (C) by not stealing, and Nature gives Mutt $1. Then Jeff can defect (D) and steal $2 from Mutt, and the game is over, or he can cooperate (C), and Nature gives Jeff $1. This continues until one or the other defects, or each player has $100. The game tree is illustrated below. Show that the only Nash equilibrium compatible with backward induction has Mutt defecting on the first round.

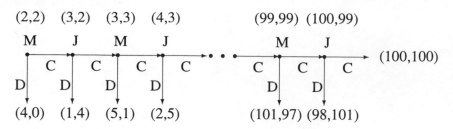

Now, of course, common sense tells you that this is not the way real players would act in this situation, and empirical evidence corroborates this intuition (McKelvey and Palfrey 1992). This issue surely merits further exploration, which we take up in chapter 5.

3

Playing It Straight: Pure Strategy Nash Equilibria

> Competition among agents . . . has merit solely as a device to extract information optimally. Competition per se is worthless.
> *Hölmstrom (1982)*

3.1 Introduction

A *pure strategy* Nash equilibrium of a game is a Nash equilibrium in which each player uses a pure, but not necessarily dominant, strategy. Not every game has a pure strategy Nash equilibrium. Indeed, there are even very simple 2×2 normal form games with no pure strategy Nash equilibria—for instance Throwing Fingers (§4.10), where the Nash equilibrium consists in throwing one finger half the time and two fingers the other half.

This chapter explores some of the more interesting applications of games with pure strategy equilibria. As you will see, we obtain extremely deep results in various branches of economic theory, including altruism in The Samaritan's Dilemma (§3.11) and The Rotten Kid Theorem (§3.12), the tragedy of the commons in The Klingons and the Snarks (§3.9), the existence of pure strategy equilibria in games of perfect information in Chess—The Trivial Pastime (§3.10), the tension between game theory and general equilibrium theory in Neoclassical Economics and Game Theory (§3.19), moral hazard in the insurance industry (§3.18), the real meaning of competition (it's not what you thought, if you've been properly socialized into neoclassical thinking) in Markets as Disciplining Devices: Allied Widgets (§3.20), honest signaling equilibria in The Truth Game (§3.21) and The Shopper and the Fish Merchant (§3.22), and the classical conception of common knowledge in Fathers and Sons (§3.23) and The Women of Sevitan (§3.24). Another feature of this chapter is its use of agent-based modeling, in Nature in Action: No-Draw, High-Low Poker (§3.16, to give students a feel for the dynamic properties of games that make the Nash equilibrium concept a plausible candidate for describing how the world works. Several

27

of these themes will be taken up in a more leisurely fashion in later chapters, but introducing them here shows the breadth of game-theoretic reasoning with an absolute minimum of technical tools.

The only materials that *must* be covered in this chapter are How to Value Lotteries (§3.14) and The Expected Utility Principle (§3.17), with Buying Fire Insurance (§3.18) being a nice application that uses up little class time. If students have not studied choice theory, it is useful to add material from §16.39 and §16.40 on the axiomatic foundations of expected utility and the so-called Allais and Ellsberg paradoxes. Also, from chapter 16, §16.41 is useful in dealing with the concepts of risk aversion and risk neutrality.

More substantively, §3.20 showcases game theory's ability to elucidate basic economic issues—in this case the nature of competition—that are totally opaque in neoclassical models (students should read the general critique in §3.19). Many of the problems are quite challenging in this chapter, so it is valuable to assign even those for which answers are available to students.

3.2 Pure Coordination Games

A *pure coordination game* is a game in which there is one pure strategy Nash equilibrium s that strictly Pareto-dominates all other Nash equilibria.[1]

a. Consider the game where you and your partner independently guess an integer between 1 and 5. If you guess the same number, you each win the amount of your guess. Otherwise you lose the amount of your guess. Show that this is a pure coordination game. HINT: Write down the normal form of this game and find the pure strategy Nash equilibria.
b. Consider a two-player game in which each player has two strategies. Suppose the payoff matrices for the two players are $\{a_{ij}\}$ for player 1 and $\{b_{ij}\}$ for player 2, where $i,j = 1,2$. Find the conditions on these payoff matrices for the game to be pure coordination game.

3.3 Competition on Main Street

The residents of Pleasantville live on Main Street, which is the only road in town. Two residents decide to set up general stores. Each can locate at any

---

[1]We say one allocation of payoffs *Pareto-dominates* another, or is *Pareto-superior* to another, if all players are at least as well off in the first as in the second, and at least one is better off. We say an allocation is *Pareto-efficient* or *Pareto-optimal* if it is not dominated by any other allocation. An allocation is *Pareto-inefficient* if it is not Pareto-efficient.

point between the beginning of Main Street, which we will label 0, and the end, which we will label 1 (if they locate at the same point, they move to opposite sides of the street). The two decide independently where to locate, and they must remain there forever. Each store will attract the customers who are closest to it, and the stores will share equally customers who are equidistant between the two. Thus, for instance, if one store locates at point x and the second at point $y > x$, then the first will get a share $x + (y - x)/2$ and the second will get a share $(1 - y) + (y - x)/2$ of the customers each day (draw a picture to help you see why). Each customer contributes $1.00 in profits each day to the general store it visits.

a. Define the actions, strategies, and daily payoffs to this game. Find the unique pure strategy Nash equilibrium.
b. Suppose there are three General Stores, each independently choosing a location point along the road (if they all choose the same point, two of them share a building). Show that there is no pure strategy Nash equilibrium.

3.4   A Pure Coordination Game

Three people independently choose an integer between zero and nine. If the three choices are the same, each person receives the amount chosen. Otherwise each person loses the amount the person chose.

a. What are the pure strategy Nash equilibria of this game?
b. How do you think people will actually play this game?
c. What does the game look like if you allow communication among the players before they make their choices? How would you model such communication, and how do you think communication would change the behavior of the players?

3.5   Twin Sisters

A mother has twin daughters who live in different towns. She tells each to ask for a certain whole number of dollars as a birthday present, and if the total of the two amounts does not exceed $101, each will have her request granted. Otherwise each gets nothing.

a. Find all the pure strategy Nash equilibria of this game.

b.   What do you think the twins will most likely do, assuming they cannot communicate? Why?

3.6   Variations on Duopoly

In a certain market there are two firms, which we label a and b. If the firms produce output q_a and q_b, then the price they will receive for their goods is given by $p = \alpha - \beta(q_a + q_b)$ or zero if p would otherwise be negative. Each firm has marginal cost $c > 0$ and no fixed costs. Suppose $\alpha > 3c$ (you'll see why we make this assumption as you go through the problem).

a.   Suppose the firms choose the quantity q_a and q_b independently in each period, without regard to their behavior in previous periods, and each maximizes profits $\pi_a = (p-c)q_a$ and $\pi_b = (p-c)q_b$. Find the unique pure strategy Nash equilibrium to this game. This is called the *Cournot duopoly* model.

b.   Suppose the two firms collude by agreeing that each will produce an amount $q^* = q_a = q_b$, and they have some way to enforce the agreement. What should they choose for q^*? What are the profits of the two firms? Compare this with the Cournot duopoly profits. This Nash equilibrium is called the *Monopoly model* or the *Cartel model*.

c.   Suppose firm a reneges on its promise in the previous part but b does not. What should a choose for q_a? What are a's profits, and what are b's profits?

d.   Suppose firm b finds out what firm a is going to do in the previous part, and chooses q_b to maximize profits, given what firm a is going to do. What is q_b now? What do you think happens if they go back and forth this way forever?

e.   Suppose the two firms choose price as opposed to quantity, where customers all go to the lowest-price firm, and the firms split the market if they choose the same price. What is the unique Nash equilibrium of this game? This is called the *Bertrand duopoly model*. Bertrand's result is often called a "paradox." In what sense do you think this is an accurate description of this solution? How do you explain the dramatic difference in outcomes between this and the Cournot model?

f.   Suppose firm a gets to choose its output first and only afterward does firm b get to choose its output. Find the equilibrium choices of q_a and q_b in this case, and compare the profits of the two firms with the Cournot duopoly case. This is called the *Stackelberg duopoly model*. HINT:

Firm a should find its profits for every q_a, given that firm b will choose q_b to maximize its profits given q_a. Then, among all these profits, firm a chooses q_a to maximize profits.

3.7 The Tobacco Market

The demand for tobacco is given by

$$q = 100000(10 - p),$$

where p is the price per pound. However, there is a government price support program for tobacco that ensures that the price cannot go under $0.25 per pound. Three tobacco farmers have each harvested 600,000 pounds of tobacco. Each must make an independent decision on how much to ship to the market and how much to discard.

a. Show that there are two Nash equilibria, one in which each farmer ships the whole crop, and a second in which each farmer ships 250,000 pounds and discards 350,000 pounds.

b. Are there any other Nash equilibria?

3.8 Price-Matching as Tacit Collusion

Bernie and Manny both sell VCRs, and both have per-unit costs of $250. They compete on price: the low price seller gets all the market, and they split the market if they have equal prices. Explain why the only Nash equilibrium has both firms charging $250, splitting the market, and making zero profit.

Suppose the monopoly price for VCRs (the price that maximizes the sum of the profits of both firms) is $300. Now suppose Bernie advertises that if a customer buys a VCR from him for $300 and discovers he or she can buy it cheaper at Manny's, Bernie will sell the customer the VCR with a rebate equal to twice the price difference between the two stores (e.g., if Manny charges $275, Bernie will give the customer a rebate of ($300 − $275) × 2 = $50). Suppose Manny does the same thing. Show that it is now Nash for both stores to charge $300. Conclusion: pricing strategies that seem to be super competitive can in fact be anticompetitive!

3.9 The Klingons and the Snarks

Two Klingons are eating from a communal cauldron of snarks. There are 1000 snarks in the cauldron, and the Klingons decide individually the rate r_i, $(i = 1, 2)$ at which they eat per eon. The net utility from eating snarks, which depends on both the amount eaten and the rate of consumption (too slow depletes the Klingon Reservoir, too fast overloads the Klingon Kishkes) is given by

$$u_i = 4q_i + 50r_i - r_i^2,$$

where q_i is the total number of snarks Klingon i eats. Since the two Klingons eventually eat all the snarks, $q_i = 1000r_i/(r_1 + r_2)$.

a. If they could agree on an optimal (and equal) rate of consumption, what would that rate be?

b. When they choose independently, what rate will they choose?

c. This problem illustrates the Tragedy of the Commons (Hardin 1968), in which a community (in this case the two Klingons, though it usually involves a larger number of individuals) overexploits a resource (in this case the bowl of snarks) because its members cannot control access to the resource. Some economists believe the answer is simple: the problem arises because no one owns the resource. So give an individual the right to control access to the resource, and let that individual sell the right to extract resources at a rate r to the users. To see this, suppose the cauldron of snarks is given to a third Master Klingon, and suppose the Master Klingon charges a diner a fixed number of Drecks (the Klingon monetary unit), chosen to maximize his profits, for the right to consume half the cauldron. Show that this will lead to an optimal rate of consumption.

This "create property rights in the resource" solution is not always satisfactory, however. First, it makes the new owner rich and everyone else poor. This could possibly be solved by obliging the new owner to pay the community for the right to control the resource. Second, it may not be possible to write a contract for the rate of resource use—the community as a whole may be better at controlling resource use than a single owner. Third, if there is unequal ability to pay among community members, the private property solution may lead to an unequal distribution of resources among community members. For a deeper analysis of these issues, see §11.4.4.

3.10   Chess—The Trivial Pastime

A *finite game* is a game with a finite number of nodes in its game tree. A game of *perfect information* is a game where every information set is a single node and Nature has no moves. In 1913 the famous mathematician Ernst Zermelo (1913) proved that in chess, either the first mover has a winning pure strategy, or the second mover has a winning pure strategy, or either player can force a draw. This proof was generalized by Harold Kuhn (1953), who proved that *every finite game of perfect information has a pure strategy Nash equilibrium*. In this problem you are asked to prove a special case of this—the game of chess.

a.   Give an example of a game that is not finite, a game that is not of perfect information, and a finite game that does not have a pure strategy Nash equilibrium.

b.   Chess is clearly a game of perfect information. It is also a finite game, since one of the rules is that if the board configuration is repeated three times, the game is a draw. Show that in chess, either Red has a winning strategy, or Black has a winning strategy, or both players have strategies that can force a draw.

So chess is formally a trivial game! But we know that this is not the case. Only brilliant and highly trained minds, or powerful computers, play chess well. The reason for this discrepancy between game theory and reality is that game theory assumes that agents can process any amount of information at zero cost. The average chess game involves about eighty moves, and the average number of possible choices at each move is about thirty, so there are roughly $30^{80} = 10^{120}$ different chess games. This amounts to about 10^{40} games for every fundamental particle in the universe (Colman 1995:294). So even the most powerful computer in the universe probably couldn't use backward induction to find a Nash equilibrium to chess.

3.11   The Samaritan's Dilemma

Many conservatives dislike Social Security and other forms of forced saving by means of which Big Brother (a.k.a. the government bureaucracy) prevents people from ending up in poverty in their old age. Some liberals respond by claiming that people are too short-sighted to manage their own retirement savings successfully. James Buchanan (1975) has made the insightful point that even if people are perfectly capable of managing their retirement savings, if we are altruistic toward others, we will force people to save more than they otherwise would.[2] Here is a simple model exhibiting his point.

A father and a daughter have current income $y > 0$ and $z > 0$, respectively. The daughter saves an amount s for her schooling next year, and receives an interest rate $r > 0$ on her savings. She also receives a transfer t from her father in the second period. Her utility function is $v(s, t) = v_1(z - s) + \delta v_2(s(1+r)+t)$, where $\delta > 0$ is a discount factor, v_1 is her first-period utility, and v_2 is her second-period utility. Her father has personal utility function $u(y)$, but he has degree $\alpha > 0$ of altruistic feeling for his daughter, so he acts to maximize $U = u(y - t) + \alpha v(s, t)$. Suppose all utility functions are increasing and concave, the daughter chooses s to maximize her utility, the father observes the daughter's choice of s, and then chooses t. Let (s^*, t^*) be the resulting equilibrium. Show that the daughter will save too little, in the sense that if the father can precommit to t^*, both she and her father would be better off. Show by example that if the father can precommit, he may precommit to an amount less than t^*.

HINT: Use backward induction, so for each s, the father chooses $t(s)$ to maximize U. Write the first-order condition for the father and differentiate totally with respect to s to show that $dt/ds < 0$. Then write the daughter's first-order condition. Suppose the equilibrium values of saving and transfer are s^* and t^*. Show that if the father can precommit to t^*, the daughter will now choose $s^{**} > s^*$, making both father and daughter better off.

For the example, let $u(\cdot) = v_1(\cdot) = v_2(\cdot) = \ln(\cdot)$.

3.12   The Rotten Kid Theorem

This problem is the core of Gary Becker's (1981) famous theory of the family. You might check the original, though, since I'm not sure I got the genders right.[3]

A certain family consists of a mother and a son, with increasing, concave utility functions $u(y)$ for the mother and $v(z)$ for the son. The son can affect

---

[2]By definition an *altruist* is an agent who takes actions that improve the fitness or material well-being of other agents when more self-interested actions are available.

[3]The Rotten Kid Theorem has been empirically tested and received some support, though the evidence falls short (often way short) of confirming that cross-generational families maximize joint income. See Cox 1987, 1990; Cox and Rank 1992; and Altonji et al. 1992, 1997.

both his income and that of the mother by choosing a level of familial work commitment a, so $y = y(a)$ and $z = z(a)$. The mother, however, feels a degree of altruism $\alpha > 0$ toward the son, so given y and z, she transfers an amount t to the son to maximize the objective function

$$u(y - t) + \alpha v(z + t). \qquad (3.1)$$

The son, however is perfectly selfish ("rotten"), and chooses the level of a to maximize his own utility $v(z(a) + t)$. However, he knows that his mother's transfer t depends on y and z, and hence on a.

a.   Use backward induction to show that the son chooses a to maximize total family income $y(a) + z(a)$.
b.   Show that t is an increasing function of α. Also, if we write $y = y(a) + \hat{y}$, then t is an increasing function of the mother's exogenous wealth $\hat{y}$.
c.   Show that for sufficiently small $\alpha > 0$, $t < 0$; i.e., the transfer is from the son to the mother.

HINT: For each a, the mother observes $y(a)$ and $z(a)$, and chooses $t = t(a)$ to maximize (3.1). This gives the first-order condition $-u' + \alpha v' = 0$. Differentiate this first-order condition with respect to a to show that the solution to the first-order condition for the maximization of $z(a) + t(a)$ is the same as for the maximization of $y(a) + z(a) = 0$.

3.13   The Illogic of Conflict Escalation

An auctioneer puts up \$$v$ >\$1, and $n > 1$ players compete for this prize as follows. Players take turns bidding in some fixed order. The bidding starts at \$0 and the player whose turn it is must either raise the bid by \$1 or drop out of the game, paying the auctioneer the amount of his last bid (or zero if he did not bid). The game ends when only one player remains. This player receives the prize, but *all* players pay their final bids to the auctioneer.

A strategy s_i for bidder i is to stay in the bidding until everyone else has dropped out, or until the level of bidding goes beyond s_i. Show that the Nash equilibria of this game all have the following form: one bidder i chooses $s_i \geq v$, and the others ($j \neq i$) all choose $s_j = 0$. Bidder i wins the prize and pays \$1.

This game was first analyzed by Martin Shubik (1971), who recognized that if two or more players were to bid positive amounts, they would continue to escalate their bids, even after the bidding goes higher than $v. Explain why this is so.

This game has been run in an experimental setting several times, and, indeed, players enter the betting and lose considerable sums of money. Moreover, even after the experience of sustaining losses, many willingly play again, and again escalate to the point of sustaining considerable losses! The history of Shubik's game is nicely analyzed by Colman (1995:191ff), who calls it the Macbeth Effect, quoting Shakespeare: "I am in blood/Stepped in so far that, should I wade no more,/Returning were as tedious as go o'er" (*Macbeth*, III, iv).

On a more prosaic note, now suppose there are two players and there is a positive probability $p \in (0, 1)$ that the game will terminate spontaneously with probability p on each bid. Upon termination, both players pay their final bids, and the higher bidder wins the prize. If you have a long weekend, or you have something like Mathematica, you can show that there is a Nash equilibrium in which both players enter the bidding and continue raising the bid until the game spontaneously ends. The condition for player 1 is simply that $v > 2/p$, while the condition for player 2 is more complicated.

3.14 How to Value Lotteries

What about games in which a stochastic event determines the payoffs to the players? While some players may know the outcome of the event, others may not. To get the payoffs for the ignorant players, we must somehow combine the various payoffs and their probabilities into one composite measure for each terminal node of the game tree. We do this using the expected utility principle, which we now describe.

The *expected value* of a lottery is the sum of the payoffs, where each payoff is weighted by the probability that the payoff will occur. Consider the lottery in pane (a) of Fig. 3.1, where p is the probability of winning amount a and $1 - p$ is the probability of winning amount b. The expected value of the lottery is then $pa + (1 - p)b$. Note that we model a lottery a lot like an extensive form game—except there is only one player.

Consider the lottery with the three payoffs shown in pane (b) of Fig. 3.1. Here p is the probability of winning amount a, q is the probability of winning amount b, and $1 - p - q$ is the probability of winning amount c. The expected value of lottery is $pa + qb + (1 - p - q)c$.

The value of a lottery with n payoffs is given in pane (c) of Fig. 3.1. The prizes are now $a_1, \ldots, a_n$ with probabilities $p_1, \ldots, p_n$, respectively. The expected value of the lottery is now $p_1a_1 + p_2a_2 + \ldots + p_na_n$. We should note that there are also *compound lotteries*, where the payoff to one lottery is another lottery, and so on. The expected value of a compound lottery is found by "pruning the lottery tree," replacing lotteries at the end by their expected values, then moving back to an earlier level, and so on until there is just one grand lottery.

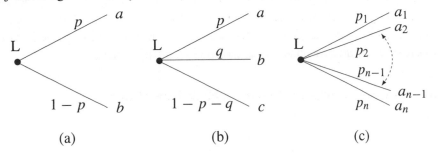

Figure 3.1. Lotteries with two, three, and n potential outcomes.

3.14.1 Where's Jack?

As an exercise in evaluating lotteries, consider the following game. Manny moves first and wins with probability 30%. If Manny does not win, Moe moves and wins with probability 1/2. If Moe does not win on this move, Manny moves again and wins with probability 40%. Otherwise, Moe wins. The winner receives $100. What is Manny's expected payoff in this game?

3.15 Payoffs in Games Where Nature Moves

In §1.3 we defined the payoff structure of an extensive form game, assuming there were no moves by Nature. We can now extend this definition to the case where there are moves by Nature. For every terminal node $t \in T$, there is a unique path $\mathbf{p}_t$ in the game tree from the root node to t. We say $\mathbf{p}_t$ is *compatible* with strategy profile s if, for every branch b on $\mathbf{p}_t$, if player i moves at b^h (the head node of b), then s_i chooses action b at b^h. If $\mathbf{p}_t$ is not compatible with s, we write $p_i(s, t) = 0$. If $\mathbf{p}_t$ is compatible with s, we define $p_i(s, t)$ to be the product of all the probabilities associated with the nodes of $\mathbf{p}_t$ at which Nature moves along $\mathbf{p}_t$, or 1 if Nature makes no moves along $\mathbf{p}_t$. We now define the payoff to player i as

$$\pi_i(s) = \sum_{t \in T} p_i(s, t) \pi_i(t). \tag{3.2}$$

Note that this is the expected payoff to player i given strategy profile s, assuming that Nature's choices are independent, so that $p_i(s, t)$ is just the probability that path $\mathbf{p}_t$ is followed, given strategy profile s. We generally assume in game theory that players attempt to maximize their expected payoffs, as defined in (3.2). This is compatible with the expected utility principle, provided the payoffs are valued in utility terms.

3.16   Nature in Action: No-Draw, High-Low Poker

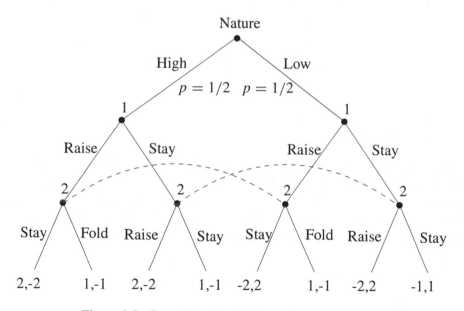

Figure 3.2. Game Tree for No-Draw, High-Low Poker

Suppose there are two card players. The deck of cards only has two types of card in equal numbers: High and Low. Each player puts \$1 in the pot. Player 1 is dealt a card (by Nature). After viewing the card, which Player 2 cannot see, he either Raises or Stays. Player 2 can Stay or Fold if Player 1 Raises, and can Raise or Stay if Player 1 Stays. If Player 1 Raises, he puts an additional \$1 in the pot. If Player 2 responds by Folding, he looses, and if he responds by Staying, he must put an additional $1 in the pot. If Player 1 Stays and Player 2 Raises, both must put an additional $1 in the pot. If the game ends without Player 2 Folding, Player 1 wins the pot if he has a High card, and loses the pot if he has a Low card. Each player's objective is to maximize the expected value of his winnings. The game tree is in fig. 3.2

We now define strategies for each of the players. Player 1 has two information sets (each one a node) and two choices at each. This gives four strategies, which we label RR, RS, SR, and SS. These mean "Raise no matter what," "Raise with High, Stay with Low," "Stay with High, Raise with Low," and "Stay no matter what." Player 2 also has two information sets, one where Player 1 Raises, and one where Player 1 Stays. We denote his four strategies SR, SS, FR, and FS. These mean "Stay if Player 1 Raises, Raise if Player 1 Stays," "Stay no matter what," "Fold if Player 1 Raises, Raise if Player 1 Stays," and "Fold if Player 1 Raises, Stay if Player 1 Stays." To find the normal form game, we first assume Nature gives Player 1 a High card. Then we have the following payoffs:

Nature Plays High

	SR	SS	FR	FS
RR	2,-2	2,-2	1,-1	1,-1
RS	2,-2	2,-2	1,-1	1,-1
SR	2,-2	1,-1	2,-2	1,-1
SS	2,-2	1,-1	2,-2	1,-1

If Nature gives Player 1 a Low card, then we have the following payoffs:

Nature Plays Low

	SR	SS	FR	FS
RR	-2,2	-2,2	1,-1	1,-1
RS	-2,2	-1,1	-2,2	-1,1
SR	-2,2	-2,2	1,-1	1,-1
SS	-2,2	-1,1	-2,2	-1,1

The expected values of the payoffs for the two players are simply the averages of the two matrices of payoffs above, since Nature chooses High or Low each with probability 1/2. We have

Expected Value Payoffs

	SR	SS	FR	FS
RR	0,0	0,0	1,-1	1,-1
RS	0,0	0.5,-0.5	-0.5,0.5	0,0
SR	0,0	-0.5,0.5	1.5,-1.5	1,-1
SS	0,0	0,0	0,0	0,0

Some strategies in this game can be dropped by the iterated elimination of weakly dominated strategies. For Player 1, RR dominates SS, and then for Player 2, SR dominates FS. It is quite straightforward to check that $\{RR,SR\}$ is a Nash equilibrium, and a box-by-box check shows that there are no other pure strategy equilibria. Note that the game is fair: Player 1 Raises no matter what, and Player 2 Stays if Player 1 Raises, and Raises if Player 1 Stays.

3.16.1   Simulating No-Draw High-Low Poker

The heavy emphasis on finding Nash equilibria in evolutionary game theory flows from two assertions. First, the equilibria of dynamic evolutionary games are always Nash equilibria (§9.6). Second, the evolutionary process does not require high-level rationality from the agents who populate dynamic evolutionary games. We can illustrate both points by simulating the dynamics of No-Draw, High-Low Poker on the computer. In this *agent-based simulation*, I created 100 Player 1 types and 100 Player 2 types, each programmed to play exactly one pure strategy, assigned randomly to them. In each round of play, Player 1's and Player 2's are randomly paired and they play No-Draw High-Low poker once. Every hundred rounds we allow reproduction to take place. Reproduction consisted in killing off five percent of the players of each type with the lowest scores, and allowing the top five percent of players with the highest score to reproduce and take the place of the defunct low scorers. However with a one percent probability, a newly-born player 'mutates' by using some randomly-chosen other strategy. The simulation ran for 50,000 rounds. The results of one run of the simulations for the distribution of player 2 types in the economy are shown in fig. 3.3. Note that the Nash strategy for Player 2 slowly but surely wins out, and the other strategies remain at very low levels, though they cannot disappear altogether because mutations constantly occur to replenish their ranks.

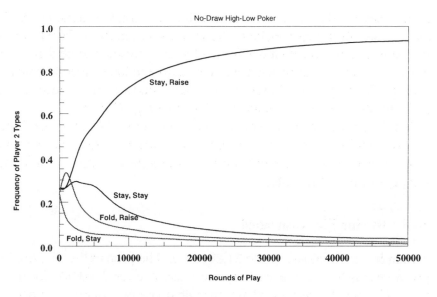

Figure 3.3. Agent-Based Simulation of No-Draw, High-Low Poker

3.17 The Expected Utility Principle

A *lottery l* is defined to be a set of *payoffs* $x_1, \ldots, x_n \in \mathbf{R}$ with probabilities $p_1, \ldots, p_n \in \mathbf{R}$, where each $p_i \geq 0$, and $\sum_i p_i = 1$. The *expected value* of the lottery l is defined to be

$$\mathbf{E}[l] = \sum_{i=1}^{n} p_i x_i.$$

Suppose an agent has a utility function $u(x)$ where $x \in \mathbf{R}$ (for instance, x could be money). The Expected Utility Principle says that the value of the lottery to the agent is given by

$$u(l) = \mathbf{E}_l[u(x)] = \sum_{i=1}^{n} p_i u(x_i),$$

in the sense that if asked to choose among a number of lotteries, the agent will choose the lottery that maximizes $u(l) = \mathbf{E}_l[u(x)]$.

The Expected Utility Principle is true, provided the agent has preferences over lotteries that satisfy a few prima facie reasonable properties, which we develop in §16.39 for the interested reader. These axioms are plausible, but there is nevertheless clear evidence that human beings systematically violate them. The culprit may well be the transitivity axiom itself. People appear to evaluate lotteries as deviations from what they consider to be their "current position," and are, for instance, more sensitive to losses than to gains. This leads to "framing effects" and other anomalies that are discussed in chapter 11 and §16.40, as well as Machina (1987) and Kreps (1990).

Despite its systematic deviation from actual human behavior, the Expected Utility Principle is the best we've got, and it will have to do until a serviceable alternative is worked out. So unless otherwise stated, we assume the Expected Utility Principle.

3.18   Buying Fire Insurance

A man has a warehouse worth $1,200,000. The probability of a fire in any given year is 5%, and he can buy fire insurance for $100,000 for the year. Should he buy the insurance? We must compare two lotteries. Suppose first the man is risk neutral, with linear utility function $u(x) = x$ (§16.41) (we say a function $f(x)$ is *linear* or *affine* if there are some constants $a, b \in \mathbf{R}$ such that $f(x) = ax + b$ holds for all $x \in \mathbf{R}$). Then the man's decision problem is as follows:

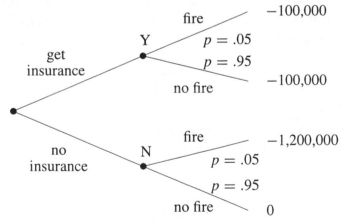

The value of the lottery if he gets insurance is −$100,000, and if he does not, it is 5% × −$1,200,000= −$60,000. Thus, he should not buy the insurance.

Suppose now the agent is risk averse (§16.41), with utility function

$$u(x) = \ln(1300000 + x).$$

Then the value of the lottery when buying insurance is $\ln(1200000) = 14.00$, and the value when not buying insurance is $5\% \times \ln(100000) + 95\% \times \ln(1300000) = 0.05(11.512925) + 0.95(14.08) = 13.95$. Since $14.00 > 13.95$, now he should buy the insurance.

3.19   Neoclassical Economics and Game Theory

By *neoclassical economics* I mean the Walrasian general equilibrium model, as developed by Kenneth Arrow, Gérard Debreu, Frank Hahn, Tjalling Koopmans, and others (Arrow 1951, Arrow and Hahn 1971, Koopmans 1957). In this model, firms and households make decisions based on commodity and factor prices, markets generate prices that equate supply and demand, and ownership rules assign the return to factor inputs to individuals. Under a suitable set of assumptions, the so-called *Fundamental Theorem of Welfare Economics* holds: Every competitive equilibrium is Pareto-optimal (i.e., there is no way to improve the welfare of one agent without lowering the welfare of some other agent), and every attainable distribution of welfare among agents can be achieved by a suitable initial distribution of property rights, followed by competitive exchange.

We present a strong critique of neoclassical economics at various points in this book (§§3.20, 6.14, 6.15, 6.16), but it is important to note that this is *not* a critique of general equilibrium theory as a field of contemporary economic research. Indeed, many contemporary general equilibrium theorists would agree with variants of this critique and are working toward better models.[4] The future may well bring us a synthesis of general equilibrium and game theory combining the strengths of the two approaches (global interdependence on the one hand, and strategic interaction on the other). Such a synthesis may look more like an ecological and/or thermodynamic system than the mechanical system envisaged by Walras and his followers.[5]

---

[4]See, for instance, Foley 1994, Geanakoplos and Polemarchakis 1996 , Geanakoplos 1996, Magill and Quinzii 1996, and especially Magill and Quinzii 1999.

[5]There currently exist certain formal relations between general equilibrium and game theory. For instance, one of the earliest general equilibrium existence theorems (Debreu 1952) models the economy as a game in which market clearing is a Nash equilibrium. Moreover, many models treat competitive equilibria as the limit of some type of game equilibrium, and the general equilibrium model is closely related to certain general bargaining and social choice models (Chichilnisky 1997).

Neoclassical economics asserts that the Walrasian general equilibrium model is an ideal type with "perfect information," and "complete contracting," of which real economies, with their "imperfect information" and "incomplete contracting," are imperfect realizations. An argument of this type is quite acceptable in physics, where the ideal type can be shown to hold in the absence of confounding factors, and where the confounding factors can themselves be modeled in terms of ideal type laws. But in economics, the ideal type laws have no independent physical or social existence, and they do not provide a basis for modeling the confounding factors. In addition, neoclassical economics generally renders the model more palatable by attributing to it qualities that it in fact does not have, such as uniqueness and stability of equilibrium, downward sloping demand curves, and a plausible price adjustment mechanism.

It might be argued that neoclassical economics deals with the "broad outline" of the economy and game theory with the "fine detail." However, neoclassical economics cannot even explain (a) why market economies require private ownership; (b) why central planning cannot substitute for private markets in allocating resources; (c) why there is generally an excess supply of labor and an excess demand for capital; (d) why most firms are quantity constrained and increase profits by expanding sales in a market where price exceeds marginal cost; and (e) why the wealthy control production and investment. Moreover, in each case game-theoretic models do much better in explaining empirical regularities. These themes are explored here and in §§3.20, 6.14, 6.15, 6.16.

The Fundamental Theorem is often considered a justification for a private-ownership market economy. In fact, as Oskar Lange and others (Barone 1935, Lange and Taylor 1938) demonstrated in the famous "socialism debate" with Friedrich von Hayek and other supporters of laissez faire capitalism (Hayek 1935) in the 1930s, these principles can just as easily be used to justify the social ownership of property and the control of the economy by the state. Indeed, the Fundamental Theorem asserts that *any* pattern of ownership is compatible with economic efficiency, so long as prices are chosen to equate supply and demand. Moreover, such prices need not be set by market interactions or any other particular mechanism—price-setting by a central planner is perfectly compatible with economic efficiency.

Lange pointed out that markets and private property play a purely metaphorical role in the neoclassical model: they are *alluded to* to account for profit maximization and market clearing, but they play no formal role, and many other institutional forms can just as easily be alluded to to account for the same events. There is, in fact, no competition in the common sense of the term, since *agents never meet other agents* and *agents do not care what other agents are doing*. The only factors determining individual behavior in the neoclassical model are prices.

Nor do markets do anything in the neoclassical model. In Léon Walras's original work (Walras 1954 [1874]), prices move to eliminate excess demand in all markets before any trade actually takes place. Thus, market clearing is not brought about by markets at all, but rather what later writers in the tradition have called an "auctioneer" who calls out prices, measures the degree of excess supply and demand in all markets, adjusts prices accordingly, and repeats the process until equilibrium prices are determined. The auctioneer then freezes these equilibrium prices, and agents are allowed to trade freely at these prices. How ironic! Not the buzzing confusion of market competition, but the cool hand of the centralized state apparatus brings about "market" equilibrium.

Well, you might reply, we've come a long way since Walras wrote down his set of equations a century and a quarter ago. Surely someone has provided a plausible decentralized, market-oriented equilibration mechanism to replace the auctioneer. But in fact, no one has succeeded in producing a plausible dynamic model of market interaction in which prices move toward their market-clearing levels. Only under implausible assumptions can even the "auctioneer" dynamic be shown to be stable (Fisher 1983). Moreover, for any possible (continuous) behavior of excess demand as a function of price— even the most chaotic and complex, stable or unstable—there is some set of preferences and an initial endowment that gives rise to this behavior, and the preferences need not be "exotic" at all to generate this behavior (Saari 1995).

The socialists won the academic debate, virtually everyone agrees. Joseph Schumpeter's classic *Capitalism, Socialism and Democracy* (1942), in which this staunch supporter of capitalism predicts its imminent demise, is perhaps the greatest tribute to the socialist victory in this debate. Hayek himself apparently concluded that it had been a mistake to conduct the debate in neoclassical terms, and in the late 1930s and early 1940s developed the analytical foundations of an alternative (Hayek 1945). But, the socialists lost the real-world conflict of economic systems. Therefore, there must be something fundamentally wrong with the neoclassical model. What?

We discuss specific problems with the neoclassical model in §3.20 and §6.14, but we might note more broadly that the general equilibrium model is inspired by field-theoretic formulations of Newtonian mechanics, in which particles create force fields (electromagnetic, gravitational, and the like), and each particle interacts with the field. In general equilibrium theory, we replace particles by people, and the field becomes the price system. But, in fact, society involves, centrally and probably irreducibly, the strategic interaction of agents. It is interesting to note that physics, too, has replaced field-theoretic models with models of particle interaction on the most fundamental level.

3.20   Markets as Disciplining Devices: Allied Widgets

The neoclassical model (§3.19) assumes contracts are costlessly enforceable. Without such contracts, and if producers have information concerning production that is not available to the Planning Board in the socialist state (or equivalently to the Walrasian auctioneer), strategic interaction in the form of market competition may be necessary to elicit the knowledge that leads to high productivity.

In effect, under the proper circumstances, market competition subjects firms to a "prisoner's dilemma" in which it is in the interest of each producer to supply high effort, even in cases where consumers and the planner cannot observe or contract for effort itself. This is the meaning of Bengt Hölmstrom's quotation at the head of this chapter.

If Hölmstrom is right—and both game-theoretic modeling and practical experience indicates that he is—the defense of competitive markets in neoclassical economics is a great intellectual irony. Since Adam Smith, supporters of the market system have defended markets on the grounds that they allocate goods and services efficiently. Much to the consternation of those who take empirical facts seriously, the estimation of the "Harberger triangles" that represent the losses from misallocation, monopoly, tariffs, quotas, and the like have little effect on per capita income or the growth rate (Browning 1997). The real benefits of competition, by contrast, have only come to light with the development of game-theoretic models of competitive interactions, of which the following problem is a fine example.

Allied Widgets has two possible constant returns to scale production techniques: fission and fusion. For each technique, Nature decides in each period whether marginal cost is 1 or 2. With probability $\theta \in (0, 1)$, marginal cost is

1. Thus, if fission is high cost in a given production period, the manager can use fusion, which will be low cost with probability θ. However, it is costly for the manager to inspect the state of Nature, and if he fails to inspect, he will miss the opportunity to try fusion if the cost of fission is high.

Allied's owner cannot tell whether the manager inspected or not, but she does know the resulting marginal cost, and can use this to give an incentive wage to the manager. Fig. 3.4 shows the manager's decision tree, assuming the manager is paid a wage w_1 when marginal costs are low and w_2 when marginal costs are high, the cost of inspecting is α, and the manager has a logarithmic utility function over income: $u(w) = \ln w$.[6]

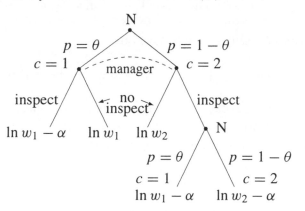

Figure 3.4. The Allied Widgets problem.

To induce the manager to inspect the fission process, the owner decides to pay the manager a wage w_1 if marginal cost is low, and $w_2 < w_1$ if marginal cost is high. But how should the owner choose w_1 and w_2 to maximize profits?[7] Suppose the manager's payoff is $\ln w$ if he does not inspect, $\ln w - \alpha$ if he inspects, and $\ln w_o$ if he doesn't take the job at all—in this case, w_o is called the manager's *reservation wage* or *fallback position*.

The expression that must be satisfied for a wage pair (w_1, w_2) to induce the manager to inspect the fission process is called the *incentive compatibility constraint*. To find this expression, note that the probability of using a low

---

[6]The logarithmic utility function is a reasonable choice, since it implies constant relative risk aversion; i.e., the fraction of wealth an agent desires to put in a particular risky security is independent of wealth.

[7]This problem introduces the *principal-agent model*, which is developed at greater length in chapter 14.

cost technique if the manager does not inspect is θ, so the payoff to the manager from not inspecting (by the Expected Utility Principle) is

$$\theta \ln w_1 + (1 - \theta) \ln w_2.$$

If the manager inspects, both techniques will turn out to be high cost with probability $(1 - \theta)^2$, so the probability that at least one of the techniques is low cost is $1 - (1 - \theta)^2$. Thus, the payoff to the manager from inspecting (again by the Expected Utility Principle) is

$$[1 - (1 - \theta)^2] \ln w_1 + (1 - \theta)^2 \ln w_2 - \alpha.$$

The incentive compatibility constraint is then

$$\theta \ln w_1 + (1 - \theta) \ln w_2 \leq [1 - (1 - \theta)^2] \ln w_1 + (1 - \theta)^2 \ln w_2 - \alpha.$$

Since there is no reason to pay the manager more than absolutely necessary to get him to inspect, we can assume this is an equality,[8] in which case the constraint reduces to $\theta(1 - \theta) \ln[w_1/w_2] = \alpha$, or

$$w_1 = w_2 e^{\frac{\alpha}{\theta(1-\theta)}}.$$

For instance, suppose $\alpha = 0.4$ and $\theta = 0.8$. Then $w_1 = 12.18 w_2$—the manager must be paid more than twelve times as much in the good state as in the bad!

But the owner must also pay the manager enough so that it is worthwhile taking the job, rather than taking the fallback w_o. The expression that must be satisfied for a wage pair (w_1, w_2) to induce the manager to take the job is called the *participation constraint*. In our case, the participation constraint is

$$[1 - (1 - \theta)^2] \ln w_1 + (1 - \theta)^2 \ln w_2 - \alpha \geq \ln w_o.$$

Assuming this is an equality, and using the Incentive Compatibility Constraint, we find $w_o = w_2 e^{\alpha/(1-\theta)}$, so

$$w_2 = w_o e^{-\frac{\alpha}{(1-\theta)}}, \qquad w_1 = w_o e^{\frac{\alpha}{\theta}}.$$

---

[8]Actually, this point may not be obvious, and is false in the case of repeated principal-agent models, such as that of §6.15. It is proved for one-shot principal-agent models in §14.7. This remark applies also to our assumption that the participation constraint, defined below, is satisfied as an equality.

Using the above illustrative numbers, and assuming $w_o = 1$, this gives

$$w_2 = 0.14, \qquad w_1 = 1.65.$$

The expected cost of the managerial incentives to the owner is

$$[1 - (1 - \theta)^2]w_1 + (1 - \theta)^2 w_2 = w_o \left[\theta(2 - \theta)e^{\frac{\alpha}{\theta}} + (1 - \theta)^2 e^{-\frac{\alpha}{(1-\theta)}} \right].$$

Again, using our illustrative numbers, this gives expected cost

$$0.96(1.65) + 0.04(0.14) = 1.59.$$

So where does competition come in? Suppose Allied has a competitor, Axis Widgets, subject to the same conditions of production. In particular, whatever marginal cost structure Nature imposes on Allied, Nature also imposes on Axis. Suppose also that the managers in the two firms cannot collude. We can show that *Allied's owner can write a Pareto-efficient contract for the manager using Axis's marginal cost as a signal, satisfying both the participation and incentive compatibility constraints, and thereby increasing profits.* They can do this by providing incentives that subject the managers to a prisoner's dilemma, in which the dominant strategy is to defect, which in this case means to inspect fission in search of a low cost production process.

To see this, consider the following payment scheme, used by both the Axis and the Allied owners, where $\phi = 1 - \theta + \theta^2$, and the parameters β and γ are defined arbitrarily, but such that $\gamma < -\alpha(1 - \theta + \theta^2)/\theta(1 - \theta)$ and $\beta > \alpha(2 - \phi)/(1 - \phi)$. This gives rise to the payoffs to the manager shown in the table, where the example uses $\alpha = 0.4$, $\theta = 0.8$, and $w_0 = 1$.

Allied Cost	Axis Cost	Allied Wage	Example
$c = 1$	$c = 1$	$w^* = w_0 e^\alpha$	$w^* = 1.49$
$c = 2$	$c = 2$	$w^* = w_0 e^\alpha$	$w^* = 1.49$
$c = 1$	$c = 2$	$w^+ = w_0 e^\beta$	$w^+ = 13.00$
$c = 2$	$c = 1$	$w^- = w_0 e^\gamma$	$w^- = 0.10$

We will show that the manager will always inspect, and the owner's expected wage payment is w^*, which merely pays the manager the equivalent of the fallback wage. Here is the normal form for the game between the two managers.

	Inspect	Shirk
Inspect	$\ln w^* - \alpha$ $\ln w^* - \alpha$	$\phi \ln w^* + (1 - \phi) \ln w^+ - \alpha$ $\phi \ln w^* + (1 - \phi) \ln w^-$
Shirk	$\phi \ln w^* + (1 - \phi) \ln w^-$ $\phi \ln w^* + (1 - \phi) \ln w^+ - \alpha$	$\ln w^*$ $\ln w^*$

Why is this so? The Inspect, Inspect box is obvious. The Inspect, Shirk box is the case where the Axis manager checks, but the Allied manager does not. Then we have the following situation (writing c_a for allied costs and c_x for Axis costs):

Event	Probability	Outcome	Allied Wage
$c = 1$	θ	$c_a = 1, c_x = 1$	$w_o e^\alpha$
$c = 2, c = 1$	$\theta(1 - \theta)$	$c_a = 2, c_x = 1$	$w_o e^\gamma$
$c = 2, c = 2$	$(1 - \theta)^2$	$c_a = 2, c_x = 2$	$w_o e^\alpha$.

Thus, the expected utility of the Allied manager who does not inspect is

$$[\theta + (1 - \theta)^2] \ln w^* + (1 - \theta)\theta \ln w^-,$$

and the expected utility of the Axis manager who does inspect, is

$$[\theta + (1 - \theta)^2] \ln w^* + (1 - \theta)\theta \ln w^+ - \alpha.$$

The Shirk, Shirk box is easier. Assuming that the managers choose their technologies in the same order, both have either low costs or high costs. Hence their payoff is $\ln w^*$.

To show that this is a prisoner's dilemma, we need only show that

$$\ln w^* - \alpha > \phi \ln w^* + (1 - \phi) \ln w^-$$

and

$$\phi \ln w^* + (1 - \phi) \ln w^+ - \alpha > \phi \ln w^* + (1 - \phi) \ln w^0.$$

The first of these becomes

$$\ln w_o > \phi \ln w_o + \phi\alpha + (1 - \phi) \ln w_o + (1 - \phi)\gamma,$$

or $\gamma < -\phi\alpha/(1 - \phi)$, which is true by assumption. The second becomes

$$\ln w^+ > \frac{\alpha}{1 - \phi} + \ln w^*.$$

or $\beta > \alpha \frac{2-\phi}{1-\phi}$, which is also true by assumption.

Note that in our numerical example the cost to the owner is $w^* = 1.49$, and the incentives for the managers are given by the normal form matrix

	Inspect	Shirk
Inspect	0 0	0.56 −1.06
Shirk	−1.06 0.55	0.224 0.224

This example shows that markets may be disciplining devices in the sense that they reduce the cost involved in providing the incentives for agents to act in the interests of their employers or clients, even where enforceable contracts cannot be written—in this case, there can be no enforceable contract for managerial inspecting. Note that in this example, even though managers are risk averse (§16.41), imposing a structure of competition between the managers means each inspects and the cost of incentives is no greater than if a fully specified and enforceable contract for inspecting could be written.

Of course, if we weaken some of the assumptions, Pareto-optimality will no longer be attainable. For instance, suppose when a technique is low cost for one firm, it is not necessarily low cost for the other, but rather is low cost with probability $q > 1/2$. Then competition between managers has an element of uncertainty, and optimal contracts will expose the managers to a positive level of risk, so their expected payoff must be greater than their fallback.

3.21 The Truth Game

A customer shows interest in a used car and asks the salesman, "Is this a good car for the money?" The salesman wants to sell the car, but doesn't want to ruin his reputation by lying. How do you model the strategies followed by the salesman in answering, and by the customer in evaluating his response? Here is one way.

Consider the following game, with players 1,2, and N (Nature). Nature flips a coin, and it comes out H with probability $p = 0.8$ and T with probability $p = 0.2$. Player 1 sees the result, but player 2 does not. Player 1 announces to player 2 that the coin came out either H or T. Then player 2 announces either h or t. The payoffs are as follows: player 1 receives $1 for telling the truth, and $2 for inducing player 2 to choose h. Player 2 receives $1 for making a correct guess, and zero otherwise.

a. Explain how this illustrates the used car salesman situation.
b. Draw a game tree for the problem, and describe the strategy sets for the two players.
c. What is the corresponding normal form game?
d. Use elimination of dominated strategies to reduce the number of viable strategies.
e. Find all the pure strategy Nash equilibria. What is the social interpretation of these equilibria? Are any Pareto-inferior to others?
f. How would you expect the set of equilibria to change if you changed the probabilities or payoffs in particular ways?

3.22   The Shopper and the Fish Merchant

A shopper encounters a fish merchant. The shopper looks at a piece of fish and asks the merchant, "Is this fish fresh?" Suppose the fish merchant knows whether the fish is fresh or not, and the shopper only knows that the probability that any particular piece of fish is fresh is 1/2. The merchant can then answer the question either "yes" or "no." The shopper, upon hearing this response, can either buy the fish or wander on.

Suppose both parties are *risk neutral* (i.e., they have linear utility functions, and hence maximize the expected value of lotteries), with utility functions $u(x) = x$, where x is an amount of money. Suppose the price of the fish is $1, the value of a fresh fish to the shopper is $2 (i.e., this is the maximum the shopper would pay for fresh fish), and the value of fish that is not fresh is zero. Suppose the fish merchant must throw out the fish if it is not sold, but keeps the $1 profit if she sells the fish. Finally, suppose the merchant has a reputation to uphold and loses $0.50 when she lies, regardless of the shopper's action.

a. Draw an extensive form for the game. Make sure the information sets are shown, as well as the payoffs.
b. Find the normal form for the game, and list all strategies. HINT: Draw the normal forms for the two separate cases good fish/bad fish, and use the expected utility principle.
c. Find the Nash equilibria of the game. HINT: Use elimination of dominated strategies.

3.23   Fathers and Sons

Classical game theory assumes that all knowledge is common knowledge, except for specific pieces of information that are known asymmetrically (e.g., which bottle has the poison in it), in the strong sense discussed in §1.5: everyone knows the rules, everyone knows that everyone knows the rules, everyone knows that everyone knows everyone knows the rules, and so on ad infinitum. There are some amusing (although questionably empirically important) games that have Nash equilibria that depend upon the depth of recursion of "who knows who knows what." This and the next problem explore this issue.

An honest but mischievous father tells his two risk-neutral sons that he has placed $10, $100, $1,000, or $10,000, all with equal probability, in an envelope, and ten times that much money in another envelope. He gives one envelope to each son. One son finds $10,000 and the second $1,000. The father takes each aside and asks him privately if he would like to switch. Each says "yes." The father reports each of these statements to the other brother. How many times must the father repeat this process before one of the sons says "no." Carefully explain your answer.

3.24   The Women of Sevitan

The Sevitan live as monogamous families in a small village where virtually everyone knows what everyone else is doing, virtually all the time. The only informational asymmetry is that no wife knows if her own husband is philandering, although every wife knows the behavior of every other husband in the village. The penalty for a philandering husband is to be branded by his wife with a purple *P* on the forehead in the middle of the night while sleeping. This penalty is only imposed by a wife who knows with certainty that her husband is guilty.

Needless to say, no husband is ever branded. But one day a woman from another village comes to visit. Upon leaving the next day, she confides in the women of Sevitan that there is at least one philanderer in the village. Nothing happens for five days. But on the sixth night a certain number of husbands are branded with the purple *P*. How many husbands are branded? How many philandering husbands are there? How could this happen, since the departing woman didn't tell the Sevitan women anything they didn't know already—that there is at least one philanderer in their midst?

4

Catching 'em Off Guard: Mixed Strategy Nash Equilibria

Float like a butterfly, sting like a bee.

Mohammed Ali

4.1 Introduction

Have you ever wondered why so many of God's creatures are bilaterally symmetric? Well, one reason is that most such creatures must chase and/or flee predators. The fox, for instance, is faster than the rabbit, but the rabbit can change direction faster than the fox. Suppose the rabbit were strong on the left side and weak on the right side. Then it would easily jump to the right, but with difficulty to the left. Thus, it would mostly jump to the right. Knowing that the rabbit will jump to the right, the fox will trail the rabbit with a bias to the right, and with a predisposition to jump right, thus making the benefit of jumping right less valuable to the rabbit. But then mutant rabbits that reversed this pattern of strength and weakness would more likely survive, driving out the existing rabbits. And so on. In equilibrium, the rabbit would be bilaterally symmetric, as would the fox. So, mixed strategies, limiting an opponent's options by mixing up one's actions, are of fundamental importance in strategic interaction.

Even though defined as though played a single time, games with mixed strategy equilibria can rarely be properly understood except in terms of repeated interactions. A few games, such as Throwing Fingers (§4.10), One-Card Two-Round Poker with Bluffing (§4.11), and Tennis Strategy (§4.18) can be thought of as the same agents playing the game repeatedly. But most are best thought of by considering a large population of agents who are randomly paired to play the game in each of many periods. In equilibrium, each agent then plays a pure strategy, but the fraction of the population playing each pure strategy is that given by the mixed strategy

54

Nash equilibrium. While such a population model is formally the subject matter of evolutionary dynamics (chapter 9), the intuition is developed in many of the models in this chapter.

After the introductory definitions, algorithms, and examples, One-Card Two-Round Poker with Bluffing is an excellent problem to present in class, explaining first the analytical derivation of the equilibrium, and then describing the agent-based simulation, which shows that low-level intelligence, in an evolutionary setting, can attain a sophisticated mixed strategy equilibrium that in classical game theory could only be justified by assuming highly sophisticated, "rational" players. A second beautiful example of population thinking is Orange-Throat, Blue-Throat and Yellow-Striped Lizards (§4.16), in which males of the lizard species *Uta stansburiana* have been shown to play Rock, Paper, and Scissors in their mating behavior. Another fine classroom example is Sex Ratios as Nash Equilibria (§4.17), which explains a deep regularity of nature that many students will never even have thought about—equal sex ratios—by showing that it is a mixed strategy equilibrium of an appropriately defined game. An instructor who prefers to stay closer to the economy could substitute Mutual Monitoring in a Partnership (§4.31) and the section following this, which nicely illustrate the interplay of cooperation and conflict in teams.

Section §4.45 develops the equivalence of mixed and behavioral strategies in extensive form games. I have found that students consider the equivalence intuitively obvious, although this cannot be the case, since it is true only assuming perfect recall. Theoretically oriented students should be urged to work through this section, but it can be skipped until behavioral strategies make a serious appearance in later chapters. For most purposes, the summary in §4.13 will suffice.

4.2 Mixed Strategies: Basic Definitions

Suppose a player has pure strategies $s_1, \ldots, s_k$ in a normal form game. A *mixed strategy* for the player is a probability distribution over $s_1, \ldots, s_k$; i.e., a mixed strategy has the form

$$\sigma = p_1 s_1 + \ldots + p_k s_k,$$

where $p_1, \ldots p_k$ are all nonnegative and $\sum_1^n p_j = 1$. By this we mean that the player chooses s_j with probability p_j, for $j = 1, \ldots, k$. We call p_j the *weight* of s_j in σ. If all the p_j's are zero except one, say $p_l = 1$, we say σ

is a *pure strategy*, and we write $\sigma = s_l$. We say that pure strategy s_j is *used* in mixed strategy σ if $p_j > 0$. We say a strategy is *strictly mixed* if it is not pure, and we say that it is *completely mixed Nash equilibrium* if all pure strategies are used in it. We call the set of pure strategies used in a mixed strategy σ_i the *support* of σ_i.

In an n-player normal form game where player i has pure strategy set S_i for $i = 1, \ldots, n$, a *mixed strategy profile* $\sigma = (\sigma_1, \ldots, \sigma_n)$ is the choice of a mixed strategy σ_i by each player. We define the *payoffs* to σ as follows. Let $\pi_i(s_1, \ldots, s_n)$ be the payoff to player i when players use the pure strategy profile $(s_1, \ldots, s_n)$, and if s is a pure strategy for player i, let p_s be the weight of s in σ_i. Then we define

$$\pi_i(\sigma) = \sum_{s_1 \in S_1} \cdots \sum_{s_n \in S_n} p_{s_1} p_{s_2} \cdots p_{s_n} \pi_i(s_1, \ldots, s_n).$$

This is a formidable expression, but the idea behind it is simple. We assume the players' choices are made independently, so the probability that the particular pure strategies $s_1 \in S_1, \ldots, s_n \in S_n$ will be used is simply the product $p_{s_1} \cdots p_{s_n}$ of their weights, and the payoff to player i in this case is just $\pi_i(s_1, \ldots, s_n)$. We get the expected payoff by multiplying and adding up over all n-tuples of mixed strategies.

We say that strategy profile $(\sigma_1^*, \ldots, \sigma_n^*)$ is a *mixed strategy Nash equilibrium* if, for each player $i = 1, \ldots, n$,

$$\pi_i(\sigma^*) \geq \pi_i(\sigma_i, \sigma_{-i}^*),$$

where σ_i is any mixed strategy for player i, and the σ_{-i} notation is as defined in §1.5. Note that this is exactly the same as in the case of pure strategies, except we use σ's instead of s's.

4.3   The Fundamental Theorem

John Nash showed that every finite game has a Nash equilibrium in mixed strategies (Nash 1950). More concretely, we have

THEOREM 4.1 Nash Existence Theorem. If each player in an n-player game has a finite number of pure strategies, then the game has a (not necessarily unique) Nash equilibrium in (possibly) mixed strategies.

The following Fundamental Theorem develops the principles for finding Nash equilibria. Let $\sigma = (\sigma_1, \ldots, \sigma_n)$ be a mixed strategy profile for an

n-player game. For any player $i = 1, \ldots, n$, let σ_{-i} represent the mixed strategies used by all the players other than player i. The *Fundamental Theorem of Mixed Strategy Nash Equilibrium* says that σ is a Nash equilibrium if and only if, for any player $i = 1, \ldots, n$ with pure strategy set S_i,

a. If $s, s' \in S_i$ occur with positive probability in σ_i, then the payoffs to s and s', when played against σ_{-i}, are equal.
b. If s occurs with positive probability in σ_i and s' occurs with zero probability in σ_i, then the payoff to s' is less than or equal to the payoff to s, when played against σ_{-i}.

The proof of the Fundamental Theorem is straightforward. Suppose σ is the player's mixed strategy in a Nash equilibrium that uses s with probability $p > 0$ and s' with probability $p' > 0$. If s has a higher payoff than s' when played against σ_{-i}, then i's mixed strategy that uses s with probability $(p + p')$, does not use s', and assigns the same probabilities to the other pure strategies as does σ, has a higher payoff than σ, so σ is not a best response to σ_{-i}. This is a contradiction, which proves the assertion. The rest of the proof is similar.

4.4 Solving for Mixed Strategy Nash Equilibria

This problem asks you to apply the general method of finding mixed strategy equilibria in normal form games. Consider the game at the right. First, of course, you should check for pure strategy equilibria, as per the previous chapter.

	U	D
L	a_1, a_2	b_1, b_2
R	c_1, c_2	d_1, d_2

To check for a completely mixed strategy equilibrium, we use the Fundamental Theorem (4.3). Suppose the column player uses the strategy $\sigma = \alpha U + (1 - \alpha)D$ (i.e., plays U with probability α). Then, if the row player uses both L and R, they must both have the same payoff against σ. The payoff to L against σ is $\alpha a_1 + (1 - \alpha)b_1$, and the payoff to R against σ is $\alpha c_1 + (1 - \alpha)d_1$. Equating these two, we find

$$\alpha = \frac{d_1 - b_1}{d_1 - b_1 + a_1 - c_1}.$$

For this to make sense, the denominator must be nonzero, and the right hand side must lie between zero and one. Note that *column* player's strategy is determined by the requirement that *row* player's two strategies be equal.

Now suppose the row player uses strategy $\tau = \beta L + (1 - \beta)R$ (i.e., plays L with probability β). Then, if the column player uses both U and D, they must both have the same payoff against τ. The payoff to U against τ is $\beta a_2 + (1 - \beta)c_2$, and the payoff to D against τ is $\beta b_2 + (1 - \beta)d_2$. Equating these two, we find

$$\beta = \frac{d_2 - c_2}{d_2 - c_2 + a_2 - b_2}.$$

Again, for this to make sense, the denominator must be nonzero, and the right-hand side must lie between zero and one. Note that now *row* player's strategy is determined by the requirement that *column* player's two strategies are equal.

a. Suppose the above really is a mixed strategy equilibrium. What are the payoffs to the two players?
b. Note that to solve a 2×2 game, we have checked for five different "configurations" of Nash equilibria—four pure and one mixed. But there are four more possible configurations, in which one player uses a pure strategy and the second player uses a mixed strategy. Show that if there is a Nash equilibrium in which the row player uses a pure strategy (say L) and the column player uses a completely mixed strategy, then *any* strategy for the column player is a best response to L.
c. How many different configurations are there to check for in a 2×3 game? In a 3×3 game?
d. Can you generalize to the number of possible configurations of Nash equilibria in an $n \times m$ normal form game?

4.5   Reviewing the Terminology

a. Define a *mixed strategy*, and write the expression for the payoff to using a mixed strategy as a function of the payoffs to the underlying pure strategies.
b. Write the condition for a set of mixed strategies to form a Nash equilibrium.
c. We say a Nash equilibrium is *strict* if the strategy used by each player in this equilibrium is the only best response to the strategies used by the other player. Define a *strictly mixed* strategy, and show that if any player in a Nash equilibrium uses a strictly mixed strategy, then the equilibrium is not strict.

4.6   Big Monkey and Little Monkey Revisited

Find the mixed strategy Nash equilibrium to the simultaneous-move Big Monkey and Little Monkey game discussed at the end of §1.2.

4.7   Dominance Revisited

Show that if a game has a solution by the iterated elimination of strictly dominated strategies (§2.2), then this solution is the only Nash equilibrium of the game. HINT: Use the Fundamental Theorem to show that each strictly dominated strategy has weight zero in a mixed strategy Nash equilibrium.

4.8   Competition on Main Street Revisited

In *Competition on Main Street* (§3.3) you showed that there is no pure strategy equilibrium with three agents. Suppose that general stores can only be set up at locations $0, 1/n, \ldots, (n-1)/n, 1$ (multiple stores can occupy the same location).

a.   Let $\pi(x, y, z)$ be the payoff to the agent choosing location x when the other two agents choose y and z. Find an expression for $\pi(x, y, z)$.

b.   Show that for $n = 4$ there is a mixed strategy Nash equilibrium in which each agent locates at points $1/4$ and $3/4$ with probability $1/7$ and point $1/2$ with probability $5/7$.

c.   Show that for $n = 6$ there is a mixed strategy Nash equilibrium in which each agent locates at points $1/3, 1/2$ and $2/3$ each with probability $1/3$.

d. * Show that for $n = 10$ there is no mixed strategy equilibrium in which all agents locate within one location of the center, but there is one in which they locate within two locations of the center. Show that locating at $3/10, 2/5, 1/2, 4/5$, and $7/10$ with equal probability is such an equilibrium.

e. * If you have the appropriate mathematical software (e.g., Mathematica or Maple), or if you have a long weekend with nothing to do, find mixed strategy equilibria for $n = 12, 14, 16$. HINT: In each case there are five locations that are occupied with nonzero probability, and the probabilities are symmetric around $n/2$.

4.9   Battle of the Sexes

Elisabetta and Alfredo love each other so much that they would rather be together than apart. But Alfredo wants to go gambling, and Elisabetta wants to go to the opera. Their payoffs are described to the right. Show that there are two pure strategy equilibria and one mixed

		Elisabetta	
Alfredo		g	o
g		2,1	0,0
o		0,0	1,2

strategy equilibrium for this game. Show that Alfredo and Elisabetta would be better off if they coordinated their activities.

4.10   Throwing Fingers

Two people play a game. Both throw down one hand with one or two fingers out. If the sum is even, player 1 wins $1 from player 2. Otherwise, player 2 wins $1 from player 1.

a. Write the normal form matrix for this game, and show that there are no pure strategy equilibria.
b. Show that each player has a mixed strategy equilibrium in which one finger is played with probability 1/2.

4.11   One-Card Two-Round Poker with Bluffing

Two card players start by each putting $2 into the "pot." Player 1 is dealt a card, which with equal probability is either H (High) or L (Low). After looking at his card (which player 2 cannot see), he either raises or folds. If he folds, the game is over and player 2 takes the pot. If he raises, he must put an additional $2 into the pot, and player 2 must now either stay or fold. If player 2 folds, the game is over, and he loses the pot. If he stays, he must put an additional $2 into the pot to meet the bet of player 1, and player 1 has another turn. Player 1 must again raise or fold. If he folds, he loses the pot, and if he plays, he must put another $2 into the pot, and player 2 has a final turn. Player 2 now must either fold or stay. If player 2 folds, he loses the pot and the game is over. If he stays, he must put an additional $2 into the pot, and player 1 must show his card. If it is H, he wins the pot, and if it is L, he loses the pot.

These rules sound complicated, but they are really simple: both players start out by *ante*'ing $2. On player 1's turn he must raise or fold, and on player 2's turn, he must see or fold. Each player has two turns. The extensive form for this game is shown in Fig. 4.1.

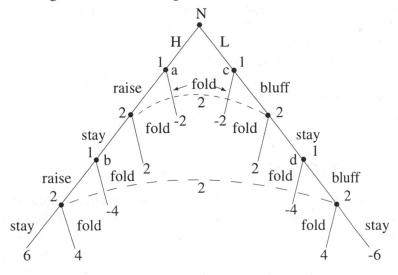

Figure 4.1. One-Card Two-Round Poker with Bluffing.

It is easy to see that player 2 has three pure strategies: *ss* (stay,stay), *sf* (stay,fold), and *f* (fold). Player 1 has nine strategies: *rrbb* (raise,raise on H, and bluff,bluff on L), *rrbf* (raise,raise on H, and bluff,fold on L), *rrf* (raise,raise on H, and fold on L), *rfbb* (raise,fold on H, and bluff,bluff on L), *rfbf* (raise,fold on H, bluff,fold on L), *fbb* (fold on H, bluff,bluff on L), *fbf* (fold on H, bluff,fold on L), *rff* (raise,fold on H, fold on L), and *ff* (fold on H, fold on L).

a. Show that Player 1 has only three undominated pure strategies, and find the optimal mixed strategy.
b. Find the optimal mixed strategy for player 2.

4.11.1   *Simulating One-Card Two-Round Poker with Bluffing*

We can simulate One-Card Two-Round Poker with Bluffing by creating in the computer *artificial life* creatures with very little information processing capacity (none, in fact). The creature's genome consists of a mixed strategy (i.e., a probability distribution over the three nondominated strategies) for player 1, and similarly for player 2. In this simulation, I created two hundred players of each type, and assigned them mixed strategies randomly. In each round of play, partners are randomly assigned, and every hundred rounds we allow reproduction to take place. In this simulation, reproduction consisted in killing off the player with the lowest score, and allowing the player with the highest score to reproduce, with mutation in the genome at rate 20%. The simulation ran for 50,000 rounds. The results of one run of the simulations for the distribution of player 2 types in the economy are shown in fig. 4.3. Note that after 25,000 rounds, the frequency of each strategy has settled down to the theoretically predicted equilibrium value.

4.12   Trust in Networks

Consider a network of many traders who are randomly paired to play a one-shot prisoner's dilemma in which each receives -1 if they both defect, each receives 1 if they both cooperate, and a defector receives 2 when playing against a cooperator, who receives -2. There are three types of agents. The first, whom we call *Defectors*, defect unconditionally against all partners. The second, whom we call *Trusters*, cooperate unconditionally with all partners. The third, whom we call *Inspectors*, monitor an imperfect signal indicating whether or not one's current partner defects against cooperators. The signal correctly identifies a Defector with probability $p > 1/2$ and correctly identifies a non-Defector with the same probability p. The Inspector then refuses to trade with a partner who is signalled as a Defector, and otherwise plays the cooperate strategy. An agent who does not trade has payoff 0. The payoff matrix for a pair of agents has the normal form shown in Figure 4.2.

	Inspect	Trust	Defect
Inspect	p^2 p^2	p p	$-2(1-p)$ $2(1-p)$
Trust	p p	1 1	-2 2
Defect	$2(1-p)$ $-2(1-p)$	2 -2	-1 -1

Figure 4.2. The Inspect-Trust-Defect Game

Think of a 'strategy' in this network as a fraction α of Inspectors, a fraction β of Trusters, and a fraction $1 - \alpha - \beta$ of Defectors, and a Nash equilibrium as a population composition (α, β) that is a best response to itself.

a. Derive the payoff matrix in Fig. 4.2.
b. Show that there are no pure strategy Nash equilibria.
c. Show that for $p \geq 3/4$, there are no Nash equilibria involving only two types of players.
d. Use §4.3 to prove that there exists a completely mixed Nash equilibrium for $p > 3/4$, and show that it is unique.
e. Show that the payoff $\pi^*(p)$ in this equilibrium is an increasing function of p, and the fraction of Defectors is a decreasing function of p.

4.13 Behavioral Strategies in Extensive Form Games

While the concept of a mixed strategy is very natural in a normal form game, the most natural definition of randomizing in an extensive form game is that of the *behavioral strategy*. A behavioral strategy for a player in an extensive form game is a probability distribution over the actions available at each point in the game where the player moves.

Lets consider, for example, One-Card Two-Round Poker with Bluffing (§4.11). If you solved this problem correctly, you found that player 1 uses the mixed strategy $(8/15)rrbb + (2/15)rrbf + (1/3)rrf$. Referring to fig. 4.1, notice that all three pure strategies involve raising at nodes a and b (since $rrbb$, $rrbf$ and rrf all start with rr). At node c, $rrbb$ and $rrbf$ involve raising and rrf involves dropping, so the player raises with probability $8/15 + 2/15 = 2/3$ at c. If we get to node d, player 1 has used either $rrbb$ or $rrbf$, and the probability of having used $rrbb$ is the conditional probability (§16.21),

$$P[\text{raise on both rounds}|\text{raise on round one}] =$$
$$\frac{P[\text{raise on both rounds}]}{P[\text{raise on round one}]} = \frac{(8/15)}{8/15 + 2/15} = 4/5,$$

which is the probability of raising at node d. We conclude that player 1 should "raise with probability 1 at a and b, raise with probability 2/3 at c, and raise with probability 4/5 at d." This defines a Nash behavioral strategy for player 1.

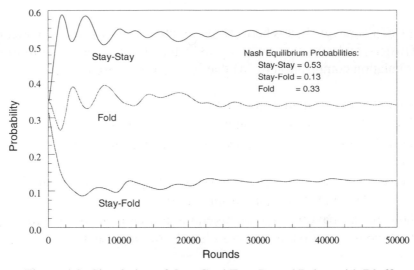

Figure 4.3. Simulation of One-Card Two-Round Poker with Bluffing

Formally, p_i is a behavioral strategy for player i in extensive form game $\mathcal{G}$ if for every information set ν of player i, if $a^\nu = \{a_1^\nu, \ldots, a_{k_\nu}^\nu\}$ is the set of actions associated with ν, then p_i is a probability distribution over a^ν.[1]

A *behavioral strategy profile* $p = (p_1, \ldots, p_n)$ for $\mathcal{G}$ is the choice of a behavioral strategy p_i for each player i. To simplify the notation, we shall also include in a behavioral strategy profile p the probability distributions over the nodes where Nature moves in $\mathcal{G}$. We assume all branches where Nature moves have strictly positive probability. Thus, a behavioral strategy profile p determines, for every player i and every information set ν $\mathcal{G}$ where i chooses, a probability distribution $p_i(a^\nu)$ over the actions a^ν at ν.

The *payoffs to a behavioral strategy profile* p are the expected payoffs to the players, assuming they use the probabilities given by p. We specify this as follows. For any two nodes a and a' in the game tree, there is either no path from a to a', or there is a unique path $(b_1, \ldots, b_k)$ from a to a'. In the former case, we write $P[a, a'|p] = 0$, and in the latter case we write

$$P[a, a'|p] = \prod_{i=1}^{k} p(b_i), \tag{4.1}$$

which is the probability of moving from a to a', given behavioral strategy p. Note that since a branch is an action, it makes sense to write $p(b_i)$.

[1]We should really say that the *restriction* of p_i to a^ν is a probability distribution over a^ν, since p_i is in fact a probability distribution over *each* information set at which i moves.

Now suppose r is the root node of $\mathcal{G}$, T is the set of terminal nodes of $\mathcal{G}$, and the payoff to player i at node $t \in T$ is $\pi_i(t)$. The payoff $\pi_i(p)$ to player i, given behavioral strategy profile p, is then

$$\pi_i(p) = \sum_{t \in T} \mathrm{P}[r, t | p] \pi_i(t).$$

There is a natural equivalence between behavioral strategies of extensive form games and mixed strategies of their normal form counterparts.[2] The following assertions, which are developed formally in §4.45, are sufficient for most purposes: (a) Suppose we are given a behavioral strategy p_i for player i. Then a pure strategy $s_i \in S_i$ for player i picks out one action from each of i's information sets. Let $p_i(s_i)$ be the product of the probabilities of each of these actions, given by p_i, and let $\sigma_i = \sum_{s_i \in S_i} p_i s_i$. Then σ_i is the mixed strategy for i corresponding to p_i. (b) Given mixed strategy σ_i and an information set ν belonging to player i, let $S_i[\nu]$ be i's pure strategies that reach ν with positive probability for some choice of strategies of the other players, and let q be the sum of the weights of the pure strategies in $S_i[\nu]$ as they occur in σ_i. Also, for each action $a_j^\nu \in \nu$, let q_j be the sum of the weights of the subset of $S_i[\nu]$ that choose a_j^ν. Finally, let $p_i(a_j^\nu) = q_j/q$, provided $q \neq 0$ (if $q = 0$, define p to be an arbitrary probability distribution on ν). Then p_i is the behavioral strategy corresponding to σ_i. (c) If σ is the mixed strategy representation of behavioral strategy p, then p is a behavioral strategy representation of σ. (d) If p is a behavioral strategy profile with mixed strategy representation σ, then the payoffs to p and to σ are the same. (e) If σ is a Nash equilibrium of the normal form representation of the extensive game $\mathcal{G}$, and if p is a behavioral strategy representation of σ, then at every information set ν, p_ν is a best response to $p_{-\nu}$, which we define to be the probability distributions over all information sets except ν, given by p.

4.14   Lions and Antelope

Two lions out hunting see Big Antelope and Little Antelope in the distance. They will surely catch whatever prey they chase, whether alone or together. However, if they pick different antelopes to chase, there is no need to share,

---

[2]This assumes perfect recall, but if using mixed strategies makes sense in an extensive form game, the game must have perfect recall, since player can refer to the pure strategy they are using to distinguish between earlier choice nodes later in the game.

whereas if they go after the same antelope, each will get only half of the kill, and the other antelope will escape. Suppose their decisions are independent, the caloric value of Big Antelope is c_b, the caloric value of Little Antelope is c_l, and $0 < c_l < c_b$.

a.   Write a normal form matrix for the game, and determine the conditions (inequality relations on c_l and c_b) under which there is at least one pure strategy equilibrium.

b.   Show that if it does not pay for them both to chase Big Antelope, then there is a mixed strategy equilibrium. Find the probability that each lion chases Big Antelope in this equilibrium.

c.   Can the payoff to the mixed strategy equilibrium exceed the payoff to catching Little Antelope in a pure strategy equilibrium? Can it fall short of the pure strategy payoff?

4.15   The Santa Fé Bar

In Santa Fé there is nothing to do at night but look at the stars or go to the local bar. Let us define the utility of looking at the stars as 0, and let the cost of walking over to the bar be 1. Suppose the utility from being at the bar is 2 if there are fewer than three people at the bar, and 1/2 if there are three or more people at the bar.

Suppose there are three people in Santa Fé.

a.   How many pure strategy equilibria are there? What is the total social surplus from a pure strategy equilibrium?

b.   Show that there is a unique symmetric mixed strategy equilibrium in which each resident goes to the bar with probability $\sqrt{6}/3 \approx 81.65\%$. Show that the total social surplus is now zero—the bar might as well not exist!

c.   Now suppose for each player $i = 1, 2, 3$ the cost of walking to the bar is c_i, the payoff when there are fewer than three people in the bar is a_i, and the payoff otherwise is b_i, where $0 < b_i < c_i < a_i$. Show that if there is any mixed strategy equilibrium, it is unique, and find the conditions under which it exists. Show that the bar might as well not exist.

d.   Generalize the problem to n people and a more general payoff structure. Show that the bar still might as well not exist.

4.16 Orange-Throat, Blue-Throat, and Yellow-Striped Lizards

The side-blotched lizard *Uta stansburiana* has three distinct male types: orange-throats, blue-throats, and yellow-striped. The orange-throats are violently aggressive, keep large harems of females (up to seven), and defend large territories. The blue-throats are less aggressive, keep small harems (usually three females), and defend small territories. The yellow-stripes are very docile but they look like females, so they can infiltrate another male's territory and secretly copulate with the females. Field researchers note that there is regular succession from generation to generation, in which orange-throated males are a majority in one period, followed by a majority of yellow-striped males, who are followed in turn by a majority of blue-throated males, and finally by a new majority of orange-throated males, thus completing the cycle.

This cycle occurs because the orange-throats have so large a territory and so large a harem that they cannot guard effectively against the sneaky yellow-striped males, who mix in with the females, and since they look a lot like females, go undetected by the orange-throats, who could easily detect the bright blue-throat males. The yellow-striped males thus manage to secure a majority of the copulations, and hence sire lots of yellow-striped males, who are very common in the next period.

	Orange Throat	Yellow Striped	Blue Throat
Orange Throat	0, 0	−1,1	1,−1
Yellow Striped	1,−1	0,0	−1,1
Blue Throat	−1,1	1,−1	0,0

When yellow-stripes are very common, however, the males of the blue-throated variety benefit, since they can detect and eject the yellow-stripes, as the blue-throats have smaller territories and fewer females to monitor. The blue-throat males thus have the greatest number of male offspring in the next period, which is thus dominated by blue-throat males. When the blue-throats predominate, the vigorous orange-throats eject them from their territories, and hence they come to dominate the succeeding period, since they acquire the blue-throat harems and territories. Thus there is a recurring three-period cycle in which each type of male dominates in one period, only to be outdone by a different male type in the succeeding period.

The game underlying this is the familiar children's game Rock, Paper, and Scissors, with the accompanying payoff structure. Note that just as in the lizard case, each "type" (rock, paper, scissors), receives zero payoff playing against itself, but is superior to one of its two dissimilar adversaries and is inferior to the other of its dissimilar adversaries (yellow-striped beats orange-throat but is beaten by blue-throat; orange-throat beats blue-throat but is beaten by yellow-striped; blue-throat beats yellow-striped but is beaten by orange-throat). Show that the only Nash equilibrium to this game is the mixed strategy equilibrium in which each strategy is played with equal probability.

After you have learned how to model game dynamics, we will return to this problem and show that under a replicator dynamic, the male lizard population does indeed cycle among the three forms in successive breeding periods (§9.12).

4.17   Sex Ratios as Nash Equilibria

Most organisms that employ sexual reproduction have two sexes: male and female. The fraction of a female's offspring that are female is determined by genetic factors and hence is heritable. In many species (e.g., most animals), the fraction is almost exactly 1/2, even if the viabilities of males and females (i.e., the probability that they mature to the point of sexual reproduction) are very different. Why is this the case?

To streamline the process of solving this problem, suppose all females breed simultaneously and their offspring comprise the next generation of birds (i.e., birds live for only one breeding period). Unless otherwise stated, you should assume (a) females "choose" a ratio u of sons to daughters born that maximizes the expected number of their genes among their grandchildren; (b) each female produces c offspring; (c) males and females contribute an equal number of genes to their offspring; (d) all males are equally likely to sire an offspring; (e) there is random mating in the next generation; and (f) the next generation is so large that no single female can affect the ratio v of males to females in the next generation.

a.   Show that $u = 1/2$ in equilibrium; i.e., a female produces half sons and half daughters. HINT: Call the birds surviving to maturity in the next generation the "breeding pool." Let s and d be the number of sons and daughters in the breeding pool. Explain why $\alpha = d/s$ is the expected number of offspring of a male in the breeding pool. Find an expression for α in terms of σ_m and σ_f, the fraction of sons and daughters, respectively, who survive to maturity, and v. Now write an expression for $f(u, v)$, the number of grandchildren of a female, in terms of α and the other parameters of the problem (u, v, s_f, s_m, and c).

Choose u to maximize $f(u, v)$, and show that the only Nash equilibrium occurs when $u = v$.

b. Suppose there are n females, and n is sufficiently small that a single female's choice *does* affect the ratio of daughters to sons. Show that an equal number of daughters and sons remains a Nash equilibrium.

c. Suppose that instead of only breeding once, a fraction δ_m of breeding males and δ_f of breeding females die in each period, and the rest remain in the mating pool. Find an expression for the equilibrium ratio of males to females and show that this ratio remains $1/2$ if $\delta_f = \delta_m$.

d. Suppose the species is haplo-diploid (many bee species are). This means that males have only one copy of each gene, which they get from their mother (i.e., males come from unfertilized eggs), while females have two copies of each gene, one from each parent. Find the equilibrium ratio of daughters to sons assuming birds live for one breeding period, and females maximize the number of copies of their genes in their grandchildren.

4.18   Tennis Strategy

In tennis, the server can serve either to the receiver's backhand or the receiver's forehand. The receiver can anticipate that the ball will come either to the forehand or backhand side. A receiver who anticipates correctly is more likely to return the ball. On the other hand, the server has a stronger backhand than forehand serve. Therefore, the receiver will return a correctly anticipated backhand serve with 60% probability and a correctly anticipated forehand serve with 90% probability. A receiver who wrongly anticipates a forehand hits a good return 20% of the time, while a receiver who wrongly anticipates a backhand hits a good return 30% of the time.

a. Write the normal form matrix for this game, and show that there are no pure strategy equilibria.

b. Find a mixed strategy equilibrium for this game. What fraction of the time does the receiver return the serve successfully?

c. Show that if the receiver's backhand gets a little better, so a correctly anticipated backhand is returned 65% of the time instead of 60%, then the server should go to the forehand more frequently and the receiver should anticipate a forehand more frequently. Find the exact rates. Show that the receiver now returns the serve successfully a greater percent of the time.

d. The moral of the story: When you improve a shot, you get to use it less, but you win more frequently.

4.19 A Mating Game

Consider a mating system in which there are males and females, 50% of each sex being *hierarchical* (H) and the other half *egalitarian* (E). When a male meets a female to mate, their sex is visible, but neither knows the other's H/E type. There are two mating strategies: *forward* (F) and *reserved* (R). Females prefer their partners to be reserved, but males prefer to be forward. In addition, when a pair of hierarchicals meet, they both prefer that one be forward and the other reserved, but when a pair of egalitarians meet, they both prefer to play the same strategy—both forward or both reserved. The payoffs are depicted in Fig. 4.4.

	F	R
F	0,0	2,1
R	1,2	0,0

H Meets *H*

	F	R
F	0,2	2,0
R	1,0	0,1

H Meets *E*

	F	R
F	1,0	0,1
R	0,2	2,0

E Meets *H*

	F	R
F	1,2	0,0
R	0,0	2,1

E Meets *E*

Figure 4.4. Mating game payoffs, where the female is the row player.

There are four pure strategies: FF (forward if H, forward if E), FR (forward if H, reserved if E), RF (reserved if H, forward if E), RR (reserved if H, reserved if E).

a. Explain why the payoffs in Fig. 4.4, where the female is the row player, reflect the preferences of the players.

b. Show that there is one pure strategy Nash equilibrium, given by RF for females and FF for males, and all players have expected payoff equal to 1.

c. Show that there is a mixed strategy equilibrium in which males play FF with probability 1/3 and RF with probability 2/3, and females play any combination of strategies leading them to be forward with probability 1/3; find the payoffs and show that this equilibrium is Pareto-dominated (§3.2) by the pure strategy equilibrium.

d. Show that there is a "mirror" mixed strategy equilibrium in which males play FF with probability 1/3 and FR with probability 2/3, and females play any combination of strategies leading them to be forward with probability 2/3; find the payoffs and show that this equilibrium is Pareto-dominated (§3.2) by the pure strategy equilibrium.

4.20 Preservation of Ecology Game

Each of three firms (1, 2, and 3) uses water from a lake for production purposes. Each has two pure strategies: purify sewage (strategy 1) or divert it back into the lake (strategy 2). We assume that if zero or one firm diverts its sewage into the lake, the water remains pure, but if two or more firms do, the water is impure and each firm suffers a loss of 3. The cost of purification is 1.

Show that the Nash equilibria can be characterized as follows:

a. One firm always pollutes and the other two never do.
b. All firms always pollute.
c. Each firm purifies with probability $1/(3 + \sqrt{3})$.
d. Each firm purifies with probability $1/(3 - \sqrt{3})$.

4.21 Hard Love

A mother wants to help her unemployed son financially, but she does not want to contribute to his distress by allowing him to loaf around. Therefore, she announces that she *may* help her son in the current period if he does not find a job. The son, however, seeks work only if he can't depend on his mother for support and may not find work even if he searches. The payoff matrix is as shown. Show that there are no pure strategy Nash equilibria, and find the unique mixed strategy equilibrium.

Son

	Seek Work	Watch Soaps
Mom		
Help Son	3,2	−1,3
Hard Love	−1,1	0,0

4.22   Coordination Failure

Determine the unique mixed Nash equilibrium of the normal form game in the insert. Show that if either player adopts any strategy other than his unique Nash strategy, the optimal response by the other player will result in a superior outcome for both. In this case, then, the Nash equilibrium is

0,0	50,40	40,50
40,50	0,0	50,40
50,40	40,50	0,0

the worst of all possible worlds. Note that in the Prisoner's Dilemma, the Nash solution is not a Pareto-minimum, since a player does worse when his partner defects and he cooperates.

4.23   Advertising Game

Three firms (players 1, 2, and 3) put three items on the market and can advertise these products either on morning or evening TV. A firm advertises exactly once per day. If more than one firm advertises at the same time, their profits are zero. If exactly one firm advertises in the morning, its profit is 1, and if exactly one firm advertises in the evening, its profit is 2. Firms must make their daily advertising decisions simultaneously.

   Show that the Nash equilibria take the following forms:

a.   One firm always chooses morning, another always chooses evening, and the third chooses morning with any probability.
b.   All firms advertise in the morning with probability $\sqrt{2} - 1$.

4.24   Colonel Blotto Game

Colonel Blotto and the Folks' Militia each try to occupy two posts by properly distributing their forces. Colonel Blotto has four regiments and the Militia has three regiments. If Colonel Blotto has more regiments than the enemy at a post, Colonel Blotto receives the enemy's regiments plus one (i.e., one is the value of occupying the post). If Colonel Blotto has fewer regiments at a post than the enemy, he loses one plus the number of regiments he has at the post. A draw gives both sides zero. The total payoff is the sum of the payoffs at the two posts.

Show that Colonel Blotto has five pure strategies and the Folks' Militia has four pure strategies. Find the payoff matrix, and find a mixed strategy Nash equilibrium for the two sides.

4.25 Number Guessing Game

You pick a number from 1 to 3. I try to guess the number. You respond (truthfully!) by saying "high," "low," or "correct." The game continues until I guess correctly. You receive a number of dollars equal to the number of guesses I took.

a. What are the Nash strategies for this game?
b. How much do you expect to win in this game?

4.26 Target Selection

There are n targets whose military values are $a_1, \ldots, a_n$, where $a_1 > a_2 > \ldots > a_n > 0$. The attacker has one attacking unit to allocate to one of the n targets, and the defender has one unit to allocate to the defense of the targets. If target k is attacked and is undefended, it will be captured, with the value a_k going to the attacker. If target k is defended, it has a probability p of being successfully held by the defender, so the expected payoff to the attacker is $(1 - p)a_k$. Show that the unique Nash equilibrium has the following characteristics:

a. There is some m such that only targets $1, \ldots, m$ are attacked and defended with positive probability.
b. If x_i is the probability of attacking target i, then

$$a_i x_i = a_j x_j \qquad i, j \leq m.$$

c. If y_i is the probability of defending target i, then

$$a_i (1 - p y_i) = a_j (1 - p y_j) \qquad i, j \leq m.$$

d.   If we define

$$A_k = \sum_{i=1}^{k} \frac{1}{a_i},$$

then the payoff of the game to the attacker is $(m - p)/A_m$, so m should be chosen to maximize this value.

4.27   A Reconnaissance Game

Attacker can either attack with all its forces (strategy 1) or attack with part of its forces, leaving the remainder as reserves and rearguards in case its forces are outflanked (strategy 2). Defender has the same two strategy options. The payoff to Attacker if Attacker uses strategy i and Defender uses strategy j is a_{ij}. We assume it is best for Attacker to use the same strategy as Defender; i.e., $a_{11} > a_{21}$ and $a_{22} > a_{12}$.

Attacker can also send out a reconnaissance force, at cost c, to find out Defender's strategy. This will surely work, unless Defender takes countermeasures at cost d (these countermeasures must be taken without knowing whether Attacker will actually reconnoiter), in which case reconnaissance will fail.

a.   How many strategies does Defender have? How many does Attacker have?
b.   Show that elimination of dominated strategies can reduce the normal form matrix to 4 × 4.
c.   If the payoff matrix is

$$A = [a_{ij}] = \begin{bmatrix} 48 & 24 \\ 12 & 36 \end{bmatrix} \qquad \text{with } c = 9 \text{ and } d = 7,$$

find a Nash equilibrium in mixed strategies, assuming the payoff to Defender is the negative of the payoff to Attacker.

4.28   Attack on Hidden Object

A defender has an object of great value that he can carry in one of two identical bombers P (protected) and F (flank). The bombers fly in formation, so to attack P, one must fly past F and run the risk α, with $0 < \alpha < 1$, of being shot down before engaging P. Once the attacker has engaged his target (whether F or P), he can destroy it with probability β, with $0 < \beta < 1$. If F is intact, it is harder to destroy P than if F is gone. If F is intact, the probability of destroying P is $\gamma = (1 - \alpha)\beta$.

Suppose the attacker has two chances to hit a target and destroy the valued object. The defender has two strategies: locate the object in F and locate the object in P. The attacker has four strategies: attack F both times, attack P both times, attack F the first time and P the second time, and vice versa. The understanding is that if the first attack was successful, the second attack is directed against the remaining target, whatever the strategy used.

Determine the payoff matrix, and find the Nash strategies.

4.29   Two-Person Zero-Sum Games

A *zero-sum game* is, appropriately enough, a game in which the sum of the payoffs to all the players is zero. Von Neumann and Morgenstern (1944), who launched modern game theory, lay great stress on zero-sum games and indeed, defined equilibrium in a way that only works for two-person zero-sum games. Nash had not yet invented the equilibrium concept that bears his name. Suppose the payoff to player 1 is $\pi(\sigma, \tau)$ when player 1 uses σ and player 2 uses τ, so the payoff to player 2 is $-\pi(\sigma, \tau)$. Von Neumann and Morgenstern defined (σ^*, τ^*) to be an equilibrium of the two-person zero-sum game if σ^* maximizes $\min_\tau \pi(\sigma, \tau)$ and τ^* minimizes $\max_\sigma \pi(\sigma, \tau)$. They showed that this *maximin solution* satisfies

$$\pi(\sigma^*, \tau^*) = \max_\sigma \min_\tau \pi(\sigma, \tau) = \min_\tau \max_\sigma \pi(\sigma, \tau). \qquad (4.2)$$

It is easy to show that *a strategy profile in a two-person zero-sum game is a Nash equilibrium if and only if it is a maximin solution*. This implies, in particular, that *all Nash equilibria of a two-person zero-sum game have the same payoffs*.

To prove a Nash equilibrium is a maximin solution, suppose (σ^*, τ^*) is a Nash equilibrium. Then, we have

$$\max_\sigma \pi(\sigma, \tau^*) \geq \min_\tau \max_\sigma \pi(\sigma, \tau) \geq \pi(\sigma^*, \tau^*)$$
$$\geq \max_\sigma \min_\tau \pi(\sigma, \tau) \geq \min_\tau \pi(\sigma^*, \tau).$$

The first inequality above is obvious, the second follows from

$$\min_\tau \max_\sigma \pi(\sigma, \tau) \geq \min_\tau \pi(\sigma^*, \tau) = \pi(\sigma^*, \tau^*),$$

the third follows from

$$\max_{\sigma} \min_{\tau} \pi(\sigma, \tau) \leq \max_{\sigma} \pi(\sigma, \tau^*) = \pi(\sigma^*, \tau^*),$$

and the fourth inequality is obvious. But the first and third terms must then be equal, since (σ^*, τ^*) is Nash, and similarly for the third and fifth terms. Thus, they are all equal, so (σ^*, τ^*) is maximin.

To show that a maximin solution is a Nash equilibrium, suppose (σ^*, τ^*) is maximin. We know that the second equation in (4.2) holds since there exists a Nash equilibrium, and we have already shown that a Nash equilibrium is maximin satisfying (4.2). But then we have

$$\pi(\sigma^*, \tau^*) \leq \max_{\sigma} \pi(\sigma, \tau^*) = \min_{\tau} \pi(\sigma^*, \tau) \leq \pi(\sigma^*, \tau^*).$$

This proves all three terms are equal, so (σ^*, τ^*) is maximin. Q.E.D.

4.30   An Introduction to Forward Induction

The little game to the right has three Nash equilibria. The first is the Pareto-efficient equilibrium (D, R), and another is the less desirable (U, L). There is also a mixed strategy Nash equilibrium, as you can easily show. How do we choose among these equilibria? Which one is the "right" one? Perhaps some natural

	U	D
L	2,2	3,0
R	0,3	4,4

Nash equilibrium refinement concept can be used to choose among them. We have found one such "refinement," that of *subgame perfection*, to be extremely insightful (see the Big Monkey and Little Monkey example in §1.2), and we return to it in chapter 5. Perhaps there are useful refinement concepts—in particular, one that can handle this little game.

Many game theorists believe that the Quest for the Correct Refinement must be unsuccessful, since which Nash equilibrium is appropriate (if any) depends on the ancillary informational conditions we expect to hold and on the specific dynamic governing the play of the game (more on this in chapters 9 and 10). This does not mean, however, that certain "plausible" refinements might not in fact select the same equilibria as certain "plausible" dynamics under certain "plausible" informational conditions. This little game gives us two interesting refinement criteria to think about: *risk dominance* and *forward induction*.

Note that the (U, L) equilibrium has the attractive property that each player does *better* if the other player in fact does *not* play the Nash strategy (receiving 3 as opposed to 2)! By contrast, in the (D, R) equilibrium each player does *much worse* if the other player chooses the "wrong" strategy (receiving 0 as opposed to 4). Thus, in a sense the (2,2) payoff is "less risky" than the (4,4) payoff. To formalize this, we say a pair of strategies is *risk dominant* (Harsanyi and Selten 1988) if each strategy is a best response to a mixed strategy of the other player that weights all the player's pure strategies equally. The justification for this concept is the Principle of Insufficient Reason (§16.28.1), which says that under conditions of complete ignorance concerning which of n outcomes will occur, you should treat the outcomes as equally likely. Armed with this definition, it is easy to show that (U, L) is indeed a risk dominant Nash equilibrium.

To illustrate forward induction, suppose player 2 has an "outside option" that pays him 3, that he can take instead of playing the game. Then, player one can reason as follows: "The only way player 2 can receive a payoff greater than 3 is if he plays R, and he believes that I will play D with greater than 75% probability. Thus, I will play R."

a. Find the mixed strategy Nash equilibrium of the 2×2 game above, and find the payoff to the two players in this equilibrium.
b. Show that (U, L) is a risk dominant Nash equilibrium.
c. Show that if we define another strategy, O (outside option), for player 2 that pays him 3, and pays player 1 some value a no matter what player one does, then there is a mixed strategy combination of R and O that strictly dominates L. But then D dominates U, and after eliminating T, R dominates O, so the iterated elimination of dominated strategies gives us the same result as forward induction.

4.31 Mutual Monitoring in a Partnership

Two agents share a resource. One agent, whom we call the "taker," gets to use the resource, and can either steal (S) or be honest (H) in the amount of resource used. The other agent, the "watcher," can monitor (M) or trust (T). We normalize the payoffs to the two players following the "cooperative" strategy (T, H) to be zero. Let b be the benefit to the taker from stealing and not getting caught, let p be the loss to the taker from getting caught stealing, and let α be the probability of getting caught if the watcher monitors. Also,

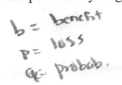
$b = $ benefit
$p = $ loss
$\alpha = $ probab.

let c be the cost to the watcher of monitoring, and let λ be the loss to the watcher if the taker steals and is not caught. We assume $b, p, \alpha, \lambda > 0$. We can normalize $b + p = 1$ (e.g., by dividing all of the payoffs to player 1 by $b + p$). The game matrix is then given in the diagram.

	T	M
H	0,0	$0,-c$
S	$b,-\lambda$	$b - \alpha, -\lambda(1 - \alpha) - c$

Let μ be the probability of monitoring in the watcher's mixed strategy, and let σ be the probability of stealing in the taker's mixed strategy.

a. Prove that if $c < \alpha\lambda$ and $b < \alpha$, then there is a completely mixed strategy Nash equilibrium with $\mu = b/\alpha$ and $\sigma = c/\alpha\lambda$. Show that the payoff to the taker is zero, and the payoff to the watcher is $-c/\alpha$.

b. Explain why the loss to the watcher depends only on c and α, and not, for instance, on λ. Explain why the return to the taker doesn't depend on any of the parameters of the problem, so long as $c < \alpha\lambda$ and $b < \alpha$.

c. What are the Nash equilibria if one or both of the inequalities $c < \alpha\lambda$ and $b < \alpha$ is violated?

4.32   Mutual Monitoring in Teams

This is a continuation of the previous problem. Now suppose there are $n + 1$ agents, where agent $n + 1$ is the "taker," agents $1, \ldots, n$ being identical "watchers." Suppose each watcher has the same probability $\alpha > 0$ of detecting stealing if monitoring, the same cost $c > 0$ of monitoring, and the same loss $\lambda > 0$ from an undetected theft. We only care about *symmetric equilibria*, in which all watchers choose the *same* probability μ of monitoring the taker.

Let $b < 1$ be the gain to the taker from stealing, and define

$$\rho = \alpha\lambda(1 - b)^{\frac{n-1}{n}}.$$

Answer the following questions, assuming $b < \alpha\lambda$ and $c < \rho$.

a. Show that there is a mixed strategy Nash equilibrium with the probability σ of stealing and the probability μ of monitoring given by

$$\sigma = \frac{c}{\rho} \qquad \mu = \frac{1 - (1-b)^{\frac{1}{n}}}{\alpha}.$$

b. Show that the payoff to a watcher is now $-c/\alpha(1-b)^{\frac{n-1}{n}}$. Why does this not depend on λ?

c. How does this solution change as the group size n increases? Why doesn't the tragedy of the commons (i.e., the free rider) result hold in this case?

d. What would happen as n increases if, for some fixed λ^*, we wrote $\lambda = \lambda^*/n$? This formulation would be reasonable if a dishonest taker imposed a fixed cost on the group no matter what its size, the cost being shared equally by the watchers.

4.33 Altruism(?) in Bird Flocks

This is an application of the results of the previous problem. Consider a flock of n birds eating in a group. A cat can catch a bird if it can sneak up behind a nearby rock without being seen. Each bird has an incentive to let the other birds look out for the cat while it conserves all its resources for eating (studies show that birds dissipate a considerable amount of energy and lose a considerable amount of time looking out for enemies). Why then do birds actually look out for predators when they eat in flocks? Are they "altruistic"? Perhaps not.[3]

Suppose it takes the cat one second out in the open to reach the rock. If seen during that one second by even one bird, the birds will all fly off, and the cat will lose $p \in (0, 1)$ in wasted time. If the cat reaches the rock, it catches one of the birds for a gain of $b = 1 - p$.

If each bird looks up from eating every $k \geq 1$ seconds, it will see the cat with probability $1/k$. Thus, we can take $\alpha = 1$ and $\mu = 1/k$ in the previous problem (T corresponds to $k = \infty$). The cost to the bird of being caught is $\lambda = 1$, and the cost of looking up once is c. Prove the following, where we define $\mu = 1 - c^{1/(n-1)}$ and $\eta = 1 - c^{n/(n-1)}$.

THEOREM: There are three types of symmetric equilibria.

[3]A similar problem arises in modeling the foraging behavior of flocks of birds in patchy environments, since if one bird finds a patch of food, all get to eat their fill (Motro 1991, Benkman 1988).

a. If $c > 1$, then no bird looks up, and the cat stalks the birds with probability 1.
b. If $c < 1$ and $b > \eta$, there is a symmetric Nash equilibrium in which the cat stalks with certainty and birds look up every $1/\mu$ seconds.
c. If $b < \eta$, then there is a symmetric Nash equilibrium where the cat stalks with probability $\sigma = c(1-b)^{-(n-1)/n}$, and the birds look up with probability $1/\mu$.

4.34   Robin Hood and Little John

Robin Hood and Little John both want to cross a rope bridge at the same time. There is only room for one. Each has two strategies: go (G) and wait (W). It takes Robin Hood and Little John times τ_r and τ_{lj}, respectively, to cross the bridge. If both go at the same time, they fight it out at cost $\delta > 0$, after which the winner crosses the bridge. The probability of winning is 1/2 for each. If both wait, they play a polite little game of Alphonse and Gaston, at a cost $\epsilon > 0$, and one of them eventually crosses first, again with probability 1/2. We assume $0 < \epsilon < \delta$, while τ_r and τ_{lj} represent the cost of waiting for the other to cross the bridge.

a. Find the payoff matrix for this game; consider each player's cost as not including the necessary crossing time for himself.
b. Find all pure and mixed strategy equilibria, and show how the relative values of τ_{lj}, τ_r, and δ determine which holds.
c. Show that the larger δ, the less likely a go-go situation emerges.
d. What is a socially optimal δ? Show that if Robin Hood always waits, he would gain by an appropriate reduction in the costs of fighting, but would not gain by an increase in the costs of fighting. What is the social significance of this?

4.35   The Motorist's Dilemma

George and Martha, traveling in opposite directions, come to an intersection and each wants to turn left, so one must wait for the other. The time to turn left is the same for both, and is equal to $\tau > 0$. The cost of both waiting is $\epsilon > 0$, and of both going at the same time is $\delta > \epsilon > 0$. In addition to the two strategies G (go) and W (wait), we add a third, C (contingent). Playing C means choosing W if the other driver chooses G, and choosing G if the other driver chooses W. If both drivers choose C, we treat this as a foul-up as serious as GG. The payoff matrix is thus as in the figure. Assuming $\tau < 2\delta$, so G is not a dominant strategy, find the Nash equilibria.

	G	W	C
G	$-\delta - \tau/2, -\delta - \tau/2$	$0, -\tau$	$0, -\tau$
W	$-\tau, 0$	$-\epsilon - \tau/2, -\epsilon - \tau/2$	$-\tau, 0$
C	$-\tau, 0$	$0, -\tau$	$-\delta - \tau/2, -\delta - \tau/2$

4.36   Family Politics

In certain species of bird (actually, this is true of many bird species) males are faithful or philanderers, females are coy or loose. Coy females insist on a long courtship before copulating, while loose females do not. Faithful males tolerate a long courtship and help rear their young, while philanderers do not wait and do not help. Suppose v is the value of having offspring to either a male or a female, $2r > 0$ is the cost of rearing an offspring, and $w > 0$ the cost of prolonged courtship to both male and female. We assume $v > r + w$. This means that if courtship leads to sharing the costs of raising an offspring, then it is worth it to both birds. The normal form matrix is shown above.

		Female	
		Coy	Loose
Male			
Faithful		$v - r - w$ $v - r - w$	$v - r$ $v - r$
Philan- derer		0 0	v $v - 2r$

a. Show that if $v > 2r$, there is one Nash equilibrium with only loose females and only philandering males.

b. Show that if $v < 2r$, there is a unique completely mixed strategy for males and females. The fraction q of females who are coy is then given by $q = r/(v - w)$, and the fraction p of males who are philanderers is given by $w/(2r + w - v)$.

4.37   Frankie and Johnny

Frankie must pay Johnny a certain amount of money as compensation for shooting Johnny's lover, but they disagree on the amount. They agree on a negotiator, who will pick whichever of Frankie's bid x_f and Johnny's bid x_j is closer to the negotiator's opinion y. Frankie and Johnny don't know y, but they know it is drawn from a distribution F such that $\Pr\{y < \tilde{y}\} = F(\tilde{y})$. What is the nature of a Nash equilibrium for this game?

4.38   A Card Game

There are two players, each of whom bets \$1 and receives a number between zero and one (uniformly distributed). Each player observes only his number. Player 1 can either fold or raise \$5. Player 2 can either fold or see. If neither folds, the player with the higher number wins. Describe a Nash equilibrium for this game.

4.39   Cheater-Inspector

There are n rounds in a game between an inspector and a "taker." The taker can cheat in any round, and the inspector can inspect in any round. If the taker cheats without getting inspected, the game stops and she gains 1 in

	trust	inspect
cheat	n	$-na$
honest	g_{n-1}	$b + g_{n-1}$

that period and in every remaining period. If the taker is inspected while cheating, the game stops, and she is fined a in that period and in every remaining period. If the taker is honest, she receives b in that round from the inspector if inspected and nothing if not inspected, and the game goes on. The game is zero-sum (i.e., whatever the taker gets the inspector loses). What is the payoff of the game to the taker, and what is an optimal strategy for taker and inspector? HINT: Let g_n be the payoff of game of length $n > 0$, and let $g_0 = 0$. Then, for any n, we have the game above. Solve it and find g_n recursively (i.e., starting with $n = 1$, then $n = 2$, and so on).

4.40   The Groucho Marx Game

Two players ante an amount $a \geq 0$, and cards numbered from 1 to n are placed in a hat. Each player draws a card, observing his own but not the other's. They simultaneously and independently decide to stay (s) or raise (r) by betting an additional $b \geq 0$. The high card wins $a + b$, or if one player raises and the other stays, the one raising wins a.

a. Show that when $n = 3$, if $a \geq b$ a Nash equilibrium involves staying
    if you pick a 1 and raising otherwise. If $a < b$, a Nash equilibrium
    is to stay unless you pick the 3. HINT: Show that staying is strictly
    dominated by raising if you pick the 3. Then, write "rr" for "raise if you
    pick a 1, raise if you pick a 2," write "rs" for "raise if you pick a 1, stay
    if you pick a 2," etc. This gives four strategies: {rr,rs,sr,ss}. The normal
    form payoff matrix is thus 4×4. Calculate the entries by finding the
    expected return to each pair of strategies. ·

b. Show that when $n = 4$ (i) if $b > a = 0$ it is Nash to stay unless you
    pick the 4; (ii) if $2b > a > 0$, it is Nash to stay unless you get a 3
    or a 4; (iii) if $a > 2b > 0$, it is Nash to stay if you get a 1, and raise
    otherwise. HINT: Eliminate strongly and weakly dominated strategies
    before forming the payoff matrix.

c. * Using probability theory (especially conditional probabilities, as devel-
    oped in §16.21), find the normal form of the Groucho Marx game for
    arbitrary $n > 0$. You may eliminate weakly dominated strategies and
    hence assume that the only undominated pure strategies take the form
    of choosing a particular number, and raising only if your card is greater
    than that number.[4]

d. * Write the matrix for the normal form game for $n = 5$, and show that
    when $a = 1$ and $b = 2$, there is exactly one Nash equilibrium, given by

$$0.125s_1 + 0.375s_3 + 0.5s_4.$$

This is difficult only because there are lots of alternatives to check. I
did this by writing a program that solves normal form games.

e. * Write the matrix for the normal form game for $n = 6$, and show that
    when $a = 1$ and $b = 2$, there is exactly one Nash equilibrium, given by

$$0.083s_1 + 0.667s_4 + 0.25s_5.$$

This is even more tiresome to verify without the appropriate computer
software.

f. * Write the matrix for the normal form game for $n = 7$, and show that
    when $a = 1$ and $b = 2$, there is exactly one Nash equilibrium, given by

$$0.063s_1 + 0.937s_5.$$

[4]Recall that starred questions are more challenging and/or more time-consuming than
others.

4.41   Real Men Don't Eat Quiche

Clem is sitting at the best seat in the sports bar minding his own business when in walks the Dark Stranger (DS). The DS would like to Bully Clem to get the seat, but only if Clem is a Wimp. If Clem is Tough, DS prefers to Defer to Clem. DS doesn't know whether Clem is a Wimp or is Tough, but he knows that with probability 1/3 Clem is Tough. If Clem is a Wimp and DS Bullies, Clem will move, but if Clem is Tough and DS Bullies, he will fight for his place at the bar. Clem gets 2 points if DS Defers to him, plus 1 point for avoiding consuming something he doesn't like. DS gets 1 point for guessing correctly.

Suppose Clem can signal whether he is Tough or a Wimp by choosing to consume either Beer or Quiche. Real men (Tough) don't like quiche and Wimps don't like beer. Find all the Nash equilibria to this game. The extensive form game, with payoffs, is shown in Fig. 4.5

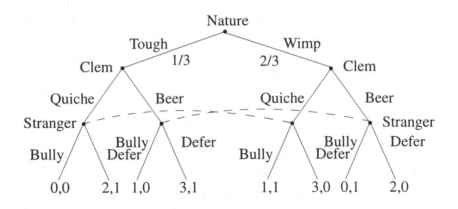

Figure 4.5. Real men don't eat quiche.

4.42   The Vindication of the Hawk

Chicken is a two-player game in which each player can either attack (A) or remain peaceful (P). Suppose at the start of the game, each player has one util of Good Stuff. If both players remain peaceful, they each get to consume

	A	W
A	$-a,-a$	0,2
W	2,0	1,1

their Stuff. If one is peaceful and the other attacks, the attacker takes the other's Stuff. But if both attack, they each lose $a > 0$ utils. this gives us the normal form matrix above.

a.   Show that there is a unique mixed strategy equilibrium, and the payoff of the game to the players *increases* when the potential loss from conflict, a, increases.
b.   Show that if there is a fixed probability $p > 0$ that a player will attack by mistake (e.g., because the wrong button got pressed), this result no longer holds.
c.   What happens if one or both of the players develops a "detector" that can give an early warning if the other player attacks?

4.43   Correlated Equilibria

Consider the Up-Down/Left-Right game played by Alphonse and Gaston, with normal form matrix shown to the right. There are two Pareto-efficient pure strategy equilibria: (1,5) and (5,1). There is also a symmetric mixed-strategy equilibrium with payoffs (2.5,2.5),

	l	r
u	5,1	0,0
d	4,4	1,5

in which Alphonse plays u with probability 0.5, and Gaston plays l with probability 0.5.

If the players can jointly observe an event with probability 1/2, they can achieve the payoff (3,3) by playing (u,l) when the event occurs, and (d,r) when it does not. Note that this is Nash, since if the event occurs and Gaston plays l, Alphonse's best response is u; if the event does not occur and Gaston plays r, then Alphonse's best response is d; and similarly for Gaston. This is called a *correlated equilibrium*.

A more general correlated equilibrium for this coordination game can be constructed as follows. Build a device that has three states: a, b, and c, with probability of occurrence α, β, and $1 - \alpha - \beta$. Allow Alphonse to have the information set $[\{a\}, \{b, c\}]$, and allow Gaston to have the information set $[\{a, b\}, \{c\}]$. For what values of α and β is the following Nash: Alphonse plays u when he sees a and plays d when he sees $\{b, c\}$; Gaston plays r when he sees c and plays l when he sees $\{a, b\}$.

Note that when a occurs, Alphonse sees a, so he knows that Gaston sees $\{a, b\}$, so Gaston plays l. Thus, Alphonse's best response is u. So far, so good. When b occurs, Alphonse sees $\{b, c\}$, so using Bayes' Rule, he knows that Gaston sees b with probability $\beta/(1-\alpha)$, and Gaston sees c with probability $(1-\alpha-\beta)/(1-\alpha)$. Thus, Alphonse knows he faces the mixed strategy l played with probability $\beta/(1-\alpha)$ and r played with probability $(1-\alpha-\beta)/(1-\alpha)$. The payoff to u in this case is $5\beta/(1-\alpha)$, and the payoff to d is $4\beta/(1-\alpha) + (1-\alpha-\beta)/(1-\alpha)$. If d is to be a best response, we must thus have $1 \geq \alpha + 2\beta$. If c occurs, the same conditions for Alphonse hold.

What about the conditions for Gaston? When c occurs, Alphonse sees $\{b, c\}$, so he plays d. Gaston's best response is r. So far, so good. When a occurs, Gaston sees $\{a, b\}$, so his Bayesian posterior for the probability that Alphonse sees a is then $\alpha/(\alpha + \beta)$. A straightforward argument, parallel to that of the previous paragraph, shows that playing l is a best response if and only if $\alpha \geq \beta$.

Any α and β that satisfy $1 \geq \alpha + 2\beta$ and $\alpha \geq \beta$ permit a correlated equilibrium. Another characterization is $\beta \leq 1/3$ and $1 - 2\beta \geq \alpha \geq \beta$.

What are the Pareto-optimal choices of α and β? Since the equilibrium is $a \rightarrow (u, l)$, $b \rightarrow (d, l)$, and $c \rightarrow (d, r)$, the payoffs to (a, b, c) are

$$\alpha(5, 1) + \beta(4, 4) + (1 - \alpha - \beta) = (1 + 4\alpha + 3\beta, 5 - 4\alpha - \beta),$$

where $\beta \leq 1/3$ and $1 - 2\beta \geq \alpha \geq \beta$. This is a linear programming problem. The solution is shown in Fig. 4.6.

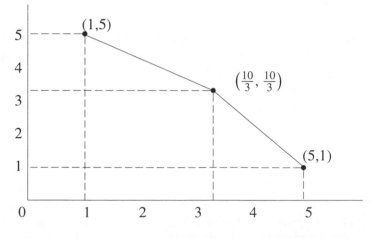

Figure 4.6. Alphonse and Gaston Correlate Their Behavior

The pair of straight lines connecting (1,5) to (10/3,10/3) to (5,1) is the set of Pareto-optimal points. Note that the symmetric point (10/3,10/3) corresponds to $\alpha = \beta = 1/3$.

4.44   Poker with Bluffing Revisited

If you have access to computer software to solve for Nash equilibria of normal form games, you can easily do the following. Doing the problem by hand is not feasible.

a. * Show that there are two Nash equilibria to Poker with Bluffing (§2.17). Ollie uses the same strategy in both, bluffing on the first round with 40% probability (i.e., he raises with H or L on the first round, and drops with M). Stan has two mixed strategy best responses to Ollie, one of which uses two pure strategies and the other uses three. The latter involves bluffing with 40% probability. The expected payoff to the game for Ollie is $1.20. (It's the same for both equilibria, since it's a zero-sum game—see §4.29).

b. * Now suppose Stan sees Ollie's first move before raising or staying. Show that there are twenty one Nash equilibria, but that Stan uses only two different mixed strategies, and both involve raising with High and raising with Medium or Low with 25% probability on the first round, and calling with High or Medium and calling with 25% probability on the second round. Stan has lots of mixed strategies, but they entail only two different behaviors at the nodes where he chooses. If Ollie raised, Stan raises with H, raises with 75% probability with Medium, and stays with Low. If Ollie stayed, Stan raises with H, and raises with 25% probability with Low. In one set of strategies, Stan raises with 50% probability with Medium, and with 25% probability in the other. In all Nash equilibria, Ollie can expect to lose $0.25.

4.45   The Equivalence of Behavioral and Mixed Strategies

How do we get from behavioral to mixed strategies? A behavioral strategy p_i for player i has a *mixed strategy representation* σ_i defined in a notationally challenged but conceptually straightforward manner. Let $\mathcal{N}_i$ be the information sets for player i, and for $v \in \mathcal{N}_i$, let $a^v = \{a_1^v, \ldots, a_{k_v}^v\}$ be the actions available to player i at information set v. Let S_i be the set of pure strategies for player i. Then, $s \in S_i$ is the choice of a particular action $s(v) = a \in a^v$ for each $v \in \mathcal{N}_i$. Using p, the probability α_s^p that the player uses pure strategy s is then defined to be

$$\alpha_s^p = \prod_{v \in \mathcal{N}_i} p(s(v)).$$

Thus, the mixed strategy representation σ_i of the behavioral strategy p_i is given by

$$\sigma_i = \sum_{s \in S_i} \alpha_s^p s.$$

You can check that σ_i is in fact a mixed strategy, i.e., $\sum_{s \in S_i} \alpha_s^p = 1$. Moreover, assuming perfect recall (§1.3), if p is a behavioral strategy profile with mixed strategy representation σ, then the payoffs to p and to σ are the same (see below).

Starting from a mixed strategy σ of the normal form game, there is also a straightforward, though again notationally challenged, way of deriving a behavioral strategy representation of σ. Let $\sigma_i = \sum_{s \in S_i} \alpha_s s$ be a mixed strategy for player i, and let $v \in \mathcal{N}_i$ with actions $a^v = \{a_1^v, \ldots, a_{k_v}^v\}$. Let $S_i[v] \subseteq S_i$ be the pure strategies that reach v with positive probability for some strategy profile of the other players, and define $P[v|\sigma_i] = \sum_{s \in S_i[v]} \alpha_s$. Thus, $P[v|\sigma_i]$ is the probability that i will choose a pure strategy that reaches v with positive probability from some choices of the other players. Now, for each $a \in a^v$, let $S_i[a] \subseteq S_i[v]$ be the pure strategies in $S_i[v]$ that choose a at v, and define $P[a|\sigma_i] = \sum_{s \in S_i[a]} \alpha_s$. Finally, let

$$p_i(a) = \frac{P[a|\sigma_i]}{P[v|\sigma_i]},$$

provided the denominator is not zero. If the denominator is zero, define $p_i(a)$ arbitrarily, just so $\sum_{a \in a^v} p_i(a) = 1$. We call p_i a *behavioral strategy representation* of σ_i. Note that p_i is uniquely defined only if all information sets are attained with positive probability.

If σ is the mixed strategy representation of behavioral strategy p, then p is a behavioral representation of σ (see below). However, there is no unique correspondence between behavioral and mixed strategies. This is because many mixed strategies can have the *same* behavioral strategy representation. For instance, in One-Card Two-Round Poker with Bluffing (§4.11), the pure strategies $rrff$ and $rrfr$ have the same behavioral strategy representation, because if you fold on the first round, it does not matter whether you fold or raise on the second round, since you never get there! Note that, in fact, in describing the game, without comment the two strategies were identified with the single strategy rrf.

For another example of multiple mixed strategy representations of the same behavioral strategy, consider the Big Monkey and Little Monkey game tree in §1.1, where Little Monkey's mixed strategy set is

$$\{\alpha ww + \beta pw + \gamma wp + \delta pp \mid \alpha, \beta, \gamma, \delta \geq 0, \ \alpha + \beta + \gamma + \delta = 1\}.$$

A typical behavioral strategy p for Little Monkey is to play w with probability μ_w if Big Monkey plays w, and play w with probability μ_p if Big Monkey plays p. For concreteness, let us assume that $\mu_w + \mu_p \leq 1$ and $\mu_w \leq \mu_p$. You can check that $\mu_p pw + \mu_w wp + (1 - \mu_w - \mu_p)pp$ is a mixed strategy representation of p. But another mixed strategy representation of p $\mu_w ww + (\mu_p - \mu_w)pw + (1 - \mu_p)pp$, and any convex combination of these two mixed strategies *also* gives rise to the same behavioral strategy p.

If this maze of symbols confuses you, try it out on the One-Card Two-Round Poker with Bluffing game. You should get the same result as we did a few paragraphs earlier.

We say a behavioral strategy profile $p = (p_1, \ldots, p_n)$ is a *Nash equilibrium in behavioral strategies* if for each player i, p_i is a best response to p_{-i}. Since behavioral strategies have the same payoffs as their mixed strategy representations (assuming perfect recall, which we do), p_i is a best response to p_{-i} if and only if the mixed strategy σ_i representation of p_i is a best response to σ_{-i}, the mixed strategy representation of p_{-i}. We conclude that *a behavioral strategy is a Nash equilibrium of the extensive form game $\mathcal{G}$ if and only if the mixed strategy representation of p is a Nash equilibrium of the normal form of $\mathcal{G}$.*

This exercise asks you to prove some of the assertions made above. Assuming perfect recall, show:

a. If p is a behavioral strategy profile for an extensive form game $\mathcal{G}$ and σ is the mixed strategy representation of p, then for any player i, σ_i is a mixed strategy, i.e., $\sum_{s \in S_i} \alpha_s^p = 1$.

b. * If σ is the mixed strategy representation of behavioral strategy p, then p is a behavioral strategy representation of σ.

c. * If p is a behavioral strategy profile with mixed strategy representation σ, then the payoffs to p and to σ are the same (Kuhn 1953).

d. If σ is a Nash equilibrium of the normal form representation of the extensive game $\mathcal{G}$, and if p is a behavioral strategy representation of σ, then at every information set ν, p_ν is a best response to $p_{-\nu}$.

5

Moving through the Game Tree: Subgames, Incredible Threats, and Trembling Hands

> Once admit that life can be guided by reason and all possibility of life is annihilated.
>
> *Leo Tolstoy*

5.1 Introduction

Backward induction can eliminate weakly dominated strategies and with them, Nash equilibria based on incredible threats (§1.2 and chapter 2). Subgame perfection and its variants generalize backward induction, eliminating Nash equilibria that use suboptimal play in parts (e.g., subgames) of the game tree. After the appropriate definitions and simple examples, I present in class the Rubinstein Bargaining Model (§5.6), both because it shows how zillions of implausible Nash equilibria can be eliminated and because it clarifies many issues in real-world bargaining. I also present Nuisance Suits (§5.9) because it neatly illustrates how agents can engage in preemptive commitment and other sophisticated behaviors well known in business, law, and politics.

At this point, however, the love story with subgame perfection ends, and we begin to investigate some anomalies. In the Finitely Repeated Prisoner's Dilemma (§5.11), subgame perfection predicts immediate defection in a hundred round Prisoner's Dilemma, but common sense and laboratory experiments tell us people will cooperate for more than ninety rounds. The standard explanation is that if there is a small probability that your partner is "irrational," you should cooperate for many rounds. Although we present this argument, it is really not plausible. For instance, if you ask two experts in game theory to play they game, they too will cooperate, but not because each thinks the other may be "irrational." The real question is: Does your opponent use backward induction to choose a strategy? If not, then you shouldn't either.

Of course, only a fool uses backward induction in this game.[1] To dramatize this point, we present agent-based simulation models of the process, showing that evolutionary dynamics approximate the subgame perfect solution only when mutation rates and the gains from defection are very low, and there is extreme evolutionary pressure against cooperative strategies. Over a broad range of conditions, cooperation prevails even in the long run.

Another very important anomaly is presented by the Ultimatum Game (§11.4.1), which shows that in some cases people will *carry out* "incredible threats." The empirical robustness of this finding has dismayed many economists, who consider it an attack on Reason. But in fact, it strongly vindicates game theory and points to a new and deeper understanding of human sociality. This anomaly is described in chapter 11, where it logically belongs, but it is pedagogically preferable to cover it at this point in the course.

This counterplay of theory, actual human behavior, and computer simulation nicely illustrates a fundamental point of evolutionary game theory: that the equilibrium properties of a game depend upon the dynamic through which behavior in the game develops. The Aristotelian urge to derive the properties of ambiguous models through reason alone should be held firmly in tow.

At this point the instructor may prefer to move on to a different topic, but important issues remain. For one, there are many cases where we would like to eliminate Nash equilibria that require that agents behave suboptimally in parts of the game that are reached with zero probability but that cannot be considered subgames. In the classical literature, this has been dealt with by defining a *sequential equilibrium* in which agents have "beliefs" that they update "rationally" as they move through the game tree (Kreps and Wilson 1982). Well, most life forms do not have anything we would be comfortable calling "beliefs" (much less ones that they "update"), and even in humans "beliefs" are things to be *explained*, not assumed. So I have coined the belief-free concept of "fuzzy subgame perfection" (§5.13) to

---

[1]This point is completely obvious, but nevertheless often contradicted. Reinhard Selten (1993), for instance, agrees that cooperation in the Finitely Repeated Prisoner's Dilemma cannot be explained by the possible "irrationality" of one's partner—the explanation given by Kreps et al. (1982)—but still considers immediate defection the only "rational" action, and not to do so is a "failure to behave according to one's rational insights" (p. 133), like not being able to stop smoking though one knows one should. Yet this is clearly incorrect. In a 100-round Prisoner's Dilemma, I *want* to cooperate with my partner; there is absolutely no "failure of will" involved.

handle some of these cases. The remainder can be dealt with in the concept of "local best responses" in behavioral strategies (§5.14). Here we show that Bayesian updating (§16.22) is not something added on to the Nash equilibrium concept, but is implied by it, so if crickets employ best response mating behaviors, they use Bayesian updating. We call a behavioral strategy profile that is a local best response at each information set a *Bayesian perfect equilibrium* (the term is used in a variety of ways in the literature).

Closely related to the concept of Bayesian perfection is Reinhardt Selten's notion of *trembling hand perfection* (§5.16), which suggests that reasonable Nash equilibria should be immune to small probabilities of error in the players' execution of choices. A "trembling hand perfect" Nash equilibrium is the limit of the equilibria of games with positive error probabilities, as these probabilities go to zero.

Selten's analysis highlights a problem with *both* trembling hand and Bayesian perfection, which we discuss in Nature Abhors Low Probability Events (§5.17). Because the cost of maintaining perceptual and behavioral systems is high, and because they can be easily misused, agents generally recognize a small set of *situational contexts* to which they have a repertoire of generally effective coping responses. When faced with a novel situation, agents fit the situation into one of these contexts. From an evolutionary standpoint *low-probability events are simply not worth worrying about*. Therefore, subgame perfection will predictably fail under a wide variety of real-life conditions.

5.2   Subgame Perfection

A *subgame* $\mathcal{H}$ of an extensive form game $\mathcal{G}$ is a part of the game that can stand alone as a game. Specifically, suppose h is a node of $\mathcal{G}$ that is a single information set. We say h and its successor nodes form a *subtree*, provided that if one node a is a successor of h, all the nodes in the same information set as a are also successors of h. Endowing this subtree with the same players, information sets, and payoffs as $\mathcal{G}$, we have a subgame $\mathcal{H}$ with root node h.

Note that we are not permitted to "break up" an information set to form a subtree, discarding some of the nodes and keeping others. For instance, consider the game tree for Selten's Horse (§5.15). This game has no proper subgames, because any subgame must include both node 3r and node 3l, and hence both node 1 and 2.[2]

---

[2]I don't know why this requirement is imposed on the definition of a subgame. I suspect

If $\mathcal{H}$ is a subgame of $\mathcal{G}$, then $\mathcal{H}$ is itself a game, and every pure strategy s_G in $\mathcal{G}$ has a counterpart s_H in $\mathcal{H}$ specifying that players in $\mathcal{H}$ make the same choices with the same probabilities as they do in $\mathcal{G}$. We call s_H the *restriction* of s_G to the subgame $\mathcal{H}$. The same idea can be expressed even more simply in terms of behavioral strategies: given a behavioral strategy profile p for $\mathcal{G}$, the corresponding behavioral strategy profile for $\mathcal{H}$ consists of the probability distributions given by p applied to the information sets in $\mathcal{H}$.

We say a Nash equilibrium of an extensive form game is *subgame perfect* if its restriction to every subgame is a Nash equilibrium of the subgame. It is clear that if s_G is a Nash equilibrium for a game $\mathcal{G}$, and if $\mathcal{H}$ is a subgame of $\mathcal{G}$ whose root node is reached with positive probability using s_G, then the restriction s_H of s_G to $\mathcal{H}$ must be a Nash equilibrium in $\mathcal{H}$. But if $\mathcal{H}$ is *not* reached using s_G, then it doesn't matter what players do in $\mathcal{H}$—their choices in $\mathcal{H}$ can be completely arbitrary, so long as these choices do not alter the way people play in parts of the game that *are* reached with positive probability. But how, you might ask, could this make a difference in the larger game? To see how, consider the following Microsoft-Netscape Game.

Microsoft and Netscape are planning to introduce a new type of Web browser. They must choose between two platforms, Java and ActiveX. If they introduce different platforms, their profits are zero. If they introduce the same platform, their profits are 1, plus Microsoft gets 1 if the platform is ActiveX and Netscape gets 1 if the platform is Java. The game tree is as shown in Fig. 5.1, where we assume that Microsoft chooses first.

Since Microsoft has one information set and two choices at that information set, we can write its pure strategy set as {ActiveX,Java}. Since Netscape has two information sets and two choices at each, its pure strategy set has four elements $\{JJ, JA, AJ, AA\}$. Here, the first letter says what Netscape

---

it is because in classical game theory the game must be "common knowledge" to the players, and if you break up information sets, some players think they're playing one game, while others think they are playing another. This is no problem for evolutionary game theory, in which what players "think" is of no importance. But I fear being prosecuted for the corruption of youth if I drop this standard requirement.

I am reminded of the story of the man who went for lunch at a Jewish delicatessen on Delancy Street in New York in about the year 1910. An Asian waiter came over and asked him in fluent Yiddish what he would like to eat. They had a pleasant conversation in Yiddish, and the man had a wonderful lunch. Curious about the Asian's linguistic talents, he asked the owner: "How does it happen that an Asian speaks fluent Yiddish?" "Shhhh," the owner replied, "I taught it to him—he thinks it's English!"

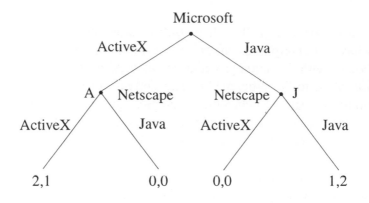

Figure 5.1. The Microsoft-Netscape game.

does if Microsoft plays ActiveX, and the second says what Netscape does if Microsoft plays Java. Thus, "*AJ*" means "play ActiveX if Microsoft plays ActiveX, and play Java if Microsoft plays Java."

It is easy to see that $\{A, AA\}$, $\{A, AJ\}$, and $\{J, JJ\}$ are all Nash equilibria (prove this formally!), but only the second is subgame perfect, because the first is not a Nash equilibrium when restricted to the subgame starting at J, and the third is not a Nash equilibrium when restricted to the subgame at A. The outcomes from $\{A, AA\}$ and $\{A, AJ\}$ are the same, since ActiveX is chosen by both players in either equilibrium. But the outcome from $\{J, JJ\}$ is that Java is chosen by both players. This is obviously to the benefit of Netscape, but it involves an *incredible threat:* Netscape threatens to choose Java *no matter what Microsoft does*, but Microsoft knows that when it actually comes time to choose at A, Netscape will in fact choose ActiveX, not Java.[3]

It is easy to see that a simultaneous move game has no subgames—actually, no *proper* subgames, since a game is always a subgame of itself—since all the nodes are in the same information set for at least one player, no matter how the extensive form game is depicted. Similarly, a game in which Nature

[3]If you are Netscape, you might try to convince Microsoft that you are *crazy*, or that you have already precommitted to Java (e.g., by building a factory for producing Java software). There are interesting examples of both strategies. Daniel Ellsberg once related that the Nixon administration executed a massive disinformation campaign to convince the Russians that President Nixon had lost his mind. The campaign included stories that Nixon was alcoholic and wandered the halls of the White House in the wee hours in his bathrobe, muttering to himself and poking at a big red (imaginary) button. The goal was to convince the Russians to back down on a nuclear missile placement dispute.

makes the first move and the outcome is not known by at least one other player (see chapter 12 for examples), also has no proper subgames.

At the other extreme, in a game of complete information (i.e., for which all information sets are singletons), *every* nonterminal node is the root node of a subgame. This allows us to find the subgame perfect Nash equilibria of such games by backward induction, as described in §2.3.

The notions of incredible threats and their counterpart *incredible promises* have contributed strongly to the theory of social interaction. But, the evidence on how people actually play games (see chapter 11) indicates clearly that *people rarely backward induct for more than a few rounds*, so the correct place of the notion of subgame perfection in a theory of strategic behavior has yet to be discovered. We previewed this issue in §2.18, and we develop it further in §11.4.1 and §15.8.

5.3 Stackelberg Leadership

A Stackelberg leader is a player who can precommit to following a certain action, so other players effectively consider the leader as "going first," and they predicate their actions on the preferred choices of the leader. Stackelberg leadership is a form of power flowing from

	t_1	t_2
s_1	0,2	3,0
s_2	2,1	1,3

the capacity to precommit. To see this, note that a form of behavior that would be an incredible threat or promise without the capacity to precommit becomes part of a subgame perfect Nash equilibrium when precommitment is possible. Formally, consider the normal form game to the right.

a. Write an extensive form game for which this is the corresponding normal form, and find all Nash equilibria.

b. Suppose the row player chooses first and the column player sees the row player's choice, but the payoffs are the same. Write an extensive form game, list the strategies of the two players, write a normal form game for this new situation, and find the Nash equilibria.

c. On the basis of these two games, comment on the observation "The capacity to precommit is a form of power."

5.4   The Subway Entry Deterrence Game

Subway has a monopoly on foot-long submarine sandwiches and makes a yearly profit of $100,000. Metro, a Canadian firm, contemplates entering the market, incurring setup costs of $25,000, which will force Subway to share its profits 50-50 with them. Subway vows to sell subs at cost, if necessary, to preserve its monopoly position. Metro's strategy choices are {enter,keep out} and Subway's choices are {fight price war,accommodate new entrant}. Draw the game tree, including the payoffs. Show that Subway's threat to fight is not credible.

You might think the answer would be different if Subway had stores in one hundred different cities, since Subway could then foster a "reputation" for underselling new entrants, which, while costly in one city, would deter potential entrants in the other ninety nine. But consider the following argument (Selten 1978). Suppose Subway had stores in two different cities. Then Subway's actions in the first city would not affect Subway's behavior in the second, since there are no more cities on which to use the reputation. Then suppose Subway had stores in three cities. Whatever it does in the first, after it is finished there, only two more cities remain, and we already know Subway cannot gain from price cutting in the two-city case, so neither can it do so in the three-city case. And so on, up to one hundred cities. What do you think of this argument?

5.5   The Dr. Strangelove Game

In the Cold War days, the USA and the Soviet Union had both conventional ground and nuclear forces. The Soviets had superior conventional forces. If the Soviets launched a ground attack on NATO countries in Europe, the USA could decide to use either nuclear or conventional ground forces to retaliate. A conventional retaliation would leave the Soviet Union better off and the USA worse off by an equal amount. If the USA retaliated with nuclear force, a nuclear war would ensue and the USA would be one hundred times worse off than in the conventional case. The Soviet Union would suffer just as much as the USA in the nuclear case.

a.   Draw a game tree for this problem, show the payoffs (set the status quo, in which the Soviet Union does not attack, to a payoff of zero for both sides), and find an equilibrium for the game.

b. Repeat the above, supposing the USA can precommit to using nuclear deterrence.

5.6 The Rubinstein Bargaining Model

Suppose two players bargain over the division of a dollar.[4] Player 1 goes first and offers player 2 a share x of the dollar. If player 2 accepts, the payoffs are $(1 - x, x)$, and the game is over. If player 2 rejects, the pie "shrinks" to $\delta < 1$, and player 2 offers player 1 a share y of this smaller pie. If player 1 accepts, the payoffs are $(y, \delta - y)$. Otherwise, the pie shrinks to δ^2, and it is once again player 1's turn to make an offer. The game continues until they settle, or if they never settle, the payoff is (0,0). The game tree is shown in Fig. 5.2.

Clearly, for any $x \in [0, 1]$ there is a Nash equilibrium in which the payoffs are $(1 - x, x)$, simply because if player 2 accepts nothing less than x, then it is Nash for player 1 to offer x to player 2, and conversely. But these equilibria are not all subgame perfect. What are the subgame perfect Nash equilibria?

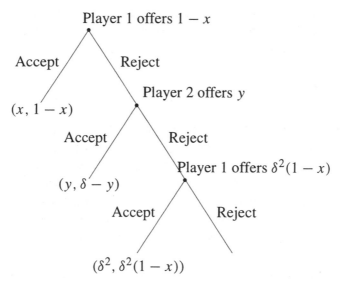

Figure 5.2. Payoffs for the Rubinstein bargaining model.

---

[4]This way of modeling bargaining was initiated by Ingolf Ståhl (1971) and Ariel Rubinstein (1982).

For the subgame perfect case, let z be the *most* player 1 can possibly get in any subgame perfect Nash equilibrium. Then the most player 1 can get on his second turn to offer is $\delta^2 z$, so on player 2's first turn, the most he must offer player 1 is $\delta^2 z$, so the least player 2 gets when it is his turn to offer is $\delta - \delta^2 z$. But then, on his first turn, player 1 must offer player 2 at least this amount, so his payoff is at most $1 - \delta + \delta^2 z$. But this must equal z, so we have

$$z = \frac{1 - \delta}{1 - \delta^2} = \frac{1}{1 + \delta}.$$

Now let z' be the *least* player 1 can possibly get in any subgame perfect Nash equilibrium. Then the least player 1 can get on his second turn to offer is $\delta^2 z'$, so on player 2's first turn, the least he must offer player 1 is $\delta^2 z'$, so the most player 2 gets when it is his turn to offer is $\delta - \delta^2 z'$. But then, on his first turn, the most player 1 must offer player 2 is this amount, so his payoff is at least $1 - \delta + \delta^2 z'$. But this must equal z', so we have

$$z' = \frac{1 - \delta}{1 - \delta^2} = \frac{1}{1 + \delta}.$$

Since $z = z'$, the *least* player 1 can earn and the *most* player 1 can earn in a subgame perfect Nash equilibrium are equal, so there is a *unique* subgame perfect Nash equilibrium, in which the payoffs are

$$\left(\frac{1}{1 + \delta}, \frac{\delta}{1 + \delta} \right).$$

Note that there is a small first-mover advantage, which disappears as $\delta \to 1$.

Do people actually find this subgame perfect equilibrium? Since it requires only two levels of backward induction, we might expect people to do so. But in fact, the game tree is *infinite*, and our trick to reducing backward induction to two steps is purely formal. Thus, we might *not* expect people to settle on the Rubinstein solution. Indeed, experimental evidence indicates that they do not (Neelin, Sonnenschein, and Spiegel 1988, Babcock, Loewenstein, and Wang 1995). Part of the reason is that *fairness* issues enter into many bargaining situations (see chapter 11). These issues are usually not important in the context of the current game, since unless the discount factor is very low, the outcome is almost a fifty-fifty split. But if we complicated the model a bit, for instance by giving players unequal "outside options" that occur with positive probability after each rejected offer, very unequal outcomes become possible. Also, the Rubinstein model predicts that all bargaining will be Pareto-optimal, since the first offer is in fact never refused. In real-world bargaining, however, breakdowns often occur (strike, war, divorce). Generally, we need models of bargaining with asymmetric information to have breakdowns with positive probability (see chapter 15 and §12.3).

5.7   Huey, Dewey, and Louie Split a Dollar

Huey, Dewey, and Louie have a dollar to split. Huey gets to offer first, and offers shares d and l to Dewey and Louie, keeping h for himself (so $h + d + l = 1$). If both accept, the game is over and the dollar is divided accordingly. If either Dewey or Louie rejects the offer, however, they come back the next day and start again, this time Dewey making the offer to Huey and Louie, and if this is rejected, on the third day Louie gets to make the offer. If this is rejected, they come back on the forth day with Huey again making the offer. This continues until an offer is accepted by both players, or until the universe winks out, in which case they get nothing. However, the present value of a dollar tomorrow for each of the players is $\delta < 1$.

Show that there exists a unique symmetric, stationary (i.e., players make the same offers on each round), subgame perfect equilibrium (interestingly enough, there exist other, nonsymmetric subgame perfect equilibria, but they are difficult to describe and could not occur in the real world).

5.8   The Little Miss Muffet Game

While eating her curds and whey, Miss Muffet confronted a spider sitting on her tuffet. Unphased, she informed the spider that they would engage in a bargaining game in which she would offer the spider a certain share x of the curds and whey. If the spider accepts, they will divide the food accordingly, and proceed on their merry ways. If the spider rejects, neither gets any of the food. Miss Muffet knows that spiders are both rational and benevolent: they only reject offers if they can gain something by doing so. Show that Muffet gets all of the curds and whey.

Now suppose the spider has enough of a scary countenance to force another game: if he rejects the first offer, he gets to make a counter offer to Miss Muffet, under the same conditions. He knows Miss Muffet is rational and benevolent as well, and hence will accept any offer unless she can do better by rejecting it. *But* the sun is hot, and bargaining takes time. By the time the second offer is accepted or rejected, the curds and whey have melted to half their original size. Show that Miss Muffet offers a 50-50 split, and the spider accepts immediately.

Now suppose there are a maximum of three rounds of bids and the food shrinks by one-third for each rejected offer. Show that Miss Muffet will offer the spider 1/3 of the food, and the spider will accept.

Now suppose there are an even number n of rounds, and the curds and whey shrink by $1/n$ per rejected offer. Show that Miss Muffet still offers the spider 1/2 of the food, and the spider will accept. But if there is an odd number n of rounds, and the curds and whey shrink by $1/n$ per rejected offer, then Miss Muffet offers the spider a share $1/2 - 1/2n$ of the food, the spider accepts, and Miss Muffet keeps the rest. As the number of periods increases, they converge to the Just Solution, sharing 50-50.

5.9 Nuisance Suits

Suppose a party contemplates suing another party over some purported Evil Thing the second party did. Call the first party the "plaintiff" and the second party the "defendant." Suppose the plaintiff's court cost for initiating a suit is c, the plaintiff's legal costs for going to trial are p, and the defendant's costs of defending himself is d. Suppose both sides know these costs and also share the knowledge that the probability that the plaintiff will win the suit is γ and the expected amount of the settlement is x. We assume $\gamma x < p$, so the suit is a frivolous "nuisance suit" that would not be pursued if the goal were to make money. Finally, suppose that before the case goes to trial (but after the suit is initiated), the parties can settle out of court for an amount s. We assume s is given, though clearly we could derive this value as well with the appropriate assumptions.

A consideration of the game tree for the problem, which is depicted in Fig. 5.3, shows that the only subgame perfect equilibrium is for the plaintiff to do nothing, since the threat of carrying through with the trial is not credible. For rolling back the game tree, we see that Drop Suit dominates Pursue Suit, so Reject Settlement dominates Accept Settlement, in which case No Offer and Offer Settlement are both inferior to Do Nothing.

The plaintiff's problem is that the threat to sue is not credible, since the suit is frivolous. But suppose the plaintiff puts his lawyer on *retainer*, meaning that he pays the amount p *in advance*, whether or not the suit is taken to trial. We show this in Fig. 5.4.

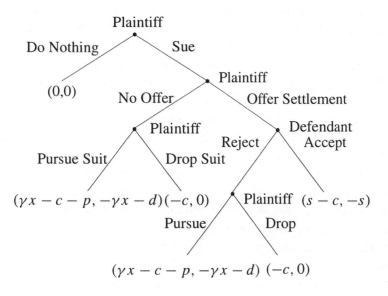

Figure 5.3. Nuisance suits.

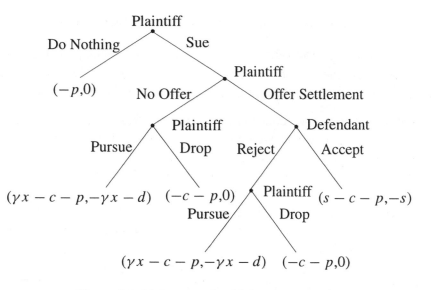

Figure 5.4. Nuisance suit with lawyer on retainer.

Then the payoffs at the Drop Suit leaf are $(-c - p, 0)$, so now Pursue Suit dominates Drop Suit. If $s > \gamma x$, plaintiff will Offer Settlement rather than No Offer, and if $\gamma x + d > s$, defendant prefers to Accept rather than Reject. Thus, the settlement is made and the payoffs are $(s - c - p, -s)$, since the plaintiff has to pay his lawyer's retainer fee p. Thus, this solution is better than Do Nothing for the plaintiff if $s > c + p$.

Note that if $\gamma = 0$ this is a perfect nonsense suit: the plaintiff has no chance of winning the suit, but he can offer to settle for $s = d$, which the defendant will accept, and this works as long as $d > c + p$.

Note that the plaintiff never gets to use the lawyer, so he can sue lots of people, settle all out of court, and still pay the single retainer p. If he can carry out n suits, the condition for profitability if $\gamma = 0$ is then $d > c + p/n$, which is a less demanding constraint.

How can the defendant protect himself against such nuisance suits? Pay his lawyer the retainer d before the fact. Then there is no gain from settling out of court. But of course if you face only *one* plaintiff, this is not a profitable solution. If you potentially face *many* plaintiffs, having a lawyer on retainer is a good idea, since otherwise you will settle out of court many times.

5.10   Cooperation in an Overlapping-Generations Economy

Consider a society in which there is a public good to which each member can contribute either zero or one unit of effort each period. The value of the public good to each member is the total amount of effort contributed to it.

a. Suppose the cost of contributing a unit of effort is α. Show that if $0 < \alpha < 1$, a dominant strategy for each member is to contribute a unit of effort, but if $\alpha > 1$, then a dominant strategy is to contribute no effort.

b. Suppose there are N members of this society. Show that if $1 < \alpha < N$, the unique Nash equilibrium is Pareto-inefficient, but that if $\alpha > N$ the equilibrium is efficient. Suppose for the rest of this problem that $1 < \alpha < N$, so members would benefit from erecting incentives that induced people to contribute to the public good.

c. At a town meeting, one member observed: "By the end of a period, we know which members contributed to the public good that period. Why don't we exclude a member from sharing in the public good in the next period if they failed to contribute in the current period?" Another said: "That seems like a good idea, but as we all know, we each live exactly T years, and with your plan, the eldest generation will certainly not contribute." A third person responded: "Well, we revere our elders anyway, so why not tolerate some indolence on their part? Indeed, let us agree to an 'age of veneration' T^* such that any member who fails to contribute in the first T^* periods of life is banished from ever enjoying the public good, but members who are older than T^* need not contribute." The first speaker queried: "How shall we determine the proper age of veneration?" The proposer responded: "We should choose T^* to maximize our net lifetime gain from the public good." They all agree.

d. Suppose there are n members of each generation, so $N = nT$, and they do not discount the future. Suppose also that $n(T - 1) \geq \alpha$. Show that

$$T^2 \geq \frac{4(\alpha - 1)}{n} \tag{5.1}$$

is necessary and sufficient for there to be a T^* such that the strategy in which each agent contributes up to age T^* and shirks thereafter is a Nash subgame perfect equilibrium.

e. Show that the optimal T^* is the largest integer satisfying equation (5.1).

5.11 The Finitely Repeated Prisoner's Dilemma

You are a subject in an experiment. You are brought into a room and seated at one end of a rickety wooden table, at the other end of which is a nebbishy little guy with a Hard Rock Café tee shirt and what looks like the flu. The experimenter comes in wearing Armani sunglasses. She hands each of you a sheet of paper and gives you a few minutes to read. The paper says:

> I will give you each $5.00, plus whatever you earn, for participating today. You see in front of you two cards. On the hidden side of one card is a C and on the other, a D. You will each hold up one of these cards. If you both choose the D (defect), you each get nothing, but if you each choose the C (cooperate), you each get $1.00. If you choose different cards, the person with the D gets $1.01 and the person with the C loses $0.01. You will repeat this interaction exactly one hundred times, after which you collect your money and go home.

You quickly note that each round (which we call a *one-shot game*, and the *stage game* for the *finitely repeated game* in which you have been thrust) is a Prisoner's Dilemma, D being a strictly dominant strategy for both players. But what is the effect of repeating play one hundred times? Obviously, there are a *lot* more pure strategies, since at each stage of the game your move depends upon the whole previous history of the game. For instance, on the last play, there are $2^{99} \times 2^{99} \approx 4 \times 10^{59}$ previous histories, so the number of pure strategies on the last play alone is two to this power, which is a Really Big Number.

But then you remember backward induction (pruning the game tree—§2.3). Starting on the last round, you realize that now you truly do have a Prisoner's Dilemma, since nothing you or the other player does can affect any future play of the game. You also realize that your partner, appearances not withstanding, is "rational" in the sense that he will never play a strictly dominated strategy. Therefore, he will play D on the final round, so your best response is to do the same. But then nothing you can do on round 99 can affect the outcome of round 100, so you will both defect on round 99. And so on right back to round 1. The conclusion is Elephants all the way down: you both play D on each round and go home poor.[5]

Despite the fact that game theory has reduced the gazillions of possible strategies to a unique subgame perfect Nash equilibrium, we all know this is *not* how you or almost anyone else would actually play this game.[6] You would say to yourself, "Why don't I just play C for a few rounds and see if Mr. Diseased over there does the same? It would only cost me a few cents, and the payoff if he cooperates would be fantastic. If he does cooperate, we could continue the whole thing until we get very near the end of the game. Since the temptation is so small (he only gains one cent by defecting), in fact I will cooperate almost until the last round." So game theory does not predict well in this case.

You might want to chalk this up to the fact that people, for one reason or another, simply do not go beyond a few iterations in eliminating dominated strategies (§2.16). But this is not really the problem. Suppose I said to

---

[5]"Elephants all the way down" refers to a famous story of relevance to the theory of repeated games. A renowned astronomer is explaining to a rapt audience that the Earth is held in its orbit about the Sun by gravitational and inertial forces. An outraged listener protests: "Sir, you are preposterous. The Earth is sustained in its ordained position in the Universe on the back of a mighty elephant." "And what," asks the astronomer, "holds up the mighty elephant?" The interlocutor appears taken aback, but thinks for a minute and finally replies: "Don't be impudent, young man. It's elephants all the way down."

[6]For experimental evidence, see Andreoni and Miller 1993 and Kahn and Murnigham 1993.

myself,

> I am perfectly rational, and my partner probably is as well.
> Therefore, he should play D on the first round. But if I play C
> on the first round, he will know either that I am not rational, or
> that I *am* rational but I am trying to fool him into believing I
> am *not* rational. Either way, if he is rational, he will play C on
> following rounds, at least until near the end of the game. But
> of course if he is rational, he will think like me, and hence he
> too will play C from the beginning. So I actually have nothing
> to lose by cooperating on the first round.

For this reasoning to work, there must be a positive probability of one of
us in fact not being rational (in the limited sense of always discarding strictly
dominated strategies). For otherwise, when I play C, my partner will simply
think I made a mistake and will keep on playing D. Suppose that there is
a probability $\epsilon > 0$ that a random person is a Tit-for-Tatter rather than a
rational player. A Tit-for-Tatter cooperates on the first round, then does what
the other player did on the previous round. If I defect on the first round, my
partner knows I am rational and will defect thereafter. But if I cooperate on
the first round, with probability ϵ I am a Tit-for-Tatter. If my partner is a
Tit-for-Tatter, he will simply cooperate as well. If he is "rational," he then
reasons:

> This guy could be either a Tit-for-Tatter or "rational." If the
> former, my best response is to cooperate up to the last round,
> then defect. If he is rational, at some point he will defect on
> me. Let's assume the worst-case scenario, that we are in round
> k and I *know* that if "rational," he will defect in this round. By
> cooperating rather than defecting, I lose $0.01, since we will
> both defect forever after, either way. However if my partner is
> a Tit-for-Tatter, by defecting on round k I lose $100 - k$, since I
> get my $1.01 now instead of on round 100, but I lose $100 - k$
> rounds of cooperation returns. So as long as $(100-k)\epsilon > 0.01$,
> I should cooperate on round k. Now I believe that $\epsilon > 1\%$, so
> I should cooperate right up to round 99 for certain.

If I reason the same way, then we both cooperate up to the last round,
provided we both believe that at least one person out of one hundred is a
Tit-for-Tatter.[7] And we should, since there is overwhelming evidence that

lots of people are Tit-for-Tatters (Fehr and Tyran 1996, Fehr, Gächter, and Kirchsteiger 1997), a point we shall elaborate upon in chapter 11.

Why does backward induction give such a seemingly absurd result? We can gain insight into this question through an agent-based simulation of the game. Fig. 5.5 shows a simulation in which two players play a 100-stage prisoner's dilemma in which the players receive one dollar for each stage played, and at the first defect (if any), the defecting player receives $1.01, the player's partner losing $0.01, and the game is terminated. The game is simulated with a population of one thousand agents who are hard-wired with a "gene" to cooperate for a certain number of rounds before defecting. We call this the agent's *defection point*. Each agent is initially randomly assigned a gene with a value between 1 and 100. The agents are then randomly paired on each round, and paired agents play the 100-stage Prisoner's Dilemma game. After each round, the lowest 0.50% of scorers die, an equal number of the highest scorers reproduce, with a mutation rate (where an agent's defection point is randomly altered) of 0.001.

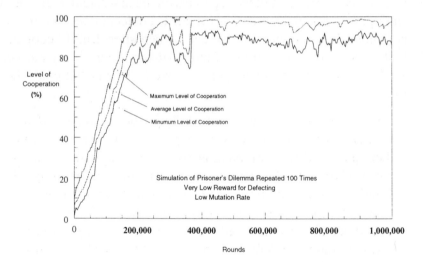

Figure 5.5. Simulation of the finitely repeated prisoner's dilemma with a very low incentive to defect (1%) and low mutation rate (0.1%).

It is clear that the simulation, rather than the logic of backward induction, confirms our intuition. At the start of play, the average level of cooperation

[7]For a more complete treatment of this model, see Kreps, Milgrom, Roberts, and Wilson 1982.

(i.e., the average defection point of the agents) is about 5. By round 200,000, most of the low-cooperation (low defection point) agents have been replaced by high-cooperation (high defection point) agents, so the average level of cooperation is in the 95 range, and the least cooperative agents defect only after round 85. Fig. 5.5 shows that, despite some bouncing around, even after 1,000,000 rounds the level of cooperation remains above the 90% level.

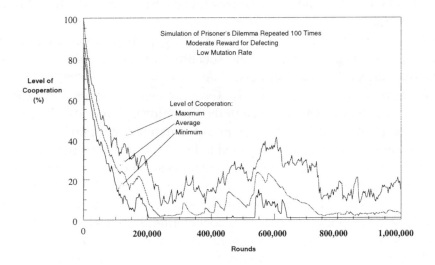

Figure 5.6. Simulation of the finitely repeated prisoner's dilemma with a moderate incentive to defect (100%) and low mutation rate (0.1%).

A plausible explanation of emergence of cooperation is that the mutation rate is sufficiently high that more cooperators are created in each round than are killed for their excess altruism. If we increase the reward for defection, the dynamic exhibited in Fig. 5.5 might be reversed. In Fig. 5.6 we increase the reward for defection and the penalty for being defected upon to one (the value of cooperating for one round), and cooperation is indeed severely attenuated over time. In this simulation, we used 2000 agents, randomly programmed with defection points between 1 and 100, with an average of about 50. Cooperation at first increases rapidly to the 95 level (barely perceptible in the figure, since this occurs in the first 3000 rounds), and then declines to very low levels. There are surges of cooperation (e.g., at round 550,000 or so) up to 20, but the average generally hovers below 5.

To see why cooperation declines, note that the highest cooperators are relatively less fit than the next highest, and in this case this disadvantage is not offset by mutations. The maximum level of cooperation thus declines over time. This reduces the gains from cooperation for the other players, so the average declines in turn.

We conclude that our intuition concerning the absurdity of the backward induction solution is thus probably due to the fact that we do not face the relentless process of "weeding out" cooperators in daily life that is depicted in the simulation. If we did, we would not find the backward induction solution strange, and we would experience life in our world, to paraphrase Thomas Hobbes, as brutish, nasty, and short. Luckily, perhaps, there wouldn't be many of us, since it is precisely our sociality as a species that accounts for our stunning evolutionary success.

We have, of course, discovered a force countering the tendency for co-operators to be weeded out through the evolutionary process—the force is mutation itself! A sufficiently high rate of mutation can support a long-term high level of cooperation, as depicted in Fig. 5.7, even when the gains from defection and the costs of being defected upon are very large (in this case 5). In this simulation we increase mutation to the extremely high rate of 30%.

Note in this case that after about 400,000 rounds the population oscillates wildly, with dips down to about 15% cooperation, and then recovery to about 60% cooperation. It is clear that the high rate of mutation prevents the pop-ulation from attaining an approximately steady state with cooperation near zero, since near zero cooperation, mutations are biased in the positive direc-tion; with nonnegligible probability, a series of mutational shocks pushes the cooperation up to a fairly high level, after which the selection process again pressures the average in a downward direction.

At first glance, the game-theoretic analysis of the Finitely Repeated Pris-oner's Dilemma is a dramatic failure for game theory, since its equilibrium predictions are wildly at variance with reality. It is easy to see why, however: in real life we don't play very many finitely repeated games. I actually can't think of any of even minimal importance. However, *we do not expect a Nash equilibrium to be approximated in real life unless there is some plausible dynamic for which the Nash equilibrium is a stable stationary point*. The Finitely Repeated Prisoner's Dilemma has no such dynamic.

We routinely play many games, however, with an *indefinite* number of repetitions (work, family life, going to the supermarket, having your house painted). So perhaps the indefinite repetitions version of the repeated game is better behaved. We turn to this scenario in chapter 6.

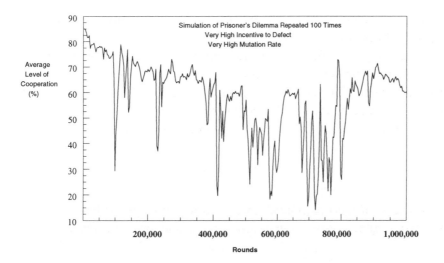

Figure 5.7. Simulation of the finitely repeated Prisoner's Dilemma with a high mutation rate.

5.12   The Finitely Repeated Prisoner's Dilemma II

	C	D
C	1,1	$-b,a$
D	$a,-b$	0,0

Our argument in §5.11 was actually pretty fast and loose. We showed that if there is an $\epsilon >$ 0 probability that your partner in the 100-round Prisoner's Dilemma is a reciprocator, then you should cooperate on any round k satisfying $(100-k)\epsilon > 0.01$. But this does not give us a full-fledged strategy for the game. The general argument is a bit delicate but worth going through (Guttman 1996). We use the game to the right, where $a > 1, b > 0$ and $a - b < 2$, and we assume there are n rounds to the game. For convenience we also assume that $(1 - \epsilon)a < 1$, where ϵ is the probability that a random player is a reciprocator (Tit-for-Tatter) rather than a best responder. A similar but slightly more complex argument is needed when $(1 - \epsilon)a > 1$, which we will not deal with here. There is no discounting.

a. Show that a best responder can never gain by defecting before the last round on a reciprocator.

b. Let us define *preemption* by a player as playing D on a round where neither player played D on the previous round. Show that if player 1 preempts at round k, player 2 will play D at least until such time as player 1 returns to playing C.

c. Show that player 1 cannot gain by defecting on some round and returning to cooperation on some later round.

d. Show that even if a player expects her partner, if a best responder, to preempt at stage k, she should not preempt at stage $k - 1$.

e. Show that in any equilibrium, neither player will defect before round

$$k^* = n - \frac{b(1 - \epsilon)}{\epsilon}.$$

f. Show that if all best responders expect other best responders to defect on round n, then cooperating up to round n is a Nash equilibrium.

5.13   Fuzzy Subgame Perfection

Myron and Bob, the Hedge Fund Gang, decide to use their sophisticated knowledge of game theory to rob ten billion dollars from a bank. Robbing the bank, they discover, is easy, but enforcing an equal split of the loot is hard. They agree that Bob, who is handy with a gun, will cover for Myron, who will snatch the cash, while Bob will take an incriminating photograph of the two of them robbing the bank. Unless he receives half the money, Bob will send the photograph to his lawyer, with instructions to set up an escrow account in his name, send the account number to Myron, and send the picture to the police unless there is five billion dollars in the escrow account within twenty-four hours.

Myron and Bob stand to lose their reputations if caught stealing, and being very prominent economists, their reputations are worth one billion dollars each. Using the criterion of subgame perfection, Bob concludes that Myron must give him half the loot. Satisfied with the arrangement, they rob the bank.

Myron, however, notices that Bob has *two* lawyers, Ethel and Fred, and could send the photo to either one. He therefore takes the whole ten billion, and disappears, sending Bob a note with the following message: "I am keeping the whole ten billion. If you send a letter to either Ethel or Fred, I will still keep the whole ten billion, and we will both be caught. You may think that this violates subgame perfection, but it does not. The game tree (Fig. 5.8) shows that there are no proper subgames, and hence the Nash equilibrium in which I take all the money and you do not send the photo is

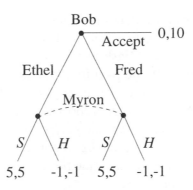

Figure 5.8. Fuzzy subgame perfection.

subgame perfect. So my threat must be credible." Bob, realizing Myron is absolutely correct, does not send the photo, and ends up making his fortune by dabbling in securities.

Of course, had Bob sent the photo to one of the lawyers, Myron would have surely split the money, since subgame or not, Myron is better off by gaining five billion rather than losing one billion.

The failure of subgame perfection to provide a plausible solution to this problem stems from the arbitrary decision to require that a subgame start with an information set that contains a single node. Suppose we drop this requirement, and define a *fuzzy subgame* $\mathcal{F}$ of a game $\mathcal{G}$ as follows. Let v be an information set of $\mathcal{G}$ such that if a node A is a successor to a node in v, then all the nodes in the same information set as A are also successors of nodes in v (this ensures that we do not "chop up" information sets in forming fuzzy subgames). The nodes of the fuzzy subgame corresponding to v consists of a new root node r_v, plus the nodes in v and all of the successor nodes in $\mathcal{G}$ to the nodes in v. We then assign Nature to the root node r_v, with a branch from r_v to each of the nodes in v. The information sets, assignments of players to information sets, and payoffs in $\mathcal{F}$ are then taken to be the same as in $\mathcal{G}$.

To assign probabilities to Nature's move at r_v, let s be a strategy profile in $\mathcal{G}$, and suppose the nodes in v are $v_1, \ldots, v_k$. Let $p_i(s)$ be the probability that the path through the game tree of $\mathcal{G}$ induced by s goes through v_i, for $i = 1, \ldots, k$, and let $p_v(s) = p_1(s) + \ldots + p_k(s)$. If $p_v(s) > 0$, we assign the branch from r_v to v_i the probability $p_i(s)/p_v(s)$, for $i = 1, \ldots, k$. If $p_v(s) = 0$, we assign a probability distribution to the branches at r_v however we please.

A strategy profile s in $\mathcal{G}$ induces a strategy profile s_v in $\mathcal{F}$ in the obvious fashion, and if $p_v(s) > 0$, it is not too hard to show that if s is a Nash equilibrium in $\mathcal{G}$, then s_v is a Nash equilibrium in $\mathcal{F}$, and the payoffs to the players in $\mathcal{F}$ coincide with the payoffs to the players in $\mathcal{G}$, conditional on passing through the information set v. If $p_v(s) = 0$, however, s_v need not be a Nash equilibrium of $\mathcal{F}$, since information set v is never reached in $\mathcal{G}$. We may define s to be *fuzzy subgame perfect* if it is a Nash equilibrium in every fuzzy subgame. Clearly, the arguments recommending the rejection of Nash equilibria that are not subgame perfect extend to equilibria that are not fuzzy subgame perfect.

The Nash equilibrium for the Hedge Fund Gang in which Myron takes everything and Bob does not send the photo is *not* fuzzy subgame perfect, since no matter how we assign probabilities to the two nodes in Myron's information set, splitting the money (S) dominates holding out (H). The Nash equilibrium in which Bob sends the photo to Ethel with probability p and Fred with probability $1 - p$, and Myron deposits the five billion in the escrow account, by contrast, is fuzzy subgame perfect for any $p \in [0,1]$.[8]

5.14   Perfect Behavioral Nash Equilibria

In §4.45, we found that a Nash equilibrium in behavioral strategies p has the property that for each player i, and for each information set v belonging to i, p_v is a best response to p_{-v}. While a satisfying result, from the behavioral point of view it is quite awkward, since it says nothing about i's behavior at v if v is not along the game path (i.e., p assigns probability zero to reaching v). You may say "who cares what happens with probability zero?" but as we have stressed before, other players may have avoided v precisely because they fear what i would do there, so treating i's behavior there as arbitrary leads to a faulty analysis of the game. Here is a partial way around this problem—we cannot avoid it completely, since sometimes the only way to analyze an equilibrium is by specifying the precise out-of-equilibrium behavior of the system.

---

[8]We write $[a, b]$ to mean the set of numbers $\{x \mid a \leq x \leq b\}$, and we call this the *closed interval* $[a, b]$.

Suppose i chooses at node $a \in v$. The expected payoff to using p_v given p_{-v}, is then

$$\pi_i(p_v, p_{-v}|a) = \sum_{t \in T} P[a, t|(p_v, p_{-v})]\pi_i(t),$$

where T is the set of terminal nodes, $\pi_i(t)$ is the payoff to i at terminal node $t \in T$, and $P[a, t|p]$ is the probability of reaching t from a given p (see equation 4.1 in §4.45). If we have the probability $P[r, a|p, v]$ of being at node a, given that i is choosing at v and p is being played, then i should choose p_v to maximize

$$\pi_i(p_v, p_{-v}|v) = \sum_{a \in v} P[a|v, p_{-v}]\pi_i(p_v, p_{-v}|a),$$

where $P[a|v, p_{-v}]$ is the probability of reaching a from the root, given p_{-v} (this does not depend on p_v). To find $P[a, t|p]$, we note that

$$P[v|p] = \sum_{a \in v} P[r, a|p]$$

is the probability of reaching v, given p. If this is nonzero, then for $a \in v$, the conditional probability (§16.21 and §16.22)

$$P[a|v, p] = \frac{P[r, a|p]}{P[v|p]} \tag{5.2}$$

represents the probability of being at node a, given that i is choosing at v and players are using behavioral profile p. We call this *Bayesian updating* because i uses the fact that v has been attained to derive the probability of various nodes in v. If $P[v|p] = 0$, however, i gains no additional information, and we define the probability distribution $\{P[a|v, p]|a \in v\}$ arbitrarily.

We conclude that the expected payoff to player i using p_v at v, given p_{-v}, is

$$\pi_i(p_v, p_{-v}|v) = \sum_{a \in v} P[a|v, p_{-v}] \sum_{t \in T} P[a, t|(p_v, p_{-v})]\pi_i(t).$$

We say that p_v^* is a *local best response* to p_{-v} if p_v^* maximizes $\pi_i(p_v, p_{-v}|v)$ over all probability distributions p_v over v.

We then have the following Fundamental Theorem on Bayesian Updating in Extensive Form Games: *If p is a Nash equilibrium in behavioral strategies* *of the extensive form game $\mathcal{G}$ and if v is an information set that is reached with positive probability given p, then p_v is a local best response to p_{-v}.*

The proof of this theorem is straightforward. Clearly,

$$\pi_i(p_v, p_{-v}) = \pi_i(p_v, p_{-v}|v)P[v|p] + \text{ terms not involving } p_v.$$

Moreover, $P[v|p]$ does not depend on p_v. Thus, if $P[v|p] > 0$, p_v maximizes $\pi_i(\cdot, p_{-v}|v)$, so p_v is a local best response at v. Q.E.D.

For an example of Bayesian updating, consider Real Men Don't Eat Quiche (§4.41). If you solved this correctly, you found that the probability α that Clem uses BB is 1/2, and the probability β that the Dark Stranger uses BB is also 1/2. This is a complete solution without using Bayesian updating. The answer must be *compatible* with Bayesian updating. Let $T = $ Tough, $B = $ Beer, $W = $ Wimp. Then we have $P[T] = 1/3$ and $P[W] = 2/3$. Also $P[B|T] = 1$ and $P[B|W] = 1/2$, since we found that $\alpha = 1/2$. Thus,

$$P[T|B] = \frac{P[B|T]P[T]}{P[B|T]P[T] + P[B|W]P[W]}$$

$$= \frac{1/3}{1/3 + (1/2)(2/3)} = \frac{1}{2}.$$

Thus, the payoff to Bully is 1/2 and the payoff to Defer is also 1/2, allowing the Dark Stranger to randomize.

If v is reached with probability zero given p, the above analysis may of course fail, since p_v need not be a best response to p_{-v} even if p is a Nash equilibrium. We then confront a situation similar to that of incredible threats: should v be reached, what will player i actually do? Note that we cannot depend on subgame perfection here, or even on fuzzy subgame perfection, because the various players' information sets may be so intertwined that v is not even the root of a fuzzy subgame. But given the behavioral strategies of the other players, we can still expect i to play a local best response at v. We say a Nash equilibrium in behavioral strategies is a *perfect Bayesian Nash equilibrium* if players use local best responses at all information sets. The perfect Bayesian criterion can eliminate implausible equilibria, as we see in the next problem.

5.15   Selten's Horse

Suppose Franz, Gustav, and Walter play the game illustrated in Fig. 5.9 (named after Reinhardt Selten). There are clearly two pure strategy Nash

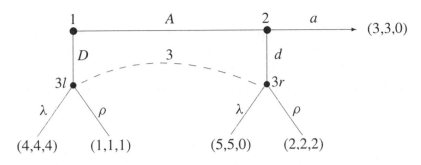

Figure 5.9. Selten's Horse

equilibria to this game: (A, a, ρ) and (D, a, λ). Moreover, there is a set M of mixed strategy equilibria given by

$$M = \{(A, a, p_\lambda \lambda + (1 - p_\lambda)\rho)|0 \le p_\lambda \le 1/3\},$$

where p_λ is the probability that Walter chooses λ, all of which of course have the same payoff (3,3,0). There is also a set N of mixed strategy equilibria given by

$$N = \{(D, p_a a + (1 - p_a)d, \lambda)|1/2 \le p_a \le 1\},$$

where p_a is the probability that Gustav chooses a, all of which have the same payoff (4,4,4). Now (D, a, λ), and indeed the whole set N, are pretty suspicious, since if Gustav were given a chance to move, he would obviously play d. This looks like a case of a Nash equilibrium that is not subgame perfect, but in fact this game *has* no proper subgames so (D, a, λ) is subgame perfect. There is a fuzzy subgame beginning with Walter's move, but this does not affect the analysis of Gustav's behavior. However, it is easy to see that a is not a local best response, so (D, a, λ) is not a perfect Nash equilibrium of the extensive form game.

By contrast, (A, a, ρ), and indeed all equilibria in M, are perfect Bayesian equilibria, as long as we use a probability distribution over Walter's information set that assigns a probability of less than 2/5 to $3l$, which we are free to do.

Show that (a) a is not a local best response, and (b) there are no Nash equilibria other than those in M and N.

5.16   Trembling Hand Perfection

Suppose an information set ν with more than one node is attained with probability zero in a Nash equilibrium using behavioral profile p. Nash equilibrium places no restrictions on p_v, while the perfect Bayesian criterion requires that p_v be a local best response given an arbitrary probability distribution over the nodes in v. But in place of arbitrary assignment, we should enrich the model in a manner that better reflects the reality we are trying to portray. *Trembling hand perfection* is an enrichment that can be defended in some circumstances. We begin with an example.

Suppose that in Selten's Horse (§5.15) when Franz intends A with probability p_A, he chooses A with probability $\epsilon_1 + (1 - 2\epsilon_1)p_A$ (where $\epsilon_1 < 1/2$); in effect, Franz has a *trembling hand*, and with probability $2\epsilon_1$ he makes a mistake, in which case he moves A or D with equal probability. Similarly, suppose when Gustav intends a with probability p_a, he chooses a with probability $\epsilon_2 + (1 - 2\epsilon_2)p_a$ (where $\epsilon_2 < 1/2$). Under these given assumptions, all information sets are reached with positive probability when $\epsilon_1, \epsilon_2 > 0$, so Gustav and Walter must choose local best responses and Walter is subject to Bayesian updating.

a.   Calculate the actual probability p_{3l} of being at $3l$ when Walter chooses.

b.   Find the perfect Bayesian Nash equilibria in behavioral strategies of this new game, and show that when we let $\epsilon_1, \epsilon_2 \to 0$, the equilibrium tends to the perfect Bayesian Nash equilibria in the game without trembles. HINT: You must use the fact that with trembles, every information set is reached, so Nash equilibria must be local best responses and hence, must use Bayesian updating.

In general, we say a Nash equilibrium p of an n-player extensive form game $\mathcal{G}$ is *trembling hand perfect* (not to be confused with subgame perfect or perfect Bayesian, which are distinct concepts) if the following condition holds (Selten 1975). For each player i, let $0 < \epsilon_i < 1$ and suppose that for every information set v, if i chooses at v, then i is constrained to choose p_v such that $p_v(a) \geq \epsilon_i$ for all $a \in v$. We call this the *perturbed game* $\mathcal{G}(\epsilon)$, where $\epsilon = (\epsilon_1, \ldots, \epsilon_n)$. Since in $\mathcal{G}(\epsilon)$ each player uses each strategy with positive probability, each information set must be reached, and hence every Nash equilibrium $p(\epsilon)$ is perfect Bayesian. We say p is trembling hand perfect if it is the limit of a sequence of perfect Bayesian equilibria $\{p(\epsilon^k)\}$ for some sequence of error vectors $\{\epsilon^k\}$ that converges to zero.

5.17   Nature Abhors Low Probability Events

Both trembling hand and Bayesian perfection presume that agents play optimally at very low probability events. Other considerations suggest that under evolutionarily relevant conditions, agents will not play optimally in such circumstances.

Biologists stress that living beings are governed by the Four F's: feeding, fighting, fleeing, and mating. These are all high probability events, and the number of variants in the behavioral repertoire of an agent in each of these spheres is generally small. Upon encountering a set of environmental stimuli, an agent first assigns the situation to one of a limited number of pre-given *situational contexts*, and then refers to the behavioral repertoire appropriate for that context for the proper choice of action. When an agent comes upon a new and strange situation, the agent does not create a new context, but rather relates the situation to one of the situational contexts for which the agent already possesses heretofore effective coping responses. Therefore, *all events encountered by living beings are high probability events*.

The number of situational contexts an agent recognizes and the number of behavioral responses appropriate to each are governed by the principle of evolutionary fitness. Adding a context, or a response within a context, has two costs that are "fixed" in the sense that they have minimum levels independent of frequency of use. First, an expanded discriminatory or behavioral repertoire requires additional neurological and physiological mechanisms. These mechanisms must be fueled and maintained in good repair at all times. Second, such responses can be deployed when they are inappropriate, causing harm to the organism (Heiner 1983, 1993). Therefore, the lower the probability of use, the less likely will the expanded responsive capacities contribute to fitness.

Since low probability events are evolutionarily unimportant, evolutionary game theory suggests that violations of subgame perfection and related refinement criteria may be common social events. They are.

6

Repeated Games, Trigger Strategies, and Tacit Collusion

> An economic transaction is a solved political problem. Economics has gained the title of Queen of the Social Sciences by choosing solved political problems as its domain.
>
> *Lerner (1972)*

> Money confers short-side power.
>
> *Bowles and Gintis (1993b)*

6.1 Introduction

When a game is repeated an indefinite number of times by the same players, the anomalies associated with finitely repeated games (§5.11) disappear. Moreover, such games are of great practical importance—we go to work every day for the same boss, we wake up every morning with the same spouse, we buy the same products, the same firms compete in the same markets, and so on. Except, in each case, sometimes we don't—which is why the repeated game is so strategically important.

The central result in the theory of repeated games is the Folk Theorem, which is an essentially negative result in classical game theory saying that repeated games have zillions of equilibria. Of course, the Folk Theorem has virtually no standing in evolutionary game theory, because few of the equilibria it supports are stable with respect to a plausible evolutionary dynamic. Nevertheless, it is worth presenting this theorem in some detail, since it exemplifies the logic of repeated games. I also present Tacit Collusion (§6.3) in class, because of its practical importance in industrial regulation and economic policy. Tit-for-Tat (§6.11) is also a classroom topic, because it is analytically challenging and historically important.

The chapter closes with an extended analysis of Contingent Renewal Contracts (§6.14), which summarizes some of my own research with Samuel Bowles, expanding on Bowles and Gintis (1993b).

6.2   Big Fish and Little Fish

Many species of fish are attacked by parasites that attach themselves to gills and inner mouth parts. Often such fish will form a symbiotic relationship with a smaller species of fish for whom the parasite is a major food source. Mutual trust is involved, however, since the larger fish must avoid the temptation of eating the smaller fish, and the smaller fish must avoid the temptation of taking a chunk out of the larger fish, thereby obtaining a meal with much less work than picking around for the tiny parasites. This scenario, which is doubtless even more common and more important for humans than for fish, is explored in the following problem.

Suppose Big Fish and Little Fish play the Prisoner's Dilemma shown on the right at times $t = 0, 1, 2, \ldots$ The payoff to each is the sum of the payoffs over all periods, weighted by

	C	D
C	5,5	-3,8
D	8,-3	0,0

discount factor δ, with $0 < \delta < 1$—a *discount factor* δ relates to a *discount rate* ρ by the formula $\delta = 1/(1 + \rho)$. We call the game played in each period the *stage game* of a *repeated game* in which at each period the players can condition their moves on the complete previous history of the various stages. A strategy that dictates following one course of action until a certain condition is met and then following a different strategy for the rest of the game is called a *trigger strategy*.

THEOREM 6.1   *The cooperative solution (5,5) can be achieved as a subgame perfect Nash equilibrium of the repeated game if δ is sufficiently close to unity and each player uses the trigger strategy of cooperating as long as the other player cooperates, and defecting forever if the other player defects on one round.*

PROOF: We use the fact that for any discount factor δ with $0 < \delta < 1$,

$$1 + \delta + \delta^2 + \ldots = \frac{1}{1 - \delta}.$$

To see this, write

$$x = 1 + \delta + \delta^2 + \ldots$$
$$= 1 + \delta(1 + \delta + \delta^2 + \ldots) = 1 + \delta x,$$

from which the result follows.

By the way, there is a faster way of arriving at the same result. Consider a repeated game that pays 1 now and in each period to a certain player, and the discount factor is δ. Let x be the value of the game to the player. The player receives 1 now and then gets to play exactly the same game in the next period. Since the value of the game in the next period is x, its present value is δx. Thus $x = 1 + \delta x$, so $x = 1/(1 - \delta)$.

Now suppose both agents play the trigger strategy. Then, the payoff to each is $5/(1 - \delta)$. Suppose a player uses another strategy. This must involve cooperating for a number (possibly zero) of periods, then defecting forever; for once the player defects, his opponent will defect forever, the best response to which is to defect forever. Consider the game from the time t at which the first player defects. We can call this $t = 0$ without loss of generality. A fish that defects receives 8 immediately and nothing thereafter. Thus the cooperate strategy is Nash if and only if $5/(1 - \delta) \geq 8$, or $\delta \geq 3/8$. When δ satisfies this inequality, the pair of trigger strategies is also subgame perfect, since the situation in which both parties defect forever is Nash subgame perfect. Q.E.D.

This gives us an elegant solution to the problem, but in fact there are lots of other subgame perfect Nash equilibria to this game. For instance, Big Fish and Little Fish can trade off trying to bite and eat each other:

THEOREM 6.2 *Consider the following trigger strategy for Little Fish: alternate $C, D, C, \ldots$ as long as Big Fish alternates $D, C, D, \ldots$. If Big Fish deviates from this pattern, defect forever. Suppose Big Fish plays the complementary strategy: alternate $D, C, D, \ldots$ as long as Little Fish alternates $C, D, C, \ldots$. If Little Fish deviates from this pattern, defect forever. These two strategies form a subgame perfect Nash equilibrium for δ sufficiently close to unity.*

PROOF: The payoffs are now $-3, 8, -3, 8, \ldots$ for Little Fish and $8, -3, 8, -3, \ldots$ for Big Fish. Let x be the payoffs to Little Fish. Little Fish gets -3 today, 8 in the next period and then gets to play the game all over again starting two periods from today. Thus, $x = -3 + 8\delta + \delta^2 x$. Solving this, we get $x = (8\delta - 3)/(1 - \delta^2)$. The alternative is for Little Fish to defect at some point, the most advantageous time being when it is his turn to get -3. He then gets zero in that and all future periods. Thus, cooperating is Nash if and only if $x \geq 0$, which is equivalent to $8\delta - 3 \geq 0$, or $\delta \geq 3/8$. Q.E.D.

The above equilibrium is pretty silly, because both fish do worse here than by fully cooperating, which they are capable of doing exactly when they can sustain this equilibrium. The value of the game to Big Fish is x, and it is easy to check that this is always less than $5/(1 - \delta)$. Little Fish does even worse. Despite being silly, at least this pair of strategies resonates with us—it is similar to the spiteful quarrels that family members often manage to sustain over long periods of time. But there are many other subgame perfect Nash equilibria that simply defy any semblance of reality. Consider, for instance:

THEOREM 6.3 *Suppose both Little Fish and Big Fish alternate* $C, D, C, \ldots$ *as long as the other does the same, so the payoffs are* $5, 0, 5, 0, \ldots$ *, both players otherwise using the trigger strategy of defecting forever. This pair of strategies forms a subgame perfect Nash equilibrium for suitably low discount rates.*

PROOF: The present value of the stream $5, 0, 5, 0, \ldots$ is the solution x to $x = 5 + 0\delta + x\delta^2$, which gives

$$x = \frac{5}{1 - \delta^2}.$$

By defecting instead of cooperating, a player gets 8 immediately and zero forever after, for a total payoff of 8. Thus, cooperating is Nash if and only if $x \geq 8$, which gives $\delta \geq \sqrt{3/8} \approx 0.61$.

Can you think of other creative subgame perfect Nash equilibria? Here is one: Little Fish plays C except on her birthday and any time the time period t is a multiple of 7777; Big Fish plays C except on Greek Orthodox (fish) holidays. Each tolerates the other's play, but responds to a deviation by defecting forever. Here is another: Little Fish defects and Big Fish cooperates on the first round, then cooperates while Big Fish defects for just enough rounds that Little Fish's gain is zero (the last round might need a mixed strategy on the part of Big Fish). Then, we repeat it all over again, with Big Fish defecting on the first round, then cooperating, and Little Fish defecting until any of Big Fish's gain is wiped out. And so on, ad infinitum. Thus, the game is worth exactly zero to each. But it is Nash subgame perfect!

6.3 Tacit Collusion

Consider a duopoly operating over an infinite number of periods $t = 1, 2, \ldots$. Suppose the duopolists are price setters, so a pure strategy for firms 1 and 2 in period t are prices $p_1^t, p_2^t \geq 0$, respectively, conditioned on the history of prices in previous time periods, and a pure strategy for the whole game is a sequence of strategies, one for each period t. Suppose the profits in period t are given by $\pi_1(p_1^t, p_2^t)$ for firm 1 and $\pi_2(p_1^t, p_2^t)$ for firm 2. The payoff to the firms for the whole game are then

$$\pi_1 = \sum_{t=0}^{\infty} \delta^t \pi_1(p_1^t, p_2^t), \qquad \pi_2 = \sum_{t=0}^{\infty} \delta^t \pi_2(p_1^t, p_2^t),$$

where δ is the common discount factor for the firms.

To specify the function $\pi_i(p_1^t, p_2^t)$, suppose the two firms have no fixed cost and constant marginal cost c, the firms face a downward-sloping demand curve, and the lowest price producer gets the whole market. Also, if the two producers have the same price, they share the market equally.

THEOREM 6.4 *There is a subgame perfect Nash equilibrium of this game in which $p_1^t = p_2^t = c$ for $t = 1, 2, \ldots$.*

Note that this is the "competitive" equilibrium in which profits are zero and price equals marginal cost. The existence of this Nash equilibrium is called Bertrand's Paradox because it seems implausible (though hardly paradoxical!) that two firms in a duopoly actually behave this way.

THEOREM 6.5 *Suppose $\delta > 50\%$, p^m is the monopoly price (i.e., the price that maximizes the profits of a monopolist), and $c \leq p \leq p^m$. Let s be a strategy profile which firm 1 sets $p_1^t = p$, firm 2 sets $p_2^t = p$, $t = 1, 2, \ldots$ and each firm responds to a deviation from this behavior on the part of the other firm by setting price equal to c forever. Then s is a subgame perfect Nash equilibrium.*

We call a Nash equilibrium of this type *tacit collusion*.

PROOF: Choose p satisfying the conditions of the theorem. Let $\pi(p)$ be total industry profits if price p is charged by both firms, so $\pi(p) \geq 0$. Suppose firm 2 follows the specified strategy. The payoff to firm 1 for following this strategy is

$$\pi^1(p) = \frac{\pi(p)}{2}\left(1 + \delta + \delta^2 + \ldots\right) = \frac{\pi(p)}{2(1 - \delta)}. \tag{6.1}$$

The payoff to firm 1 for defecting on the first round by charging an amount $\epsilon > 0$ less than p is $\pi^1(p - \epsilon)$. Thus, $2(1 - \delta) < 1$ is sufficient for Nash.

Clearly, the strategy is subgame perfect, since the Bertrand solution in which each firm charges marginal cost is Nash. Q.E.D.

Intuition tells us that tacit collusion is more difficult to sustain when there are many firms. The following theorem, the proof of which we leave to the reader (just replace the "2" in the denominators of equation (6.1) by "*n*") shows that this is correct.

THEOREM 6.6 *Suppose there are n > 1 firms in the industry, but the conditions of supply and demand remain as before, the set of firms with the lowest price in a given time period sharing the market equally. Then, if* $\delta > 1 - 1/n$ *and* $c \le p \le p^m$, *the trigger strategies in which each firm sets a price equal to p in each period, and each firm responds to a deviation from this strategy on the part of another firm by setting price equal to c forever, form a subgame perfect Nash equilibrium.*

Another market condition that reduces the likelihood that tacit collusion can be sustained is incomplete knowledge on the part of the colluding firms. For instance, we have the following.

THEOREM 6.7 *Suppose there is an n-firm oligopoly, as described above, but a firm that has been defected upon cannot implement the trigger strategy until k > 1 periods have passed. Then, tacit collusion can hold only if* $\delta^{k+1} > 1 - 1/n$.

This theorem shows that *tacit collusion is less likely to hold the more easily a firm can "hide" its defection.* This leads to the counterintuitive, but quite correct, conclusion that making contractual conditions public knowledge ("putting all your cards on the table") may *reduce* rather than *increase* the degree of competition in an industry.

PROOF: If it takes *k* periods after a defection to retaliate, the gain from defection is

$$\pi(p)(1 + \delta + \delta^2 + \ldots + \delta^k) = \frac{\pi(p)}{1 - \delta}\left(1 - \delta^{k+1}\right),$$

from which the result immediately follows, since the present value of cooperating forever is $\pi(p)/n(1 - \delta)$. Q.E.D.

THEOREM 6.8 *Suppose in each period* $t = 1, 2, \ldots$ *industry demand is either low,* $q = D(p)$, *or high,* $q = D(p) + \alpha$, *where* $\alpha > 0$, *with equal probability. Then, under conditions of monopoly, the price* p_h^m *in the high demand period exceeds the price* p_l^m *in the low demand period. However, under some conditions a duopoly engaging in tacit collusion to maximize their total profits may charge lower prices in the high demand period than in the low demand period.*

PROOF: Suppose a monopolist maximizes $\pi = (p-c)(D(p)+\beta)$, giving first-order condition $\pi_p = D(p) + \beta + (p-c)D'(p) = 0$. Differentiating this totally with respect to β gives

$$\pi_{pp}\frac{dp}{d\beta} + \pi_{p\beta} = 0.$$

However, $\pi_{pp} < 0$ by the second-order condition, and $\pi_{p\beta} = 1$, so $dp/d\beta > 0$. This shows that $p_h^m > p_l^m$ (let β go from zero to α).

The payoff to the trigger strategy in which each firm chooses the monopoly price in each period is

$$V = \sum_{t=0}^{\infty} \delta^t \left[\frac{1}{2}\frac{\pi_l^m}{2} + \frac{1}{2}\frac{\pi_h^m}{2} \right] = \frac{\pi_l^m + \pi_h^m}{4(1-\delta)}.$$

When is this a Nash equilibrium? Clearly, if a firm does not benefit from defecting in the high demand period, it also does not benefit by defecting in the low demand period. So we need only find out when defecting in the high demand period is not profitable. The additional payoff from defecting in the high demand period is $\pi_h^m/2$, and the cost is δV (since the firm loses V, but starting in the next period), so for tacit collusion to be Nash, we must have $\delta \geq \pi_h^m/2V$, which simplifies to

$$\delta \geq \frac{2\pi_h}{3\pi_h^m + \pi_l^m}. \tag{6.2}$$

It is easy to see that the right-hand side of this expression lies in the interval (1/2,2/3). Thus, tacit collusion is harder in this case than in the case where demand does not fluctuate.

Suppose, however, that δ lies in the interval (1/2,2/3) but inequality (6.2) is *violated*. Then, it may be possible to maintain tacit collusion by charging *less* than the monopoly price in one or both periods, thus lowering the temptation to defect. Let $V(p_l, p_h)$ be the return to each firm when both firms charge p_l in the low demand state and p_h in the high demand state. Let us choose p_l and p_h to maximize $V(p_l, p_h)$ subject to the constraints that ensure that tacit collusion is Nash. If π_l and π_h are profits in the low and high demand states, we must have

$$\frac{\pi_s}{2} \leq \delta V(p_l, p_h) \qquad \text{for } s = l, h. \tag{6.3}$$

We shall show that this requires setting $p_l = p_l^m$ and setting

$$\pi_h = a\pi_l^m,$$

where $a = \frac{\delta}{2-3\delta}$, provided $\pi_h \leq \pi_h^m$. To see this, we rewrite the constraints (6.3) as

$$\pi_s \leq \delta \frac{\pi_l + \pi_h}{2(1-\delta)} \qquad \text{for } s = l, h,$$

which reduce to

$$\pi_l \leq a\pi_h, \qquad \pi_h \leq a\pi_l.$$

Note that $a \geq 1$, since $1/2 < \delta < 2/3$. The two possible cases are exhibited in Fig. 6.1.

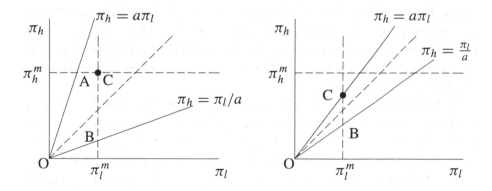

Figure 6.1. Tacit collusion under conditions of variable demand. In the left pane the discount rate is sufficiently low that the monopoly price can be sustained in each period (at C), and the right pane is the case where the discount rate is so high that price must be set below the monopoly price in periods of high demand to deter defection.

Note that in Fig. 6.1 the pair of prices (π_l, π_h) must lie to the right of $\pi_l = \pi_l^m$, below $\pi_h = \pi_h^m$, below $\pi_h = a\pi_l$, and above $\pi_h = \pi_l/a$; i.e., in the quadrilateral OACB in the left pane. Clearly, total profits are maximized at C, where the monopoly price is charged in both periods. But if a is close to unity (i.e., δ is close to 1/2), the set of feasible prices reduces to the triangle OCB in the right pane, with a maximum again at C. In this case, the firms charge the monopoly price in the low demand state, but something *below* the monopoly price in the high demand state.

6.4   The Folk Theorem: An Embarras de richesses

The *Folk Theorem for Repeated Games* is so called because no one can discover who first thought of it—it is just part of the "folklore" of game theory. We shall first present a stripped-down analysis of the Folk Theorem with an example and provide a somewhat more complete discussion in the next section.

Consider the stage game in §6.2. There is of course one subgame perfect Nash equilibrium in which each player gets zero. Moreover, neither player can be forced to receive a negative payoff in the repeated game based on this stage game, since zero can be assured simply by playing D. Also, any point in the region OEABCF in Fig. 6.2 could be attained in the stage game, assuming the players could agree on a mixed strategy for each. To see this, notice that if Big Fish uses C with probability α and Little Fish uses C with probability β, then the expected payoff to the pair is $(8\beta - 3\alpha, 8\alpha - 3\beta)$, which traces out every point in the quadrilateral OEABCF for $\alpha, \beta \in [0, 1]$ (check it out!). Only the points in OABC are superior to the universal defect equilibrium (0,0), however.

The Folk Theorem says that *any point in the region OABC can be sustained as a subgame perfect Nash equilibrium of the repeated game based on the stage game in §6.2, provided the discount rates of the players are sufficiently low*.[1] To implement a particular point in OABC, let (α, β) be C-probabilities for the two players associated with the point. Allow a random number generator to choose a sequence of choices for Big Fish in which the frequency of C is α, and similarly for Little Fish. Give both players a copy of the list, and instruct both players to (a) play their strategy, and (b) if their partner

---

[1] It is worth repeating that the Folk Theorem is a staple of classical game theory but is widely disrespected in evolutionary game theory because few of the equilibria it supports are stable with respect to a plausible evolutionary dynamic.

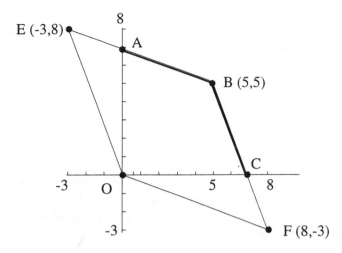

Figure 6.2. The Folk Theorem: any point in the region OABC can be sustained as the subgame perfect Nash equilibrium of the repeated game based on the stage game in §6.2.

does not play the appropriate corresponding strategy, to defect (play D) forever. Clearly, these strategies are Nash subgame perfect. There is an obvious generalization of this result.

THEOREM 6.9 The Folk Theorem. *Consider any two-player stage game with a Nash equilibrium with payoffs (a, b) to the two players. Suppose there exists a pair of strategies for the two players that gives the players (c, d). Then, if $c \geq a$ and $d \geq b$, and the discount factors of the players are sufficiently close to unity, there is a subgame perfect Nash equilibrium of the repeated game with expected payoffs (c, d) in each period.*

6.5 Variations on the Folk Theorem

Consider an n-player game with player strategy sets S_i for $i = 1, \ldots, n$, so the set of strategy profiles for the game is $S = \{(s_1, \ldots, s_n) | s_i \in S_i, i = 1, \ldots, n\}$. The payoff for player i is $\pi_i(s)$, where $s \in S$. For any $s \in S$ we write s_{-i} for the vector obtained by dropping the ith component of s, and for any $i = 1, \ldots, n$ we write $(s_i, s_{-i}) = s$. For a given player j, suppose the other players choose strategies m^j_{-j} such that j's best response m^j_j gives j the lowest possible payoff in the game. We call the resulting strategy profile

m^j the *maximum punishment payoff* for j. Then, $\pi_j^* = \pi_j(m^j)$ is j's payoff when everyone else "gangs up on him." We call $\pi^* = (\pi_1^*, \ldots, \pi_n^*)$ the *minimax point* of the game. Now define

$$\Pi = \{(\pi_1(s), \ldots, \pi_n(s)) | s \in S, \pi_i(s) \geq \pi_i^*, i = 1, \ldots, n\},$$

so Π is the set of strategy profiles in the stage game with payoffs at least as good as the maximum punishment payoff for each player.

We let this be the stage game for a repeated game with discount factor δ, common to all the agents. If the stage game is played in periods $t = 0, 1, 2, \ldots$, and if the sequence of strategy profiles used by the players is $s(1), s(2), \ldots$, then the payoff to player j is

$$\tilde{\pi}_j = \sum_{t=0}^{\infty} \delta^t \pi_j(s(t)).$$

With these definitions behind us, we have the following theorem.

THEOREM 6.10 The Folk Theorem. *For any $\pi = (\pi_1, \ldots, \pi_n) \in \Pi$, if δ is sufficiently close to unity, there is a Nash equilibrium of the repeated game such that π_j is j's payoff for $j = 1, \ldots, n$ in each period.*

The proof of the theorem is straightforward. For any such $\pi \in \Pi$, each player j uses the strategy s_j that gives payoffs π in each period, provided the other players do likewise. If one player deviates, however, all other players play the strategies that impose the maximum punishment payoff on j forever. Since $\pi_j \geq \pi_j^*$, player j cannot gain from deviating from s_j, so the profile of strategies is Nash.

Note that this Folk Theorem says nothing about subgame perfection. Indeed, the strategies that impose the maximum punishment on player j may be far from a Nash equilibrium, so the punishment threat is not credible. However, we have the following.

THEOREM 6.11 The Folk Theorem with Subgame Perfection. *Suppose $y = (y_1, \ldots, y_n)$ is the vector of payoffs in a Nash equilibrium of the underlying one-shot game, and $\pi \in \Pi$ with $\pi_i \geq y_i$ for $i = 1, \ldots, n$. Then, if δ is sufficiently close to unity, there is a subgame perfect Nash equilibrium of the repeated game such that π_j is j's payoff for $j = 1, \ldots, n$ in each period.*

The proof of this theorem is also straightforward. For any such $\pi \in \Pi$, each player j uses the strategy s_j that gives payoffs π in each period, provided the other players do likewise. If one player deviates, however, all players play the strategies that give payoff vector y forever.

This theorem is of course much more plausible than the first Folk Theorem, since it does not involve incredible threats. Fudenberg and Maskin (1986) have shown that subgame perfection is possible even when π does *not* dominate any one-shot Nash equilibrium, but this requires a great deal more coordination among the players, since players must be punished for not punishing defectors, and players must be punished for not punishing players who have not punished when they were supposed to, and so on.

There is no doubt but that the repeated game helps us understand social cooperation and reveals some of the central factors upon which the capacity of a society to sustain cooperation depends—such factors as the discount rate, the probability that the stage game will be replayed, the expected time between plays, the degree of informational completeness, and the like. However, the existence of vast numbers of subgame perfect Nash equilibria renders the repeated game framework virtually useless. By explaining practically anything, the model in fact explains nothing.

It is tempting simply to reject the Pareto-inefficient equilibria out of hand, after which most of the multiplicity disappears. The problem is that even when there is cooperation in repeated interactions, this cooperation is usually less than perfect and often breaks down. Moreover, while trigger strategies are sometimes plausible (e.g., when a couple breaks up, or a boss fires a worker, or a client switches suppliers), they are often not plausible, because the gains from "renegotiating" a cooperative solution are often quite large. This leads players to defect, expecting that the breakdown of cooperation can be repaired in the not-too-distant future—that the "poor repentant sinner" will be taken back into the fold.

6.6 The One-Stage Deviation Principle

Suppose s is a strategy profile for players in a repeated game, so s specifies what move each player makes at each stage of the game, depending on the prior history of moves in the game. We say s satisfies the One-Stage Deviation Principle if no player can gain by deviating from s, either on or off the equilibrium path of the game tree, in a single stage and conforming to s thereafter. The following theorem is often very useful in analyzing repeated games, since it says that a strategy profile is subgame perfect if it satisfies the One Stage Deviation Principle. Clearly, it is a lot simpler to check single stage deviations than arbitrary alternative strategy profiles.

THEOREM 6.12 The One-stage Deviation Principle. *A strategy profile s for a repeated game with positive discount rates, based on a stage game with bounded payoffs, is a subgame perfect Nash equilibrium if and only if it satisfies the one-stage deviation principle.*

For a proof of this theorem (it's not difficult) and some extensions see Fudenberg and Tirole (1991).

6.7   A Trembling Hand, Cooperative Equilibrium

Suppose the acts involved in cooperating in §6.2 are in fact complex and demanding, so there is some probability $\epsilon > 0$ that a player will make a mistake, playing D instead of C. Of course, trigger strategies are devastating in such a situation, since with probability 1 eventually one player will make a mistake, and both will defect for ever after. If it were possible to distinguish mistakes from intentional defection, there would be no difficulty in sustaining cooperation. Suppose, however, that there is not. There may nevertheless be a *trembling hand* cooperative equilibrium of the following form: if either player defects, both defect for k rounds, and then both return to cooperation (no matter what happened in the defection rounds). Given ϵ, of course k should be chosen to be the *smallest* integer such that it pays to cooperate rather than defect.

Does such a k exist? Let v be the value of the game when both players use the following "trembling hand" strategy. There are two "phases" to the game. In the "cooperate" phase, (try to) play C, and in the "punishment" phase, play D. If the game is in the cooperate phase and either agent plays D (on purpose or by mistake), the game moves to the punishment phase. If the punishment phase has lasted for k rounds, the game moves to the cooperate phase. The game starts in the cooperate phase.

It is clear that there is no gain from playing C in the punishment phase. Can there be a gain from playing D in the cooperate phase?

Here is where the One-Stage Deviation Principle becomes useful. If the above strategies do not form a subgame perfect Nash equilibrium, then playing D in the cooperate phase and then returning to the trembling hand strategy has a higher payoff than cooperating. The payoff to playing D in the cooperate phase and then returning to the trembling hand strategy is just $8(1-\epsilon)+d^{k+1}v$, since your partner also plays D with probability ϵ, in which case you get nothing but still must wait k periods to resume cooperating. Thus, cooperating is Nash when $8(1-\epsilon)+d^{k+1}v$, is less than v, or

$$v(1-\delta^{k+1}) > 8(1-\epsilon). \tag{6.4}$$

But what is v? Well, v must satisfy the equation

$$v = (1-\epsilon)\epsilon(-3+\delta^{k+1}v)+(1-\epsilon)^2(5+\delta v)+\epsilon[(1-\epsilon)8+\delta^{k+1}v]. \tag{6.5}$$

To see this, note that if you both cooperate at the start of the game, with probability $(1-\epsilon)\epsilon$, you play C and your partner plays D, in which case you get -3 now and after $k+1$ periods, you're back into the cooperate phase, the present value of which is $\delta^{k+1}v$. This is the first term in (6.5). With probability $(1-\epsilon)^2$ you both play C, so you get 5 and v again in the next period. This is the second term. With probability ϵ you play D, in which case you get 8 if your partner plays C, zero if your partner plays D, and in either case, you get v after $k+1$ periods. This is the final term in (6.5).

Solving (6.5) for v, we get

$$v = \frac{5(1-\epsilon)}{1-\delta(1-\epsilon)^2-\delta^k\epsilon(2-\epsilon)}.$$

Suppose, for instance, $\epsilon = 15\%$ and $\delta = 95\%$. It is easy to check by hand calculation that $v = 85$ if there is no punishment phase ($k = 0$), but the payoff to defecting is $87.55 > v$. For one round of punishment ($k = 1$), $v = 67.27$, but the value of defecting is $8(1-\epsilon)+\delta^2 v = 67.51$, so punishment is still not sufficiently severe. For two rounds of punishment ($k = 2$), $v = 56.14$, and $8(1-\epsilon)+\delta^3 v = 54.93$, so two rounds of punishment are needed to sustain cooperation. Note that if we could assume players were "honest" (always cooperated), then the value of the game would be 85, but the cost of inducing cooperation when we cannot assume "honesty" reduces the value to 54.93.

6.8 Death and Discount Rates in Repeated Games

Suppose an agent plays a repeated game in which the payoff in each period is π, the agent's discount rate is ρ, and the probability that the agent dies at the end of each period is $\sigma > 0$. Prove that the present value of the game to the agent is the same as the present value of the game would be if the probability of death were zero and the discount rate were $\rho + \sigma$.

6.9   The Strategy of an Oil Cartel

Suppose there are two oil-producing countries, Iran and Iraq. Both can operate at either of two production levels: 2 or 4 million barrels a day. Depending on their decisions, the total output on the world market will be 4, 6, or 8 million barrels a day, and the price per barrel in these three cases is $25, $15, and $10, respectively. Costs of production are $2 per barrel for Iran and $4 per barrel for Iraq.

a.   Draw a normal form matrix of this game and its payoffs.
b.   Show that this matrix is a Prisoner's Dilemma and the equilibrium is for both to produce high output.
c.   Now suppose this game is repeated every day, and both countries agree to cooperate by producing the low output, each one threatening the other with a *trigger strategy:* "If you produce high output, even once, I will produce high output forever." Show that cooperation is a Nash equilibrium if the discount rate is sufficiently low. Do you think this threat is *really* credible? Wouldn't one of the countries try to renegotiate the deal after a while? Wouldn't both sides know this and take it into account? How could they take it into account?

6.10   Manny and Moe

Manny and Moe play the game in the figure an indefinite number of times. They do not discount the future. Show that if the probability p of continuing the game in each period is sufficiently large, then it is Nash for both Manny and Moe to cooperate (play C) in each period. What is the smallest value of p for which this is true?

	Manny	
Moe	C	D
C	3,3	0,5
D	5,0	1,1

6.11   Tit-for-Tat

Consider a repeated Prisoner's Dilemma with two players. The payoffs are (r, r) for mutual cooperation, (p, p) for mutual defection, (t, s) when player one defects and player 2 cooperates, and (s, t) when player one cooperates and player two defects, where $t > r > p > s$ and $2r > s + t$. A Tit-for-Tat player cooperates on the first round of a repeated Prisoner's Dilemma and thereafter does what the other player did on the previous round.

a. Show that for a sufficiently low discount rate for each of the players, Tit-for-Tat is a Nash equilibrium.
b. What is the largest discount rate that can support a Tit-for-Tat Nash equilibrium?
c. Show that Tit-for-Tat is not subgame perfect. HINT: If a player defects on a particular round, Tit-for-Tat specifies that the two players will exchange cooperate/defect forever, which has a lower payoff than cooperating forever. You might think that it can't possibly matter, since a player using a trigger strategy will *never* be the first to defect. But this is irrelevant—the definition of a strategy in a game requires that a move be chosen for *every node in the game tree where the player moves*, whether or not the node can be reached with positive probability in a Nash equilibrium. In fact, often what happens at unreachable nodes—nodes that are not hit if players play a particular Nash strategy profile—is critical to specifying the equilibrium. Subgame perfection is a case in point (if you don't understand this, review chapter 5).
d. Revise the Tit-for-Tat strategy to make it subgame perfect. HINT: define *contrite Tit-for-Tat* (Boyd 1989) as follows. A player is either in *good standing* or *bad standing*. In period 1 both players are in good standing. A player is in good standing in period $t > 1$ only if in period $t - 1$ (i) he cooperated and his partner was in good standing; (ii) he cooperated and he was in bad standing; or (iii) he defects and he was in good standing, while his partner was in bad standing. Otherwise the player is in bad standing in period $t > 1$. Contrite Tit-for-Tat says to cooperate unless one is in good standing and one's partner is in bad standing. Use the one-shot deviation principle to show that contrite Tit-for-Tat is subgame perfect.

6.12 A Public Goods Experiment

A group of ten economics students in a game theory class play the following game. Each student is given $1 and is handed the following instructions:

> You may anonymously deposit any portion of your $1 in a "public account." Whatever you do not deposit in the public account, you may keep for yourself. The money in the public account will be multiplied by five and shared among the ten of you.

Thus, each student gets $5 if all cooperate (contribute everything to the public good), and each student gets only $1 if all defect (contribute nothing to the public account).

a.   Show that this is a ten-player Prisoner's Dilemma.
b.   What are the Nash equilibria to this game if it is repeated a finite number of times?
c.   What are the equilibria if the game is repeated indefinitely with probability $p = 0.99$, assuming the players have discount rate zero?
d.   What do you think really happens when this game is played (see chapter 11)?

6.13   Reputational Equilibrium

Consider a firm that can produce a good at any quality level $q \in [0, 1]$. If consumers anticipate quality q_a, their demand x is given by

$$x = 4 + 6q_a - p.$$

Suppose the firm knows this demand curve and takes q_a as given, but can set the quality q supplied. The firm has no fixed costs, and the cost of producing one unit of the good of quality q is $2 + 6q^2$.

   In each period $t = 1, 2, \ldots$ the firm chooses a quality level q and a price p. Consumers see the price but do not know the quality until they buy the good. Consumers follow a trigger strategy, in which they buy the good in each period in which $q \geq q_a$, but if $q < q_a$ in some period, they never buy from the firm again.

a.   If the firm uses discount factor $\delta = 0.9$, for what levels of q_a is there a viable *reputational equilibrium*, i.e. an equilibrium in which the firm produces quality q_a in each period?
b.   If consumers know the firm's cost function and discount factor, and anticipate quality q_a that maximizes the firm's profits, show that the equilibrium level of q_a is 0.5, and show that this is a reputational equilibrium.

6.14   Contingent Renewal Contracts

In §3.19 we criticized the neoclassical model for purporting to explain the economy without strategic interaction, and in §3.20 we sharpened this criticism by questioning the plausibility of complete contracting. In this section we develop some game-theoretic mechanisms that substitute for complete contracting.

In many exchanges, including those between (a) employer and employee, (b) lender and borrower, and (c) firm and customer, the agent on one side of the exchange gives money (employer, lender, customer), while the agent on the other side of the exchange gives a promise (employee, borrower, firm). The employee promises to work hard, the borrower promises to repay the loan, and the firm promises to provide high-quality products. Rarely, however, is this promise subject to a contract that can be enforced at reasonably low cost.

Let us call the player who gives money the *principal*, and the player who gives promises the *agent*. In the absence of an enforceable contract, why do agents keep their promises? Of course, some agents are just honest, but there are doubtless enough dishonest people, and enough people who can convince themselves that they are Doing the Right Thing by *not* keeping their promise, that exchange would break down if enforcement were based purely on the integrity of the agents.

Perhaps the threat of suing is sufficient to secure agent compliance. But generally such threats are not credible. The idea of taking an employee to court for not working hard enough is ludicrous. A lender can sue a borrower for nonpayment, but if the borrower was imprudent, winning the suit is a Pyrrhic victory—there is not much to collect! A customer can sue a firm for faulty goods, of course, but very few of us have ever done such a thing, and it is not reasonable to suppose that, except in special cases (for instance, products that cause personal injury), firms satisfy customers' needs because they are afraid of being taken to court. So why, then, do agents generally keep their promises?

The answer is, of course, that if agents don't keep their promises, principals dump them: employers fire workers who shirk, lenders refuse future loans to borrowers who have defaulted, and customers switch to new suppliers when dissatisfied. All three actions represent *trigger strategies in a repeated game:* the exchange between principal and agent is renewed indefinitely (perhaps with some exogenous probability of dissolution), the principal using the threat of nonrenewal to secure compliance. We call these *contingent renewal* exchanges.[2]

---

[2]There are also one-shot principal agent relationships, of course; we discuss these extensively in chapter 14. Such relationships are probably not very important in the case of firm-consumer or employer-employee exchanges, but they *are* in the case of lender-

Contingent renewal exchanges are among the most prevalent exchanges in market economies. In my humble opinion, the contingent renewal model should be taught to students in chapter 2 of their Introductory Economics texts, right after supply and demand. Only the dead weight of tradition prevents it from being so treated. But this, of course, is obvious, so let's move on.

6.14.1   Costless Contract Enforcement: Achilles' Heel of Neoclassical Economics

At the heart of neoclassical economics is the notion that the price mechanism equates supply and demand. The *Fundamental Theorem of Welfare Economics*, in particular, says that in a general equilibrium model, under appropriate conditions every competitive equilibrium is Pareto-optimal, and every feasible distribution of utility among agents can be attained by a suitable initial distribution of property rights, followed by competitive exchange (§3.19). There have been many critiques of this model, and despite its enormous contribution to economic theory, it is no longer on the cutting edge of research these days.[3] Nonconvexity, externalities, multiple equilibria, and the absence of equilibration mechanisms entailing local stability, as well as other arcane issues, are often mentioned as the problem with the neoclassical model. But the biggest problem, easily trumping the others, is that the model assumes that *agents can write costlessly enforceable contracts for all goods exchanged on markets*. This may be reasonable for standardized goods (for instance, raw materials, basic chemicals, and easily graded agricultural goods) but, as we have seen, is misleading when applied to labor, credit, and consumer goods markets.

6.14.2   Contingent Renewal Markets Do Not Clear in Equilibrium

A *contingent renewal market* is a market in which exchanges between buyers and sellers are regulated by contingent renewal relationships. Since the principal (employer, lender, consumer) in such markets uses a trigger strategy (the threat of nonrenewal) to elicit performance from the agent (worker, borrower, firm), the loss of the relationship must be costly to the agent. But

---

borrower exchanges, where reputation and equity sharing are often more important than contingent renewal in protecting the interests of lenders.

[3]That it is still taught to students as the "ideal case" from which the real world is an imperfect realization strikes me as scandalous.

if the price is set in such markets to equate supply and demand, the cost to an agent of being cut off by the principal is zero, since the agent will secure another position in the next period at the prevailing price. Hence, if the principal uses a trigger strategy, there must be a positive probability that there is an excess supply of agents. It follows that *in a Nash equilibrium of a contingent renewal market, there is an excess supply of agents.*

Note how nicely this conclusion explains some of the most pervasive facts about market economies.

- **Labor markets.** In the neoclassical model, the wage rate adjusts to equate the supply of and the demand for labor. The general condition of labor markets, however, is *excess supply*. Often this takes the form of explicit unemployment, which neoclassical economists explain using complex models involving search costs, friction, adaptive expectations, exotic intertemporal elasticities, and the like. Using Occam's razor (always opt for the simplest explanation first), a contingent renewal labor market does the job. There simply cannot be full employment in such models (Gintis 1976, Shapiro and Stiglitz 1984, Bowles 1985, Bowles and Gintis 1993b). Excess supply in labor markets takes the form not only of unemployment, but "under-employment": workers hold one position but are capable and willing to fill a "better" position, even at the going wage or a bit below, but cannot secure such a position.
- **Credit markets.** In the neoclassical model, the interest rate adjusts to equate the supply of and the demand for loans. The general condition of credit markets, however, is excess demand. Why does the interest rate not rise to cut off this excess demand? There are two basic reasons (Stiglitz and Weiss 1981, Stiglitz 1987). First, an increase in the interest rate will drive borrowers who have low-risk, low-expected-return projects out of the market, and increase the expected riskiness of the remaining pool of borrowers. Second, an interest rate increase will induce borrowers to increase the riskiness of their investment projects, thus lowering the lender's expected return.

  Since risksharing—requiring the borrower to put up a fraction of the equity in a project—is the most widely used and effective means of endogenous contract enforcement in credit markets, it follows that *lending is directed predominantly toward wealthy agents.* This basic fact of life, which seems so perverse from the neoclassical standpoint (loans should be from the wealthy to the nonwealthy), is perfectly comprehensible from the standpoint of models in which contract enforcement is endogenous, even without contingent renewal. Contingent renewal (making available a line of credit, contingent on performance) adds the dimension that a certain subset of nonwealthy borrowers with good projects can get loans, facing the threat of falling into the pool of unemployed "creditseekers" should their credit line be terminated.[4]

- **Consumer goods markets.** In the neoclassical model, price adjusts until supply and demand are equal. This implies that firms can sell as much as they want, subject to the market price, and choose how much to produce according to cost considerations. Everyday observation tells a different story: firms try to Sell More Stuff, and except in their wildest dreams, they can produce with ease however much stuff they manage to sell. Only under the threat of a failing grade can we convince our students that the commonsense view is wrong. Of course, there are sophisticated neoclassical models in which firms have "differentiated products" and "downward-sloping demand curves," but this is not really what is happening. What's really happening is that firms do not have their own, private demand curves—they want to Sell More Stuff at the prevailing price, in head-to-head competition with other firms trying to do the same thing. For instance, automobile manufacturers all serve the same array of markets, and buyers frequently shift among firms. They also sell at about the same price, for a given quality product, and can produce as much as they can sell at constant marginal cost. Downward-sloping demand curves do not capture this reality.

  If the commonsense view is correct, so that sellers want to Sell More Stuff in equilibrium, price must exceed marginal cost in equilibrium. How can this be? The simplest explanation is that *where product quality cannot be ensured by explicit contract, goods are in excess supply*. Consumers typically pay a price *in excess* of marginal cost, the implicit threat to switch suppliers if dissatisfied, inducing firms to

[4]There is a wonderful joke illustrating this point. Sol and his lawyer Manny are riding down the Avenue of the Americas in New York, and Sol sees a beautiful office building. "Manny," he says, "find out how much they want for that office building." The next day Manny calls Sol and says, "I have good news and bad news. The good news is they only want $27,000,000, and they'll take 25% of this in the form of stock options." "What's the bad news?" asks Sol. "They want a cash down payment of $50,000," Manny replied.

supply high-quality products (Klein and Leffler 1981, Gintis 1989).[5]

6.14.3 Money Confers Short-Side Power

Power? That's politics, not economics. Or is it? Suppose we say a principal *P* has power over an agent *A* if *P* can impose, or credibly threaten to impose, sanctions on *A*, but *A* has no such capacity vis-à-vis *P* (Bowles and Gintis 1992). This definition is doubtless incomplete and unnuanced, but conforms to standard notions in analytical political theory (Simon 1953, Dahl 1957, Harsanyi 1962). In the neoclassical model there is no power, because all markets clear and contracts are costlessly enforced. In contingent renewal markets, however, principals have power over agents because they can impose costs on agents by terminating them. Since agents are in excess supply, without collusion agents can exercise no parallel threat over their principals. It follows that employers have power over employees, lenders have power over borrowers, and consumers have power over the firms from which they buy. We may call this *short-side power* because it always lies with the transactor on the short side of the market—i.e., the side for which the quantity of desired transactions is the lesser.

So, *contingent renewal markets do not clear, and in equilibrium they allocate power to agents located on the short side of the market.*

6.14.4 When Money Talks, People Listen

If we review the cast of characters in our various contingent renewal markets, we find a strong regularity: the principal gives money to the agent, and the principal is on the short side of the market. For instance, the employer, the lender, and the consumer hand over money to the worker, the borrower, and the supplying firm, and the latter are all short-siders. The reason for this is clear: the money side of contracts is relatively easy to enforce. As you will see in chapter 14 (or you can turn to this chapter now), this important regularity is implicit in all principal-agent models, where it is assumed that the principal can make credible promises (to wit, the incentive scheme), while the agent cannot.

[5]Is this threat credible? A "rational actor model" is developed below in which the threat is credible because switching suppliers is costless. Even where switching is costly, however, our analysis of retaliation in chapter 11 can plausibly be extended to cover the case of costly switching.

The application of the notion that "money talks" is particularly dramatic in the case of consumer goods markets. In neoclassical theory, consumer sovereignty means that free markets (under the appropriate conditions) lead to efficient allocations. What the term *really* means in people's lives is that since firms are on the long side of the market (they are quantity constrained), consumers can tell producers how to behave—people are truly sovereign. Probably nowhere in the daily lives of ordinary people do they feel more power, and gain more respect, than when acting as consumers, constantly pandered to by obsequious suppliers interested in staying in their good graces—and benefiting from the difference between price and marginal cost.

6.14.5   The Economy Is Controlled by the Wealthy

If you ask average college students whether they agree with the statement that "the wealthy control production and investment in the economy," most will probably reply with some quip like, "Does water run downhill?" "Is the Pope Catholic?" or perhaps with something about the excretory behavior of a bear in the woods. Of course, the wealthy control the economy. This is not a criticism, and it's not profound. It's just true.

Economists basing their intuitions on neoclassical economics (§3.19), of course, disagree. The wealthy have great *purchasing power*, they opine, but this does not translate into power in any *political* sense. As Paul Samuelson (1957:894) has noted, "in a perfectly competitive market it really doesn't matter who hires whom; so let labor hire capital." The result, expressed long ago by Joseph Schumpeter (1934), is a decentralization of power to consumers: "The people who direct business firms only execute what is prescribed for them by wants." These views taken together imply the touchingly apolitical conception of the competitive economy expressed by Abba Lerner at the head of this chapter. Unfortunately, it is not always plausible, as we illustrate in the next two examples—one from labor markets and the other from consumer goods markets.

6.15   Contingent Renewal Labor Markets

In this section we develop a repeated game between employer and employee in which the employer pays the employee a wage higher than the expected value of his next best alternative, using the threat of termination (a trigger strategy) to induce a high level of effort, in a situation where it is infeasible to write and enforce a contract for labor effort. When all employers behave in this manner, we have a nonclearing market in equilibrium.

Suppose an employer's income per period is $q(e)$, an increasing, concave function of the effort e of an employee. The employee's payoff per period $u = u(w, e)$ is an increasing function of the wage w and a decreasing function of effort e. Effort is known to the employee but is only imperfectly observable by the employer. In each period, the employer pays the employee w, the employee chooses effort e, and the employer observes a signal that registers the employee as "shirking" with probability $f(e)$, where $f'(e) < 0$. If the employee is caught shirking, he is dismissed and receives a fallback with present value z. Presumably z depends on the value of leisure, the extent of unemployment insurance, the cost of job search, the startup costs in another job, and the present value of the new job. The employer chooses w to maximize profits. The tradeoff the employer faces is that a higher wage costs more, but it increases the cost of dismissal to the employee. The profit-maximizing wage equates the marginal cost to the marginal benefit.

The employee chooses $e = e(w)$ to maximize the discounted present value v of having the job, where the flow of utility per period is $u(w, e)$. Given discount rate ρ and fallback z, the employee's payoff from the repeated game is

$$v = \frac{u(w, e) + [1 - f(e)]v + f(e)z}{1 + \rho},$$

where the first term in the numerator is the current period utility, assumed for convenience to accrue at the end of the period, and the others measure the expected present value obtainable at the end of the period, the weights being the probability of retaining or losing the position. Simplifying, we get

$$v = \frac{u(w, e) - \rho z}{\rho + f(e)} + z.$$

The term ρz in the numerator is the forgone flow of utility from the fallback, so the numerator is the net flow of utility from the relationship, while $f(e)$ in the denominator is added to the discount rate ρ, reflecting the fact that future returns must be discounted by the probability of their accrual as well as by the rate of time preference.

The employee varies e to maximize v, giving the first-order condition

$$\frac{\partial u}{\partial e} - \frac{\partial f}{\partial e}(v - z) = 0, \tag{6.6}$$

which says that the employee increases effort to the point where the marginal disutility of effort is equal to the marginal reduction in the expected loss occasioned by dismissal. Solving (6.6) for e gives us the employee's best response $e(w)$ to the employer's wage offer w.

We assume that the employer can hire any real number n of workers, all of whom have the effort function $e(w)$, so the employer solves

$$\max_{w,n} \; \pi = q(ne(w)) - wn.$$

The first-order conditions on n and w give $q'e = w$, and $q'ne' = n$, which together imply

$$\frac{\partial e}{\partial w} = \frac{e}{w}. \tag{6.7}$$

This is the famous *Solow condition* (Solow 1979).

The best response function and part of the employer's choice of an optimal enforcement strategy (w^*) are shown in Fig. 6.3, which plots effort against salary. The iso-v function v^* is one of a family of loci of effort levels and salaries that yield identical present values to the employee. Their slope, $-(\partial v/\partial w)/(\partial v/\partial e)$, is the marginal rate of substitution between wage and effort in the employee's objective function. Preferred iso-v loci lie to the right.

By the employee's first-order conditions (6.6), the iso-v loci are vertical where they intersect the best response function (because $\partial v/\partial e = 0$). The negative slope of the iso-v functions below $e(w)$ results from the fact that in this region the contribution of an increase in effort, via $(\partial f/\partial e)(v - z)$, to the probability of keeping the job outweigh the effort-disutility effects. Above $e(w)$, the effort-disutility effects predominate. Because v rises along $e(w)$, the employee is unambiguously better off at a higher wage. One of the employer's iso-cost loci is labeled $e = m^*w$, where m^* is the profit-maximizing effort per dollar. The employer's first-order condition identifies the equilibrium wage w^* as the tangency between the employer's iso-cost function, $e = m^*w$, and the employee's effort function, with slope e', or point x in the figure.

It should be clear that the contingent renewal equilibrium at x is not first-best, since if the parties could write a contract for effort, any point in the lens-shaped region below the employee's indifference curve v^* and above the employer's iso-cost line $e = m^*w$ makes both parties strictly better off than at x. Note that if we populated the whole economy with firms like this, we would in general have $v > z$ in market equilibrium, since if $v = z$,

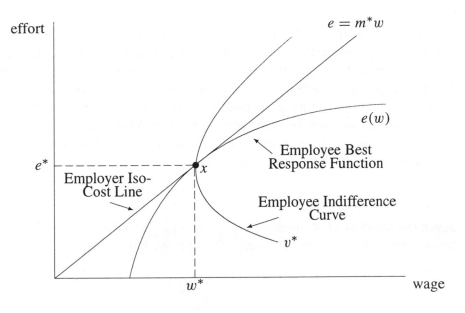

Figure 6.3. The employee's best response function.

(6.6) shows that $\partial u/\partial e = 0$, which is impossible so long as effort is a disutility. This is one instance of the general principle enunciated above, that *contingent renewal markets do not clear in (Nash) equilibrium*, and the agent whose promise is contractible (usually the agent paying money) is on the long side of the market.

Perhaps an example would help visualize this situation. Suppose the utility function is given by

$$u(w, e) = w - \frac{1}{1-e}$$

and the shirking signal is given by

$$f(e) = 1 - e.$$

You can check that $e(w)$ is then given by

$$e(w) = 1 - a - \sqrt{a^2 + \rho a},$$

where $a = 1/(w - \rho z)$. The reader can check that this function indeed has the proper shape: it is increasing and concave, is zero when $w = 2 + \rho(1+z)$, and approaches unity with increasing w. The solution for the employer's optimum w, given by the Solow condition (6.7), is very complicated, so I will approximate the solution. Suppose $\rho = 0.05$ and the employment rate is $q \in [0, 1]$. An employee dismissed at the end of the current period therefore has a probability q, of finding a job right away (we assume all firms are alike) and so regains the present value v. With probability $1 - q$, however, the ex-employee remains unemployed for one period, and tries again afterward. Therefore we have

$$z = qv + (1 - q)z/(1 + \rho),$$

assuming the flow of utility from being unemployed (in particular, there is no unemployment insurance) is zero. Solving, we have

$$z = \frac{(1 + \rho)q}{q + \rho}v.$$

For a given unemployment rate q, we can now find the equilibrium values of w, e, v, and z, and hence the employer's unit labor cost e/w. Running this through Mathematica, the equilibrium values of w and e as the employment rate q goes from zero to 0.67 are depicted in Fig. 6.4.

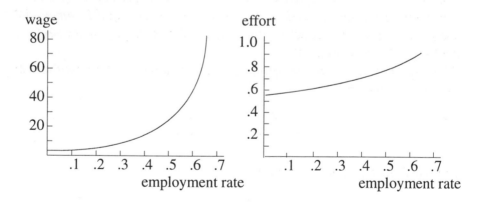

Figure 6.4. Wage and effort as functions of the employment rate in a contingent renewal labor market.

Note that while effort increases only moderately as the unemployment rate drops from 100% to 33%, the wage rate increases exponentially as the unemployment rate approaches 33%. I could not find a solution for

$q > 0.67$. The actual unemployment rate can be fixed by specifying the firm's production function and imposing a zero profit condition. However this is accomplished, there will be positive unemployment in equilibrium.

6.16   I'd Rather Switch than Fight

In this section we develop a repeated game between firm and consumer, in which product quality cannot be contracted for and can be verified only by consuming the good. The consumer pays a price greater than marginal cost using the threat of brand-switching (a trigger strategy) to induce a high level of quality on the part of the firm. The result is a nonclearing product market, with firms enjoying price greater than marginal cost. Thus they are quantity constrained in equilibrium (i.e., they want to Sell More Stuff).

Every Monday, families in Pleasant Valley wash their clothes. To ensure brightness, they all use bleach. Low-quality bleach can, with low but positive probability, ruin clothes, destroy the washing machine's Bleach Delivery Gizmo, and irritate the skin. High-quality bleach is therefore deeply pleasing to Pleasant Valley families. However, high-quality bleach is also costly to produce. Why should firms supply high quality?

Since people have different clothes, washing machines, and susceptibility to skin irritation, buyers cannot depend on a supplier's reputation to ascertain quality. Moreover, a firm could fiendishly build up its reputation for delivering high-quality bleach, and then, when it has a large customer base, supply low quality for one period and then close up shop (this is called "milking your reputation"). Aggrieved families could of course sue the company if they have been hurt by low-quality bleach, but such suits are hard to win and very costly to pursue. So no one does this.

If the quality q of bleach supplied by any particular company can only be ascertained after having purchased the product, and if there is no way to be compensated for being harmed by low-quality bleach, how can high quality be assured?

Suppose the cost to a firm of producing a gallon of the bleach of quality q is $b(q)$, where $b(0) > 0$ and $b'(q) > 0$ for $q \geq 0$. Each consumer is a customer of a particular supplier and purchases exactly one gallon of bleach each Friday at price p from this supplier. If dissatisfied, the customer switches to another supplier at zero cost. Suppose the probability of being dissatisfied, and hence of switching, is given by the decreasing function $f(q)$. We assume an infinite time horizon with a fixed discount rate ρ.

a.   Considering both costs $b(q)$ and revenue q as accruing at the end of the period, show that the value $v(q)$ to a firm from having a customer is

$$v(q) = \frac{p - b(q)}{f(q) + \rho}.$$

b.   Suppose the price p is set by market competition, so it is exogenous to the firm. Show that the firm chooses quality q so that

$$p = b(q) + b'(q)g(q)$$

where $g(q) = -[f(q) + \rho]/f'(q)$, provided $q > 0$.

c.   Show that quality is an increasing function of price.

Notice that in this case firms are quantity constrained, since price is greater than marginal cost in a market (Nash) equilibrium, and that consumers are on the long side of the market. This illustrates the general arguments in §6.14.4.

This model raises an interesting question. What determines firm size? In the standard perfect competition model, firm size is determined by the condition that average costs be at a minimum. This is of course just silly, since a firm can always produce at any multiple of the "optimal firm size" simply by working the production process, whatever it might be, in parallel.[6] The monopolistic competition model, in which a firm has a downward-sloping demand curve, is better, but it doesn't apply to a case like ours, where firms are price takers, as in the perfect competition model, and firm size is determined by the dynamic process of movement of customers among firms. Here is one plausible model of such a process.

Suppose there are n firms in the bleach industry, all selling at the same price p. Suppose firm j has market share m^t_j in period t. Suppose for $j = 1, \ldots, n$, a fraction f_j of firm j's customers leave the firm in each period, and a fraction a_j of customers who have left firms are attracted to firm j. We say the bleach industry is *in equilibrium* if the market share of each firm is constant over time. We have the following.

[6]Why they teach the standard model to students these days is quite beyond me—it's totally bogus, since it's a model of *plant* size, not *firm* size. The important questions of vertical and horizontal integration, the real determinants of firm size, are virtually orthogonal to the question of plant size. Industrial economists have known this for a very long time. For a contemporary review of the literature on the subject, see Sutton (1997).

THEOREM 6.13 *There is a unique asymptotically stable equilibrium in the bleach industry.*

PROOF: We normalize the number of customers in Pleasant Valley to one. Then, the number of customers leaving firm j is $m_j^t f_j$, so the total number of customers looking for new suppliers is $\sum_j m_j^t f_j$. A particular firm j attracts a fraction a_j of these. This assumes a firm can woo back a fraction a_j of its recently departed customers; the argument is the same if we assume the opposite. Thus, the net customer loss of firm j in period t is

$$f_j m_j^t - a_j \sum_{k=1}^n f_k m_k^t. \tag{6.8}$$

In equilibrium this quantity must be zero and $m_k^t = m_k$ for all t and for $k = 1, \ldots, n$. This gives the equilibrium condition

$$m_j = \mu_j \sum_{k=1}^n f_k m_k, \tag{6.9}$$

where we have defined $\mu_k = a_k / f_k$. Note also that if we add up the n equations in (6.8), we get zero, so $\sum_k m_k^t = 1$ for all t, implying $\sum_k m_k = 1$. Summing (6.9), we arrive at the equilibrium conditions

$$m_j = \frac{\mu_j}{\sum_k \mu_k}.$$

Thus, there exists a unique industry equilibrium. To prove asymptotic stability, we define the $n \times n$ matrix $B = (b_{ij})$, where $b_{ij} = a_i f_j$ for $i \neq j$, and $b_{ii} = a_i f_i + (1 - f_i)$, $i, j = 1, \ldots, n$. Then, writing the column vector $m^t = (m_1^t, \ldots, m_n^t)$, we have $m^{t+1} = Bm^t$, and hence $m^t = B^t m^0$, where B^t is the tth power of B. The matrix B is a positive matrix, and it is easy to check that it has eigenvalue 1 with corresponding positive eigenvector $m = (m_1, \ldots, m_n)$. By Perron's Theorem (see, for instance, Horn and Johnson, 1985, Section 8.2), 1 is the unique maximal eigenvalue of B. Also $(1, 1, \ldots, 1)$ is a right eigenvector of B corresponding to the eigenvalue 1. It follows that B^t tends to the matrix whose columns are each m (see Horn and Johnson, 1985, Theorem 8.2.8), which proves the theorem. Q.E.D.

7

Biology Meets Economics: Evolutionary Stability and the Birth of Dynamic Game Theory

There is but a step between the sublime and the ridiculous.

Leo Tolstoy

7.1 The Birth of Evolutionary Stability

In 1973 the biologist John Maynard Smith and the mathematician G. R. Price wrote an article in *Nature* showing how game theory applies to the behavior of animals (§7.11). Maynard Smith went on to write a book on the subject (Maynard Smith 1982), which has become a classic. The idea of applying game theory to animals—and not just the higher primates, but fish, dung beetles, fireflies, and pond scum as well—seemed strange at the time, since game theory had always been the preserve of hyperrationality. Animals hardly fit the bill. Maynard Smith made three critical shifts—one in the concept of a strategy, the second in the concept of equilibrium, and a third in the nature of agent interactions.

Strategy. In classical game theory, *players* have strategy sets from which they choose particular strategies. In biology, *species* have strategy sets (genotypic variants), of which *individuals* inherit one or another variant (perhaps mutated), which they then play in their strategic interactions. This extends nicely to the treatment of culture in human society. We say that *society* has the strategy set (the set of alternative cultural forms) and *individuals* inherit or choose among them.

Equilibrium. In place of the Nash equilibrium, Maynard Smith and Price used the *evolutionarily stable strategy* (ESS) concept. A strategy is evolutionarily stable if a whole population using that strategy cannot be invaded by a small group with a mutant genotype. Similarly, a cultural form is evolutionarily stable if, upon being adopted by all members of a society (firm, family, etc.), no small group of individuals using an alternative cultural form can invade. We thus move from explaining the actions of individuals to modeling the diffusion of forms of behavior ("strategies") in society.

Player interactions. In place of the one-shot and repeated games of classical game theory, Maynard Smith introduced the notion of the *repeated, random pairing of agents* who play strategies based on their genome but not on the previous history of play.

Evolutionary stability is particularly useful because it says something about the dynamic properties of a system without being committed to any particular dynamic model. As we shall see, however, the precise relationship with dynamic stability is by no means straightforward (§9.7).

7.2 Properties of Evolutionarily Stable Strategies

Consider a two-player normal form game in which both players have the set $S = \{s_1, \ldots, s_n\}$ of pure strategies, and the payoffs to an agent playing $s_i \in S$ and another agent playing $s_j \in S$ are π_{ij} for the first and π_{ji} for the second. We call such a game *symmetric in payoffs*. In addition, we assume the agents cannot condition their play on whether they are "player 1" or "player 2." We call such a game *symmetric in strategies*. If a game is symmetric in both payoffs and strategies, we simply call the game *symmetric*. We call $A = (\pi_{ij})$ the *matrix* of the symmetric game. Notice that A represents only the payoffs for the row player, since the payoffs to the column player are just the transpose of A.

Let $\mathcal{G}$ be a symmetric game with matrix A (we'll call it the *stage game*) and large population of agents. In each period $t = 1, 2, \ldots$, agents are randomly paired and they play the stage game $\mathcal{G}$. Each agent is of type i for some $s_i \in S$, meaning that the agent uses strategy s_i in the stage game. If the proportion of agents of type j is p_j at a particular time, we say the *state* of the population is $\sigma = p_1 s_1 + \ldots + p_n s_n$. The payoff at that time to a player of type i when the state of the population is σ is defined by

$$\pi_{i\sigma} = \sum_{j=1}^{n} \pi_{ij} p_j,$$

which is the player's expected payoff before being assigned a particular partner. These conditions define a new game, called the *evolutionary game* corresponding to the stage game $\mathcal{G}$. In some evolutionary games individuals can play mixed strategies, in which case an agent who plays a mixed strategy

$\tau = q_1 s_1 + \ldots + q_n s_n$ is called of "type τ", and has payoff

$$\pi_{\tau\sigma} = \sum_{i,j=1}^{n} q_i \pi_{ij} p_j,$$

when the state of the population is σ.

Suppose the state of the population is $\sigma = p_1 s_1 + \ldots + p_n s_n$. The expected payoff to a randomly chosen member of the population is thus just $\pi_{\sigma\sigma}$. If we replace a fraction $\epsilon > 0$ of the population with a "mutant" of type j, the new state of the population is

$$\tau = (1 - \epsilon)\sigma + \epsilon s_j,$$

so the payoff to a randomly chosen nonmutant is

$$\pi_{\sigma\tau} = (1 - \epsilon)\pi_{\sigma\sigma} + \epsilon\pi_{\sigma j},$$

and the payoff to a mutant is

$$\pi_{j\tau} = (1 - \epsilon)\pi_{j\sigma} + \epsilon\pi_{jj}.$$

We say the mutant type can *invade* the population if $\sigma \neq \tau$ and for sufficiently small $\epsilon > 0$,

$$\pi_{j\tau} \geq \pi_{\sigma\tau},$$

which says that a mutant does at least as well against the new population as does a nonmutant. We say σ is an *evolutionarily stable strategy* if it cannot be invaded by any mutant type.

A Nash equilibrium in an evolutionary game can consist of a *monomorphic* population of agents, each playing the same mixed strategy, or a *polymorphic* population, a fraction of the population playing each of the underlying pure strategies in proportion to its contribution to the mixed Nash strategy. The two interpretations are interchangeable under many conditions, and we shall not commit ourselves exclusively to either interpretation. We will, however, assume that mutants can employ mixed strategies in applying the evolutionary stability criterion, because as we shall see later (§9.6), with this assumption evolutionarily stable strategies have powerful dynamic properties.

The following exercise asks you to derive some of the more important properties of evolutionarily stable strategies:

a. Show that σ is evolutionarily stable if and only if, for any mutant type τ, we have

$$\pi_{\sigma\sigma} \geq \pi_{\tau\sigma},$$

and if $\pi_{\sigma\sigma} = \pi_{\tau\sigma}$, then

$$\pi_{\sigma\tau} > \pi_{\tau\tau}.$$

This says that σ is evolutionarily stable if and only if a mutant cannot do better against an incumbent than an incumbent can do against another incumbent, and if a mutant does as well as an incumbent against another incumbent, then an incumbent must do better against a mutant than a mutant does against another mutant. Note here that we are assuming mutants can use mixed strategies.

b. Show that an evolutionarily stable strategy is a Nash equilibrium.

c. Show that every strict Nash equilibrium (§4.5) in an evolutionary game is evolutionarily stable.

d. Suppose the stage game has two pure strategies. Show that if $\pi_{11} \neq \pi_{21}$ and $\pi_{12} \neq \pi_{22}$, then the game has an evolutionarily stable strategy.

e. Using the same notation, show that the stage game has a strictly mixed Nash equilibrium if and only if $\pi_{11} > \pi_{21}$ and $\pi_{22} > \pi_{12}$, or $\pi_{11} < \pi_{21}$ and $\pi_{22} < \pi_{12}$. The equilibrium is evolutionarily stable only if the second set of inequalities holds.

f. * Show that an evolutionary game whose stage game has a finite number of pure strategies can have only a finite number of evolutionarily stable strategies.

g. * Show that σ is evolutionarily stable if and only if there is some $\epsilon > 0$ such that $\pi_{\sigma\tau} > \pi_{\tau\tau}$ for all τ within distance ϵ of σ.[1] This implies that an evolutionarily stable strategy σ is an *isolated Nash equilibrium*, in the sense that there is an $\epsilon > 0$ such that no strategy $\tau \neq \sigma$ within distance ϵ of σ is a Nash equilibrium. It also clearly proves f.

h. Show that if $\sigma \in S$ is a completely mixed evolutionarily stable strategy (i.e., it uses all pure strategies with positive probability), then it is the unique Nash equilibrium of the game and the condition

$$\pi_{\sigma\tau} > \pi_{\tau\tau}$$

holds for all mixed strategies τ, $\tau \neq \sigma$.

---

[1]By the *distance* between two strategies $\sigma = \sum_i p_i s_i$ and $\tau = \sum_i q_i s_i$ we mean the distance in $\mathbf{R}^n$ between the points $(p_1, \ldots, p_n)$ and $(q_1, \ldots, q_n)$. If your are stumped, see Hofbauer and Sigmund 1998.

7.3   Are Evolutionarily Stable Strategies Unbeatable?

It is easy to show that x is evolutionarily stable in the game shown at the right. We shall see later that it is also asymptotically stable in the replicator dynamic (§9.7). Nevertheless, it is not an *unbeatable strategy*, in the sense of always having the highest payoff when invaded by multiple mutants.

	x	y	z
x	1,1	1,1	0,0
y	1,1	0,0	1,0
z	0,0	0,1	0,0

a. Show that x is evolutionarily stable.
b. Show that if a fraction ϵ_y of y-players and a fraction $\epsilon_z > \epsilon_y$ of z-players simultaneously invade, then y has a higher payoff than x.

To complicate the picture, some game theorists have *defined* evolutionary stability as "unbeatability" in the above sense. In a famous article, Boyd and Lorberbaum (1987) showed that "no pure strategy is evolutionarily stable in the repeated prisoner's dilemma game," and Farrell and Ware (1989) extended this by showing that no mixed strategy using a finite number of pure strategies is evolutionarily stable. Finally, Lorberbaum (1994) extended this to all nondeterministic strategies, and Bendor and Swistak (1995) showed that for a sufficiently low discount rate, no pure strategy is evolutionarily stable in any nontrivial repeated game. In all cases, however, evolutionary stability is interpreted as "unbeatability" in the above sense. But unbeatability is not a very important concept, since as far as I know, it has no interesting dynamic properties.

7.4   Trust in Networks II

Show that the completely mixed Nash equilibrium found in Trust in Networks (§4.12) is not evolutionarily stable, and can be invaded by Trusters. In case you think this means this equilibrium is dynamically unstable, think again! See Trust in Networks III (§9.8).

7.5   Cooperative Fishing

In a certain fishing village, two fisherman gain from having the nets put out in the evening. However, the fishermen benefit equally whether or not they share the costs of putting out the nets. Suppose the expected catch is v, the cost of putting out the nets to each is c_1 if each fisherman does it alone, and the cost to each is $c_2 < c_1$ if they do it together. We assume $v/2 > c_1$, so it is worthwhile for a fisherman to put out the nets even if he has to do it alone. But since $c_2 < c_1$, he prefers help. On the other hand, by free-riding on the first fisherman's effort (i.e., by not helping), the other fisherman gets $v/2$ anyway.

What is the normal form game, where each fisherman has the available strategies Put Out (P) and Free Ride (F)? Show that there is a unique mixed strategy equilibrium and that this strategy is evolutionarily stable.

7.6 A Nash Equilibrium That Is Not Evolutionarily Stable

Suppose agents consume each other's products, but not their own. An agent can produce one or two units per period at cost 1, and then meets another consumer. They can agree to exchange either one or two units. The utility of consump-

	1	2
1	1,1	1,1
2	1,1	2,2

tion is 2 per unit consumed. The first strategy is thus "exchange equal for equal, but at most one unit of the good," and strategy two is "exchange equal for equal, but at most two units of the good." The payoff matrix is shown at the right. Show that one of the Nash equilibria consists of evolutionarily stable strategies, but the other does not. What does this say about evolutionary stability and the elimination of weakly dominated strategies?

7.7 Rock, Paper, and Scissors Is Not Evolutionarily Stable

A Nash equilibrium that is not evolutionarily stable may nevertheless be quite important. Consider, for instance, Rock, Paper, and Scissors (§4.16). Show that the unique, completely mixed Nash equilibrium to this game is not evolutionarily stable. We will see later (§9.12) that under a replicator dynamic, Rock, Paper, and Scissors traces out closed orbits around the equilibrium (1/3, 1/3, 1/3), as suggested in the example of the lizard *Uta stansburiana* (§4.16).

7.8 Sex Ratios as Evolutionarily Stable Strategies

The sex ratio game in §4.17 is not an evolutionary game, strictly speaking, since females do not meet pairwise and play a stage game. But it has a payoff structure like an evolutionary game, since $f(u, v)$ is the payoff to a female using sex ratio u when the population is using v. Show that in this sense, the strategies used in the mixed strategy Nash equilibrium found in the first part of §4.17 are evolutionarily stable.

7.9   Invasion of the Pure Strategy Mutants

It is possible that a Nash equilibrium be immune to invasion by any pure strategy mutant, but not by an appropriate *mixed* strategy mutant. This is the case with respect to the game at the right, assuming $a > 2$. Here the first strategy is evolutionarily stable if only pure strategy mutants are allowed, but not if mixed strategy

1,1	1,1	1,1
1,1	0,0	a,a
1,1	a,a	0,0

mutants are allowed. Show that a mixed strategy using pure strategies 2 and 3 each with probability 1/2 can invade a Nash equilibrium consisting of strategy 1 alone. Is there an evolutionarily stable strategy using pure strategies 2 and 3? Since mutants are normally considered to be rare, it is often plausible to restrict consideration to single mutant types or to mixed strategies that include only pure strategies used in the Nash equilibrium, plus at most one mutant.

7.10   Multiple Evolutionarily Stable Strategies

Using the matrix to the right, show that there are two evolutionarily stable strategies, one using the first two rows and columns, and the second using the second and third strategies. Show that there is also a completely

5,5	7,8	2,1
8,7	6,6	5,8
1,2	8,5	4,4

mixed Nash equilibrium that is stable against invasion by pure strategies, but not evolutionarily stable. Prove the latter either by finding a mixed strategy that does invade HINT: Try one of the evolutionarily stable strategies or use a previously proved theorem. If you want to cheat, look up a paper by Haigh (1975), which develops a simple algorithm for determining whether a Nash equilibrium is evolutionarily stable.

7.11   The Logic of Animal Conflict

In many species throughout the animal kingdom, males compete for access to females. Since the result of this competition is reproductive success, it is not surprising that males in many species are bigger and stronger than females, and often have awesome fighting and reproductive equipment (Alcock 1993). Is it not surprising, then, that so few animals have developed truly *deadly* instruments to use against their compatriots? Venomous snakes wrestle, but they do not bite each other in combat. Deer have impressive antlers and butt heads furiously, but their antlers are not lethal weapons, and they rarely kill each other. Horns in many species point backwards, or are so tightly curled up that they cannot inflict much damage. Even animals that have very dangerous equipment (e.g., the chimpanzee's bite or the elephant's tusks) deploy it rarely.

The common view among animal behaviorists, brilliantly developed in Wynne-Edwards's 1962 book *Animal Dispersion in Relation to Social Behavior*, was that limitations on intraspecies warfare evolved because it was "for the good of the species." This explanation never sat well with many biologists, however, because it is not clear how the "good of the species" becomes encoded in the genes of individuals. Provoked by Wynne-Edwards, George C. Williams published *Adaptation and Natural Selection* in 1966, a devastating attack on the notion of *group selection* implicit in Wynne-Edwards's argument. The fact that a species exists, Williams noted, of course means that the males of the species do not kill each other off. But we cannot use the existence of the species as an *explanation* of why they don't kill each other off.

There were two types of response to Williams's challenge. One was to develop analytically rigorous models of group selection, specify the conditions under which they are operative, and argue that these conditions are biologically plausible. We touch on this body of research in §11.7. The more influential response, however, was to assert that what appears to be altruistic behavior is in fact self-interest in disguise. Prominent among those holding this position were Maynard Smith and Price, whose "The Logic of Animal Conflict" (1973) gave birth to evolutionary game theory.[2]

---

[2]Actually, Maynard Smith and Price did not explicitly use game theory in this paper, though they employ strategies and a payoff matrix, and did not define an evolutionarily stable strategy appropriately. Moreover, they did not investigate the equilibria of their model in any systematic way and made incorrect inferences from their own model. Nevertheless,

In Maynard Smith and Price's model, pairs of individuals meet randomly and play a stage game repeated for a fixed number of rounds. Players have three possible actions, "dangerous" (D), "conventional" (C), and "retreat" (R). By playing D, the opponent receives serious injury (payoff -100) with 10% probability, and minor injury (payoff -2) with probability 90%. A player whose opponent retreats (R) has a payoff of 60, and the stage game is over. The "Mouse" strategy is to play C until seriously injured, then retreat. The "Hawk" strategy is to play D until seriously injured, then retreat. The "Bully" strategy is to play D until the opponent plays D twice, then retreat. The "Retaliator" strategy is to play C, then do what your opponent did on the last move (Tit-for-Tat). The "Prober-Retaliator" strategy is to act like the Retaliator, except that with some positive probability, play D, and continue to play D unless the opponent retaliates by playing D. They came up with the payoff matrix shown in Fig. 7.1. Since the game is symmetric, only the payoffs for the row player are shown.

	Mouse	Hawk	Bully	Retaliator	Prober-Retaliator
Mouse	29.0	19.5	19.5	29.0	17.2
Hawk	80.0	-19.5	74.6	-18.1	-18.9
Bully	80.0	4.9	41.5	11.9	11.2
Retaliator	29.0	-22.3	57.1	29.0	23.1
Prober-Retaliator	56.7	-20.1	59.4	26.9	21.9

Figure 7.1. Average payoffs in simulated intraspecific contests.

To find the Nash equilibria and evolutionarily stable strategies in the game determined by this payoff matrix, I used computer software that I wrote to solve two-player normal form games. You should check the following:

a. There is a symmetric Nash equilibrium that is immune to invasion by pure strategies in which the population consists of 57.6% Hawk and

this paper is a brilliant classic. "What can be said," said Wittgenstein, "can be said clearly." But the *first time* something is said, it is rarely said clearly, and researchers who insist on clarity at all costs rarely make important discoveries.

42.4% Bully. This equilibrium is in fact evolutionarily stable, but that is quite hard to check. Using the techniques of chapters 8 and 9, we can show that this equilibrium is asymptotically stable in the replicator dynamic, which implies that it is evolutionarily stable. Alternatively, you can use the technique described in Haigh (1975).

b. There is a symmetric Nash equilibrium that is not evolutionarily stable, with 38.9% Hawk, 44.1% Bully, and 17.0% Prober-Retaliator.

c. (Retaliator,Retaliator) is a symmetric Nash equilibrium, but it is not evolutionarily stable since it can be invaded by Mouse.

d. (Mouse,Hawk) is a Nash equilibrium, but since the game is symmetric and the players cannot tell whether they are row or column players, this stage game equilibrium cannot occur in the evolutionary game. There is another such asymmetric equilibrium of the stage game, in which one player uses (Hawk, Bully, Prober-Retaliator) with probabilities (0.366,0.327,0.308) and the other player uses (Mouse,Bully,Prober-Retaliator) with probabilities (0.377,0.296,0.326).

Note that there is a *unique* evolutionarily stable mixed strategy in this game, consisting of Hawks and Bullies. Maynard Smith and Price do not find this evolutionarily stable strategy, and speculate that the species would evolve into mainly Retaliators and Prober-Retaliators, which is not the case.

7.12   Hawks, Doves, and Bourgeois

Consider a population of birds that fight over valuable territory. There are two possible strategies. The "hawk" (H) strategy is to escalate battle until injured or your opponent retreats. The "dove" (D) strategy is to display

	H	D
H	$(v-w)/2$	v
D	0	$v/2 - t$

hostility but retreat before sustaining injury if your opponent escalates. The payoff matrix is given in the figure, where v is the value of territory, w is the cost of injury, and t is the cost of protracted display when D plays against D. In this and the next figure we have included only the payoff to player 1, since the payoff to player 2 is the payoff to player 1 symmetrically across the diagonal. The birds can play mixed strategies, but they are physically indistinguishable.

a. Justify the entries in the payoff matrix.

b. Show that if $w > v$, neither H nor D is an evolutionarily stable strategy.

c. Suppose the birds all play $\alpha H + (1 - \alpha)D$. Show that if $t > 0$ and $w > v$, there is a unique $\alpha \in (0, 1)$ such that this mixed strategy is evolutionarily stable.

d. Suppose a new mutant comes along, a "bourgeois" (B) who plays H if it was the first to occupy the territory, and plays D if it comes upon another bird's territory. Show that, under plausible conditions, when we add B to the birds' repertoire, we get the payoff matrix in Fig. 7.2. What relations among v, w, and t must obtain in order for B to be evolutionarily stable?

	H	D	B
H	$(v - w)/2$	v	$3v/4 - w/4$
D	0	$v/2 - t$	$v/4 - t/2$
B	$(v - w)/4$	$3v/4 - t/2$	$v/2$

Figure 7.2. Hawks, doves, and bourgeois.

7.13   Trogs and Farfel

Trogs float in a primordial ooze. They make farfel, which is the only food they eat. But a trog cannot eat its own farfel. Rather, each trog secretes a unit of farfel, then floats around in the ooze until it encounters another trog, after which they exchange their farfel. A trog can make either Good farfel or Bad farfel. It costs a trog x ergs to make a unit of bad farfel and y ergs to make a unit of good farfel $(y > x)$, and the energy derived from consuming good farfel is z and from consuming bad farfel is w $(z > w)$. A trog's payoff from a transaction is the net number of ergs obtained.

a. Show that the trogs face a prisoner's dilemma if and only if $z - w > y - x$.

The trogs can recognize one another, so each encounter between trogs is one in a series of such encounters, and thus is part of a repeated Prisoner's Dilemma between the two trogs. Trogs are genetically wired to play strategies in the normal form of the repeated prisoner's dilemma.

Tit-for-Tat is a strategy defined as follows. The first time you meet a new trog, give it Good farfel. Each time you meet this particular trog again, give the trog the same type of farfel it gave you in your previous encounter (§5.11).

Trogs use a discount factor δ, with $0 < \delta < 1$, to add up energy over time: an erg in the next period is worth δ ergs today, because the trog might die before the next period arrives. Assume the expected length of time before a trog meets its current partner again is one time period.

b. Show that Tit-for-Tat is not evolutionarily stable and can be invaded by the strategy "always give good farfel."

We say a particular strategy is *weakly evolutionarily stable* if, when all trogs follow this strategy, no mutant following a different strategy can invade it in the sense of doing better than the incumbent trogs in exchanges.

c. Show that Tit-for-Tat is weakly evolutionarily stable if and only if

$$\delta > \frac{y - x}{z - w}.$$

HINT: Let G and B represent "give Good farfel" and "give Bad farfel," respectively. First show that playing B forever against Tit-for-Tat is not a best response if and only if the above condition holds. Then show that playing B for a certain number of rounds, followed by playing G, is not a best response if and only if the above condition holds.

d. Show that "always give Bad farfel" is evolutionarily stable.

e. If you are musically literate, compose and sing the song "You Give Good Farfel."

7.14 Evolutionary Stability in Finite Populations

Consider a population in which agents are randomly paired in each period and each pair plays a 2×2 game. Let $r_{\mu\nu}$ be the payoff to playing μ when your partner plays ν. Suppose agents are "hardwired" to play a particular strategy, and let $r(\mu)$ and $r(\nu)$ be the expected payoffs to an μ-type and a ν-type agent, respectively.

Suppose there are n agents, m of which play the "mutant" strategy μ, the rest playing the "incumbent" strategy ν. Then we have

$$r(\mu) = \left(1 - \frac{m-1}{n}\right) r_{\mu\nu} + \frac{m-1}{n} r_{\mu\mu}$$

$$r(\nu) = \left(1 - \frac{m}{n}\right) r_{\nu\nu} + \frac{m}{n} r_{\nu\mu}.$$

It follows that

$$r(\nu) - r(\mu) = \left(1 - \frac{m}{n}\right)(r_{\nu\nu} - r_{\mu\nu})$$
$$+ \frac{m}{n}(r_{\nu\mu} - r_{\mu\mu}) + \frac{1}{n}(r_{\mu\mu} - r_{\mu\nu}). \qquad (7.1)$$

We say a strategy ν is *noninvadable* if there is an $\epsilon > 0$ such that for all feasible mutants $\mu \neq \nu$ and all positive m such that $m/n < \epsilon$, $r(\nu) > r(\mu)$. When this condition fails, we say ν is *invadable*. We say a strategy ν is *Nash* if ν is a best reply to itself, or equivalently, if there is a Nash equilibrium in which only ν is played. We say a strategy ν is *evolutionarily stable* if there is a population size n such that ν is noninvadable for all populations of size n or greater.

a. Show that it is possible for a non-Nash strategy to be noninvadable, even by a Nash strategy.
b. Show that it is possible for a Nash strategy to be invadable.
c. Show that strategy ν is evolutionarily stable if and only if ν is a Nash strategy, and for any μ that is a best reply to ν, ν is a better reply to μ than μ is to itself, or if μ is as good a reply to itself as ν is to μ, then μ is a better reply to itself than μ is to ν. Equivalently, for any mutant μ, either $r_{\nu\nu} > r_{\mu\nu}$, or $r_{\nu\nu} = r_{\mu\nu}$ and $r_{\nu\mu} > r_{\mu\mu}$, or $r_{\nu\nu} = r_{\mu\nu}$ and $r_{\nu\mu} = r_{\mu\mu}$ and $r_{\mu\mu} > r_{\mu\nu}$.
d. The above conditions are not those of Maynard Smith, which state that ν is evolutionarily stable if and only if ν is Nash and for any μ that is a best reply to n, ν is a better reply to μ than μ is to itself, or equivalently, for any mutant μ, either $r_{\nu\nu} > r_{\mu\nu}$, or $r_{\nu\nu} = r_{\mu\nu}$ and $r_{\nu\mu} > r_{\mu\mu}$. Show that we can derive Maynard Smith's conditions by letting $m, n \to \infty$ in (A7.1) in such a manner that $m/n = \epsilon$, but the limit argument cannot be used to conclude that $r(\nu) > r(\mu)$ in the "large finite" case.

e. Let $p = m/n$, $a = r_{vv} - r_{\mu v}$, $b = r_{v\mu} - r_{\mu\mu} - r_{vv} + r_{\mu v}$, and $c = r_{\mu\mu} - r_{\mu v}$. Then (A7.1) becomes

$$r(v) - r(\mu) = \frac{1}{n}(na + mb + c). \tag{7.2}$$

Suppose v can be invaded by mutant strategy μ, and the system follows any dynamic in which a strategy with a higher payoff increases in frequency. Show that if $n(a + b) > c$, μ will invade until μ is the largest integer less than $-(na + c)/b$. Otherwise μ will invade until v is extinct.

In the case of partial invasion in the last example, we say μ is *quasi-evolutionarily stable*. Note that μ is quasi-evolutionarily stable with respect to v for very large n if and only if μ and v are part of a completely mixed Nash equilibrium (assuming there are no other feasible pure strategies).

7.15 Evolutionary Stability in Asymmetric Games

Many situations can be modeled as evolutionary games, except for the fact that the two players are not interchangeable. For instance, in One-Card Two-Round Poker with Bluffing (§4.11), the player going first has a completely different set of strategies from the player going second. Yet, despite the lack of symmetry, we simulated the game quite nicely as an evolutionary game. Analogous situations include interactions between predator and prey, boss and worker, male and female, incumbent and intruder, among a host of others.

This is not simply a technicality—it makes no sense to say that a "mutant meets its own type" when the game is asymmetric, so evolutionary stability has no meaning. The obvious way around this problem is to define a homogeneous set of players who in each period are paired randomly, one of the pair being randomly assigned to be player 1, and the other to be player 2. We may call this the "symmetric version" of the asymmetric evolutionary game. However, *an evolutionarily stable strategy in the symmetric version of an asymmetric evolutionary game must be a strict Nash equilibrium*— that is, each type in the asymmetric game must use exactly *one* pure strategy (Selten 1980). To see this, suppose there is a Nash equilibrium $u = (\sigma_1, t_2)$ of the symmetric version, where a player uses strictly mixed strategy σ_1 when assigned to be player 1, and uses t_2 (pure or mixed) when assigned

Frequency

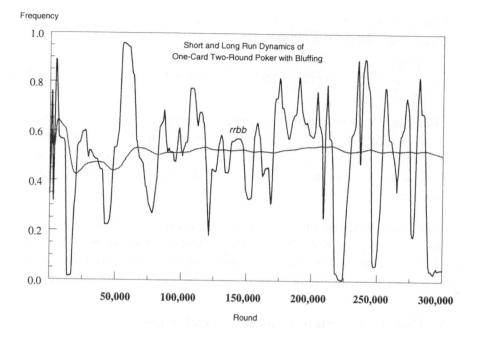

Figure 7.3. Simulation of One-Card Two-Round Poker with Bluffing.

to be player 2. Consider a mutant that uses $v = (s_1, t_2)$, where s_1 is a pure strategy that appears with positive weight in σ_1. Then v does as well against u as u does against itself, and v does as well against v as u does against v. All this is true because the payoff to s_1 against t_2 in the asymmetric game is equal to the payoff to σ_1 against t_2 by the Fundamental Theorem (§4.3).

It follows that *mixed strategy Nash equilibria in asymmetric evolutionary games are never evolutionarily stable in the symmetric version of the game.* As we shall see later, this situation reflects the fact that mixed strategy Nash equilibria in asymmetric evolutionary games with a replicator dynamic are never asymptotically stable (§9.15). Some game theorists consider this a weakness of evolutionary game theory (Mailath 1998), but in fact it reflects a deep and important regularity of social interaction—in asymmetric evolutionary games, the frequency of different types of behavior goes through periodic cycles through time.

For a dramatic example of this important insight, we return to our simulation of One-Card Two-Round Poker with Bluffing (Fig. 4.3). In this simulation I lowered the mutation rate to 1% and ran the simulation for

300,000 rounds. The results are shown in Fig. 7.3 for one of the player 1 types, *rrbb* (bluff all the way). Note that the *average frequency* of each strategy settles down to the theoretically predicted equilibrium value, but the *round-to-round frequencies* fluctuate wildly in the medium run. Strategy *rrbb*, which has the equilibrium frequency of about 50%, sometimes goes for thousands of rounds with frequency under 5% or over 90%.

8

Dynamical Systems and Differential Equations

> History is Spirit at war with itself.
>
> *Georg Wilhelm Friedrich Hegel*

8.1 Introduction

We have studied Nash equilibria of games, but *do* games reach Nash equilibrium, and if so, by what process? If there are several Nash equilibria, to which one does the game go? Indeed, what are Nash equilibria equilibria of? To answer these questions we will study the behavior of *dynamical systems* that are generally not in equilibrium but which, under appropriate conditions, approach a state of equilibrium over time, or orbit equilibria the way planets orbit the sun, or have some other love-hate relationship with equilibria (e.g., strange attractors).

We can apply several analytical tools in treating strategic interactions as dynamical systems, including difference equations, stochastic processes (such as Markov chains and diffusion processes), statistical mechanics, and differential equations. The differential equation approach is the most basic and has the quickest payoff, so that is what we will develop in this chapter.

We begin with the definition of a dynamical system, followed by examples with one independent variable (population growth models) that can be solved explicitly, and with two independent variables (the Lotka-Volterra model) for which there is a full characterization in phase space (§8.2-§8.5). We follow by characterizing local stability (§8.6), which we apply in systems with one and two independent variables. I spend a fair amount of class time on Dynamical Systems in Two Dimensions (§8.8), which includes a full characterization and complete analytical solution for the linear case, as well as the use of the Jacobian matrix to reduce the nonlinear to the linear case in hyperbolic systems. Sections 8.9 to 8.12 make good problem sets. The remainder of the chapter deals with more advanced topics (the

Hartman-Grobman, Poincaré-Bendixson, and Liapunov Theorems), which can be referred to when needed in later chapters.

8.2 Dynamical Systems

Suppose $x = (x_1, \ldots, x_n)$ is a point in n-dimensional space $\mathbf{R}^n$ that traces out a curve through time. We can describe this as

$$x = x(t) = (x_1(t), \ldots, x_n(t)) \qquad \text{for } -\infty < t < \infty.$$

Often we do not know $x(t)$ directly, but we do know the forces determining its rate and direction of change in some region of $\mathbf{R}^n$. We thus have

$$\frac{dx_1}{dt} = f^1(x_1, \ldots, x_n),$$
$$\frac{dx_2}{dt} = f^2(x_1, \ldots, x_n),$$
$$\vdots$$
$$\frac{dx_n}{dt} = f^n(x_1, \ldots, x_n),$$

or more succinctly,

$$\dot{\mathbf{x}} = f(\mathbf{x}) \qquad \mathbf{x} \in \mathbf{R}^n, \tag{8.1}$$

where the "dot" indicates the derivative with respect to t, so $\dot{\mathbf{x}} = dx/dt$. We always assume f has continuous partial derivatives.

We call this a set of *first order ordinary differential equations* in n unknowns. It is "first order" because no derivative higher than the first appears. It is "ordinary" as opposed to "partial" because we want to solve for a function of the single variable t, as opposed to solving for a function of several variables.

We call $\mathbf{x}(t)$ a *dynamical system* if it satisfies such a set of ordinary differential equations, in the sense that $\dot{\mathbf{x}}(t) = f(\mathbf{x}(t))$ for t in some (possibly infinite) interval. A *fixed point*, also called a *critical point*, or a *stationary point*, is a point $\mathbf{x}^* \in \mathbf{R}^n$ for which $f(\mathbf{x}^*) = 0$.

8.3   Population Growth

Suppose the rate of growth of fish in a lake is r. Then the number y of fish in the lake is governed by the equation

$$\dot{y} = ry.$$

We can solve this equation by "separation of variables," bringing all the expressions involving t on the right, and all the expressions involving y on the left. This is not possible for just any differential equation, of course, but it is possible in this case. This gives

$$\frac{dy}{y} = r\,dt.$$

Now we integrate both sides, getting

$$\ln y = rt + a,$$

where a is a constant of integration. Taking the antilogarithm of both sides, we get

$$y = be^{rt},$$

where $b = e^{a}$ is another constant of integration.

We determine the constant of integration by noting that if the number of the fish in the lake at time $t = 0$ is y_0, then we must have $b = y_0$. This gives the final solution

$$y = y_0 e^{rt}. \tag{8.2}$$

This function is graphed in Fig. 8.1.

8.4   Population Growth with Limited Carrying Capacity

Equation (8.2) predicts that the fish population can grow without bounds. More realistically, suppose that the more fish, the lower the rate of growth of fish. Let η be the "carrying capacity" of the lake—the number of fish such that the rate of growth of the fish population is zero. The simplest expression for the growth rate of the fish population, given that the growth rate is r when $y = 0$, is then $r(1 - y/\eta)$. Our differential equation then becomes

$$\dot{y} = r\left(1 - \frac{y}{\eta}\right)y \qquad \eta, r > 0. \tag{8.3}$$

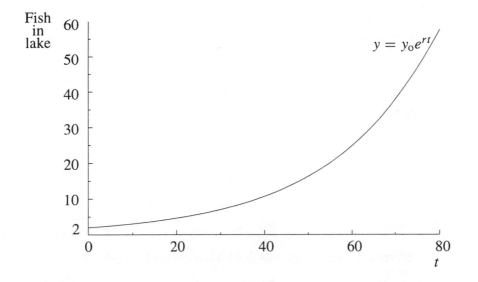

Figure 8.1. Exponential growth of fish in lake. The initial population is $y_0 = 2$, and the rate of growth is $r = 4.2\%$.

Note that the dynamical system given by this equation has two fixed points: $y^* = 0$, where the fish population is zero, and $y^* = \eta$, where the population is just equal to the carrying capacity.

To solve the equation, we separate variables, getting

$$\frac{dy}{y(\eta - y)} = \frac{r}{\eta} dt.$$

We now integrate both sides, getting

$$\int \frac{dy}{y(\eta - y)} = \frac{r}{\eta} t + a, \tag{8.4}$$

where a is a constant of integration. We use the method of partial fractions to write

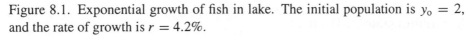

Thus, we have

$$\int \frac{dy}{y(\eta - y)} = \frac{1}{\eta} \left[\int \frac{dy}{\eta - y} + \int \frac{dy}{y} \right]$$

$$= \frac{1}{\eta} \ln \frac{y}{\eta - y}.$$

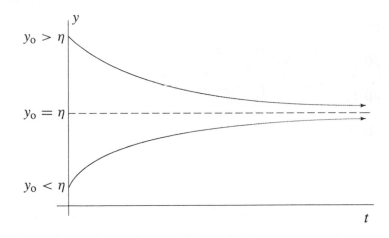

Figure 8.2. Population growth with limited carrying capacity.

Substituting into (8.4), we get

$$\ln \frac{y}{\eta - y} = rt + a\eta.$$

Taking antilogarithms of both sides, this becomes

$$\frac{y}{\eta - y} = be^{rt},$$

where $b = e^{a\eta}$ is another constant of integration. If the number of fish in the lake at time $t = 0$ is y_0, then we must have $b = y_0/(\eta - y_0)$, which can be either positive or negative, depending on whether the initial fish population is larger or smaller than the stationary population size η.

Now we can solve this equation for y, getting

$$y = \frac{\eta}{Ae^{-rt} + 1},$$

where $A = (\eta - y_0)/y_0$. Note that this equation predicts a smooth movement from disequilibrium to stationarity as $t \to \infty$. A picture of the process is given in Fig. 8.2.

8.5   The Lotka-Volterra Predator-Prey Model

Consider a society in which weary travelers stay for the night at roadside inns. Some innkeepers are dishonest, robbing and murdering their guests in the middle of the night. But some travelers arm themselves to fend off dishonest innkeepers. Let x be the fraction of travelers who are unarmed, and let y be the fraction of innkeepers who are dishonest. Suppose dishonest innkeepers grow at the rate $\delta_1 x$ but are put out of business at the rate $\gamma_1(1-x)$. These equations reflect the fact that dishonesty has a higher reward the more unarmed travelers there are, and a higher penalty the more armed travelers there are. The net growth rate is then $\dot{y}/y = \delta_1 x - \gamma_1(1-x)$, which we can write more simply as

$$\dot{y} = \delta y(x - \gamma), \qquad \delta > 0, 1 > \gamma > 0, \tag{8.5}$$

where we have written $\delta = \delta_1 + \gamma_1$ and $\gamma = \gamma_1/(\delta_1 + \gamma_1)$. Equation (8.5) expresses the rate of growth $\dot{y}/y$ as a function of the frequency of unarmed travelers in the population.

Suppose the natural rate of growth of unarmed travelers is $g > 0$, perhaps because "trusting" behaviors tend to spread when people are not robbed in their sleep. But being robbed reduces the rate of growth of unarmed travelers by the rate μy, so

$$\dot{x} = x(g - \mu y). \tag{8.6}$$

Now, (8.5) and (8.6) form a pair of differential equations in two unknowns (x and y), the solution to which is a dynamical system known as the *Lotka-Volterra predator-prey model*.

How do we solve this equation? There is no solution in closed form (e.g., using polynomials, trigonometric functions, logarithms, and exponentials). We can, however, discover the properties of such equations without solving them explicitly.

We begin such an analysis with a *phase diagram* of the differential equations. The phase diagram for the Lotka-Volterra model is depicted in Fig. 8.3.

The horizontal dotted line represents the condition $dx/dt = 0$, and the vertical dotted line represents the condition $dy/dt = 0$. The fixed point is at $(\gamma, g/\mu)$, where the two intersect. The little arrows show in which direction the flow of the dynamical system moves for that particular point (x, y). The arrows point northward when $dy/dt > 0$ and southward when $dy/dt < 0$, and they point eastward when $dx/dt > 0$ and westward when $dx/dt < 0$. The arrows are vertical where $dx/dt = 0$ because motion is purely north-south instantaneously at such a point, and are horizontal where $dy/dt = 0$, since motion is purely east-west at such a point. In each of the four quadrants marked off by the dotted lines, the direction of the flow is qualitatively similar. Thus to the northeast of the fixed point, the flow

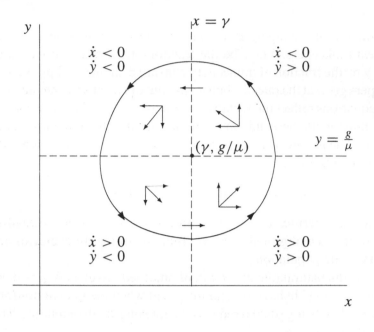

Figure 8.3. Phase diagram of Lotka-Volterra system.

is northwest; to the northwest, the flow is southwest; to the southwest, the flow is southeast; and to the southeast of the fixed point, the flow is to the northeast. So it is clear that the flow circles counterclockwise about the fixed point. However, we cannot tell prima facie whether the flow circles into the fixed point or forms closed circuits about the fixed point.

We can actually show that Lotka-Volterra does have closed orbits. To do this, we find a function that is constant on any trajectory of the dynamical system, and show that this function is monotonic (strictly increasing or decreasing) along a ray starting from the fixed point and pointing northeast.[1]

Suppose we have such a function f and consider a path starting at a point **x** on the ray, making one complete revolution around the fixed point and hitting the ray again, say at **y**. Since f is constant on the path, $f(\mathbf{x}) = f(\mathbf{y})$. But since f is monotonic on the ray, we must have $\mathbf{x} = \mathbf{y}$, so the path is a closed orbit. First, we eliminate t from (8.5) and (8.6) by dividing the first

---

[1]We say a function $f(x)$ is (1) *increasing* if $x > y$ implies $f(x) \geq f(y)$; (2) *strictly increasing* if $x > y$ implies $f(x) > f(y)$; (3) *decreasing* if $x > y$ implies $f(x) \leq f(y)$; (4) *strictly decreasing* if $x > y$ implies $f(x) < f(y)$.

by the second, getting

$$\frac{dy}{dx} = \frac{\delta y(x - \gamma)}{x(g - \mu y)}.$$

Now we separate variables, pulling all the x's to the right, and all the y's to the left:

$$\frac{g - \mu y}{y}dy = \frac{\delta(x - \gamma)}{x}dx.$$

Now we integrate both sides, getting

$$g \ln y - \mu y = \delta x - \delta \gamma \ln x + C,$$

where C is an arbitrary constant of integration. Bringing all the variables over to the left, and taking the antilogarithm, we get

$$y^g x^{\delta \gamma} e^{-(\mu y + \delta x)} = e^C. \tag{8.7}$$

So now we have an expression that is constant along any trajectory of the Lotka-Volterra dynamical system.

Now, consider a point (x, y) that starts at the fixed point $(\gamma, g/\mu)$ and moves to the northeast in a direction heading away from the origin. We can write this as $x = \gamma s$, $y = (g/\mu)s$, where s is a parameter measuring the distance from the fixed point. Note that when $s = 1$, (x, y) is at the fixed point. Substituting in (8.7), we get

$$\left(\frac{g}{\mu}\right)^g \gamma^{\delta \gamma} s^{g + \delta \gamma} e^{-(g + \delta \gamma)s} = e^C.$$

This looks forbidding, but it's really not. We pull the first two terms on the left over to the right, and then take the $(g + \delta \gamma)$-th root of both sides. The right-hand side is a complicated constant, which we can abbreviate by D, and the left is just se^{-s}, so we have

$$se^{-s} = D. \tag{8.8}$$

If we can show that the left-hand side is strictly decreasing for $s > 1$, we are done, since then any $s > 1$ that satisfies (8.8) must be unique. We take the derivative of the left-hand side, getting

$$e^{-s} - se^{-s} = (1 - s)e^{-s},$$

which is negative for $s > 1$. This shows that the dynamical system moves in closed orbits around the fixed point.

It follows from this analysis that if the system begins out of equilibrium, both the fraction of unarmed travelers and the fraction of dishonest innkeepers will go through constant-amplitude oscillations around their equilibrium values forever. We shall later characterize this as an *asymmetric evolutionary game* (§9.15) for which this oscillatory behavior is quite typical.

8.6   Dynamical Systems Theory

With these examples under our belt, we can address the basic theory of dynamical systems (a.k.a. differential equations).[2]

Suppose a dynamical system is at a point x_0 at time t_0. We call the locus of points through which the system passes as $t \to \infty$ the *forward trajectory* of the system through x_0, or the *trajectory* of the system starting at x_0. The *backward trajectory* of the system through x_0 is the locus of points through which the system passes as $t \to -\infty$. The forward and backward trajectories are together called the trajectory *through* x_0.

Clearly if a dynamical system is at a fixed point x^*, it will stay there forever, so the trajectory starting at x^* is simply x^* itself. However, if we perturb the system a little from x^* by choosing a new initial point x_0 at time $t = 0$, there are several things that can happen. We begin with a couple of definitions. If $x \in \mathbf{R}^n$, and $r > 0$, we define a *ball of radius r* around x, which we write $B_r(x)$, as the set of points $y \in \mathbf{R}^n$ whose distance from x is less than r. We define a *neighborhood* of x to be any subset of $\mathbf{R}^n$ that contains some ball around x. Finally, we say a set in $\mathbf{R}^n$ is an *open set* if it is a neighborhood of each of its points. Note that a set is open if and only if it contains a ball of some positive radius around each of its points.

We define an ϵ-*perturbation* of the dynamical system at a fixed point x^* to be a trajectory of the system starting at some $x_0 \in B_\epsilon(x^*)$, where $\epsilon > 0$ and $x_0 \neq x^*$. We say a trajectory $x(t)$ *approaches* x^* if $x(t) \to x^*$ as $t \to \infty$. We say a trajectory $x(t)$ ϵ-*escapes* x^* if there is some t_0 such that $x(t) \notin B_\epsilon(x^*)$ for $t > t_0$; i.e., after some point in time, the trajectory never gets closer than ϵ to x^*.

---

[2]There are many excellent texts on differential equations. Some of my favorites are Perko 1991, Hirsch and Smale 1974, Epstein 1997, and Hofbauer and Sigmund 1998. The last of these is a beautiful summary of recent advances in evolutionary dynamics.

If there is some $\epsilon > 0$ such that for any $\mathbf{x}_0 \in B_\epsilon(\mathbf{x}^*)$, the trajectory through $\mathbf{x}_0$ approaches $\mathbf{x}^*$, we say the fixed point at $\mathbf{x}^*$ is *asymptotically stable*. The set of points $\mathbf{x}_0 \in \mathbf{R}^n$ such that a trajectory through $\mathbf{x}_0$ approaches $\mathbf{x}^*$ is called the *basin of attraction* of the fixed point $\mathbf{x}^*$. If every point where the differential equation is defined is in the basin of attraction of $\mathbf{x}^*$, we say the fixed point is *globally stable* .

If $\mathbf{x}^*$ is not asymptotically stable, but for any ball $B_\epsilon(\mathbf{x}^*)$ there is another ball $B_\delta(\mathbf{x}^*)$ such that for any point $\mathbf{x}_0 \in B_\delta(\mathbf{x}^*)$, the trajectory starting at $\mathbf{x}_0$ never leaves $B_\epsilon(\mathbf{x}^*)$, we say the fixed point at $\mathbf{x}^*$ is *neutrally stable*. Neutral stability means that a sufficiently small perturbation about the fixed point never leads the system too far away from the fixed point. A special case is when any trajectory through $\mathbf{x}_0 \in B_\epsilon(\mathbf{x}^*)$ is a *closed orbit*; i.e., the trajectory starting at $\mathbf{x}_0$ eventually returns to $\mathbf{x}_0$.

If $\mathbf{x}^*$ is neither asymptotically stable nor neutrally stable, we say $\mathbf{x}^*$ is *unstable*. Thus, $\mathbf{x}^*$ is unstable if there is an $\epsilon > 0$ such that for any ball $B_\delta(\mathbf{x}^*)$, there is a point $\mathbf{x}_0 \in B_\delta(\mathbf{x}^*)$ such that the trajectory starting at $\mathbf{x}_0$ ϵ-escapes $\mathbf{x}^*$.

8.6.1 Existence and Uniqueness

THEOREM 8.1 Existence, Uniqueness, and Continuous Dependence on Initial Conditions. *Suppose that f in equation (8.1) has continuous derivatives on an open set D containing a point x_0. Then there is some interval $I = [-t_0, t_0]$ and a unique trajectory $\mathbf{x}(t)$ satisfying (8.1) defined on I with $\mathbf{x}(0) = x_0$. Moreover, $\mathbf{x}(t)$ depends smoothly upon x_0 in the following sense: there is some $\delta > 0$, and a unique function $\mathbf{x}(t, \mathbf{y})$ that satisfies (8.1) on an interval $[-t_1, t_1]$ with $\mathbf{x}(0, \mathbf{y}) = \mathbf{y}$, for all $\mathbf{y} \in B_\delta(\mathbf{x}_0)$. Moreover, $\mathbf{x}(t, \mathbf{y})$ has continuous partial derivatives, and continuous second partial derivatives with respect to t.*

This theorem says that if $f(\mathbf{x})$ is suitably well behaved, the dynamical system (8.1) has a unique, twice differentiable trajectory through each point $\mathbf{x}_0$, and the trajectory varies differentiably as we vary $\mathbf{x}_0$. In particular, two trajectories can never cross.

THEOREM 8.2 Continuous Dependence on Parameters. *Let $\mu \in \mathbf{R}^k$ be a set of k parameters, and suppose $f(\mathbf{x}, \mu)$ has continuous partial derivatives in a neighborhood of $(\mathbf{x}_0, \mu_0) \in \mathbf{R}^{n+k}$. Then there is a $t_1 > 0$, a $\delta > 0$, an*

$\epsilon > 0$, and a unique function $\mathbf{x}(t, \mathbf{y}, \mu)$ that satisfies

$$\dot{\mathbf{x}} = f(\mathbf{x}(t, \mathbf{y}, \mu), \mu) \tag{8.9}$$

with $\mathbf{x}(0, \mathbf{y}, \mu) = \mathbf{y}$, for $t \in [-t_1, t_1]$, $\mathbf{y} \in B_\delta(\mathbf{x}_0)$, and $\mu \in B_\epsilon(\mu_0)$. Moreover, $\mathbf{x}(t, \mathbf{y}, \mu)$ has continuous partial derivatives.

This theorem says that if $f(\mathbf{x}, \mu)$ is suitably well behaved, the trajectories of the dynamical system (8.9) vary differentiably as we vary the parameters μ.

8.6.2 The Linearization Theorem

Given a dynamical system (8.1), we define the *Jacobian* of f at a point $\mathbf{x} \in \mathbf{R}^n$ to be the $n \times n$ matrix $Df(\mathbf{x}) = (a_{ij})$ where

$$a_{ij} = \frac{\partial f^i}{\partial x_j}(\mathbf{x}) \qquad \text{for } i, j = 1, \ldots, n.$$

Suppose $\mathbf{x}^*$ is a fixed point of the dynamical system (8.1), and let $A = Df(\mathbf{x}^*)$ be the Jacobian of the system at $\mathbf{x}^*$. We define the *linearization* of the original dynamic system (8.1) at $\mathbf{x}^*$ to be the linear dynamical system

$$\dot{x}_1 = a_{11}x_1 + a_{12}x_2 + \ldots + a_{1n}x_n,$$
$$\dot{x}_2 = a_{21}x_1 + a_{22}x_2 + \ldots + a_{2n}x_n,$$
$$\vdots$$
$$\dot{x}_n = a_{n1}x_1 + a_{n2}x_2 + \ldots + a_{nn}x_n,$$

or, more succinctly,

$$\dot{\mathbf{x}} = A\mathbf{x} \qquad \mathbf{x} \in \mathbf{R}^n. \tag{8.10}$$

Note that the fixed point of linearization has been moved from $\mathbf{x}^*$ to 0 (we could keep the fixed point at $\mathbf{x}^*$ by defining the linearization as $\dot{\mathbf{x}} = A(\mathbf{x} - \mathbf{x}^*)$, but this needlessly complicates the notation).

We define the *eigenvalues* of the matrix A in (8.10) to be the set of (possibly complex) numbers λ that satisfy the equation

$$A\mathbf{x} = \lambda\mathbf{x} \tag{8.11}$$

for some vector $\mathbf{x} \neq 0$. This equation can be rewritten as $(A - \lambda I)x = 0$, which holds for $x \neq 0$ only if the determinant of $A - \lambda I$ is zero. This determinant is given by

$$|A - \lambda I| = \begin{vmatrix} a_{11} - \lambda & a_{12} & \cdots & a_{1n} \\ a_{21} & a_{22} - \lambda & \cdots & a_{2n} \\ \vdots & \vdots & \vdots & \vdots \\ a_{n1} & a_{n2} & \cdots & a_{nn} - \lambda \end{vmatrix}$$

Since this is a polynomial of degree n, we know from linear algebra—you can refer to Hirsch and Smale (1974) for details—there are exactly n (possibly complex) eigenvalues, if we account properly for their "multiplicity." At any rate, we shall only deal in this book with dynamical systems in one or two dimensions, where the calculation of the eigenvalues is very simple.

We call the dynamical system (8.1) *hyperbolic* at a fixed point $\mathbf{x}^*$ if every eigenvalue of the Jacobian matrix $Df(x^*)$ has nonzero real part. We then have the following.

THEOREM 8.3 Linearization Theorem. *Suppose the dynamical system (8.1) is hyperbolic at fixed point $\mathbf{x}^*$. Then $\mathbf{x}^*$ is asymptotically stable if its linearization (8.10) is asymptotically stable, and is unstable if its linearization is unstable. As a partial converse, if $\mathbf{x}^*$ is asymptotically stable, then no eigenvalue of the Jacobian matrix $Df(x^*)$ has strictly positive real part.*

When no eigenvalue has a strictly positive real part at $\mathbf{x}^*$, but one or more eigenvalues have a zero real part, $\mathbf{x}^*$ may be either stable or unstable.

8.7 Dynamical Systems in One Dimension

If $n = 1$, equation (8.1) becomes

$$\dot{x} = f(x), \qquad x \in \mathbf{R}. \tag{8.12}$$

Suppose $f(x)$ has the shape shown in Fig. 8.4. We call a diagram like the one in Fig. 8.4 a *phase diagram*—a depiction of the state space of the dynamic system with little arrows showing the direction of movement of the system at representative points in the state space.

It is obvious that fixed points x_a and x_c are stable, while fixed point x_b is unstable. To see that this agrees with Linearization Theorem 8.3, note that the Jacobian at a point x is just the one-dimensional matrix $(f'(x))$, and the

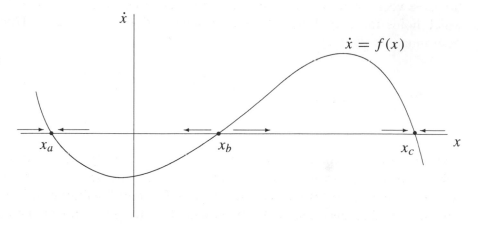

Figure 8.4. Stable and unstable fixed points.

eigenvalue of this matrix is just $f'(x)$. Thus, the system has a fixed point at x^* if $f(x^*) = 0$, and this fixed point is hyperbolic if $f'(x^*) \neq 0$. Note that in Fig. 8.4 all three fixed points are hyperbolic, since $f'(x) < 0$ at x_a and x_c, and $f'(x) > 0$ at x_b. The linearization of (8.12) at fixed point x^* is $\dot{x} = f'(x^*)x$, which has solution

$$x(t) = x(0)e^{f'(x^*)t},$$

which is obviously stable when $f'(x^*) < 0$ and unstable when $f'(x^*) > 0$. Applying the Linearization Theorem, we find that the fixed points at x_a and x_c are stable, while fixed point x_b is unstable.

We can also apply the Linearization Theorem to the Population Growth with Limited Carrying Capacity dynamical system (8.3). This system has two fixed points, $y = 0$ and $y = \eta$. The Jacobian at a point y is just

$$r\left(1 - \frac{2y}{\eta}\right),$$

which has the value $r > 0$ at $y = 0$ and the value $-r < 0$ at $y = \eta$. The linearization of the dynamical system at $y = 0$ is thus

$$\dot{y} = ry,$$

which has the solution $y = ae^{rt}$. This explodes to infinity, so $y = 0$ is unstable.

The linearization of the dynamical system at $y = \eta$ is

$$\dot{y} = -ry$$

with solution $y = ae^{-rt}$. This converges to zero so $y = \eta$ is an asymptotically stable fixed point.

We conclude that in this model, the fixed point $y = \eta$ is globally stable, and is approached exponentially from any $y > 0$.

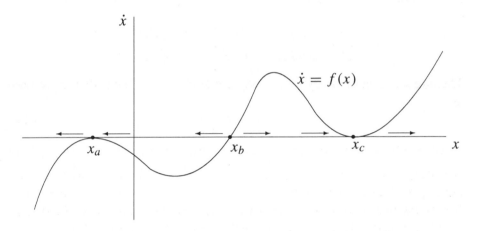

Figure 8.5. Phase diagram of non-hyperbolic fixed points in a one-dimensional system. Note that x_a is unstable to the left and locally stable to the right, B is unstable, and C is locally stable to the left, unstable to the right.

If (8.12) is not hyperbolic at a fixed point x^* (i.e., $f'(x^*) = 0$), then we cannot apply the Linearization Theorem. We illustrate this in the phase diagram shown in Fig. 8.5. Here the fixed point at x_b is unstable, just as before. But at fixed points x_a and x_c, the Jacobians are zero (i.e., $f'(x_a) = f'(x_c) = 0$), so the fixed points are not hyperbolic. Note that linearization has the solution $x(t) = 0$, which of course tells us nothing about the dynamical system. In fact, we can easily see that the system approaches the fixed point from the right of x_a, but ϵ-escapes the fixed point to the left of x_a for small ϵ. At x_c the system approaches the fixed point from the left of x_c, but ϵ-escapes the fixed point from right of x_c for small ϵ.

8.8 Dynamical Systems in Two Dimensions

We can write the equations for a dynamical system in two dimensions as

$$\dot{x} = f(x, y),$$
$$\dot{y} = g(x, y). \tag{8.13}$$

Suppose this has a fixed point at a point (x^*, y^*). We can write the Jacobian of the system at this point as

$$A = \begin{bmatrix} a_{11} & a_{12} \\ a_{21} & a_{22} \end{bmatrix} = \begin{bmatrix} f_x(x^*, y^*) & f_y(x^*, y^*) \\ g_x(x^*, y^*) & g_y(x^*, y^*) \end{bmatrix}.$$

The linearization of the dynamical system about (x^*, y^*) can then be written as

$$\dot{\mathbf{x}} = A\mathbf{x}, \tag{8.14}$$

where $\mathbf{x}$ is the column vector $\begin{bmatrix} x \\ y \end{bmatrix}$. Let $\alpha = \text{trace of } A/2 = (a_{11} + a_{22})/2$, let $\beta = \det(A) = a_{11}a_{22} - a_{21}a_{12}$, and let $\gamma = \alpha^2 - \beta$. It is easy to check that the eigenvalues of (8.14) are $\lambda_1 = \alpha + \sqrt{\gamma}$ and $\lambda_2 = \alpha - \sqrt{\gamma}$. Note that if $\beta = 0$, the two equations in (8.14) are multiples of each other, so the system is indeterminate. Thus we assume that $\beta \neq 0$. We have the following.

THEOREM 8.4 *If $\gamma > 0$, the dynamical system (8.14) is governed by the equations*

$$x(t) = ae^{\lambda_1 t} + be^{\lambda_2 t} \tag{8.15}$$
$$y(t) = ce^{\lambda_1 t} + de^{\lambda_2 t} \tag{8.16}$$

for some constants a, b, c, and d. If the system starts at $(x(0), y(0)) = (x_0, y_0)$, then

$$a = \frac{(a_{11} - \lambda_2)x_0 + a_{12}y_0}{2\sqrt{\gamma}}, \quad b = -\frac{(a_{11} - \lambda_1)x_0 + a_{12}y_0}{2\sqrt{\gamma}} \tag{8.17}$$

$$c = \frac{a_{21}x_0 + (a_{22} - \lambda_2)y_0}{2\sqrt{\gamma}}, \quad d = -\frac{a_{21}x_0 + (a_{22} - \lambda_1)y_0}{2\sqrt{\gamma}}. \tag{8.18}$$

It follows that

a. The unique fixed point of the system is (0,0).

b. The dynamical system is hyperbolic with eigenvalues $\lambda_1 = \alpha + \sqrt{\gamma}$ and $\lambda_2 = \alpha - \sqrt{\gamma}$.

c. If $\lambda_1, \lambda_2 < 0$, which occurs precisely when $\alpha < 0$ and $\beta > 0$, the fixed point at $(0,0)$ is globally stable. This is called a stable node.

d. If $\lambda_1, \lambda_2 > 0$, which occurs precisely when $\alpha, \beta > 0$, the fixed point at $(0,0)$ is unstable and every trajectory starting at a nonfixed point (x_0, y_0) approaches ∞ as $t \to \infty$. This is called an unstable node .

e. If $\lambda_1 > 0$ and $\lambda_2 < 0$, which occurs precisely when $\beta < 0$, the system is unstable, but if (x_0, y_0) lies on the straight line

$$(a_{11} - \lambda_2)x + a_{12}y = 0,$$

the system converges to the fixed point as $t \to \infty$. This line is called the stable manifold of the system. Also, if (x_0, y_0) lies on the straight line

$$(a_{11} - \lambda_1)x + a_{12}y = 0,$$

the system converges to the fixed point as $t \to -\infty$. This line is called the unstable manifold of the system. The fixed point is called a saddle point.

The proof of this theorem, which is left to the reader, is simple. The main point is to show that the answer satisfies (8.14). By Theorem 8.1, there are no other solutions. The constants a, b, c, and d are solutions to the four equations

$$x(0) = x_0 = a + b$$
$$y(0) = y_0 = c + d$$
$$\dot{x}(0) = a_{11}x_0 + a_{12}y_0 = a\lambda_1 + b\lambda_2$$
$$\dot{y}(0) = a_{21}x_0 + a_{22}y_0 = c\lambda_1 + d\lambda_2,$$

which follow directly from (8.14), (8.15), and (8.16).

The phase diagram for a stable node in the case $\gamma > 0$ is elementary: the trajectories all converge to the fixed point; in the case of an unstable node, the trajectories all move away from the fixed point. But the case of a saddle point is more interesting and is depicted in Fig. 8.6.

THEOREM 8.5 *If $\gamma < 0$, the dynamical system (8.14) is satisfied by the equations*

$$x(t) = e^{\alpha t}[a \cos \omega t + b \sin \omega t] \qquad (8.19)$$
$$y(t) = e^{\alpha t}[c \cos \omega t + d \sin \omega t], \qquad (8.20)$$

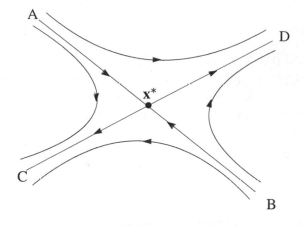

Figure 8.6. The stable and unstable manifolds of a saddle point. Note that AB is the stable manifold and CD is the unstable manifold of the saddle point.

where $\omega = \sqrt{-\gamma}$. If the system starts at $(x(0), y(0)) = (x_0, y_0)$, then

$$a = x_0 \quad b = \frac{(a_{11} - a_{22})x_0 + 2a_{12}y_0}{2\omega} \tag{8.21}$$

$$c = y_0 \quad d = \frac{2a_{21}x_0 + (a_{22} - a_{11})y_0}{2\omega}. \tag{8.22}$$

It follows that

a. *The unique fixed point of the system is (0,0).*
b. *The system is hyperbolic if and only if $\alpha \neq 0$, and its eigenvalues are $\lambda = \alpha \pm \omega\sqrt{-1}$.*
c. *Nonfixed point trajectories circle around the fixed point with period ω.*
d. *If $\alpha < 0$, the fixed point is globally stable. This is called a* stable focus.
e. *If $\alpha > 0$, the fixed point is unstable. This is called an* unstable focus.
f. *If $\alpha = 0$, the fixed point is neutrally stable, and all trajectories are closed orbits. This is called a* center.

THEOREM 8.6 *If $\gamma = 0$, the dynamical system (8.14) satisfies the equations*

$$x(t) = e^{\alpha t}(at + b) \tag{8.23}$$
$$y(t) = e^{\alpha t}(ct + d), \tag{8.24}$$

and if the system starts at $(x(0), y(0)) = (x_0, y_0)$, we have

$$a = (a_{11} - \alpha)x_0 + a_{12}y_0 \quad b = x_0 \tag{8.25}$$
$$c = a_{21}x_0 + (a_{22} - \alpha)y_0 \quad d = y_0. \tag{8.26}$$

Then the system has the single eigenvalue α, and

a. *The unique fixed point of the system is (0,0).*
b. *The system is hyperbolic if and only if α ≠ 0.*
c. *If α ≥ 0, the origin is an unstable node.*
d. *If α < 0, the origin is an stable node.*

Fig. 8.7 summarizes the behavior of the linear two-dimensional system of differential equations. Note that we have not said what happens when $\beta = \det(A) = 0$. This is called a *degenerate critical point* and is not of much interest. It means one of the differential equations is a multiple of the other, so there is really only one equation.

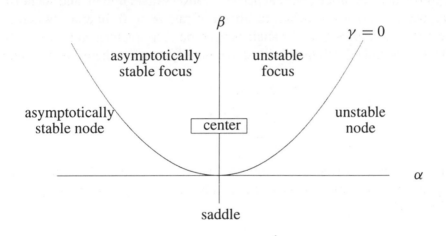

Figure 8.7. A summary of types of fixed points in a two-dimensional dynamical system.

8.9   Exercises in Two-Dimensional Linear Systems

For each of the following differential equations, draw a phase diagram, write out the general solution, and use the results of §8.8 to determine analytically the nature of the fixed point.

a $\dot{x} = \lambda x, \dot{y} = \mu y$ for $\lambda, \mu > 0$.
b $\dot{x} = \lambda x, \dot{y} = \mu y$ for $\lambda > 0, \mu < 0$.
c $\dot{x} = \lambda x, \dot{y} = \mu y$ for $\lambda, \mu < 0$.

d $\dot{x} = \lambda x + y$, $\dot{y} = \lambda y$ for $\lambda > 0$.

e $\dot{x} = \lambda x + y$, $\dot{y} = \lambda y$ for $\lambda < 0$.

f $\dot{x} = ax - by$, $\dot{y} = bx + ay$ for $a, b > 0$.

g $\dot{x} = -x - y$, $\dot{y} = x - y$.

h $\dot{x} = 3x - 2y$, $\dot{y} = x + y$.

i $\dot{x} = 3x + y$, $\dot{y} = -x + y$.

j $\dot{x} = y$, $\dot{y} = -x + 2y$.

8.10 Cultural Dynamics

Suppose there are three political parties: conservative, liberal, and socialist. Suppose conservatives switch to liberal at rate $\alpha > 0$, liberals switch to socialist at rate $\beta > 0$, and socialists become conservatives at rate $\gamma > 0$. The differential equations for this dynamical system are therefore given by

$$\dot{x} = -\alpha x + \gamma z$$
$$\dot{y} = \alpha x - \beta y$$
$$\dot{z} = \beta y - \gamma z,$$

where x, y, and z are the proportions of conservatives, liberals, and socialists, respectively. Assume that at time zero $x(0) > 0$, $y(0) > 0$, $z(0) > 0$ and $x(0) + y(0) + z(0) = 1$.

a. Explain why $x(t) \geq 0$, $y(t) \geq 0$, $z(t) \geq 0$ and $x(t) + y(t) + z(t) = 1$ for all $t \geq 0$.

b. Find the equilibrium of the dynamic system.

c. Find the Jacobian of the system and show that the equilibrium is neutrally stable.

d. Use the equation $z = 1 - x - y$ to eliminate z from the dynamical system, reducing it to a two equation system.

e. Find the equilibrium of the two dimensional system, and show that it is asymptotically stable.

f. Under what conditions is the equilibrium a stable node as opposed to a stable focus?

g. Explain why the system is neutrally stable when viewed one way but asymptotically stable when viewed another way.

8.11 Lotka-Volterra with Limited Carrying Capacity

The general Lotka-Volterra model (see §8.5 for a specific case) has the form

$$\dot{x} = x(a - by),$$
$$\dot{y} = y(-c + dx). \tag{8.27}$$

This model has the absurd property that if the predator is absent, the prey grows at the constant rate a forever. Suppose we add a limited carrying capacity term (§8.4), so the first equation in (8.27) becomes

$$\dot{x} = x(a - by - \epsilon x),$$

where $\epsilon > 0$, corresponding to capacity a/ϵ. Show that the fixed point of this system is a stable focus for small ϵ and a stable node for large ϵ.

8.12 Take No Prisoners

Two firms share a nonmarketable, nonexcludable resource R that lowers production costs but is subject to overcrowding and depletion. Suppose that when firm 1 has size x and firm 2 has size y, the profits of the two firms are given by

$$\pi^x(x, y) = \gamma_x(R - x - y) - \alpha_x,$$
$$\pi^y(x, y) = \gamma_y(R - x - y) - \alpha_y,$$

where $\gamma_x, g_y > 0$. Suppose also that the firms' growth rates are equal to their profit rates, so

$$\dot{x} = x(\gamma_x(R - x - y) - \alpha_x),$$
$$\dot{y} = y(\gamma_y(R - x - y) - \alpha_y).$$

We assume that $\gamma_x R > \alpha_x$, $\gamma_y R > \alpha_y$, and $\gamma_x/\alpha_x > \gamma_y/\alpha_y$.

a. Show that if $y = 0$ the model has an unstable fixed point at $x = 0$ and an asymptotically stable fixed point at $x = x^* = R - a_x/g_x$.
b. Show that if $x = 0$ the model has an unstable equilibrium at $y = 0$ and an asymptotically stable fixed point at $y = y^* = R - a_y/g_y$.
c. Show that the complete model has three fixed points, $(0,0)$, $(x^*, 0)$, and $(0, y^*)$, of which only the second is asymptotically stable.

We conclude that both firms cannot coexist in equilibrium.

8.13 The Hartman-Grobman Theorem

The Linearization Theorem 8.3 tells us that we can determine whether a hyperbolic fixed point of a dynamical system is asymptotically stable or unstable by looking at its linearization. This is a fairly weak statement, since we have discovered a lot more about the nature of equilibria than just stability. We have, for instance, distinguished nodes, foci, and saddles, and in the latter case, we have found that there are always stable and unstable manifolds. It turns out that in the hyperbolic case, each of these properties of the linearization of a dynamical system is also possessed by the system itself. This is the famous *Hartman-Grobman Theorem*. To state the theorem, however, we need a new definition.

Suppose the dynamical system defined by $\dot{\mathbf{x}} = f(\mathbf{x})$ has a fixed point at $\mathbf{x}^*$, and the dynamical system defined by $\dot{\mathbf{y}} = f(\mathbf{y})$ has a fixed point at $\mathbf{y}^*$. We say that the two systems are *topologically equivalent* at these fixed points if there are balls $B_\epsilon(\mathbf{x}^*)$ and $B_\delta(\mathbf{y}^*)$ around the two fixed points and a continuous one-to-one mapping $\phi : B_\epsilon(\mathbf{x}^*) \to B_\delta(\mathbf{y}^*)$ with a continuous inverse that takes trajectories of the dynamical system lying in $B_\epsilon(\mathbf{x}^*)$ into trajectories of the dynamical system lying in $B_\delta(\mathbf{y}^*)$ and preserves the direction of time.

Intuitively, two dynamical systems are topologically equivalent at $\mathbf{x}^*$ and $\mathbf{y}^*$ if we can perform the following operation. Draw the phase diagram in the neighborhood of $\mathbf{x}^*$ on a rubber sheet, including trajectories and arrows indicating the direction of time. Now stretch the rubber sheet without tearing or folding until it looks just like the phase diagram for the second dynamical system in a neighborhood of $\mathbf{y}^*$. If this is possible (you may need lots of fingers!), then the systems are topologically equivalent.

THEOREM 8.7 Hartman-Grobman. *If $\mathbf{x}^*$ is a hyperbolic fixed point of the dynamical system given by $\dot{\mathbf{x}} = f(\mathbf{x})$, then this fixed point is topologically equivalent to the fixed point at the origin of the linearization of the system $\dot{\mathbf{x}} = A\mathbf{x}$, where $A = Df(\mathbf{x}^*)$ is the Jacobian matrix of the system evaluated at $\mathbf{x}^*$.*

This means that we can determine the qualitative behavior of a dynamical system in a neighborhood of a hyperbolic fixed point by looking at its linearization, which is of course much easier to analyze. Indeed, we have fully characterized such equilibria for one- and two-dimensional systems. Higher-dimensional linear systems are harder to analyze, but they too can be completely characterized and are essentially combinations of one- and two-dimensional systems, placed at angles to each other in higher dimensions.

8.14 Special Features of Two-Dimensional Dynamical Systems

Two-dimensional dynamical systems have lots of nice properties not shared by higher-dimensional systems. This appears to be due to the famous *Jordan Curve Theorem*, which says that any continuous, non-self-intersecting, closed curve divides the plane into two connected pieces—an "inside" and an "outside." Trajectories of a dynamical system are of course continuous and non-self-intersecting, though not generally closed.

Let $\mathbf{x}(t)$ be a trajectory of the dynamical system (8.1). We say a point $\mathbf{y} \in \mathbf{R}^n$ is an *ω-limit point* of the trajectory if there is a sequence $t_n \to \infty$ such that

$$\lim_{n \to \infty} \mathbf{x}(t_n) = \mathbf{y}.$$

For instance, if $\mathbf{x}^*$ is an asymptotically stable fixed point, then $\mathbf{x}^*$ is the ω-limit of every trajectory starting at a point in the basin of attraction of $\mathbf{x}^*$. In some cases, a trajectory can actually have lots of ω-limit points. For instance, suppose the fixed point $\mathbf{x}^*$ is an unstable spiral, but there is a closed orbit at some distance from $\mathbf{x}^*$. Then a trajectory starting at a point near $\mathbf{x}^*$ can spiral out, getting closer and closer to the closed orbit. Each point on the closed orbit is thus an ω-limit of the trajectory. If a trajectory is bounded (i.e., is contained in some ball), then it must have at least one ω-limit point.

THEOREM 8.8 Poincaré-Bendixson. *Suppose $\mathbf{x}(t)$ is a bounded trajectory of (8.13), and Ω is the set of ω-limit points of the trajectory. Then if Ω contains no fixed points of (8.13), Ω is a periodic orbit of (8.13).*

The following theorem is also often useful.

THEOREM 8.9 *Suppose equation (8.13) has a closed orbit Γ and let U be the interior region bounded by Γ. Then U contains a fixed point of (8.13).*

8.15 A Non-Hyperbolic Dynamical System

Here is another example, in two dimensions, of the breakdown of linearization when the linear equations are neutrally stable in some direction. Consider the pair of equations

$$\dot{x} = v \tag{8.28}$$

$$\dot{v} = -x - \epsilon x^2 v. \tag{8.29}$$

This has one fixed point at $(x, v) = (0, 0)$. The linearized equations are then simply

$$\dot{x} = v$$
$$\dot{v} = -x,$$

which gives $\ddot{x} = \dot{v} = -x$, where we write $\ddot{x} = d^2x/dt^2$. This has the solution $x = a \cos t + b \sin t$, where a and b are chosen so that the equation satisfies the initial condition $(x(0), v(0)) = (x_0, v_0)$. Since $x(0) = a$, we have $a = x_0$. Also, $v = -a \sin t + b \cos t$, so $v(0) = b$, giving $b = v_0$. Thus, the general solution is

$$x = x_0 \cos t + v_0 \sin t,$$

which is periodic (i.e., makes ellipses or circles) with period 2π. Since this is neutrally stable, it tells us nothing about how the nonlinear system behaves. How does the nonlinear system behave? We use the following theorem.

8.16   Liapunov's Theorem

THEOREM 8.10 Liapunov.   *Suppose* $\mathbf{x}^*$ *is a fixed point of the dynamical system (8.1), which has the solution* $\mathbf{x} = \mathbf{x}(t)$. *Suppose* $V : \mathbf{R}^n \to \mathbf{R}$ *is defined in some open neighborhood* U *around* $\mathbf{x}^*$, *and has the following properties:*

a. $V(\mathbf{x}^*) = 0.$
b. $V(\mathbf{x}) > 0$ *for* $\mathbf{x} \neq \mathbf{x}^*, \mathbf{x} \in U.$
c. $\frac{dV(\mathbf{x}(t))}{dt} \leq 0$ *for* $\mathbf{x} \neq \mathbf{x}^*, \mathbf{x} \in U.$

Then $\mathbf{x}^*$ *is asymptotically or neutrally stable. Moreover, if the inequality in (c) is strict, then* $\mathbf{x}^*$ *is asymptotically stable.*

A function $V(\mathbf{x})$ with the properties listed in Liapunov's Theorem is called a *Liapunov function*.

How do we find a Liapunov function for equations (8.28) and (8.29)? There is no recipe for doing this, so we must experiment. Perhaps the simplest such function is $V(x, v) = x^2 + v^2$. Then

$$\dot{V} = V_x \dot{x} + V_v \dot{v}$$
$$= 2x(v) + 2v(-x - \epsilon x^2 v)$$
$$= -2\epsilon x^2 v^2.$$

Note that this is negative for $\epsilon > 0$, so the nonlinear system is asymptotically stable in this case, even though the linearized system is neutrally stable. If $\epsilon < 0$, it is easy to see that the system is unstable. HINT: Run the system backwards in time, and show that it crosses the level curve $V(x) = v_0 > 0$.

9

Evolutionary Dynamics

> Through the animal and vegetable kingdoms, nature has scattered the
> seeds of life abroad with the most profuse and liberal hand; but has
> been comparatively sparing in the room and nourishment necessary
> to rear them.
>
> *T. R. Malthus*

> Fifteen months after I had begun my systematic enquiry, I happened
> to read for amusement "Malthus on Population" . . . it at once
> struck me that . . . favorable variations would tend to be preserved,
> and unfavorable ones to be destroyed. Here, then, I had at last got a
> theory by which to work.
>
> *Charles Darwin*

9.1 Introduction

Our study of evolutionary dynamics is built solidly around the replicator
equations. We begin by defining the replicator dynamic, deriving it in several
distinct ways, and exploring its major characteristics (§9.2–§9.4). The next
several sections make good on our promise to justify Nash equilibrium in
terms of dynamical systems, as we exhibit the relationship between dynamic
stability of evolutionary models on the one hand, and dominated strategies
(§9.5), Nash equilibria (§9.6), evolutionarily stable strategies (§9.7), and
perfect Bayesian equilibria (§9.9) on the other. While many of the results
we obtain remain valid in more general settings (e.g., when the dynamic has
an aggregate tendency toward favoring more fit strategies, but not necessarily
as strongly as the replicator dynamic), sacrificing generality for simplicity
is desirable in a first course. There are plenty of good homework exercises,
from Invasion of the Pure Strategy Mutants (§9.10) to Replicator Dynamics,
the Lotka-Volterra Model, and Biodiversity (§9.14).

We next turn to asymmetric evolutionary games (§9.15), which have the
surprising property—one extremely important from the point of view of
understanding real-world evolutionary dynamics—that strictly mixed Nash
equilibria are never asymptotically stable, but are often neutrally stable,

leading to generically stable orbits (the Lotka-Volterra model has orbits, but it is not generic, as small changes in the coefficients lead to the equilibrium being either a stable or an unstable focus). In asymmetric games, the limit points of dynamic processes are generally Nash equilibria, but virtually nothing stronger than this can be asserted, including the elimination of weakly dominated strategies (Samuelson and Zhang 1992).

We close with The Replicator Dynamic, Cultural Transmission, and Social Imitation (§9.19), which is a forward-looking critique of the replicator dynamic from the point of view of human cultural dynamics. This section should not be skipped, for it is virtually certain that the next generation of game theorists who model cultural equilibrium and change will be occupied with reintegrating the standard sociological notions of vertical, horizontal, and oblique transmission (Lumsden and Wilson 1981, Cavalli-Sforza and Feldman 1981, Boyd and Richerson 1985), social imitation (Bandura 1977), and structural-functionalism (Parsons 1964) with the types of instrumental cultural change associated with the replicator and related dynamics.

9.2   The Origins of Evolutionary Dynamics

The central actor in an evolutionary system is the *replicator*—an entity having some means of making approximately accurate copies of itself. The replicator can be a gene, an organism (defining "accurate copy" appropriately in the case of sexual reproduction), a strategy in a game, a belief, a technique, a convention, or a more general institutional or cultural form. A *replicator system* is a set of replicators in a particular environmental setting with a structured pattern of interaction among agents. An *evolutionary dynamic* of a replicator system is a process of change over time in the frequency distribution of the replicators (and in the nature of the environment and the structure of interaction, though we will not discuss these here), in which strategies with higher payoffs reproduce faster in some appropriate sense. We call an asymptotically stable fixed point of an evolutionary dynamic an *evolutionary equilibrium*, and we call a neutrally stable fixed point (§8.6) of an evolutionary dynamic an *evolutionary focal point*.

In addition to having an evolutionary dynamic, evolutionary systems may generate novelty if random errors ("mutations") occur in the replication process, allowing new replicators to emerge and diffuse into the population if they are relatively well adapted to the replicator system.

The stunning variety of life forms that surround us, as well as the beliefs, practices, techniques, and behavioral forms that constitute human culture, are the product of evolutionary dynamics.

Evolutionary dynamics can be applied to a variety of systems, but we will consider here only two-player *evolutionary games*; which consist of a *stage game* played by pairs of agents in a large population, each "wired" to play some pure strategy. In each time period, agents are randomly paired, they play the stage game, and the results determine their rate of replication.[1] For the moment, we restrict consideration to symmetric evolutionary games (§7.2) in which the players cannot condition their actions on whether they are player 1 or player 2.

There are various plausible ways to specify an evolutionary dynamic— see Friedman (1991) and Hofbauer and Sigmund (1998) for details. Here we will discuss only *replicator dynamics*, which are quite representative of evolutionary dynamics in general. Our first task is to present a few of the ways a replicator dynamic can arise.

9.2.1 Strategies as Replicators

Consider an evolutionary game where each player follows one of n pure strategies s_i for $i = 1, \ldots, n$. The play is repeated in periods $t = 1, 2, \ldots$. Let p_i^t be the fraction of players playing s_i in period t, and suppose the payoff to s_i is $\pi_i^t = \pi_i(p^t)$, where $p = (p_1, \ldots, p_n)$. We look at a given time t, and number the strategies so that $\pi_1^t \leq \pi_2^t \leq \ldots \leq \pi_n^t$.

Suppose in every time period dt, each agent with probability $\alpha dt > 0$ learns the payoff to another randomly chosen other agent and changes to the other's strategy if he perceives that the other's payoff is higher. However, information concerning the difference in the expected payoffs of the two strategies is imperfect, so the larger the difference in the payoffs, the more likely the agent is to perceive it, and change. Specifically, we assume the

---

[1]The reader should note the *restrictive character of the random pairing assumption*. The fact that pairing is random (often called "panmictic pairing" in the biological literature) precludes fundamental processes in behavioral ecology that depend upon *local interactions*, including kinship, allopatric (spatially isolated) speciation, and frequency-dependent interactions in human communities. The fact that interactions are limited to pairs precludes the forms of organized sociality exhibited by the eusocial insects and primates, including, of course, humans. We accept this assumption because not much is known about more general evolutionary games, though it is currently a hot topic of research.

probability p_{ij}^t that an agent using s_i will shift to s_j is given by

$$p_{ij}^t = \begin{cases} \beta(\pi_j^t - \pi_i^t) & \text{for } \pi_j^t > \pi_i^t \\ 0 & \text{for } \pi_j^t \leq \pi_i^t \end{cases}$$

where β is sufficiently small that $p_{ij} \leq 1$ holds for all i, j. The expected fraction $\mathbf{E}p_i^{t+dt}$ of the population using s_i in period $t + dt$ is then given by

$$\mathbf{E}p_i^{t+dt} = p_i^t - \alpha dt \, p_i^t \sum_{j=i+1}^{n} p_j^t \beta(\pi_j^t - \pi_i^t) + \sum_{j=1}^{i} \alpha dt \, p_j^t p_i^t \beta(\pi_i^t - \pi_j^t)$$

$$= p_i^t + \alpha dt \, p_i^t \sum_{j=1}^{n} p_j^t \beta(\pi_i^t - \pi_j^t)$$

$$= p_i^t + \alpha dt \, p_i^t \beta(\pi_i^t - \bar{\pi}^t),$$

where $\bar{\pi}^t = \pi_1^t p_1^t + \ldots + \pi_n^t p_n^t$ is the average return for the whole population. If the population is large, we can replace $\mathbf{E}p_i^{t+dt}$ by p_i^{t+dt}. Subtracting p_i^t from both sides, dividing by dt, and taking the limit as $dt \to 0$, we get

$$\dot{p}_i^t = \alpha\beta p_i^t(\pi_i^t - \bar{\pi}^t), \qquad \text{for } i = 1, \ldots, n, \tag{9.1}$$

which is called the *replicator dynamic*. Since the constant factor $\alpha\beta$ merely changes the rate of adjustment to stationarity but leaves the stability properties and trajectories of the dynamical system unchanged, we often simply assume $\alpha\beta = 1$ (§9.3).

Several points are worth making concerning the replicator dynamic. First, *under the replicator dynamic, the frequency of a strategy increases exactly when it has above average payoff*. In particular, this means that *the replicator dynamic is not a best reply dynamic*; i.e., agents do not adopt a best reply to the overall frequency distribution of strategies in the previous period. Rather, the agents in a replicator system have limited and localized knowledge concerning the system as a whole. Some game theorists call such agents "boundedly rational," but this term is very misleading, since the real issue is the distribution of information, not the degree of rationality (whatever that might mean, which is probably not very much).

Second, if we add up all the equations, we get $\sum_i \dot{p}_i^t = 0$, so if $\sum_i p_i^t = 1$ at one point in time, this remains true forever. Moreover, while a particular replicator can become extinct, a replicator that is not represented in the population at one point in time will never be represented in the population at any later point in time. So, replicator dynamics deal poorly with mutation and innovation. A more general system adds a term to the replicator equation expressing the spontaneous emergence of replicators.

Third, our derivation assumes that there are no "mistakes"—players never switch from a better to a worse strategy. However, it is not hard to see that if we added a small probability of switching from a better to a worse strategy, the behavior of the system would be much the same. In particular, the expected error in the neighborhood of the Nash equilibrium would be zero, so the Nash equilibrium would still be a fixed point of the dynamical system.

But there is a more serious criticism: Why are we allowed to take expected values? Taking expected values allows us to *average* over the possible behaviors of an agent, so that even if there is a positive probability that a player will switch from better to worse, on average the player will not. This justifies the use of the replicator dynamic, which compels a dynamical system *always* to increase the frequency of a strategy with above average payoff. If we do *not* take expected values, this property fails. For instance, if there is a probability $p > 0$, no matter how small, that a player will go from better to worse, and if there are n players, then there is a probability $p^n > 0$ that *all* players will switch from better to worse. We would have a "stochastic dynamic" in which movement over time probably, but not necessarily, increases the frequency of successful strategies. If there is a single stable equilibrium, this might not cause much of a problem, but if there are several, such rare accumulations of error will inevitably displace the dynamical system from the basin of attraction of one equilibrium to that of another (see chapter 10).

We conclude that *the replicator dynamic, by abstracting from stochastic influences on the change in frequency of strategies, is an idealized version of how systems of strategic interaction develop over time*, and is accurate only if the number of players is very large in some appropriate sense, compared to the time interval of interest. To model the stochastic dynamic, we use stochastic processes—Markov chains and their continuous limits, diffusion processes. We provide an introduction to such dynamics in chapter 10.

It is some satisfaction to note that as the rate of error becomes small, the deviation of the stochastic dynamic from the replicator dynamic becomes arbitrarily small with arbitrarily high probability; see Freidlin and Wentzell (1984) chap. 2. But the devil is in the details. For instance, as long as the probability of error is positive, under quite plausible conditions a stochastic system with a replicator dynamic will make regular transitions from one evolutionary equilibrium to another, and superior mutant strategies will be driven to extinction with high probability; see chapter 10, as well as Samuelson (1997) and Foster and Young (1990) for examples and references. But as long as we don't look too closely or wait too long, replicator dynamics do just fine.

9.2.2   *A Dynamic Hawk/Dove Game*

There is a desert that can support n raptors. Raptors are born in the evening and are mature by morning. There are always at least n raptors alive each morning. They hunt all day for food, and at the end of the day, the n raptors that remain search for nesting sites (all raptors are female and reproduce by cloning). There are two types of nesting sites: good and bad. On a bad nesting site, a raptor produces an average of u offspring per night, and on a good nesting site, she produces an average of $u + 2$ offspring per night. However, there are only $n/2$ good nesting sites, so the raptors pair off and vie for the good sites.

There are two variants of raptor: *hawk raptors* and *dove raptors*. When a dove raptor meets another dove raptor, they do a little dance and with equal probability one of them gets the good site. When a dove raptor meets a hawk raptor, the hawk raptor takes the site without a fight. But when two hawk raptors meet, they fight to the point that the expected number of offspring for each is one less than if they had settled for a bad nesting site. Thus the payoff to the two "strategies" Hawk and Dove are as shown in the diagram.

	Hawk	Dove
Hawk	$u - 1$ $u - 1$	$u + 2$ u
Dove	u $u + 2$	$u + 1$ $u + 1$

Let p be the fraction of hawk raptors in the population of n raptors. Assuming n is sufficiently large that we can consider p to be a continuous variable, and suppose the number of days in the year is sufficiently large that we can treat a single day as an infinitesimal dt of time. We can then show that *there is a unique equilibrium frequency p^* of hawk raptors and the system is governed by a replicator dynamic.*

In time period dt, a single dove raptor expects to give birth to

$$f_d(p)dt = (u + 1 - p)dt$$

$$u(p-1) + (u+1)p$$
$$up - u + up + p$$
$$?$$

little dove raptors overnight, and there are $n(1 - p)$ dove raptors nesting in the evening, so the number of dove raptors in the morning is

$$n(1 - p)(1 + (u + 1 - p)dt) = n(1 - p)(1 + f_d(p)dt).$$

Similarly, the number of hawk raptors in the evening is np and a single hawk raptor expects to give birth to

$$f_h(p)dt = (u + 2(1 - p) - p)dt$$

little hawk raptors overnight, so there are

$$np(1 + (u + 2(1 - p) - p)dt) = np(1 + f_h(p)dt)$$

hawk raptors in the morning. Let

$$f(p) = (1 - p)f_d(p) + pf_h(p),$$

so $f(p)dt$ is the total number of raptors born overnight and $n(1 + f(p)dt)$ is the total raptor population in the morning. We then have

$$p(t + dt) = \frac{np(t)(1 + f_h(p)dt)}{n(1 + f(p))dt} = p(t)\frac{1 + f_h(p)dt}{1 + f(p)dt},$$

which implies

$$\frac{p(t + dt) - p(t)}{dt} = p(t)\left\{\frac{f_h(p) - f(p)}{1 + f(p)dt}\right\}.$$

If we now let $dt \to 0$, we get

$$\frac{dp}{dt} = p(t)[f_h(p) - f(p)]. \tag{9.2}$$

This is of course a replicator dynamic. Note that $p(t)$ is constant (i.e., the population is in equilibrium) when $f_h(p) = f(p)$, which means $f_h(p) = f_d(p) = f(p)$.

If we substitute values in equation (9.2), we get

$$\frac{dp}{dt} = p(1 - p)(1 - 2p). \tag{9.3}$$

This equation has three fixed points: $p = 0, 1, 1/2$. From our discussion of one-dimensional dynamics (§8.7), we know that a fixed point is an evolutionary equilibrium (i.e., is asymptotically stable) if the derivative of the right-hand side is negative, and is unstable if the derivative of the right-hand side is positive. It is easy to check that the derivative of $p(1 - p)(1 - 2p)$ is positive for $p = 0, 1$ and negative for $p = 1/2$. Thus, a population of all dove raptors or all hawk raptors is stationary, but the introduction of even one raptor of the other type will drive the population toward the heterogeneous evolutionary equilibrium.

9.2.3 Sexual Reproduction, Biological Fitness, and the Replicator Dynamic

Suppose the *fitness* (i.e., the expected number of offspring) of members of a certain population depends on a single *genetic locus*, at which there are two genes (such creatures, which includes most of the "higher" plants and animals, are called *diploid*). Suppose there are n alternative types of genes (called *alleles*) at this genetic locus, which we label $g_1, \ldots, g_n$. An individual whose gene pair is (g_i, g_j), whom we term an "ij-type," then has fitness w_{ij}, which we interpret as being its probability of surviving to sexual maturity.

Suppose sexually mature individuals are randomly paired off once in each time period, and for each pair (g_i, g_j) of genes, g_i taken from the first and g_j taken from the second member of the pair, a number of offspring of type ij are born, of which w_{ij} reach sexual maturity. The parents then die.

THEOREM 9.1 *For each $i = 1, \ldots, n$ let $p_i(t)$ be the frequency of g_i in the population. Then, fitness of a g_i allele is given by $w_i(t) = \sum_{j=1}^{n} w_{ij} p_j(t)$, the average fitness in the population is given by $w(t) = \sum_{i=1}^{n} p_i w_i(t)$, and the following replicator equations hold:*

$$\dot{p}_i = p_i[w_i(t) - w(t)] \qquad for \ i = 1, \ldots, n. \tag{9.4}$$

PROOF: For any $i = 1, \ldots, n$, let y_i be the number of alleles of type g_i, and let y be the total number of alleles, so $y = \sum_{j=1}^{n} y_j$ and $p_i = y_i/y$. Since p_j is the probability that a g_i allele will meet a g_j allele, the expected number of g_i genes in the offspring of a g_i gene is just $\sum_j w_{ij} p_j$, and so the total number of g_i alleles in the next generation is $y_i \sum_j w_{ij} p_j$. This gives the differential equation

$$\dot{y}_i = y_i \sum_{j=1}^{n} w_{ij} p_j.$$

Differentiating the identity $\ln p_i = \ln y_i - \ln y$ with respect to time t, we get

$$\frac{\dot{p}_i}{p_i} = \frac{\dot{y}_i}{y_i} - \sum_{j=1}^{n} \frac{\dot{y}_j}{y}$$

$$= \sum_{j=1}^{n} w_{ij} p_j - \sum_{j=1}^{n} \frac{\dot{y}_j}{y_j} p_j$$

$$= \sum_{j=1}^{n} w_{ij} p_j - \sum_{j,k=1}^{n} w_{jk} p_j p_k,$$

which is the replicator dynamic. Q.E.D.

The following important theorem was discovered by the famous biologist R. A. Fisher.

THEOREM 9.2 Fundamental Theorem of Natural Selection. *The average fitness $w(t)$ of a population increases along any trajectory of the replicator dynamic (9.4), and satisfies the equation*

$$\dot{w} = 2 \sum_{i=1}^{n} p_i (w_i - w)^2.$$

Note that the right-hand side of this equation is twice the fitness variance.

PROOF: Let W be the $n \times n$ matrix (w_{ij}) and let $p(t) = (p_1(t), \ldots, p_n(t))$ be the column vector of allele frequencies. The fitness of allele i is then

$$w_i = \sum_{j=1}^{n} w_{ij} p_j,$$

and the average fitness is

$$w = \sum_{i=1}^{n} p_i w_i = \sum_{i,j=1}^{n} p_i w_{ij} p_j.$$

Then,

$$\dot{w} = 2 \sum_{i,j=1}^{n} p_j w_{ji} \dot{p}_i = 2 \sum_{i,j=1}^{n} p_j w_{ji} p_i (w_i - w)$$

$$= 2 \sum_{i=1}^{n} p_i (w_i - w) w_i$$

$$= 2 \sum_{i=1}^{n} p_i (w_i - w)^2,$$

where the last equation follows from $\sum_{i=1}^{n} p_i (w_i - w) w = 0$. Q.E.D.

The above model can be extended in a straightforward manner to a situation in which the parents live more than one generation, and the Fundamental Theorem can be extended to include many genetic loci, provided they do not interact. However, it is a bad mistake to think that the Fundamental Theorem actually holds in the real world (this is often referred to as the *Panglossian fallacy*, named after Voltaire's Dr. Pangloss, who in *Candide* declared that "all is for the best in this, the best of all possible worlds"). Genes *do* interact, so that the fitness of an allele depends not just on the allele, but on the other alleles in the individual's genetic endowment. Such genes, called *epistatic genes*, are actually quite common. Moreover, the fitness of populations may be *interdependent* in ways that reduce fitness over time (see, for instance, §8.5, which describes the Lotka-Volterra predator-prey model). Finally, stochastic effects ignored in replicator dynamics can lead to the elimination of very fit genes and even populations.

9.3 Properties of the Replicator System

Given the replicator equation (9.1), show the following:

a. For $1 \le i < j \le n$, show that

$$\frac{d}{dt}\left(\frac{p_i}{p_j}\right) = \left(\frac{p_i}{p_j}\right)(\pi_i - \pi_j).$$

b. Suppose that there is an $n \times n$ matrix $A = (a_{ij})$ such that for each $i = 1, \ldots, n$, $\pi_i = \sum_j a_{ij} p_j$; i.e., a_{ij} is the payoff to player i when paired with player j in the stage game. Show that adding a constant to a column of A does not change the replicator equation and hence does not change the dynamic properties of the system. Note that this allows us to set the diagonal of A to consist of zeros, or set the last row of A to consiste of zeros, in analyzing the dynamics of the system.

c. How does the column operation described in the previous question affect the Nash equilibria of the stage game? How does it affect the payoffs?

d. A more general form of (9.1) is

$$\dot{p}_i^t = a(p, t) p_i^t (\pi_i^t - \bar{\pi}^t) \qquad \text{for } i = 1, \ldots, n, \qquad (9.5)$$

where $p = (p_i, \ldots, p_n)$, π_i^t and $\bar{\pi}^t$ are defined as in (9.1) and $a(p, t) > 0$ for all p, t. Show that for any trajectory $p(t)$ of (9.5) there is an increasing function $b(t) > 0$ such that $q(t) = p(b(t))$ is a trajectory of the original replicator equation (9.1). Thus, multiplying the replicator equations by a positive function preserves trajectories and the direction of time, altering only the time scale.

9.4   Characterizing the Two-Variable Replicator Dynamic

Consider the replicator dynamic in two variables given by

$$\dot{w} = Aw, \qquad (9.6)$$

where $w = (p, q)$, $p + q = 1$, and A is the 2×2 matrix $\{\alpha_{ij}\}$.

a. Use §9.3 to show that we can assume $\alpha_{21} = \alpha_{22} = 0$, and then explain why the differential equation governing the dynamics of the system can be written

$$\dot{p} = p(1 - p)(a + bp), \qquad (9.7)$$

where $a = \alpha_{12}$ and $b = \alpha_{11} - \alpha_{12}$.

b. Show that in addition to the fixed point $p = 0$ and $p = 1$, there is an interior fixed point p^* of this dynamical system (i.e., a p^* such that $0 < p^* < 1$) if and only if $0 < -a < b$ or $0 < a < -b$.

c. Suppose p^* is an interior fixed point of (9.7). Find the Jacobian of the system and show that p^* is an evolutionary equilibrium if and only if $b < 0$, so $0 < -b < a$. Show in this case that both of the other fixed points of (9.7) are unstable.

d. If p^* is an unstable interior fixed point of (9.7), show that the fixed points $p = 0$ and $p = 1$ are both evolutionary equilibria.

e. Show that if $z = p/q$, then $w = (p, q)$ satisfies (9.6) if and only if

$$\dot{z} = qz(\alpha_{11}z + \alpha_{12}), \tag{9.8}$$

and this has an interior evolutionary equilibrium $z^* = -\alpha_{12}/\alpha_{11}$ if and only if $\alpha_{11} < 0 < \alpha_{12}$.

f. Now use §9.3 to show that this has the same trajectories as the simpler differential equation

$$\dot{z} = z(\alpha_{11}z + \alpha_{12}). \tag{9.9}$$

Show that the general solution to (9.9) is given by $z(t) = \alpha_{12}(ce^{-\alpha_{12}t} - a_{11})$, where $c = \alpha_{12}/z(0) + \alpha_{11}$. In this case we can verify directly that there is an interior evolutionary equilibrium if and only if $\alpha_{11} < 0 < \alpha_{12}$.

9.5 Do Dominated Strategies Survive under a Replicator Dynamic?

All Nash equilibria of a game survive the iterated elimination of strongly dominated strategies, but not of weakly dominated strategies (see chapter 1). Not surprisingly, strongly dominated strategies do not survive in a replicator dynamic. Suppose there are n pure strategies in the stage game of an evolutionary game in which $p_i(t)$ is the fraction of the population playing strategy i at time t. Recall that a strategy is *completely mixed* if $p_i(t) > 0$ for all i. We have the following theorem.

THEOREM 9.3 *Let* $p(t) = (p_1(t), \ldots, p_n(t))$ *be a completely mixed trajectory of the replicator dynamic (9.1) and suppose strategy i does not survive the iterated elimination of strictly dominated strategies. Then, strategy i does not survive the replicator dynamic; i.e.,* $\lim_{t \to \infty} p_i(t) = 0$.

To see this, first suppose i is strictly dominated by p^0. We write $\pi(p, q)$ for the payoff to strategy p against strategy q. Then, $\pi(p^0, p) > \pi_i(p)$ for all mixed strategies p. Since the set of mixed strategies is closed and bounded, $\epsilon = \min_p(\pi(p^0, p) - \pi_i(p))$ is strictly positive. Let

$$f(p) = \ln(p_i) - \sum_{j=1}^{n} p_j^0 \ln(p_j).$$

It is easy to check that $df(p(t))/dt \le -\epsilon$, so $p_i(t) \to 0$.

It is intuitively obvious that this proof can be extended to the case of iterated domination. For instance, suppose strategy j is not strictly dominated until strictly dominated strategy i has been eliminated. By the above argument, when t is sufficiently large, i is used with vanishingly small probability, so now j is strictly dominated, and hence we can apply the above argument to j. And so on. The theorem is proved in Samuelson and Zhang (1992).

What about weakly dominated strategies? If the pure strategies against which a weakly dominated strategy does poorly are *themselves* driven out of existence by a replicator dynamic, then the weakly dominated strategy may persist in the long run. However, we do have the following theorem.

THEOREM 9.4 *Let $p(t) = (p_i(t), \ldots, p_n(t))$ be a completely mixed trajectory of the replicator dynamic (9.1), and suppose pure strategy s_i is weakly dominated by p^o, so $\pi(p^o, s_j) > \pi(s_i, s_j)$ for some pure strategy s_j. Suppose $\lim_{t \to \infty} p_j(t) > 0$. Then, $\lim_{t \to \infty} p_i(t) = 0$.*

It is worthwhile thinking about the implications of this theorem for the persistence of a non-subgame-perfect Nash equilibrium under a replicator dynamic. Consider the little game to the right. Clearly, there are two Nash equilibria. The first is (l,l), where each player gets 1. But if player 2 is greedy, he can threaten to play r, the best response to which on the part of player 1 is r. Thus, (r,r) is a second Nash equilibrium.

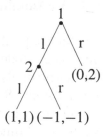

This equilibrium is, however, not subgame perfect, since player 2's threat of playing r is not credible.

a. Construct the normal form game and show that strategy r for player 2 is weakly dominated by strategy l.
b. Write the replicator equations for this system and find all the fixed points of the replicator dynamic. Note that the underlying game is not symmetric in this case.
c. Find the Jacobian of the dynamical system at each of the fixed points, draw a phase diagram for the system, and show that any trajectory that does not start at a fixed point tends to the subgame perfect equilibrium as $t \to \infty$.
d. If you are inquisitive, study some other non-subgame-perfect Nash equilibria of various games and try to generalize as to (1) the relationship between non-subgame perfection and weakly dominated strategies, and (2) the conditions under which a non-subgame perfect Nash equilibrium can persist in a replicator dynamic.

9.6   Equilibrium and Stability with a Replicator Dynamic

Consider an evolutionary game with n pure strategies and stage game payoff π_{ij} to an i-player who meets a j-player. If $p = (p_1, \ldots, p_n)$ is the frequency of each type in the population, the expected payoff to an i-player is then $\pi_i(p) = \sum_{j=1}^{n} p_j \pi_{ij}$, and the average payoff in the game is $\bar{\pi}(p) = \sum_{i=1}^{n} p_i \pi_i(p)$. The replicator dynamic for this game is then given by

$$\dot{p}_i = p_i(\pi_i(p) - \bar{\pi}(p)). \tag{9.10}$$

We are now at the point of motivating the importance of the Nash equilibrium as the fundamental equilibrium concept of game theory. You will recall that in the early chapters of this book (see, for instance, §1.5), we rejected classical game-theoretic justifications of Nash equilibrium, on grounds that they required too much "rationality" on the part of agents, and the required that rationality be "common knowledge," although, in fact, it is common to find players who are not "rational" in the classical sense. Rather, we suggested, equilibria of dynamic evolutionary games are Nash equilibria of their underlying stage games. We can now justify this argument.

THEOREM 9.5 *The following hold, provided an evolutionary game satisfies the replicator dynamic (9.10).*

a. *If p^* is a Nash equilibrium of the evolutionary game, p^* is a fixed point of the replicator dynamic.*

b. *If p^* is an evolutionary equilibrium or a focal point of the replicator dynamic, then it is a Nash equilibrium.*

The first of these assertions follows directly from the Fundamental Theorem of mixed strategy Nash equilibrium (§4.3). To prove the second assertion, assume p^* is *not* a Nash equilibrium. Then, there is an i and an $\epsilon > 0$ such that $\pi_i(p^*) - \bar{\pi}(p^*) > \epsilon$ in a ball around p^*. But then the replicator dynamic implies p_i grows exponentially along a trajectory starting at any point in this ball, which means p^* is not an evolutionary equilibrium or focal point. Q.E.D.

In general, the converse of these assertions is false. Clearly, there are fixed points of the replicator dynamic that are not Nash equilibria of the evolutionary game, since if an i-player does not exist in the population at one point in time, it can never appear in the future under a replicator dynamic.

Therefore, for any i, the state $p_i = 1$, $p_j = 0$ for $j \neq i$ is a fixed point under the replicator dynamic.

Also, a Nash equilibrium need not be an evolutionary equilibrium of the replicator dynamic. Consider, for instance, the two-player pure coordination game that pays each player one if they both choose L or R, but zero otherwise. There is a Nash equilibrium in which each chooses L with probability 1/2. If p is the fraction of L-choosers in the population, then the payoff to an L-player is $\pi_L(p) = p$ and the payoff to an R-player is $\pi_R(p) = 1 - p$. The average payoff is then $\bar{\pi}(p) = p^2 + (1 - p)^2$, so $\pi_L(p) - \bar{\pi}(p) = p - p^2 - (1 - p)^2$. The Jacobian is then $3 - 4p$, which is positive at $p^* = 1/2$, so the fixed point is unstable. This is of course intuitively clear, since if there is a slight preponderance of one type of player, then all players gain from shifting to that type.

9.7   Evolutionary Stability and Evolutionary Equilibrium

Consider the replicator dynamic (9.10) for the evolutionary game described in §9.6. We have the following theorem.

THEOREM 9.6 *If p^* is an evolutionarily stable strategy, then p^* is an evolutionary equilibrium of the replicator dynamic (9.10). Moreover, if p^* uses all strategies with positive probability, then p^* is a globally stable fixed point of the replicator dynamic.*

This theorem, which is due to Taylor and Jonker (1978), is proved nicely in Hofbauer and Sigmund (1998:70–71).

Evolutionary equilibrium does *not* imply evolutionary stability, however. The matrix to the right represents the normal form of the stage game of an evolutionary game that has a locally stable fixed point that is not evolutionarily stable. Show the following:

2,2	1,5	5,1
5,1	1,1	0,4
1,5	4,0	3,3

a.   The game has a unique Nash equilibrium, in which the three strategies are used in proportions $(15/35, 11/35, 9/35)$.

b.   This Nash equilibrium is not evolutionarily stable, since it can be invaded by the third strategy.

c.   The eigenvalues of the Jacobian of the replicator dynamic equations are $3(-3 \pm 2i\sqrt{39})/35$, so the fixed point is a stable focus.

d. Section §7.3 exhibits an evolutionarily stable strategy that is not "unbeatable." By calculating the eigenvalues of the Jacobian, show that this strategy is asymptotically stable in the replicator dynamic.

9.8 Trust in Networks III

In Trust in Networks (§4.12), we found a completely mixed Nash equilibrium, which in Section 7.4 we found to be evolutionarily unstable, since in could be invaded by Trusters. Now show that this equilibrium is in fact globally stable under the replicator dynamic. We illustrate this dynamic in Fig. 9.1. Note that south of the equilibrium, the fraction of Trusters increases, but eventually the path turns back on itself and the fraction of Trusters again increases. This is another example of an evolutionary equilibrium that is not an evolutionary stable strategy: near the equilibrium, the dynamic path moves away from the equilibrium before veering back towards it.

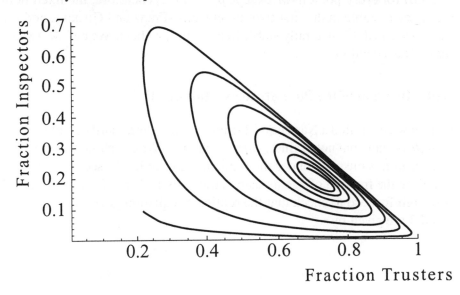

Figure 9.1. A typical path of the Trust in Networks dynamic system.

9.9 Bayesian Perfection and Stable Sets

In Selten's Horse (§5.15) we found a connected set M of perfect Bayesian equilibria, all involving the same behaviors of the three players: Franz chooses A, Gustav chooses a, and Walter never gets to choose.

Assuming a replicator dynamic, and letting (p_A, p_a, p_λ) be the vector of probabilities of using A, a, and λ respectively, you can check that the replicator equations (section §9.2) are

$$\dot{p}_A = p_A(1 - p_A)(1 - p_a(3p_\lambda - 1))$$
$$\dot{p}_a = p_a(1 - p_a)(1 - 3p_\lambda)$$
$$\dot{p}_\lambda = p_\lambda(1 - p_\lambda)(3 - p_A(5 - 2p_a)).$$

If we evaluate the Jacobian of this set of differential equations at (D, a, λ) (corresponding to $p_A = 0$, $p_a = 1$, and $p_\lambda = 1$), we find the eigenvalues $(3, -1, -2)$. Therefore, the fixed point (D, a, λ) is unstable—this corresponds to the fact that (D, a, λ) is not perfect Bayesian. If we evaluate the Jacobian at (A, a, ρ) (corresponding to $p_A = 1$, $p_a = 1$, and $p_\lambda = 0$), we find that the eigenvalues are $(-2, -1, 0)$. Indeed, the eigenvalues have signs $(-, -, 0)$ for every point in M except $p_\lambda = 1/3$. Therefore, the fixed point (A, a, ρ) is stable in the first two dimensions (Franz and Gustav), and it is easy to see that it is neutrally stable in the third (Walter). We call M a *stable set* of Nash equilibria.

9.10 Invasion of the Pure Strategy Mutants, II

In §7.9 we exhibited a Nash equilibrium that is evolutionarily stable against a *single* mutant, but not against *pairs* of mutants. We can show that this Nash equilibrium is unstable under the replicator dynamic. To see this, let γ, α, and β be the fraction of agents using strategies 1, 2, and 3, respectively. It is straightforward to check that the replicator equation governing strategies 2 and 3 are given by

$$\dot{\alpha} = \alpha(-\alpha + \beta(a - 1) + (\alpha + \beta)^2 - 2\alpha\beta a)$$
$$\dot{\beta} = \beta(-\beta + \alpha(a - 1) + (\alpha + \beta)^2 - 2\alpha\beta a).$$

The Jacobian of the equations is the zero matrix at the fixed point $\gamma = 1$, i.e., where $\alpha = \beta = 0$. Thus, linearization does not help us. However, we can easily calculate that when α, β, $\gamma > 0$ the maximum of $\dot{\alpha} + \dot{\beta}$ is $\gamma a(a - 2)$. This is strictly positive under our assumption $a > 2$, so $\dot{\gamma} < 0$. This proves that the Nash equilibrium using strategy 1 is unstable. Note that the Nash equilibrium using strategies 2 and 3 with probability 1/2 is evolutionarily stable, and stable under the replicator dynamic.

Use the same method to check that the two evolutionarily stable equilibria in §7.10 are evolutionary equilibria, and the completely mixed Nash equilibrium, which you showed was resistant to invasion by pure but not mixed strategies, is a saddle point under the replicator dynamic.

9.11   A Generalization of Rock, Paper, and Scissors

	R	P	S
R	α,α	$1,-1$	$-1,1$
P	$-1,1$	α,α	$1,-1$
S	$1,-1$	$-1,1$	α,α

The game to the right, where we assume $-1 < \alpha < 1$ and $\alpha \neq 0$, is a generalization of Rock, Paper, and Scissors in which agents receive a nonzero payoff α if they meet their own type. We will show that the game has a unique Nash equilibrium in which each player chooses each strategy with probability 1/3. This equilibrium is not evolutionarily stable for $\alpha > 0$. The Nash equilibrium is a hyperbolic fixed point under the replicator dynamic. It is a stable focus for $\alpha < 0$ and an unstable focus for $\alpha > 0$.

To prove these assertions, note first that no pure strategy is Nash. If one player randomizes between two pure strategies, the other can avoid the -1 payoff, so only strictly mixed solutions can be Nash. We can check directly that the only such strategy σ that is Nash uses probabilities $(1/3,1/3,1/3)$. This is not evolutionarily stable for $\alpha < 0$, however, since the pure strategy R has payoff $\alpha/3$ against σ, which is also the payoff to σ against σ, and has payoff α against itself.

The payoff of the strategies against $(x_1, x_2, 1 - x_1 - x_2)$ are

$$
\begin{aligned}
R: &\quad \alpha x_1 + x_2 - (1 - x_1 - x_2) &=&\quad (1+\alpha)x_1 + 2x_2 - 1 \\
P: &\quad -x_1 + \alpha x_2 + (1 - x_1 - x_2) &=&\quad -2x_1 - (1-\alpha)x_2 + 1 \\
S: &\quad x_1 - x_2 + \alpha(1 - x_1 - x_2) &=&\quad (1-\alpha)x_1 - (\alpha+1)x_2 + \alpha
\end{aligned}
$$

The average payoff is then $2\alpha(x_1^2 + x_1 x_2 + x_2^2 - x_1 - x_2) + \alpha$, and the fitnesses of the three types are

$$
\begin{aligned}
f_1: &\quad (1 + 3\alpha)x_1 + 2(1+\alpha)x_2 - (1+\alpha) - 2\alpha(x_1^2 + x_1 x_2 + x_2^2) \\
f_2: &\quad -2(1-\alpha)x_1 - (1 - 3\alpha)x_2 + (1-\alpha) - 2\alpha(x_1^2 + x_1 x_2 + x_2^2) \\
f_3: &\quad (1+\alpha)x_1 - (1-\alpha)x_2 - 2\alpha(x_1^2 + x_1 x_2 + x_2^2).
\end{aligned}
$$

Note that $x_1 = x_2 = 1/3$ gives $f_1 = f_2 = f_3 = 0$, so this is our Nash equilibrium. For the replicator dynamic, we have $\dot{x}_1 + \dot{x}_2 + \dot{x}_3 = 0$, so we only need the first two equations. Assuming $x_1, x_2 > 0$, we get

$$\frac{\dot{x}_1}{x_1} = -(2\alpha(x_1^2 + x_1 x_2 + x_2^2) - (1 + 3\alpha)x_1 - 2(1 + \alpha)x_2 + (1 + \alpha))$$

$$\frac{\dot{x}_2}{x_2} = -(2\alpha(x_1^2 + x_1 x_2 + x_2^2) + 2(1 - \alpha)x_1 + (1 - 3\alpha)x_2 - (1 - \alpha)).$$

It is straightforward to check that $x_1 = x_2 = 1/3$ is the only fixed point for this set of equations in the positive quadrant.

The Jacobian of this system at the Nash equilibrium is

$$\frac{1}{3} \begin{bmatrix} 1 + \alpha & 2 \\ -2 & -1 + \alpha \end{bmatrix}.$$

This has determinant $\beta = 1/3 + \alpha^2/9 > 0$, the trace is $\text{Tr} = 2\alpha/3$ and the discriminant is $\gamma = \text{Tr}^2/4 - \beta = -1/3$. The eigenvalues are thus $\alpha/3 \pm \sqrt{-3}/3$, which have nonzero real parts for $\alpha \neq 0$. Therefore, the system is hyperbolic. By Theorem 8.5, the dynamical system is a stable focus for $\alpha < 0$ and an unstable focus for $\alpha > 0$.

9.12   *Uta stansburia* in Motion

We shall now determine the dynamic behavior of the male lizard population in §4.16 under a replicator dynamic. It is easy to check that if the frequencies of orange-throats (Rock), blue-throats (Paper), and yellow-striped (Scissors) are α, β, and $1 - \alpha - \beta$, respectively, the payoffs to the three strategies are $1 - \alpha - 2\beta$, $2\alpha + \beta - 1$, and $\beta - \alpha$, respectively. The average payoff is zero (check this!), so the replicator dynamic equations are

$$\begin{aligned} \frac{d\alpha}{dt} &= \alpha(1 - \alpha - 2\beta) \\ \frac{d\beta}{dt} &= \beta(2\alpha + \beta - 1). \end{aligned} \tag{9.11}$$

The Jacobian matrix at the fixed point $\alpha = \beta = 1/3$ is given by

$$\begin{bmatrix} -1/3 & -2/3 \\ 2/3 & 1/3 \end{bmatrix}.$$

The trace of the Jacobian is thus zero, the determinant is $1/3 > 0$, and the discriminant is $-1/3 < 0$. By Theorem 8.5 the eigenvalues are imaginary so the system is not hyperbolic. It is easy to solve for the trajectories of this system—by Theorem 8.5 they are closed orbits and the fixed point is a center. But this tells us nothing about the original, nonlinear system (9.11), since the fixed point is not hyperbolic (see Theorem 8.3). So, back to the drawing board.

Let $V(\alpha, \beta, \gamma) = \ln(\alpha) + \ln(\beta) + \ln(\gamma)$. Along a trajectory of the dynamical system we have

$$\dot{V} = \frac{\dot{\alpha}}{\alpha} + \frac{\dot{\beta}}{\beta} + \frac{\dot{\gamma}}{\gamma}$$
$$= (1 - \alpha - 2\beta) + (2\alpha + \beta - 1) + (\beta - \alpha) = 0.$$

Thus, V is constant on trajectories. This implies that trajectories are bounded and bounded away from $(0, 0)$ so the set Γ of ω-limit points of a trajectory contains no fixed points, and hence by the Poincaré-Bendixson Theorem (Theorem 8.8), Γ is a periodic orbit. But then by Theorem 8.9, Γ must contain $(0, 0)$. Hence, trajectories also must spiral around $(0, 0)$, and since V is increasing along a ray going northeast from the fixed point, trajectories must be closed orbits.

9.13 The Dynamics of Rock-Paper-Scissors and Related Games

Consider the rock-paper-scissors type game to the right, where r and s are nonzero. Suppose α, β, and $\gamma = 1 - \alpha - \beta$ are the fraction of the population playing the three strategies, and suppose in each period members are randomly

	α	β	γ
α	0,0	r,s	s,r
β	s,r	0,0	r,s
γ	r,s	s,r	0,0

paired and they play the game. What is the replicator dynamic for the game? How does the behavior of the system depend on r and s? Prove the following:

The Rock, Paper, and Scissors game has the unique mixed strategy Nash equilibrium $(\alpha, \beta) = (1/3, 1/3)$ with the following dynamic properties:

a. The fixed point cannot be a saddle point.
b. The fixed point is an evolutionary equilibrium if $r + s > 0$ and unstable if $r + s < 0$.
c. The fixed point is a focus if $r \neq s$, and a node if $r = s$.
d. If $r + s = 0$, as in the traditional Rock, Paper and Scissors game, the fixed point of the linearized system is a center, so the system is not

hyperbolic. Thus, we cannot determine the dynamic for this case from the Hartman-Grobman theorem. However, we can show that the fixed point is a center, so all trajectories of the system are periodic orbits.

9.14 The Lotka-Volterra Model and Biodiversity

Suppose two species interact in a fixed environment. If u and v represent the number of individuals of species A and B respectively, the system follows the differential equations

$$\dot{u} = u \left[a \frac{u}{u+v} + b \frac{v}{u+v} - k(u+v) \right]$$
$$\dot{v} = v \left[c \frac{u}{u+v} + d \frac{v}{u+v} - k(u+v) \right],$$

where $k > 0$ and $(d-b)(a-c) > 0$. We interpret these equations as follows: the growth rate of each species is frequency dependent, but they share an ecological niche and hence are subject to overcrowding, the intensity of which is measured by k. For instance, suppose individuals meet at random. Then, an A meets another A with probability $u/(u+v)$, and they may reproduce at rate a, while an A meets a B with probability $v/(u+v)$, in which case the A eats the B ($b > 0$) or vice-versa ($b < 0$). Show the following.

a. Let $w = u + v$, the size of the total population, and $p = u/w$, the fraction of species A in the population. The stationary fraction p^* of species A is given by

$$p^* = \frac{d-b}{a-c+d-b},$$

which is strictly positive and independent of the crowding factor k.

b. If we think of w as the whole population, then the payoff π_A to species A, the payoff π_B to species B, and the mean payoff $\bar{\pi}$ to a member of the population, *abstracting from the overcrowding factor k*, are given by

$$\pi_A = ap + b(1-p),$$
$$\pi_B = cp + d(1-p),$$
$$\bar{\pi} = p\pi_A + (1-p)\pi_B.$$

Show that p satisfies the replicator dynamic

$$\dot{p} = p(\pi_A - \bar{\pi}),$$

even taking into account the overcrowding factor. This equation indicates that the frequency of species A in the population is independent of the crowding factor in the dynamic interaction between the two species. Moreover, the stability conditions for p are also independent of k, so we conclude: *If neither species can become extinct when the crowding factor k is low, the same is true no matter how large the crowding factor k.*

c. We can generalize this result as follows. Suppose there are n species, and let u_i be the number of individuals in species i, for $i = 1, \ldots, n$. Define $w = \sum_j u_j$ and for $i = 1, \ldots, n$ let $p_i = u_i/w$, the relative frequency of species i. Suppose the system satisfies the equations

$$\dot{u}_i = u_i [a_{i1} p_1 + \ldots + a_{in} p_n - ku]$$

for $k > 0$. We assume the $\{a_{ij}\}$ are such that there is a positive stationary frequency for each species. Show that the system satisfies the differential equations

$$\frac{\dot{p}_i}{p_i} = \sum_{j=1}^{n} a_{ij} p_j - \sum_{j,k=1}^{n} a_{jk} p_j p_k$$

for $i = 1, \ldots, n$. Show that this represents a replicator dynamic if the payoffs to the various species abstract from the crowding factor k. Once again we find that the frequency of each species is independent of the crowding factor, and if the ecology is sustainable with low crowding factor (i.e., no species goes extinct), then it remains so with high crowding factor.

This result is surprising, perhaps. How do we account for it? It is easy to see that the *absolute* number of individuals in each species in equilibrium is proportional to $1/k$. Thus, when k is large, the justification for using a replicator dynamic is no longer valid: with considerable probability, the stochastic elements abstracted from in the replicator dynamic act to reduce some p_i to zero, after which it cannot ever recover unless the ecological system is repopulated from the outside. For an example of dynamics of this type, see Durrett and Levin (1994).

9.15   Asymmetric Evolutionary Games

Consider two populations of interacting agents. In each time period, agents from one population (row players) are randomly paired with agents from the other population (column players). The paired agents then play a game in which row players have pure strategies $S = \{s_1, \ldots, s_n\}$ and column players have pure strategies $T = \{t_1, \ldots, t_m\}$. Agents are "wired" to play one of the pure strategies available to them, and the payoffs to an i-type (i.e., a row player wired to play s_i) playing a j-type (i.e., a column player wired to play t_j) are α_{ij} for the i-type and β_{ij} for the j-type. We call the resulting game an *asymmetric evolutionary game*.

Suppose the frequency composition of strategies among column players is $q = (q_1, \ldots, q_m)$, where q_j is the fraction of j-types among column players. Then, the payoff to an i-type row player is

$$\alpha_i(q) = \sum_{j=1}^{m} q_j \alpha_{ij}.$$

Similarly if the frequency composition of strategies among row players is $p = (p_1, \ldots, p_n)$, where p_i is the fraction of i-types among row players, then the payoff to a j-type column player is

$$\beta_j(p) = \sum_{i=1}^{n} p_i \beta_{ij}.$$

We say $s_i \in S$ is a *best response* to $q \in Q$ if $\alpha_i(q) \geq \alpha_k(q)$ for all $s_k \in S$, and we say $t_j \in T$ is a *best response* to $p \in P$ if $\beta_j(p) \geq \beta_k(p)$ for all $t_k \in T$. A *Nash equilibrium* in an asymmetric evolutionary game is a frequency composition $p^* \in P$ of row players and $q^* \in Q$ of column players such that for all $s_i \in S$, if $p_i^* > 0$, then s_i is a best response to q^*, and for all $s_j \in T$, if $q_j^* > 0$, then t_j is a best response to p^*.

Note that there is a natural correspondence between the mixed strategy Nash equilibria of a two-player normal form game as defined in §4.2 and the Nash equilibria of an asymmetric evolutionary game. Thus, if we take an arbitrary two-player game in which row players and column players are distinguished and place the game in an evolutionary setting, we get an asymmetric evolutionary game. Hence, the dynamics of asymmetric evolutionary games more or less represent the dynamics of two-player games in general.[2]

A replicator dynamic for an asymmetric evolutionary game is given by the $n + m - 2$ equations

$$
\begin{aligned}
\dot{p}_i &= p_i(\alpha_i(q) - \alpha(p, q)) \\
\dot{q}_j &= q_i(\beta_j(p) - \beta(p, q)),
\end{aligned}
\tag{9.12}
$$

where $\alpha(p, q) = \sum_i p_i \alpha_i(q)$, $\beta(p, q) = \sum_j q_j \beta_j(p_i)$, $i = 1, \ldots, n - 1$, and $j = 1, \ldots, m - 1$. Note that while the *static* game pits the row player against the column player, the *evolutionary* dynamic pits row players against themselves and column players against themselves. This aspect of an evolutionary dynamic is often misunderstood. We see the conflict between a predator and its prey, or between a pathogen and its host, and we interpret the "survival of the fittest" as the winner in this game. But, in fact, in an evolutionary sense predators fight among themselves for the privilege of having their offspring occupy the predator niche in the next period and improve their chances by catching more prey. Meanwhile the prey are vying among themselves for the privilege of having their offspring occupy the prey niche, and they improve their chances by evading predators for an above average period of time.

What nice properties does this dynamic have? Well, it is not hard to see that Theorem 9.3 continues to hold: only strategies that survive the iterated elimination of strictly dominated strategies survive the replicator dynamic. A version of Theorem 9.5 also holds in this case: a Nash equilibrium of the evolutionary game is a fixed point under the replicator dynamic, a limit point of a trajectory under the replicator dynamic is a Nash equilibrium, and an evolutionary equilibrium or a focal point of the replicator dynamic is a Nash equilibrium. Even Theorem 9.6 continues to hold: an evolutionarily stable strategy is an evolutionary equilibrium under the replicator dynamic. However, as we have seen in §7.15, *an evolutionarily stable strategy of an asymmetric evolutionary game must be a strict Nash equilibrium*; i.e., both row and column players must be monomorphic in equilibrium, there being only one type of player on each side. So, in all but trivial cases, evolutionary stability does *not* obtain in asymmetric evolutionary games. Since evolutionary stability is closely related to being an evolutionary equilibrium

---

[2]I say more or *less* because in fact the assumption of random pairings of agents is not at all characteristic of how agents are paired in most strategic interaction settings. More common is some form of *assortative interaction*, in which agents with particular characteristics have a higher than chance probability of interacting. Assortative interactions, for instance, are a more favorable setting for the emergence of altruism than panmictic interactions.

under the replicator dynamic the following theorem (Hofbauer and Sigmund 1998) is not surprising.

THEOREM 9.7 *A strictly mixed strategy Nash equilibrium of asymmetric evolutionary games is not an evolutionary equilibrium under the replicator dynamic.*

Actually, this situation applies to a much larger class of evolutionary dynamics than the replicator dynamic. See Samuelson and Zhang (1992) for details.

For a simple example of Theorem 9.7, consider the case where $n = m = 2$; i.e., row and column players each have two pure strategies. We have the following theorem.

THEOREM 9.8 *In the asymmetric evolutionary game in which each player has two pure strategies, a mixed strategy Nash equilibrium (p^*, q^*) is either unstable or an evolutionary focal point. In the latter case, all trajectories are closed orbits around the fixed point, and the time average of the frequencies $(p(t), q(t))$ around an orbit is (p^*, q^*):*

$$
\frac{1}{T} \int_0^T q(t)dt = \frac{\alpha}{\gamma} = q^*
$$

$$
\frac{1}{T} \int_0^T p(t)dt = \frac{\beta}{\delta} = p^*. \tag{9.13}
$$

When the time average of a dynamical system equals its equilibrium position, we say the system is *ergodic*.

PROOF: Check out the following fact. If a constant is added to each entry in a column of the matrix $A = \{\alpha_{ij}\}$, or to each row of the matrix $B = \{\beta_{ij}\}$, the replicator equations 9.12 remain unchanged. We can therefore assume $\alpha_{11} = \alpha_{22} = \beta_{11} = \beta_{22} = 0$. Writing $p = p_1$ and $q = q_1$, the replicator equations then become

$$
\dot{p} = p(1 - p)(\alpha - \gamma q)
$$

$$
\dot{q} = q(1 - q)(\beta - \delta p),
$$

where $\alpha = \alpha_{12}$, $\beta = \beta_{12}$, $\gamma = \alpha_{12} + \alpha_{21}$, and $\delta = \beta_{12} + \beta_{21}$. A mixed strategy equilibrium then occurs when $0 < \alpha/\gamma, \beta/\delta < 1$, and is given by $p^* = \beta/\delta, q^* = \alpha/\gamma$. The Jacobian at the fixed point is

$$
J(p^*, q^*) = \begin{bmatrix} 0 & -\gamma p^*(1 - p^*) \\ -\delta q^*(1 - q^*) & 0 \end{bmatrix}.
$$

Note that if α and β (or equivalently γ and δ) have the same sign, this is a saddle point (Theorem 8.4) and hence unstable. You can check that in this case at least one of the monomorphic fixed points is an evolutionary equilibrium. Since the mixed strategy equilibrium is hyperbolic, the fixed point is also a saddle under the replicator dynamic, by the Hartman-Grobman Theorem (Theorem 8.7). In case this argument whizzed by you, make a phase diagram to get a feel for this very common situation.

If α and β have opposite signs, the linearized system is neutrally stable, so the mixed strategy equilibrium is not hyperbolic. Although we cannot apply the Hartman-Grobman Theorem, a sketch of the phase diagram shows that trajectories spiral around the fixed point. We can then determine that trajectories are closed orbits by exhibiting a function that is constant on trajectories. To see this, we divide the second replicator equation by the first, getting

$$\frac{dq}{dp} = \frac{(\beta - \delta p)q(1 - q)}{(\alpha - \gamma q)p(1 - p)}.$$

Separating variables, we get

$$\frac{\alpha - \gamma q}{q(1 - q)}dq = \frac{\beta - \delta p}{p(1 - p)}dp.$$

Integrating both sides and simplifying, we get

$$\alpha \ln(q) - (\alpha - \gamma)\ln(1 - q) - \beta \ln(p) + (\beta - \delta)\ln(1 - p) = C,$$

for some constant C. Suppose $\alpha > \gamma$. Then, this function is monotonic in the q direction, so the spirals must in fact be closed orbits. If $\alpha \leq \gamma$, then we must have $\beta > \delta$, so the function is monotonic in the p direction, so again the spirals are closed orbits.

To check the ergodic property of the system in the case of neutral stability, consider a trajectory $(p(t), q(t))$ starting at a point $(p(0), q(0)) = (p_0, q_0)$. We integrate both sides of the equation $\dot{p}/p(1 - p) = \alpha - \gamma q$ with respect to time, getting

$$\ln(p(t)) + \ln(1 - p(t)) = A + \alpha t - \gamma \int_0^t q(\tau)d\tau,$$

where the constant of integration A satisfies $A = \ln(p_0) + \ln(1 - p_0)$. If the period of the trajectory is T, so $p(T) = p_0$ and $q(T) = q_0$, then letting

$t = T$ in the previous expression gives

$$\frac{1}{T} \int_0^T q(t)dt = \frac{\alpha}{\gamma} = q^*.$$

A similar argument justifies the second equation in (9.13) as well. This proves the theorem. Q.E.D.

9.16 Asymmetric Evolutionary Games: Reviewing the Troops

To gain some feeling for the argument in §9.15, check out the dynamic properties of the asymmetric evolutionary game versions of the following games. HINT: In most cases the results follow easily from performing the row and column manipulations that leave zeros on the diagonals of the two payoff matrices.

a. Draw the phase diagram in §9.15.
b. The mixed strategy equilibrium of the Big Monkey and Little Monkey game (§1.2).
c. The mixed strategy equilibrium of the Battle of the Sexes (§4.9).
d. The Family Politics game (§4.36).
e. In the Real Men Don't Eat Quiche game (§4.41), each player has four strategies, but two are dominated. Looking only at the remaining two strategies for each player, show that the mixed strategy Nash equilibrium has closed trajectories.
f. The Vindication of the Hawk game (§4.42).
g. A Mating Game (§4.19).

9.17 The Evolution of Trust and Honesty

Consider an asymmetric evolutionary game with buyers and sellers. Each seller can be either honest (H) or dishonest (D), and each buyer can either inspect (I) or trust (T). Let p

	H	D
I	3,2	2,1
T	4,3	1,4

be the fraction of buyers who inspect and let q be the fraction of sellers who are honest. Suppose the payoff matrix for an encounter between a buyer and a seller is given as in the figure to the right. The payoff to inspect is then $3q + 2(1 - q) = q + 2$, the payoff to trust is $4q + (1 - q) = 3q + 1$, the payoff to be honest is $2p + 3(1 - p) = -p + 3$, and the payoff to be dishonest is $p + 4(1 - p) = -3p + 4$.

Suppose we have a replicator dynamic, such that the fraction of inspectors grows at a rate equal to its fitness minus the average fitness of buyers. Buyer average fitness is $p(q + 2) + (1 - p)(3q + 1) = 3q + 1 - p(2q - 1)$, so the inspector growth rate is $q + 2 - [3q + 1 - p(2q - 1)] = (1 - p)(1 - 2q)$, and we have the replicator equation

$$\dot{p} = p(1 - p)(1 - 2q). \tag{9.14}$$

Similarly, the fraction of honest sellers grows at a rate equal to its fitness minus the average fitness among sellers, giving

$$\dot{q} = q(1 - q)(2p - 1). \tag{9.15}$$

a. Show that these two coupled differential equations have five fixed points, $(0,0)$, $(0,1)$, $(1,0)$, $(1,1)$, and $(1/2,1/2)$.
b. Show that the first four fixed points are unstable.
c. Show that the equilibrium at $(1/2,1/2)$ is not hyperbolic: its linearization is a center. It follows that we cannot use the Hartman-Grobman Theorem to ascertain the type of fixed point.
d. Draw a phase diagram and show that the trajectories are spirals moving counterclockwise around the fixed point.

How might we prove that the fixed point is a center? Suppose we could find a function $f(p, q)$ that is constant on trajectories of the system. If we could then show that f is strictly increasing along an appropriate ray from the fixed point to the northeast, we would be done, since only closed orbits are then possible. This is precisely what we did to show that the trajectories of the Lotka-Volterra equations are orbits around the fixed point (§8.5). See also (§9.12) and (§9.15).

Eliminating t from (9.14) and (9.15), we get

$$\frac{dq}{dp} = \frac{(q - q^2)(2p - 1)}{(p - p^2)(1 - 2q)}.$$

Separating the variables, this becomes

$$\frac{1 - 2p}{p - p^2}dp = -\frac{1 - 2q}{q - q^2}dq.$$

Integrating both sides and combining terms, we get $\ln{(p - p^2)(q - q^2)} = C$ for some constant C. We simplify by taking the antilogarithm of both sides, getting $(p - p^2)(q - q^2) = e^C$. Thus, $f(p, q) = p(1 - p)q(1 - q)$ is constant on trajectories of the dynamical system. Consider a ray from the origin through the fixed point. We may parametrize this by $p = q = s$, which hits the fixed point when $s = 1/2$. Then, $f(p(s), q(s)) = s^2(1 - s)^2$, so $df(p(s), q(s))/ds = 2s(1 - s)(1 - 2s)$. This is strictly positive for $1/2 < s < 1$. If the trajectory were not a center, it would hit this ray more than once, and $f(p(s), q(s))$ would have a larger value the second time than the first, which is impossible. This proves that (1/2,1/2) is a center.

9.18   The Loraxes and Thoraxes

In the Great Blue Lagoon, there are little fish called Loraxes that pick parasites from the mouth and gills of big fish called Thoraxes.[3] This is of great benefit to both, since the Lorax gets a meal and the Thorax lowers its parasite count. The problem is that the Thorax can eat a Lorax who happens to be foraging in and around its mouth. The Lorax can either trust (T) the Thorax and pick away, or flee (F) the Thorax and seek dinner elsewhere. The Thorax can either cooperate (C) with a trusting Lorax, or eat it (E). If the Lorax flees, the payoff to each is $s > 0$ (life is sweet). If the Lorax trusts, and the Thorax eats, the payoff to the Lorax is 0 (death is nothingness) and to the Thorax is 1 (dinner is bliss). However, if the Thorax cooperates, they each have payoff r, where $s < r < 1$.

We suppose that Thoraxes are wired either to cooperate with Loraxes or to eat them, and Loraxes are similarly programmed either to trust or to flee Thoraxes, however brimming with parasites. We suppose that the frequency of the various strategies can change over time through Darwinian evolution, so we can think of this as a game in which the concept of Nash equilibrium, evolutionarily stable strategy, and replicator dynamics might apply. In this spirit, show the following:

a. If Thoraxes have a visible mark that indicates whether they cooperate with or eat Loraxes, there is a unique Nash equilibrium in which all Thoraxes cooperate and all Loraxes trust.

b. If Loraxes know only the fraction p of cooperators among the Thoraxes, but cannot tell an individual cooperator from an eater, there is a unique

---

[3]This account is fanciful. For more on *cleaner fish*, see §6.2 and Trivers 1985.

Nash equilibrium in which all Thoraxes eat Loraxes, and all Loraxes flee all Thoraxes.

c. Suppose a cooperative Thorax gives some sign of its nature, but it is difficult to determine, so a Lorax must pay an inspection cost of $\delta > 0$ to find out. We call this action "inspecting" (I). If a Lorax does not inspect (NI), it uses the fraction of cooperating Thoraxes (p) to decide whether to trust or flee. Show that if $s/r > \delta/(r - s)$ there is a unique mixed strategy Nash equilibrium in which Loraxes inspect with probability $q^* = 1 - r$ and Thoraxes cooperate with probability $p^* = 1 - \delta/s$. If $s/r < \delta/(r - s)$, the only Nash equilibrium is the trivial one in which all Loraxes flee Thoraxes and all Thoraxes eat Loraxes.

d. Suppose out of equilibrium the system moves according to a linear dynamic, whereby the probability p of cooperating is proportional to the difference between the payoffs to C and E, and the probability q of inspecting is proportional to the difference between the payoffs to I and NI. Show that if $s/r > \delta/(r - s)$ and we start with $p > s/r$, the system moves in elliptical orbits around the mixed strategy equilibrium (p^*, q^*).

9.19 Cultural Transmission and Social Imitation

When payoffs represent individual reproductive fitness, the replicator equation is a natural first cut at modeling evolutionary dynamics. The basic behavioral repertoire of *Homo sapiens* (sociality, language, brain size, emotional predispositions) has doubtless evolved in this manner. But when payoffs are less directly related to reproductive fitness, as is usually the case in human cultural evolution, the replicator dynamic is rarely a plausible model of behavioral change. This is especially the case in analyzing cultural change in the biological shortrun—say 5000 years or less.

We motivated the use of the replicator equation in cultural models by positing that individuals change their behavior by imitating others who are more successful (§9.2.1). However, the main way individuals acquire behavioral traits is by *transmission from others*, including parents (*vertical transmission*), peers (*horizontal transmission*), and influential individuals and institutions (*oblique transmission*). The pioneers in modeling evolutionary cultural theory (Lumsden and Wilson 1981, Cavalli-Sforza and Feldman 1981, Boyd and Richerson 1985) developed these and related terms to analyze the interplay of forces guiding cultural change. These contributions appeared largely before evolutionary game theory matured (starting with Maynard Smith 1982), so there is a lot of work to be done in integrating their insights with those of this chapter.

Even when individuals seek new behavioral traits, it is not always obvious what attributes of others are valid indicators of their success and hence should be adopted. Often the wisest action is simply to emulate a (perhaps weighted) majority behavior. Several models of such *frequency dependent selection* have been developed, none of which predicts the general adoption of more fit behaviors (Banerjee 1992, Bikhchandani, Hirshleifer, and Welsh 1992, Harrington 1999).

Taking into account these and related forces can lead to substantially different conclusions from those inferred from a replicator dynamic. Consider, for instance, the following cultural dynamic. There are two traits, A (ethnic identity) and B (cosmopolitan identity). Suppose cosmopolitans (B) are more successful in life than ethnics (A), so ethnics have a tendency to be emulated equal to $1 - s$ compared to tendency 1 for cosmopolitans, where $0 < s < 1$. If α and $1 - \alpha$ are the frequencies of ethnics and cosmopolitans in the population prior to emulation, after emulation the frequencies become $\alpha(1 - s)/(1 - \alpha s)$ and $(1 - \alpha)/(1 - \alpha s)$. Suppose families consist of two parents who are paired randomly with respect to ethnic vs. cosmopolitan orientation, so the frequency of AA families (both parents ethnic) is $f_{AA} = \alpha^2(1 - s)^2/(1 - \alpha s)^2$, the frequency of AB families (one parent of each type) is $f_{AB} = 2\alpha(1 - \alpha)(1 - s)/(1 - \alpha s)^2$, and the frequency of BB families (both cosmopolitan) is $f_{BB} = (1 - \alpha)^2/(1 - \alpha s)^2$. To model vertical transmission, suppose all the children of AA families are ethnic, a fraction γ of children from AB families are ethnic, and none of the children from BB families is ethnic. If all families have the same expected number of offspring, the frequency of ethnic orientation A in the next generation will be $\alpha' = f_{AA} + \gamma f_{AB}$, which is

$$\alpha' = \frac{\alpha(1 - s)}{(1 - \alpha s)^2}\left[\alpha(1 - s) + 2\gamma(1 - \alpha)\right].$$

Note that for genetic inheritance $\gamma = 1/2$, in which case $\alpha' < \alpha$, the less fit trait will disappear as predicted by the replicator dynamic. However, suppose it is easier for a child to acquire an ethnic than a cosmopolitan orientation. Then, we might expect $\gamma > 1/2$. As long as

$$\frac{1 + s}{2} < \gamma < \frac{1}{2(1 - s)},$$

there is an equilibrium with a positive level of the less fit trait A. For instance, suppose the offspring of AB families are always A, so $\gamma = 1$. In this case $\alpha' - \alpha$ has the sign of $\alpha(1 - \alpha)(1 - 2s + s^2\alpha)$, which is strictly positive for $s \leq 1/2$, so in equilibrium $\alpha = 1$, despite its lower fitness according to the replicator dynamic. We conclude that *traits that are less fit but readily transmitted culturally can persist in equilibrium*. Interestingly, a similar phenomenon, called *meiotic drive*, occurs in genetic evolution, when a gene ensures that it will be overrepresented in zygotes despite its being harmful to the organism.

In fact, we can say more:

a. Show that the "extended" replicator equation, including both genetic and cultural inheritance, can be written as

$$\frac{d\alpha}{dt} = \frac{\alpha(1 - \alpha)(s^2\alpha + 2\gamma(1 - s) - 1)}{(1 - s\alpha)^2}.$$

b. Evaluate the Jacobian of this differential equation at the interior equilibrium $\alpha^* = (1 - 2\gamma)(1 - s)/s^2$ and show that it is always positive, so the equilibrium is unstable.

c. Describe how the final steady state of the system depends on the initial frequency α_0 of ethnics in the population.

d. How does the basin of attraction of the more fit equilibrium depend on the fitness penalty s of ethnics and the cultural transmission coefficient γ?

Behavioral traits that are only weakly linked to the basic sociological mechanisms of vertical, horizontal, and oblique transmission are probably best modeled by a variant of the replicator dynamic. More complex traits will require correspondingly more complex modeling. Perhaps the dominant cultural transmission mechanisms, and our epigenetic predisposition to be influenced by them, can be modeled evolutionarily, but this task remains to be done.

10

Markov Economies and Stochastic Dynamical Systems

Riverrun, past Eve and Adam's, from swerve of shore to bend of bay,
brings us to a commodius vicus.

James Joyce

10.1   Introduction

Markov chains, and more generally stochastic processes, are immensely powerful tools for characterizing aspects of dynamical systems that cannot be captured using systems of ordinary differential equations. While the topic is far too broad to deal with in any detail in this book, I have found that some introduction to such models, which may be called *stochastic dynamical systems*, is important if students are to develop a mature sense of how one models probabilistic social systems. Students who like what they see here can proceed to a more leisurely study in Karlin and Taylor (1975, 1981) which gives many examples from economics, finance, and biology.

This chapter samples the literature by presenting two examples. The first is a model of my own that generalizes a famous paper by Kiyotaki and Wright (1989) concerning the emergence of money in a barter economy. This model is an interesting hybrid of Markov chain theory and game theory, since we use the ergodic theorem for finite Markov chains (§16.38) to define the payoffs to the game under a variety of conditions, and investigate the properties of Nash equilibria subject to these payoffs without specifying out-of-equilibrium behavior of the model. The Nash equilibria are thus "rational expectations equilibria," in which the expectations are stationary distributions of the Markov chain. To show that the model has plausible disequilibrium behavior, we present an agent-based simulation of the theoretical results.

Our second example is a Markov model of adaptive learning that illustrates the concept of stochastic stability, as developed in Young (1998). After

220

developing some of the theoretical results, we again provide an agent-based simulation of the model.

10.2   The Emergence of Money in a Markov Economy

The neoclassical general equilibrium model is limited by its failure to model strategic interactions among agents (§3.19,§6.14.1, and §6.14.3). Typical of this weakness is its difficulty in modeling money. General equilibrium theory has generally treated money as an asset that is held because of its low risk and high liquidity. But money is dominated by demand deposits that have the same risk and liquidity characteristics as money, but unlike money are also interest bearing (Chang, Hamberg, and Hirata 1983). In fact, *money lowers transactions costs in a world in which it is expensive to write and enforce two-sided exchanges of goods.* Using game theory, we can develop a stochastic model of production and exchange that illustrates the transactions demand for money and that shows how money might emerge through a dynamic evolutionary process (Gintis 1997).

Consider a game with a large but finite number of players, each of whom lives a finite but uncertain number of periods. In each period, players are randomly paired and engage in bilateral exchange. Each player produces some goods, consumes others, and holds an inventory of untraded goods. We show that under plausible conditions a Nash equilibrium exists in which a good is a medium of exchange, accepted in trade by players who value it only for its ability to facilitate future trades with other agents.[1]

Each player has a strategy specifying which trades are acceptable from a given pre-trade inventory, and what the player consumes and produces from a given post-trade inventory. Players meet randomly in each period with their accumulated inventories, they trade, and they then produce and consume, given their post-trade inventories. We assume each player has a constant probability ρ of living to the next period, and a player who dies is immediately replaced by an identical player with an empty inventory, who inherits the strategy of its predecessor.

Let G be the (finite) set of goods in the economy, each available in an integral number of units, and let K be a finite set of players. Each player $k \in K$ consumes goods $C_k \subset G$ and produces goods $P_k \subset G$. Players do not consume the goods they produce—whence the need for trade. Each

---

[1]This model is inspired by Kiyotaki and Wright 1989. See also Kiyotaki and Wright 1991, 1993, and Aiyagari and Wallace 1991, 1992.

player $k \in K$ has an increasing utility function u_k over C_k. Each good $g \in P_k$ has unit production cost $\kappa_g > 0$, measured in utility units, and we assume every player k has some good $g_k \in P_k$ such that $\kappa_{g_k} < u(g)$ for some $g \in C_k$, so gains from trade are possible. If p is a bundle of goods consisting of n_g units of each good $g \in G$, we write $p = \sum_{g \in G} n_g g$. The cost of producing $p = \sum_{g \in P_k} n_g g$ is then

$$\kappa(p) = \sum_{g \in P_k} n_g \kappa_g.$$

In addition, each player $k \in K$ incurs a storage cost $\alpha_g > 0$ in each trading period for each unit of a good g held in inventory. Thus, the cost of holding inventory $\mathbf{i} = \sum_{g \in G} n_g g$ is

$$\alpha(\mathbf{i}) = \sum_{g \in G} n_g \alpha_g.$$

We assume inventories can hold a maximum of n_{max} items. The utility accruing to player $k \in K$ in one round is

$$v_k = u_k(c_k) - \kappa(\gamma_k) - \alpha(\mathbf{i}_k), \tag{10.1}$$

where c_k is the set of goods consumed, γ_k is the set of goods produced, and $\mathbf{i}_k$ is the inventory k takes into the next trading period.

Players are randomly paired for trade in each period. A pure strategy $s_k \in S_k$ for player $k \in K$ consists of the following for each inventory $\mathbf{i}$: a trading function $A_k(\mathbf{i})$ such that if inventory $\mathbf{j} \in A_k(\mathbf{i})$, then k is willing to trade so as to move from inventory $\mathbf{i}$ to inventory $\mathbf{j}$; a consumption function $c_k(\mathbf{j})$ that indicates what k consumes (if anything) from post-trade inventory $\mathbf{j}$; and a production function $\gamma_k(\mathbf{j})$ that indicates what goods k produces to add to post-trade inventory $\mathbf{j}$. Note that there are only a finite number of pure strategies for a player, since there are only a finite number of inventories.

If players k and k' using strategies $s_k \in S_k$ and $s_{k'} \in S_{k'}$ meet and hold inventories $\mathbf{i}_k$ and $\mathbf{i}_{k'}$ respectively, their trading functions A_k and $A_{k'}$ define a (possibly empty) set of mutually acceptable trades $G(s_k, \mathbf{i}_k, s_{k'}, \mathbf{i}_{k'})$. If this set is nonempty, a trade is chosen randomly from among its Pareto-efficient members.

If $s = \{s_k | k \in K\}$ is a pure strategy for the game, and if we start off each agent with an empty inventory, the model will generate a time path of consumption, production, exchange, and inventories for each player in each future time period, depending on the random assignment of players to trade and the choice of trades from the sets of mutually acceptable trades. This can be a very large game with a huge number of strategies and lots of moves by Nature.

However, there is an easy way to make the model tractable: we ask what happens in long-run equilibrium, when the patterns of consumption, production, and trade have become in some appropriate sense *time independent*. In such a situation, we can assume each player knows the probability distribution over player types and inventories, and chooses production, consumption, and trading strategies to maximize long-run expected utility, where expectations are taken relative to this probability distribution.

But how do we obtain such a probability distribution? We define the *state* of the game at a point in time to be the inventory holdings $\mathbf{I} = \{\mathbf{i}_k | k \in K\}$ of each of the players. Then the game strategy s generates a finite probability transition matrix P^s such that $P^s(\mathbf{I}, \mathbf{I}')$ is the probability of moving from $\mathbf{I}$ to $\mathbf{I}'$. The random variable $\mathbf{I}$ determined by P^s is then a *finite Markov chain*, and by the *ergodic theorem for finite Markov chains* (see Theorem 16.2), there is a stationary distribution $\mathcal{P}^s$ over inventories that is constant from the current to the next period. Specifically, for any inventory $\mathbf{I}$ the probability $P^+(\mathbf{I})$ that $\mathbf{I}$ occurs in the next period, which is given by

$$P^+(\mathbf{I}) = \sum_{\mathbf{I}'} P^s(\mathbf{I}') P^s(\mathbf{I}', \mathbf{I}),$$

satisfies $P^+(\mathbf{I}) = P^s(\mathbf{I})$.[2] The ergodic theorem also states that after the game is run for a sufficiently long time, the expected distribution of inventories will be equal to the stationary distribution P^s, so it is reasonable for a player to use P^s to plan an optimal production, trading, and consumption strategy.

These definitions extend directly to the case where each player uses a mixed strategy σ_k, giving rise to the game-level mixed strategy $\sigma = \{\sigma_k | k \in K\}$, and the ergodic distribution P^σ over inventories. We then define the payoff to player $k \in K$, given σ, to be the player's expected return from using strategy σ_k where the probability distribution of moving from inventory $\mathbf{i}_k$ to $\mathbf{i}'_k$ is given by the marginal probability distribution induced by P^σ on $k's$ inventories.

[2]Since by construction every state in the Markov chain has a nonzero probability of transition to the zero state, the set of states attainable from the zero state is an irreducible aperiodic persistent set, so the ergodic theorem applies.

We have in principle defined a normal form game. I say 'in principle' because the relevant equations have not been written out in detail. The reader is encouraged to do so. Clearly there is a *no trade Nash equilibrium* in which no player produces, consumes, or trades anything. However, there are lots of other Nash equilibria, which is suggested by the following theorem, which follows trivially from Nash's theorem that finite games always have at least one Nash equilibrium (§4.3).

THEOREM 10.1 *Suppose each player $k \in K$ is constrained to a nonempty pure strategy set $U_k \subseteq S_k$. Then there exists a Nash equilibrium in mixed strategies based on the pure strategies in $\{U_k \mid k \in K\}$.*

For instance, we have the following theorem.

THEOREM 10.2 *Suppose each player produces exactly one good, and for any two goods g and h there is a producer of g that consumes h. If the utility of consumption is sufficiently great for each good, there is a Nash equilibrium in which all goods are traded with positive probability.*

We leave the proof of this theorem, which is straightforward, to the reader, or see Gintis (1997). HINT: Constrain the pure strategies of the players by saying that each player must hold a unit of some good in its inventory in each period, and a player must offer to trade its production good g_k unit for unit against any consumption good $c_k \in C_k$. By Theorem 10.1 there exists a Nash equilibrium for the resulting "constrained" game. Then, show that when the constraints are relaxed, the players have no incentive to change their strategies.

What about money? We say a good $m \in G$ is a *universal medium of exchange*, or simply is *money*, if m is accepted in trade by all agents against all other goods $g \neq m$. We say a good $m \in G$ has *low storage costs* if for each $k \in K$, $s_m \leq s_g$ for all $g \in G$. We then have the following theorem.

THEOREM 10.3 *Suppose each player $k \in K$ produces exactly one good g_k, and let $m \in G$ have low storage costs. Suppose that for each $g \in G$ there is a player who produces m and consumes g. Then, if the utility of consumption is sufficiently high, there is a Nash equilibrium of the economy in which m is a universal medium of exchange.*

We again leave the proof to the reader. HINT: Suppose $m \in G$ satisfies the conditions of the theorem. Add three constraints to the players' pure trade strategies. First, constrain each player to hold a unit of some good in its inventory in each period. Second, for each player $k \in K$, admit only those trade preferences A_k for which k's post-trade inventory is no smaller than k's pre-trade inventory. Third, require all players to choose strategies in which one unit of m is accepted in exchange for each good $g \neq m$ that they currently hold in their inventories. Then show that when the constraints are relaxed, players have no incentive to change their strategies.

What about *fiat money*, which is a money that is neither produced nor consumed by players (presumably it is produced by some outside agent, such as the government)? We assume there is a fiat good that may be traded and, upon the death of a player, is passed on to the player's successor. We say the good is fiat money if it is accepted in trade by all agents.

THEOREM 10.4 *Suppose there is a fiat good m, each player produces exactly one good, each good except m is produced by at least one player, and for any two goods $g, h \neq m$ there is a producer of g that consumes h. If the amount of m is sufficiently small, the storage cost of m is sufficiently low, and the utility of consumption is sufficiently high, then there is an equilibrium in which each good $g \neq m$ trades for m with positive probability in each period; i.e., m is fiat money.*

We leave the proof to the reader. HINT: Add three constraints to players' pure trade strategies. First, constrain each player to hold a unit of some good in its inventory in each period. Second, constrain players to offer only one unit of a good in trade. Third, require all agents to accept a unit of m in exchange for some good $g \neq m$ currently held in inventory. Show that in the resulting equilibrium, no agent gains by deviating from its constrained strategy.

10.2.1 Simulating a Monetary Economy

It is nice to show that trading systems with money exist, but it is quite another to show that among the myriad of Nash equilibria of such systems, equilibria with money have some privileged position. The strongest such statement would be that under a suitable dynamic there is convergence to a Nash equilibrium with money for a reasonable range of initial conditions. The emergence of money need not be a high-probability event, since trading systems with money will outperform barter and nontrade systems, and hence will have a tendency to expand at their expense. But local stability over a range of initial conditions would be highly desirable.

Unfortunately, we lack the analytical machinery to prove local stability in the context of the above model, but we can show through simulations that money always emerges when the appropriate conditions are present. To show this, we construct an economy with five goods $g_1, \ldots g_5$, ordered from highest to lowest in storage costs. We assume that, except in the case of a fiat good, for each pair of goods there is a type of player in the economy producing the first good and consuming the second. There are thus twenty player types, since we assume that for each good g, the utility of consumption u_g, the cost of production κ_g, and the storage cost s_g are the same for all players who consume, produce, and store g, respectively.

For simplicity we assume that a player's maximum inventory is one unit, and we constrain each player to consume when it has acquired its consumption good, and to produce a unit of its production good when its inventory is empty. Dropping these constraints merely lengthens the time to convergence, since players who act otherwise are eventually driven into extinction. This reduces a player's strategy to its trading function—the specification of which goods the player will accept in exchange for its inventory. We call such a trading strategy the player's *genotype*, and we assign genotypes randomly to the initial population. We represent the genotype by a 5×5 matrix $\gamma = (\gamma_{ij})$, where $\gamma_{ij} = 1$ if the player accepts good g_j in trade for g_i and $\gamma_{ij} = 0$ if the player refuses such a trade.

With five goods there are $2^{25} = 33,554,432$ distinct trading strategies. We can reduce this number to $2^{16} = 65,536$ by eliminating dominated strategies. For instance, strategies that involve not accepting a consumption good in trade, or trading a good for itself. Equating behaviorally equivalent strategies—for instance, strategies that differ on what to accept in trade when a player sells her consumption good, which can never occur—reduces this to $2^{12} = 4,096$ distinct strategies. Since there are twenty types of agents, and assuming all players of the same type use the same strategies, there are $4096^{20} \approx 10^{72}$ pure strategies for the economy, an astronomically large figure. However, simulations with 1000 to 2000 players—50 to 100 agents of each of the twenty types—exhibit quite rapid convergence. Repeated runs of the model with different random draws of the population exhibit converges to roughly the same equilibrium after about 6,000 generations, which is about 60,000 trading sessions.

A simulation begins by creating a population of agents with randomly generated genomes, empty inventories, and zero wealth. In each round of trade, each player chooses a good from inventory to sell, and trading partners are assigned randomly. If they agree to trade, each player's wealth is augmented by u_c if the player acquires its consumption good, and decremented by k_p if it must produce its production good. Whether or not trade takes place, each player's wealth is debited an amount equal to the storage costs on the good it holds in inventory.

Every ten rounds, which we call a "generation," some agents die and others are born. The lowest scorers of each type dies, and are replaced by the offspring of the highest-scoring players of that type, and the offspring is endowed with the average wealth for that type. In addition, elderly players— defined as those who have lived for more than ten generations—die at a given rate and are replaced by offspring of the more successful agents. Reproduction takes the form of asexual replication with mutation (one entry in the trading matrix is randomly chosen to mutate for each new player).

A typical simulation used 100 agents of each of the twenty types, with storage costs for the five goods $(g_1, g_2, g_3, g_4, g_5)$ set to $(40,30,20,10,2)$. The simulation ran for 553 generations before all player types stabilized, in the sense that the frequencies of the various strategies remained constant over time except for the random perturbations induced by mutation. As expected, *the low-storage-cost good g_5 emerged as a universal medium of exchange*.

It may be suspected that the simulation is simply picking out agents who are partial to goods with low storage cost. Two additional simulations dispel this suspicion. In the first, we increase the frequency of g_4-consumers from 20% to 44% of the total population and reduce the frequency of g_5-consumers to 4% of the population. Since the probability of finding a buyer for g_4 is now significantly higher than for any other good, it is possible that g_4 serve as money for other agents, despite a storage cost that is higher than that of g_5 (for this simulation, the storage cost of g_4 was set to 3 and that of g_5 remained at 2). Using 2000 agents, the strategies stabilized after 935 generations, all agents accept g_4 as money, except g_3-producers who consume g_1, and only g_1-producers and/or consumers accept g_5 as money. This pattern of trade has an intuitive interpretation: storage costs are so high for g_1-producers that they will accept g_5 in trade, despite its drawbacks; g_1-consumers therefore accept g_5 because they can trade it with g_1-producers (that g_3-producers who consume g_1 do not accept g_4 is an anomaly that did not appear in other runs). This shows that *both storage costs and frequency of use enter into the specification of media of exchange*.

In our second simulation, we increase the frequency of g_5-producers from 20% to 68% of the total population, and we reduce the frequency of all other producer types equally to 8% of the population each. There is now a glut of the low-storage-cost good g_5, so we would expect agents to reject g_5 in trade, and move toward using g_4 as a money good. Again for this simulation, the storage cost of g_4 was set to 3 and that of g_5 remained at 2. Using 4000 agents, the strategies stabilized after 760 generations, all agents accept g_4 as money, and only g_1-producers and some g_1-consumers accept g_5 as money. As in the previous simulation, storage costs are sufficiently high for g_1-producers that they will accept g_5 in trade despite its oversupply, and some g_1-consumers accept g_5 because they can trade it with g_1-producers. This shows that *in addition to storage costs the frequency of production affects whether a good is accepted as money:* a good must be scarce as well as low cost to serve as a medium of exchange.

What about fiat money? In this case, intuition (and perhaps some familiarity with monetary history) suggests that using fiat money involves a *self-fulfilling prophecy*, in the sense that if enough of the population expects a fiat good to be accepted as money, then everyone will accept it. Our simulations show that this is indeed the case. If m is a fiat good, and if the initial fraction of players willing to accept m in trade is sufficiently large, then in equilibrium m is fiat money. In one simulation we set the amount of fiat money per player to one unit for every five players, and we set the player genotypes so that initially 50% of players accept m in exchange. Then, in equilibrium we find that m serves as fiat money. Other simulations give the same result when the fiat good/player ratio is as low as one unit per ten players and as high as six units per ten agents, and when as little as 25% of the initial stock of agents are genetically constrained, at least in the initial period, to accept m in exchange. Under random assignment of genomes to players, however, the fiat good does not generally emerge as fiat money.

10.3   Good Vibrations

Consider the pure coordination game at the right. We can check using the techniques of chapter 3 that there are two pure strategy equilibria, *ll* and *rr*, as well as a mixed strategy equilibrium. If we represent the out-of-equilibrium dynamics of the game using a

	l	r
l	5,5	0,0
r	0,0	3,3

replicator process (see chapter 9), the pure strategy equilibria will be stable and the mixed strategy equilibrium unstable. But the concept of stability that is used, while at first glance compelling and intuitive, is actually quite unrealistic. The idea is that if we start at the equilibrium *ll*, and we subject the system to a small disequilibrium shock, the system will move back into equilibrium. But in the real world, dynamical systems are *constantly* subject to shocks, and if the shocks come frequently enough, the system won't have time to move back into equilibrium before the next shock comes.

The evolutionary models considered in chapters 7 and 9 are certainly subject to continual random "shocks," since agents are paired randomly, play mixed strategies with stochastic outcomes, and update their strategies by sampling the population. We avoided considering the stochastic nature of these processes by implicitly assuming that random variables can be replaced by their expected values, and mutations occur infrequently compared with the time to restore equilibrium. But what if we are not sure that these approximations are reasonable or, even worse, what if we know they are not?

One way to go is to move from deterministic to stochastic differential equations, where we add an appropriate stochastic error term to the right-hand-side of an equation such as (8.1). This approach turns out to be very fruitful but involves sophisticated mathematical techniques, including stochastic processes and partial differential equations.[3] Moreover, applications have been confined mainly to financial economics. Applying the approach to game theory is very difficult, since stochastic differential equations with more than one independent variable virtually never have a closed form solution—so it's computer simulation all the way! Consider the following, completely different, and much more accessible approach, based on the work of H. Peyton Young (1998) and others. We start by modeling adaptive learning with and without errors.

10.4 Adaptive Learning

How does an agent decide what strategy to follow in a game? We have described three distinct methods so far in our study of game theory. The first is to determine the expected behavior of the other players and choose a best response ("rational expectations"). The second is to inherit a strategy (e.g., from one's parents) and blindly play it. The third is to mimic another player by switching to the other player's strategy, if it seems to be doing

---

[3]For relatively accessible expositions, see Dixit 1993 and Karlin and Taylor 1981.

better than one's own. But there is a fourth, and very commonly followed, modus operandi: follow the history of how other players have played in the past, and choose a strategy for the future that is a best response to the past play of others. We call this *adaptive learning*, or *adaptive expectations*.

To formalize this, consider an evolutionary game in which each player has limited memory, remembering only $h = \{h_1, h_2, \ldots, h_m\}$, the last m moves of the players with whom he has been paired. If the player chooses the next move as a best response to h, we say the player follows adaptive learning.

Suppose, for instance, two agents play the coordination game in §10.3, but the payoffs to ll and rr are both 5,5. Let $m = 2$, so the players look at the last two actions chosen by their opponents. The best response to ll is thus l, the best response to rr is r, and the best response to rl or lr is any combination of l and r. We take this combination to be: play l with probability 1/2 and r with probability 1/2. There are clearly sixteen distinct "states" of the game, which we label $abcd$, where each of the letters can be l or r, b is the last move by player 1, a is player 1's move previous to this, d is the last move by player 2, and c is player 2's move previous to this. For instance, $llrl$ means player 1 moved l on the previous two rounds, while player 2 moved first r and then l.

We can reduce the number of states to ten by recognizing that since we don't care about the order in which the players are counted, a state $abcd$ and a state $cdab$ are equivalent. Eliminating redundant states, and ordering the remaining states alphabetically, the states become $llll$, $lllr$, $llrl$, $llrr$, $lrlr$, $lrrl$, $lrrr$, $rlrl$, $rlrr$, and $rrrr$. Given any state, we can now compute the probability of a transition to any other state on the next play of the game. For instance, $llll$ (and similarly $rrrr$) is an *absorbing* state in the sense that, once it is entered, it stays there forever. The state $lllr$ goes to states $llrl$ and $lrlr$, each with probability 1/2. The state $llrl$ goes either to $llll$ where it stays forever, or to $lllr$, each with probability 1/2. The state $lrlr$ goes to $rlrl$ and $rrrr$ each with probability 1/4, and to $rlrr$ with probability 1/2. And so on.

We can summarize the transitions from state to state in a 10×10 matrix $M = (m_{ij})$, where $m_{abcd,efgi}$ is the probability of moving from state $abcd$ to state $efgi$. We call M a *probability transition matrix*, and the dynamic process of moving from state to state is a *Markov chain* (§16.38). Since matrices are easier to describe and manipulate if their rows and columns are numbered, we will assign numbers to the various states, as follows: $llll = 1$, $lllr = 2$, ...$rrrr = 10$. This gives us the following probability transition matrix:

$$
M = \begin{pmatrix}
1 & 0 & 0 & 0 & 0 & 0 & 0 & 0 & 0 & 0 \\
0 & 0 & 0.5 & 0 & 0 & 0.5 & 0 & 0 & 0 & 0 \\
0.5 & 0.5 & 0 & 0 & 0 & 0 & 0 & 0 & 0 & 0 \\
0 & 0 & 0 & 0 & 0 & 1 & 0 & 0 & 0 & 0 \\
0 & 0 & 0 & 0 & 0 & 0 & 0 & 0.25 & 0.5 & 0.25 \\
0 & 0 & 0.25 & 0.25 & 0 & 0.25 & 0.25 & 0 & 0 & 0 \\
0 & 0 & 0 & 0 & 0 & 0 & 0 & 0 & 0.5 & 0.5 \\
0.25 & 0.5 & 0 & 0 & 0.25 & 0 & 0 & 0 & 0 & 0 \\
0 & 0 & 0 & 0 & 0 & 0.5 & 0.5 & 0 & 0 & 0 \\
0 & 0 & 0 & 0 & 0 & 0 & 0 & 0 & 0 & 1
\end{pmatrix}
$$

Also, if we represent the ten states by the ten ten-dimensional row vectors $\{v_1, \ldots, v_{10}\}$, where $v_1 = (1,0,\ldots,0)$, $v_2 = (0,1,0,\ldots,0)$, and so on, then it is easy to see that if we are in state v_i in one period, the probability distribution of states in the next period is just $v_i M$, meaning the product of v_i, which is a 1×10 row vector, and M, which is a 10×10 matrix, so the product is another 1×10 row vector. It is also easy to see that the sum of the entries in $v_i M$ is unity and that each entry represents the probability that the corresponding state will be entered in the next period.

   If the system starts in state i at $t = 0$, $v_i M$ is the probability distribution of the state it's in at $t = 1$. Can we calculate the probability distribution of the state the system is in at $t = 2$? Well, let's write

$$
v_i M = p_1 v_1 + \ldots + p_{10} v_{10}.
$$

Then, with probability p_j the system has probability distribution $v_j M$ in the second period, so the probability distribution of states in the second period is

$$
p_1 v_1 M + \ldots + p_{10} v_{10} M = v_i M^2.
$$

Similar reasoning shows that the probability distribution of states after k periods is simply $v_i M^k$. Thus, just as M is the probability transition matrix for one period, so is M^k the probability transition matrix for k periods. To find out the long-run behavior of the system, we therefore want to calculate

$$
M^* = \lim_{k \to \infty} M^k.
$$

I trust you understand that this cannot be calculated by hand! Even calculating M^2 by hand is a royal drag. However, there are ways of computing M^* without actually calculating the limit (see any book on Markov chains).

I let Mathematica, the computer algebra software package, calculate M^k for larger and larger k until the entries in the matrix stopped changing or became vanishingly small, and I came up with the following matrix:

$$
M = \begin{pmatrix}
1 & 0 & 0 & 0 & 0 & 0 & 0 & 0 & 0 & 0 \\
2/3 & 0 & 0 & 0 & 0 & 0 & 0 & 0 & 0 & 1/3 \\
5/6 & 0 & 0 & 0 & 0 & 0 & 0 & 0 & 0 & 1/6 \\
1/2 & 0 & 0 & 0 & 0 & 0 & 0 & 0 & 0 & 1/2 \\
1/3 & 0 & 0 & 0 & 0 & 0 & 0 & 0 & 0 & 2/3 \\
1/2 & 0 & 0 & 0 & 0 & 0 & 0 & 0 & 0 & 1/2 \\
1/6 & 0 & 0 & 0 & 0 & 0 & 0 & 0 & 0 & 5/6 \\
2/3 & 0 & 0 & 0 & 0 & 0 & 0 & 0 & 0 & 1/3 \\
1/3 & 0 & 0 & 0 & 0 & 0 & 0 & 0 & 0 & 2/3 \\
0 & 0 & 0 & 0 & 0 & 0 & 0 & 0 & 0 & 1
\end{pmatrix}.
$$

In other words, no matter where you start, you end up in one of the absorbing states, which is a Pareto-optimal Nash equilibrium. We call pure strategy Nash equilibria in which all players choose the same strategy *conventions* (Young 1998). We conclude that *adaptive learning leads with probability 1 to a convention.*

10.4.1   The Steady State of a Markov Chain

There is a simpler way to compute M^* in the previous case. The computation also gives a better intuitive feel for the steady state solution to the adaptive learning dynamical system generated by a pure coordination game. We know that whatever state we start the system in, we will end up in either state *llll* or state *rrrr*. For state *abcd*, let P[*abcd*] be the probability that we end up in *llll* starting from *abcd*. Clearly, P[*llll*] = 1 and P[*rrrr*] = 0. Moreover, P[*lllr*] = P[*llrl*]/2 + P[*lrrl*]/2, since *lllr* moves to either *llrl* or to *lrrl* with equal probability. Generalizing, you can check that, if we define

$$v = (\text{P}[llll], \text{P}[lllr], \ldots, \text{P}[rrrr])',$$

the column vector of probabilities of being absorbed in state *llll*, then we have

$$Mv = v.$$

If we solve this equation for v, subject to $v[1] = 1$, we get

$$v = (1, 2/3, 5/6, 1/2, 1/3, 1/2, 1/6, 2/3, 1/3, 0)',$$

which then must be the first column of M^*. The rest of the columns are zero, except for the last, which must have entries so the rows each sum up to unity. By the way, I wouldn't try to solve the equation $Mv = v$ by hand unless you're a masochist. I let Mathematica do it (v is called an *eigenvector* of M, so Mathematica has a special routine for finding v easily).

10.5   Adaptive Learning When Not All Conventions Are Equal

Now consider the pure coordination game illustrated in §10.3, where the *ll* convention Pareto-dominates the *rr* convention. How does adaptive learning work in such an environment? We again assume each player finds a best response to the history of the other player's previous two moves. The best response to *ll* and *rr* are still *l* and *r*, respectively, but now the best response to *rl* or *lr* is also *l*. Now, for instance, *lllr* and *lrlr* both go to *llll* with probability 1. The probability transition matrix now becomes as shown.

$$M = \begin{pmatrix}
1 & 0 & 0 & 0 & 0 & 0 & 0 & 0 & 0 & 0 \\
0 & 0 & 1 & 0 & 0 & 0 & 0 & 0 & 0 & 0 \\
1 & 0 & 0 & 0 & 0 & 0 & 0 & 0 & 0 & 0 \\
0 & 0 & 0 & 0 & 0 & 1 & 0 & 0 & 0 & 0 \\
0 & 0 & 0 & 0 & 0 & 0 & 0 & 1 & 0 & 0 \\
0 & 0 & 1 & 0 & 0 & 0 & 0 & 0 & 0 & 0 \\
0 & 0 & 0 & 0 & 0 & 0 & 0 & 0 & 1 & 0 \\
1 & 0 & 0 & 0 & 0 & 0 & 0 & 0 & 0 & 0 \\
0 & 0 & 0 & 0 & 0 & 1 & 0 & 0 & 0 & 0 \\
0 & 0 & 0 & 0 & 0 & 0 & 0 & 0 & 0 & 1
\end{pmatrix}$$

To calculate

$$M^* = \lim_{k \to \infty} M^k$$

is relatively simple, since in this case $M^k = M^4$ for $k \geq 4$. Thus, we have

$$M = \begin{pmatrix}
1 & 0 & 0 & 0 & 0 & 0 & 0 & 0 & 0 & 0 \\
1 & 0 & 0 & 0 & 0 & 0 & 0 & 0 & 0 & 0 \\
1 & 0 & 0 & 0 & 0 & 0 & 0 & 0 & 0 & 0 \\
1 & 0 & 0 & 0 & 0 & 0 & 0 & 0 & 0 & 0 \\
1 & 0 & 0 & 0 & 0 & 0 & 0 & 0 & 0 & 0 \\
1 & 0 & 0 & 0 & 0 & 0 & 0 & 0 & 0 & 0 \\
1 & 0 & 0 & 0 & 0 & 0 & 0 & 0 & 0 & 0 \\
1 & 0 & 0 & 0 & 0 & 0 & 0 & 0 & 0 & 0 \\
1 & 0 & 0 & 0 & 0 & 0 & 0 & 0 & 0 & 0 \\
0 & 0 & 0 & 0 & 0 & 0 & 0 & 0 & 0 & 1
\end{pmatrix}.$$

In other words, if you start in state *rrrr*, you stay there; otherwise, after four steps you arrive at *llll* and remain there forever. We conclude that *with adaptive learning, if the system starts in a nonconventional state, it always ends up in the Pareto-efficient conventional state.*

10.6 Adaptive Learning with Errors

We now investigate the effect on a dynamic adaptive learning system when players are subject to error. Consider the pure coordination game illustrated in §10.3, but where the payoffs to *ll* and *rr* are equal. Suppose each player finds a best response to the history of the other player's previous two moves with probability $1 - \epsilon$, but chooses incorrectly with probability $\epsilon > 0$. The probability transition matrix now becomes

$$
M = \begin{pmatrix}
a & 2b & 0 & 0 & e & 0 & 0 & 0 & 0 & 0 \\
0 & 0 & c & d & 0 & c & d & 0 & 0 & 0 \\
c & 1/2 & 0 & 0 & d & 0 & 0 & 0 & 0 & 0 \\
0 & 0 & b & e & 0 & a & b & 0 & 0 & 0 \\
0 & 0 & 0 & 0 & 0 & a & 0 & 1/4 & 1/2 & 1/4 \\
0 & 0 & 1/4 & 1/4 & 0 & 1/4 & 1/4 & 0 & 0 & 0 \\
0 & 0 & 0 & 0 & 0 & 0 & 0 & d & 1/2 & c \\
1/4 & 1/2 & 0 & 0 & 1/4 & 0 & 0 & 0 & 0 & 0 \\
0 & 0 & d & d & 0 & c & c & 0 & 0 & 0 \\
0 & 0 & 0 & 0 & 0 & 0 & 0 & e & 2b & a
\end{pmatrix},
$$

where $a = (1 - \epsilon)^2$, $b = \epsilon(1 - \epsilon)$, $c = (1 - \epsilon)/2$, $d = \epsilon/2$, and $e = \epsilon^2$. Note that now *there are no absorbing states*. To see what happens in the long run, suppose $\epsilon = 0.01$, so errors occur one percent of the time. Using Mathematica to calculate M^*, we find *all the rows are the same*, and each row has the entries

(0.442 0.018 0.018 0.001 0.0002 0.035 0.018 0.0002 0.018 0.442)

In other words, you spend about 88.4% of the time in one of the conventional states, and about 11.6% of the time in the other states.

It should be intuitively obvious how the system behaves. If the system is in a conventional state, say *llll*, it remains there in the next period with probability $(1 - \epsilon)^2 = 98\%$. If one player makes an error, the state moves to *lllr*. If there are no more errors for a while, we know it will return to *llll* eventually. Thus, it requires multiple errors to "kick" the system to a new convention. For instance, $llll \rightarrow lllr \rightarrow lrrr \rightarrow rrrr$ can occur with just two errors: $llll \rightarrow lllr$ with one error, $lllr \rightarrow lrrr$ with one error, and $lrrr \rightarrow rrrr$ with no errors, but probability 1/2. We thus expect convention flips about every two hundred plays of the game.

To test our 'informed intuition,' I simulated one thousand repetitions of this stochastic dynamical system using Mathematica. Fig. 10.1 reports on the result.

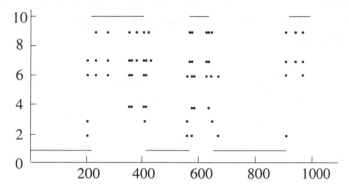

Figure 10.1. Simulating adaptive learning with errors.

10.7 Stochastic Stability

We define a state in a stochastic dynamical system to be *stochastically stable* if the long-run probability of being in that state does not become zero or vanishingly small as the rate of error ϵ goes to zero. Clearly, in the previous example $llll$ and $rrrr$ are both stochastically stable and no other state is. Consider the game in §10.3. It would be nice if the Pareto-dominant equilibrium ll were stochastically stable, and no other state were stochastically stable. We shall see that is the case. Now the probability transition matrix becomes

$$M = \begin{pmatrix} a & 2b & 0 & 0 & e & 0 & 0 & 0 & 0 & 0 \\ 0 & 2b & a & 0 & e & 0 & 0 & 0 & 0 & 0 \\ a & 2b & 0 & 0 & e & 0 & 0 & 0 & 0 & 0 \\ 0 & 0 & b & e & 0 & a & b & 0 & 0 & 0 \\ 0 & 0 & 0 & 0 & 0 & 0 & 0 & b & a & b \\ 0 & 0 & a & b & 0 & b & e & 0 & 0 & 0 \\ 0 & 0 & 0 & 0 & 0 & 0 & 0 & b & a & b \\ a & 2b & 0 & 0 & e & 0 & 0 & 0 & 0 & 0 \\ 0 & 0 & b & e & 0 & a & b & 0 & 0 & 0 \\ 0 & 0 & 0 & 0 & 0 & 0 & 0 & e & 2b & a \end{pmatrix},$$

where $a = (1-\epsilon)^2$, $b = \epsilon(1-\epsilon)$, and $e = \epsilon^2$. Again there are no absorbing states. If $\epsilon = 0.01$, we calculate M^*, again finding that we find *all the rows are the same*, and each row has the entries

$$(0.9605 \quad 0.0198 \quad 0.0198 \quad 0 \quad 0 \quad 0 \quad 0 \quad 0 \quad 0 \quad 0).$$

In other words, the system spends 96% of the time in the Pareto-dominant conventional states and virtually all of the remaining time in "nearby states." It is clear (though it should be formally proved) that *ll* is the only stochastically stable state.

11

Homo reciprocans, *Homo egualis*, and Other Contributors to the Human Behavioral Repertoire

> The Americans . . . are fond of explaining almost all the actions of their lives by the principle of self-interest rightly understood. . . . In this respect I think they frequently fail to do themselves justice.
> *Alexis de Tocqueville*

> My motive for doing what I am going to do is simply personal revenge. I do not expect to accomplish anything by it. . . . Of course, I would like to get revenge on the whole scientific and bureaucratic establishment . . . but that being impossible, I have to content myself with just a little revenge.
> *Theodore Kaczynski (the Unabomber)*

11.1   Introduction

This chapter is probably the most important in the book in terms of the contribution of game theory to our understanding of what is specifically human about human sociality. It also represents an area of quite active contemporary research. While this material will be attractive to students, it presents a problem for instructors who, in all likelihood, have neither studied nor taught in this area. For this reason, I have presented the novel material at a more leisurely pace than the material in other chapters, and have supplied more descriptive details and a greater number of references to the literature. The first time one teaches this material, class presentations and discussions may be preferable to a formal lecture format.

This chapter has three main points. First, in many decision-making and strategic settings people do not behave like the self-interested "rational" actor depicted in neoclassical economics and classical game theory. Second, despite its increased complexity in comparison with traditional *Homo economicus*, human behavior can be modeled using game theory and optimization subject to constraints. Third, there are plausible models of human cultural and genetic evolution that explain how we have gotten to be the way we are. Our analytical and evolutionary models, however, leave considerable room for improvement, and we are presently on the steep portion of the learning curve in developing analytical models of human behavior.

We begin with an overview of the experimental method and its results, including methodological discussions concerning the interpretation of experimental results (§3.15) and the meaning of "rationality" (§11.2.2). While it is easy to discuss such topics in excess, I have found some class time devoted to these issues to be amply rewarded.

Section §11.3, Behavioral Economics: Games against Nature and against Ourselves, presents the results of some thirty years of brilliant research by Daniel Kahneman, Amos Tversky, and their associates into individual decision-making processes. This material is important for the microeconomics of individual choice but does not appear in our models of strategic interaction, so it can be relegated to assigned reading if the instructor is pressed for time. Section §11.4, subtitled The Laboratory Meets Strategic Interaction, is an overview of the basic empirical studies of social interaction upon which our analytical models are based and is worthy of careful study and discussion.

The next two sections represent attempts to model some of the experimental results. In *Homo egualis* (§11.5) we show that if individuals have inequality aversion, we can explain some experimental results, including why altruism appears in ultimatum and public goods games but not in marketlike interactions. In *Homo reciprocans:* Modeling Strong Reciprocity (§11.6) we model some of the experimental results that depend on the tendency of people to cooperate and punish as forms of prosocial behavior.

Economists are fond of explaining a complex social division of labor involving cooperation among individuals with low biological relatedness using models of complete contracting (neoclassical economics) or repeated games (classical game theory). Of course *reciprocal altruism* (Trivers 1971), which is self-interested cooperation using trigger strategies and reputation-building in a repeated game (§6.10, and chapter 6 in general) is important in humans, probably occurs a bit among primates (Byrne and Whiten 1988), and perhaps in a few other species (Pusey and Packer 1997). But as we suggest below, it is not plausible to model human sociality based on self-interested behavior alone.

This leads us to evolutionary models of non-*Homo economicus* behavior. Economists often argue that only self-interested behavior is evolutionarily viable. Yet living organisms routinely sacrifice resources that could be used for self-preservation for the sake of producing, nurturing, and protecting offspring(Daly and Wilson 1983). Self-interested agents are therefore rare mutants with low fitness and no evolutionary future. Perhaps then economists take "self-interest" to mean "family interest." Using William Hamilton's principle of *kin selection* we can indeed explain much of the apparent altruism in most species (Wilson 1975, Grafen 1984, Krebs and Davies 1993). But not so in humans.

In Altruism and Assortative Interactions (§11.7) we sketch an approach to the study of altruism that has proven illuminating and draws on standard notions from game theory and population biology. This approach is based on *Price's equation*, which, while intimately related to the replicator equation, is not yet widely known to economists. In The Evolution of Strong Reciprocity (§11.8) we apply Price's equation to a game-theoretic model explaining the evolutionary emergence of *Homo reciprocans*.

In *Homo parochius:* Modeling Insider/Outsider Relations (§11.9) we close with a model of the evolutionary emergence of ethnic and other preferences in which agents act in a distinctive prosocial manner with respect to "insiders" and correspondingly antisocial behavior toward "outsiders."

I have included few exercises in this chapter, in the belief that the material is new and exploratory and the student would do better to delve into some of the source material rather than solve problems. The instructor might assign additional readings from the references and ask students to write short papers based on such readings.

11.2   Modeling the Human Actor

When the same object of knowledge is modeled in different ways, the models should agree where they overlap—as, for example, in the smooth transitions from physics to chemistry to biology. This principle has been routinely violated in the social sciences, which maintain mutually incompatible theories across various disciplines. Economists hold that individuals are self-interested and maximize utility subject to constraints. Sociologists hold that individuals conform to societal norms. Social psychologists hold that individuals identify with groups and further their interests. Animal behaviorists derive behavior from the morphology and evolutionary history of a species. Correspondingly incongruous models are affirmed by anthropologists, psychologists, and political scientists.

This is a great scandal, and game theory is an important tool for moving beyond it.[1]

Game theory is a general lexicon that applies to the behavior of life forms, providing the tools for carefully modeling the conditions of social interaction, the characteristics of players, the rules of the game, the informational structure, and the payoffs associated with particular strategic interactions. This fosters a unified behavioral theory and also allows *experimental game theory* to use the same language and techniques, whether in biology, anthropology, social psychology, or economics. Since game-theoretic predictions can be systematically tested, the results can be replicated by different laboratories (Plott 1979, V. Smith 1982, Sally, 1995).

While many of the predictions of neoclassical economic theory (§3.19) have been verified experimentally, many others have been decisively disconfirmed. What distinguishes success from failure?

- When modeling market processes with well specified contracts, such as double continuous auctions (supply and demand) and oligopoly, game-theoretic predictions are verified under a wide variety of social settings (Davis and Holt 1993, Kachelmaier and Shehata 1992).[2]

- Where contracts are incomplete and agents can engage in strategic interaction, with the power to reward and punish the behavior of other players, the neoclassical predictions generally fail (§11.4).

In other words, *precisely* where standard neoclassical models do well *without* the intellectual baggage of game theory, game theory predicts well, but where game theory has something really *new* to offer, its predictions fail.

The culprit is the representation of the human actor—the so-called *rational actor model*—adopted by game theory. We will call this the *Homo economicus* model, because there is nothing particularly "rational" (or "irrational") about it. Neoclassical economics has accepted this model because when faced with market conditions—anonymous, nonstrategic interactions—people behave like self-interested, outcome-oriented actors

[1] Edward O. Wilson has mounted a powerful contemporary plea for the unity of the sciences. Wilson maintains that physics is the basis for such unity. However, since physics has no concept of strategic interaction, a concept central to all life forms, game theory is a more plausible unifying force for the behavioral sciences.

[2] Even here experimental economics sheds much new light, particularly in dealing with price dynamics and their relationship to buyer and seller expectations (Smith and Williams 1992).

(although probably not time consistent). In other settings, especially in the area of strategic interactions, people behave quite differently.

11.2.1   Interpreting the Results of Experimental Game Theory

When the results of experiments contradict received wisdom in economics, many economists reject the experiments rather than the received wisdom. For instance, in the ultimatum game (§11.4.1), individuals offered a small share of the pie frequently choose a zero payoff when a positive payoff is available. Critics claim that subjects have not learned how to play the game and are confused by the unreality of the experimental conditions, so their behavior does not reflect real life. Moreover, whatever experimentalists do to improve laboratory protocols (e.g., remove cues and decontextualize situations), the critics deem as insufficient, and the experimentalists complain among themselves that the critics are simply dogmatic enemies of the "scientific method."

To move beyond this impasse we must recognize that the critics are correct in sensing some fundamental difference between experiments in social interaction and the traditional experimental method in natural science, and that experimental results must be interpreted more subtly than is usually done. The upshot is, however, an even stronger vindication of the experimental method and an even deeper challenge to the received wisdom.

Laboratory experiments are a means of controlling the social environment so that experiments can be replicated and the results from different experiments can be compared. In physics and chemistry, the experimental method has the additional goal of *eliminating all influences on the behavior of the object of study except those controlled by the experimenter.* This goal can be achieved because elementary particles, and even chemical compounds, are completely interchangeable, given a few easily measurable characteristics (atomic number, energy, spin, chemical composition, and the like). Experiments in human social interaction, however, *cannot* achieve this goal, even in principle, because experimental subjects bring their personal history with them into the laboratory. Their behavior is therefore *ineluctably* an interaction between the subject's personal history and the experimenter's controlled laboratory conditions.

This observation is intimately related to the basic structure of evolutionary game theory (as well as human psychology, as stressed by Loewenstein 1999). As we have seen (§5.17), in strategic interaction nature abhors low probability events, and for an experimental subject, *the experiment is precisely a low probability event!* Neither personal history nor general cultural/genetic evolutionary history has prepared subjects for the Ultimatum, Dictator, Common Pool Resource, and other games that they are asked to confront. As we have suggested in §5.17, an agent treats a low probability event as a high probability event by assigning a novel situation to one of a small number of pre-given *situational contexts*, and then deploying the behavioral repertoire—payoffs, probabilities, and actions—appropriate to that context. We may call this *choosing a frame* for interpreting the experimental situation. This is how subjects bring their history to an experiment.[3]

The results of the ultimatum game (§11.4.1), for instance, suggest that in a two-person bargaining situation, in the absence of other cues, the situational context applied by most subjects dictates some form of "sharing." Suppose we change the rules such that both proposer and respondent are members of different *teams* and each is told that their respective winning will be paid to the team rather than the individual. A distinct situational context, involving "winning," is now often deemed appropriate, dictating acting on behalf of one's team and suppressing behaviors that would be otherwise individually satisfying—such as "sharing." In this case, proposers offer much less, and respondents very rarely reject positive offers (Shogren 1989). Similarly, if the experimenters introduce notions of property rights into the strategic situation (e.g., that the proposer in an ultimatum game has "earned" or "won" the right to this position), then motivations concerning "fairness" are considerably attenuated in the experimental results (Hoffman, McCabe, Shachat, and Smith 1994, Hoffman, McCabe, and Smith 1996).

In short, laboratory experiments (a) elucidate how subjects identify situational contexts, and then (b) describe how agents react to the formal parameters and material payoffs, subject to the situational contexts they have identified.

---

[3]For a similar view, see Hoffman, McCabe, and Smith (1996). A caveat: It is incorrect to think that the subjects are "irrational" or "confused" because they drag their history into an experimental situation. In fact, they are acting normally on the basis of the preferences they exhibit in daily life. Of course, if this low probability event (being a subject in an experiment) turns into a high probability event (e.g., by being repeatedly asked to be a subject), agents may change their framing or even create a wholly new situational context for the purpose at hand. The process is not well understood.

11.2.2 Self-Interest and Rationality

The culture surrounding economics as a discipline fosters the belief that rationality implies self-interest, outcome-orientation, and time-consistency.[4] No such implication can be supported. A *rational agent* draws conclusions logically from given premises, has premises that are defensible by reasoned argument, and uses evidence dispassionately in evaluating factual assertions. This is reflected in economic theory by a rational agent having transitive preferences and maximizing an appropriate objective function over an appropriate choice set (§11.3.2). Since rationality does not presuppose unlimited informational processing capacities and perfect knowledge, even Herbert Simon's (1982) concept of *bounded rationality* is consistent with a fully rational agent.[5]

I have never seen a serious argument supporting the assertion that rationality in either the everyday sense, or in the narrower sense of optimizing subject to constraints, implies self-interest, outcome-orientation, or time-consistency. Perhaps Milton Friedman's (1953) suggestion that assumptions are justified by the conclusions they support is the most worthy of notice. But since the *Homo economicus* model does not predict well outside of impersonal market situations, his argument is no help here. The most common "informal" argument is reminiscent of Louis XIV's après moi le déluge defense of the monarchy: drop these assumptions and we lose the ability to predict altogether. The models developed recently in the professional literature, some of which are presented below, show that we have little to fear from the Flood.

In neither the everyday nor the narrower economic sense of the term does rationality imply self-interest. It is just as "rational" for me to prefer to have *you* enjoy a fine meal as for me to enjoy the meal myself. It is just as "rational" for me to care about the rain forests as to care about my beautiful cashmere sweater. And it is just as "rational" to reject an unfair offer as it is to discard an ugly article of clothing.

Evolutionary game theory treats agents' objectives as a matter of fact, not logic, with a presumption that these objectives must be compatible with

---

[4]I use the term "self-interested" to mean *self-regarding*. Self-regarding agents evaluate alternative states of the world by considering only their impact on themselves, narrowly construed.

[5]Indeed, it can be shown (Zambrano 1997) that every boundedly rational agent is a fully rational agent subject to an appropriate set of Bayesian priors concerning the state of nature.

an appropriate evolutionary dynamic. We can just as well build models of regret, altruism, vindictiveness, status-seeking, and addiction as of choosing a bundle of consumption goods subject to a budget constraint (Gintis 1972a, 1972b, 1974, 1975, Bowles and Gintis 1993b, Becker and Murphy 1988, Becker 1996, Becker and Mulligan 1997). As suggested below, evolutionary models do not predict self-interested behavior.

Far from being the norm, people who are self-interested are in common parlance called *sociopaths*. A sociopath treats others instrumentally, either without regard for their feelings (e.g., a sexual predator, a cannibal, or a professional killer), or evaluates the feelings of others only according to their effect on the sociopath (e.g., a sadist or a bully). A neoclassical economist may respond that the postulate of self-interest applies only to the market phenomena that economists normally study—even Adam Smith, the architect of the *invisible hand*, was also the author of the Theory of Moral Sentiments, according to which the principle of *sympathy* guides the social relations among people. But social interactions, even in economics, are not restricted to impersonal market contexts. Moreover, by deploying the appropriate game-theoretic models (§11.5), we shall see that we can predict when non-self-interested agents will behave in a self-interested manner. We need not assume self-interest from the outset.

11.3   Behavioral Economics: Games against Nature and against Ourselves

Problems with the *Homo economicus* model arise even prior to strategic interactions among multiple agents, with *games against Nature* and *games against ourselves*.[6] A "game against nature" involves a single agent choosing under conditions of uncertainty, where none of the uncertainty is strategic—that is, either the uncertainty is due to natural acts (crop loss, death, and the like) or, if other people are involved, the others do not behave strategically toward the agent being modeled. A "game against oneself" is a choice

---

[6]For pedagogical reasons I am giving this experimental material the benefit of the doubt. Many of the situations subjects face in behavioral experiments are precisely the "zero probability events" for which we expect individuals to be evolutionarily unprepared. Thus, as Ken Binmore (1999) stresses, we cannot presume that because human subjects do not find the optima in complex decision problems in the laboratory, they are incapable of finding the optima in the everyday-life situations that use the same analytical principles. Indeed, under appropriate conditions we would expect roughly optimal solutions to replicate and diffuse in a population without individuals ever having to "solve" the underlying problems.

situation in which an agent optimizes over time, but cannot automatically precommit to carrying out in the future the plans being made in the present. Experimental evidence supports the following generalizations concerning such games:

- People appear to have higher discount rates over payoffs in the near future than in the distant future. It follows that people often favor short term gains that entail long term losses. We often term this "impulsivity" or "weakness of will." Technically this is called *hyperbolic discounting*.
- People often have inconsistent preferences over lotteries and do not know and cannot apply the laws of probability consistently without extensive formal training. Rather, people use informal heuristics and socially acquired rules to choose among risky alternatives.
- The *Homo economicus* model assumes that people react to the absolute level of payoffs, whereas in fact they tend to privilege the status quo (their current position) and are sensitive to changes from the status quo. In particular, people tend to exhibit *loss aversion*, making them risk-loving over losses and risk-averse over gains at the same time (§16.41).

11.3.1   Time Inconsistency and Hyperbolic Discounting

"Time consistency" means that the future actions required to maximize the current present value of utility remain optimal in the periods when the actions are to be taken.[7] The central theorem on choice over time is that time consistency requires that utility be additive and independent across time periods, with future utilities discounted to the present at a fixed rate (Strotz

---

[7]I do not know why it is considered "rational" to be time consistent. There are no plausible models within which time consistency has optimal welfare-enhancing properties. In a strategic setting, time consistency can entail lower payoffs. For instance, if I cannot control my temper (getting angry today has a higher value than paying the costs tomorrow), and you know this, you may give me my way, whereas if I were time consistent, you would know that I won't actually blow a fuse.

Of course, if you are not time consistent, and if you know this fact, you will not commit yourself to future choices that you know you will not make, or you will precommit yourself to making certain future choices, even at a cost. For instance, if you are saving in year 1 for a purchase in year 3, but you know you will be tempted to spend the money in year 2, you can put it in a bank account that cannot be accessed until the year after next. My former teacher Leo Hurwicz called this the "piggy bank effect."

1955).[8] Are people time consistent? Take, for instance, impulsive behavior. Economists are wont to argue that what appears to be "impulsive"—cigarette smoking, drug use, unsafe sex, overeating, dropping out of school, punching out your boss, and the like—may in fact be welfare-maximizing for people who have high time discount rates or who prefer acts with high future costs. Controlled experiments in the laboratory cast doubt on this explanation, indicating that people exhibit a systematic tendency to discount the near future at a higher rate than the distant future (Chung and Herrnstein 1967, Loewenstein and Prelec 1992, Herrnstein and Prelec 1992, Fehr and Zych 1994, Kirby and Herrnstein 1995). In fact, observed intertemporal choice appears to fit the model of *hyperbolic discounting* (Ainslie and Haslam 1992, Ainslie 1975, Laibson 1997), first observed by Richard Herrnstein in studying animal behavior (Laibson and Rachlin 1997). In addition, agents have different rates of discount for different types of outcomes (Loewenstein 1987, Loewenstein and Sicherman 1991).

We should not ask why these anomalies occur, because there is no reason to expect time consistency in human behavior in the first place. Since humans appear to share hyperbolic discounting with other species, there is probably an evolutionary explanation for the phenomenon. Impulsiveness may reduce fitness and personal welfare under contemporary environmental circumstances, but it may have contributed to success, or at least imposed little harm, in the conditions under which *Homo sapiens* evolved (Cosmides and Tooby 1992b).

Neurological research suggests that that balancing current and future payoffs involves adjudication among structurally distinct and spatially separated modules that arose in different stages in the evolution of *Homo sapiens*. Long term decision-making capacity is localized in specific neural structures in the prefrontal lobes and functions improperly when these areas are damaged, despite the fact that subjects with such damage appear to be otherwise completely normal in brain functioning (Damasio 1994). *Homo sapiens* may be structurally predisposed, in terms of brain architecture, toward a systematic present-orientation.

---

[8]Actually, as Lones Smith has pointed out (personal communication), this result assumes that discounting at time t of consumption that occurs at time $s > t$ depends only on the horizon length $s - t$. In general, time consistency does not imply either additivity or a constant discount rate. For instance, aging implies that the probability of death increases with time, so people should apply higher discount rates to the future than to the present (comedian George Burns once exclaimed, when in his nineties, that he never buys green bananas). This behavior does not necessarily imply time inconsistency.

11.3.2   *Choice under Uncertainty*

The centerpiece of the theory of choice under uncertainty is the *expected utility principle*, which says that "rational" agents choose among lotteries to maximize the expected utility of the payoffs (§3.14, Kreps 1988). Von Neumann and Morgenstern (1944), Friedman and Savage (1948), Savage (1954), and Anscombe and Aumann (1963) showed that the expected utility principle can be derived from the assumption that agents have consistent preferences over an appropriate set of lotteries. By "consistency" we mean *transitivity* and *independence from irrelevant alternatives*, plus some plausible technical conditions. We say preferences are *transitive* if, whenever A is preferred to B, and B is preferred to C, then A is preferred to C.

Why should agents have transitive preferences? An agent who optimizes subject to constraints will certainly have transitive preferences. But the expected utility principle models agents *as if* they were optimizing, when in fact they are *not*, just as we model expert billiards players by assuming that they solve certain systems of differential equations, which of course they do not. If choices are easily reversed, one could fool a nontransitive agent with the "money pump": sell him A, then induce him to pay for B, which he prefers to A, then induce him him to pay for C, which he prefers to B, then induce him to pay for A again. Such an agent fits any plausible definition of "irrational." But lots of choices are *not* reversible, so it is not obviously irrational to be intransitive over such choices.[9]

Independence from irrelevant alternatives is some variation of the following (the particulars depend on the model): suppose two lotteries l_1 and l_2 have the same outcomes with the same probabilities, except for one particular outcome, where the l_1 outcome is preferred to the l_2 outcome. Then lottery l_1 is preferred to lottery l_2. Another version of this is Leonard Savage's *sure-thing principle*, which states that if you prefer l_1 to l_2 when state of the world A occurs, and you also prefer l_1 to l_2 when A does *not* occur, then you prefer l_1 to l_2.[10]

Laboratory testing of the *Homo economicus* model of choice under uncertainty was initiated by the psychologists Daniel Kahneman and Amos

---

[9]One plausible theory of intransitivity with some empirical support is *regret theory* (Loomes 1988, Sugden 1993).

[10]It is plausible that a rational agent would subscribe to the sure-thing principle. However, people systematically violate the principle because they do not reason well logically over disjunctions without extensive training (Shafir and Tversky 1992, Tversky and Shafir 1992, Shafir 1994).

Tversky. In a famous article in the journal *Science*, Tversky and Kahneman (1974) summarized their early research as follows:

> How do people assess the probability of an uncertain event or the value of an uncertain quantity? . . . people rely on a limited number of heuristic principles which reduce the complex tasks of assessing probabilities and predicting values to simpler judgmental operations. In general, these heuristics are quite useful, but sometimes they lead to severe and systematic errors.

Subsequent research has strongly supported this assessment (Kahneman, Slovic, and Tversky 1982, Shafir and Tversky 1992, Shafir and Tversky 1995). Although we still do not have adequate models of these heuristics, we do know the following:

a. In judging whether an event or object A belongs to a class or process B, one heuristic that people use is to consider whether A is *representative* of B but to consider no other relevant facts, such as the frequency of B. For instance, if informed that an individual has a good sense of humor and likes to entertain friends and family, and asked if the individual is a professional comic or a clerical worker, people are more likely to say the former. This is despite the fact that a randomly chosen person is much more likely to be a clerical worker than a professional comic, and many people have a good sense of humor, so there are many more clerical workers satisfying the description than professional comics.

b. A second heuristic is that in assessing the frequency of an event, people take excessive account of information that is easily *available* or highly *salient*, even though a selective bias is obviously involved. For this reason, people tend to overestimate the probability of rare events, since such events are highly newsworthy while nonoccurrences are not reported.

c. A third heuristic in problem solving is to start from an initial guess, chosen for its representativeness or salience, and adjust upward or downward toward a final figure. This is called *anchoring* because there is a tendency to underadjust, so the result is too close to the initial guess.

d. Probably as a result of anchoring, people tend to overestimate the probability of conjunctions (p and q) and underestimate the probability of disjunctions (p or q). For an instance of the former, a person who knows an event occurs with 95% probability will overestimate the probability that the event occurs ten times in a row. The actual probability is about 60%. In this case the individual starts with 95% and does not adjust downward sufficiently. Similarly, if a daily event has a failure one time in a thousand, people will underestimate the probability that a failure occurs at least once in a year. The actual probability is 30.5%. Again, the individual starts with 0.1% and doesn't adjust upward enough.

e. People prefer objective probability distributions to subjective distributions derived from applying probabilistic principles, such as the Principle of Insufficient Reason (§16.28.1), which says that if you are completely ignorant as to which of several outcomes will occur, you should treat them as equally probable. For example, if you give a subject a prize for drawing a red ball from an urn containing red and white balls, the subject will pay to have the urn contain 50% red balls rather than contain an indeterminate percentage of red balls.

Choice theorists often express dismay over the failure of people to apply the laws of probability and conform to the axioms of choice theory. This is a strange reaction. People are doubtless applying rules that serve them well in daily life. It takes many years of study to feel at home with the laws of probability, the understanding of which is the product of the last couple of hundred years of scientific research. Moreover, it is costly, in terms of time and effort, to apply these laws even if we know them. Of course, if the stakes are high enough, it is worthwhile to go to the effort, or engage an expert who will do it for you. But generally, as Kahneman and Tversky suggest, we apply a set of heuristics that more or less get the job done. Among the most prominent heuristics is simply *imitation:* decide what class of phenomenon is involved, find out what people "normally do" in that situation, and do it. If there is some mechanism leading to the survival and growth of relatively successful behaviors (see chapter 9), and if the problem in question recurs with sufficient regularity, the choice-theoretic solution will describe the winner of a dynamic social process of trial, error, and imitation.

Should we expect people to conform to the axioms of choice theory—transitivity, independence from irrelevant alternatives, the sure-thing principle, and the like? Where we know that agents are really optimizing, and have expertise in decision theory, we doubtless should. But this only applies to a highly restricted range of human actions. In more general settings we should not. We might have recourse to Darwinian analysis, demonstrating that under the appropriate conditions agents who are genetically constituted to obey the axioms of choice theory will be better fit to solve general decision-theoretic problems, and hence will emerge triumphant through an evolutionary dynamic. But human beings did not evolve facing general decision-theoretic problems, but rather a few specific decision-theoretic problems associated with survival in small social groups. We may have to settle for modeling these specific choice contexts to discover how our genetic constitution and cultural tools interact in determining choice under uncertainty.

11.3.3   Loss Aversion and Status Quo Bias

It appears that people value gains and losses not according to their absolute levels, but rather according to their deviation from their current position (Helson 1964). The most venerable expression of this principle is the *Weber-Fechner Law* that initiated the science of psychophysics. According to this law, a just-noticeable change in a stimulus is a fixed ratio of the level of the stimulus. The assumption that utility functions are concave, and hence individuals are risk-averse, is of course based on similar reasoning, as is the notion that individuals "adjust" to an accustomed level of income (§16.41), so that subjective well-being is associated more with *changes* in income rather than with the *level* of income.   See, for instance Easterlin (1974, 1995), Lane (1991, 1993), and Oswald (1997).

Experimental evidence supports an even stronger assertion: *people are about twice as averse to taking losses as to enjoying an equal level of gains* (Kahneman, Knetch, and Thaler 1990, Tversky and Kahneman 1981b). This means, for instance, that an individual may attach zero value to a lottery that offers an equal chance of winning $1000 and losing $500. This also implies people are *risk-loving over losses*, while they remain risk-averse over gains. For instance, many individuals will choose a 25% probability of losing $2000 rather than a 50% chance of losing $1000 (both have the same expected value, of course, but the former is riskier).

One implication of loss aversion is the *endowment effect* (Kahneman, Knetch, and Thaler 1991), according to which people place a higher value on what they possess than they place on the same things when they do not possess them. For instance, if you win a bottle of wine that you could sell for $200, you may drink it rather than sell it, but you would never think of buying even a $100 bottle of wine. Not only does the endowment effect exist, but there is evidence that people underestimate it and hence cannot rationally correct for it in their choice behavior (Loewenstein and Adler 1995).

Another implication is the existence of a *framing effect*, whereby one form of a lottery is strictly preferred to another, even though they have the same payoffs with the same probabilities (Tversky and Kahneman 1981a). For instance, people prefer a price of $10 plus a $1 discount to a price of $8 plus a $1 surcharge. Framing is of course closely associated with the endowment effect, since framing usually involves privileging the initial state from which movements are assessed.

Yet another implication is a *status quo bias*, according to which people often prefer the status quo over any of the alternatives, but if one of the alternatives becomes the status quo, that too is preferred to any of the alternatives (Kahneman, Knetch, and Thaler 1991). The status quo makes sense if we recognize that any change can involve a loss, and since on the average gains do not offset losses, it is possible that any one of a number of alternatives might be preferred if it is the status quo.

11.4   Experimental Game Theory: The Laboratory Meets Strategic Interaction

Many of the anomalies in testing game-theoretic predictions of strategic interaction flow from two observations:

- The *Homo economicus* model assumes preferences are *self-regarding* and *outcome-regarding*, whereas preferences are also *other-regarding* and *process-regarding*.   In particular, people care about fairness (§11.5), reciprocity (§11.6), and group membership (§11.9).
- The *Homo economicus* model assumes preferences are *exogenous:* they are determined outside of, and substantially unaffected by, the structure of strategic interaction or any other substantive aspect of the economy.   However, preferences are partly *endogenous*, depending both on the agent's personal history and the nature of the strategic interaction in which the agent is engaged. In particular, by *choosing a frame* (§11.2.1), an agent chooses to act according to a particular pattern of subjective payoffs.

As a basis for interpreting a broad range of experiments, I will introduce several new *personas*, the most novel of whom I call *Homo reciprocans*. *Homo reciprocans'* behavior in market situations, in which punishing and rewarding are impossible or excessively costly, is much like that of *Homo economicus*. But *Homo reciprocans* comes to strategic interactions with a propensity to cooperate, responds to cooperative behavior by maintaining or increasing his level of cooperation, and responds to noncooperative behavior by retaliating against the "offenders," even at a cost to himself, and even when he could not reasonably expect future personal gains to flow from such retaliation. When other forms of punishment are not available, *Homo reciprocans* responds to defection with defection, leading to a downward spiral of noncooperation. *Homo reciprocans* is thus neither the selfless altruist of utopian theory, nor the selfish hedonist of neoclassical economics. Rather, he is a conditional cooperator whose penchant for reciprocity can be elicited under circumstances in which personal self-interest would dictate otherwise.[11] A second, probably more familiar, persona is *Homo egualis*, who cares not only about his own payoff, but also about how it compares with the payoff of others. *Homo egualis* may be willing to reduce his own payoff to increase the degree of equality in the group (whence widespread support for charity and social welfare programs). But he is especially displeased when subjected to *relative deprivation*, by being placed on the losing end of an unequal relationship. Indeed, *Homo egualis* may be willing to reduce his own payoff if that reduces the payoff of relatively favored players even more (Loewenstein, Thompson, and Bazerman 1989).

A third and also quite familiar persona is *Homo parochius*, who divides the world into *insiders* and *outsiders* according to context-dependent and even apparently arbitrary characteristics, values insiders' welfare more highly than that of outsiders, evaluates insiders' personal qualities more highly than that of outsiders, and partially suppresses personal goals in favor of the goals of the group of insiders. Race, ethnicity, common language, and nationality are well-known examples of characteristics that are used to distinguish "insiders" from "outsiders." But in experimental settings, subjects exhibit parochial preferences even when the basis of group membership is explicitly random or arbitrary, and there is no a priori reason for subjects to care about others in their own as opposed to other groups (Turner 1984).

11.4.1   The Ultimatum Game

The *ultimatum game*, first studied by Werner Güth, Rolf Schmittberger, and Berndt Schwarze (1982), is a showcase for costly retaliation in a one-shot

[11]Another aspect of reciprocity is commonly known as "gift exchange," in which one agent behaves more kindly than required toward another, with the hope and expectation that the other will respond kindly as well (Akerlof 1982). For instance, in an laboratory-simulated work situation in which "employers" can pay higher than market-clearing wages in hopes that "workers" will reciprocate by supplying a high level of effort, see Fehr, Gächter, Kirchler, and Weichbold 1998 and Fehr, Gächter, and Kirchsteiger 1997.

situation. Under conditions of anonymity, one player, called the "proposer," is handed a sum of money, say $10, and is told to offer any number of dollars, from $1 to $10, to the second player, who is called the "responder." The responder, again under conditions of anonymity, can either accept the offer or reject it. If the responder accepts the offer, the money is shared accordingly. If the responder rejects the offer, both players receive nothing.

There are *lots* of Nash equilibria in this game. In fact, there are $2^{10} - 1 = 1023$ Nash equilibria, since every pattern of "accept/reject" of the ten numbers $1, \ldots, 10$, except "reject every offer" is part of a Nash equilibrium, and the best response for the proposer to such a strategy is the smallest number in that pattern that the responder will accept ("reject every offer" is never a best response). For instance, one Nash equilibrium is for the responder to accept (3,7,10) and reject all other offers, and for the proposer to offer 3.

But, there is only *one* responder strategy that is subgame perfect: accept anything you are offered. However, when actually played by people, *the subgame perfect outcome is almost never attained or even approximated.* In fact, as many replications of this experiment have documented, under varying conditions and with varying amounts of money, proposers routinely offer respondents very substantial amounts (50% of the total being the modal offer), and respondents frequently reject offers below 30% (Camerer and Thaler 1995, Güth and Tietz 1990, Roth, Prasnikar, Okuno-Fujiwara, and Zamir 1991). These results are obtained in experiments with stakes as high as three months' earnings.[12]

Are these results culturally dependent? Do they have a strong genetic component, or do all "successful" cultures transmit similar values of reciprocity to individuals? Roth et al. (1991) conducted ultimatum games in four different countries (United States, Yugoslavia, Japan, and Israel) and found that while the level of offers differed a bit in different countries, the probability of an offer being rejected did not. This indicates that both proposers and respondents share the same notion of what is considered "fair" in that society, and that proposers adjust their offers to reflect this common notion. The differences in level of offers across countries, by the way, were relatively small.

---

[12]For analyses of ultimatum games, see Forsythe, Horowitz, Savin, and Sefton 1994, Hoffman, McCabe, Shachat, and Smith 1994, Hoffman, McCabe, and Smith 1998, Cameron 1995, and Fehr and Tougareva 1995.

By contrast, Henrich (2000) carried out ultimatum games among the Machiguenga Indians, a Peruvian Amazon hunter-gatherer tribe, and found significant differences. Among the Machiguenga, average offers were much lower, the median offer being about 20%, offers of 15% were often accepted, and the rejection rate was very low. These anthropological results are currently being extended by studying additional societies in various parts of the world (Bowles, Boyd, Fehr, and Gintis 1997).

In the United States and other complex societies, when asked why they offer more than the lowest possible amount, proposers commonly say that they are afraid that respondents will consider low offers unfair and reject them. When respondents reject offers, they give virtually the same reasons for their actions.[13]

11.4.2   The Public Goods Game

Another important experimental setting in which strong reciprocity has been observed is that of the *public goods game,* designed to illuminate such problems as the voluntary payment of taxes and contribution to team and community goals. Public goods experiments have been run many times, under varying conditions, beginning with the pioneering work of the sociologist G. Marwell, the psychologist R. Dawes, the political scientist J. Orbell, and the economists R. Isaac and J. Walker in the late 1970s and early 1980s.[14] The following is a common variant of the game. Ten subjects are told that $1 will be deposited in each of their "private accounts" as a reward for participating in each round of the experiment. For every $1 that a subject moves from his "private account" to the "public account," the experimenter will deposit one half dollar in the private accounts of each of the subjects at the end of the game. This process will be repeated ten times, and at the end the subjects can take home whatever they have in their private accounts.

If all ten subjects are perfectly cooperative, each puts $1 in the public account at the end of each round, generating a public pool of $10; the experimenter then puts $5 in the private account of each subject. After ten rounds of this, each subject has $50. Suppose, by contrast, that one subject is perfectly selfish, while the others are cooperative. The selfish one keeps his

---

[13]In all of the above experiments a significant fraction of subjects (about a quarter, typically) conform to the self-interested preferences of *Homo economicus*, and it is often the self-serving behavior of this minority that, when it goes unpunished, unravels initial generosity and cooperation when the game is repeated.

[14]For a summary of this research and an extensive bibliography, see Ledyard (1995).

$1-per-round in his private account, whereas the cooperative ones continue to put $1 in the public pool. In this case, the selfish subject who takes a free ride on the cooperative contributions of others ends up with $55 at the end of the game, while the other players will end up with $45 each. But if all players opt for the selfish payoff, then no one contributes to the public pool, and each ends up with $10 at the end of the game. And if one player cooperates, while the others are all selfish, that player will end up with $5 at the end of the game while the others will get $15. It is thus clear that this is indeed an "iterated Prisoner's Dilemma"—whatever other players do on a particular round, a player's highest payoff comes from contributing nothing to the public account. If others cooperate, it is best to take a free ride; if others are selfish, it is best to join them. But if no one contributes, all receive less than they would if all had cooperated.

Public goods experiments show that only a fraction of subjects conform to the *Homo economicus* model, contributing nothing to the public account. Rather, in a one-stage public goods game, people contribute on average about half of their private account. The results in the early stages of a repeated public goods game are similar. In the middle stages of the repeated game, however, contributions begin to decay, until at the end they are close to the *Homo economicus* level—i.e., zero.

Could we not explain the decay of public contribution by *learning*: the participants really do not understand the game at first, but once they hit upon the free-riding strategy, they apply it? Not at all. One indication that learning does not account for the decay of cooperation is that increasing the number of rounds of play (when this is known to the players) leads to a decline in the rate of decay of cooperation (Isaac, Walker, and Williams 1994). Similarly, Andreoni (1988) finds that when the whole process is repeated with the same subjects but with different group composition, the initial levels of cooperation are restored, but once again cooperation decays as the game progresses. Andreoni (1995) suggests a *Homo reciprocans* explanation for the decay of cooperation: public-spirited contributors want to retaliate against free-riders, and the only way available to them in the game is by not contributing themselves.

11.4.3 The Public Goods Game with Retaliation

Could the decay of cooperation in the public goods game be due to cooperators retaliating against free-riders by free-riding themselves? Subjects often report this behavior retrospectively. More compelling, however, is the fact that when subjects are given a more constructive way of punishing defectors, they use it in a way that helps sustain cooperation (Dawes, Orbell, and Van de Kragt 1986, Sato 1987, Yamagishi 1988a, 1988b, 1992).

For instance, in Ostrom, Walker, and Gardner (1992) subjects interacted for about twenty-five periods in a public goods game, and by paying a "fee," subjects could impose costs on other subjects by "fining" them. Since fining costs the individual who uses it but the benefits of increased compliance accrue to the group as a whole, the only subgame perfect Nash equilibrium in this game is for no player to pay the fee, so no player is ever punished for defecting, and all players defect by contributing nothing to the public account. However, the authors found a significant level of punishing behavior. The experiment was then repeated with subjects being allowed to communicate, without being able to make binding agreements. In the framework of the *Homo economicus* model, such communication is called *cheap talk* and cannot lead to a distinct subgame perfect equilibrium. But in fact such communication led to almost perfect cooperation (93%) with very little sanctioning (4%).

The design of the Ostrom-Walker-Gardner study allowed individuals to engage in strategic behavior, since costly retaliation against defectors could increase cooperation in future periods, yielding a positive net return for the retaliator. It is true that backward induction rules out such a strategy, but we know that people do not backward induct very far anyway. What happens if we remove any possibility of retaliation being strategic? This is exactly what Fehr and Gächter (2000) studied. They set up a repeated public goods game with the possibility of costly retaliation, but they ensured that group composition changed *in every period* so subjects knew that costly retaliation could not confer any pecuniary benefit to those who punish. Nonetheless, punishment of free-riding was prevalent and gave rise to a large and sustainable increase in cooperation levels.

11.4.4   The Common Pool Resource Game

In 1968 Garrett Hardin wrote a famous article in the journal *Science* entitled "The Tragedy of the Commons" (Hardin 1968). The term "commons" referred originally to the region of an English village that belonged to the villagers as a group and on which villagers were permitted to graze their sheep or cows. The "tragedy" in the tragedy of the commons was that the commons tended to be overgrazed, since each villager would graze to the point where the *private* costs equal the benefits, whereas grazing imposed additional *social* costs on the rest of the community. We explored this phenomenon rather fancifully in Klingon and Snarks (§3.9), but in fact it applies to what are termed *common pool resources* in general. Some involve social problems of the highest importance, including air and water pollution, overfishing, overuse of antibiotics, traffic congestion, excessive groundwater use, overpopulation, and the like.

The general implication from Hardin's analysis was that some centralized entity, such as a national government or international agency, had to step in to prevent the tragedy by regulating the common. The historical experience in regulating the commons, however, has been a patchwork of successes and failures. In 1990 Elinor Ostrom published an influential book, *Governing the Commons*, suggesting that the Hardin analysis did not apply generally, since local communities often had ways of self-organizing and self-governing to prevent overexploitation of the commons, and that government policy often exacerbated rather than ameliorated the problem by undermining the social connections on which local regulation was based.

When formalized as a game, the common pool resource problem is simply an n-person repeated Prisoner's Dilemma, in which each player hopes the other players will cooperate (not take too much of the common resource), but will defect (take too much) no matter what the other players do. Since the public goods game (§11.4.2) is also an n-person repeated prisoner's dilemma, it is not surprising that both in the real world and in experimental settings, under the appropriate conditions, we see much more cooperation than predicted by the *Homo economicus* model.

Ostrom, Gardner, and Walker (1994) used both experimental and field data to test game-theoretic models of common pool resources. They found more spontaneous cooperation in the field studies than predicted, and when communication and sanctioning were permitted in the laboratory, the level of cooperation became quite high.

While common pool resource and public goods games are equivalent for *Homo economicus,* people treat them quite differently in practice. This is because the status quo in the public goods game is the individual keeping all the money in the private account, while the status quo in the common pool resource game is that the resource is not being used at all. This is a good example of a *framing effect* (§11.3.3), since people measure movements from the status quo and hence tend to undercontribute in the public goods game and overcontribute (underexploit) in the common pool resource game, compared to the social optimum (Ostrom 1998).

In the real world, of course, communities often do *not* manage their common pool resources well. The point of Ostrom's work is to identify the sources of failure, not to romanticize small communities and informal organization. Among other reasons, the management of common pool resources fails when communities are so large that it pays to form a local coalition operating against the whole community, and when resources are so unequally distributed that it pays the wealthy to defect on the nonwealthy and conversely (Hackett, Schlager, and Walker 1994, Bardhan, Bowles, and Gintis 2000).

11.5   *Homo egualis*

Homo egualis exhibits a *weak* urge to reduce inequality when on top, and a *strong* urge to reduce inequality when on the bottom. Since the advent of hierarchical societies that are based on settled agriculture, societies have attempted to inculcate in its less fortunate members precisely the opposite values—subservience to and acceptance of the status quo. The widely observed distaste for relative deprivation is thus probably a genetically based behavioral characteristic of humans. Since small children spontaneously share (even the most sophisticated of primates, such as chimpanzees, fail to do this), the urge of the fortunate to redistribute may also be part of human nature, though doubtless a weaker impulse in most of us.

Support for *Homo egualis* comes from the anthropological literature. *Homo sapiens* evolved in small hunter-gatherer groups. Contemporary groups of this type, although widely dispersed throughout the world, display many common characteristics. This commonality probably reflects their common material conditions. From this and other considerations we may tentatively infer the social organization of early human society from that of these contemporary foraging societies.[15]

Such societies have no centralized structure of governance (state, judicial system, church, Big Man), so the enforcement of norms depends on the voluntary participation of peers. There are many unrelated individuals, so

---

[15]See Woodburn 1982, Boehm 1982, 1993, Blurton-Jones 1987, Cashdan 1980, Knauft 1991, Hawkes 1992, 1993, Kaplan and Hill 1985a,b, Kaplan, Hill, Hawkes, and Hurtado 1984, Lee 1979, Woodburn and Barnard 1988, Endicott 1988, Balikci 1970, Kent 1989, Damas 1972, Wenzel 1995, Knauft 1989.

cooperation cannot be explained by kinship ties. Status differences are very circumscribed, monogamy is widely enforced,[16] members who attempt to acquire personal power are banished or killed, and there is widespread sharing of large game and other food sources that are subject to substantial stochasticity, independent of the skill and/or luck of the hunters. Such conditions are, of course, conducive to the emergence of *Homo egualis*.

We model *Homo egualis* following Fehr and Schmidt (1999). Suppose the monetary payoffs to n players are given by $x = (x_1, \ldots, x_n)$. We take the utility function of player i to be

$$u_i(x) = x_i - \frac{\alpha_i}{n-1} \sum_{x_j > x_i} (x_j - x_i) - \frac{\beta_i}{n-1} \sum_{x_j < x_i} (x_i - x_j). \qquad (11.1)$$

A reasonable range of values for β_i is $0 \leq \beta_i < 1$. Note that when $n = 2$ and $x_i > x_j$, if $\beta_i = 0.5$ then i is willing to transfer income to j dollar for dollar until $x_i = x_j$, and if $\beta_i = 1$ then i is willing to throw away money until $x_i = x_j$. We also assume $\beta_i < \alpha_i$, reflecting the fact that people are more sensitive to inequality when on the bottom than when on the top.

We shall show that with these preferences, we can reproduce some of the salient behaviors in ultimatum and public goods games, where fairness appears to matter, as well as in market games where it does not.

Consider first the ultimatum game. Let y be the share the proposer offers the respondent, so the proposer gets $x = 1 - y$. Since $n = 2$, we can write the two utility functions as

$$u(x) = \begin{cases} x - \alpha_1(1 - 2x) & x \leq 0.5 \\ x - \beta_1(2x - 1) & x > 0.5 \end{cases} \qquad (11.2)$$

$$v(y) = \begin{cases} y - \alpha_2(1 - 2y) & y \leq 0.5 \\ y - \beta_2(2y - 1) & y > 0.5 \end{cases} \qquad (11.3)$$

We have the following theorem.

THEOREM 11.1 *Suppose the payoffs in the ultimatum game are given by (11.2) and (11.3), and α_2 is uniformly distributed on the interval $[0, \alpha^*]$. Writing $y^* = \alpha^*/(1 + 2\alpha^*)$, we have the following:*

a.   *If $\beta_1 > 0.5$ the proposer offers $y = 0.5$.*

---

[16]Monogamy in considered to be an extremely egalitarian institution for men, since it ensures that virtually all adult males will have a wife.

b.   *If $\beta_1 = 0.5$ the proposer offers $y \in [y^*, 0.5]$.*
c.   *If $\beta_1 < 0.5$ the proposer offers y^*.*

In all cases the respondent accepts. We leave the proof, which is straightforward, to the reader.

Now suppose we have a public goods game $\mathcal{G}$ with $n \geq 2$ players. Each player i is given an amount 1 and decides independently what share x_i to contribute to the public account, after which the public account is multiplied by a number a with $1 > a > 1/n$ and shared equally among the players. The monetary payoff for each player then becomes $1 - x_i + a \sum_{j=1}^{n} x_j$ and the utility payoffs are given by (11.1). We then have this theorem.

THEOREM 11.2 *In the n-player public goods game $\mathcal{G}$,*

a.   *If $\beta_i < 1 - a$ for player i, then contributing nothing to the public account is a dominant strategy for i.*
b.   *If there are $k > a(n-1)/2$ players with $\beta_i < 1 - a$, then the only Nash equilibrium is for all players to contribute nothing to the public account.*
c.   *If there are $k < a(n-1)/2$ players with $\beta_i < 1 - a$ and if all players i with $\beta_i > 1 - a$ satisfy $k/(n-1) < (a + \beta_i - 1)/(\alpha_i + \beta_i)$, then there is a Nash equilibrium in which the latter players contribute all their money to the public account.*

Note that if a player has a high β and hence could possibly contribute, but also has a high α so the player strongly dislikes being below the mean, then condition $k/(n-1) < (a + \beta_i - 1)/(\alpha_i + \beta_i)$ in part (c) of the theorem will fail. In other words, cooperation with defectors requires that contributors not be excessively sensitive to relative deprivation.

The proof of the theorem is a bit tedious but straightforward, and will be left to the reader. We prove only (c). We know from (a) that players i with $\beta_i < 1 - a$ will not contribute. Suppose $b_i > 1 - a$, and assume all other players satisfying this inequality contribute all their money to the public account. By reducing his contribution by $\delta > 0$, player i saves $(1-a)\delta$ directly plus receives $k\alpha_i\delta/(n-1)$ in utility from the higher returns compared to the noncontributors, minus $(n - k - 1)\delta\beta_i$ in utility from the lower returns compared with the contributors. The sum must be nonpositive in a Nash equilibrium, which reduces to the inequality in (c).

Despite the fact that players have egalitarian preferences given by (11.1) if the game played has sufficiently marketlike qualities, the unique Nash equilibrium may settle on the competitive equilibrium, however "unfair" this appears to be to the participants. Consider the following.

THEOREM 11.3 *Suppose preferences are given by (11.1) and $1 is to be shared between player 1 and one of the players $i = 2, \ldots, n$, who submit simultaneous bids y_i for the share they are willing to give to player 1. The highest bid wins, and among equal highest bids, the winner is drawn at random. Then, for any set of (α_i, β_i), in every subgame perfect Nash equilibrium player 1 receives the whole $1.*

The proof is left to the reader. Show that at least two bidders will set their $y_i's$ to 1, and the seller will accept this offer.

11.6 *Homo reciprocans:* Modeling Strong Reciprocity

While models of *Homo egualis* can explain many experimental results that are anomalous in terms of *Homo economicus*, other experiments suggest that agents care about the *intentions* of their partners as well as the distributional outcomes. For instance, if offers in an ultimatum game are generated by a computer rather than proposers, and if respondents knows this, low offers are much less likely to be rejected (Blount 1995). This suggests that players are motivated by *reciprocity*, reacting to a violation of behavioral norms rather than simply seeking a more equitable distribution of outcomes (Greenberg and Frisch 1972).

The importance of reciprocity in strategic interaction is common to many forms of life, as has been stressed by Robert Trivers (1971) in his seminal work on reciprocal altruism. The robustness of reciprocal behavior appears in computer simulations as well, as in the work of Robert Axelrod and W. D. Hamilton (1981) on Tit-for-Tat strategies (§6.11). Agent-based simulations of repeated-interaction prisoner's dilemma games also show the robustness of strategies that are "nice" by never defecting first, "punishing" by always punishing defection, and "forgiving" by returning to cooperation after a short period of punishing, if the other player is cooperating.[17]

---

[17]Nowak and Sigmund (1992) show that when players can make mistakes, a more forgiving version of Tit-for-Tat, called Generous Tit-for-Tat, drives out Tit-for-Tat. Nowak and Sigmund (1993) show that when players can respond to their own as well as their opponents' moves, strategies that repeat moves when successful and switch when unsuccessful (Pavlov) outcompete Tit-for-Tat under the same simulation conditions as present in the original computer contests run by Axelrod. Laboratory experiments with humans

However, as we know from the theory of repeated games (§6.4), reciprocity in the above sense is just "enlightened self-interest," which is fully compatible with the *Homo economicus* model, as long as discount rates are sufficiently low. In effect, Trivers's reciprocal altruist and the Axelrod-Hamilton Tit-for-Tatter behave little differently from *Homo economicus* with an appropriate time discount rate. The *Homo reciprocans* who emerges from laboratory experiments, by contrast, provides a more robust basis for prosocial behavior, since he does not depend upon frequently repeated interactions to induce him to cooperate and punish defectors.

Homo reciprocans exhibits what may be called *strong reciprocity*, by which we mean a propensity to cooperate and share with others similarly disposed, even at personal cost, and a willingness to punish those who violate cooperative and other social norms, even when punishing is personally costly, and even when there are no plausible future rewards or benefits from so behaving.

Critics of the notion of strong reciprocity suggest that reciprocal behavior in one-shot games is just a confused carryover of the subject's extensive experience with repeated games in everyday life to the rare experience of the one-shot game in the laboratory. This is incorrect. Human beings in contemporary society are engaged in one-shot games with very high frequency—virtually every interaction we have with strangers is of this form. Major rare events in people's lives (fending off an attacker, battling hand-to-hand in wartime, experiencing a natural disaster or major illness) are one-shots in which people appear to exhibit strong reciprocity much as in the laboratory. Moreover, *the fact that humans often "confuse" one-shots and repeated interactions, when they clearly have the cognitive mechanisms to distinguish, suggests that the "confusion" may be fitness-enhancing.* It is therefore misleading to suggest that conflating one-shot and repeated games is a regrettable human weakness.

Consider a two-person extensive form game $\mathcal{G}$, where a fairness norm (a situational context that players may or may not apply to the game) suggests equal payoffs to all players—examples include the Prisoner's Dilemma, the ultimatum game, and the Common Pool Resources game.[18] Let $\pi_i(p_1, p_2)$ be the payoff to player $i = 1, 2$ when i uses behavioral strategy p_i (§4.13), and let $\pi_i(p_1, p_2|v)$ be the payoff to i, conditional on being at information

(Wedekind and Milinski 1993) show that human subjects use Generous Tit-for-Tat and Pavlov, as well as more sophisticated Pavlov-like strategies.

[18]This model of strong reciprocity follows Falk and Fischbacher 1998.

set v. The *fairness* $f_j(p_1, p_2|v)$ of j if it is $i \neq j$'s move at v is defined by

$$f_j(p_1, p_2|v) = \pi_i(p_1, p_2|v) - \pi_j(p_1, p_2|v).$$

Thus, at v, j has been relatively generous if $f_j > 0$, and relatively selfish if $f_j < 0$.

For every pure action a available to i at v, let $p_i(a)$ be the behavioral strategy for i that is the same as p_i everywhere except at v, where i takes action a. We then define i *kindness* from taking action a at v to be

$$k_i(p_1, p_2, a|v) = \pi_j((p_i(a), p_j)|v) - \pi_j(p_1, p_2|v),$$

where $(p_i(a), p_j) = p_1(a), p_2$ if $i = 1$ and $(p_i(a), p_j) = p_1, p_2(a)$ if $i = 2$. In other words, given the pair of strategies (p_1, p_2), player i who moves at node v is being "kind" when choosing move a if this gives j a greater payoff than that indicated by p_i.

The total payoff to i at a terminal node $t \in T$ of $\mathcal{G}$ is then

$$u_i(t) = \pi_i(t) + \rho_i \sum_{v \in N_i(t)} f_j(p_1, p_2|v) k_i(p_1, p_2, a_v|v), \qquad (11.4)$$

where $N_i(t)$ is the set of information sets where i moves on the path to t, and a_v is the action at v on the path to t. Note that if $f_j > 0$ at a certain node, then *ceteris paribus* player i gains from exhibiting positive kindness, while if $f_j < 0$, the opposite is the case. Note also that these payoffs are relative to a specific pair of behavioral strategies (p_1, p_2). This aspect of (11.4) reflects the fact that *Homo reciprocans* cares not only about payoffs, but also about the actions of the other player. We say that a pair of strategies (p_1^*, p_2^*) of $\mathcal{G}$ is a *reciprocity equilibrium* if (p_1^*, p_2^*) is a Nash equilibrium of (11.4) when (p_1, p_2) is replaced by (p_1^*, p_2^*) on the right-hand side of (11.4).[19]

THEOREM 11.4 *Suppose both players in an ultimatum game have preferences given by (11.4), where $\rho_1, \rho_2 > 0$ are known by both players, and let s be the share the proposer offers the respondent. Let $p^*(s)$ be the respondent's best reply to the offer s, and let $(p^*(s^*), s^*)$ be a reciprocity*

---

[19]Following Rabin (1993), Falk and Fischbacher (1998) use the concept of a *psychological game* (Geanakoplos, Pearce, and Stacchetti 1989) to formulate the notion of a reciprocity equilibrium. Our formulation accomplishes the same end without requiring a notion of "subjective beliefs," which lack explanatory value in an evolutionary model.

equilibrium. Then the respondent surely accepts (i.e., $p^*(s^*) = 1$), and the proposer chooses

$$s^* = \max \left[\frac{1 + 3\rho_2 - \sqrt{1 + 6\rho_2 + \rho_2^2}}{4\rho_2}, \frac{1}{2}\left(1 - \frac{1}{\rho_1}\right) \right].$$

The theorem also holds when either or both of ρ_1, ρ_2 is zero, and if both are zero, we have the *Homo economicus* equilibrium. Note that the second expression for the equilibrium offer s^* will hold when the proposer is highly motivated by fairness, while the first expression holds if the proposer is motivated to make an offer sufficiently high so as not to be rejected.

To prove Theorem 11.4, suppose that in equilibrium the proposer offers s^* and the respondent accepts with probability p^*. Then the fairness term for the respondent is $f_2 = p^*(s^* - (1 - s^*)) = p^*(2s^* - 1)$. If the respondent accepts, then the kindness term is $k_2 = (1 - s^*) - p^*(1 - s^*)$, so the total utility from accepting is $s^* + \rho_2 p^*(2s^* - 1)(1 - p^*)(1 - s^*)$. If the respondent rejects, then $k_2 = 0 - p^*(1 - s^*)$, so the total utility is $0 - \rho_2 p^*(2s^* - 1)p^*(1 - s^*)$. The net gain from accepting is thus $\Delta_a = s^* + \rho_2 p^*(2s^* - 1)(1 - s^*)$, which is positive if $s^* \geq 1/2$. Suppose $s^* < 1/2$. Then if $\Delta_a > 0$ for $p^* = 1$, the responder will still choose $p = 1$. Otherwise let $\hat{p} = s^*/\rho_2(1 - 2s^*)(1 - s^*)$, which equates the payoffs to accepting and rejecting the offer. If $p^* < \hat{p}$, then the payoff to accepting exceeds the payoff to rejecting, so $p^* = 1$, which is a contradiction. Similarly, if $p^* > \hat{p}$, then rejecting dominates accepting, so $p^* = 0$, which is a contradiction. Thus, $p^* = \hat{p}$.

To determine s^*, let $p(s)$ be the responder's probability, derived above. Then the proposer's fairness term is $f_1 = p(s^*)(1 - s^* - s^*)$, and his kindness term is $k_1 = p(s)s - p(s^*)s^*$, so his payoff to proposing s is

$$u_1(s) = p(s)(1 - s) + \rho_1 p(s^*)(1 - 2s^*)(p(s)s - p(s^*)s^*).$$

Clearly, $u_1(s)$ is decreasing for $s > 1/2$, $s^* \leq 1/2$. Note that the smallest s such that $p(s) = 1$ satisfies $s = \rho_2(1 - 2s)(1 - s)$, which is given by $\hat{s} = \left(1 + 3\rho_2 + \sqrt{1 + 6\rho_2 + \rho_2^2}\right)/4\rho_2$. Moreover, it is easy to see that both $p(s)(1 - s)$ and $p(s)s$ are increasing so long as $p(s) < 1$, so $\hat{s} \leq s^* \leq 1/2$. This means that $p^*(s^*) = 1$. The derivative of $u_1(s)$ is $\rho_1(1 - 2s^*) - 1$, so if this is negative, then we must have $s^* = \hat{s}$. But we cannot have

$\rho_1(1 - 2s^*) - 1 > 0$, or $s^* = 1$, which is a contradiction. Therefore, the alternative is $\rho_1(1 - 2s^*) - 1 = 0$, which means $s^* = (1 - 1/\rho_1)/2$, completing the proof. Q.E.D.

This theorem assumes the proposer knows the respondent's ρ_2, which accounts for the fact that offers are never refused. It is not difficult to see how to modify this by assuming the proposer knows only the probability distribution over respondent types.

As another example of a reciprocity equilibrium, let the game $\mathcal{G}$ be the Prisoner's Dilemma (§2.6, §6.11), with cooperative payoffs (b, b), mutual defect payoffs (c, c), and where a cooperator receives 0 against a defector and a defector receives a against a cooperator. We assume $a > b > c > 0$. Suppose $\mathcal{G}$ is *sequential*, with One going first and choosing "cooperate" with probability p, then Two choosing "cooperate" with probability q if One cooperated, and choosing "cooperate" with probability r if One defected. We have this theorem.

THEOREM 11.5 *Suppose players in the sequential Prisoner's Dilemma game $\mathcal{G}$ have utility functions given by (11.4), where $\rho_1, \rho_2 > 0$ are known by both players. Then there is a unique reciprocity equilibrium (p^*, q^*, r^*) with the following characteristics.*

a. $r^* = 0$.
b. *q^* is the larger of zero and $q^* = 1 - (a - b)/(\rho_2 ab)$.*
c. *Let $\hat{p} = (q^*b - c)/(\rho_1 a(1 - q^*)(q^*b + (1 - q^*)a - c))$. Then $p^* = \hat{p}$ provided this quantity is between zero and one. If $\hat{p} < 0$, then $p^* = 0$, and if $\hat{p} > 1$, then $p^* = 1$.*

Part (a) says that if One defects, Two defects as well. Part (b) says that if One cooperates and if the strength of Two's reciprocity motive ρ_2 is sufficiently strong, Two cooperates with positive probability. Also, this probability is increasing in the strength of Two's reciprocity motive, but it never reaches 100%. Part (c) is a little more complicated. The numerator is the expected gain from cooperation q^*b over defection c. If this is positive, the denominator is as well, so a selfish One (low ρ_1) will cooperate with certainty, whereas a reciprocator (high ρ_1) may not, because he is averse to giving Two a high payoff from defecting. The denominator is necessarily positive, so if the numerator is negative, no proposer will cooperate.

To prove Theorem 11.5, suppose One defected. Two's fairness term is then $f_2 = r^*(-a) + (1 - r^*)(c - c) = -ar^*$. His kindness term from cooperating is $k_2 = a - \pi_1^*$, where π_1^* is One's equilibrium payoff given that One defected. Two's kindness term from defecting is $k_2 = c - \pi_1^*$. Two's payoff from cooperating is thus $u_2 = 0 - \rho_2 a r^*(a - \pi_2^*)$, where π_2^* is the equilibrium payoff given that One defected, and Two's payoff from defecting is $u_2 = c - \rho_2 a r^*(c - \pi_2^*)$, so clearly Two will defect with probability 1, giving $r^* = 0$. This proves (a).

Now suppose One cooperated. Two's fairness term is then $f_2 = q^*(b - b) + (1 - q^*)a = a(1 - q^*)$. His kindness term from cooperating is $k_2 = b - \pi_1^*$, where π_1^* is One's equilibrium payoff. His kindness term from defecting is $k_2 = 0 - \pi_1^*$. Two's payoff from cooperating is thus $u_2 = b + \rho_2 a(1 - q^*)(b - \pi_1^*)$. Two's payoff from defecting is $u_2 = a - \rho_2(1 - q^*)\pi_1^*$. Let $\hat{q}$ be the value of q^* that equates the two, so $\hat{q} = 1 - (a - b)/\rho_2 ab$. Clearly, $q^* < \hat{q}$ is impossible since in this case Two always cooperates, so $q^* = 1$, which is a contradiction. If $q^* > \hat{q}$, Two always defects, so $q^* = 0$, which is impossible unless $\hat{q} < 0$. We conclude that if $\hat{q} \geq 0$, then $q^* = \hat{q}$, and if $\hat{q} < 0$ then $q^* = 0$. This proves (b).

One's fairness term is

$$f_1 = p^* q^* b + (1 - p^*)q_1 - (p^* q_2 + (1 - p^*)(1 - r^*)c),$$

where $q_1 = r^* a + (1 - r^*)c$ and $q_2 = q^* b + (1 - q^*)a$. Since $r^* = 0$, this reduces to $f_1 = -p^*(1 - q^*)a$. If One cooperates, his kindness term is $k_1 = q^* b + (1 - q^*)a - \pi_2^*$, and if One defects, his kindness term is $k_1 = (1 - r^*)c - \pi_2^* = c - \pi_2^*$. Therefore, One's payoff from cooperating is $q^* b - \rho_1 p^*(1 - q^*)a(q^* b + (1 - q^*)a - \pi_2^*)$, and One's payoff from defecting is $r^* a + (1 - r^*)c - \rho_1 p^*(1 - q^*)a(c - \pi_2^*) = c - \rho_1 p^*(1 - q^*)a(c - \pi_2^*)$. Let $\hat{p}$ be the value that equates these two, so $\hat{p} = (q^* b - c)/\rho_1 a(1 - q^*)(q^* b + (1 - q^*)a - c)$. Now, if $p^* < \hat{p}$, then $p^* = 1$ since cooperating dominates defecting, and this requires $\hat{p} > 1$. If $p^* > \hat{p}$ then $p^* = 0$, so $\hat{p} < 0$. It follows that if $0 < \hat{p} < 1$, then $p^* = \hat{p}$, which completes the proof of the theorem. Q.E.D.

11.7   Altruism and Assortative Interactions

In an evolutionary model we equate welfare with fitness—the capacity to produce offspring with one's own characteristics. The altruist, by definition, becomes less fit in the process of rendering the group more fit, so evolution should entail the disappearance of the altruist. This argument has been applied to biological models where "offspring" means "children," but it applies equally to cultural models where successful behaviors are adopted by other agents. A culturally altruistic behavior is one that confers benefits on the group but is less likely to be copied by other group members than the nonaltruistic behavior.

This argument does not completely rule out altruism. Suppose there are many groups, and the altruists so enhance the fitness of the groups they are in, compared to the groups without altruists, that the former outcompete the latter, so that the average fitness of the altruist is higher than that of the selfish agent. Altruism can then proliferate. For instance, platoons with brave soldiers may survive in a situation where platoons with selfish soldiers are defeated, *despite* the fact that the brave soldiers have higher mortality than the selfish soldiers within the "brave" platoons. Overall, then, the frequency of brave soldiers in the army may increase.

To formalize this idea, suppose there are groups $i = 1, \ldots, n$, and let f_i be the fraction of the population in group i. Let π_i be the mean fitness of group i, so $\bar{\pi} = \sum_i f_i \pi_i$ is the mean fitness of the whole population. We assume groups grow from one period to the next in proportion to their relative fitness, so if f_i' is the fraction of the population in group i in the next period, then

$$f_i' = f_i \frac{\pi_i}{\bar{\pi}}.$$

Now, suppose there is a trait with frequency x_i in group i, so the frequency of the trait in the whole population is $\bar{x} = \sum_i f_i x_i$. If π_i' and x_i' are the fitness of group i and the frequency of the trait in group i in the next period, then $\bar{x}' = \sum_i f_i' x_i'$, and writing $\Delta x_i = x_i' - x_i$, we have

$$
\begin{aligned}
\bar{x}' - \bar{x} &= \sum f_i' x_i' - \sum f_i x_i = \sum f_i \frac{\pi_i}{\bar{\pi}} x_i' - \sum f_i x_i \\
&= \sum f_i \frac{\pi_i}{\bar{\pi}} (x_i + \Delta x_i) - \sum f_i x_i \\
&= \sum f_i \left(\frac{\pi_i}{\bar{\pi}} - 1 \right) x_i + \sum f_i \frac{\pi_i}{\bar{\pi}} \Delta x_i.
\end{aligned}
$$

Now, writing $\Delta \bar{x} = \bar{x}' - \bar{x}$, we can rewrite this as

$$\bar{\pi} \Delta \bar{x} = \sum f_i (\pi_i - \bar{\pi}) x_i + \sum f_i \pi_i \Delta x_i. \tag{11.5}$$

The second term is just $\mathbf{E}[\pi \Delta x]$, the expected value of $\pi \Delta x$, over all groups, weighted by the relative size of the groups. If the trait in question renders individuals bearing it less fit than other group members, this term will be negative, since $\Delta x_i < 0$ within each group. To interpret the first term, note that the *covariance* between the variables π and x is given by

$$\text{cov}[\pi, x] = \sum f_i (\pi_i - \overline{\pi})(x_i - \overline{x}),$$

and since $\sum f_i (\pi_i - \overline{\pi})\overline{x} = 0$, we can write (11.5) as

$$\overline{\pi} \Delta x = \text{cov}[\pi, x] + \mathbf{E}[\pi \Delta x]. \tag{11.6}$$

This is a very famous relationship in biology, called *Price's equation*(Price 1970). Note that even if the expectation term $\mathbf{E}[\pi \Delta x]$ is negative, so individuals with the trait are disfavored within groups, the overall effect on the growth Δx of the trait in the population can be positive, provided that the covariance term $\text{cov}[\pi, x]$ is positive and sufficiently large. But the covariance will be positive precisely when *groups with high average values of the trait also have above-average fitness*—i.e., when the trait improves the fitness of the group in which it is expressed at high levels.

For an example of Price's equation, consider an evolutionary game with the stage game $\mathcal{G}$ depicted here. There are two types of agents, "selfish" and "altruist." By cooperating, an agent produces a payoff (fitness increment)

	C	D
C	$b - c, b - c$	$-c, b$
D	$b, -c$	$0, 0$

$b > 0$ for his partner, at personal cost $c < b$, and by defecting an agent produces zero at zero cost. This is thus a Prisoner's Dilemma in which defection is a dominant strategy. Suppose the players pair off in each period, and each type is likely to meet its own type with probability $r \geq 0$, and a random member of the population with probability $1 - r$. If $r > 0$ we say there is *assortative interaction*. We then have *Hamilton's Law* (Hamilton 1963).

THEOREM 11.6 *Consider the evolutionary game with stage game $\mathcal{G}$, in which the degree of assortative interaction is $r \geq 0$. A small number of cooperators can invade a population of selfish actors if and only if $br \geq c$.*

To prove this theorem,[20] note that there are three types of groups, aa, as, and ss, all of size 2 at the beginning of the period. Since Price's equation

---

[20]There is a proof using the replicator dynamic equations, but that would not illustrate Price's equation.

remains the same if we aggregate all groups with the same internal composition, we can assume there are three groups whose fraction of total membership are f_{aa}, f_{as}, and f_{ss}, with mean fitness $\pi_{aa} = b - c$, $\pi_{as} = (b - c)/2$, and $\pi_{ss} = 0$, respectively.

To determine f_{aa}, f_{as}, and f_{ss}, let f be the fraction of altruists in the population. If r is the level of assortative interaction, the frequency of aa pairs is $f_{aa} = f(r + (1 - r)f)$ and the frequency of ss pairs is $f_{ss} = (1 - f)(r + (1 - r)(1 - f))$, so the frequency of as pairs must be $f_{as} = 1 - f_{aa} - f_{ss} = 2f(1 - f)(1 - r)$. Note that $f_{aa} + f_{as}/2 = f$ and $f_{ss} + f_{as}/2 = 1 - f$, as expected.

Let the trait measured by x be the "frequency of altruism." Then $x_{aa} = 1$, since in aa groups all members are altruists, and similarly $x_{as} = 1/2$, $x_{ss} = 0$. Since the fraction of altruists in aa remains 1 at the end of the period, we have $\Delta x_{aa} = 0$, and for the same reason $\Delta x_{ss} = 0$. However, the expected number of altruists in as groups at the end of the period is

$$\text{fraction of altruists} \;\times\; \frac{\text{fitness of altruists}}{\text{mean fitness}} = \frac{1}{2}\frac{-c}{(b - c)/2}.$$

Thus, $\Delta x_{as} = -c/(b - c) - 1/2 = -(b + c)/2(b - c)$. The expectation term in Price's equation then becomes

$$\mathbf{E}[\pi, \Delta x] = f_{aa}\pi_{aa}\Delta x_{aa} + f_{as}\pi_{as}\Delta x_{as} + f_{ss}\pi_{ss}\Delta x_{ss}$$

$$= f(r + (1 - r)f)(b - c) \times 0$$

$$+ 2f(1 - f)(1 - r)\frac{b - c}{2}\left(-\frac{(b + c)}{2(b - c)}\right)$$

$$+ (1 - f)(r + (1 - r)(1 - f)) \times 0 \times 0$$

$$= -\frac{b + c}{2}f(1 - f)(1 - r).$$

This is negative, as expected, becomes more negative with increasing cost c of altruism, and less negative when the degree r of assortative interaction increases. The expectation term also becomes more negative when the benefit b conferred increases, because the altruist becomes less fit by comparison with the selfish agent.

Note that

$$\bar{x} = f_{aa}x_{aa} + f_{as}x_{as} + f_{ss}x_{ss}$$

$$= f(r + (1 - r)f) \times 1 + 2f(1 - f)(1 - r) \times 1/2$$
$$+ (1 - f)(r + (1 - r)(1 - f)) \times 0$$
$$= f(r + (1 - r)f) + f(1 - f)(1 - r) = f,$$

so the covariance term in Price's equation becomes in this example

$$\text{cov}[\pi, x] = f_{aa}(\pi_{aa} - \overline{\pi})(x_{aa} - \overline{x}) + f_{as}(\pi_{as} - \overline{\pi})(x_{as} - \overline{x})$$
$$+ f_{ss}(\pi_{ss} - \overline{\pi})(x_{ss} - \overline{x})$$
$$= f_{aa}\pi_{aa}(x_{aa} - \overline{x}) + f_{as}\pi_{as}(x_{as} - \overline{x}) + f_{ss}\pi_{ss}(x_{ss} - \overline{x})$$
$$= f(r + (1 - r)f)(b - c)(1 - f)$$
$$+ 2f(1 - f)(1 - r)\frac{b - c}{2}(1/2 - f)$$
$$+ (1 - f)(r + (1 - r)(1 - f)) \times 0 \times (0 - f)$$
$$= (1 + r)(1 - f)f(b - c)/2.$$

Note that the covariance term increases when the level r of assortative interaction increases and when the social value $b - c$ of altruism increases. The condition for the altruistic trait to increase is $\text{cov}[\pi, x] + \mathbf{E}[\pi, \Delta x] > 0$ which reduces to

$$r \geq r_* = \frac{c}{b}. \tag{11.7}$$

It follows that *a small number of altruists can invade a population of selfish agents, provided $r \geq r_*$*, so a positive level of assortative interaction is necessary for altruism to invade. This proves the theorem. Q.E.D.

Hamilton applied this model to altruism among kin by treating r as the biological degree of relatedness between two individuals, which can be defined as follows. Suppose individual A inherited a rare one-of-a-kind mutant from an ancestor. The *degree of relatedness* of A and another individual B is the probability that B has the same rare mutant gene.[21] For instance, since humans inherit half their genes from their fathers and half from their mothers[22] a father and a son have relatedness $r = 0.5$. This is because a rare mutant inherited by the son is equally likely to have come from his

---

[21]The usual definition is that the degree of relatedness is the number of genes two individuals share by common descent (i.e., inherited from the same ancestor). The two definitions are the same, when properly interpreted.

[22]Actually, this is true except for a small number of sex-related genes, which we will ignore for simplicity. We also assume that mothers and fathers are not related (i.e., there is no "inbreeding").

father or his mother. Similarly, two siblings have relatedness $r = 0.5$, since a rare gene possessed by one came from one parent, who transmitted it to the other sibling with probability $1/2$. You can check that grandparents and grandchildren are related $r = 0.25$, and so on.

Suppose, then, that two individuals have a degree of biological relatedness r, and one has an altruistic mutation that leads it to cooperate, increasing its partner's fitness by b at a fitness cost c to himself. Since the partner has the same mutant gene with probability r, the expected change in the frequency of the altruistic gene is $rb - c$, so the altruistic gene increases precisely when $rb > c$.

The important point of this analysis is that *the same mechanism that accounts for altruism among kin can account for altruism among unrelated individuals, if we replace the biological process of genetic inheritance by some social process that maintains the frequency r of assortative interaction at a sufficiently high level.*

11.8   The Evolution of Strong Reciprocity

The stunning success of *Homo sapiens* is based on the ability of its members to form societies consisting of large numbers of biologically unrelated cooperating individuals. Neoclassical economic theory explains such cooperation using models of exchange with complete contracting. We have argued that such models do not yet adequately depict current economies (§3.19), much less those more rudimentary economies that accompanied the evolutionary emergence of our species, when the biological basis for our behavior and preferences were formed.

Game theory gives us more plausible models of social cooperation with incomplete or nonexistent contracting, in which *Homo economicus* agents build reputations by cooperating and punishing noncooperators, and in repeated interactions use threats of punishment, such as trigger strategies, to induce cooperation (see chapter 6). Reciprocal altruism of this type probably accounts for a good deal of human cooperation but is in fact quite rare among other species. How do we explain this fact? Intelligence alone is not the answer. Reciprocal altruism does require a high level of cognitive development, but since this behavior occurs in some species of vampire bats, its absence in species with at least this level of cognitive development, which includes a large number of birds and mammals, remains to be explained.

A critical weakness of reciprocal altruism is that when a social group is threatened with extinction or dispersal, say through war, pestilence, or famine, cooperation is most needed for survival. But the discount rate, which depends inversely on the probability of future interactions, increases sharply when the group is threatened. Thus, *precisely when society is most in need of prosocial behavior, cooperation based on reciprocal altruism will collapse*, for the simple reason that the discount rate will rise to levels where cooperation is no longer a Nash equilibrium. The rarity of reciprocal altruism can then be explained by the fact that *for most members of most species enough of the time, the discount rate is very high* because individual death rates are high, rates of group extinction and dispersal are high, and migration across groups occurs at a high rate.

But might not the same be said of human society during most of its evolutionary history? Since primates have not developed more than rudimentary levels of reciprocal altruism despite extremely high levels of cognitive ability, such is likely to have been the case. Perhaps the development of strong reciprocity, which leads agents to cooperate and punish noncooperators *independent of the future benefits and costs of such action*, took place precisely as a solution to the problem of high discount rates. Here is a suggestion as to how this might have occurred.

Homo reciprocans is an altruist in the sense that he improves the welfare of a group of unrelated individuals at the expense of his personal welfare. For unlike *Homo economicus*, who cooperates and punishes only if it is in his long term interest to do so, *Homo reciprocans* behaves prosocially even at personal cost. If *Homo reciprocans* is an evolutionary adaptation, it must be a considerable benefit to a group to have strong reciprocators, and the group benefits must outweigh the individual's costs in the sense of Price's equation (11.6); i.e., we must have $\text{cov}[\pi, x] > -\text{E}[\pi, \Delta x]$, where x is the frequency of the strong reciprocity trait and π is group fitness.

Consider an n-player public goods game (§11.4.2) in which each player has an amount c that may be kept or contributed to the "common pool." If the money is contributed, an amount $b > c$ is distributed equally among the members of the group. Thus, if k players contribute, each contributing player receives kb/n, and each noncontributing member receives $c + kb/n$. If $b/n < c$, the only Nash equilibrium is universal defection, in which each player keeps c. The Folk Theorem (§6.4) states that if this game is repeated indefinitely, full cooperation becomes a subgame perfect Nash equilibrium, provided the discount rate is sufficiently low.

We model early human society as a collection of small communities, each of which is engaged in this public goods game. Defecting is always detected and is common knowledge. When the discount factor is high enough to induce cooperation, defectors are excluded from participation in the community for a number of periods just sufficient to make defecting a suboptimal strategy, at zero cost to the community.

We suppose that in each "good" period the community will persist into the next period with probability δ^*, so δ^* is the discount factor (§6.2). In each "bad" period there is a high probability $1 - \delta_*$ that the community will disband, so the discount factor is $\delta_* < \delta^*$. We suppose that the "bad" state occurs with small probability $p > 0$, and for simplicity, we suppose that the threat to the community does not affect the cost c or the return b. Suppose at the beginning of each period, prior to agents deciding whether or not to cooperate, the state of the community for that period is revealed to the members. Let π^* be the present value (total fitness) of a member if all members cooperate forever and the state of the community is "good," and let π_* be the present value of universal cooperation if the state is "bad." Then the present value before the state is revealed is $\pi = p\pi_* + (1 - p)\pi^*$, and we have the following recursion equations:

$$\pi^* = b - c + \delta^*\pi$$
$$\pi_* = b - c + \delta_*\pi,$$

which we can solve, giving

$$\pi^* = \frac{1 + p(\delta^* - \delta_*)}{1 - \delta^* + p(\delta^* - \delta_*)}(b - c) \qquad (11.8)$$

$$\pi_* = \frac{1 - (1 - p)(\delta^* - \delta_*)}{1 - \delta^* + p(\delta^* - \delta_*)}(b - c) \qquad (11.9)$$

$$\pi = \frac{1}{1 - \delta^* + p(\delta^* - \delta_*)}(b - c). \qquad (11.10)$$

Note that $\pi^* - \pi_* = \pi(\delta^* - \delta_*)$, which is strictly positive, as expected. These equations assume that the fitness of a member of a community that disbands is zero, which is thus the benchmark for all fitness values, and to which we must add an exogenous "baseline fitness" to account for the change in population of the set of communities.

When can cooperation be sustained? Clearly, if it is worthwhile for an agent to cooperate in a bad period, it is worthwhile to cooperate in a good period, so we need only check the bad-period case. The current cost of co-operating is $c - b/n$, which we approximate by c for notational convenience (the approximation is good for a large community), so the condition for co-operation is $c < \delta_* \pi$. There is a Nash equilibrium in which members thus cooperate in the good state but not in the bad when the following inequalities hold:

$$\delta^* \pi > c > \delta_* \pi, \tag{11.11}$$

which will be the case if δ^* is near unity and δ_* is near zero. We assume these inequalities hold.

Suppose community i has a fraction f_i of strong reciprocators who co-operate and punish defectors independent of the state of the community. Suppose each cooperator inflicts a total amount of harm $l_r < 1$ on defectors, at a cost $c_r < 1$ to themselves. Because of (11.11), in a bad state selfish agents always defect unless punished by strong reciprocators. If there are n_i community members, in a bad state $n_i(1 - f_i)$ defect, and the total harm inflicted on those caught is $n_i f_i l_r$, so the harm per defector imposed by strong reciprocators is $f_i l_r / (1 - f_i)$. The gain from defecting in (11.11) now becomes $c - f_i l_r / (1 - f_i)$. Thus, if the fraction f_i of strong reciprocators is at least

$$f_* = \frac{c - \pi \delta_*}{c - \pi \delta_* + l_r}, \tag{11.12}$$

complete cooperation will hold. Note that f_* is strictly between zero and one, since the numerator, which is the gain from defecting prior to being punished by reciprocators, is positive. Also, the larger l_r, the smaller the minimum fraction f_* of reciprocators needed to induce cooperation.

If $f_i < f_*$, there will be no cooperation in a bad period (we continue to assume the parameters of the model are such that there is always cooperation in the good period). In this situation the community disbands and each member takes the fallback fitness 0. The fitness π_s of members of such "selfish" communities then satisfies the recursion equation $\pi_s = (1 - p)(b - c + \delta^* \pi_s)$, which becomes

$$\pi_s = \frac{(1 - p)}{1 - (1 - p)\delta^*}(b - c). \tag{11.13}$$

Our assumption that there is always cooperation in the good state requires that $\delta^* \pi_s > c$, which becomes

$$\frac{\delta^*(1 - p)}{1 - (1 - p)\delta^*}(b - c) > c,$$

which we will assume holds. Note that the relative fitness benefit from being in a cooperative community is

$$d\pi = \pi - \pi_s = p\pi \frac{1 - (1 - p)(\delta^* - \delta_*)}{1 - (1 - p)\delta^*} > 0. \qquad (11.14)$$

We suppose that the fraction of strong reciprocators in a community is common knowledge, and strong reciprocators punish defectors only in communities where $f_i \geq f^*$, and in doing so they each incur the fixed fitness cost c_r. We shall interpret c_r as a surveillance cost, and since punishment is unnecessary except in "bad" periods, strong reciprocators will incur this cost only with probability p, so the expected fitness cost of being a strong reciprocator is pc_r.

We will use Price's equation to chart the dynamics of strong reciprocity, which in this case says the change Δf in the fraction of strong reciprocators in the population is given by

$$\Delta f = \frac{1}{\bar{\pi}}\text{cov}[\pi, x] + \frac{1}{\bar{\pi}}\mathbf{E}[\pi \Delta x], \qquad (11.15)$$

where $\bar{\pi}$ is the mean fitness of the population. Let q_f be the fraction of the population in cooperative communities, so

$$q_f = \sum_{f_i \geq f_*} q_i,$$

where q_i is the fraction of the population in community i. The fitness of each member of a community with $f_i \geq f_*$ (resp. $f_i < f_*$) is π (resp. π_s), so the average fitness is $\bar{\pi} = q_f \pi + (1 - q_f)\pi_s$. Note that

$$\frac{1}{\bar{\pi}}\mathbf{E}[\pi \Delta x] = \sum_{f_i \geq f^*} q_i f_i \frac{\pi}{\bar{\pi}}(-pc_r). \qquad (11.16)$$

Let $f_c = \sum_{f_i \geq f_*} q_i f_i / q_f$, which is the mean fraction of strong reciprocators in cooperative communities. Note that

$$\pi - \bar{\pi} = (1 - q_f)(\pi - \pi_s)$$
$$= (1 - q_f)\left[\frac{1}{1 - \delta^* + p(\delta^* - \delta_*)} - \frac{1 - p}{1 - \delta^* + p\delta^*}\right](b - c)$$
$$\approx (1 - q_f)p\pi.$$

This approximation will usually be very good, since $p\delta_*$ is very small compared to $1 - \delta^*(1 - p)$, and it is harmless anyway, so we will assume that $\pi - \overline{\pi} = (1 - q_f)p\pi$. But then $\pi/\overline{\pi} = 1/(1 - p(1 - q_f))$, so (11.16) becomes

$$\frac{1}{\overline{\pi}}\mathbf{E}[\pi \Delta x] = -\frac{pc_r q_f f_c}{1 - p(1 - q_f)}. \tag{11.17}$$

To evaluate the covariance term, we define $f_s = \sum_{f_i < f_*} q_i f_i/(1 - q_f)$, which is the mean frequency of strong reciprocators in noncooperative communities. Also, $\pi(1 - p(1 - q_f)) = \overline{\pi}$, so

$$\frac{\pi}{\overline{\pi}} - 1 = \frac{(1 - q_f)p}{1 - p(1 - q_f)}.$$

Similarly, we have $\pi_s - \overline{\pi} = -q_f(\pi - \pi_s) = -q_f p\pi$, so

$$\frac{\pi_s}{\overline{\pi}} - 1 = -q_f p\frac{\pi}{\overline{\pi}} = \frac{-q_f p}{1 - p(1 - q_f)}.$$

Therefore, we can evaluate the covariance term as

$$\frac{1}{\overline{\pi}}\mathrm{cov}(\pi_i, f_i) = \sum_{f_i \geq f_*} q_i \left(\frac{\pi}{\overline{\pi}} - 1\right) f_i + \sum_{f_i < f_*} q_i \left(\frac{\pi_s}{\overline{\pi}} - 1\right) f_i$$

$$= q_f f_c\frac{(1 - q_f)p}{1 - p(1 - q_f)} - (1 - q_f)f_s\frac{-q_f p}{1 - p(1 - q_f)}$$

$$= \frac{q_f(1 - q_f)p}{1 - p(1 - q_f)}(f_c - f_s).$$

Thus, the condition for the increase in strong reciprocity is

$$(1 - q_f)\left(1 - \frac{f_s}{f_c}\right) - c_r > 0, \tag{11.18}$$

and equilibrium occurs when the left-hand side of the equation is zero.

From (11.18) we get the following.

THEOREM 11.7 *Under the condition stated above, the fraction of strong reciprocators in the population lies strictly between zero and one in equilibrium. Moreover, a small number of strong reciprocators can invade a population of selfish types, provided f_s/f_c is sufficiently small, i.e., provided the strong reciprocators have a sufficiently strong tendency to associate with one another.*

Suppose communities are of size n and form randomly, the overall frequency of strong reciprocators being f. Then the expected frequency of strong reciprocators in each community will be f, with variance $f(1-f)/n$. Therefore, if $f < f_*$ and if n is large (say 100), with high probability no communities will have $f_i > f_*$, and even if some such communities exist, f_s/f_c will be very close to unity. Therefore, we have the following.

THEOREM 11.8 *Without a positive level of assortative interactions, strong reciprocators cannot invade a population of selfish types.*[23]

So let us assume that there is some way that strong reciprocators can recognize one another. Without attempting to model community formation too closely, let us simply say that communities are of equal size, and that a fraction g are formed by assortative interactions, consisting of a fraction r of strong reciprocators and a fraction $1 - r$ drawn randomly from the population. If the fraction of strong reciprocators in the population is f, then the assortative groups have a fraction $f_c = r + f(1 - r)$ of strong reciprocators. To determine f_s, note that the fraction of strong reciprocators in assortative groups is gf_c, so the fraction in randomly formed groups is $f - gf_c$, and since such groups form a fraction $1 - g$ of the total, the fraction of strong reciprocators in a randomly formed group is $f_s = (f - gf_c)/(1 - g)$. Then if assortative groups are cooperative while randomly mixed groups are not, we have $g = q_f$, and (11.18) becomes

$$\frac{r(1 - f)}{r + f(1 - r)} - c_r > 0. \tag{11.19}$$

This inequality holds for any value of $r > 0$ when f is very small, which is thus the condition for the invadability of strong reciprocators *however small the level of assortative interaction*. The level r of assortative interaction does, however, determine the equilibrium frequency of strong reciprocators. Setting the left-hand side of (11.19) to zero and solving for the equilibrium frequency $\hat{f}$ of strong reciprocators, we get

$$\hat{f} = \frac{r(1 - c_r)}{r(1 - c_r) + c_r}. \tag{11.20}$$

[23]One may think that a pattern of outmigration from cooperative groups might allow strong reciprocity to increase, but extensive analysis by population biologists fails to turn up any plausible models of this type. For an important contribution and review of the literature, see Rogers 1990.

The fraction of strong reciprocators thus varies from zero when $r = 0$ to $1 - c_r$ when $r = 1$. We may summarize this argument by saying the following.

THEOREM 11.9 *Suppose there is a degree $r > 0$ of assortative interaction among strong reciprocators. Then a small number of reciprocators can invade a population of selfish types, and the equilibrium fraction of reciprocators is given by $\hat{f}$ in (11.20).*

11.9 *Homo parochius:* Modeling Insiders and Outsiders

From the point of view of classical political philosophy, personas such as *Homo reciprocans* and *Homo egualis* are anomalous, because the behaviors they support are of ambiguous ethical value. *Homo reciprocans* is a spontaneous and often unconditional cooperator (ethically positive), but is morally judgmental and vindictive (ethically negative, at least according to liberal ethics). *Homo egualis* seeks equality, but even at the expense of pulling down everyone if that hurts the well-off more than himself. *Homo parochius*, who divides the world into *insiders* and *outsiders* according to race, ethnicity, and other ascriptive attributes of individuals, is universally condemned in modern ethical systems (although heartily affirmed in the Old Testament and other religious documents) while being embraced by a good fraction of ordinary individuals without sufficient "moral training."

Everyday observation is sufficient to convince one that the ability and willingness to divide the world into "insiders" and "outsiders" is virtually universal in us, although many good souls refuse to participate in forms of parochialism that compromise individual rights—such as racial, ethnic, and religious intolerance, or stereotyping based on gender, sexual preference, and social class. But even where such forms of discriminatory behavior are severely frowned upon, *Homo parochius* emerges in force in the form of hometown favoritism. For every New Yorker who is a fan of the Chicago White Sox, for instance, there are doubtless a thousand who are fans of the New York Yankees. And as we have suggested, such "insider-outsider" behavior is extremely easy to invoke in an experimental setting (Turner 1984).[24]

[24]Unlike the other exotic behaviors described in this chapter, that of *Homo parochius* does exist in other highly social species, such as ants, termites, and bees, where nest-mates can be clearly distinguished by chemical markers. While it is doubtful that anything akin to

By *parochialism* we mean favoring members of one's own group over members of other groups at a net material cost to oneself. The following model of parochial behavior, based on a model of reciprocity developed in Sethi and Somanathan (1999), shows that parochial behavior can be the stable outcome of an evolutionary dynamic (we do not distinguish between cultural and genetic mechanisms).

Suppose a group of n fishers share a lake that has a carrying capacity of one ton of fish per fisher per season. If fisher i exerts effort x_i, his net profit, measured in tons of fish in a season is given by

$$\pi(x_i) = x_i \left(1 - \frac{1}{n} \sum_{i=1}^{n} x_i \right) - ax_i^2, \tag{11.21}$$

where $a > 0$ is a measure of the cost of effort. Note that when total community effort is small, a unit of effort yields nearly a unit of fish, but when total effort is close to n, a unit of effort yields almost no fish. This is thus an example of the "tragedy of the commons" (§3.9, §11.4.4). If the fishers are "selfish" and choose best responses, you can easily show the following.

THEOREM 11.10 *There is a unique Nash equilibrium, in which each fisher chooses effort level*

$$x_i^* = \frac{1}{1 + 2a + n^{-1}}$$

and receives payoff

$$\pi(x_i^*) = \frac{(a + n^{-1})}{(1 + 2a + n^{-1})^2}.$$

If the community members could agree to share the catch equally and could enforce a socially optimal effort level x° for each fisher, they would set

$$x^\circ = \frac{1}{2(1 + a)},$$

and each fisher would have payoff

$$\pi(x^\circ) = \frac{1}{4(1 + a)}.$$

"race" or "ethnicity" exists in nonhuman animals, groups of primates do offer preferential treatment to their own members.

Clearly, for large n, the lake is severely overfished, unless a is so large that the x_i^* is small, i.e., unless there is no tendency for the community to press upon the capacity limits of the lake. Note that when $a = 0$, $\pi(x^*) = n/(n+2)^2$, which is close to zero for large n. More generally, $\lim_{n\to\infty} \pi(x_i^*) = a/(1+2a)^2 \approx a$.

Suppose a fraction f of fishers are *discriminators* in the sense that instead of maximizing $\pi(x)$, they attach a positive weight α to the payoff of other discriminators, and a negative weight β to the payoff of selfish types. The "selfish" fishers (a fraction $1 - f$ of the total) simply maximize their personal material payoffs. We will consider only symmetric Nash equilibria in which all discriminators choose the same effort level x_r, and all selfish types choose the same effort level x_s. Actually, as an exercise you can prove that there are no other Nash equilibria. To determine x_r and x_s, we define

$$\pi(x, y, z) = z\left(1 - \frac{(nf-1)x_r + (n(1-f)-1)x_s - x - y}{n}\right) - az^2.$$
(11.22)

Thus, for instance, $\pi(x, y, x)$ is the net payoff of a fisher with effort x when one other fisher has effort level y, and the remaining fishers produce at the equilibrium level. Then a selfish type chooses x to maximize $\pi(x, x_r, x)$. Solving the first-order condition for x and setting $x = x_s$, we find that the selfish fisher's optimal effort is

$$x_s^* = \frac{n(1 - fx_r)}{(1 + 2a - f)n + 1}.$$
(11.23)

We find x_r by maximizing the following expression with respect to y:

$$u_r(y) = \pi(x_s^*, y, y) + \alpha(fn-1)\pi(x_s^*, y, x_r) - \beta(1-f)n\pi(x_s^*, y, x_s^*),$$
(11.24)

where we set $x_s = x_s^*$ in (11.22). In this equation, the first term is the catch of the discriminator who is choosing y; the second term is the catch of the other discriminators, weighted by α; and the third term is the catch of selfish types, weighted negatively by β. Solving the first-order condition $u_r'(y) = 0$, we find

$$x_r^* = \frac{n(n\beta(1 + 2a - f) + 1)}{d_2 n^2 + 2d_1 n + d_0},$$
(11.25)

where $d_2 = 4a^2 + 2\alpha(1 + f\alpha) + (1 - f)n(\alpha + \beta)$, $d_0 = (1 - \alpha)(n + !)$, and $d_1 = (a(2 - \alpha) + f\alpha)$. Note that when $f = 1$, $x_r^* = n/((1 - \alpha)(n +$

$1) + 2an + 1)$, which gives the socially optimal level of $x_r^* 1/2(1+a)$ when $\alpha = 1$, as we would expect. Substituting 11.25 in the expression for x_s^*, we find

$$x_s^* = x_r^* \frac{1 + 2an + (fn-1)\alpha}{1 + 2an + (1-f)n\beta}. \tag{11.26}$$

We assume a replicator dynamic (§9.2), in which the fraction f of discriminators increases when its payoff is greater than that of selfish types. The payoff to discriminators is then $\rho_r(f) = \pi(x_s, x_r, x_r)$, and the payoff to selfish types is $\pi(x_s, x_r, x_s) = \rho_s(f)$. We then can calculate that the difference in payoffs to discriminators and selfish types is given by

$$\rho_r(f) - \rho_s(f) = \frac{n((1-f)n\beta - (fn-1)\alpha)f_1}{d_2 n^2 + 2d_1 n + d_o}, \tag{11.27}$$

where $f_1 = (1 + (fn-1)\alpha + an(2 + (fn-1)\alpha - (1-f)n\beta))$. The equal payoff condition $\rho_s(f^*) = \rho_r(f^*)$ is then satisfied by two values:

$$f_1^* = \frac{\alpha + n\beta}{n(\alpha + \beta)} \qquad f_2^* = -\frac{1 - \alpha + an(2 - \alpha - n\beta)}{n\alpha + an^2(\alpha + \beta)}. \tag{11.28}$$

To check for stability, we form the replicator equation

$$\dot{f} = f(\rho_r(f) - \bar{\rho}(f)),$$

where $\bar{\rho}(f) = f\rho_r(f) + (1-f)\rho_s(f)$ is the mean fitness of the population. The Jacobian of this expression is quite complicated, but Mathematica calculated it without much complaint, and evaluating this at f_1^* we find that the equilibrium is stable, while evaluating at f_2^* (which may in fact be negative, and hence behaviorally meaningless) we find f_2^* is unstable.

Can discriminators invade a monomorphic population of self-interested fishers? We find that the Jacobian at $f = 0$ is given by

$$J_{f=0} = \frac{n(\alpha + n\beta)(1 - \alpha + an(2 - \alpha - n\beta))}{(1 + n + 2an)^2(1 - \alpha + 2an)^2},$$

which is positive when

$$\beta < \frac{1 - \alpha + (2 - \alpha)an}{an^2}. \tag{11.29}$$

A similar analysis of the case where $f = 1$ shows that the Jacobian is always strictly positive, so a monomorphic community of discriminator fishers cannot be invaded by self-interested fishers. In both the $f = 0$ and $f = 1$ cases, our inference holds only for sufficiently large n, since we assume the Jacobian does not change sign when a small number of mutants invade. We thus arrive at the following theorem.

THEOREM 11.11 *There is an evolutionary equilibrium in which the frequency of discriminators is given by f_1^* in (11.28) and hence is strictly positive. The effort levels of all agents are equal and are the same as the Nash equilibrium with self-interested agents exhibited in Theorem 11.10. When the frequency of discriminators is greater than f_1^*, the Nash equilibrium with discriminators is more efficient than the Nash equilibrium with self-interested agents. Conversely, when the frequency of discriminators is positive but less than f_1^*, the Nash equilibrium with discriminators is less efficient than the Nash equilibrium with self-interested agents.*

If n is sufficiently large, a monomorphic population of self-interested fishers can be invaded by a small number of discriminators provided they are not "too prejudiced," in the sense of (11.29).

Finally, if n is sufficiently large, a monomorphic population of reciprocating fishers cannot be invaded by a small number of self-interested fishers.

How might α and β move if they are subject to a replicator dynamic in the case of the heterogeneous equilibrium? Consider a community with a fraction f of discriminators characterized by parameters α and β. Suppose one discriminator "mutates" to a slightly larger value of α. I will not present the equations here because the calculations are complicated but (by now) straightforward (thank the Lord for Mathematica!). We have the following.

THEOREM 11.12 *If $f > f_1^*$, a mutant with a lower α has a relatively higher payoff, so under a replicator dynamic α will fall when the fraction of discriminators is in the efficiency-enhancing region. Conversely, if $f < f_1^*$, a mutant with a higher α has a relatively higher payoff, so under a replicator dynamic α will rise when the fraction of discriminators is in the efficiency-reducing region. At $f = f_1^*$, α-mutants have the same payoff as other discriminators.*

The parallel question for the parameter β has the following answer.

THEOREM 11.13 *If $f > f_1^*$, a mutant with a higher β has a relatively higher payoff, so under a replicator dynamic β will rise when the fraction of discriminators is in the efficiency-enhancing region. Conversely, if $f < f_1^*$,* *under a replicator dynamic β will fall when the fraction of discriminators is in the efficiency-reducing region. At $f = f_1^*$, β-mutants have the same payoff as other discriminators.*

Note that mutations in α and β move the dynamical system toward the equilibrium at $f = f_1^*$. However, the system is only *neutrally stable* in α and β at the equilibrium, so conditions other than those discussed in the model determine their equilibrium values, and, with them, the equilibrium f in a system in which α and β are endogenous.

a. Prove Theorem 11.10.
b. Prove Theorem 11.11 under the condition $a = 0$.
c. Prove Theorem 11.12 under the condition $a = 0$.
d. Prove Theorem 11.13 under the condition $a = 0$.

12

Learning Who Your Friends Are: Bayes' Rule and Private Information

> The philosophers kick up the dust and then complain that they cannot see.
>
> *Spinoza*

12.1 Private Information

Occasionally we have come across a game in which there is *private information*: some pieces of relevant information are known by some players but not by others *even before any player has made a move in the game*.[1] For instance in The Truth Game (§3.21) the car dealer knows the quality of the car but the prospective buyer does not. In One-card Two-round Poker with Bluffing (§4.11), One knows whether the card is high or low, but Two does not. In Real Men Don't Eat Quiche (§4.41), Clem knows whether he is Tough or a Wimp, but the Dark Stranger does not.

Private information can take several forms. First, the payoffs to a particular player may depend on the player's type, as in the case of Clem, who likes quiche only if he's a Wimp. Second, a player's type may affect the payoffs to other players, so, for instance, a strong opponent may inflict more harm than a weak opponent. Third, various states of the world may be known to some players but not others, as in the Truth Game, where only the dealer knows the quality of the car. Finally, some players may be precommited to making some choices and precluded from making others. For instance, in Predatory Pricing: Pooling and Separating Equilibria (§12.10), a "sane" firm may share the market with a new entrant if it is profitable to do so, while a "crazy" incumbent always preys on a new entrant, even if this leads to a lower payoff.

---

[1] Such games are usually called games of *incomplete information* in the literature. But this seems misleading, since unless information is private in the sense of being *asymmet-*

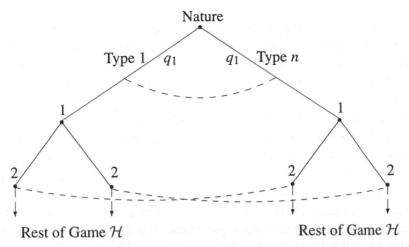

Figure 12.1. Modeling games with private information: the Harsanyi transformation.

There is a straightforward way to model games with private information, due to Harsanyi (1967). Notice that in all three games mentioned above (§3.21, §4.11, §4.41), Nature moves first, determining the private information available to one of the players (high or low quality, high or low card, Wimp or Tough). Then a complete copy of a game tree $\mathcal{H}$ describing the player's moves is attached to the tail of each branch corresponding to Nature's moves and the nodes from each copy of $\mathcal{H}$ where a player is ignorant of Nature's move are collected into a single information set for that player. In the general case we do exactly the same thing.

Formally describing the general case leads to a flurry of mathematical symbols that belies the simplicity of the procedure, so I will describe only the case where only Player One has private information. Let $\mathcal{H}$ be a game in which Player One may be one of a number of *types*, each "type" representing the private information One possesses. We make a new game $\mathcal{G}$ as illustrated in Fig. 12.1.

First, at the root node of $\mathcal{G}$, Nature chooses a type $\{1, \ldots, n\}$ for Player One, using a probability distribution $\{q_1, \ldots, q_n\}$ over types that is common knowledge to all the players. For each such choice—i.e., for each branch emanating from the root node—we append a copy of $\mathcal{H}$. Second, for each player i other than Nature and Player One, we note that each information set of player i in $\mathcal{H}$ has as many copies in $\mathcal{G}$ as there are Player One types. We collect all these information sets into one information set of $\mathcal{G}$ and assign

rically distributed among players, the reasoning we are about to undertake is vacuous.

this to player i. Thus, Player One now knows his type, but other players only know the frequency distribution of Player One types.[2] Finally, we define a strategy for Player One in $\mathcal{G}$ to be a choice of a strategy of $\mathcal{H}$ for each of the types Player One can have. The strategies for the other players in $\mathcal{G}$ are the same as in $\mathcal{H}$.

Games with private information often have many implausible Nash equilibria, and subgame perfection (as well as its mild generalization fuzzy subgame perfection—see §5.13) is rarely available to reject them because information sets are so pervasive that games with private information rarely have subgames. Moreover, there are often many mixed strategies that dictate exactly the same player choices, so the standard normal form notation obscures the game's behavioral regularities. For these reasons, in analyzing games with private information we often use the concept of a *perfect Nash equilibrium in behavioral strategies* in place of the Nash equilibrium in mixed strategies. This equilibrium concept is developed in §4.45 and §5.14, so if you have not yet studied those sections, now is the time to do so. For the impatient, however, a brief summary should suffice. We assume perfect recall (§1.3) throughout.

A *behavioral strategy* p_i for player i in an extensive form game $\mathcal{G}$ is a probability distribution p_ν over the player's action set at each of the player's information sets $\nu \in \mathcal{N}_i$, and a *behavioral strategy profile* p is the choice of a behavioral strategy for each player. Also included in p are the probability distributions over the nodes where Nature moves in $\mathcal{G}$. The *payoffs to a behavioral strategy profile* p are the expected payoffs to the players, assuming they use the probabilities given by p.

Starting from a mixed strategy σ of the normal form of $\mathcal{G}$, there is a natural way of deriving a *behavioral strategy representation* p of σ, such that the probabilities with which nodes are chosen from information sets are the same for p and σ, and p and σ have the same payoffs. Moreover, any behavioral strategy p has a *mixed strategy representation* σ that (a) induces the same probabilities on information sets, and (b) has the same payoffs as p. The association between mixed strategies and behavioral strategies is not one-to-one, however, because many mixed strategies can have the same behavioral representation.

---

[2]It may sound silly to say that Player One does not know such personal characteristics as sex and age until "revealed" by Nature's choice, but this "veil of ignorance" assumption is in fact purely formal.

We say a behavioral strategy profile $p = (p_1, \ldots, p_n)$ is a *Nash equilibrium in behavioral strategies* if, for each player i, p_i is a best response to p_{-i}. This is equivalent to saying that the mixed strategy representation σ of p is a Nash equilibrium of the normal form of $\mathcal{G}$.

The behavioral strategy concept allows us to define a new and often appropriate best response concept, called the *local best response*. Suppose i is chosen at node $a \in \nu$. The expected payoff to using p_ν given $p_{-\nu}$, is then

$$\pi_i(p_\nu | a, p_{-\nu}) = \sum_{t \in T} P[a, t | p_\nu, p_{-\nu}] \pi_i(t),$$

where T is the set of terminal nodes, $\pi_i(t)$ is the payoff to i at terminal node $t \in T$ and $P[a, t | p]$ is the probability of reaching t from a given p. If $P[a | p_{-\nu}, \nu]$ is the probability of being at node a, given that i is choosing at ν and p is being played, then i should choose p_ν to maximize

$$\pi_i(p_\nu | p_{-\nu}, \nu) = \sum_{a \in \nu} P[a | \nu, p_{-\nu}] \sum_{t \in T} P[a, t | p_\nu, p_{-\nu}] \pi_i(t).$$

Moreover, $P[a | p, \nu]$ is given by *Bayesian updating*:

$$P[a | \nu, p_{-\nu}] = \frac{P[a | p_{-\nu}]}{P[\nu | p_{-\nu}]}$$

where $P[\nu | p_{-\nu}] = \sum_{a \in \nu} P[a | p_{-\nu}]$. Note that when $P[\nu | p_{-\nu}] = 0$ (i.e., ν is not reached using $p_{-\nu}$), this definition does not make any sense, and we define $P[a | \nu, p_{-\nu}]$ arbitrarily. We then have the following *Fundamental Theorem on Bayesian Updating in Extensive Form Games*.

THEOREM 12.1 *If p is a Nash equilibrium of the extensive form game $\mathcal{G}$ and if ν is an information set that is reached with positive probability given p, then p_ν is a local best response to $p_{-\nu}$.*

This theorem gives us a quite convenient way of calculating Nash equilibria in behavioral strategies. In fact, in the literature this Nash equilibrium concept is called a *perfect Bayesian Nash equilibrium*, and I will do so as well, henceforth.

If an information set ν is not reached under p, it is still plausible that the local best response condition should hold at ν for all, or for an "appropriate subset" of probability distributions $P[a | \nu, p_{-\nu}]$ over the nodes at ν. The reasons for this are the same as for subgame perfection: should an agent in fact choose at v, he may use a best response, so other agents will do well not to heed incredible threats that entail avoiding v. How we determine "appropriate subsets" of probability distributions over unreachable information sets is, however, a gray area of game theory. One strong criterion is Selten's trembling hand perfection (§5.16), which implies that agents always behave as though there is a slight probability that an information set will be reached and play best responses even to very highly improbable states of affairs.

The trembling hand criterion is, however, much too strong in many situations, because *evolutionary processes ignore low probability events*. It follows a fortiori that evolutionary processes ignore zero probability events. For a codfish, the probability of being impaled on a fish hook is such a low probability event that it is simply not registered in the fish's perceptual or behavioral repertoire. It is folly to represent this situation as one in which the cod does not know which node (prey versus fishhook) it occupies in an information set. Reed warblers raise cuckoo eggs as their own not because they occupy an information set at which there is a very low probability that an egg is not their own, but because evolutionary pressures have not driven the species to make such distinctions. Nor is there any strong reason to believe that such pressures will develop, since cuckoos have evolved to change their hosts frequently. Human beings may be more susceptible to trembling hand perfection, but I would not bet my bank account on it. If you give people offers they cannot refuse, they often refuse anyway. If you put people in unfamiliar situations and depend on their reacting optimally, or even well, to these situations, you are not long for this world.

These considerations should not be taken as asserting that there are certain inherent limitations to game theory, but rather that we need new modeling concepts to deal with low probability events. For instance, perhaps we should assume that players partition the event world into sets whose probability is at least p_* and choose best responses based on these partitions. A mutant, however, can repartition the event space without violating the p_* minimum, to "invade" a Nash equilibrium based on a given partition. Since the strategy space is no longer finite (or closed and bounded), there need not necessarily be a Nash equilibrium of the metagame where partitions evolve, so the description of strategic interaction becomes one of temporary equilibria with shifting ways of carving up reality.

12.2 The Role of Beliefs in Games with Private Information

If you have previously studied game theory, you will no doubt have noticed that our treatment of Bayesian updating in games with private information has not relied at all on the concept of "beliefs." This is not an oversight but rather a natural side-effect of our evolutionary perspective. Classical game theory takes the decision processes of the *rational actor* as central, whereas evolutionary game theory takes the *behavior* of corporeal actors as central and models the game's evolution using replicator dynamics, diffusion processes and other population-level phenomena. Beliefs in such a framework are the *explicandum,* not the *explicans*—a shorthand way of expressing a behavioral regularity rather than the source of the regularity. There is absolutely no need to introduce the concept of beliefs into the general theory of games with private information.[3]

It may be comforting to the classically minded to have a notion that agents have beliefs at the start of the game (called *priors*), which they update using Bayes' rule in the course of the game and use to describe the process as *sequential rationality*, but the notion is completely unnecessary. The assumption that agents know the frequency distribution of types is no more or less in need of justification than the assumption that they know the rules of the game, the payoffs and the decision tree. It is an assumption that is justified by its ability to explain the behavior of agents in social life. Moreover, the "belief" concept invites all sorts of philosophical nonsense of the type parodied in the Spinoza quote at the head of the chapter.

Consider, for example, the great debate over the status of the assumption that "priors" are common knowledge. Harsanyi and other venerable game theorists (for instance, Aumann 1987a) have defended this *common prior assumption* on the grounds that "rational agents" faced with the same information must have the same priors. Others dispute this (e.g., Kreps 1990), and indeed there may be compelling technical arguments as to why, even in the case of costless information processing with no informational capacity constraints, identical information need not entail identical beliefs (Kurz 1997). Moreover, people appear to have consistent and predictable judgmental biases. There is, for instance, a considerable body of evidence that in bargain-

---

[3]There is one well-known equilibrium refinement concept that depends integrally upon a concept of beliefs, that of *sequential equilibrium* (Kreps and Wilson 1982), but the concept is virtually identical to (actually slightly weaker than) that of trembling hand perfection, which does not use a concept of beliefs.

ing and litigation, people have "self-serving biases" that do not simply reflect informational heterogeneity (Loewenstein, Issacharoff, Camerer, and Babcock 1992, Babcock, Loewenstein, Issacharoff, and Camerer 1995, Babcock and Loewenstein 1997).

The common prior assumption has also been defended by arguing that when there are differences in priors among agents, we should expand the number of agent types to include such differences—Mertens and Zamir (1985) show that this is always possible—so common priors then hold in the larger game. However, if we create new types to capture heterogeneous beliefs, the game becomes correspondingly more complex, and the assumption that the game structure and the frequency distribution of types are common knowledge becomes correspondingly less plausible. There may be cases where people do not have common priors over the parameters of the game, but they *do* have common priors concerning the frequency distribution of *differences* in priors, but probably not on this planet.

From the evolutionary perspective, there is no clear value in using game theory to analyze situations that have not been subjected to an extensive evolutionary process, after which it might be plausible that agents have *correct* and hence *common* priors, on grounds that agents that have inaccurate maps of the world are less likely to survive than agents who have accurate maps. But then again, perhaps not.

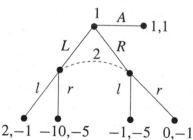

As an example of these ideas, consider the little game at the right, adapted from Kreps and Wilson (1982). There are two perfect Bayesian equilibria, (A,r) and (L,l), where the former requires weighting the probability of being at left-hand node of player 2's information set at least 0.5. It might be thought that the former equilibrium is "irrational," since if player 2 does indeed choose, then player 1 must have played L, since by playing R, player 1 cannot do as well as playing A, whatever player 2 does. But this is to force more structure on the game than it in fact possesses. It might be argued that if player 2 in fact chooses at all, then player 1 must have played L, since playing R ensures that player 1 does worse than when playing A. Therefore, the only "rational" move for player 2 is l. Knowing this, player 1 should play L and the (A,r) equilibrium cannot be played.

However, consider Fig. 12.2, which shows a simulation of the game with five hundred randomly programmed agents of each type who are randomly

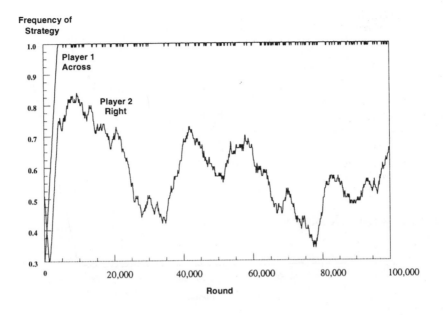

Figure 12.2. Simulation with random mutations.

paired in each period and 2% of which die and are replaced by more "fit" agents (i.e., ones with higher-payoff strategies) after every 100 periods. With random mutations, the (A,r) equilibrium eventually emerges. This outcome is typical of the random mutation case. If we bias mutations in favor of L, then we do obtain the (L,l) equilibrium as exhibited in Fig. 12.3. We could develop a model in which the mutation rate is itself subject to evolutionary forces, in which either equilibrium could predominate, depending on the precise structure of the larger model.

12.3 Haggling at the Bazaar

Consider a seller facing a buyer in a two-period game. In period 1 the seller makes an offer to sell at price p_1, and the buyer accepts or rejects. If the buyer accepts, the exchange is made, and the game is over. Otherwise, the seller makes another offer p_2, and the buyer accepts or rejects. If he accepts in the second period, the exchange is made. Otherwise, no trade occurs. The game tree is depicted in Fig. 12.4.

Suppose the reservation price of the good to the seller is s and the value to the buyer is b. Suppose buyer and seller have discount factors δ_s and δ_b

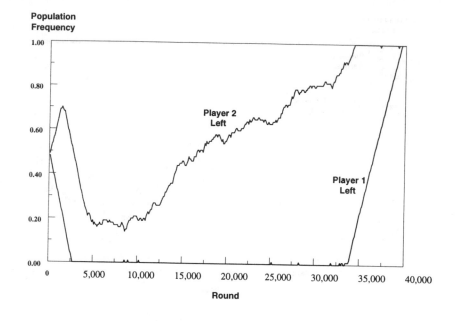

Figure 12.3. Simulation with mutations biased toward *L*.

for trades that are made in the second period. The value *b* to the buyer is unknown to the seller, but the seller believes that with probability π it is b_h and with probability $1 - \pi$ it is b_l, where $b_h > b_l > s$ (so the seller would gain from transacting with either type). Suppose that the parameters of the problem are such that if the seller did not get a second chance to make an offer, he would charge the lesser amount b_l, since otherwise the seller will ask the higher price in both periods and the problem is uninteresting.

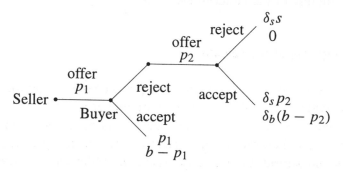

Figure 12.4. Haggling at the bazaar.

a.   Show that the payoffs are $[p_1, b - p_1]$, $[\delta_s p_2, \delta_b(b - p_2)]$ and $[\delta_s s, 0]$ in case the buyer accepts on the first round, the second round, and neither round, respectively.

b. Explain why the statement "if the seller did not get a second chance to make an offer, he would charge the lesser amount b_l" is equivalent to the statement that $\pi b_h + (1 - \pi)s \le b_l$, or simply $\pi \le (b_l - s)/(b_h - s)$.

c. Suppose $b_h \ge p_1 > b_l$, so there is some chance of getting to the second round. Let $\mu(p_1)$ be the seller's posterior probability that $b = b_h$, given that the buyer refused on round 1 at price p_1. Show that $\mu(p_1) = x\pi/(x\pi + 1 - \pi)$ where x is probability that a buyer for whom $b = b_h$ refuses price p_1. Show that this implies $\mu(p_1) \le \pi$; i.e., if we get to the second round, the seller's posterior probability of the event $\{b = b_h\}$ cannot increase.

d. Thus, conclude that if we reach a second round, the seller will offer $p_2 = b_l$.

e. Now roll back the game tree to the one-stage game in which the seller offers price p_1, the payoff for the buyer strategy "accept the offer" is $(p_1, b - p_1)$, and the payoff to the buyer strategy "reject the offer" is $(\delta_s b_l, \delta_b(b - b_l))$.

f. Define $p^* = b_h - \delta_b(b_h - b_l)$. Show that the only undominated strategies for the seller are $p_1 = b_l$ and $p_1 = p^*$.

g. Show that the seller chooses $p_1 = b_l$ if b_l is greater than $\pi p^* + (1 - \pi)\delta_s b_l$, chooses $p_1 = p^*$ if the opposite inequality holds, and otherwise is indifferent between the two choices. Show that the first case reduces to the inequality

$$b_h > \left(\frac{1 - \delta_s}{\pi} - (\delta_b - \delta_s)\right)\frac{b_l}{1 - \delta_b}. \tag{12.1}$$

h. Conclude that there is a unique perfect Bayesian equilibrium. What does equation (12.1) tell you about the conditions favoring the buyer or the seller?

i. Suppose the parameters of the problem are such that if the seller did not get a second chance to make an offer, he would charge the *greater* amount b_h. Show that there is no Bayesian perfect Nash equilibrium in pure strategies. Can you see intuitively why this would be the case? If you are ambitious, see if you can find a Bayesian perfect Nash equilibrium in mixed strategies.

12.4   Adverse Selection

In traditional models of the market for a good, supply and demand schedules intersect, determining the price. But in traditional models the characteristics of the good being traded are contractually specified or otherwise guaranteed fixed as the price is varied. The real world is often not so accommodating. Where the characteristics cannot be fixed, it is possible that some valued aspect of the good, which we may call its *quality*, will vary systematically with the price. We say there is *adverse selection* if the quality of the supply declines as the price declines. Here are some possible examples.

Labor: The wage in a traditional labor market is set to equate supply and demand. But this assumes the quality of workers is known by employers. Suppose not and a firm wishing to hire an employee must incur costs to evaluate applicants. The firm advertises a wage w for the job and evaluates applicants until a successful applicant is found. If the firm increases the wage offer, the pool of qualified applicants could increase, because some qualified workers who would not apply at the lower wage do apply at the higher. Thus, there is adverse selection in the labor market. The profit-maximizing firm will raise the wage offer to the point where the costs of paying a higher wage are just offset by the gains from lower transactions costs. Note that the wage will be higher than the market-clearing wage in this case, so there will be an *excess supply of labor* in (Nash) equilibrium.

Capital: The interest rate on a loan adjusts to equate demand and supply only if the quality of a borrower (the probability that the borrower will repay the loan) is contractually specifiable or otherwise known to a lender. Suppose a bank posts an interest rate r. If there is an excess demand for loans at that interest rate, the bank may be tempted to raise the interest rate. By so doing, some relatively low risk, low expected return projects would drop out of the demand, since they could not make a positive profit at a higher interest rate. But high risk, high expected return projects would remain in the applicant pool. If such a high-risk borrower is successful, the loan is repaid; if not, the lender simply gets stuck. This is adverse selection in the capital market. At some point, the gains from a higher interest rate will be offset by the losses because of the lower quality of the borrower pool, at which the (Nash) equilibrium interest rate will be determined. Note that there is an excess demand for credit at this interest rate.

Consumer Goods: In a traditional consumer good market, the price is set to equate supply and demand. But suppose the quality of the good is difficult to measure and the higher the price, the higher the expected quality of the good. Then consumers will be willing to pay a higher than market clearing price for the good, trading off the higher price for the higher expected quality. Once again, the (Nash) equilibrium involves an excess supply of the good.

For an overview of adverse selection models and other failures of markets to clear because of private information, see Stiglitz (1987). Such models have been successfully applied to building a microeconomic foundation for some of the macroeconomic phenomena described by John Maynard Keynes (Mankiw and Romer 1991). The analytical theory of adverse selection was initiated by George Akerlof's (1970) famous "The Market for 'Lemons'." The next example is in the spirit, but not in the letter of Akerlof's contribution.

12.5   A Market for Lemons

Consider a used-car market, in which the sellers all know the value of the cars they want to sell, but the buyers only know the distribution of car values. Suppose all agents are risk neutral (§16.41), and the value v of a used car is a random variable uniformly distributed on the interval $[v_*, v^*]$, where $0 < v_* < v^*$ and the reservation price for the seller of a car of value v is fv, where $0 < f < 1$. For simplicity, we assume this is the same for all sellers, and all buyers know f.

A pure strategy for a buyer is thus the choice of a price offer p. Clearly, it is a best response for a seller to accept any price $p \geq fv$. Assume there is perfect competition, so each buyer offers a price $p = \mathbf{E}[v|p]$; i.e., the price equals the expected value of the car, assuming the seller is willing to trade at that price.

For what values of f is this market Pareto-efficient? For what values of f are no cars bought or sold? What fraction of cars are sold in general?

To answer these questions, we first show that the allocation is Pareto-efficient if and only if

$$f \leq \frac{1 + v_*/v^*}{2}.\tag{12.2}$$

PROOF: If the equilibrium is Pareto-optimal, then all cars must be sold, so $p \geq fv^*$ must hold. The expected value of a car in this case is $\mathbf{E}[v|p] = (v^* + v_*)/2$, so $p = (v^* + v_*)/2$. Thus, $p = (v^* + v_*)/2 \geq fv^*$, or $f \leq (1 + v_*/v^*)/2$.

Now suppose $f \leq (1 + v_*/v^*)/2$ and let $p = (v^* + v_*)/2$. Then $fv^* \leq (v^* + v_*)/2 = p$, so $\mathbf{E}[v|p] = p$, and the equilibrium is Pareto-optimal. Q.E.D.

We also can show that if (12.2) fails, then the equilibrium price is given by

$$p = \frac{v_*}{2 - 1/f}.$$

The range of cars on the market will be $[v_*, v_*/(2f - 1)]$. In particular, as f approaches 1, this interval shrinks to zero length. This is Gresham's law in action: bad cars drive out good.

PROOF: If (12.2) fails (i.e., if cars are relatively valuable to their owners), then we can show that for a price $p \geq v_*$, the cars offered for sale will be uniformly distributed on $[v_*, p/f]$. To see this, we use Bayes' Rule. Let $V(\tilde{v})$ be the event "true value of car $\leq \tilde{v}$" and let $S(p)$ be the event "owner willing to sell car for price p." Then, for $fv_* \leq p < fv^*$, we have

$$
\begin{aligned}
P[V(\tilde{v})|S(p)] &= \frac{P[V(\tilde{v}) \& S(p)]}{P[S(p)]} \\
&= \frac{P[S(p)|V(\tilde{v})]P[V(\tilde{v})]}{P[S(p)]} \\
&= \frac{P[S(p)|V(\tilde{v})](\tilde{v} - v_*)/(v^* - v_*)}{(p/f - v_*)/(v^* - v_*)} \\
&= \frac{P[S(p)|V(\tilde{v})](\tilde{v} - v_*)}{p/f - v_*}
\end{aligned}
$$

which is zero for $\tilde{v} > p/f$ and $(\tilde{v} - v_*)/(p/f - v_*)$ for $fv_* \leq \tilde{v} \leq p/f$. This is the uniform distribution on $[v_*, p/f]$.

Prospective buyers in this case will purchase if and only if $p \leq (p/f + v_*)/2$, so the only possible Nash equilibrium has $p = (p/f + v_*)/2$, or

$$p = \frac{v_*}{2 - 1/f}.$$

The range of cars on the market will be $[v_*, v_*/(2f - 1)]$, as asserted.

12.6   Choosing an Exorcist

If your body is inhabited by an evil spirit, you go to an exorcist. Suppose there are two types of exorcists: thorough and casual. Exorcists know their type. The possessed (or their loved ones) can costlessly inspect exorcists and with probability $q = 10\%$ inspection reveals a thorough exorcist to be thorough, while with probability $1 - q$ the inspection of a thorough exorcist is inconclusive. Inspecting a casual exorcist is always inconclusive. Casual exorcism is worth $100 to the buyer and costs the seller $50 to provide, while thorough exorcism is worth $600 to the buyer and costs the seller $300 to provide. If an exorcist offers spells at price p and if the buyer accepts, the buyer's payoff is the difference between the value of the spells and p, and the payoff to the exorcist is p minus the cost of conjuring the spells.

Suppose that the equilibrium price p^* of exorcism that is claimed to be thorough is determined by the condition that the return to all exorcists from an encounter with a possessed buyer be equal. Suppose also that buyers and sellers of exorcist spells meet randomly.

By eliminating dominated strategies, we need consider only the following. Buyers accept any price $\leq \$100$. A buyer who discovers (with probability q) that a seller is thorough always accepts p^* and, in addition, of buyers who do not know the type of a seller asking p^*, a fraction α accept p^* and the remaining fraction $1 - \alpha$ reject p^*. Thorough exorcists all offer to sell at p^*, but a fraction β of casual exorcists also offer to sell at p^*, misrepresenting their spells as thorough, while the remaining fraction $1 - \beta$ of casual exorcists market their services truthfully. It so happens and it is common knowledge that 25% of exorcists are casual.

We can find the appropriate values of p^*, α, and β such that the above represents a Nash equilibrium as follows. First, we represent the expanded game tree in Fig. 12.5. Note that we have pruned the game tree according to the characteristics of the three types of exorcists in order to keep the diagram manageable.

We can find α by noting that the payoff to honest casual, dishonest casual, and thorough exorcists must be equal. The payoff to honesty is $\$100 - \$50 = \$50$, so the payoff to selling at p^* must also be $50 for the dishonest exorcist. But this payoff is just $\alpha(p^* - \$50)$, so $\alpha = 50/(p^* - 50)$. The payoff to a thorough exorcist is then $(q + (1 - q)\alpha)(p^* - 300)$, which must also equal 50. This gives the quadratic equation $qp^2 - 400qp + 30000q - 12500 = 0$ for p^*, with solution

$$p^* = 200 + 100\sqrt{1 + 1.25/q}.$$

Now we have

$$\alpha = 50 \bigg/ \left(150 + 100\sqrt{1 + 1.25/q}\right).$$

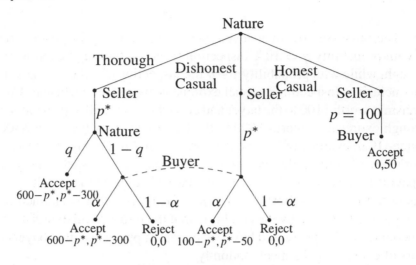

Figure 12.5. Choosing an exorcist.

With $q = 10\%$, this gives $p^* = 567.42$ and $\alpha = 9.66\%$.

To find β—the fraction of cheaters among the casual exorcists—we proceed as follows. Suppose inspection of a seller reveals nothing. Let $\pi(p)$ be the probability that the spells are casual given the asking price is p. Using Bayes' Rule, we find

$$\pi(p) = \mathrm{P}[\text{casual}|p]$$
$$= \frac{\mathrm{P}[p|\text{casual}]\,\mathrm{P}[\text{casual}]}{\mathrm{P}[p|\text{casual}]\,\mathrm{P}[\text{casual}] + \mathrm{P}[p|\text{thorough}]\,\mathrm{P}[\text{thorough}]}.$$

Using the fact that 25% of exorcists are casual, we get

$$\pi(p^*) = \frac{\beta \times \frac{1}{4}}{\beta \times \frac{1}{4} + 1 \times \frac{3}{4}} = \frac{\beta}{\beta + 3}, \tag{12.3}$$

and of course $\pi(\$100) = 1$ (an exorcist selling services for \$100 is surely casual). Since only a fraction of buyers accept p^*, the payoff to accept and reject must be equal. The payoff to reject is zero, so the payoff to accept must also be zero. But the expected payoff to accept is

$$100\pi(p^*) + 600(1 - \pi(p^*)) - p^*,$$

so

$$\pi(p^*) = \frac{4}{5} - \frac{1}{5}\sqrt{1 + 1.25/q},$$

so $\pi(p^*) = 6.51\%$. Substituting this in (12.3), we get $\beta = 3\pi(p^*)/(1 - \pi(p^*)) = 20.90\%$: a casual exorcist is dishonest with probability 20.9%.

12.7   A First-Price Sealed-Bid Auction

An object is to be sold to the highest bidder in a *first-price sealed-bid auction* (i.e., bids are submitted simultaneously, the highest bidder wins and pays the highest bid). Suppose there are two bidders, for each of whom the value v of the object is uniformly and independently distributed on the unit interval. This is thus a Bayesian game where the type of each player is the value of the object. Suppose both players choose a strategy of bidding $f(v)$, an increasing differentiable function of v. Given value v_1, Bidder 1 wants to choose b_1 to maximize

$$(v_1 - b_1)\mathrm{P}[b_1 > f(v_2)] = (v_1 - b_1)\mathrm{P}[g(b_1) > v_2] = (v_1 - b_1)g(b_1),$$

where $g(b) = f^{-1}(b)$, which exists since $f(v)$ is strictly increasing. Thus, given v_1, b_1 satisfies the first-order condition $g(b_1) = (v_1 - b_1)g'(b_1)$. By the symmetry of the problem, however, we must have $v_1 = g(b_1)$, so we have the differential equation

$$g(b_1) = (g(b_1) - b_1)g'(b_1).$$

This equation is satisfied by the linear function $g(b) = 2b$.[4] It follows that each bidder will bid $b = v/2$.

Now suppose there are k bidders, each with an independently distributed value v on the unit interval. Bidder 1 chooses b_1 to maximize

$$
\begin{aligned}
(v_1 - b_1)\mathrm{P}[b_1 &< \min\{f(v_2), \ldots, f(v_n)\}] \\
&= (v_1 - b_1)\mathrm{P}[g(b_1) < \min\{v_2, \ldots, v_n\}] \\
&= (v_1 - b_1)g(b_1)^{k-1}.
\end{aligned}
$$

The first-order condition, after a bit of simplification, is now

$$g(b_1) = (k - 1)(g(b_1) - b_1)g'(b_1).$$

This is satisfied by $g(b) = kb/(k - 1)$, so the optimal bid is $f(v) = (k - 1)v/k$. Note that as the number of bidders increases, the optimal bid approaches v.

[4]To arrive at this equation, assume $g(b)$ is a polynomial of some low degree and equate the coefficients of b on both sides of the differential equation to show that $2b$ works. Michael Mesterson-Gibbon has shown (personal communication) that this is not the only solution, but it is the unique solution with $g'(b_1) > 0$ and $0 \le g(b_1) \le 1$ for all b_1.

12.8   A Common Value Auction: The Winner's Curse

In the second-price auction (§2.8), the increasing-bid auction (§2.11), and the first-price sealed-bid auction (§12.7), each bidder has a private value for the object under contention and this value is known with certainty. The *common value auction* is a first-price, sealed-bid auction in which the object has the same value for all bidders, but they do not know that value—for instance, bidding for oil-drilling rights.

It is easy to see that in a common value auction, bidding your *measured value* will get you into trouble, since if you win, you are more likely than any other bidder to have overestimated the value! For instance, suppose there are n bidders, each of whom is allowed to take one "measurement" of the value, and suppose the measured value is $\tilde{v} = v + \epsilon$, where v is the actual value and ϵ is an error term that is uniformly distributed on the closed interval $[-a, a]$. Suppose all bidders bid their measured values and suppose you win. Prove that your expected loss is

$$a\frac{n-1}{n(n+1)} > 0, \tag{12.4}$$

so you lose by winning! This is called the *winner's curse*. Note that while the expected loss per bidder falls to zero as the number n of bidders increases, the total loss of all bidders is approximately a.

Since professional bidders are not usually stupid, they must bid less than their measured value in a common value auction. One possibility is to bid a constant amount less. But it is easy to see that this does not work. For instance, suppose everyone but you bids an amount b less than the measured value and you bid c less than your measured value, choosing c to maximize your expected profit. You can check that your profit is proportional to

$$-(2a + b - c)^n(a(n-1) - b + c) - (b - c)^n(a(n+1) + b - c).$$

Since all bidders make the same calculation, we must have $b = c$, in which case this expression becomes $-2^n a^{n+1}(n-1)$, which is negative. So this does not solve the problem of how to bid. You might check the literature to see what solutions are proposed to the Winner's Curse.

12.9   A Common Value Auction: Quantum Spin Decoders

The government ordered a quantum spin decoder built for its SETI (Search for Extra Terrestrial Intelligence) project and put it up for auction when the project was abandoned. The decoder is commercially useless, but it has two potentially valuable parts, a kramel inhibitor and a beta-phase detector. General Electric and Martin Marietta sent technicians to check out the decoder prior to the auction, but the GE technician didn't know much about beta-phase detectors and reported back that the kramel inhibitor is worth x on the market and the beta-phase detector is worth at most $\beta > 0$. The Martin Marietta technician didn't know much about kramel inhibitors and reported back that the beta-phase detector is worth y on the market and the kramel inhibitor is worth at most $\alpha > 0$.

So, suppose the value of the decoder is $\tilde{x} + \tilde{y}$, where $\tilde{x}$ is uniformly distributed on $[0, \alpha]$ and $\tilde{y}$ is uniformly distributed on $[0, \beta]$. Suppose GE knows the precise value x of the kramel inhibitor and Martin Marietta knows the precise value y of the beta-phase detector. Suppose, moreover, that these facts are common knowledge to both firms.

a. Suppose Martin Marietta sends an industrial spy to the economics division of GE and returns triumphantly with GE's bidding formula:

$$\left(\frac{\alpha + \beta}{2}\right) \frac{x}{\alpha}. \tag{12.5}$$

"But what is x?" asks her boss. "That I could not find out," she replies. Similarly, GE sends out a spy who returns with the formula

$$\left(\frac{\alpha + \beta}{2}\right) \frac{y}{\beta} \tag{12.6}$$

but does not know y. Show that these strategies form a linear Bayesian Nash equilibrium, find the value of the auction to the two firms and find the probability that each wins.

b. How do you make sense of the two strategies?

c. It looks like we are getting somewhere with this problem, but we're really not. To see this, suppose GE's spy came back and said, "Well, you know how our economists came up with the number $\delta > 1$ such that we should bid δx? Well, I found out Martin Marietta also has a magic number γ, which they use. They will bid γy and, moreover, you can check that $\gamma = \delta/(2\delta - 1)$." Strange but true. The Martin Marietta spy comes back with a similar story of having found out GE's δ and $\delta = \gamma/(2\gamma - 1)$.

Show that these two strategies form a linear Bayesian Nash equilibrium, whatever $\gamma > 1$ is.

d. Things are a bit better if there are three bidders. Show that in this case the strategy of each firm bidding 5/3 times its observation is a linear Bayesian Nash equilibrium.

e. Show that if there are four bidders, there is a unique linear Bayesian Nash equilibrium where each firm bids 9/4 times its observation. Only do this if you have a computer algebra program or a very sharp pencil.

f. Show that if there are five bidders, there is a linear Bayesian Nash equilibrium where each firm bids 14/5 times its observation. Only do this if you have a sophisticated computer algebra program or a very sharp pencil. I could not prove that this is unique, though I didn't try very hard.

12.10   Predatory Pricing: Pooling and Separating Equilibria

There are two firms, the "incumbent" and the "entrant." There are also two periods. The incumbent had a monopoly in the industry previous to period 1, earning monopoly profits m in each period. But the entrant decided to enter the market in period 1. The incumbent takes an action during period 1, either "prey" (charge a very low price to drive the entrant out of the market) or "accommodate" (charge a profit-maximizing price). The entrant's profit is $d_2 > 0$ if the incumbent accommodates and his loss is $p_2 > 0$ if the incumbent preys, with $m > d_2$. The incumbent may be either "sane" or "crazy." When sane, the incumbent makes d_1 by accommodating and loses p_1 when preying, with $d_1, p_1 > 0$. If the incumbent is crazy, he loses money by preying but reaps the psychic reward of punishing the entrant for disturbing his monopoly (or perhaps he has a different assessment of the costs and benefits of maintaining the monopoly, or has a reputation to uphold). Thus, if the incumbent is crazy he always preys.

However, even a sane incumbent might decide to prey, to try to convince the entrant that the incumbent is crazy and drive him out of the market in the second period. Let π_1 be the entrant's prior probability that the incumbent is sane (this is a Bayesian subjective probability, perhaps based on the frequency of sane incumbents in the economy), before the incumbent takes an action, and let π_2 be the entrant's posterior judgment that the incumbent is sane if he preyed in the first period. We assume that an incumbent is sane with probability 1 if he accommodated in the first period.

In period 2, the entrant chooses an action, either "stay" or "exit." If the incumbent is sane, he will not prey in period 2, since it can have no effect on the entrant's behavior. So, by staying the entrant will earn d_2 if the incumbent is sane and lose p_2 if the incumbent is crazy. If the incumbent is sane, he earns d_1 in period 2 if the entrant stays and $m > d_1$ if the entrant exits.

Fig. 12.6 shows a partial game tree for the problem, showing only the part of the game tree where the incumbent is sane and assuming that the discount factor for second period payoffs is δ.

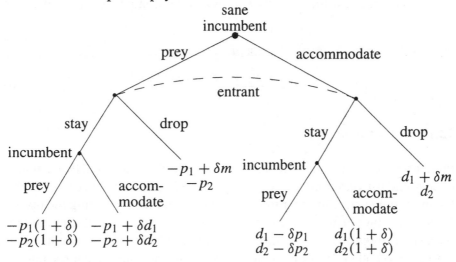

Figure 12.6. The predatory pricing model: This shows the part of the game tree starting from the Sane Incumbent. Note that all the nodes for the Entrant are part of two-node information sets, the other node of which is "Crazy Incumbent," who always preys.

We say a perfect Bayesian equilibrium is *separating* if the sane firm accommodates in the first period. Otherwise, the equilibrium is *pooling*. A separating equilibrium is one in which the "type" of a player (e.g., sane/crazy) is revealed by the player's behavior, whereas a pooling equilibrium is one in which different types of players behave in the same way. In a separating equilibrium for this game, the entrant has perfect knowledge in the second period.

a. Show that the condition for a separating equilibrium is

$$-p_1 + \delta m \leq d_1(1 + \delta). \tag{12.7}$$

b. Show that the condition for a pooling equilibrium is

$$\pi_1 \leq \frac{p_2}{d_2 + p_2} \tag{12.8}$$

c. If neither of these conditions holds, show that we may have a "hybrid" perfect Bayesian equilibrium, in which incumbent and entrant both randomize their choices. Show that this mixed strategy equilibrium is given as follows. Let α be the probability that a sane incumbent preys in the first period, and let β be the probability that the entrant stays in the second period if the incumbent preys in the first period. Then we have

$$\alpha = \frac{(1 - \pi_1)p_2}{\pi_1 d_2}, \tag{12.9}$$

$$\beta = \frac{-p_1 + \delta m - d_1(1 + \delta)}{m - d_1}. \tag{12.10}$$

12.11 Limit Pricing

Pre-game-theoretic industrial organization theorists often held that a monopolist would use *anticipatory pricing*, maintaining a product price lower than the monopoly price, in order to deter competition from entering the market. In antitrust law, it was hard to apply that argument against a monopolist because it suggested that the monopolist should be forced to raise his price!

But why bother lowering your price *before* an entrant comes into the market? Perhaps predatory pricing is a good idea, but it is certainly not clear that anticipatory pricing is as well. But suppose the incumbent wants to signal to a potential entrant that his costs of production are so low that the entrant couldn't make a profit by entering the market. Could this be a reasonable strategy? Let's see.

Suppose there is an incumbent firm with monopoly power in period 1, and this firm chooses first period price p. Then, in period 2, firm 2 decides whether to enter or to stay out. If firm 2 enters, there is a duopoly for that period and the game is over. Otherwise, firm 1 remains a monopoly.

Suppose both firms have constant marginal costs and no fixed costs. Moreover, marginal cost takes two values, high ($c = c_h$) or low ($c = c_l$). The entrant has high costs and the incumbent can have low costs with probability q, or high costs with probability $1 - q$. Let $m^h(p)$ be the incumbent's monopoly profit when he charges p and $c = c_h$ and let $m^l(p)$ be the incumbent's monopoly profit when he charges p and $c = c_l$. Let p_m^l and p_m^h

denote the monopoly prices charged by the incumbent when marginal cost is low or high (i.e., the monopolist's profit-maximizing price).

Let $m^l = m^l(p^l_m)$ and $m^h = m^h(p^h_m)$ be the incumbent's profit when he maximizes short run profits, depending on his type. Suppose the incumbent knows his cost, and the entrant learns the incumbent's cost after entering the market and committing himself to production. Thus, the duopoly price is independent of first-period prices. We denote the entrant's duopoly profits by d^h when costs are high and d^l when costs are low. We assume that $d^h > 0 > d^l$, so the entrant would enter only if the incumbent's costs are high (otherwise the problem is trivial).

The only way the incumbent can signal low cost is by charging a low price p^l. If $c = c_l$ and $p^l = p^l_m$, this is clearly optimal. But even if $c = c_h$, by charging p^l, the monopolist might convince the entrant not to enter, so the monopolist could charge the monopoly price in the second period. Thus, the l-firm might charge $p^l < p^l_m$ to deter the h-firm from entering. This is known as *limit pricing*.

Of course, if the entrant believes that a monopolist would charge a low price even if $c = c_h$, then observing the low price would have no effect on the entrant's decision. As before, we say a perfect Bayesian equilibrium is a *separating equilibrium* if the incumbent's action reveal his type; otherwise we say the equilibrium is a *pooling equilibrium*.

a. Prove that $p^l_m < p^h_m$, so it is plausible that a monopolist charging a low price has low costs.
b. Under what conditions do we have a separating equilibrium?
c. Give an example of a separating equilibrium.

We conclude from this analysis that when there is a separating equilibrium (a) because there is limit pricing (the incumbent manipulates his price to prevent pooling), the entrant knows the type of the incumbent perfectly; and (b) consumers are better off than if the incumbent were prevented from using limit pricing, since they get a lower price in the first period and entry still occurs when it should (i.e., when the incumbent is a high-cost producer).

12.12   A Simple Limit-Pricing Model

Consider a two-period game in which in the first period firm A has a monopoly position in an industry in which demand is $q = m - p$ where p is price and q is quantity. Suppose the firm has constant marginal cost

c, which can either be high (c_h) or low $(c_l < c_h)$. Firm A maximizes profits $\pi = (p - c)q = (m - q - c)q$ by setting $q = (m - c)/2$ and $p = m - q = (m + c)/2$.

Suppose, however, there is a firm B which has constant marginal cost c_h and fixed cost f and which could enter the market in the second period. Should B enter, the Cournot duopoly price will obtain in the second period. We assume that A knows B's production costs, but B does not know whether A is a high-cost (c_h) or a low-cost (c_l) producer. If A charges the monopoly price in the first period, then of course B can use this price to infer whether or not A is a low-cost or high-cost producer. To make the problem interesting, we assume that B would have negative profits competing against A if A is a low-cost producer and positive profits if A is a high-cost producer. But of course A could charge a price different from his monopoly price in the first period to deter B from entering in the second period.

Under what conditions will there be a separating equilibrium in which A charges his monopoly price in the first period? NOTE: You can leave your solution in the form of inequalities that must be satisfied in a separating equilibrium. Be sure to define separating and pooling equilibria, including the belief assumptions involved.

13

When It Pays to Be Truthful: Signaling in Games with Friends, Adversaries, and Kin

> Each discipline of the social sciences rules comfortably within its own chosen domain . . . so long as it stays largely oblivious of the others.
>
> *Edward O. Wilson (1998):191*

13.1 Signaling as a Coevolutionary Process

A Thompson's gazelle who spots a cheetah, instead of fleeing, will often "stott," which involves an 18-inch vertical jump, with legs stiff and white rump patch fully displayed to the predator. The only plausible explanation for this behavior (Alcock 1993) is that the gazelle is signaling the cheetah that it would be a waste of both their times and energies for the cheetah to chase the gazelle, since the gazelle is obviously very fit. Of course, if the cheetah could not understand this signal, it would be a waste of time and energy for the gazelle to emit it. Also, if the signal could be easily falsified and the ability to stott had nothing to do with the probability of being caught, cheetahs would never have evolved to heed the signal in the first place.[1]

A *signal* is a special sort of physical interaction between two agents. Like other physical interactions, a signal changes the physical constitution of the agents involved. But unlike interactions among nonliving objects, or between a nonliving object and a living agent, a signal is the product of a *strategic dynamic* between sender and receiver, each of whom is pursuing distinct but interrelated objectives. Moreover, a signal is a specific *type* of strategic physical interaction, one in which the content of the interaction is determined by the sender, and it changes the receiver's behavior by altering the way the receiver evaluates alternative actions.

[1] For a recent review of evidence for costly signaling in birds and fish in the form of colorful displays that indicate health and vigor, see Olson and Owens 1998. On the more general topic of costly signaling, see Zahavi and Zahavi 1997 and §13.6.

The most important fact about a signal is that it is generally the result of a *coevolutionary process between senders and receivers* in which both benefit from its use. For if a signal is costly to emit (and if its use has been stable over time), then the signal is most likely both *beneficial to the sender* and *worthy of belief for the receiver*—a sender is better off sending that signal rather than none, or some other, and a receiver is better off acting on it the way receivers traditionally have, rather than ignoring it or acting otherwise. The reason is obvious: if the receiver were *not* better off acting this way, a mutant who ignored (or acted otherwise to) the signal would be more fit than the current population of receivers, and would therefore increase its frequency in the population. Ultimately, so many receivers would ignore (or act otherwise on) the signal that, being costly to the sender, it would not be worth sending—unless, of course, the "otherwise" were also beneficial to the sender.

Signaling systems are not always in equilibrium and potentially beneficial mutations need not occur. Moreover, human beings are especially adept both at dissimulating (emitting "false" signals) and detecting such dissimulation (Cosmides and Tooby 1992a). However, human beings are disposed to taking the signals around them at face value unless there are good reasons for doing otherwise (Gilbert 1991). The treatment of signals as emerging from a coevolutionary process, and persisting as a Nash equilibrium of the appropriate game, is the starting point for a theory of signaling.

13.2   A Generic Signaling Game

Signaling games are special cases of Bayesian games, presented in chapter 12. In Bayesian games, players have "types" which may be partially or wholly revealed in the course of play. In signaling games, player 1 has a "type" that is revealed to player 2 *via* a special "signal," to which player 2 responds by choosing an "action," the payoffs to the two players being a function of player 1's type and signal and player 2's action. Thus, the stage game that played so prominent a role in the general Bayesian game framework collapses, in the case of signaling games, to a pair of payoff functions.

Specifically, there are players Sender, Receiver, and Nature. Nature begins by choosing from a set T of possible *types* or *states of affairs*, choosing $t \in T$ with probability $\rho(t)$. Sender observes t but Receiver does not. Sender then transmits a *signal* $s \in S$ to Receiver, who uses this signal to choose an *action* $a \in A$. The payoffs to the two players are $u(t, s, a)$ and $v(t, s, a)$, respectively. A pure strategy for Sender is thus a function $f : T \to S$, where $s = f(t)$ is the signal sent when Nature reveals type t, and a pure strategy for Receiver is a function $g : S \to A$, where $a = g(s)$ is the action taken when Receiver receives signal s. A mixed strategy for Sender is a probability distribution $p_1(s; t)$ over S for each $t \in T$, and a mixed strategy for Receiver is a probability distribution $p_2(a; s)$ over A for each signal s received. A Nash equilibrium for the game is thus a pair of probability distributions $(p_1(\cdot; t), p_2(\cdot, s))$ for each pair $\{(t, s) | t \in T, s \in S\}$ such that each agent uses a best response to the other, given the probability distribution $\rho(t)$ used by Nature to choose the type of Sender.

We say a signal $s \in S$ is *along the path of play*, given the strategy profile $(p_1(\cdot; t), p_2(\cdot; s))$, if there is a strictly positive probability that Sender will transmit s, i.e., if

$$\sum_{t \in T} \rho(t) p_1(s; t) > 0.$$

If a signal is not along the path of play, we say it is *off the path of play*. If s is along the path of play, we know from our argument in §12.1 that a best response for Receiver maximizes Receiver's expected return, with a probability distribution over T given by

$$P[t|s] = \frac{p_1(s; t)\rho(t)}{\sum_{t' \in T} p_1(s; t')\rho(t')}.$$

We thus require of p_1 and p_2 that

a. For every state $t \in T$ and all signals $s' \in S$ such that $p_1(s'; t) > 0$, s' maximizes

$$\sum_{a \in A} u(t, s', a) p_2(a; s)$$

over all $s \in S$.

b. For every signal $s \in S$ along the path of play, and all actions $a' \in A$ such that $p_2(a'; s) > 0$, a' maximizes

$$\sum_{t \in T} v(t, s, a) P[t|s]$$

over all $a \in A$.

c. if a signal $s \in S$ is not along the path of play, we may choose $P[t|s]$ arbitrarily such that (b) still holds. See the discussion of zero probability information sets in §5.17 and §12.1.

13.3   Introductory Offers

A product comes in two qualities, high and low, at unit costs c_h and c_l, with $c_h > c_l > 0$. Consumers purchase one unit per period, and a consumer only learns the quality of a firm's product by purchasing it in the first period. Consumers live for two periods, and a firm cannot change its quality between the first and second period. Thus, a consumer can use the information concerning product quality gained in the first period to decide whether to buy from the firm again in the second period. Moreover, firms can discriminate between first- and second-period consumers and offer different prices in the two periods, for instance, by extending an *introductory offer* to a new customer.

Suppose the value of a high-quality good to the consumer is h, the value of a low-quality good is zero, a consumer will purchase the good only if this does not involve a loss, and a firm will sell products only if it makes positive profits. We say that the industry is in a *truthful signaling equilibrium* if the firms' choice of sale prices accurately distinguishes high-quality from low-quality firms. If the firms' choices do not distinguish high from low quality, we have a *pooling equilibrium*. In the current situation, this means that only the high-quality firms will sell. Let δ be the consumer's discount factor on second-period utility.

a. Show that if $h > c_h + (c_h - c_l)\delta$, there is a truthful signaling equilibrium, and not otherwise.
b. What is the high-quality firm's price structure in a truthful signaling equilibrium?
c. Show that each consumer gains $h - c_l$ in the truthful signaling equilibrium, and firms gain $c_l - c_h + \delta(h - c_h)$ per customer.

13.4   Web Sites (for Spiders)

In the spider *Agelenopsis aperta*, individuals search for desirable locations for spinning webs. The value of a web is $2v$ to its owner. When two spiders come upon the same desirable location, the two invariably compete for it.

Spiders can be either strong or weak, but it is impossible to tell which type a spider is by observation. A spider may rear onto two legs to indicate that it is strong, or fail to do so, indicating that it is weak. However, spiders do not have to be truthful. Under what conditions will they in fact signal truthfully whether they are weak or strong? Note that if it is in the interest of both the weak and the strong spider to represent itself as strong, we have a "pooling equilibrium," in which the value of the signal is zero, and it will be totally ignored—hence, it will probably not be issued. If only the strong spider signals, we have a truthful signaling equilibrium.

Assume that when two spiders meet, each signals the other as strong or weak.[2] Based on the signal, each spider independently decides to attack or retreat. If two strong spiders attack each other, they each incur a cost of c_s, and each has a 50% chance of gaining/keeping the territory. Thus, the expected payoff to each is $v - c_s$. If neither spider attacks, each has a 50% chance of gaining the territory, so their expected payoff is v for each. If one spider attacks and the other retreats, the attacker takes the location, and there are no costs. So the payoffs to attacker and retreater are $2v$ and 0, respectively. The situation is the same for two weak spiders, except they have a cost c_w. If a strong and a weak spider attack each other, the strong wins with probability 1, at a cost b with $c_s > b > 0$, and the weak spider loses, at a cost $d > 0$. Thus, the payoff to the strong spider against the weak is $2v - b$, and the payoff to the weak against the strong is $-d$. In addition, strong spiders incur a constant cost per period of e to maintain their strength. The table shows a summary of the payoffs for the game.

Type 1,Type 2	Action 1,Action 2	Payoff 1,Payoff 2
strong,strong	attack,attack	$v - c_s, v - c_s$
weak,weak	attack,attack	$v - c_w, v - c_w$
strong,weak	attack,attack	$2v - b, -d$
either,either	attack,retreat	$2v, 0$
either,either	retreat,retreat	$0, 0$

Each spider has eight pure strategies: signal that it is strong or weak (s/w), attack/retreat if the other spider signals strong (a/r), attack/retreat if

---

[2]Note that this is a signaling game in which there is *bilateral signaling*: Sender sends a signal to Receiver, Receiver simultaneously sends a signal to Sender, and they each choose actions simultaneously. The conditions for a Nash equilibrium in such games are straightforward generalizations of the conditions developed in §13.2.

the other spider signals weak (*a/r*). We may represent these eight strategies as *saa, sar, sra, srr, waa, war, wra, wrr*, where the first indicates the spider's signal, the second indicates the spider's move if the other spider signals strong, and the third indicates the spider's move if the other spider signals weak (for instance, *sra* means "signal strong, retreat from a strong signal and attack a weak signal"). This is a complicated game, since the payoff matrix for a given pair of spiders has sixty-four entries, and there are four types of pairs of spiders. Rather than use brute force, let us assume there is a truthful signaling equilibrium and see what that tells us about the relationships among v, b, c_w, c_s, d, e, and the fraction p of strong spiders in the population.

Suppose $v > c_s, c_w$, and the proportion p of strong spiders is determined by the condition that the payoffs to the two conditions of being strong and being weak are equal.

a. What strategies are used in a truthful signaling equilibrium?
b. Use (a) to find the proportion p of strong spiders in a truthful signaling equilibrium. Find bounds for v in terms of e, c_w, and c_s for there to exist both strong and weak spiders in equilibrium.
c. What conditions on the parameters must hold for the equilibrium to foster truthful signaling?
d. Show that as long as both strong and weak spiders exist in equilibrium, an increase in the cost e of being strong leads to an increase in payoff to all spiders, weak and strong alike. Explain in words why this "counterintuitive" result is true.
e. Show that for some range of values of the parameters, an increase in the payoff v to the location can entail a *decrease* in the payoff to the spiders. For what value of the parameters is this the case? What value v^* maximizes the payoff to the spiders? Explain in words why this strange-seeming situation can occur.

13.5   Sex and Piety: The Darwin-Fisher Model of Sexual Selection

In most species, females invest considerably more in raising their offspring than do males—for instance, they produce a few large eggs as opposed to the male's millions of small sperm. So, female fitness depends more on the *quality* of inseminations, whereas male fitness depends more on the *quantity* of inseminations (§4.17). Hence, in most species there is an *excess demand for copulations* on the part of males, for whom procreation is very cheap, and therefore there is a *nonclearing market for copulations*, with the males on the long side of the market (§6.14). In some species this imbalance leads to violent fights among males (dissipating the rent associated with achieving a copulation), with the winners securing the scarce copulations. But in many species, *female choice* plays a central role, and males succeed by being attractive rather than ferocious.

What criteria might females use to choose mates? We would expect females to seek mates whose appearance indicates they have genes that will enhance the survival value of their offspring. This is indeed broadly correct. But in many cases, with prominent examples among insects, fish, birds, and mammals, females appear to have *arbitrary prejudices* for dramatic, ornamental, and colorful displays even when such accoutrements clearly reduce male survival chances—for instance, the plumage of the bird of paradise, the elaborate structures and displays of the male bowerbird, and the stunning coloration of the male guppy. Darwin speculated that such characteristics improve the mating chances of males at the expense of the average fitness of the species. The great biologist R. A. Fisher (1915) offered the first genetic analysis of the process, suggesting that an arbitrary female preference for a trait would enhance the fitness of males with that trait and hence the fitness of females who pass that trait to their male offspring, so the genetic predisposition for males to exhibit such a trait could become common in a species. More recent analytical models of sexual selection, called *Fisher's runaway process* include Lande (1981), Kirkpatrick (1982), Pomiankowski (1987), and Bulmer (1989). We will follow Pomiankowski (1987), who showed that *as long as females incur no cost for being choosy, the Darwin-Fisher sexual selection process works, but even with a slight cost of being choosy, costly ornamentation cannot persist in equilibrium.*

We shall model runaway selection in a way that is not dependent on the genetics of the process, so it applies to cultural as well as genetic evolution. Consider a community in which there are an equal number of males and females and there is a cultural trait which we will call *pious fasting*. While both men and women can have this trait, only men act on it, leading to their death prior to mating with probability $u > 0$. However, both men and women pass the trait to their children through family socialization. Suppose a fraction t of the population have the pious-fasting trait.

Suppose there is another cultural trait, a *religious preference for pious fasting*, which we call being "choosy" for short. Again, both men and women can carry the choosy trait and pass it on to their children, but only women can act on it, by choosing mates who are pious fasters at rate $a > 1$ times that of otherwise equally desirable males. However, there may be a cost of exercising this preference, since with probability $k \geq 0$ a choosy woman may fail to mate. Suppose a fraction p of community members bears the religious preference for pious fasters.

We assume parents transmit their values to their offspring in proportion to their own values—for instance, if one parent has the pious-fasting trait and the other does not, then half their children will have the trait. Males who are pious fasters then exercise their beliefs, after which females choose their mates, and a new generation of young adults is raised (the older generation moves to Florida to retire).

Suppose there are n young adult males and an equal number of young adult females. Let x_{tp} be the fraction of young adults who are "choosy fasters," x_{-p} the fraction of "choosy nonfasters," x_{t-} the fraction of "nonchoosy fasters," and x_{--} the fraction of "nonchoosy nonfasters." Note that $t = x_{tp} + x_{t-}$ and $p = x_{tp} + x_{-p}$. If there is no correlation between the two traits, we would have $x_{tp} = tp$, $x_{t-} = t(1-p)$, and so on. But we cannot assume this, so we write $x_{tp} = tp + d$, where d (which biologists call *linkage disequilibrium*) can be either positive or negative. It is easy to check that we then have

$$x_{tp} = tp + d$$
$$x_{t-} = t(1-p) - d$$
$$x_{-p} = (1-t)p - d$$
$$x_{--} = (1-t)(1-p) + d.$$

While male and female young adults have equal fractions of each trait—since their parents pass on traits equally to both—pious fasting and mate choosing can lead to unequal frequencies in the "breeding pool" of parents in the next generation. By assumption, a fraction k of choosy females do not make it to the breeding pool, so if t^f is the fraction of pious-faster females in the breeding pool, then

$$t^f = \frac{t - kx_{tp}}{1 - kp},$$

where the denominator is the fraction of females in the breeding pool, and the numerator is the fraction of pious-faster females in the breeding pool. Similarly, if p^f is the fraction of choosy females in the breeding pool, then

$$p^f = \frac{p(1-k)}{1 - kp},$$

where the numerator is the fraction of choosy females in the breeding pool.

We now do the corresponding calculations for males. Let t^m be the fraction of pious-faster males and p^m the fraction of choosy males in the breeding pool, after the losses associated with pious fasting are taken into account. We have

$$t^m = \frac{t(1-u)}{1-ut},$$

where the denominator is the fraction of males, and the numerator is the fraction of pious-faster males in the breeding pool. Similarly,

$$p^m = \frac{p - ux_{tp}}{1-ut},$$

where the numerator is the fraction of choosy males in the breeding pool.

By assumption, all $n^f = n(1-kp)$ females in the breeding pool are equally fit. We normalize this fitness to 1. The fitnesses of pious and nonpious males in the breeding pool are, however, unequal. Suppose each female in the breeding pool mates once. There are then $n^f(1-p^f)$ nonchoosy females, so they mate with $n^f(1-p^f)(1-t^m)$ nonpious males and $n^f(1-p^f)t^m$ pious males. There are also $n^f p^f$ choosy females, who mate with $n^f p^f(1-t^m)/(1-t^m+at^m)$ nonpious males and $n^f p^f at^m/(1-t^m+at^m)$ pious males (the numerators account for the $a:1$ preference for pious males and the denominator is chosen so that the two terms add to $n^f p^f$). If we write

$$r_- = (1-p^f) + \frac{p^f}{1-t^m+at^m},$$

and

$$r_t = (1-p^f) + \frac{ap^f}{1-t^m+at^m},$$

then the total number of matings of nonpious males is $n^f(1-t^m)r_-$ and the total number of matings of pious males is $n^f t^m r_t$. The probability that a mated male is pious is therefore $t^m r_t$. Since the probability that a mated female is pious is t^f and both parents contribute equally to the traits of their offspring, the fraction of pious traits in the next generation is $(t^m r_t + t^f)/2$. If we write $\beta_t = t^m r_z - t$ and $\beta_p = p^f - p$, then the change Δt in the frequency of the pious trait can be written as

$$\Delta t = \frac{t^m r_t + t^f}{2} - t = \frac{1}{2}\left(\beta_t + \frac{d\beta_p}{p(1-p)}\right). \tag{13.1}$$

What about the change in p across generations? The fraction of mated, choosy females is simply p^f, since all females in the breeding pool mate. The number n^m of males in the breeding pool is $n^m = n(1 - ut)$, of which nx_{-p} are nonpious and choosy, while $n(1-u)x_{tp}$ are pious and choosy. Each nonpious male has $n^f r_-/n^m$ offspring, and each pious male has $n^f r_t/n^m$ offspring, so the total number of choosy male offspring per breeding female is just

$$p^{m'} = nx_{-p}r_-/n^m + n(1 - u)x_{tp}r_t/n^m.$$

A little algebraic manipulation shows that this can be written more simply as

$$p^{m'} = p + \frac{d\beta_t}{t(1 - t)}.$$

Then the change Δp in the frequency of the choosy trait can be written as

$$\Delta p = \frac{p^{m'} + p^f}{2} - p = \frac{1}{2}\left(\beta_p + \frac{d\beta_t}{t(1 - t)}\right). \tag{13.2}$$

Let us first investigate (13.1) and (13.2) when choosy females are not less fit, so $k = 0$. In this case, $p^f = p$, so $\beta_p = 0$. Therefore, $\Delta t = \Delta p = 0$ exactly when $\beta_t = 0$. Solving this equation for t, we get

$$t = \frac{(a - 1)p(1 - u) - u}{u(a(1 - u) - 1)}. \tag{13.3}$$

This shows that there is a range of values of p for which an equilibrium frequency of t exists. Checking the Jacobian of the right-hand sides of (13.1) and (13.2), we find that stability requires that the denominator of (13.3) be positive (do it as an exercise). Thus, the line of equilibria is upward-sloping, and t goes from zero to one as p goes from $u/(a - 1)(1 - u)$ to $au/(a - 1)$ (you can check that this defines an interval contained in $(0, 1)$ for $0 < u < 1$ and $a(1 - u) > 1$). This set of equilibria is shown in Fig. 13.1. This shows that the Darwin-Fisher sexual selection process is plausible, even though it lowers the average fitness of males in the community—in essence, the condition $a(1 - u) > 1$ ensures that the benefit of sexual selection more than offsets the cost of the ornamental handicap.

Suppose, however, $k > 0$. If we then solve for $\Delta t = \Delta p = 0$ in (13.1) and (13.2), we easily derive the equation

$$d^2 = t(1 - t)p(1 - p).$$

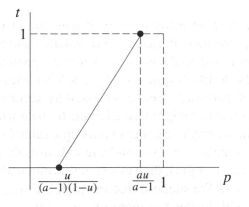

Figure 13.1. Equilibria in Darwin-Fisher sexual selection model when there is no selection against choosy females.

But $t(1-t)p(1-p) = (x_{t-}+d)(x_{-p}+d)$, which implies $x_{t-} = x_{-p} = 0$. But then, nonchoosy females must mate only with nonpious males, which is impossible so long as there is a positive fraction of pious males. We conclude that *when choosiness is costly to females, sexual selection cannot exist.* Since in most cases we can expect some positive search cost to be involved in favoring one type of male over another, we conclude that sexual selection probably does not occur in equilibrium in nature. Of course, random mutations could lead to a disequilibrium situation in which females prefer certain male traits, leading to increased fitness of males with those traits. But when the fitness costs of such choices kick in, choosy females will decline until equilibrium is restored.

13.6 Biological Signals as Handicaps

Zahavi (1975), based on close observation of avian behavior, proposed an alternative to the Darwin-Fisher sexual selection mechanism—a notion of costly signaling which he called the *handicap principle.* According to the handicap principle, a male who mounts an elaborate display is in fact signaling his good health and/or good genes, since an unhealthy or genetically unfit male lacks the resources to mount such a display. The idea was treated with skepticism for many years, since it proved difficult to model or empirically validate the process. This situation changed when Grafen (1990b) developed a simple analytical model of the handicap principle. Moreover, empirical evidence has grown in favor of the costly signaling approach to sexual selection, leading many to favor it over the Darwin-Fisher sexual selection model, especially in cases where female mate selection is costly.

Grafen's model is a special case of the generic signaling model presented in §13.2. Suppose a male's type $t \in [t_{min}, \infty)$ is a measure of male vigor (e.g., resistance to parasites). Females do best by accurately determining t, since an overestimate of t might lead a female to mate when she should not, and an underestimate might lead her to pass up a suitable mate. If a male of type t signals his type as $s = f(t)$, and a female uses this signal to estimate the male's fitness as $a = g(s)$, then in an equilibrium with truthful signaling we will have $a = t$. We suppose that the male's fitness is $u(t, s, a)$, with $u_t > 0$ (a male with higher t is more fit), $u_s < 0$ (it is costly to signal a higher level of fitness), and $u_a > 0$ (a male does better if a female thinks he's more fit). We assume the male's fitness function $u(t, s, g(s))$ is such that a more vigorous male will signal a higher fitness; i.e., $ds/dt > 0$. Given $g(s)$, a male of type t will then choose s to maximize $U(s) = u(t, s, g(s))$, which has first-order condition

$$U_s(s) = u_s(t, s, g(s)) + u_a(t, s, g(s))\frac{dg}{ds} = 0. \qquad (13.4)$$

If there is indeed truthful signaling, then this equation must hold for $t = g(s)$, giving us the differential equation

$$\frac{dg}{ds} = -\frac{u_s(g(s), s, g(s))}{u_a(g(s), s, g(s))}, \qquad (13.5)$$

which, together with $g(s_{min}) = t_{min}$, uniquely determines $g(s)$. Since $u_s < 0$ and $u_a > 0$, we have $dg/ds > 0$, as expected.

Differentiating the first-order condition (13.4) totally with respect to t, we find

$$U_{ss}\frac{ds}{dt} + U_{st} = 0.$$

Since $U_{ss} < 0$ by the second-order condition for a maximum, and since $ds/dt > 0$, we must have $U_{st} > 0$. But we can write

$$U_{st} = u_{st} + u_{at}g'(s)$$

$$= \frac{u_{st}u_a(g(s), s, g(s)) - u_{at}u_s(g(s), s, g(s))}{u_a} > 0.$$

Therefore,

$$\frac{d}{dt}\left[\frac{u_s(t, s, g(s))}{u_a(t, s, g(s))}\right] = \frac{U_{st}}{u_a} > 0. \tag{13.6}$$

We can now rewrite (13.4) as

$$u_a(t, s, g(s))\left[\frac{u_s(t, s, g(s))}{u_a(t, s, g(s))} + g'(s)\right] = 0. \tag{13.7}$$

Since the fraction in this expression is increasing in t, and the expression is zero when $t = g(s)$, this shows $s = g^{-1}(t)$ is a local maximum, so the male maximizes fitness by truthfully reporting $s = g^{-1}(t)$, at least locally.

For an example of the handicap principle, suppose $u(t, s, a) = a^r t^s$, $0 < t < 1$, so (13.5) becomes $g'/g = -(1/r)\ln g$, which has solution $\ln g = ce^{-s/r}$. Using $g(s_{min}) = t_{min}$ this gives

$$g(s) = t_{min}^{e^{-\frac{s-s_{min}}{r}}},$$

and

$$f(t) = s_{min} - r\ln\frac{\ln t}{\ln t_{min}}.$$

The reader will note an important element of unrealism in this model: it assumes that the cost of female signal processing and detection is zero, and hence signaling is perfectly truthful and reliable. If we allow for costly female choice, we would expect that signal detection would be imperfect and there would be a positive level of dishonest signaling in equilibrium, and the physical process of signal development should involve an evolutionary dynamic intimately related to receiver neurophysiology (Dawkins and Guilford 1991; Guilford and Dawkins 1991, 1993). In contrast with the Darwin-Fisher model of sexual selection, we would not expect a small amount of costly female choice to undermine a signaling equilibrium, since there are direct fitness benefits to females in locating vigorous males.

13.7 The Shepherds Who Never Cry Wolf

Since we value truthfulness, one might have the impression that when both a truthful signaling and a nonsignaling equilibrium exist, the truthful signaling equilibrium should entail higher payoffs for at least some of the players. But that need not be the case. Here is a counterexample.

Two shepherds take their flocks each morning to adjoining pastures. Sometimes a wolf will attack one of the flocks, causing pandemonium among the threatened sheep. A wolf attack can be clearly heard by both shepherds, allowing a shepherd to come to the aid of his companion. But unless the wolf is hungry, the cost of giving aid exceeds the benefits, and only the shepherd guarding the threatened flock can see if the wolf is hungry.

There are three pure strategies for a threatened shepherd: never signal (N), signal if the wolf is hungry (H), and always signal (A). Similarly, there are three pure strategies for the shepherd who hears a wolf in the other pasture: never help (N), help if signalled (H), and always help (A).

We make the following assumptions. The payoff to a day's work when no wolf appears is 1 for each shepherd. The cost of being attacked by a hungry wolf and a nonhungry wolf is a and $b < a$, respectively. The cost of coming to the aid of a threatened shepherd is d, and doing so prevents the loss to the threatened shepherd, so his payoff is still 1. Finally, it is common knowledge that the probability that a wolf is hungry is $p > 0$.

We assume the shepherds' discount rates are too high, or wolf visits too infrequent, to support a repeated-game cooperative equilibrium using trigger strategies, so the game is a one-shot. If the shepherds are self-interested, of course neither will help the other, so we assume that they are brothers, and the total payoff to shepherd 1 (the threatened shepherd) is his own-payoff π_1 plus $k\pi_2$, where π_2 is the own-payoff of shepherd 2, and similarly, the total payoff to shepherd 2 (the potential helper) is $\pi_2 + k\pi_1$.

If $ka > d > kb$, a shepherd prefers to aid his threatened brother when, and only when, the wolf is hungry (why?). So we assume this is the case. We also assume that $a - dk > c > b - dk$, which means that a threatened shepherd would only want his brother to come to help if the wolf is hungry (why?). So there ought to be a signaling equilibrium in this case. Note, however, that this signaling equilibrium will exist whether p is small or large, so for very large p, it might be worthwhile for a brother *always* to help, thus saving the cost c of signaling to his brother, and saving the cost kc to himself. This, in fact, is the case. While this can be proved in general, you are asked in this problem to prove a special case.

Assume $k = 5/12$ (note that $k = 1/2$ for full brothers, but the probability that two brothers that *ostensibly* have the same father *in fact* have the same father is probably about 80% in human populations). Also assume $a = 3/4$, $b = 1/4$, $c = 19/48$, and $d = 1/4$. Finally, assume $p = 3/4$. After verifying that the above inequalities hold, do the following:

a. Show that there is a signaling equilibrium, and find the payoffs to the shepherds.

b. Show that there is pooling equilibrium in which a threatened shepherd never signals, and a shepherd always helps his threatened brother. Show that this equilibrium is Pareto-superior to the signaling equilibrium.

c. There is also a mixed strategy Nash equilibrium (truthful signaling occurs, but not with certainty) in which the threatened shepherd sometimes signals, and the other shepherd sometimes helps without being asked. Find this equilibrium and its payoffs, and show that the payoffs are slightly better than the signaling equilibrium but not as high as the pooling equilibrium.

13.8 My Brother's Keeper

Consider the following elaboration on the theme of §13.7. Suppose the threatened shepherd, whom we will call the Sender, is either healthy, needy, or desperate, each of which is true with probability 1/3. His brother, whom we will call the Donor, is either healthy or needy, each with probability 1/2. Suppose there are two signals that the threatened shepherd can give: a low-cost signal costing 0.1, and a high-cost signal costing 0.2. If he uses either one, we say he is "asking for help." We assume that the payoff for each brother is his own fitness plus 3/4 of his brother's fitness. The Sender's fitness is 0.9 if healthy, 0.6 if needy, and 0.3 if desperate, minus whatever he pays for signaling. The Donor's fitness is 0.9 if healthy and 0.7 if needy. However, the Donor has a resource that ensures his fitness is 1 if he uses it, and the fitness of the Sender is 1 (minus the signaling cost) if he transfers it to the Sender. The resource is perishable, so either he or his brother must use it in the current period.

a. Show that after eliminating "unreasonable" strategies (define carefully what you mean by "unreasonable"), there are six pure strategies for the Sender, in each of which a healthy sender never signals: Never Ask; Signal Low If Desperate; Signal High If Desperate; Signal Low If Desperate or Needy; Signal Low If Needy, High If Desperate; and Signal High If Needy or Desperate. Similarly, there are ten strategies for Donor: Never Help; Help If Healthy and Signal Is High; Help If Healthy and Asked; Help If Healthy; Help If Signal Is High; Help If Healthy and Asked, or Needy and Signal Is High; Help If Healthy or

Signal Is High; Help If Asked; Help If Healthy or Asked; and Help
Unconditionally.

b. * If you have a lot of time on your hands, or if you know a computer
programming language, derive the 6 × 10 normal form matrix for the
game.

c. * Show that there are seven pure strategy equilibria. Among these there is
one completely pooling equilibrium: Never Ask, Always Help. This, of
course, affords the Sender the maximum possible payoff. However, the
pooling equilibrium maximizes the sum of the payoffs to both players,
so it will be preferred by both if they are equally likely to be Sender
and Donor. This is asocial optimum even among the mixed strategy
equilibria, but that is even harder to determine—my Normal Form Game
Solver and Gambit are useful here.

d. Show that the truthful signaling strategies (Signal Low If Needy, High If
Desperate, Help If Healthy and Asked or Needy and Signal Is High) form
a Nash equilibrium, but that this equilibrium is strictly Pareto-inferior
to the pooling (nonsignaling) equilibrium.

This model shows that there can be many signaling equilibria, but all may be
inferior to complete altruism (Never Ask, Always Help). This is doubtless
because the coefficient of relatedness is so high (3/4 is the coefficient of
relatedness between sisters in many bee species, where the queen mates
with a single haploid male).

Simulating the model gives an entirely surprising result, as depicted in
Fig. 13.2. For this simulation, I created seven hundred players, each randomly programmed to play one strategy as Sender and another as Donor.
The players were randomly paired on each round, and one was randomly
chosen to be Sender, the other Donor. After every ten rounds, the strategies
with the highest scores reproduced, and their offspring replaced those with
the lowest scores. Figure 13.2 shows the outcome for the two strongest
strategies. For the Donor, this involved using Help If Healthy or If Asked,
and for Sender, either Signal Low If Desperate or Needy, or Signal Low
If Desperate. After 20,000 rounds, the only remaining strategy (except for
occasional mutations), is the latter, the other fifty-nine strategies having
disappeared. This is the signaling equilibrium that is best for the Donor
but whose total fitness is inferior to the pooling equilibrium Never Ask,
Always Help. Nor is this a fluke outcome: I ran the simulation ten times
with different seeds to the random number generator, and this equilibrium
emerged every time. The implication is clear: *a signaling equilibrium can*

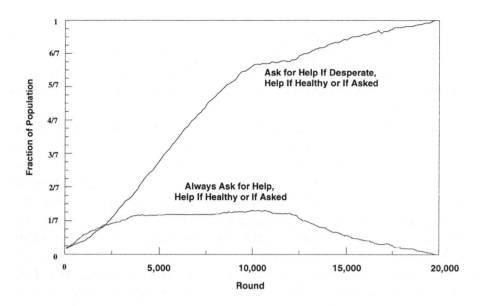

Figure 13.2. A signaling equilibrium in the Brother's Helper game.

emerge from an evolutionary process even when it is inferior to a pooling equilibrium.

13.9   Honest Signaling among Partial Altruists

In a certain fishing community, each fisher works alone on the open sea, earning a payoff that we will normalize to 1. A fisher occasionally encounters threatening weather. If the fisher does not escape the weather, his payoff is zero. If a threatened fisher has sufficient energy reserves, he can escape the bad weather, and his expected payoff is u, where $0 < u < 1$. We call such a fisher *secure*. However, with a certain probability p ($0 < p < 1$) a threatened fisher does *not* have sufficient energy reserves. We say he is *in distress*.

If a threatened fisher sees another fisher on the horizon, he can send a signal to ask for help, at cost t, with $0 < t < 1$. If the fisher is in distress and a potential helper comes to his aid (we assume the potential helper is not threatened), the payoff to the distressed fisher is 1, but the cost to the helper is $c > 0$. Without the help, however, the distressed fisher succumbs to the bad weather and has payoff 0.

To complicate matters, a threatened fisher who is helped by another fisher but who is *not* distressed has payoff v, where $1 > v > u$. Thus, threatened fishers have an incentive to signal that they are in distress even when they are not. Moreover, fishers can tell when other fishers are threatened, but only the threatened fisher himself knows his own reserves, and hence whether or not he is in distress.

We assume that encounters of this type among fishers are one-shot affairs, because the probability of meeting the same distressed fisher again is very small. Clearly, unless there is an element of altruism, no fisher will help a threatened fisher. So let us suppose that in an encounter between fishers, the nonthreatened fisher receives a fraction $r > 0$ of the total payoff, including signaling costs, received by the threatened fisher (presumably because r is the degree of genetic or cultural relatedness between fishers). However, the helper bears the total cost c himself.

For example, if a fisher is in distress and signals for help and receives help, the distressed fisher's payoff is $1 - t$ and the helper's payoff is $r(1 - t) - c$.

The nonthreatened fisher (Fisher 1) who sees a threatened fisher (Fisher 2) has three pure strategies: Never Help, Help If Asked, and Always Help. Fisher 2 also has three strategies: Never Ask, Ask When Distressed, Always Ask. We call the strategy pair {Help If Asked, Ask If Distressed} the *Honest Signaling* strategy pair. If this pair is Nash, we have an Honest Signaling equilibrium. This is called a *separating equilibrium* because agents truthfully reveal their situation by their actions. Any other equilibrium is called a *pooling equilibrium*, since agents' actions do not always reveal their situations.[3]

The reasoning you are asked to perform below shows that when there are potential gains from helping distressed fishers (i.e., $(1 + r)(1 - t) > c$), then if fishers are sufficiently altruistic and signaling is sufficiently costly but not excessively costly, an Honest Signaling equilibrium can be sustained as a Nash equilibrium. The idea that signaling must be costly (but not too costly) to be believable was championed by Amotz Zahavi (1975) and modeled by Grafen (1990a), Maynard Smith (1991), Johnstone and Grafen (1992, 1993), and others in a notable series of papers. The general game-theoretic point is simple, but extremely important: if a signal is not on balance truthful, it will not be heeded, so if it is costly to emit, it will not be emitted. Of course, there is much out-of-equilibrium behavior, so there is lots of room for duplicity in biology and economics.

---

[3]For more on separating and pooling equilibria, see §12.10 and §12.11.

a. Show that if

$$(1+r)\left[v - u + \frac{pt}{1-p}\right] < c < (1+r)(1-t), \qquad (13.8)$$

then Honest Signaling is socially efficient (i.e., maximizes the sum of the payoffs to the two fishers)? HINT: Set up the 3×3 normal form for the game, add up the entries in each box, and compare. For the rest of the problem, assume that these conditions hold.

b. Show that there is always a pooling equilibrium in which Fisher 2 uses Never Ask. Show that in this equilibrium, Fisher 1 Never Helps if

$$c > r[p + (1-p)(v-u)] \qquad (13.9)$$

and Always Helps if the opposite inequality holds.

c. Show that if

$$v - u < \frac{c}{r} < 1$$

and

$$v - u < t < 1,$$

Honest Signaling is a Nash equilibrium.

d. Show that if t is sufficiently close to 1, Honest Signaling can be a Nash equilibrium even if it is not socially efficient.

e. Show that if Honest Signaling and {Never Ask, Never Help} are both Nash equilibria, then Honest Signaling has a higher total payoff than {Never Ask, Never Help}.

f. Show that if Honest Signaling and {Never Ask, Always Help} are both Nash equilibria, then Honest Signaling has a higher total payoff than {Never Ask, Always Help}.

13.10   Educational Signaling

Suppose there are two types of workers, high-ability (h) and low-ability (l), and the proportion of high-ability workers in the economy is $\alpha > 0$. Suppose workers invest in acquiring a level of schooling s, which is both costly to obtain and productive. Specifically, suppose that a high-ability worker incurs a cost $c_h(s)$ of obtaining s years of schooling, while a low-ability workers incurs a cost of $c_l(s)$. We also assume schooling is more costly for low-ability workers than for high, so $c_h'(s) < c_l'(s)$ for all $s \geq 0$.

Schooling is also productive, so the marginal productivity of a high-ability worker with s years of schooling is $y_h(s)$, and the corresponding value for a low-ability worker is $y_l(s)$. We assume $y_h(0) = y_l(0) = 0$ and $y_h'(s) > y_l'(s) > 0$ for all $s \geq 0$, which means that high-ability workers have higher marginal products than low-ability workers, and schooling increases the productivity of high-ability workers more than low. To simplify the diagrams, we assume y_h and y_l are linear functions of s.

Suppose employers cannot observe ability, but they do observe s, and if workers with different abilities obtain different amounts of schooling, they may offer a wage based on s. We assume the labor market is competitive, so all firms must offer a wage equal to the expected marginal product of labor.

A truthful signaling equilibrium in this case involves high- and low-ability workers choosing different amounts of schooling, so employers know their type by their schooling choices. They thus pay wages $y_h(s)$ to the high-ability workers and $y_l(s)$ to the low. Assuming workers know this, high-ability workers will choose s to maximize $y_h(s) - c_h(s)$ and low-ability workers will choose s to maximize $y_l(s) - c_l(s)$. This is depicted in Fig. 13.3. Agents maximize their payoff by choosing the highest indifference curve that intersects their wage curve, which means tangency points between wage curves and indifference curves as illustrated. Moreover, neither type of agent would prefer to get the amount of schooling chosen by the other, since this would involve a lower level of utility; i.e., the equilibrium point for each type lies below the indifference curve for the other type.

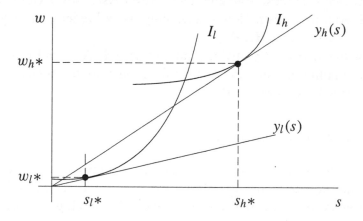

Figure 13.3. A truthful signaling equilibrium.

a. Explain why there cannot be a truthful signaling equilibrium if the costs of schooling are the same for the two ability levels. Draw a diagram to illustrate your argument. HINT: Indifference curves for the same utility function cannot cross.

b. Modify Fig. 13.3 to illustrate the following assertion: If the optimum schooling level for the high-ability worker lies inside the optimal indifference curve for the low-ability worker, then the low-ability worker will mimic the high-ability worker and destroy the truthful signaling equilibrium.

c. However, high-ability workers may have a response to this: they may be able to increase their educational level to a point sufficiently high that it will no longer benefit the low-ability workers to imitate them. This is called an "Educational Rat Race." Make a diagram illustrating this rat race and another in which it is not worthwhile for high-ability workers to signal their quality.

d. Analyze the case of a pooling equilibrium, in which both high- and low-ability workers choose the same schooling level. Show that in this case employers do not use either the $y_h(s)$ or the $y_l(s)$ schedules, but rather set wages so that

$$w(s) = \alpha y_h(s) + (1 - \alpha)y_l(s) \qquad (13.10)$$

for both types of workers. Show that in a pooling equilibrium, high-ability workers maximize their payoff subject to hitting the wage curve $w(s)$, and low-ability workers imitate their choice of educational level. Draw a diagram illustrating this result, and make sure the curves are drawn so neither high- nor low-ability workers have an incentive to switch unilaterally to the truthful signaling equilibrium.

This analysis does not exhaust the possibilities for a signaling equilibrium. There could also exist mixed strategy equilibria in which some low-ability workers imitate the high-ability workers and others do not. There could also be strange Bayesian priors for the employers that would lead to strange pooling equilibria. For instance, if employers believe that a worker who does not choose $s = s_0$ for some given s_0 is "crazy" and must be low-ability. Then every worker may choose s_0 to get the pooling wage, which is higher than the low-ability wage. Such behavior by employers would be stupid, and they might be driven out of existence in a dynamic adjustment process.

13.11   Education as a Screening Device

Suppose a worker can be of high ability a_h with probability α, or low ability $a_l < a_h$ with probability $1 - \alpha$. Workers know their own ability, but employers do not. Workers can also choose to acquire high as opposed to low education, and this is observable by employers. Moreover, it costs c/a ($c > 0$) for a worker of ability a to acquire high education, so high education is more costly for the low-ability worker. We assume that workers are paid their expected marginal product, and the marginal product of a worker of ability a is just a, so high education does not improve worker productivity—education is at best a screening device, informing employers which workers are high ability. Suppose e_l is the event "worker chose low education" and e_h is the event "worker chose high education." Then, if w_l and w_h are the wage paid to low- and high-education workers, respectively, we have

$$w_k = P[a_h|e_k]a_h + P[a_l|e_k]a_l, \qquad k = l, h, \qquad (13.11)$$

where $P[a|e]$ is the conditional probability that the worker has ability a in the event e.

A Nash equilibrium for this game consists of a choice $e(a) \in \{e_l, e_h\}$ of education level for $a = a_h, a_l$ and a set of probabilities $P[a|e]$ for $a = a_h, a_l$ and $e = e_h, e_l$ that are consistent in the sense that if $P[e] > 0$, then $P[a|e]$ is given by Bayesian updating.

a. Show that there is a pooling equilibrium in which $e(a_h) = e(a_l) = e_l$, $w_h = w_l = \alpha a_h + (1 - \alpha)a_l$, and $P[a_l|e_l] = P[a_l|e_h] = 1 - \alpha$. In other words, employers disregard the education signal, and workers choose low education.

b. Show that there is some range of values for c such that there is a truthful signaling equilibrium in which $e(a_h) = e_h$, $e(a_l) = e_l$, $w_l = a_l$, $w_h = a_h$, $P[a_l|e_l] = 1$, and $P[a_l|e_h] = 0$. In other words, despite the fact that education does not increase worker productivity, workers can signal high ability by acquiring education, and employers reward high-ability workers with relatively high wages.

c. In the spirit of trembling hand perfection (§5.16 and §12.1), suppose that with a small probability $\epsilon > 0$ a worker is given a free education, regardless of ability. Show that the pooling equilibrium does not have to specify arbitrarily the probabilities $P[a_l|e_h]$ off the path of play, since $P[e_h] = \epsilon > 0$, and since both ability types are equally likely to get a free education, we have $P[a_l|e_h] = 1 - \alpha$.

d. Show that if c is sufficiently small, there are two pooling equilibria and no truthful signaling equilibrium. The first pooling equilibrium is as before. In the second pooling equilibrium, both ability types choose to be educated. Specifically, $e(a_h) = e(a_l) = e_h$, $w_l = a_l$, $w_h = \alpha a_h + (1 - \alpha)a_l$, $P[a_l|e_l] = 1$, and $P[a_l|e_h] = 1 - \alpha$. Note that this requires specifying the probabilities for e_l, which are off the path of play. The truthful signaling equilibrium is inefficient and inegalitarian, while the pooling equilibrium is inefficient but egalitarian. The pooling equilibrium is not very plausible, because it is more reasonable to assume that if a worker gets education, he is high ability.

e. Show that if we added a small exogenous probability $\epsilon > 0$ that a worker of either type is denied an education, all outcomes are along the path of play, and the posterior $P[a_l|e_l] = 1 - \alpha$ follows from the requirement of Bayesian updating.

f. Now suppose the educational level is a continuous variable $e \in [0, 1]$. Workers then choose $e(a_h)$, $e(a_l) \in [0, 1]$, and employers face probabilities $P[a_h|e]$, $P[a_l|e]$ for all education levels $e \in [0, 1]$.

Show that for $e \in [0, 1]$, there is a $\bar{e} > 0$ such that for any $e^* \in [0, \bar{e}]$, there is a pooling equilibrium where all workers choose educational level e^*. In this equilibrium, employers pay wages $w(e^*) = \alpha a_h + (1 - \alpha)a_l$ and $w(e \neq e^*) = a_l$. They have the conditional probabilities $P[a_l|e \neq e^*] = 1$ and $P[a_l|e = e^*] = 1 - \alpha$.

g. Show that when $e \in [0, 1]$, if c is sufficiently large, there is a range of values of e^* such that there is a truthful signaling equilibrium where high-ability workers choose $e = e^*$ and low-ability workers choose $e = 0$. In this equilibrium, employers pay wages $w(e^*) = a_h$ and $w(e \neq e^*) = a_l$. They face the conditional probabilities $P[a_l|e \neq e^*] = 0$ and $P[a_l|e \neq e^*] = 1$.

13.12 Capital as a Signaling Device

Suppose there are many producers, each with a project to fund. There are two types of projects, each of which requires capital investment k. The "good" project returns 1 at the end of the period, and the "bad" project returns 1 with probability p $(0 < p < 1)$ at the end of the period, and otherwise returns 0. There are also many lenders. While each producer knows the type of his own project, the lenders only know that the frequency of good projects in the economy is q $(0 < q < 1)$.

We assume the capital market is perfect and all agents are risk neutral (§16.41). Thus, each lender's reservation position is the risk-free interest rate $\rho > 0$, so a producer can always obtain financing for his project if he offers to pay an interest rate r that allows a lender to earn expected return ρ on his capital investment k.

We call a project with capital cost k *socially productive* if its expected return is greater than $k(1 + \rho)$. This corresponds to the idea that while individual agents may be risk averse, the law of large numbers applies to creating a social aggregate, so a social surplus is created on all projects that return at least the risk-free interest rate.

a. Show that for any $p, q > 0$ there is a nonempty interval (k^g_{min}, k^g_{max}) of capital costs k such that no project is funded, despite the fact that a fraction q of the projects are socially productive.

b. Show that for any $p, q > 0$ there is a nonempty interval (k^b_{min}, k^b_{max}) of capital costs k such that all projects are funded, despite the fact that a fraction $1 - q$ of the projects are not socially productive.

This is a sorry state of affairs, indeed! But is there not some way that an owner of a good project could signal this fact credibly? In a suitably religious society, perhaps the requirement that borrowers swear on a stack of Bibles that they have good projects might work. Or if producers have new projects available in each of many periods, we may have a "reputational equilibrium" in which producers with bad projects are not funded in future periods, and hence do not apply for loans in the current period. Or society might build debtors' prisons and torture the defaulters.

But suppose none of these is the case. Then equity comes to the rescue! Suppose each producer has an amount of capital $k^p > 0$. Clearly, if $k^p \geq k$, there will be no need for a credit market, and producers will invest in their projects precisely when they are socially productive (prove it!). More generally,

c. Show that for all $p, q, k > 0$ such that good projects are socially productive and bad projects are socially unproductive, there is a wealth level $k^p_{min} > 0$ such that if all producers have wealth $k^p > k^p_{min}$; a producer's willingness to invest k^p in his project is a perfect indicator that the project is good. In this situation, exactly the good projects are funded, and the interest rate is the risk-free interest rate ρ.

The previous result says that if producers are sufficiently wealthy, there is a truthful signaling equilibrium, in which producers signal the quality of their projects by the amount of equity they are willing to put in them. But if there are lots of nonwealthy producers, many socially productive investments may go unfunded (Bardhan, Bowles, and Gintis 2000).

14

Bosses and Workers, Landlords and Peasants, and Other Principal-Agent Models

> Men plan and God laughs.
>
> *Yiddish proverb*

14.1 Introduction to the Principal-Agent Model

In the *principal-agent model*, the payoff to the *principal* depends on an action taken by the *agent*. The principal cannot contract for the action, but can compensate the agent based on some observable signal that is *correlated* with the action. The principal is *first mover* as in a Stackelberg duopoly model (§3.6) and chooses an incentive scheme for paying the agent that depends on the observed signal. The principal offers this incentive scheme as a contract to the agent. The agent then (a) determines the optimal action to take, given the incentives, and then (b) decides whether or not to accept the contract, based on the expected payment and the subjective cost of performing the action. Upon accepting the contract, the agent performs the optimal action, the principal observes the signal correlated with the action, pays the agent according to the incentive scheme, and receives a payoff dependent upon the signal.[1]

For example, suppose the principal is an employer. The agent is then a worker, the worker's action is a level of work effort, the signal may be the employer's profits or a supervisor's report on the worker's behavior, the incentive scheme is a wage that depends on the signal, and the employer's payoff is expected profits, which depend on the worker's effort level. For another example, suppose the principal is an insurance company. The agent may be the owner of a warehouse who purchases fire insurance from the

---

[1]Note that the *incentive scheme* is contractible, even though the agent's *action* is not. If the principal cannot precommit to pay the incentives, or if the agent's actions can affect the incentive scheme itself, then some other model must be used (e.g., a bargaining model).

company, the owner's action may be a degree of care in avoiding a fire, the incentive scheme may be a percentage of co-insurance for the owner, and the signal may be an observed level of fire damage.

In case you've never heard of co-insurance, it goes like this: if the warehouse would cost \$1,000,000 to replace and the co-insurance rate is 20%, then if the warehouse were totally destroyed by fire, the insurance company would pay only \$800,000. Note that if the market value of the warehouse dipped below \$800,000 for some reason, the owner would pray for a fire.[2] You have seen principal-agent problems before, including Contingent Renewal Contracts (§6.14), which discusses a variety of models, Markets as Disciplining Devices: Allied Widgets (§3.20), in which the principal is the firm's owner and the agent is the firm's manager, and I'd Rather Switch than Fight (§6.16), in which the principal is the consumer and the agent is the supplier.[3] Here we study such problems more systematically and in greater depth.

14.2   Labor Discipline with Monitoring

An employer hires supervisors to watch the workers, docking the pay of any worker who is caught shirking. Worker effort takes the form of working a certain fraction e of the time, so if there are N workers and each worker works at effort level e for one hour, then total labor supplied is eN. The employer's revenue in this case is $q(eN)$, where $q(\cdot)$ is an increasing function. All workers have the same utility function $u(w, e) = (1 - e)w$, where w is the wage rate and e is the effort level. The worker, who is normally paid w, is paid $z < w$ if caught shirking.

Suppose that a worker who chooses effort level e is caught shirking with probability $p(e) = 1 - e$, so the harder the worker works, the lower the

---

[2]Or perhaps more than pray, as in the following anecdote: Manny is taking his morning constitutional and bumps into his old friend Sol, who exclaims, "Manny, I heard about the terrible fire at your warehouse. I'm so sorry for you." "Shhhh!" replies Manny, "It's tomorrow!" As a gruesome example of the same phenomenon, a few years back the bottom dropped out of the race-horse market, so the insurance value of a thoroughbred horse far exceeded its market value. Many owners saw to it that their horses suffered "accidental" broken legs, recovering their losses at the expense of the insurance companies (and the horses).

[3]Arguably, principal-agent models best describe the most important transactions in a market economy, involving capital, labor, and product markets alike. See §6.14 for an analysis of the broad implications of this fact.

probability of being caught shirking. The game tree for this problem is depicted in Fig. 14.1

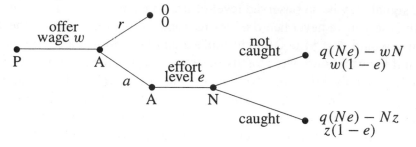

Figure 14.1. Labor discipline with monitoring.

a. Show that $w(1 - e)e + z(1 - e)^2$ is the payoff to a worker who chooses effort level e.

b. Show that if the employer offers wage $w > 2z$, the worker's best response is to choose

$$e(w) = \frac{w - 2z}{2(w - z)}.$$

Show that this worker's *best response schedule* is increasing and concave, as depicted in Fig. 14.2.

c. If the employer chooses w and N to maximize profits, show that the choice of w in fact maximizes $e(w)/w$, the amount of effort per dollar of wages, which is the slope of the employer iso-cost line in Fig. 14.2.

d. Show that Nash equilibrium (w^*, e^*) satisfies the *Solow condition* (Solow 1979),

$$e'(w^*) = \frac{e(w^*)}{w^*}.$$

This is where the employer iso-cost line is tangent to the worker's best response schedule at (w^*, e^*) in Fig. 14.2.

e. Show that

$$w^* = (2 + \sqrt{2})z \approx 3.41z, \qquad e^* = \frac{1}{\sqrt{2}(1 + \sqrt{2})} \approx 0.29.$$

f. Suppose the worker's reservation utility is $z_0 > 0$, so the worker must be offered expected utility z_0 to agree to come to work. Show that the employer will set $z = 2z_0/(1 + \sqrt{2}) \approx 0.83z_0$.

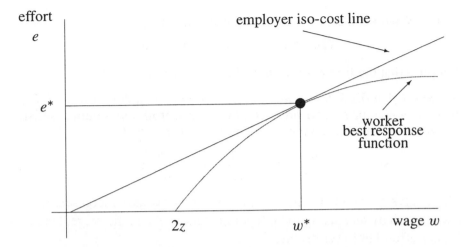

Figure 14.2. Equilibrium in the labor discipline model.

14.3 Labor as Gift Exchange

In a famous paper, "Labor Contracts as Partial Gift Exchange," George Akerlof (1982) suggested that when employers pay workers more than absolutely necessary, workers often reciprocate by working harder or more carefully than they otherwise would. He called this *gift exchange*. Economists generally ignored this possibility until Ernst Fehr, working at the University of Zurich, showed that laboratory experiments strongly confirm the existence of Akerlof's gift exchange phenomenon. See also Fehr's related work on reciprocity in §11.4.1 and §11.4.2. Specifically, whereas under competitive experimental conditions *without* the opportunity for buyers and sellers to reciprocate, prices and quantities converge to the competitive equilibrium, when reciprocation *can* be expressed, many buyers and sellers behave reciprocally, driving a competitive experimental market permanently away from the competitive outcome (Fehr, Gächter, Kirchler, and Weichbold 1998, Fehr, Kirchsteiger, and Riedl 1998).

This section analyzes a simple model of gift exchange in labor markets. A firm hires N identical workers, each of whom supplies effort level $e(w - z)$, where $e(\cdot)$ is increasing and concave, w is the wage, and z is a benchmark wage such that $w > z$ indicates that the employer is being generous, and conversely $w < z$ indicates that the boss is a skinflint. The firm's revenue is an increasing and concave function $f(eN)$ of total amount of effort supplied by the N workers, so the firm's net profit is given by

$$\pi(w, N) = f(e(w - z)N) - wN.$$

Suppose that the firm chooses w and N to maximize profits.

a. Show that the *Solow condition*, $de/dw = e/w$, holds (Solow 1979).
b. Show that the second-order condition for a profit maximum is satisfied.
c. Show that the following comparative static results hold:

$$\frac{de}{dz} > 0; \quad \frac{d\pi}{dz} < 0 \quad ; \frac{dw}{dz} > 0.$$

This analysis shows that when workers' reference wage z increases, employers respond by *increasing* the gift component $w - z$ in the wage, leading to higher effort but lower profits.

14.4   Labor Discipline with Profit Signaling

An employer hires a worker to do a job. There are two possible levels of profits for the employer, high (π_H) and low ($\pi_L < \pi_H$). The worker can affect the probability of high profits by choosing to work with either high or low effort. With high effort, the probability of high profits is p_h, and with low effort the probability of high profits is p_l, where $0 < p_l < p_h < 1$.

If the employer could see the worker's choice of effort, he could simply write a contract for high effort, but he cannot. The only way he can induce A to work hard is to offer the proper *incentive contract*: pay a wage w_H if profits are high, and $w_L < w_H$ if profits are low.

How should the employer choose the incentives w_L and w_H to maximize expected profits? The game tree for this situation is shown in Fig. 14.3, where we assume the utility of the wage is $u(w)$, the cost of high effort to the worker is d_h, and the cost of low effort is $d_l < d_h$. By working hard, the worker faces a lottery with payoffs $u(w_H) - d_h$, $u(w_L) - d_h$ with probabilities $(p_h, 1 - p_h)$, the expected value of which is

$$p_h(u(w_H) - d_h) + (1 - p_h)(u(w_L) - d_h)$$
$$= p_h u(w_H) + (1 - p_h)u(w_L) - d_h.$$

With low effort, the worker faces a lottery with payoffs $u(w_H) - d_l$, $u(w_L) - d_l$ with probabilities $(p_l, 1 - p_l)$, the expected value of which is

$$p_l(u(w_H) - d_l) + (1 - p_l)(u(w_L) - d_l)$$
$$= p_l u(w_H) + (1 - p_l)u(w_L) - d_l.$$

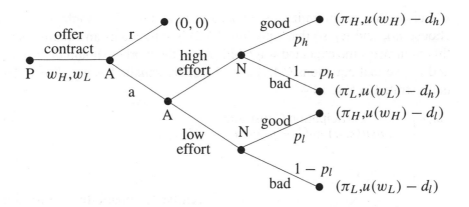

Figure 14.3. Labor incentives.

Thus, the worker will choose high effort over low effort only if the first of these expressions is at least as great as the second. For this to be the case, we must have $p_h u(w_H) + (1-p_h)u(w_L) - d_h > p_l u(w_H) + (1-p_l)u(w_L) - d_l$, which simplifies to

$$(p_h - p_l)(u(w_H) - u(w_L)) \geq d_h - d_l. \tag{14.1}$$

This is called the *incentive compatibility constraint* for eliciting high effort.

The incentive compatibility constraint (14.1) shows that the larger the cost to the worker of supplying high effort $(d_h - d_l)$, the larger the wage differential $(w_H - w_L)$ must be. Also, the smaller the difference in the probability of affecting the outcome $(p_h - p_l)$, the larger the wage differential must be. This makes sense, since if $p_h - p_l$ is very small, the worker's payoff is not very different whether choosing high or low effort, unless the wage differential is very large.

Now suppose the worker's next best job prospect has expected value z. Then to get the worker to take the job, the employer must offer the worker at least z. This the following *participation constraint:*

$$p_h u(w_H) + (1 - p_h)u(w_L) - d_h \geq z, \tag{14.2}$$

assuming the principal wants the worker to work hard.

The expected profit of the employer, assuming the worker works hard, is given by

$$p_h(\pi_H - w_H) + (1 - p_h)(\pi_L - w_L). \tag{14.3}$$

It's clear that to minimize the expected wage bill, the employer should choose w_H and w_L so that equation (14.2) is satisfied as an equality, since this minimizes the expected wage bill. Also, the worker should choose w_H and w_L so that equations (14.1) and (14.2) are satisfied as equalities. This is illustrated in Fig. 14.4.

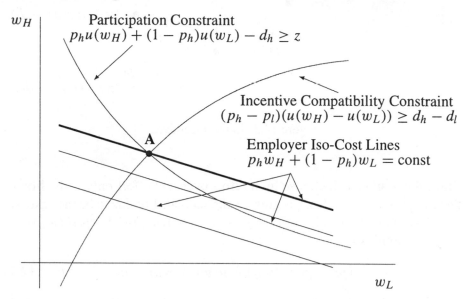

Figure 14.4. Minimizing the cost of inducing an action, given participation and incentive compatibility constraints.

Using this figure, prove the following:

a.   Employer iso-cost lines are of the form $p_h w_H + (1 - p_h)w_L = $ const.
b.   The participation constraint is decreasing and convex.
c.   The incentive compatibility constraint is increasing and cuts the w_L-axis for some $w_L > 0$. If the agent is weakly decreasingly risk averse (i.e., if $u''' > 0$), then the incentive compatibility constraint is concave.
d.   If the agent is strictly risk averse (§16.41), the slope of the iso-cost lines is less than the slope of the participation constraint at its intersection A with the incentive compatibility constraint.

It follows that the solution is at **A** in Fig. 14.4.

14.4.1 Properties of the Labor Discipline Model

The above exercise shows that the unique Nash equilibrium in the model is the solution to the two equations $p_h u(w_H) + (1 - p_h)u(w_L) - d_h = z$ and $(p_h - p_l)(u(w_H) - u(w_L)) = d_h - d_l$. Solving simultaneously, we get

$$u(w_L) = z + \frac{p_h d_l - p_l d_h}{p_h - p_l} \tag{14.4}$$

$$u(w_H) = u(w_L) + \frac{d_h - d_l}{p_h - p_l}. \tag{14.5}$$

Note that the worker in this case is no better off than if he did not take the job—this is a one-shot incentive model, not a realistic labor discipline model, in which the employer pays the worker a wage higher than his fallback and hires the worker for an indefinite number of periods, using the threat of dismissal to elicit effort from the worker (§6.15).

As we might expect, if z rises, so do the two wage rates w_L and w_H. If d_h rises, you can check that w_H rises and w_L falls. Similar results hold when p_h and p_l vary.

Now that we know the cost to the principal of inducing the agent to take each of the two actions, we can determine which action the principal should ask the agent to choose. If H and L are the expected profits in the good and bad states, respectively, then the return $\pi(a)$ for inducing the agent to take action $a = h, l$ is given by

$$\pi(h) = Hp_h + L(1 - p_h) - \mathbf{E}_h w,$$
$$\pi(l) = Hp_l + L(1 - p_l) - \mathbf{E}_l w,$$

where $\mathbf{E}_h w$ and $\mathbf{E}_l w$ are the expected wage payments if the agent takes actions h and l, respectively; i.e., $\mathbf{E}_h w = p_h w_H + (1 - p_h)w_L$ and $\mathbf{E}_l w = p_l w_H + (1 - p_l)w_L$.

Is it worth inducing the worker to choose high effort? For low effort, only the participation constraint $u(w_l) = d_l + z$ must hold, where w_l is the wage paid independent of whether profits are H or L, with expected profit $p_l H + (1 - p_l)L - w_l$. Choose the incentive wage if and only if $p_h(H - w_H) + (1 - p_h)(L - w_L) \geq p_l H + (1 - p_l)L - w_l$. This can be written

$$(p_h - p_l)(H - L) \geq p_h w_H + (1 - p_h)w_L - w_l. \tag{14.6}$$

We have seen that, in general, if the worker is risk neutral and it is worth exerting high effort, then the optimum is to make the principal the fixed claimant and the agent the residual claimant (§14.7). To see this for the current example, we can let $u(w) = w$ (why is this okay?). The participation constraint is $p_h u(w_H) + (1 - p_h)u(w_L) = p_h w_H + (1 - p_h)w_L = z + d_h$, the employer's profit is then $A = p_h H + (1 - p_h)L - (z + d_h)$. Suppose we give A to the employer as a fixed payment, and let $w_H = H - A$, $w_L = L - A$. Then the participation constraint holds, since

$$p_h w_H + (1 - p_h)w_L = p_h H + (1 - p_h)L - A = z + d_h.$$

Since high effort is superior to low effort for the employer, equation (14.6) must hold, giving

$$(p_h - p_l)(H - L) \geq p_h w_H + (1 - p_h)w_L - (z + d_l)$$
$$= z + d_h - (z + d_l) = d_h - d_l.$$

But then,

$$w_H - w_L = H - L \geq \frac{d_h - d_l}{p_h - p_l},$$

which says that the incentive compatibility constraint is satisfied.

Figure 14.5 is a graphical representation of the principal's problem. Note that in this case there are many profit-maximizing contracts—any point on the heavy solid line in the figure maximizes profits.

14.5   Peasants and Landlords

A landlord hires a peasant to plow, sow, and reap a cornfield. The landlord's profit is H if the crop is good, and $L < H$ if the crop is poor. The peasant can either work at high effort h or low effort l, and the probability p_h of a good crop when he exerts high effort is greater than the probability p_l of a good crop when he expends low effort, with $0 < p_l < p_h < 1$. The landowner cannot observe the peasant's effort.

Suppose the peasant's utility function when the wage is w is given by $u(w) - d_h$ with high effort and $u(w) - d_l$ with low effort. We assume $d_h > d_l$, so unless given some inducement, the peasant will not work hard, and $u' > 0, u'' < 0$, so the peasant has diminishing marginal utility of the wage. The peasants fallback utility is z.

To induce the peasant to work hard, the landlord chooses a pair of wages w_H and w_L, and pays the peasant w_H if profit is H and w_L if profit is L. This is called an *incentive wage*.

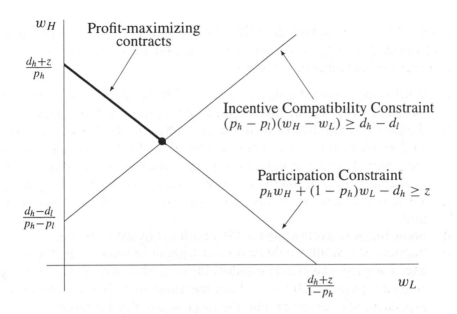

Figure 14.5. The principal's problem when the agent is risk neutral.

a. What should the landlord pay the peasant if he wants to minimize the expected wage $Ew = p_h w_H + (1 - p_h) w_L$, subject to eliciting high effort?

b. Using the appropriate Kuhn-Tucker conditions, prove that both the PC and the ICC must hold as equalities.

c. Prove that the optimal incentive wage for the landlord is given by

$$u(w_L) = d_h - p_h(d_h - d_l)/(p_h - p_l) + z$$
$$u(w_H) = d_h + (1 - p_h)(d_h - d_l)/(p_h - p_l) + z.$$

d. Suppose now that the peasant is risk neutral but the landlord is risk averse (§16.41). Show that if high effort produces a surplus over low effort, the landlord's profit-maximizing solution involves getting a fixed rent from the peasant, who becomes the residual claimant, bearing all the risk and taking all the profits and losses.

14.6 Mr. Smith's Car Insurance

Mr. Smith wants to buy theft insurance for his car, which is worth $1,200. If Smith is careful, the probability of theft is 50%, and if he is careless, the probability of theft is 75%. Smith is risk averse with utility function

$u(x) = \ln(x + 1)$, and the disutility of being careful is $\epsilon > 0$. To keep the problem simple, suppose the car lasts one period and is either stolen or not stolen at the beginning of the period.

a. What is the expected utility of the car to Mr. Smith? For what range of values of ϵ is it worthwhile for Smith to be careful without insurance?
b. Suppose Mr. Smith buys an insurance contract for premium x that pays $1,200 if his car is stolen. Show that Smith will not be careful, and find the premium to the insurance company, assuming the company is risk neutral and competition forces the insurance policy to be a fair lottery.
c. What is the expected utility of the car plus the insurance policy for Smith?
d. Show that it is worthwhile for Mr. Smith to buy the insurance.
e. Suppose Mr. Smith would be careful without insurance, and the insurance company can charge a deductible of z, so if the car is stolen, the company pays $1,200 - z$. Find the value of z that maximizes the expected utility of the car plus the insurance policy for Smith.
f. Show that Smith is now careful with insurance.

Note that this problem, while clearly in the spirit of a principal-agent model, differs from the generic case in one crucial way: the principal rather than the agent is forced to his reservation position (a zero-profit condition), since we assume a competitive market for insurance.

14.7 A Generic One-Shot Principal-Agent Game

Principal-agent games are variations of the following scenario. The agent has a set $A = \{a_1, \ldots, a_n\}$ of available actions. The principal receives one of a set $S = \{s_1, \ldots, s_m\}$ of signals that depend on the action chosen by the agent. Let $p_{ij} = P[s_j|a_i]$ be the conditional probability of signal s_j when the agent takes action a_i. Note that we must have

$$\sum_{j=1}^{m} p_{ij} = 1 \qquad \text{for } i = 1, \ldots, n.$$

The agent has utility function $u(w, a)$, where w is money, and $a \in A$ is the action the agent performs, and has a reservation utility is u_o, which is the minimum expected utility that would induce the agent to work for the principal. The principal has payoff $\pi(a) - w$ for $a \in A$.[4]

[4]We assume $\pi(a)$ has a stochastic component, so the principal cannot infer a from $\pi(a)$.

To maximize his payoff, the principal must determine the payoff associated with getting the agent to perform each action $a_i \in A$ and then choose the largest of the n payoffs. Thus, for each $i = 1, \ldots, n$ the principal must find incentives $w_{ij}, j = 1, \ldots, m$ such that the principal agrees to pay the agent w_{ij} if he observes the signal s_j, and the incentive scheme $w_i = \{w_{i1}, \ldots, w_{im}\}$ induces the agent to choose a_i. The principal must then choose the index i that maximizes his return

$$\pi(a_i) - \mathbf{E}_i w_i = \pi(a_i) - \sum_{j=1}^{m} p_{ij} w_{ij},$$

where $\mathbf{E}_i$ is expectation with respect to the probabilities that obtain when the agent chooses a_i.

Suppose the principal wants to induce the agent to choose action a_k. There are two constraints to the problem.

Participation Constraint. The expected utility to the agent must be enough to induce the agent to participate: $\mathbf{E}_k u(w_k, a_k) \geq u_o$, or

$$\sum_{j=1}^{m} p_{kj} u(w_{kj}, a_k) \geq u_o.$$

Incentive Compatibility Constraint. The chosen action a_k must maximize the payoff to the agent, among all actions $a_i \in A$, so $\mathbf{E}_k u(w_k, a_k) \geq \mathbf{E}_i u(w_k, a_i)$ for $i = 1, \ldots, n$, or

$$\sum_{j=1}^{m} p_{kj} u(w_{kj}, a_k) \geq \sum_{j=1}^{m} p_{ij} u(w_{kj}, a_i) \qquad \text{for } i = 1, \ldots, n.$$

Having determined the minimum expected cost $\mathbf{E}_k w_k$ of inducing the agent to choose action a_k, the principal chooses the index k to maximize $\pi(a_k) - \mathbf{E}_k w_k$.

Prove the following.

THEOREM 14.1 Fundamental Theorem of the One-Shot Principal-Agent Model. *Every solution to the principal-agent problem has the following characteristics:*

a. *The agent is indifferent between participating and taking the reservation utility u_o.*

b. *If the agent is strictly risk averse and the principal's optimal action a_k is not the agent's most preferred action, then*

   1. *At least one of the incentive compatibility constraints holds as an equality.*

   2. *The principal's payoff is strictly lower than it would be if he could write an enforceable contract for the delivery of action a_k.*

c. *If the agent is risk neutral, and if the return $\pi(a)$ is transferable (i.e., it can be assigned to the agent), the contract that maximizes the principal's payoff is that which gives the agent a fixed payment and makes the agent the residual claimant on $\pi(a)$.*

The last finding is one of the most important in all of game theory, I believe. It says that individual agents (e.g., farmers, workers, managers) should always be residual claimants on their projects, as long as they are risk neutral and the return $\pi(a)$ to their actions is transferable. In practice, however, such agents are normally *not* residual claimants on their projects—managers may have salaries plus stock options and farmers may have sharecropping contracts, but these contractual forms do not render the principals fixed claimants. What is wrong? It could be that principals (landlords, stockholders) do not choose optimal contracts. More likely, however, agents are risk averse, so that they would not want to be residual claimants, or they are credit constrained, so they cannot credibly promise to make good on the project's losses in bad times. Moreover, $\pi(a)$ is often *not* transferable (e.g., in a large work team, it is difficult to isolate the contribution of a single worker). At any rate, the theory of who controls productive activity is brightly illuminated by the principal-agent model.

15

Bargaining

> There is no such thing as Islamic science, just as there is no Hindu
> science, no Jewish science, no Confucian science.
>
> *Abdus Salam*

15.1 Introduction

A *bargaining model* is a game in which two or more players stand to gain
by cooperating, but they must negotiate an acceptable procedure for sharing the gains from cooperation. A model of bargaining specifies whether
and when agreement will be reached, and how the gains will be divided, depending on the bargaining rules and the characteristics of the bargainers. We
have encountered several bargaining models already—the Ståhl-Rubinstein
bargaining model in §5.6, a finite bargaining game solvable by backward
induction in §5.8, and an incomplete information bargaining game with a
Pareto-inefficient outcome in §12.3

Game theory has made especially important contributions in the area of
bargaining. As the following models illustrate, there are several plausible
implications of analytical bargaining models, including the following:

a. Where all parties have complete knowledge, there are generally Pareto-
    efficient bargaining equilibria, in which there are no impasses, strikes,
    or wars, and all divorces are amicable.
b. A bargainer with an improved fallback position (the payoff if agreement
    cannot be reached) receives a larger payoff. Thus if there is near full em-
    ployment, workers do better in bargaining with employers, even though
    being dismissed occurs with zero probability in equilibrium. Similarly,
    a country with an imposing standing army does better in negotiations,
    even though the probability of war is zero.
c. A bargainer who becomes less risk averse receives a larger payoff. Since
    the wealthy tend to be the least risk averse, because utility functions
    tend to display decreasing absolute risk aversion (§16.41), the relatively
    wealthy bargainer does better.

345

d. A bargainer who discounts the future less heavily receives a higher pay-off. Thus, workers with a large strike fund can bargain more effectively, and a person who needs a plumber in a hurry to fix a leak is in a weak bargaining position.

There is, of course, much more to learn about bargaining. For one thing, when there is incomplete knowledge, outcomes are generally not Pareto-efficient and may be strongly dependent upon details of the bargaining process (Kennan and Wilson 1990). Moreover, we have stressed that people rarely choose strategies by relying on many levels of backward induction, and they (correctly) assume the players they face are similarly disinclined (§2.18). Where evolutionary pressures are brought to bear on particular bargaining situations, and if mutation and error rates are sufficiently low, we might expect subgame perfect equilibria to dominate in the long run. But there is no reason to believe that these conditions hold in the real-world bargaining situations we are modeling. Moreover, contrary to standard bargaining models, people care about the *process* of bargaining as well the *outcome*, much as they do to dictator, ultimatum, and public goods games (see chapter 11), where issues of fairness and the intentions of other players strongly affect behavior. We need models that reflect these realities.

15.2 The Nash Bargaining Model

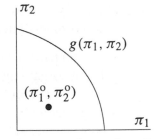

Two players bargain over a division (π_1, π_2), where π_1 and π_2 satisfy the differentiable relationship $g(\pi_1, \pi_2) = 0$. Suppose the two players have utility functions $u(\pi_1)$ and $v(\pi_2)$, respectively. If the two players cannot come to an agreement, the players have fallback payoffs π_1^o and π_2^o, respectively. For instance, the players may be splitting an amount of money M, so $\pi_1 + \pi_2 = M$, and $\pi_1^o = \pi_2^o = 0$, since if they cannot agree on a split each gets nothing. We assume the curve defined by $g(\pi_1, \pi_2)$ is downward sloping and convex, as in the diagram to the right.

John Nash showed that under certain (sometimes plausible) conditions, the two will agree to a pair (π_1^*, π_2^*) that maximizes the expression $(u(\pi_1) - u(\pi_1^o))(v(\pi_2) - v(\pi_2^o))$ subject to the constraint $g(\pi_1, \pi_2) = 0$. This is called the *Nash bargaining solution*. This solution is illustrated in the diagram below, where we have moved from (π_1, π_2) axes to (u, v) axes, so the Nash bargaining solution is the point $(u^*, v^*) = (u(\pi_1^*), v(\pi_2^*))$ where the Pareto frontier $\{(u(\pi_1), v(\pi_2)) \mid g(\pi_1, \pi_2) = 0\}$ is tangent to the isoquant $(u - u^\circ)(v - v^\circ)$. Note that in utility space, the fallback becomes $(u^\circ, v^\circ) = (u(\pi_1^\circ), v(\pi_2^\circ))$. Here is a rigorous statement of Nash's theorem.

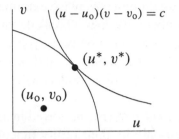

A *bargaining problem* (S, d_1, d_2) consists of a set $S = \{(x, y) \mid x, y \in \mathbf{R}\}$ of ordered pairs of feasible payoffs to two agents, and a pair of points $(d_1, d_2) \in S$ representing the agents' fallback payoffs if they cannot agree. Agreement consists of choosing a point $(\pi_1, \pi_2) \in S$ so that the first agent gets π_1 and the second gets π_2.

A *bargaining solution* is a pair of functions $\pi_1 = f_1(S, d_1, d_2)$ and $\pi_2 = f_2(S, d_1, d_2)$ that assign to a bargaining problem (S, d_1, d_2) a pair of payoffs (π_1, π_2), one to each of the two agents. Suppose a bargaining problem has the following four properties:

a. *Invariance to Equivalent Utility Representations:* If we replace $u(\pi_1)$ by $\alpha u(\pi_1) + \beta$ or $v(\pi_2)$ by $\alpha v(\pi_2) + \beta$, for $\alpha > 0$, the solution does not change.
b. *Pareto-Efficiency:* Suppose

$$(f_1(S, d_1, d_2), f_2(S, d_1, d_2)) = (\pi_1, \pi_2) \in S,$$

and let $(t_1, t_2) \in S$. Then if $u(t_1) > u(\pi_1)$, we must have $v(t_2) < v(\pi_2)$.
c. *Symmetry:* If $(\pi_2, \pi_1) \in S$ whenever $(\pi_1, \pi_2) \in S$, if $d_1 = d_2$, and if $u(\pi) = v(\pi)$ for all $s \in S$, then $f_1(\pi_1, \pi_2, d_1, d_2) = f_2(\pi_1, \pi_2, d_1, d_2)$.
d. *Independence from Irrelevant Alternatives:* If (S, d_1, d_2) and (T, d_1, d_2) are bargaining problems with $S \subseteq T$ and

$$(f_1(T, d_1, d_2), f_2(T, d_1, d_2)) \in S,$$

then $f_1(S, d_1, d_2) = f_1(T, d_1, d_2)$ and $f_2(S, d_1, d_2) = f_2(T, d_1, d_2)$.

Invariance says that the outcome cannot depend on the arbitrary units in which we measure utility, and *Pareto-efficiency* says that any bargaining solution exhausts all opportunities for making both players better off. Critics often claim that Pareto-efficiency is unrealistic, since bargaining breaks down all the time in the real world (strikes, wars, bitter divorces, expensive litigation). However, bargaining takes place extremely frequently in social and economic life, and only rarely does it break down. Breakdowns, though, are highly salient events that cannot be portrayed within the framework of the Nash bargaining model. Bargaining breakdown can be addressed, however, using game-theoretic bargaining models with asymmetric information (§15.9).

Symmetry says that neither player is preferred in any way to the other, so players are distinguished only by their utility functions and fallback positions. *Independence from irrelevant alternatives* is the most subtle assumption. This property says that the outcome of a bargain cannot depend on the availability of alternative bargains that are not in fact chosen when players have the option to do so. One common form of asymmetry in bargaining is the fact that in alternating offer bargaining models (§5.6, §5.7, and §5.8), the player who goes first often has an advantage.

THEOREM 15.1 Nash Bargaining Theorem. *There is a unique bargaining solution*

$$(\pi_1, \pi_2) = (f_1(S, d_1, d_2), f_2(S, d_1, d_2))$$

that satisfies the properties a.–d. This solution defines (π_1, π_2) as the payoff pair (s_1, s_2) that maximizes $(u(s_1) - u(d_1))(v(s_2) - v(d_2))$ subject to the constraint $(s_1, s_2) \in S$.

This solution is called the *Nash bargaining solution*. The proof of Nash's Bargaining Theorem is not difficult (see Osborne and Rubinstein 1990 for details). Discovering the theorem, on the other hand, is a stroke of genius.

Note that the Nash bargaining model is neither a normal nor an extensive form game. The question then arises as to whether there are plausible games that satisfy the Nash axioms. We explore this issue below.

a. Prove that in a Nash bargaining situation, a player whose fallback position improves gains at the expense of the other player.
b. Show that this fact remains true when we extend the Nash bargaining

solution to $n > 2$ players. In this case, $\pi_1^*, \ldots, \pi_n^*$ maximizes

$$\max_{\pi_1,\ldots,\pi_n} \prod_{i=1}^{n} (u_i(\pi_i) - u_i(\pi_i^o))$$

subject to the constraint $g(\pi_1, \ldots, \pi_n) = 0$.

15.3 Risk Aversion and the Nash Bargaining Solution

In the Nash bargaining model, the more risk averse (§16.41) an agent is, the worse the agent does in bargaining. To see this, suppose the Pareto frontier of the bargaining set is given by $y = g(x)$, where $g(x)$ is decreasing and concave, the agents have concave utility functions $u_1(x)$ and $u_2(y)$, and the fallback is $u_1 = u_2 = 0$. Maximizing $u_1(x)u_2(y)$ gives $u_1'(x)/u_1(x) = -u_2'(y)y'/u_2(y)$. The curve $u_1'(x)/u_1(x)$ is downward sloping, since its derivative is $(u_1''u_1 - (u')^2)/u_1^2 < 0$. Similarly, the curve $u_2'(y)y'/u_2(y)$ is upward sloping, since its derivative is $-(u_2''(y)(y')^2 + u_2'y'')u_2'(y) - u_2'(y)^2(y')^2/u_2(y)^2$, which is positive. This gives the Nash bargaining equilibrium at z^* in Fig. 15.1.

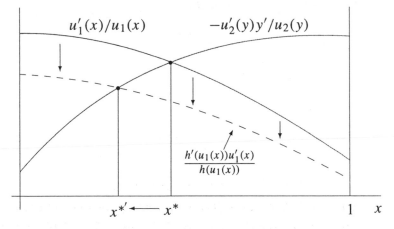

Figure 15.1. Bargaining with risk averse agents.

Now suppose the first agent becomes more risk averse. What does this mean for the agent's utility function? Specifically, suppose the original utility function $u_1(x)$ with $u_1(0) = 0$ becomes the more risk averse utility function $v_1(x)$ with $v_1(0) = 0$.

The Arrow-Pratt measure of risk aversion is

$$\lambda_u(x) = -\frac{u''(x)}{u'(x)}$$

for utility function $u(x)$. The higher is $\lambda_u(x)$, the greater the risk premium the agent must receive to be willing to accept a small lottery around x, rather than have the expected value of the lottery. We say $v(x)$ is *uniformly more risk averse* than $u(x)$ if $\lambda_v(x) > \lambda_u(x)$ for all x (§16.41).

Utility function $v(x)$ with $v(0) = 0$ is uniformly more risk averse than utility function $u(x)$ with $u(0) = 0$ if and only if there is a strictly concave function $h(\cdot)$ with $v(x) = h(u(x))$ for all x and $h(0) = 0$. Using this fact, we can write the agent's new utility function as $v_1(x) = h(u_1(x))$, where $h : \mathbf{R} \to \mathbf{R}$ is increasing and concave. Now the curve $u'_1(x)/u_1(x)$ is replaced by $h'(u_1(x))u'_1(x)/h(u_1(x))$, which is the former curve shifted downward. To see this, we need only show that $h'(t) < h(t)/t$. This is obvious geometrically (see Fig. 15.2), but using calculus, we see that $th'(t) = h(t)$ when $t = 0$, and $(th')' = h' + th'' < h'$, so $th'(t)$ increases more slowly than $h(t)$.

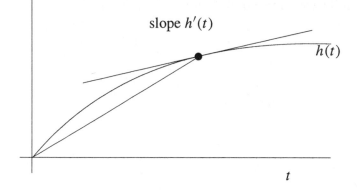

Figure 15.2. Increasing risk aversion.

Since the curve $u'_1(x)/u_1(x)$ shifts down when agent 1 becomes more risk averse, her share decreases (from x^* to $x^{*'}$ in Fig. 15.2). This proves the assertion.

15.4   Rubinstein Bargaining with Outside Options

Two agents bargain over splitting a dollar using the Ståhl-Rubinstein alternating offer bargaining model with common discount rate δ (§5.6). Suppose that, as a respondent, player i can accept or reject the offer. If the offer is rejected, an outside option worth s_i materializes with probability $p > 0$. If the offer materializes, the respondent can accept or reject the outside offer. If the outside offer is accepted, the respondent's payoff is s_i, and the proposer's payoff is zero. Otherwise, the proposer and the respondent exchange roles and the game continues. The game tree is depicted in Fig. 15.3.

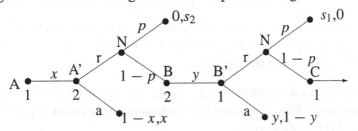

Figure 15.3. Rubinstein bargaining with outside options.

The following exercise derives a subgame perfect Nash equilibrium of this bargaining game. Using the technique of §5.6, you can show that this is the *unique* subgame perfect Nash equilibrium. Use the One-Stage Deviation Principle (§6.6) to do the following problem.

a. Show that if $s_i > (1 - (1 - p)\delta)/p$, player i would do better not to bargain and simply wait for the outside option in each period. We assume in the rest of the problem that the reverse inequality holds.

b. Suppose $s_1, s_2 < \delta/(1+\delta)$. Show that the equilibrium coincides with the Rubinstein model without outside options: the proposer offers $\delta/(1 + \delta)$, and the respondent accepts anything greater than $\delta/(1 + \delta)$ while rejecting anything less than this amount. The payoffs are $\pi_1 = 1/(1+\delta)$ and $\pi_2 = \delta/(1 + \delta)$.

c. Let

$$\pi_1 = \frac{1 - (1 - p)\delta - ps_2}{1 - (1 - p)\delta^2},$$

and suppose $s_1 < \delta\pi_1$ and $\delta/(1+\delta) < s_2$. Show that there is a subgame perfect Nash equilibrium in which player 1 offers $1 - \pi_1$, player 2 accepts, and the payoffs are $(\pi_1, 1 - \pi_1)$.

d. Let

$$\pi_1 = \frac{1 - \delta + \delta p s_1}{1 - (1 - p)\delta^2},$$

and suppose $s_2 < \delta\pi_1$ and $\delta/(1+\delta) < s_1$. Show that there is a subgame perfect Nash equilibrium in which player 1 offers $1 - \pi_1$, player 2 accepts, and the payoffs are $(\pi_1, 1 - \pi_1)$.

e. Let

$$\pi_1 = \frac{1 - (1 - p)\delta(1 - ps_1) - ps_2}{1 - (1 - p)^2\delta^2},$$

and suppose $s_1, s_2 > \delta\pi_1$. Then there is a subgame perfect Nash equilibrium in which each player offers $1 - \pi_1$ and seeks the outside option if offered less than this amount.

This solution looks complicated, but if we graph it the result is very straightforward. Fig. 15.4 shows the relationship between π_1 and s_2 when $0 < s_1 < \delta/(1+d) < s_1/\delta$.

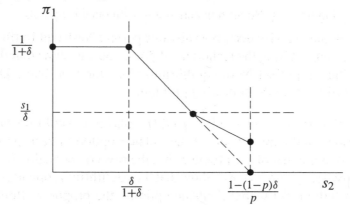

Figure 15.4. The effect of outside options on payoffs in the Rubinstein bargaining model.

15.5   Bargaining with Two-Sided Outside Options

The previous problem assumes that the respondent has an outside option available. One would think that the same variety of equilibria would obtain if the proposer had an outside option, but such is not at all the case (Ponsati and Sákovics 1998). Suppose One and Two bargain for $1, where One has an outside option x_1 and Two has an outside option x_2, where $0 \leq x_1 \leq 1 - x_2 \leq 1$. If an offer is rejected, either player can take the outside option, forcing the other to take the outside option as well. Note that this includes $x_1 = x_2 = 0$, so the outside option is not available, but the players are not forced to continue bargaining. Show the following:

a. If One is first to offer, there is a subgame perfect equilibrium in which One offers x_2 and Two accepts. Note that this implies that if $x_2 = 0$ then One gets the whole dollar!

b. Suppose One's discount factor is $\delta_1 \in (0, 1)$ and Two's discount factor is $\delta_2 \in (0, 1)$, and suppose $x^* \in [1 - \delta_2(1 - x_1/\delta_1), 1 - x_2]$. Then there is a subgame perfect equilibrium in which One offers Two $1 - x^*$ and Two accepts. HINT: Show that Two will accept an offer on the first round only if (1) Two is indifferent to accepting vs. waiting until the next period; (2) both players (weakly) prefer the agreement to the outside options; and (3) One (weakly) prefers continuing to taking the option.

c. For any period $t > 0$, suppose $x^* \in [(1 - \delta_2(1 - x_1/\delta_1))/\delta_1, (1 - \delta_1(1 - x_2/\delta_2))/\delta_2^{t-1}]$. Then there is a subgame perfect equilibrium in which offers are refused for the first $t - 1$ rounds, and on the tth One receives x^* and Two receives $1 - x^*$.

15.6   Rubinstein Bargaining and Nash Bargaining

The Nash bargaining model is useful only if there are plausible games that satisfy the Nash bargaining axioms. The Rubinstein model does not accomplish this, because it violates the symmetry axiom—player 1 has a first-mover advantage. We could correct this by having the players flip a fair coin to see who goes first, but we still have the problem that the Rubinstein model uses player discount factors rather than utility functions. In this and the following section we explore models that do implement Nash bargaining.

Suppose two agents bargain over the choice of an allocation $s \in S$, where $S \subset \mathbf{R}^2$ is a closed, bounded, convex set. We write the Pareto frontier of this set as $y = g(x)$, and we assume $g'(x)$ exists and is negative. Let δ be the discount factor, and suppose the agents take turns making an offer of a pair $(x, y) = (x, g(x))$, until one of the agents accepts the other's offer. We suppose that the value of the payoff declines by a factor of δ per period, and if an offer is rejected, then with a probability $p > 0$ bargaining ends and the agents get their fallback positions (d_1, d_2). We call the subgame perfect Nash equilibrium to this game the Rubinstein bargaining solution for discount factor δ and probability of breakdown p (§5.6).

Show that if the discount factor $\delta = 1$, then as $p \to 0$, the Rubinstein bargaining solution approaches the Nash bargaining solution.

15.7   Zeuthen Lotteries and the Nash Bargaining Solution

The following implementation of the Nash bargaining model is due to Zeuthen (1930), whose work predates game theory. While Zeuthen's model is not exactly an extensive form game, it could be made into one with little difficulty.

Suppose two players are bargaining over the choice of an allocation s in a set S of feasible payoffs. We say an allocation $s \in S$ is "on the table" if one player proposed s. If the other player accepts s, the game is over, and the allocation is implemented. If the other player rejects s, then there is a probability $1 - p$ that bargaining will break down and the players will get a fallback allocation $d \in S$. Otherwise, with probability p, the other agent proposes an alternative $s' \in S$. The game continues until both agree to an allocation, or bargaining breaks down.

We write (p, s) for the *Zeuthen lottery* that pays $s \in S$ with probability p and d with probability $1 - p$ (see the diagram to the right), and we assume agents $i = 1, 2$ have utility functions $u_i : S \to \mathbf{R}$ over the lotteries, and for any two lotteries (p, s) and (p', s') we say player i prefers the first to the second if $u(p, s) > u(p', s')$, and we say i is indifferent between the two lotteries if $u(p, s) = u(p', s')$. We identify an allocation $s \in S$ that is on the table with the Zeuthen lottery $(1, s)$ that gives s with probability 1; i.e., we write s and $(1, s)$ interchangeably. This is because if s is on the table, then the players can obtain s with certainty.

We say an allocation $s^* \in S$ is a *Zeuthen equilibrium* to the bargaining problem if the following condition holds: when s^* is on the table and (p, s) is any Zeuthen lottery, then if one player strictly prefers (p, s) to s^*, the other agent prefers (p, s^*) to s. In other words, if one player rejects s^* and puts s on the table in the next period, then the other player will reject s and put s^* on the table again. Hence, the respondent cannot gain by rejecting s^*.

Note that Zeuthen bargaining is very close to the Rubinstein bargaining model, except that it does not specify a first mover and hence treats the players symmetrically. Moreover, a Zeuthen equilibrium is clearly Pareto-efficient and is independent of equivalent utility representations. Show that if $s^* \in S$ is a Zeuthen equilibrium, then s^* is an equilibrium to the Nash bargaining problem; i.e., s^* maximizes

$$(u_1(s) - u_1(d))(u_2(s) - u_2(d)) \qquad s \in S.$$

15.8   Bargaining with Fixed Costs

Mutt and Jeff bargain over splitting $1 using alternating offers, but it costs Mutt c_1 and Jeff c_2 per period if an offer is rejected. Suppose $c_1 < c_2 < c_1 + c_2 < 1$. We will show that there is a unique subgame perfect Nash equilibrium in which, if Mutt goes first, he offers Jeff nothing and Jeff accepts (as usual, we assume the *nice guy principle* that a player only rejects an offer if doing so strictly increases the player's expected payoff), and if Jeff goes first, he offers Mutt $1 - c_2$ and Mutt accepts.

a. Use the One-Stage Deviation Principle (§6.6) to show that Mutt's strategy of offering Jeff nothing and Jeff accepting is a subgame perfect Nash equilibrium.
b. Let m_1 be the most Mutt can get in any subgame perfect Nash equilibrium. Suppose $c_1 \leq m_1 < 1$. Show that this leads to a contradiction.
c. Suppose $0 < m_1 < c_1$. Show that this leads to a contradiction.
d. It follows that $m_1 = 1$, so clearly, if Jeff goes first, the best he can do is to offer Mutt $1 - c_1$, and keep c_1.

Of course, this solution, while mathematically rigorous, is intuitively bizarre, since it predicts an extremely one-sided division no matter how small the costs are, and no matter how small the difference in costs between the two players. Once again, backward induction leads to an absurdity.

15.9   Bargaining with Incomplete Information

Suppose a seller has a perishable good whose value to a prospective buyer is v, which is distributed uniformly on an interval $[0, v_1]$. The seller has two chances to make a deal with the buyer, but if the first offer is rejected, the payoffs to both parties after the second offer must be discounted by $\delta < 1$ (§12.3). The seller's strategy set thus consists of price pairs (p_1, p_2), where p_1 is the first-period offer and p_2 is the second-period offer, assuming the first-period offer is rejected. The buyer's strategies consist of accepting and/or rejecting various prices in the two periods. We consider only subgame perfect equilibria, and since the buyer has all the information available to the seller, the buyer also knows the seller's optimal (possibly mixed) strategy. Finally, we assume a buyer will accept an offer unless the buyer can do strictly better by rejecting it (this is the *nice guy principle*).

The following question asks you to show that the seller will set $p_1 = v_1(2-\delta)/4$ and $p_2 = v_1/4$. Thus, once again we find that asymmetry leads to inefficient bargaining, since if $v < v_1/4$ no bargain will be struck between the two.

a. Suppose the seller knows that if the first offer is rejected, then the value to the prospective buyer is uniformly distributed on $[0, v_2]$. Show that it is optimal for the buyer to set $p_2 = v_2/2$.

b. Show that if p_1 is rejected, then either $v < p_1, p_2$ or

$$v < \frac{p_1 - \delta p_2}{1 - \delta}. \tag{15.1}$$

c. Show that either $v < p_1, p_2$, or $v_2 = 2p_1/(2-\delta)$ and hence $p_2 = p_1/(2-\delta)$, so the buyer's payoff in the second round is $\delta(v - p_1/(2-\delta))$.

d. Show that either $v < p_1, p_2$ or $p_1 = v_1(2-\delta)/4$ and $p_2 = v_1/4$.

It follows that the seller sets $p_1 = v_1(2-\delta)/4$ and $p_2 = v_1/4$. If $v \geq v_1/4$, the first bid is accepted with probability 1/2; if the first bid is rejected, then v is uniformly distributed on $[0, v_1/2]$, and the second bid is also accepted with probability 1/2. If $v < v_1(2-\delta)/4$, no deal is made. Note that if the buyer is very impatient ($\delta = 0$), $p_1 = v_1/2$, whereas if the buyer is very patient ($\delta = 1$), $p_1 = v_1/4$. Patient buyers do better.

16

Probability and Decision Theory

> Doubt is disagreeable, but certainty is ridiculous.
>
> *Voltaire*

16.1 Probability Spaces

We assume a *universe* or *sample space* X, and a set $\mathcal{E}$ of subsets $A, B, C, \ldots$ of X, called *events*. We assume $\mathcal{E}$ is closed under countable unions (if $A_1, A_2, \ldots$ are events, so is $\cup_{i=1}^{\infty} A_i$), finite intersections (if $A_1, \ldots, A_n$ are events, so is $\cap_{i=1}^{n} A_i$), and complementation (if A is an event so is the set of elements of X that are not in A, which we write A^c). If A and B are events, we interpret $A \cap B = AB$ as the event "A and B both occur," $A \cup B$ as the event "A or B occurs," and A^c as the event "A does not occur."

For instance, suppose we flip a coin twice, the outcome being HH (heads on both), HT (heads on first and tails on second), TH (tails on first and heads on second), and TT (tails on both). The sample space is then $X = \{HH, TH, HT, TT\}$. Some events are $\{HH, HT\}$ (the coin comes up heads on the first toss), $\{TT\}$ (the coin comes up tails twice), and $\{HH, HT, TH\}$ (the coin comes up heads at least once).

The *probability* of an event $A \in \mathcal{E}$ is a real number $P[A]$ such that $0 \leq P[A] \leq 1$. We assume that $P[X] = 1$, which says that with probability 1 *some* outcome occurs, and we also assume that if $A = \cup_{i=1}^{\infty} A_i$, where $A_i \in \mathcal{E}$ and the $\{A_i\}$ are disjoint (i.e., $A_i \cap A_j = \emptyset$ for all $i \neq j$), then $P[A] = \sum_{i=1}^{\infty} P[A_i]$, which says that probabilities are countably additive over disjoint unions.

16.2 DeMorgan's Laws

Show that for any two events A and B, we have

$$(A \cup B)^c = A^c \cap B^c$$

and

$$(A \cap B)^c = A^c \cup B^c.$$

These are called *deMorgan's Laws*. Express the meaning of these formulas in words.

Show that if we write p for proposition "A occurs" and q for "B occurs," then

$$\text{not } (p \text{ or } q) \Leftrightarrow (\text{ not } p \text{ and not } q),$$

$$\text{not } (p \text{ and } q) \Leftrightarrow (\text{ not } p \text{ or not } q).$$

The formulas are also deMorgan laws. Give examples of both rules.

16.3   Interocitors

An interocitor consists of two kramels and three trums. Let A_k be the event "the kth kramel is in working condition," and B_j is the event "the jth trum is in working condition." An interocitor is in working condition if at least one of its kramels and two of its trums are in working condition. Let C be the event "the interocitor is in working condition." Write C in terms of the A_k and the B_j.

16.4   The Direct Evaluation of Probabilities

THEOREM 16.1   *Given $a_1, \ldots, a_n$ and $b_1, \ldots, b_m$, there are $n \times m$ distinct ways of choosing one of the a's and one of the b's. If we also have $c_1, \ldots, c_r$, there are $n \times m \times r$ distinct ways of choosing one of the a's, one of the b's, and one of the c's.*

Apply this Theorem to determine how many different elements there are in the sample space of

a.   the double coin flip.
b.   the triple coin flip.
c.   rolling a pair of dice.

16.5   Probability as Frequency

Suppose the sample space X consists of a finite number n of equally probable elements. Suppose the event A contains m elements. Then the *probability of the event A* is defined as m/n.

A second definition: Suppose an experiment has n distinct outcomes, all of which are equally likely. Let A be a subset of the outcomes, and $n(A)$ the number of elements of A. We define the *probability* of A as $P[A] = n(A)/n$.

For example, in throwing a pair of dice, there are $6 \times 6 = 36$ mutually exclusive equally likely events, each represented by an ordered pair (a, b) where a is the number of spots showing on the first die and b the number on the second. Let A be the event that both dice show the same number of spots. Then $n(A) = 6$ and $P[A] = 6/36 = 1/6$.

A third definition: Suppose an experiment can be repeated any number of times, each outcome being independent of the ones before and after it. Let A be an event that either does or does not occur for each outcome. Let $n_t(A)$ be the number of times A occurred on all the tries up to and including the tth try. We define the *relative frequency* of A as $n_t(A)/t$, and we define the *probability of A* as

$$P[A] = \lim_{t \to \infty} \frac{n(A)}{t}.$$

We say two events A and B are *independent* if $P[A]$ does not depend on whether B occurs or not, and conversely, $P[B]$ does not depend on whether A occurs or not. If events A and B are independent, the probability that both occur is the product of the probabilities that either occurs: i.e.,

$$P[A \text{ and } B] = P[A] \times P[B].$$

For example, in flipping coins, let A be the event "the first ten flips are heads." Let B be the event "the eleventh flip is heads." Then the two events are independent.

For another example, suppose there are two urns, one containing 100 white balls and 1 red ball, and the other containing 100 red balls and one white ball. You do not know which is which. You choose two balls from the first urn. Let A be the event "The first ball is white," and let B be the event "The second ball is white." These events are not independent, since if you draw a white ball the first time, you are more likely to be drawing from the urn with 100 white balls than the urn with 1 white ball.

Determine the following probabilities. Assume all coins and dice are "fair" in the sense that H and T are equiprobable for a coin, and $1, \ldots, 6$ are equiprobable for a die.

a. At least one head occurs in a double coin toss.
b. Exactly two tails occur in a triple coin toss.

c. The sum of the two die equals 7 or 11 in rolling a pair of dice.
d. All six dice show the same number when six dice are thrown.
e. A coin is tossed seven times. The string of outcomes is HHHHHHH.
f. A coin is tossed seven times. The string of outcomes is HTHHTTH.
g. A player rolls two dice, winning if the sum is 7 or 11, and losing if the sum is 2 or 3. For any other outcome, the player continues rolling the dice until either winning by matching the first number rolled, or losing by the sum being 2, 7 or 12. What is the probability of winning?

16.6   Sampling

The mutually exclusive outcomes of a random action are called *sample points*. The set of sample points is called the *sample space*. An *event A* is a subset of a sample space Ω. The event A is *certain* if $A = \Omega$ and *impossible* if $A = \emptyset$. The *probability* of an event A is $P[A] = n(A)/n(\Omega)$, assuming Ω is finite.

a. Suppose we choose r object in succession from a set of n distinct objects $a_1, \ldots, a_n$, each time recording the choice and returning the object to the set before making the next choice. This gives an ordered sample of the form $(b_1, \ldots, b_r)$, where each b_j is some a_i. We call this *sampling with replacement*. Show that in sampling r times with replacement from a set of n objects, there are n^r distinct ordered samples.
b. Six dice are thrown. What is the probability all six die show the same number?
c. Suppose we choose r objects in succession from a set of n distinct objects $a_1, \ldots, a_n$, without returning the object to the set. This gives an ordered sample of the form $(b_1, \ldots, b_r)$, where each b_j is some unique a_i. We call this *sampling without replacement* . Show that in sampling r times without replacement from a set of n objects, there are

$$n(n-1)\ldots(n-r+1) = \frac{n!}{(n-r)!}$$

distinct ordered samples, where $n! = n \times n - 1 \times \ldots \times 2 \times 1$.

16.7   Self-presentation

A group of n people agree to exchange presents by putting their names in a hat. Each then draws one name and gives a present to the person on the slip. What is the probability that each gives a present to herself?

16.8   Social Isolation

A subway train made up of n cars is boarded by r passengers $(r \leq n)$, each entering a car at random. What is the probability of the passengers all ending up in different cars?

16.9   Aces Up

A deck of fifty-two cards has four aces. A player draws two cards randomly from the deck. What is the probability that both are aces?

16.10   Mechanical Defection

A shipment of 7 machines has two defective machines. An inspector checks two machines randomly drawn from the shipment, and accepts the shipment if neither is defective. What is the probability the shipment is accepted?

16.11   Double Orders

An industry has n firms, and in any one day has orders from r customers $(r \leq n)$. Each firm is equally likely to receive each order. What is the probability no firm gets more than one order on a given day?

16.12   Combinations and Sampling

The number of *combinations* of n things taken r at a time is the number of subsets of size r, taken from the n things without replacement. We write this as $\binom{n}{r}$. In this case we do not care about the order of the choices. For instance, consider the set of numbers $\{1,2,3,4\}$. The number of samples of size two without replacement $= 4!/2! = 12$. These are precisely $\{12,13,14,21,23,24,31,32,34,41,42,43\}$. The combinations of the four numbers of size two (i.e., taken two at a time) are $\{12,13,14,23,24,34\}$, or six in number. Note that $6 = \binom{4}{2} = 4!/2!2!$. A set of n elements has $n!/r!(n-r)!$ distinct subsets of size r. Thus, we have

$$\binom{n}{r} = \frac{n!}{r!(n-r)!}.$$

16.13   Mass Defection

A batch of 100 manufactured items is checked by an inspector, who examines 10 items at random. If none is defective, she accepts the whole batch. What is the probability that a batch containing 10 defective items will be accepted?

16.14   An Unlucky Streak

From a lot of n items, k are defective. Find the probability that a items out of a random sample of size b selected for inspection are defective.

16.15   House Rules

Suppose you are playing the following game against the House in Las Vegas. You pick a number between one and six. The House rolls three dice, and pays you $1000 if your number comes up on one die, $2000 if your number comes up on two dice, and $3000 if your number comes up on all three dice. If your number does not show up at all, you pay the House $1000. At first glance, this looks like a *fair game* (i.e., a game in which the expected payoff is zero), but in fact it is not. How much can you expect to win (or lose)?

16.16   The Powerball Lottery

The Powerball lottery has a jackpot of $104.3 million. In the Powerball lottery you choose 5 distinct numbers from 1 to 49 for the white balls and one number from 1 to 42 for the red Powerball. To win the jackpot you must match all six numbers. 138.5 million tickets are sold. Assuming that numbers are randomly picked what is the probability that there is a winner? What is the probability that there is be more than one winner?

16.17   The Addition Rule for Probabilities

Let A and B be two events. Then $0 \leq P[A] \leq 1$ and

$$P[A \cup B] = P[A] + P[B] - P[AB].$$

If A and B are disjoint (i.e., the events are mutually exclusive), then

$$P[A \cup B] = P[A] + P[B].$$

Moreover, if $A_1, \ldots, A_n$ are mutually disjoint, then

$$P[\cup_i A_i] = \sum_{i=1}^{n} P[A_i].$$

We call events $A_1, \ldots, A_n$ a *partition* of the sample space X if they are mutually disjoint and exhaustive (i.e., their union is X). In this case for any event B, we have

$$P[B] = \sum_i P[BA_i].$$

16.18   Die, Die!

What is the probability in throwing a pair of dice that the two dice are the same, or the result adds up to 8?

16.19   Les Cinq Tiroirs

You are looking for an object in one of five drawers. There is a 20% chance that it is not in any of the drawers, but if it is in a drawer, it is equally likely to be in each one. Show that as you look in the drawers one by one, the probability of finding the object in the next drawer rises if not found so far, but the probability of eventually finding it goes down.

16.20   A Guessing Game

Each day the call-in program on a local radio station conducts the following game. A number is drawn at random from $\{1, 2, \ldots, n\}$. Callers choose a number at random, and win a prize if correct. Otherwise, the station announces whether the guess was high or low, and they move on to the next caller. What is the expected number $f(n)$ of callers before one guesses the number?

16.21   Conditional Probability

If A and B are events, and if the probability $P[B]$ that B occurs is strictly positive, we define the *conditional probability* of A given B, denoted $P[A|B]$, by

$$P[A|B] = \frac{P[AB]}{P[B]}.$$

We say $B_1, \ldots, B_n$ are a *partition* of event B if $\cup_i B_i = B$ and $B_i B_j = \emptyset$ for $i \neq j$. We have

a. If A and B are events, $P[B] > 0$, and B implies A (i.e., $A \subseteq B$), then $P[A|B] = 1$.

b. If A and B are contradictory (i.e., $AB = \emptyset$), then $P[A|B] = 0$.

c. If $A_1, \ldots, A_n$ are a partition of event A, then

$$P[A|B] = \sum_{i=1}^{n} P[A_i|B].$$

d. If $B_1, \ldots, B_n$ are a partition of the sample space X, then

$$P[A] = \sum_{i=1}^{n} P[A|B_i] P[B_i].$$

16.22   Bayes' Rule

If $B_1, \ldots, B_n$ is a partition of the sample space and if $P[A], P[B_k] > 0$, then

$$P[B_k|A] = \frac{P[A|B_k] P[B_k]}{\sum_{i=1}^{n} P[A|B_i] P[B_i]}.$$

To see this, note that the denominator on the right-hand side is just $P[A]$, and the numerator is just $P[AB_k]$ by definition.

As a special case, suppose A and B are events with $P[A], P[B], P[B^c] > 0$. Then we have

$$P[B|A] = \frac{P[A|B] P[B]}{P[A|B] P[B] + P[A|B^c](1 - P[B])}.$$

16.23 Drug Testing

Bayes' Rule is useful because often we know $P[A|B]$, $P[A|B^c]$ and $P[B]$, and we want to find $P[B|A]$. For example, suppose 5% of the population uses drugs, and there is a drug test that is 95% accurate: it tests positive on a drug user 95% of the time, and it tests negative on a drug nonuser 95% of the time. Show that if an individual tests positive, the probability of his being a drug user is 50%. HINT: Let A be the event "is a drug user," let "Pos" be the event "tests positive," let "Neg" be the event "tests negative," and apply Bayes' Rule.

16.24 A Bolt Factory

In a bolt factory, machines A, B, and C manufacture 25%, 35%, and 40% of total output and have defective rates of 5%, 4%, and 2%, respectively. A bolt is chosen at random and found to be defective. What are the probabilities that it was manufactured by machines A, B, and C?

16.25 Color Blindness

Suppose 5% of men are color-blind and 0.25% of women are color-blind. A person is chosen at random and found to be color-blind. What is the probability the person is male?

16.26 Urns

A collection of $n + 1$ urns, numbered from 0 to n, each contains n balls. Urn k contains k red and $n - k$ white balls. An urn is chosen at random and n balls are randomly chosen from it, the ball being replaced each time before another is chosen. Suppose all n balls are found to be red. What is the probability the next ball chosen from the urn will be red? Show that when n is large, this probability is approximately $(n + 1)/(n + 2)$. The last step is not obvious.

16.27 The Monty Hall Game

You are a contestant in a game show. The host says, "Behind one of those three doors is a new automobile. Behind the other two doors are goats (silent—like the automobile). You may choose any door." You choose door 1. The game host then opens door 2 and shows you that there is a goat behind it. He then asks, "Now would you like to change your guess?" We will show that the answer is "no" if the game show host randomly opened one of the two other doors, but "yes" if he simply opened a door he knew did not have a car behind it.

Suppose there are n doors ($n \geq 3$). Let A_k be the event "car is behind door k." Let B_k be the event "host chooses door k, contestant did not choose door k, and door k has a goat behind it." We write $P[E]$ for the probability of the event E and $P[E|F]$ for the conditional probability of event E, given event F. Clearly, $P[A_k] = 1/n$ for $k = 1, \ldots, n$. By Bayes' Rule,

$$P[A_j|B_k] = \frac{P[B_k|A_j]\,P[A_j]}{P[B_k]} = \frac{P[B_k|A_j]}{nP[B_k]} \qquad j, k = 1, \ldots, n. \quad (16.1)$$

provided $P[B_k] > 0$.

Suppose, without loss of generality, that the contestant chooses door 1, so he wins if A_1. Thus, $P[win] = P[A_1] = 1/n$.

Now suppose the host chooses *randomly* from all doors except door 1. He chooses door $k > 1$ with probability $1/(n-1)$, and this has a goat behind it with probability $(n-1)/n$, so $P[B_k] = 1/n$ for $k > 1$. If A_1, door k certainly has a goat behind it, so $P[B_k|A_1] = 1/(n-1)$ for $k > 1$. From equation (16.1) we get

$$P[A_1|B_k] = \frac{1/(n-1)}{n(1/n)} = 1/(n-1), \qquad k > 1.$$

If A_j for $j > 1$, then for $k \neq 1, j$, the probability of B_k conditional on A_j is $1/(n-1)$. To see this, note that since the host does not know what door has the car behind it, he chooses each of the doors $2, \ldots, n$ with equal probability. Moreover, whichever k he chooses certainly has a goat behind it, since $k \neq j$. Now, from $P[B_k|A_j] = 1/(n-1)$ for $j \neq k$, $j > 1$, and equation (16.1) we get

$$P[A_j|B_k] = \frac{1/(n-1)}{n(1/n)} = 1/(n-1), \qquad j \neq k, \quad j > 1,$$

which is the same as $P[A_1|B_k]$—the contestant does not gain from switching.

But suppose the host *never* picks the door with the car behind it. Now $P[B_k|A_1] = 1/(n-1) = P[B_k]$ for $k > 1$, so from equation (16.1) we have

$$P[A_1|B_k] = \frac{1/(n-1)}{n[1/(n-1)]} = 1/n, \qquad k > 1.$$

For $j > 1, k \neq j, P[B_k|A_j] = 1/(n-2)$, since the host must pick randomly from all doors except 1 and j. Thus, from equation (16.1) we get

$$P[A_j|B_k] = \frac{1/(n-2)}{n[1/(n-1)]} = \frac{(n-1)}{n(n-2)}, \qquad j \neq k, \quad j > 1.$$

Since $(n-1)/n(n-2) > 1/n$, the contestant should switch.

Note that if $n = 3$, these probabilities reduce to 1/3 and 2/3 in the one case and 1/2 and 1/2 in the other.

Here is another proof for the three-door case. Let C_i be the event "car behind door i." Let the doors be numbered such that contestant chose door 1 and host chose door 2. Let H be the event "host picks goat." Suppose first that the host chooses *randomly* between the two doors. Then we have $P[C_1] = P[C_2] = P[C_3] = 1/3$ since the labeling of the doors tells us nothing about what is behind them, so it is equiprobable that the animal is behind any door. Also $P[H] = 2/3$, the probability that an animal is behind a randomly chosen door. Moreover, $P[H|C_1] = 1$, since if the car is behind door 1, the host *must* pick a door with an animal behind it. By Bayes' Rule,

$$P[C_1|H] = \frac{P[H|C_1]P[C_1]}{P[H]} = \frac{1(1/3)}{2/3} = 1/2.$$

Thus, $P[C_2|H] = 1/2$, and there is no reason to change doors. Now suppose the host chooses a door he *knows* has an animal behind it. Then $P[C_2] = 0$, so $P[C_3] = 2/3$, and $P[H] = 1$. Then $P[H|C_1] = 1$, and Bayes' Rule gives

$$P[C_1|H] = \frac{P[H|C_1]P[C_1]}{P[H]} = \frac{1(1/3)}{1} = 1/3.$$

Thus, $P[C_3|H] = 2/3$, and the contestant doubles the chances of winning by switching doors.

16.28   The Logic of Murder and Abuse

Let A be the event that Nicole had been repeatedly beaten by her husband ("abused" for short), let B be the event "was murdered," and let C be the event "was murdered by her husband." Suppose we know the following facts: (a) 5% of women are abused by their husbands; (b) 0.5% of women are murdered; (c) 0.025% of women are murdered by their husbands; (d) 90% of women who are murdered by their husbands had been abused by their husbands; (e) a woman who is not murdered by her husband (whether or not she is murdered) is neither more nor less likely to have been abused by her husband than a randomly selected woman.

Nicole is found murdered, and it is ascertained that she had been abused by her husband. The defense attorneys for her husband show that the probability that a man who abuses his wife actually kills her is only 4.31%, so there is a strong presumption of innocence for him. The attorneys for the prosecution show that there is in fact a 94.74% chance the husband murdered his wife, independent from any evidence other than that he abused her. Here is how the two teams of attorneys argued. The jury was well versed in probability theory, so they had no problem understanding the reasoning.

First, from Bayes' Rule,

$$P[C|A] = \frac{P[A|C]\,P[C]}{P[A|C]\,P[C] + P[A|C^c](1 - P[C])}.$$

This is the probability that a man murders his wife if he has abused her. But from (d) above, $P[A|C] = 9/10$; from (c) $P[C] = 1/400$; from (e) and (a), $P[A|C^c] = P[A] = 1/20$; so we find $P[C|A] = 6/139 \approx 4.31\%$.

"I object!" says the chief prosecutor. "The defense ignores the fact that Nicole was *murdered*. What we *really* must know is $P[C|AB]$, the probability a *murdered* woman who was abused by her husband was murdered by him." "But," splutters the astounded judge, "how could you calculate such a complex probability?" A large overhead projector is brought into the court, and the chief prosecutor proceeds with the following calculation, the astute jurors taking mental notes. "We have," says the prosecutor,

$$P[C|AB] = \frac{P[ABC]}{P[AB]} = \frac{P[A|BC]\,P[BC]}{P[ABC] + P[ABC^c]}$$

$$= \frac{P[A|BC]\,P[C|B]\,P[B]}{P[A|BC]\,P[C|B]\,P[B] + P[A|BC^c]\,P[C^c|B]\,P[B]}$$

$$= \frac{P[A|C]\,P[C|B]}{P[A|C]\,P[C|B] + P[A](1 - P[C|B])},$$

where $P[A|BC^c] = P[A]$ by (e). From (b), $P[B] = 1/200$, so $P[C|B] = P[C]/P[B] = 1/2$, so we have $P[C|AB] = 18/19 = 94.74\%$.

16.28.1   The Principle of Insufficient Reason

The Principle of Insufficient Reason says that if you are "completely ignorant" as to which among the states $A_1, \ldots, A_n$ will occur, then you should assign probability $1/n$ to each of the states. The argument in favor of the principle is strong (see Savage 1954 and Sinn 1980 for discussions), but there are some interesting arguments against it. For instance, suppose A_1 itself consists of m mutually exclusive events $A_{11}, \ldots, A_{1m}$. If you are "completely ignorant" concerning which of these occurs, then if $P[A_1] = 1/n$, we should set $P[A_{1i}] = 1/mn$. But are we not "completely ignorant" concerning which of $A_{11}, \ldots, A_{1m}, A_2, \ldots, A_n$ occurs? If so, we should set each of these probabilities to $1/(n + m - 1)$. If not, in what sense were we "completely ignorant" concerning the original states $A_1, \ldots, A_n$?

16.29   Ah, Those Kids

You see an acquaintance strolling down the street with a boy whom he introduces as his son. You know he has another child, and he likes strolling with both children equally. What is the probability the other child is a boy?

You see an acquaintance at a father-and-son dinner for sixth graders. He introduces the boy as his son. You know he has another child, this one in the eighth grade. What is the probability the other child is a boy?

16.30   The Greens and the Blacks

The Greens and the Blacks are playing bridge. After a deal, Mr. Brown, an onlooker, asks Mrs. Black: "Do you have an ace in your hand?" She nods yes. After the next deal, he asks her: "Do you have the ace of spades?" She nods yes again. In which of the two situations is Mrs. Black more likely to have at least one other ace in her hand? Calculate the exact probabilities in the two cases.

16.31   Laplace's Law of Succession

An urn contains a large number n of white and black balls, where the number of white balls is uniformly distributed between 0 and n. Suppose you pick out m balls with replacement, and r are white. Show that the probability of picking a white ball on the next draw is approximately $(r + 1)/(m + 2)$.

16.32   The Brain and Kidney Problem

A mad scientist is showing you around his foul-smelling laboratory. He motions to an opaque, formalin-filled jar. "This jar contains either a brain or a kidney," he exclaims. Searching around his workbench, he finds a brain and adds it to the jar. He then picks one blob randomly from the jar, and it is a brain. What is the probability the remaining blob is a brain?

16.33   Sexual Harassment on the Job

Suppose you get a new supervisor every year on the job, and the probability that a new supervisor will harass you is 5% (i.e., one boss out of twenty is a slime bag). Suppose your accumulated promotion and retirement benefits are $1000 per year of service, but you receive these only if you stay at the firm for thirty years. Suppose you would be willing to pay a maximum of $10,000 to avoid being harassed. What are the odds that at some point in time you will quit your job to avoid being harassed? What are the expected number of years on the job that you can expect to be harassed?

16.34   The Value of Eyewitness Testimony

A town has one hundred taxis, eighty-five green taxis owned by the Green Cab Company and 15 blue taxies owned by the Blue Cab Company. On March 1, 1990, John Doe was struck by a speeding cab, and the only witness testified that the cab was blue rather than green. John Doe sued the Blue Cab Company. The judge instructed the jury and the lawyers at the start of the case that the reliability of a witness must be assumed to be 80% in a case of this sort, and that liability requires that the "preponderance of the evidence," meaning at least a 50% percent probability, be on the side of the plaintiff.

The lawyer for John Doe argued that the Blue Cab Company should pay, since the witness's testimonial gives a probability of 80% that Doe was struck by a blue taxi. The lawyer for the Blue Cab Company argued as follows. If the witness were shown all the cabs in town, he would have incorrectly identified 20% of the 85 green taxis (i.e., seventeen of them) as blue, and correctly identified 80% of the 15 blue taxis (i.e., twelve of them) as blue. Thus, of the 29 identifications of a taxi as blue, only twelve would be correct and seventeen would be incorrect. Thus, the preponderance of the evidence is in favor of the defendant—most likely Mr. Doe was hit by a green taxi.

Formulate the second lawyer's argument rigorously in terms of Bayes' Rule. Which argument do you think is correct, and if neither is correct, what is a good argument in this case?

16.35   The End of the World

Let A be the event "When the human race becomes extinct, fewer than 1 trillion (one million billion) persons will have lived." Let B be the event "Currently fewer than 100 billion persons have lived." Paleontological evidence tells us that $P[B] \approx 1$, and quite clearly it is reasonable to suppose that $P[A] \leq P[B]$. Thus, from Bayes' Rule we conclude that $P[A|B] \leq P[B|A]$ (prove it!). But also $P[B|A] < P[B|A'] < 10\%$, where A' is the event "When the human race becomes extinct, exactly 1 trillion persons will have lived," since if the current period is randomly chosen from among all the years that human beings are not extinct, the current period will be in the first 10% with probability 10%. This proves that $P[A|B]$, which is approximately the probability that there will be fewer than a trillion people ever existing (since B is near certainty), is less than 10%. It follows that we should limit population growth, or humanity will become extinct very soon.

Now each of these steps appears valid, but the reasoning as a whole is quite absurd, at least to the minds of many. The renowned physicist Freeman Dyson, for instance, criticizes it bitterly (*Nature* 380 [1996]:296). What do you think is wrong with the argument, if anything?

16.36   Bill and Harry

Bill and Harry each tell the truth one-third of the time. Bill says something, and Harry says, "Bill just told the truth." What is the probability that Bill told the truth?

16.37   When Weakness Is Strength

Many people have criticized the Darwinian notion of "survival of the fittest" by declaring that the whole thing is a simple tautology: whatever survives is "fit" by definition! Defenders of the notion reply by noting that we can measure fitness (e.g., speed, strength, resistance to disease, aerodynamic stability) independent of survivability, so it becomes an empirical proposition that the fit survive. Indeed, under some conditions it may be simply false, as game theorist Martin Shubik (1954) showed in the following ingenious problem.

Three marksmen, a, b, and c, are having a shootout. They draw straws to see who goes first, second, and third, and then each shoots his gun, taking turns repeatedly in that order, until only one of them is left standing. The conditions are as follows. If a marksman is hit, he is eliminated; a is a perfect shot, b has 80% accuracy, and c has 50% accuracy. For notational purposes, let $\pi_i(xyz)$ be the probability of survival for player $i = a, b, c$ when all three are still in and they are in order xyz; for instance, $\pi_a(abc)$ is the probability a wins when the order is abc. Similarly, if only two remain, let $\pi_i(xy)$ be the probability of survival for player $i = x, y$ when only x and y remain, and it is x's turn to shoot.

a. Show that when it is c's turn to shoot, he should shoot in the air rather than aim at either of the other marksmen.
b. Show that c, the least fit in terms of accuracy, is the most likely to survive, and find the probability that each of the marksmen survives.
c. You may think that this counterintuitive result has something to do with the fact that the marksmen must shoot in a specific order. Show that if the marksman who fires is picked randomly in each round (i.e., the marksmen shoot at will, but not simultaneously), then the survivability of the marksmen is perfectly inverse to their accuracy.

16.38   Markov Chains

A *finite Markov chain* is a model that in each time period $t = 0, 1, \ldots$ can be any one of n *states*, such that if the system is in state i in one time period, there is a probability p_{ij} that the system is in state j in the next time period. Thus, for each i, we must have $\sum_j p_{ij} = 1$, since the system must go somewhere in each period. We call the $n \times n$ matrix $P = \{p_{ij}\}$ the *transition probability matrix* of the Markov chain, and each p_{ij} is called a mphtransition probability. A *denumerable Markov chain* ndexMarkov chain!deng.tex umerable has an infinite number of states $t = 1, 2, \ldots$, and is otherwise the same. If we do not care whether the finite or denumerable case obtains, we speak simply of a *Markov chain*.

Many games can be viewed as Markov chains. Here are some examples:

a. Suppose two gamblers have wealth k_1 and k_2 dollars, respectively, and in each period they play a game in which each has an equal chance of winning one dollar. The game continues until one player has no more wealth. Here the state of the system is the wealth w of player 1, $p_{w,w+1} = p_{w,w-1} = 1/2$ for $0 < w < k_2$, and all other transition probabilities are zero.

b. Suppose n agents play a game in which they are randomly paired in each period, and the stage game is a prisoner's dilemma. Players can remember the last k moves of their various partners. Players are also given one of r strategies, which determine their next move, depending on their current histories. When a player dies, which occurs with a certain probability, it is replaced by a new player who is a clone of a successful player. We can consider this a Markov chain in which the state of the system is the history, strategy, and score of each player, and the transition probabilities are just the probabilities of moving from one such state to another, given the players' strategies (§10.4).

c. Suppose n agents play a game in which they are randomly paired in each period to trade. Each agent has an inventory of goods to trade and a strategy indicating which goods the agent is willing to trade for which other goods. After trading, agents consume some of their inventory and produce more goods for their inventory, according to some consumption and production strategy. When an agent dies, it is replaced by a new agent with the same strategy and an empty inventory. If there is a maximum size inventory and all goods are indivisible, we can consider this a finite Markov chain in which the state of the system is the strategy and inventory of each player and the transition probabilities are determined accordingly (§10.2).

d. In a population of beetles, females have k offspring in each period with probability f_k, and beetles live for n periods. The state of the system is the fraction of males and females of each age. This is a denumerable Markov chain, where the transition probabilities are calculated from the birth and death rates of the beetles.

We are interested in the long-run behavior of Markov chains. In particular, we are interested in the behavior of systems that we expect will attain a long-run equilibrium of some type independent from its initial conditions. If such an equilibrium exists, we say the Markov chain is *ergodic*. In an ergodic system, history does not matter—every initial condition leads to the same long-run behavior. Nonergodic systems are history dependent. It is intuitively reasonable that the repeated prisoner's dilemma and the trading model described above are ergodic. The gambler model is not ergodic, because the system could end up with either player bankrupt.[1] What is your intuition concerning the beetle population, assuming there is a positive probability that a female has no offspring in a breeding season? HINT: As John Maynard Keynes said, "In the long run, we are all dead."

It turns out that there is a very simple and powerful theorem that tells us exactly when a Markov chain is ergodic and provides a simple characterization of the long-run behavior of the system. To develop the machinery needed to express and understand this theorem, we will define a few terms. Let $p_{ij}^{(m)}$ be the probability of being in state j in m periods if the chain is currently in state i. Thus, if we start in state i at period 1, the probability of being in state j at period 2 is just $p_{ij}^{(1)} = p_{ij}$. To be in state j in period 3 starting from state i in period 1, the system must move from state i to some state k in period 2, and then from k to j in period 3. This happens with probability $p_{ik}p_{kj}$. Adding up over all k, the probability of being in state j in period 3 is

$$p_{ij}^{(2)} = \sum_k p_{ik}p_{kj}.$$

Using matrix notation, this means the matrix of two-period transitions is given by

$$P^{(2)} = \{p_{ij}^{(2)} | i, j = 1, 2, \ldots\} = P^2.$$

Generalizing, we see that the k-period transition matrix is simply P^k. What we are looking for, then, is the limit of P^k as $k \to \infty$. Let us call this limit (supposing it exists) $P* = \{p*_{ij}\}$. Now $P*$ must have two properties. First, since the long-run behavior of the system cannot depend on where it started, $p*_{ij} = p*_{i'j}$ for any two states i and i'. This means that all the rows of $P*$ must be the same. Let us denote the (common value of the) rows by $u = \{u_1, \ldots, u_n\}$, so u_j is the probability that the Markov chain will be in state j in the long run. The second fact is that

$$PP* = P \lim_{k \to \infty} P^k = \lim_{k \to \infty} P^{k+1} = P*.$$

[1] Specifically, you can show that the probability that player 1 wins is $k_1/(k_1 + k_2)$, and if player 1 has wealth w at some point in the game, the probability he will win is $w/(k_1 + k_2)$.

This means u must satisfy

$$u_j = \lim_{m \to \infty} p_{ij}^{(m)} \quad \text{for } i = 1, \ldots, n \tag{16.2}$$

$$u_j = \sum_i u_i p_{ij} \tag{16.3}$$

$$\sum_k u_k = 1, \tag{16.4}$$

for $j = 1, \ldots, n$. Note that (16.3) can be written in matrix notation as $u = uP$, so u is a *left eigenvector* of P. The first equation says that u_j is the limit probability of being in state j starting from any state, the second says that the probability of being in state j is the probability of moving from some state i to state j, which is $u_i p_{ij}$, summed over all states i, and the final equation says u is a probability distribution over the states of the Markov chain. The *recursion equations* (16.3) are often sufficient to determine u, which we call the *invariant distribution* or *stationary distribution* of the Markov chain.

A few examples are useful to get a feel for the recursion equations (16.3). Consider first the n-state Markov chain called the *random walk on a circle*, in which there are n states, and from any state $t = 2, \ldots, n - 1$ the system moves with equal probability to the previous or the next state, from state n it moves with equal probability to state 1 or state $n - 1$1, and from state 1 it moves with equal probability to state 2 and to state n. In the long run, it is intuitively clear that the system will be all states with equal probability $1/n$. To derive this from the recursion equations, note that the probability transition matrix for the problem is given by

$$P = \begin{bmatrix} 0 & 1/2 & 0 & \ldots & 0 & 0 & 1/2 \\ 1/2 & 0 & 1/2 & \ldots & 0 & 0 & 0 \\ & & & \vdots & & & \\ 0 & 0 & 0 & \ldots & 1/2 & 0 & 1/2 \\ 1/2 & 0 & 0 & \ldots & 0 & 1/2 & 0 \end{bmatrix}.$$

The recursion equations for this system are given by

$$u_1 = \frac{1}{2}u_n + \frac{1}{2}u_2$$

$$u_i = \frac{1}{2}u_{i-1} + \frac{1}{2}u_{i+1} \quad i = 2, \ldots, n - 1$$

$$u_n = \frac{1}{2}u_1 + \frac{1}{2}u_{n-1}$$

$$\sum_{i=1}^{n} u_i = 1.$$

Clearly, this set of equations has solution $u_i = 1/n$ for $i = 1, \ldots, n$ (it can be shown that there are no other solutions, but that is harder).

Consider next a closely related n-state Markov chain called the *random walk on the line with reflecting barriers*, in which from any state $2, \ldots, n-1$ the system moves with equal probability to the previous or the next state, but from state 1 it moves to state 2 with probability 1, and from state n it moves to state $n - 1$ with probability 1. Intuition in this case is a bit more complicated, since states 1 and n behave differently from the other states. The probability transition matrix for the problem is given by

$$P = \begin{bmatrix} 0 & 1 & 0 & \cdots & 0 & 0 & 0 \\ 1/2 & 0 & 1/2 & \cdots & 0 & 0 & 0 \\ & & & \vdots & & & \\ 0 & 0 & 0 & \cdots & 1/2 & 0 & 1/2 \\ 0 & 0 & 0 & \cdots & 0 & 1 & 0 \end{bmatrix}.$$

The recursion equations for this system are given by

$$u_1 = u_2$$
$$u_i = \frac{1}{2}u_{i-1} + \frac{1}{2}u_{i+1} \quad i = 2, \ldots, n-1$$
$$u_n = u_{n-1}$$
$$\sum_{i=1}^{n} u_i = 1.$$

Once again this set of equations has solution $u_i = 1/n$ for $i = 1, \ldots, n$, which represents the stationary distribution for this Markov chain.

For an example of a denumerable Markov chain, suppose a *serial mono-gamist* is in state k if he is in a marriage that will dissolve in k days and is in state 0 if he is currently mateless (yes, we can label the states starting with zero if we please). Suppose when mateless, he remains mateless with probability f_0 and finds a mate to whom he will be married for k days with probability f_k, $k = 1, \ldots, \infty$. This is a Markov chain with $p_{0k} = f_k$ for all k, and $p_{k,k-1} = 1$ for $k \geq 1$, all other transition probabilities being zero. The recursion equations in this case are

$$u_i = u_0 f_i + u_{i+1}$$

for $i \geq 0$. If we let $r_k = f_k + f_{k+1} + \ldots$ (so r_k is the probability of entering a marriage that lasts at least k days), it is easy to see that $u_k = r_k u_0$ satisfies the recursion equations, and the requirement that $\sum_i u_i = 1$ becomes $u_0 = 1/\mu$, where $\mu = \sum r_k$. It is straightforward to show that μ is the expected value of the probability distribution $\{f_k\}$ (show it!), so we conclude that if this expected value does not exist, then no stationary distribution exists. Otherwise, the stationary distribution is given by

$$u_i = r_i/\mu \qquad \text{for } i = 0, 1, \ldots.$$

Note that $\mu = 1/u_0$ is the expected number of periods between visits to u_0, since μ is the expected value of $\{f_k\}$. We can also show that $1/u_k = \mu/r_k$ is the expected number of periods μ_k between visits to state k, for any $k \geq 0$. Indeed, the fact that $u_k = 1/\mu_k$, where u_k is the probability of being in state k in the long run and μ_k is the expected number of periods between visits to state k, is a general feature of Markov chains with stationary distributions, as we show below.

Let us prove that $\mu_k = \mu/r_k$ for $k = 2$ in the above model, leaving the general case to the reader. From state 2 the Markov chain moves to state 0 in two periods, then requires some number j of periods before it moves to some state $k \geq 2$, and then in $k - 2$ states moves to state 2. Thus, if we let v be the expected value of j and we let w represent the expected value of k, we have $\mu_k = 2 + v + w - 2 = v + w$. Now v obviously satisfies the recursion equation

$$v = f_0(1 + v) + f_1(2 + v) + r_2(1),$$

since after a single move the system remains in state 0 with probability f_0 and the expected number of periods before hitting $k > 1$ is $1 + v$ (the first term), or moves to state 1 with probability f_1 and the expected number of periods before hitting $k > 1$ is $2 + v$ (the second term), or hits $k > 1$ immediately with probability r_2 (the final term). Solving, we find that $v = (1 + f_1)/r_2$. To find w, note that the probability of being in state k conditional on $k \geq 2$

is f_k/r_2. Thus $v + w = \mu/r_2$ follows from

$$w = \frac{1}{r_2}(2f_2 + 3f_3 + \ldots)$$

$$= \frac{1}{r_2}(\mu - f_0 - 2f_1 - r_2)$$

$$= \frac{1}{r_2}(\mu - 1 - f_1).$$

16.38.1   The Ergodic Theorem for Markov Chains

When are equations (16.2) true, and what exactly do they say? To answer this, we will need a few more concepts. We limit our discussion to *irreducible Markov chains*, which we define as follows. We say a state j can be *reached* from a state i if $p_{ij}^{(m)} > 0$ for some positive integer m. We say a Markov chain is *irreducible* if every state can be reached from every other state. If a Markov chain M is not irreducible, we can carve up M into sets of states each of which represents an irreducible Markov chain, and states in each subset can be reached only by states in the same subset (work this out!). Clearly, a nonirreducible chain cannot be ergodic, because where it starts out determines the set of states in which it remains forever.

If M is irreducible, then all the u_i in (16.2) are *strictly positive*. To see this, suppose some $u_j = 0$. Then by (16.3), if $p_{ij} > 0$, then $p_i = 0$. Thus, any state that reaches j in one period must also have weight zero in u. But a state i' that reaches j in two periods must pass through a state i that reaches j in one period, and since $u_i = 0$, we also must have $u_{i'} = 0$. Extending this argument, we say that any state i that reaches j must have $u_i = 0$, and since M is irreducible, all the $u_i = 0$, which violates (16.4). The fact that the u_i must be strictly positive is central to the following argument.

We say a Markov chain is *periodic* if there is some integer $k > 1$ such that $p_{ii}^{(k)} > 0$ and $p_{ii}^{(m)} = 0$ unless m is a multiple of k; i.e., the Markov chain can return to state i only after time periods that are multiples of some integer greater than 1. If a state is not periodic, we say it is *aperiodic*. Clearly, in an irreducible Markov chain M, all states must be aperiodic or the limit in (16.2) could not exist—some subsequences of $p_{jj}^{(m)}$ would have limit zero, and some would have a positive limit, so u_j could not satisfy (16.2).

Now let q_i be the probability that, starting from state i, the system returns to state i in some future period. If $q_i < 1$, then it is clear that state i can only occur a finite number of times, so in the long run $u_i = 0$, which we have seen is impossible for an irreducible Markov chain. We say a state i is *persistent* if $q_i = 1$, and *transient* otherwise.

Aperiodicity and persistence are enough for finite Markov chains, but for denumerable Markov chains another complication can arise: a state i can be persistent, but the expected number of periods μ_i before a return to state i could be infinite. We call μ_i the *mean recurrence time* of state i. If the mean recurrence time of state i is μ_i, M is in state i on average one period out of every μ_i, so we should have $u_i = 1/\mu_i > 0$. We found this to be true in the case of the serial monogamist above, and in fact it can be shown to be true in general. Then M can have a stationary distribution only if μ_i is finite. This motivates the following definition: An aperiodic persistent state i is called *ergodic* if the mean recurrence time μ_i is finite.

This argument motivates the following *ergodic theorem for Markov chains*, the proof of which can be found in Feller (1950).

THEOREM 16.2 *Let M be an irreducible Markov chain with no periodic states. If all states in M are ergodic, then the recursion equations (16.2) hold, and all $u_i > 0$. Conversely, suppose $u_1, \ldots, u_n \geq 0$ exist satisfying the recursion equations (16.3) and (16.4). Then all states are ergodic, (16.2) holds, and $u_j = 1/\mu_j > 0$ for each state j, where μ_j is the mean recurrence time for state j.*

16.38.2   The Sisyphean Markov Chain

As an exercise, consider the following *Sisyphean Markov chain*, in which Albert has a piano on his back and must climb up an infinite number of steps $k = 1, 2, \ldots$. At step k, with probability b_k, he stumbles and falls all the way back to the first step, and with probability $1 - b_k$ he proceeds to the next step. This gives the probability transition matrix

$$
P = \begin{bmatrix}
b_1 & 1-b_1 & 0 & 0 & 0 & \cdots \\
b_2 & 0 & 1-b_2 & 0 & 0 & \cdots \\
b_3 & 0 & 0 & 1-b_3 & 0 & \cdots \\
\vdots & \vdots & \vdots & \vdots & \vdots & \ddots
\end{bmatrix}.
$$

a.   Show that the recursion equations for this system are

$$
u_1 = \sum u_i b_i
$$
$$
u_{k+1} = u_k (1 - b_k).
$$

b. Show that these equations are satisfied only if

$$b_1 + (1 - b_1)b_2 + (1 - b_1)(1 - b_2)b_3 + \ldots = 1,$$

which is true unless the left-hand side is infinite. HINT: Let the left-hand side equal $x < \infty$, subtract b_1 from both sides and divide by $1 - b_1$; now the left-hand side does not depend on b_1 but the right-hand side does, unless $x = 1$.

c. Use the fact that $\sum_i u_i = 1$ to find u_1, which must satisfy

$$u_1[1 + (1 - b_1)b_2 + (1 - b_1)(1 - b_2)b_3 + \ldots] = 1.$$

d. Show that the Markov chain is ergodic if $b_k = 1/2$ and find the $\{u_i\}$.

e. Show that the Markov chain is not ergodic if $b_k = 1/k$, because the mean time between passages to state 1 is infinite.

f. What are the implications of this analysis for existentialist philosophy?

16.38.3   Andrei Andreyevich's Two-Urn Problem

After Andrei Andreyevich Markov discovered the chains for which he is named, he proved the Ergodic Theorem (see above) for finite chains. Then he looked around for an interesting problem to solve. Here is what he came up with—this problem had been solved before, but not rigorously.

Suppose there are two urns, one teal and one magenta, each containing m balls. Of the $2m$ balls, b are khaki and the remainder are olive. At each time period $t = 1, \ldots$, two balls are drawn randomly, one from each urn, and each ball is placed in the other urn. Let state i represent the event that there are $i \in [0, \ldots, b]$ khaki balls in the teal urn. What is the probability u_i of state i in the long run?

Let $P = \{p_{ij}\}$ be the $(b+1) \times (b+1)$ probability transition matrix. To move from i to $i - 1$, a khaki ball must be drawn from the teal urn, and an olive ball must be drawn from the magenta urn. This means $p_{i,i-1} = i(m-b+i)/m^2$. To remain in state i, either both balls drawn are khaki or both are teal, $p_{i,i} = (i(b - i) + (m - i)(m - b + i))/m^2$. To move from i to $i + 1$, an olive ball must be drawn from the teal urn, and a khaki ball must be drawn from the magenta urn. This means $p_{i,i+1} = (m - i)(b - i)/m^2$. All other transition probabilities are zero.

The recursion equations in this case are given by

$$u_i = u_{i-1}p_{i-1,i} + u_i p_{ii} + u_{i+1}p_{i+1,i}$$

for $i = 0, \ldots, b + 1$, where we set $u_{-1} = u_{b+2} = 0$. I do not know how Andrei solved these equations, but I suspect he guessed at the answer and then showed that it works. At any rate, that is what I shall do. Our intuition concerning the Ergodic Theorem suggests that in the long run the probability distribution of khaki balls in the teal urn are the same as if m balls were randomly picked from a pile of $2m$ balls (of which b are khaki) and put in the teal urn. If we write the number of combinations of n things taken r at a time as $\binom{n}{r} = n!/r!(n-r)!$, then u should satisfy

$$u_i = \binom{m}{i}\binom{m}{b-i} \Big/ \binom{2m}{b}.$$

The denominator in this expression is the number of ways the b khaki balls can be allocated to the $2m$ possible positions in the two urns, and the numerator is the number of ways this can be done when i khaki balls are in the teal urn. You can check that u now satisfies the recursion equations.

16.39   Preferences and Expected Utility

Game theory is based on the notion that agents maximize utility subject to constraints (e.g., in choosing a best response in a game), but no one has actually ever discovered a utility function, and most behavioral scientists do not believe they exist. Rather, the claim is that if the behavior of an agent has certain regularities, we can fully describe the agent's behavior *as if* it were the result of maximizing utility.[2] In this section we develop a set of behavioral properties (we will call them "axioms") that yield not only a utility function over outcomes but a probability distribution over states of nature, and such that the expected utility principle holds. We outline Savage's (1954) classic analysis of this problem.[3]

Let X be a set of payoffs, with characteristic elements x, y, x', y'. For ease of exposition, we shall assume X is a subset of some $\mathbf{R}^n$, though this is not strictly necessary. Suppose when faced with the choice between x and y, the agent is observed to choose x. We say x is *weakly preferred* to y, and we write $x \succeq y$. We say "weakly" because we cannot tell simply by

[2]This quite nicely parallels physics, where the behavior of a system can be described by finding the maxima or minima of a function (e.g., total energy, or the length of a path), with no implication that this actually describes the physical processes involved.

[3]For a more leisurely but still relatively informal presentation of this material, see Kreps 1988. For a complete treatment, see Savage 1954 or Fishburn 1970.

observing that x was chosen whether the agent strictly prefers x to y, or is in fact indifferent between the two and on another occasion might choose y over x under the same conditions. We call $\succeq$ a *binary relation*.[4] Indeed, we will assume $\succeq$ is *reflexive*, meaning that for all $x \in X$, $x \succeq x$.

Given $\succeq$, we can define a bunch of other binary relations, including the following: (a) $x \not\succeq y$ means "not $x \succeq y$"; (b) $x \succ y$ means "$x \succeq y$ and not $y \succeq x$," and we say "x is strictly preferred to y"; (c) $x \not\succ y$ means "not $x \succ y$"; (d) $x \sim y$ means "$x \succeq y$ and $y \succeq x$," and we say "the agent is indifferent between x and y"; (e) $x \not\sim y$ means "not $x \sim y$." These definitions introduce no new concepts, but make it easier to talk about preference relations.

As an exercise, check for yourself the following: (a) for any $x, y \in X$, exactly one of the relations $x \succ y$, $x \sim y$, and $y \succ x$ holds; (b) $x \succeq y$ is equivalent to $x \succ y$ or $x \sim y$; (c) $\sim$ and $\succ$ are transitive, but neither is complete; (d) $\succ$ is *asymmetric*, meaning $x \succ y$ implies $y \not\succ x$; (e) $\sim$ is *symmetric*, meaning $x \sim y$ implies $y \sim x$.

We say $u : X \to \mathbf{R}$ is a *utility function* representing $\succeq$ if, for any $x, y \in X$, $x \succ y$ if and only if $u(x) > u(y)$. It is clear that if $\succeq$ is represented by a utility function $u(\cdot)$, then for any $x, y \in X$, $x \succeq y$ if and only if $u(x) \geq u(y)$. Also, for any $x, y \in X$, we must have either $x \succeq y$ or $y \succeq x$, since either $u(x) \geq u(y)$ or $u(y) \geq u(x)$. If $\succeq$ has this property, we say that $\succeq$ is a *complete binary relation*. Moreover, if $x, y, z \in X$, $x \succeq y$ and $y \succeq z$, then $x \succeq z$, since if $u(x) \geq u(y)$ and $u(y) \geq u(z)$, then $u(x) \geq u(z)$. If $\succeq$ has this property, we say that $\succeq$ is a *transitive binary relation*. We say $\succeq$ is a *preference relation* if it is both complete and transitive. For the rest of this section, we assume $\succeq$ is a preference relation. To insure that the analysis is not trivial, we also assume that $x \succeq y$ is false for at least some $x, y \in X$. It is easy to show the following.

THEOREM 16.3 *A binary relation $\succeq$ on the set X of payoffs can be represented by a utility function $u : X \to \mathbf{R}$ if and only if $\succeq$ is a preference relation.*

This shows that we can use utility functions to represent choice behavior whatever the underlying mechanism driving choice may be, so long as choice

---

[4]More generally, a binary relation on X is an operator $\odot$ such that for any $x, y \in X$, $x \odot y$ is either true or false. For instance ">" is a binary relation in arithmetic, as are "<", "$\leq$", "=", "$\geq$", and "$\neq$". But "+" is not a binary relation, since $x + y$ is neither true nor false.

is complete (i.e., the agent can always choose between two payoffs) and transitive (i.e., the agent never weakly prefers x to y, weakly prefers y to z, but strongly prefers z to x). It is clear that $u(\cdot)$ is not unique, and indeed, we have the following.

THEOREM 16.4 *If $u(\cdot)$ represents the preference relation $\succeq$ and $f(\cdot)$ is a strictly increasing function, then $v(\cdot) = f(u(\cdot))$ also represents $\succeq$. Conversely, if both $u(\cdot)$ and $v(\cdot)$ represent $\succeq$, then there is an increasing function $f(\cdot)$ such that $v(\cdot) = f(u(\cdot))$.*

The first half of the theorem is true because if f is strictly increasing, then $u(x) > u(y)$ implies $v(x) = f(u(x)) > f(u(y)) = v(y)$, and conversely. For the second half, suppose $u(\cdot)$ and $v(\cdot)$ both represent $\succeq$, and for any $y \in \mathbf{R}$ such that $v(x) = y$ for some $x \in X$, let $f(y) = u(v^{-1}(y))$. Then $f(\cdot)$ is increasing (since it is the composition of two increasing functions) and $f(v(x)) = u(v^{-1}(v(x))) = u(x)$, which proves the theorem. Q.E.D.

Savage's accomplishment was to show that if the agent has a preference relation over *lotteries* that has some plausible properties, then not only can the agent's preferences be represented by a utility function, but we can infer the probabilities the agent implicitly places on various events, and the expected utility principle holds for these probabilities.

To see this, let S be a finite set of *states of nature*. We call subsets $A \subseteq S$ *events*. Also, let $\mathcal{L}$ be a set of "lotteries," where a *lottery* is a function $\pi : S \to X$ that associates with each state of nature $s \in S$ a payoff $\pi(s) \in X$. We suppose that the agent chooses among lotteries without knowing the state of nature, after which "Nature" choses the state $s \in S$ that obtains, so that if the agent chose lottery $\pi \in \mathcal{L}$, his payoff is $\pi(s)$.

Now suppose the agent has a preference relation $\succ$ over $\mathcal{L}$ (we use the same symbol $\succ$ for preferences over both outcomes and lotteries). We seek a set of plausible properties of $\succ$ over lotteries that together allow us to deduce (a) a utility function $u : X \to \mathbf{R}$ corresponding to the preference relation $\succ$ over outcomes in X; (b) a probability distribution $p : S \to \mathbf{R}$ such that the expected utility principle holds with respect to the preference relation $\succ$ over lotteries and the utility function $u(\cdot)$; i.e., if we define

$$\mathbf{E}_\pi[u; p] = \int_S p(s)u(\pi(s)), \qquad (16.5)$$

where the integral is suitably defined over S, then for any $\pi, \rho \in \mathcal{L}$

$$\pi \succ \rho \qquad \Leftrightarrow \qquad \mathbf{E}_\pi[u; p] > \mathbf{E}_\rho[u; p].$$

Our first condition is that $\pi \succ \rho$ depends only on states of nature where π and ρ have different outcomes. We state this more formally as

A1. For any $\pi, \rho, \pi', \rho' \in \mathcal{L}$ and any event $A \subseteq S$, if $\pi(s) = \rho(s)$ and $\pi'(s) = \rho'(s)$ for any $s \in A$, and $\pi(s) = \pi'(s)$ and $\rho(s) = \rho'(s)$ for any $s \in A^c$, then $\pi \succ \rho \Leftrightarrow \pi' \succ \rho'$

(recall that $A^c = \{s \in S | s \notin A\}$). This axiom allows us to define a *conditional preference* $\pi \succ_A \rho$, where $A \subseteq S$, which we interpret as "π is strictly preferred to ρ, given event A," as follows. We say $\pi \succ_A \rho$ if, for some $\pi', \rho' \in \mathcal{L}$, $\pi(s) = \pi'(s)$ and $\rho(s) = \rho'(s)$ for all $s \in A$, and $\pi'(s) = \rho'(s)$ for $s \notin A$. This allows us to define $\succeq_A$ and $\sim_A$ in a similar manner. We then define an event $A \subseteq S$ to be *null* if $\pi \sim_A \rho$ for all $\pi, \rho \in \mathcal{L}$.

Our second condition is then the following.

A2. If $A \subseteq S$ is not null, and if $\pi(s) = x$ and $\rho(s) = y$ for all $s \in A$, then $\pi \succ_A \rho \Leftrightarrow x \succ y$.

This axiom says that a natural relationship between outcomes and lotteries holds: if π pays x given event A and ρ pays y given event A, and if $x \succ y$, then $\pi \succ_A \rho$, and conversely.

Our third condition asserts that the probability that a state of nature occurs is independent from the outcome one receives when the state occurs. The difficulty in stating this axiom is that the agent cannot choose probabilities, but only lotteries. But if the agent prefers x to y, and if $A, B \subseteq S$ are events and $x \succ y$, then the agent treats A as "more probable" than B if and only if a lottery that pays x when A occurs and y when A does not occur will be preferred to a lottery that pays x when B occurs and y when B does not. However, this must be true for any $x, y \in X$ such that $x \succ y$, or the agent's notion of probability is incoherent (i.e., it depends on what particular payoffs we are talking about—for instance, "wishful thinking," where if the prize associated with an event increases, the agent thinks it is more likely to occur). More formally, we have the following.

A3. Suppose $x \succ y$, $x' \succ y'$, $\pi, \rho, \pi', \rho' \in \mathcal{L}$, and $A, B \subseteq S$. Suppose that π pays off x when $s \in A$ and y when $s \in A^c$, and ρ pays off x' when $s \in A$ and y' when $s \in A^c$. Moreover, suppose that π' pays off x when $s \in B$ and y when $s \in B^c$, and ρ' pays off x' when $s \in B$ and y' when $s \in B^c$. Then $\pi \succ \rho \Leftrightarrow \pi' \succ \rho'$.

The fourth condition is a weak version of the notion that if one lottery has a higher payoff than another for any event, then the first is preferred to the second. To state this condition, note that if $x \in X$, we can also consider $x \in \mathcal{L}$ to be the lottery that pays x for all states of nature. We then have the following.

A4. For any event A, if $\pi \succ_A \rho(s)$ for all $s \in A$, then $\pi \succeq_A \rho$.
Also, any event A, if $\rho(s) \succ_A \pi$ for all $s \in A$, then $\rho \succeq_A \pi$.

In other words, if for any event A, π pays more than the best ρ can pay, the $\pi \succ \rho$, and conversely.

Finally, we need a technical property that is something like the density property that is needed to show that a preference relation can be represented by a utility function. It says that for any $\pi, \rho \in \mathcal{L}$, and any $x \in X$, we can partition S into a number of disjoint subsets $A_1, \ldots A_n$ such that $\cup_i A_i = S$, and for each A_i, if we change π so that its payoff is x on A_i, then π is still preferred to ρ, and similarly, for each A_i, if we change ρ so that its payoff is x on A_i, then π is still preferred to ρ. This means that no payoff is "supergood," so that no matter how unlikely an event A is, a lottery with that payoff is always preferred to a lottery with a different payoff. Similarly, no payoff can be "superbad." The condition is formally as follows:

A5. For all $\pi, \rho \in \mathcal{L}$ with $\pi \succ \rho$, and for all $x \in X$, there are disjoint subsets $A_1, \ldots, A_n$ of S such that $\cup_i A_i = S$ and for any A_i (a) if $\pi'(s) = x$ for $s \in A_i$ and $\pi'(s) = \pi(s)$ for $s \in A^c$, then $\pi' \succ \rho$, and (b) if $\rho'(s) = x$ for $s \in A_i$ and $\rho'(s) = \rho(s)$ for $s \in A^c$, then $\pi \succ \rho'$.

We then have Savage's theorem.

THEOREM 16.5 *Suppose* **A1–A5** *hold. Then there is a probability function* p *on* S *and a utility function* $u : X \to \mathbf{R}$ *such that for any* $\pi, \rho \in \mathcal{L}, \pi \succ \rho$ *if and only if* $\mathbf{E}_\pi[u; p] > \mathbf{E}_\rho[u; p]$.

The proof of this theorem is somewhat arduous (it is sketched in Kreps 1988).

16.40 Exceptions to the Expected Utility Principle

Although most economists consider the expected utility principle acceptably accurate as a basis of modeling behavior—it is, after all, quite central to all of game theory—there are certainly well-established situations in which agents appear to violate it. Machina (1987) reviews this body of evidence and presents models to deal with them. We sketch here the most famous of these "anomalies," the so-called *Allais paradox* and *Ellsberg paradox*. They are, of course, not "paradoxes" at all but simply empirical regularities that do not fit the expected utility principle.

Maurice Allais (1953) offered the following scenario. There are two choice situations in a game with prizes ($2,500,000, $500,000, $0). The first is a choice between a lottery π that offers these prizes with probabilities (0,1,0) and π' that offers the prizes with probabilities (0.10,0.89,0.01). The second is a choice between a lottery ρ with probabilities (0,0.11,0.89) and ρ' with probabilities (0.10,0,0.90). Most people, when faced with these two choice situations, choose $\pi \succ \pi'$ and $\rho' \succ \rho$. What would you choose?. It is easy to see that this is not consistent with the expected utility principle. To see this, let us write $u_h = u(2500000)$, $u_m = u(500000)$, and $u_l = u(0)$. Then if the expected utility principle holds, $\pi \succ \pi'$ implies $u_m > 0.1u_h + 0.89u_m + 0.01u_l$, so $0.11u_m > 0.10u_h + 0.01u_l$, which implies (adding $0.89u_l$ to both sides) $0.11u_m + 0.89u_l > 0.10u_h + 0.9u_l$, which says $\rho \succ \rho'$.

Why do people make this "mistake"? Perhaps because of *regret*, which does not mesh well with the expected utility principle (Loomes 1988, Sugden 1993). If you choose π' in the first case and you end up getting nothing, you will feel really foolish, whereas in the second case, you are probably going to get nothing anyway (not your fault), so increasing the chances of getting nothing a tiny bit (0.01) gives you a good chance (0.10) of winning the really big prize. Or perhaps because of *loss aversion* (§11.3.3), since in the first case, the anchor point (the most likely outcome) is $500,000, while in the second case the anchor is 0. Loss-averse agents will then shun π', which gives a positive probability of loss, whereas in the second case, neither lottery involves a loss, from the point of view of the most likely outcome.

Another classic violation of the expected utility principle was suggested by Ellsberg (1961). Consider two urns. Urn A has 51 red balls and 49 white balls. Urn B also has 100 red and white balls, but the fraction of red balls is unknown. One ball is chosen from each urn but remains hidden from sight. Subjects are asked to choose in two situations. First, a subject can choose the ball from urn A or urn B, and if the ball is red, the subject wins $10. In the second situation, the subject can choose the ball from urn A or urn B, and if the ball is white, the subject wins $10. Many subjects choose the ball from urn A in both cases. This violates the expected utility principle, no matter what probability the subject places on the probability p that the ball from urn B is white. For in the first situation, the payoff to choosing urn A is $0.51u(10) + 0.49u(0)$, and the payoff from choosing urn B is $(1 - p)u(10) + pu(0)$, so strictly preferring urn A means $p < 0.49$. In the second situation, the payoff to choosing urn A is $0.49u(10) + 0.51u(0)$, and the payoff from choosing urn B is $pu(10) + (1 - p)u(0)$, so strictly preferring urn A means $p > 0.49$. This shows that the expected utility principle does not hold.

The usual explanation of this behavior is that the subject *knows* the probabilities associated with the first urn, while the probabilities associated with the second urn are *unknown*. People prefer the known to the unknown, then, in a way that violates the expected utility principle.

16.41 Risk Behavior and the Shape of the Utility Function

If $\succeq$ is defined over X, we can say nothing about the *shape* of a utility function $u(\cdot)$ representing $\succeq$, since by Theorem 16.4, any increasing function of $u(\cdot)$ also represents $\succeq$. However, if $\succeq$ is represented by a utility function $u(x)$ satisfying the expected utility principle, then $u(\cdot)$ is determined up to an arbitrary constant and unit of measure.[5] Specifically, we have the next theorem.

THEOREM 16.6 *Suppose the utility function $u(\cdot)$ represents the preference relation $\succeq$ and satisfies the expected utility principle. If $v(\cdot)$ is another utility function representing $\succeq$, then there are constants $a, b \in \mathbf{R}$ with $a > 0$ such that $v(x) = au(x) + b$ for all $x \in X$.*

For a proof of this theorem, see Mas-Colell, Whinston, and Green (1995), p. 173.

If $X = \mathbf{R}$, so the payoffs can be considered to be "money," and utility satisfies the expected utility principle, what shape do such utility functions have? It would be nice if they were linear in money, in which case expected utility and expected value would be the same thing (why?). But the famous Swiss mathematician Daniel Bernoulli (1700–1782), who participated in the birth of probability theory, showed that linear utility is highly implausible in his famous *St. Petersberg Paradox*. Consider a lottery in which I toss a fair coin repeatedly until it comes up tails. If the total number of heads is k,

---

[5] According to a long-standing tradition that has little foundation in mathematics, we say utilities over outcomes are *ordinal*, while utilities over lotteries are *cardinal*.

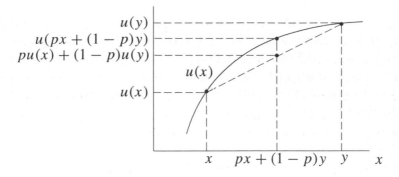

Figure 16.1. A concave utility function.

then you win 2^k dollars. How much would you pay me to play this lottery? Notice that if the coin comes up tails on the first toss, you get nothing. But if I toss ten heads in a row before a tail, you get $2^{10} = \$1,024$. I have found that most students are willing to pay between \$2 and \$10 to play this game. But, as Bernoulli showed, the expected value of the lottery is *infinite*, since the payoff is

$$\frac{1}{2} \times 2 + \frac{1}{4} \times 4 + \frac{1}{8} \times 8 + \ldots = 1 + 1 + 1 + \ldots = \infty.$$

This example shows that utility must grow less fast than a linear function, which means it is probably concave, as illustrated in Fig. 16.1. We say a function $u : X \rightarrow \mathbf{R}$ is *strictly concave* if, for any $x, y \in X$, and any $p \in (0, 1)$, we have $pu(x) + (1-p)u(y) < u(px + (1-p)y)$. We say $u(x)$ is *weakly concave*, or simply *concave*, if $u(x)$ is either strictly concave or linear, in which case the above inequality is replaced by $pu(x) + (1 - p)u(y) = u(px + (1 - p)y)$. Notice that if we define the lottery π as paying x with probability p and y with probability $1 - p$, then the condition for strict concavity says that *the expected utility of the lottery is less than the utility of the expected value of the lottery*, as depicted in Fig. 16.1.

What *are* good candidates for $u(x)$? It is easy to see that strict concavity means $u''(x) < 0$, providing $u(x)$ is twice differentiable (which we assume). But there are lots of functions with this property. According to the famous *Weber-Fechner Law* of psychophysics, for a wide range of sensory stimuli, and over a wide range of levels of stimulation, a just-noticeable change in a stimulus is a constant fraction of the original stimulus. If this holds for money, then the utility function is logarithmic. Using a convenient scaling (cf. Theorem 16.6), we can write $u(x) = \ln(x)$, so $u(1) = 0$ and

$u(0) = -\infty$. This utility function is certainly strictly concave, since $u''(x) = -1/x^2 < 0$ for $x > 0$. The expected utility of Daniel Bernoulli's lottery for this utility function is then

$$\sum_{k=1}^{\infty} \frac{\ln(2^k)}{2^k} = \ln(2),$$

so a person with this utility function would only be willing to pay \$2 to play this game![6] Another plausible concave utility function is $u(x) = x^a$, where $a \in (0, 1)$. This is increasing and $u''(x) = a(a-1)x^{a-2} < 0$, so it is concave. In this case the Bernoulli lottery is

$$\sum_{k=1}^{\infty} \frac{2^{ak}}{2^k} = \frac{1}{1 - 2^{a-1}} - 1,$$

so, for instance, if $a = 1/2$, so $u(x) = \sqrt{x}$, the utility of the lottery is $\sqrt{2} + 1$, and the amount you would pay to play the lottery would be the square of this number, which is about \$5.83.

We say an agent is *risk averse* if the agent prefers the expected value of a lottery to the lottery itself (provided, of course, the lottery does not offer a single payoff with probability 1, which we call a "sure thing"). We know, then, that an agent with utility function $u(\cdot)$ is risk averse if and only if $u(\cdot)$ is concave.[7] Similarly, we say an agent is *risk loving* if he prefers any lottery to the expected value of the lottery, and *risk neutral* if he is indifferent between a lottery and its expected value. Clearly, an agent is risk neutral if and only if he has linear utility.

Does there exist a measure of risk aversion that allows us to say when one individual is more risk averse than another, or how an agent's risk aversion changes with changing wealth? We may define agent A to be *more risk averse* than agent B if whenever A prefers a lottery to an amount of money

[6]Where did the ln(2) answer come from? You can take my word for it, or write out the first ten terms and see what you get. Or, if you like math, you can replace the 2 by x in the sum, integrate the series, find the sum, differentiate the series, and let $x = 2$.

[7]One may ask why people play government-sponsored lotteries, or spend money at gambling casinos, if they are generally risk averse. The most plausible explanation is that people enjoy the act of gambling. The same woman who will have insurance on her home and car, both of which presume risk aversion (§3.18), will gamble small amounts of money for recreation. An excessive love for gambling, of course, leads an individual either to personal destruction or wealth and fame (usually the former).

x, B will also prefer the lottery to x. We say A is *strictly* more risk averse than B if he is more risk averse, and there is some lottery that B prefers to an amount of money x, but such that A prefers x to the lottery.

Clearly, the degree of risk aversion depends on the curvature of the utility function (by definition the *curvature* of $u(x)$ at x is $u''(x)$), but since $u(x)$ and $v(x) = au(x) + b$ $(a > 0)$ describe the same behavior, but $v(x)$ has curvature a time that of $u(x)$, we need something more sophisticated. The obvious candidate is $\lambda_u(x) = -u''(x)/u'(x)$, which does not depend on scaling factors. This is called the *Arrow-Pratt coefficient of absolute risk aversion*, and it is exactly the measure that we need. We have the following theorem.

THEOREM 16.7 *An agent with utility function $u(x)$ is more risk averse than an agent with utility function $v(x)$ if and only if $\lambda_u(x) > \lambda_v(x)$ for all x.*

For example, the logarithmic utility function $u(x) = \ln(x)$ has Arrow-Pratt measure $\lambda_u(x) = 1/x$, which decreases with x; i.e., as the agent becomes wealthier, he becomes less risk averse. Studies show that this property, called *decreasing absolute risk aversion*, holds rather widely (Rosenzweig and Wolpin 1993, Saha, Shumway, and Talpaz 1994, Nerlove and Soedjiana 1996). Another increasing concave function is $u(x) = x^a$ for $a \in (0, 1)$, for which $\lambda_u(x) = (1 - a)/x$, which also exhibits decreasing absolute risk aversion. Similarly, $u(x) = 1 - x^{-a}$ $(a > 0)$ is increasing and concave, with $\lambda_u(x) = -(a + 1)/x$, which again exhibits decreasing absolute risk aversion. This utility has the additional attractive property that *utility is bounded*: no matter how rich you are, $u(x) < 1$.[8] Yet another candidate for a utility function is $u(x) = 1 - e^{-ax}$, for some $a > 0$. In this case $u(x) = a$, which we call *constant absolute risk aversion*.

Another commonly used term is the *coefficient of relative risk aversion*, $\mu_u(x) = \lambda_u(x)/x$. Notice that for any of the utility functions $u(x) = \ln(x)$, $u(x) = x^a$ for $a \in (0, 1)$, and $u(x) = 1 - x^{-a}$ $(a > 0)$, $\mu_u(x)$ is constant, which we call *constant relative risk aversion*. For $u(x) = 1 - e^{-ax}$ $(a > 0)$, we have $\mu_u(x) = a/x$, so we have *decreasing relative risk aversion*.

As an exercise, consider the utility function

$$u(x) = 1 - e^{-ax^b},$$

where $b < 1$ and $ab > 0$.

---

[8]If utility is unbounded, it is easy to show that there is a lottery that you would be willing to give all your wealth to play, no matter how rich you are. This is not plausible behavior.

a. Show that $u(x)$ is increasing and concave.
b. Find the Arrow-Pratt measures of absolute and relative risk aversion for this utility function.
c. Show that $u(x)$ exhibits decreasing absolute risk aversion for $a < 0$, constant relative risk aversion for $a = 0$, and increasing relative risk aversion for $a > 0$.

II

Answers and Hints

2

Leading from Strength: Eliminating Dominated Strategies

2.8 Second-Price Auction

Suppose first you win, and let v_s be the second-highest bid. If you had bid more than v_i, you still would have won, and your gain would still be the same, namely $v_i - v_s \geq 0$. If you had bid lower than v_i, there are three subcases: you could have bid more than, equal to, or less than v_s. If you had bid more than v_s, you would have had the same payoff, $v_i - v_s$. If you had bid equal to v_s, you could have lost the auction in the playoff among the equally high bidders, and if you had bid less than v_s, you certainly would have lost the auction. Hence, nothing beats bidding v_i in case you win.

But suppose you bid v_i and lost. Let v_h be the highest bid and v_s be the second-highest bid. Since you lost, your payoff is zero, so if you had bid less than v_i, you would still have lost, so you couldn't improve your payoff this way. If had you bid more than v_i, it wouldn't matter unless you had bid enough to win the auction, in which case your gain would have been $v_s - v_i$. Since $v_i \neq v_h$, we must have $v_i \leq v_s$, as v_s is the second-highest offer. Thus, you could not have made a positive gain by bidding higher than v_i.

Hence, bidding v_i is a best response to any set of bids by the other players.

2.10 Hagar's Battles

Each side should deploy its troops to the most valuable battlefields. To see this suppose player 1 does not. Let x_j be the highest value battlefield unoccupied by player 1, and let x_i be the lowest value battlefield occupied by player 1. What does player 1 gain by switching a soldier from x_i to x_j? If both are occupied by player 2, there is no change. If neither is occupied by player 2, player 1 gains $a_j - a_i > 0$. If player 2 occupies x_j but not x_i, player 1 loses a_i by switching, and player 2 loses a_j, so player 1 gains $a_j - a_i > 0$. Similarly if player 2 occupies x_i but not x_j.

Another explanation: Suppose you occupy a_i but not a_j, where $a_j > a_i$. The figure below shows that the gain from switching from a_i to a_j is positive in all contingencies.

Enemy Occupies

	a_i not a_j	a_j not a_i	a_i and a_j	neither
loss	lose i	lose i	lose i	lose i
gain	gain j	gain j	gain j	gain j
net gain	$j - i$	$j - i$	$j - i$	$j - i$

2.14 A Military Strategy Game

First we can eliminate all Country I strategies that don't arrive at A. This leaves six strategies, which we can label fcb, feb, fed, hed, heb, and hgd. We can also eliminate all Country A strategies that stay at A at any time, or that hit h or f. This leaves the six strategies bcb,beb,bed,ded,deb,dgd. Here is the payoff matrix:

	bcb	beb	bed	ded	deb	dgd
fcb	−1	−1	1	1	−1	1
feb	−1	−1	−1	−1	−1	1
fed	1	−1	−1	−1	−1	−1
hed	1	−1	−1	−1	−1	−1
heb	−1	−1	−1	−1	−1	1
hgd	1	1	−1	−1	1	−1

Now feb is weakly dominated by fcb, as is heb. Moreover, we see that fed and hed are weakly dominated by hgd. Thus there are two remaining strategies for Country I, "south" (hgd) and "north" (fcb).

Also bcb is dominated by beb and dgd is dominated by ded, so we may drop them. Moreover, beb and deb are the same "patrol north", while bed and ded are the same "patrol south." This gives us the following reduced game:

	patrol north	patrol south
attack north	$-1,1$	$1,-1$
attack south	$1,-1$	$-1,1$

So this complicated game is just the heads-tails game, which we will finish solving when we do mixed strategy equilibria!

2.15 Strategic Voting

We can solve this by pruning the game tree. We find that player 1 chooses "no,' and players 2 and 3 choose "yes," with payoff $(b, b - c, b - c)$. It is best to go first. The game tree is:

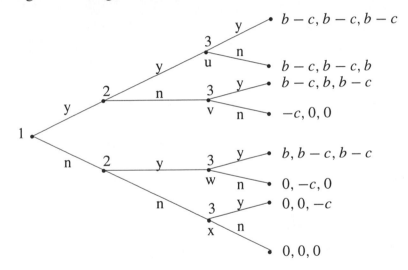

Note that this does not give a full specification of the strategies, since player 2 has four strategies and player 3 has sixteen strategies. The above description says only what players 2 and 3 do "along the game path," i.e., as the game is actually played.

To describe the Nash equilibrium in full, let us write player 3's strategies as "uvwx," where u, v, w, and x are each either y ("yes") or n ("no") and indicate the choice at the corresponding node in the game tree, starting from the top. Then the third player's choice is nyyn. Similarly, player 2's choice is ny, and the first player's is, of course, n.

If player 3 chooses nnnn, player 2 chooses yn, and player 1 chooses y, we have another Nash equilibrium (check it out!), in which player 3 now gets b and the other two get $b - c$. The equilibrium is strange because it means that player 3 should make suboptimal choices at nodes v and w—he says he will choose "no" but in fact he will choose "yes" at these nodes, since this gives him a higher payoff. The strategy nnnn is called an *incredible threat*, because it involves player 3 threatening to do something that he in fact will not do when it comes time to do it. But if the others believe him, he will never have to carry out his threat! We say such a Nash equilibrium violates *subgame perfection*, a phenomenon of great importance that we have touched upon in the Big Monkey and Little Monkey game (§1.2), and we will take it up systematically in chapter 5.

3

Playing It Straight: Pure Strategy Nash Equilibria

3.7 The Tobacco Market

a. Let's not use numbers until we need to. We can write $p = a - bq$, where $q = q_1 + q_2 + q_3$, and q_i is the amount sent to market by farmer i. Farmer 1 maximizes $pq_1 = (a-bq)q_1$. If there is an interior solution, the first-order condition on q_1 must satisfy

$$a - b(q_2 + q_3) - 2bq_1 = 0.$$

If all farmers ship the same amount of tobacco, then $q_2 = q_3 = q_1$, so this equation becomes $4bq_1 = a$, which gives $q_1 = q_2 = q_3 = a/4b$, and $q = 3a/4b$, so $p = a/4$. The profit of each farmer is $pq = a^2/16b$. In our case $a = 10$ and $b = 1/100000$, so the price is \$2.50 per pound, and each farmer ships 250,000 pounds and discards the rest. The price support doesn't matter, since $p > \$0.25$. Each farmer has profit \$625,000.

If the second and third farmers send their whole crop to market, then $q_2 + q_3 = 1,200,000$. In this case even if farmer 1 shipped nothing, the market price would be $10 - 1,2000,000/100,000 = -2 < 0.25$, so the price support would kick in. Farmer 1 should then also ship all his tobacco at \$0.25 per pound, and each farmer has profit \$150,000.

b. You can check that there are no other Nash equilibria. If one farmer sends all his crop to market, the other two would each send 400,000/3 pounds to market. But then the first farmer would gain by sending less to market.

3.9   The Klingons and the Snarks

Suppose the Klingons choose a common rate r of consumption. Then each eats 500 snarks, and each has payoff

$$u = 2000 + 50r - r^2.$$

Setting the derivative u' to zero, we get $r = 25$, so each has utility $u = 2000 + 50(25) - 25^2 = 2625$.

Now suppose they choose their rates separately. Then

$$u_1 = \frac{4000r_1}{r_1 + r_2} + 50r_1 - r_1^2.$$

Setting the derivative of this to zero, we get the first-order condition

$$\frac{\partial u_1}{\partial r_1} = \frac{4000r_2}{(r_1 + r_2)^2} + 50 - 2r_1 = 0,$$

and a symmetrical condition holds for the second Klingon:

$$\frac{\partial u_2}{\partial r_2} = \frac{4000r_1}{(r_1 + r_2)^2} + 50 - 2r_2 = 0.$$

These two imply

$$\frac{r_2}{r_1} = \frac{r_1 - 25}{r_2 - 25},$$

which has solutions $r_1 = r_2$ and $r_1 + r_2 = 25$. The latter, however, cannot satisfy the first-order conditions. Setting $r_1 = r_2$, we get

$$\frac{4000}{4r_1} + 50 - 2r_1 = 0,$$

or $1000/r_1 + 50 - 2r_1 = 0$. This is a quadratic that is easy to solve. Multiply by r_1, getting $2r_1^2 - 50r_1 - 1000 = 0$, with solution $r = (50 + \sqrt{(2500 + 8000)})/4 = 38.12$. So the Klingons eat about 50% faster than they would if they cooperated! Their utility is now $u = 2000 + 50r_1 - r_1^2 = 2452.87$, lower than if they cooperated.

3.10 Chess—The Trivial Pastime

a. The game in §3.9 is not finite and is not a game of perfect information. The game of Throwing Fingers (§4.10)'has no pure strategy Nash
equilibrium.

b. We will have to prove something more general. Let's call a game *Chessian* if it is a finite game of perfect information in which players take
turns, and the outcome is either (win,lose), (lose,win), or (draw,draw),
where win is preferred to draw, and draw is preferred to lose. Let us call
a game *certain* if it has a solution in pure strategies. If a Chessian game
is certain, then clearly either one player has a winning strategy, or both
players can force a draw. Suppose there were a Chessian game that is
not certain. Then there must be a *smallest* Chessian game that is not
certain (i.e., one with fewest nodes). Suppose this has k nodes. Clearly,
$k > 1$, since it is obvious that a Chessian game with one node is certain.
Take any node all of whose child nodes are terminal nodes (why must
this exist?). Call this node A. Suppose Red (player 1) chooses at A (the
argument is similar if Black chooses). If one of the terminal nodes from
A is (win,lose), label A (lose,win); if all of the terminal nodes from A
are (lose,win), label A (win,lose); otherwise label A (draw,draw). Now
erase the branches from A, along with their terminal nodes. Now we
have a new, smaller, Chessian game, which is certain, by our induction
assumption. It is easy to see that if Red has a winning strategy in the
smaller game, it can be extended to a winning strategy in the larger
game. Similarly, if Black has a winning strategy in the smaller game, it
can be extended to a winning strategy in the larger game. Finally, if both
players can force a draw in the smaller game, their respective strategies
must force a draw in the larger game.

3.11 The Samaritan's Dilemma

The father's first-order condition is

$$U_t(t, s) = -u'(y - t) + \alpha\delta v_2'(s(1 + r) + t) = 0,$$

and the father's second-order condition is

$$U_{tt} = u''(y - t) + \alpha\delta v_2''(s(1 + r) + t) < 0.$$

If we treat t as a function of s (backward induction!), then the equation $U_t(t(s), s) = 0$ is an identity, so we can differentiate totally with respect to s, getting

$$U_{tt}\frac{dt}{ds} + U_{ts} = 0.$$

But $U_{ts} = \alpha\delta(1+r)v_2'' < 0$, so $t'(s) < 0$; i.e., the more the daughter saves, the less she gets from her father in the second period.

The daughter's first-order condition is

$$v_s(s, t) = -v_1' + \delta v_2'(1 + r + t'(s)) = 0.$$

Suppose the daughter's optimal s is s^*, and so the father's transfer is $t^* = t(s^*)$. If the father precommits to t^*, then $t'(s) = 0$ would hold in the daughter's first-order condition. Therefore, in this case $v_s(s^*, t^*) > 0$, so the daughter is better off by increasing s to some $s^{**} > s^*$, and hence the father is better off as well, since he is a partial altruist.

For the example, if $u(\cdot) = v_1(\cdot) = v_2(\cdot) = \ln(\cdot)$, then it is straightforward to check that

$$t^* = \frac{y(1 + \alpha\delta(1 + \delta)) - \delta(1 + r)z}{(1 + \delta)(1 + \alpha\delta)}$$

$$s^* = \frac{\delta(1 + r)z - y}{(1 + r)(1 + \delta)}.$$

If the father can precommit, solving the two first-order conditions for maximizing $U(t, s)$ gives

$$t^f = \frac{\alpha(1 + \delta)y - (1 + r)z}{1 + \alpha + \alpha\delta},$$

$$s^f = \frac{(1 + r)(1 + \alpha\delta)z - \alpha y}{(1 + r)(1 + \alpha + \alpha\delta)}.$$

We then find

$$t^* - t^f = \frac{y + (1 + r)z}{(1 + \delta)(1 + \alpha\delta)(1 + \alpha + \alpha\delta)} > 0,$$

$$s^f - s^* = \frac{y + (1 + r)z}{(1 + r)(1 + \delta)(1 + \alpha + \alpha\delta)} > 0.$$

3.12   The Rotten Kid Theorem

a.   Mom's objective function is

$$V(t, a) = u(y(a) - t) + \alpha v(z(a) + t),$$

so her first-order condition is

$$V_t(t, a) = -u'(y(a) - t) + \alpha v'(z(a) + t) = 0$$

If we treat t as a function of a in the above equation (this is where backward induction comes in!), it becomes an identity, so we can differentiate with respect to a, getting

$$-u''(y' - t') + \alpha v''(z' + t') = 0. \tag{A3.1}$$

Therefore, $z' + t' = 0$ implies $y' - t' = y' + z' = 0$. Thus the first-order conditions for the maximization of $z + t$ and $z + y$ have the same solutions.

b.   Note that since a satisfies $z'(a) + y'(a) = 0$, a does not change when α changes. Differentiating the first-order condition $V_t(t(\alpha)) = 0$ totally with respect to α, we get

$$V_{tt} \frac{dt}{d\alpha} + V_{t\alpha} = 0.$$

Now $V_{tt} < 0$ by the second-order condition for a maximum, and

$$V_{t\alpha} = v' > 0,$$

which proves that $dt/d\alpha > 0$. Since a does not depend on $\hat{y}$, differentiating $V_t(t(y)) = 0$ totally with respect to $\hat{y}$, we get

$$V_{tt} \frac{dt}{d\hat{y}} + V_{t\hat{y}} = 0.$$

But $V_{t\hat{y}} = -u'' > 0$ so $dt/d\hat{y} > 0$.

c.   Suppose t remains positive as $\alpha \to 0$. Then v' remains bounded, so $\alpha v' \to 0$. From the first-order condition, this means $u' \to 0$, so $y - t \to \infty$. But y is constant, since a maximizes $y + z$, which does not depend on α. Thus $t \to -\infty$.

3.13   The Illogic of Conflict Escalation

We do only the last part of the problem. Each player in effect faces a decision problem against Nature where staying in round k wins \$$v$ with probability p, loses k with probability $p(1-p)$, and leads to round $k+2$ with probability $(1-p)^2$. Dropping in round k for $k > 2$ costs $k-2$. The pure strategies are s_k, which says "bid until round k, then drop if you have not already won or lost." We calculate the expected payoff to s_k. Consider player 1, who bids first. The probability that the game terminates spontaneously at round n is $(1-p)^{n-1}p$. Player 1 wins \$$v-n$ if the game terminates spontaneously on an odd round $n < k$, loses $n-1$ if the game terminates spontaneously on an even round $n < k$, and loses $k-2$ if the game continues to round k. The expected return from winning is 0 for $k = 1$ and for $k \geq 3$ is given by

$$v_{+k} = (v-1)p + (v-3)p(1-p)^2 + \ldots + (v-k+2)p(1-p)^{k-3}$$

Note that this also holds for $k = 1$. The expected cost of losing by spontaneous termination is

$$v_{-k} = p(1-p) + 3p(1-p)^3 + \ldots + (k-2)p(1-p)^{k-2}.$$

Finally, the expected loss from dropping out at round k is $k-2$ times the probability of reaching round k, or $(k-2)(1-p)^{k-1}$. Thus the total value of strategy s_k for $k > 1$ is $v_{+k} - v_{-k} - (k-2)(1-p)^{k-1}$. This can be summed by hand, but it is very tedious. Mathematica calculated it for me, giving the value v_k of stopping on round k equal (after some simplification) to

$$v_k = \frac{p^3 - p^2(v+3) + 4p + (vp-2)(1-(1-p)^k)}{(2-p)(1-p)p}.$$

The derivative of v_k is $-\ln(1-p)(pv-2)(1-p)^{k-1}/p(2-p)$, which is positive if $v > 2/p$. Since $v_1 = 1$, this shows that Player 1 should never stop. The analysis for player 2 is similar.

3.14   How to Value Lotteries

3.14.1   Where's Jack?

Let A be the event "Manny wins on the first round," B the event "Moe wins on the second round," and C the event "Manny wins on the third round." We have $p(A) = 0.3$, $p(B) = (1 - p(A))(0.5) = 0.35$, and $p(C) = (1 - p(B) - p(A))(0.4) = 0.14$. Thus, the probability Manny wins is $p(A) + p(C) = 0.44$, so Manny's expected payoff is \$44.

3.21 The Truth Game

b. Here is the game tree, written "sideways":

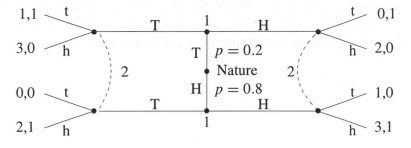

Player 1 has strategy set {HH,HT,TH,TT}, where HH means announce H if you see H, announce H if you see T, HT means announce H if you see H, announce T if you see T, etc. Thus, HH = always say H, HT = tell the truth, TH = lie, TT = always say T. Player 2 has strategy set {hh,ht,th,tt}, where hh means say h if you are told h, and say h if you are told t, ht means say h if you are told h and say t if you are told t, etc. Thus, hh means always say h, ht means trust player 1, th means distrust player 1, and tt means always say t.

c. Here are the payoffs to the two cases, according to Nature's choice:

	hh	ht	th	tt
HH	2,0	2,0	0,1	0,1
HT	3,0	1,1	3,0	1,1
TH	2,0	2,0	0,1	0,1
TT	3,0	1,1	3,0	1,1

Payoff when coin is T

	hh	ht	th	tt
HH	3,1	3,1	1,0	1,0
HT	3,1	3,1	1,0	1,0
TH	2,1	0,0	2,1	0,0
TT	2,1	0,0	2,1	0,0

Payoff when coin is H

The actual payoff matrix is $0.2 \times$ first matrix $+ 0.8 \times$ second:

	hh	ht	th	tt
HH	2.8,0.8	2.8,0.8	0.8,0.2	0.8,0.2
HT	3.0,0.8	2.6,1.0	1.4,0.0	1.0,0.2
TH	2.0,0.8	0.4,0.0	1.6,1.0	0.0,0.2
TT	2.2,0.8	0.2,0.8	2.2,0.8	0.2,0.2

d. tt is dominated by hh, so we can drop tt. There are no other dominated pure strategies.

e. (TT,th) and (HH,ht) are both Nash. In the first, 1 always says T and 2 assumes 1 lies; in the second, 1 always says H and 2 always believes 1. The first equilibrium is Pareto-inferior to the second.

3.22   The Shopper and the Fish Merchant

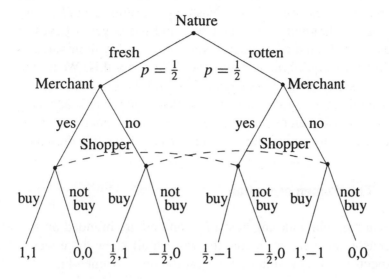

Here is the normal form for each of the two cases Good Fish/Bad Fish, and their expected value:

	bb	bn	nb	nn
yy	1,1	1,1	0,0	0,0
yn	1,1	1,1	0,0	0,0
ny	$\frac{1}{2}$,1	$-\frac{1}{2}$,0	$\frac{1}{2}$,1	$-\frac{1}{2}$,0
nn	$\frac{1}{2}$,1	$-\frac{1}{2}$,0	$\frac{1}{2}$,1	$-\frac{1}{2}$,0

Good Fish

	bb	bn	nb	nn
yy	$\frac{1}{2}$, -1	$\frac{1}{2}$, -1	$-\frac{1}{2}$, 0	$-\frac{1}{2}$, 0
yn	1, -1	0, 0	1, -1	0, 0
ny	$\frac{1}{2}$, -1	$\frac{1}{2}$, -1	$-\frac{1}{2}$, 0	$-\frac{1}{2}$, 0
nn	1, -1	0, 0	1, -1	0, 0

Bad Fish

	bb	bn	nb	nn
yy	$\frac{3}{4}$, 0	$\frac{3}{4}$,0	$-\frac{1}{4}$,0	$-\frac{1}{4}$, 0
yn	1,0	$\frac{1}{2}$, $\frac{1}{2}$	$\frac{1}{2}$,$-\frac{1}{2}$	0,0
ny	$\frac{1}{2}$, 0	0, $-\frac{1}{2}$	0, $\frac{1}{2}$	$-\frac{1}{2}$, 0
nn	$\frac{3}{4}$,0	$-\frac{1}{4}$,0	$\frac{3}{4}$,0	$-\frac{1}{4}$,0

$\frac{1}{2}$ Good Fish + $\frac{1}{2}$ Bad Fish

Applying the successive elimination of dominated strategies, we have *yn* dominates *ny*, after which *bn* dominates *bb*, *nb*, and *nn*. But then *yy* dominates *yn* and *nn*. Thus, a Nash equilibrium is *yy/bn*: the merchant says the fish is good no matter what, and the buyer believes him. Since some of the eliminated strategies were only weakly dominated, there could be other Nash equilibria, and we should check for this. We find that another is for the seller to use pure strategy *nn* and the buyer to use pure strategy *nb*. Note that this equilibrium only works if the buyer is a "nice guy" in the sense of choosing among equally good responses that maximizes the payoff to the seller. The equilibrium *yy/bn* does not have this drawback.

3.24   The Women of Sevitan

There are six philandering husbands, and all are branded on the sixth day. The reason this happens is that the women all knew there was at least one philanderer, but they didn't know that the other women knew this. That is, the fact that each woman knows there is a philanders is not known to the other five women until six rounds of the game are played. Here is a sketch of the general argument.

Suppose there is one philanderer. Then all women but one would see one philanderer. The wife of the philanderer would see no philanderers. Thus when the visitor informs the village that there is a philanderer, the wife of the philanderer knows it must be her husband, so she would brand him on night 1.

Suppose there are two philanderers: All women but two see two philanderers, but the wives of the philanderers each sees one philanderer. Each of deceived wives reasons that if her husband were not a philanderer, she would be in the previous case. But since no wife brands on night one, both deceived wives must brand on night 2. The new information in this case is that each of the deceived wives knew there was one philanderer, but did not know that the other deceived wife knew there was at least one, until the second night.

Suppose there are three philanderers. All women but three see three philanderers. Each of the three deceived wives sees two philanderers. Each of them reasons that if her husband were not a philanderer, this would be the previous case. But that is impossible after night 2. Thus, each deceived wife brands on night 3. The new information in this case is that each of the deceived wives knew there were at least two philanderers, and hence knew that each of the others knew there was at least one philanderer. Each deceived woman thinks, "If I am not deceived, then I have learned that each of the two deceived women knows the other knows there is at least one philanderer." This is new information. After the first night, this new information implies each deceived woman knows she is deceived.

This argument can be extended any number of rounds. Since no husband is branded in the first five nights, they must all be philanderers, and hence will be branded on the sixth night.

4

Catching 'em Off Guard: Mixed Strategy Nash Equilibria

4.9 Battle of the Sexes

b. Let α be the probability of Alfredo going to the opera, and let β be the probability of Elisabetta going to the opera. Since in a mixed strategy equilibrium, the payoff to gambling and opera must be equal for Alfredo, we must have

$$\beta = 2(1 - \beta),$$

which implies $\beta = 2/3$. Since the payoff to gambling and opera must also be equal for Elisabetta, we must have

$$2\alpha = 1 - \alpha,$$

so $\alpha = 1/3$. The payoff of the game to each is then

$$\frac{2}{9}(1,2) + \frac{5}{9}(0,0) + \frac{2}{9}(2,1) = \left(\frac{2}{3}, \frac{2}{3}\right),$$

since both go gambling $(1/3)(2/3) = 2/9$ of the time, both go to the opera $(1/3)(2/3) = 2/9$ of the time, and otherwise they miss each other.

c. Both do better if they can coordinate, since $(2,1)$ and $(1,2)$ are both better than $(2/3,2/3)$.

Note that we get the same answer if we find the Nash equilibrium by finding the intersection of the players' best response function. To see this, note that the payoffs to the two players are

$$\pi_1 = \alpha\beta + 2(1 - \alpha)(1 - \beta) = 3\alpha\beta - 2\alpha - 2\beta + 2$$
$$\pi_2 = 2\alpha\beta + (1 - \alpha)(1 - \beta) = 3\alpha\beta - \alpha - \beta + 1.$$

Thus,

$$\frac{\partial \pi_1}{\partial \alpha} = 3\beta - 2 \begin{cases} > 0 & \text{if } \beta > 2/3 \\ = 0 & \text{if } \beta = 2/3 \,, \\ < 0 & \text{if } \beta < 2/3 \end{cases}$$

so the optimal α is given by

$$\alpha = \begin{cases} 1 & \text{if } \beta > 2/3 \\ [0, 1] & \text{if } \beta = 2/3 \,. \\ 0 & \text{if } \beta < 2/3 \end{cases}$$

Similarly,

$$\frac{\partial \pi_2}{\partial \alpha} = 3\alpha - 1 \begin{cases} > 0 & \text{if } \alpha > 1/3 \\ = 0 & \text{if } \alpha = 1/3 \,, \\ < 0 & \text{if } \alpha < 1/3 \end{cases}$$

so the optimal β is given by

$$\beta = \begin{cases} 1 & \text{if } \alpha > 1/3 \\ [0, 1] & \text{if } \alpha = 1/3 \,. \\ 0 & \text{if } \alpha < 1/3 \end{cases}$$

This gives the following diagram,

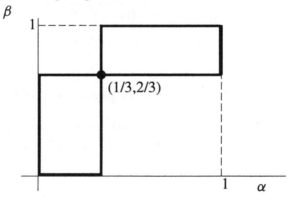

4.11   One-Card Two-Round Poker with Bluffing

The normal form is as follows:

	ss	sf	f
rrbb	0,0	4,−4	2,−2
rrbf	1,−1	0,0	2,−2
rrf	2,−2	1,−1	0,0
rfbb	−5,5	0,0	2,−2
rfbf	−4,4	4,−4	2,−2
rff	−3,3	−3,3	0,0
fbb	−4,4	1,−1	0,0
fbf	−3,3	−3,3	0,0
ff	−2,2	−2,2	−2,2

The last six strategies for player 1 are weakly dominated by rrbb. Eliminating these strategies gives the following reduced normal form.

	ss	sf	f
rrbb	0,0	4,−4	2,−2
rrbf	1,−1	0,0	2,−2
rrf	2,−2	1,−1	0,0

If 2 uses α ss $+ \beta$ sf $+ (1 - \alpha - \beta)$ f, the payoffs to 1's strategies are:

$$\text{rrbb:} \quad 4\beta + 2(1 - \alpha - \beta) = -2\alpha + 2\beta + 2$$
$$\text{rrbf:} \quad \alpha + 2(1 - \alpha - \beta) = -\alpha - 2\beta + 2$$
$$\text{rrf:} \quad 2\alpha + \beta$$

If rrbb and rrbf are used, we have $\beta = \alpha/4$; if rrbb and rrf are used, we have $4\alpha = \beta + 2$. If rrbf and rrf are used we have $\alpha + \beta = 2/3$. Thus, if all three are used, we have $\alpha = 8/15$, $\beta = 2/15$, and $1 - \alpha - \beta = 1/3$. The payoff is $18/15 = 6/5$.

If 1 uses γ rrbb $+ \delta$ rrbf $+ (1 - \gamma - \delta)$ rrf, the payoffs to 2's strategies are

$$\text{ss:} \quad -\delta - 2(1 - \gamma - \delta) = 2\gamma + \delta - 2$$
$$\text{sf:} \quad -4\gamma - (1 - \gamma - \delta) = -3\gamma + \delta - 1$$
$$\text{f:} \quad -2\gamma - 2\delta.$$

Thus, if ss and sf are used, $\gamma = 1/5$. If ss and f are both used, $4\gamma + 3\delta = 2$, so if all are used, $3\delta = 2 - 4/5 = 6/5$, and $\delta = 2/5$. Then $1 - \gamma - \delta = 2/5$. The payoff is $4/5 - 2 = -1/5 - 1 = -6/5$, so it all works out.

There is a Nash equilibrium

$$\frac{8}{15}ss + \frac{2}{15}sf + \frac{1}{3}f,$$

$$\frac{1}{5}rrbb + \frac{2}{5}rrbf + \frac{2}{5}rrf,$$

with a payoff of 6/5 to player 1.

Note that we have arrived at this solution by eliminating weakly dominated strategies. Have we eliminated any Nash equilibria this way?

4.15 The Santa Fé Bar

For the first part, let p be the probability of going to the bar for each resident. The payoff to not going to the bar and the payoff to going to the bar must be equal. Thus, the payoff to going to the bar must be zero. This already proves that the social surplus must be zero. To find p, note that the probability that the other two people go to the bar is p^2, so the expected payoff to going to the bar is

$$2(1 - p^2) + \frac{1}{2}p^2 - 1 = 0,$$

the solution to which is $p = \sqrt{6}/3$.

For the second part, let p_i be the probability of player i going to the bar, for $i = 1, \ldots, 3$. In a mixed strategy equilibrium, the payoff for each player to going to the bar and staying home must be the same. It is easy to show that this is equivalent to

$$p_i p_j = \frac{a_k - c_k}{a_k - b_k} \qquad i \neq j \neq k \neq i.$$

Let $\alpha_k = p_i p_j$ for $i \neq j \neq k$, and define $\beta = \sqrt{\alpha_1 \alpha_2 \alpha_3}$. Note that $\beta = p_i \alpha_i$ for $i = 1, 2, 3$, which requires $\beta < \alpha_i$ for $i = 1, \ldots, 3$. This means

$$\alpha_1 \alpha_2 < \alpha_3$$

$$\alpha_1 \alpha_3 < \alpha_2$$

$$\alpha_2 \alpha_3 < \alpha_1.$$

This is always the case when $\alpha_1 = \alpha_2 = \alpha_3$.

4.17   Sex Ratios as Nash Equilibria

a.   We have

$$\alpha = \frac{d}{s} = \frac{\sigma_f(1-v)}{\sigma_m v} \tag{A4.1}$$

and

$$f(u, v) = \sigma_f(1-u)c^2 + \sigma_m u c^2 \alpha \tag{A4.2}$$

To understand this expression, note that $\sigma_f(1-u)c$ is the number of daughters who survive to maturity, and so $\sigma_f(1-u)c^2$ is the number of grandchildren born to daughters. Similarly, $\sigma_m uc$ is the number of sons, and $\sigma_m uc(c\alpha)$ is the number of grandchildren sired by sons.

Substituting equation (A4.1) into equation (A4.2) and simplifying, we get

$$f(u, v) = c^2\sigma_f\left\{1 + u\left(\frac{1-2v}{v}\right)\right\}.$$

Thus, if $v \neq 1/2$, there cannot be a mixed strategy equilibrium: if the fraction of males in the population is less than 50%, each female should produce all males (i.e., set $u = 1$), and if the fraction of males in the population is greater than 50%, each female should produce all females (i.e., set $u = 0$). The only possible Nash strategy is therefore $u = v = 1/2$, since such a strategy must be symmetric (the same for all agents) and mixed (since all pure strategies are clearly not Nash).

b.   Now suppose there are n females. It is easy to check that (A4.1) becomes

$$\alpha = \frac{d}{s} = \frac{\sigma_f[n - u - (n-1)v]}{\sigma_m[(n-1)v + u]}.$$

The number of grandchildren (A4.2) then becomes

$$f(u, v) = \sigma_f(1-u)c^2 + \sigma_m u c^2 \frac{\sigma_f[n - u - (n-1)v]}{\sigma_m[(n-1)v + u]}$$

$$= \frac{c^2\sigma_f}{(n-1)v + u}\{-2u^2 - u[2(n-1)v - (n+1)] + (n-1)v\}.$$

The first-order condition on u for maximizing $f(u, v)$ then gives

$$2(n-1)v = n + 1 - 4u.$$

In a symmetric equilibrium, we must have $u = v$, which implies $u = v = 1/2$.

c.   Now suppose a fraction δ_m of males and δ_f of females die in each period, and the rest remain in the mating pool. Let m be the number of males and let n be the number of females in the first period. Then the ratio α of females to males in the breeding pool in the next period is given by

$$\alpha = \frac{d + n(1 - \delta_f)}{s + m(1 - \delta_m)} = \frac{\sigma_f cn(1 - v) + n(1 - \delta_f)}{\sigma_m cnv + m(1 - \delta_m)}. \qquad (A4.3)$$

The number of grandchildren of one female who has fraction u of males and $1 - u$ of females, when the corresponding fraction for other breeding females is v, is given by

$$f(u, v) = c^2 \left[\sigma_f(1 - u) + \sigma_m u \alpha \right] = c^2 \left\{ 1 + u \left[\frac{\sigma_m}{\sigma_f} \alpha - 1 \right] \right\}.$$

Hence, a mixed strategy Nash equilibrium requires

$$\alpha = \frac{\sigma_f}{\sigma_m}. \qquad (A4.4)$$

Solving (A4.3) and (A4.4) and simplifying, we get

$$v = \frac{1}{2} \left[1 - \frac{\sigma_f \gamma(1 - \delta_m) - \sigma_m(1 - \delta_f)}{\sigma_m \sigma_f c} \right], \qquad (A4.5)$$

where we have written $\gamma = m/n$. But in the second period m is simply the denominator of (A4.3) and n is the numerator of (A4.3), so (A4.4) implies $\gamma = m/n = \sigma_m/\sigma_f$. Substituting this expression for γ in (4.5), we get

$$v = \frac{1}{2} \left[1 - \frac{\delta_f - \delta_m}{\sigma_f c} \right],$$

from which the result follows.

d.   Now suppose males are haploid and females are diploid. Then, for a female who has fraction u of sons and $1 - u$ of daughters, when the corresponding fraction for other breeding females is v, the fraction of genes in daughters is $c(1 - u)/2$, and the fraction in sons is cu. The number of genes (normalizing the mother's gene complement to unity) in daughters of daughters is $c^2(1 - u)(1 - v)/4$, the number of genes in sons of daughters is $c^2(1 - u)v/2$, and the number of genes in daughters of sons is $c^2 u \alpha(1 - v)$. None of the female's genes are in sons of sons, since only the mother passes genetic material to her sons. The number of genes in the mother's grandchildren is the sum of these three components, which simplifies to

$$f(u, v) = c^2 \left\{ \frac{1+v}{4} - u \left[\frac{1+v}{4} - (1-v)\alpha \right] \right\},$$

so we must have

$$\alpha = \frac{1+v}{4(1-v)}. \tag{A4.6}$$

But by our assumption that individuals live for only one breeding period, (A4.1) still holds. Solving (A4.1) and (A4.6) simultaneously, and defining $v = \sigma_f/\sigma_m$, we get

$$v = \frac{8v \pm \sqrt{64v^2 + 5}}{2(4v - 1)},$$

where the sign of the square root is chosen to ensure $0 < v < 1$. This implies that, for instance, if $\sigma_f = \sigma_m$, then $v \approx 0.096$; i.e., the ratio of daughters to sons should be about ten to one.

4.19   A Mating Game

A mixed strategy for a female is a pair of probabilities (α_H, α_E), where α_H is the probability of being forward when she is H, and α_E is the probability of being forward when she is E. A mixed strategy for a male is a pair of probabilities (β_H, β_E), where β_H is the probability of being forward when he is H, and β_E is the probability of being forward when he is E. Let $\alpha = \alpha_H + \alpha_E$, and $\beta = \beta_H + \beta_E$. You can check that the payoffs for males are (a) $\pi_{FF}^m = 1$; (b) $\pi_{FR}^m = 3(2 - \alpha)/4$; (c) $\pi_{RF}^m = 3\alpha/4$; (d) $\pi_{RR}^m = 1$. The payoffs for females are (a) $\pi_{FF}^f = 1 - \beta/4$; (b) $\pi_{FR}^f = 2 - \beta$; (c) $\pi_{RF}^f = \beta/2$; (d) $\pi_{RR}^f = 1 - \beta/4$. Also, $\alpha, \beta = 2$ for FF, $\alpha, \beta = 1$ for FR and RF, and $\alpha, \beta = 0$ for RR. Now you can form the 4×4 normal form matrix, and the rest is straightforward.

4.20   Preservation of Ecology Game

The first two parts are easy. For the third and fourth, suppose x, y and z are the probabilities the three firms purify. If firm 3 purifies, its expected payoff is $-xy - x(1-y) - y(1-x) - 4(1-x)(1-y)$. If firm 3 pollutes, its payoff is $-3x(1-y) - 3(1-x)y - 3(1-x)(1-y)$. If firm 3 is to use a mixed strategy, these must be equal, so after simplification we have $(1-3x)(1-3y) = 3xy$. Solving, and repeating for the other two firms, we get the two desired solutions.

4.22   Coordination Failure

We'll do the second part. Suppose 1 uses the three pure strategies with probabilities α, β, and $\gamma = 1 - \alpha - \beta$, respectively, and 2 uses the pure strategies with probabilities a, b, and $c = 1 - a - b$. We can assume without loss of generality that $\alpha > \beta \geq \gamma$. The payoffs to a, b, and c are

$$\pi_a = 50\beta + 40(1 - \alpha - \beta) = 40 - 40\alpha + 10\beta,$$
$$\pi_b = 40\alpha + 50(1 - \alpha - \beta) = 50 - 10\alpha - 50\beta,$$
$$\pi_c = 50\alpha + 40\beta.$$

We have $\alpha + 2\beta > 1$, so $\beta > (1 - \alpha)/2$. Then,

$$\pi_c - \pi_a = 50\alpha + 40\beta - [40 - 40\alpha + 10\beta] = 90\alpha + 30\beta - 40$$
$$> 90\alpha + 30(1 - \alpha)/2 - 40 = 15 + 75\alpha - 40 = 75\alpha - 25 > 0.$$

Thus, c is better than a. Also,

$$\pi_c - \pi_b = 50\alpha + 40\beta - [50 - 10\alpha - 50\beta] = 60\alpha + 90\beta - 50$$
$$> 60\alpha + 90(1 - \alpha)/2 - 50 = 45 + 15\alpha - 50 = 15\alpha - 5 > 0,$$

so c is better than b. Thus, player 2 will use c, and his payoff is $50\alpha + 40\beta > 50\alpha + 20(1 - \alpha) = 20 + 30\alpha > 30$. The payoff to 1 is then $40\alpha + 50\beta > 40\alpha + 25(1 - \alpha) = 25 + 15\alpha > 30$. Thus, both are better off than with the 30 payoff of the Nash equilibrium.

4.23   Advertising Game

a. It is clear that the strategies described are Nash. We will show that these are the *only* Nash equilibria in which at least one firm uses a pure strategy. Suppose first that firm 1 chooses the pure strategy M (morning). If both firms 2 and 3 choose mixed strategies, then one of them could gain by shifting to pure strategy E (evening). To see this, let the two mixed strategies be $\alpha M + (1 - \alpha)E$ for firm 2 and $\beta M + (1 - \beta)E$ for firm 3. Let $\pi_i(s_1 s_2 s_3)$ be the payoff to player i when the three firms use pure strategies $s_1 s_2 s_3$. Then, the payoff to M for firm 2 is

$$\pi_2 = \alpha\beta\pi_2(MMM) + \alpha(1 - \beta)\pi_2(MME) + (1 - \alpha)\beta\pi_2(MEM)$$
$$+ (1 - \alpha)(1 - \beta)\pi_2(MEE)$$
$$= \alpha\beta(0) + \alpha(1 - \beta)(0) + (1 - \alpha)\beta(2) + (1 - \alpha)(1 - \beta)(0)$$
$$= 2(1 - \alpha)\beta.$$

Since $0 < \beta$ by definition, this is maximized by choosing $\alpha = 0$, so firm 2 should use pure strategy E. This contradicts our assumption that both firms 1 and 2 use mixed strategies.

A similar argument holds if firm 1 uses pure strategy E. We conclude that if firm 1 uses a pure strategy, at least one of the other two firms will use a pure strategy. The firm that does will not use the same pure strategy as firm 1, since this would not be a best response. Therefore, two firms use opposite pure strategies, and it doesn't matter what the third firm does.

Now we repeat the whole analysis assuming firm 2 uses a pure strategy, with clearly the same outcome. Then, we do it again for firm 3.

This proves that if one firm uses a pure strategy, at least two firms use a pure strategy, which concludes this part of the problem.

b. Let x, y, and z be the probabilities of advertising in the morning for firms 1, 2, and 3. The expected return to 1 of advertising in the morning is $(1 - y)(1 - z)$, and in the evening it is $2yz$. If these are equal, any choice of x for firm 1 is Nash. But equality means $1 - y - z - yz = 0$, or $y = (1 - z)/(1 + z)$. Now repeat for firms 2 and 3, giving the equalities $y = (1 - z)/(1 + z)$ and $z = (1 - x)/(1 + x)$. Solving simultaneously, we get $x = y = z = \sqrt{2} - 1$. To see this, substitute $y = (1 - z)/(1 + z)$ in $x = (1 - y)/(1 + y)$, getting

$$x = \frac{1 - y}{1 + y} = \frac{1 - \frac{1-z}{1+z}}{1 + \frac{1-z}{1+z}} = z.$$

Thus, $x = (1 - x)/(1 + x)$, which is a simple quadratic equation, the only root of which between 0 and 1 is $\sqrt{2} - 1$. Thus, this is Nash.

To show that there are no other Nash equilibria, suppose $0 < x < 1$ and $0 < y < 1$. We must show $0 < z < 1$, which reproduces equilibrium (b). But $0 < x < 1$ implies $(1 + y)(1 + z) = 2$ (*why?*), and $0 < y < 1$ implies $(1 + x)(1 + z) = 2$. If $z = 0$, then $x = y = 1$, which we assumed is not the case. If $z = 1$ then $x = y = 0$, which is also not the case. This proves it.

4.24   Colonel Blotto Game

The payoff matrix, giving Colonel Blotto's return (the enemy's payoff is the negative of this) is as follows:

		Enemy Strategies			
		(3,0)	(0,3)	(2,1)	(1,2)
	(4,0)	4	0	2	1
Colonel	(0,4)	0	4	1	2
Blotto	(3,1)	1	−1	3	0
Strategies	(1,3)	−1	1	0	3
	(2,2)	−2	−2	2	2

Suppose the enemy uses all strategies. By symmetry, 1 and 2 must be used equally, and 3 and 4 must be used equally. Let p be the probability of using (3,0), and q be the probability of using (2,1). The expected return to Colonel Blotto is then

$$
\begin{aligned}
4p + 2q + q &= 4p + 3q \\
4p + q + 2q &= 4p + 3q \\
p - p + 3q &= 3q \\
-p + p + 3q &= 3q \\
-2p - 2p + 2q + 2q &= -4p + 4q.
\end{aligned}
$$

Colonel Blotto cannot use all strategies in a mixed strategy, since there is no p that makes all entries in this vector equal. Suppose we drop Colonel Blotto's (3,1) and (1,3) strategies and choose p to solve $4p + 3q = -4p + 4q$ and $2p + 2q = 1$. Thus, $p = 1/18$ and $q = 4/9$. There are other Nash equilibria.

4.25 Number Guessing Game

Clearly, the game is determined in the first two rounds. Let us write my strategies as (g,h,l), for "guess g, if high guess h and if low guess l." Then, we have the payoff matrix, where 0 means "not applicable."

		My Choices			
	(102)	(103)	(213)	(310)	(320)
1	1	1	2	2	3
2	2	3	1	3	2
3	3	2	2	1	1

(Your Choices: 1, 2, 3)

Suppose you choose 1, 2 and 3 with probabilities α, β, and $1 - \alpha - \beta$. Then, I face $[-2\alpha - \beta + 3, -\alpha + \beta + 2, 2 - \beta, \alpha + 2\beta + 1, 2\alpha + \beta + 1]$. Clearly, I can't use all actions. Suppose I drop (102) and (320). Then, equating the costs of the other three, I get $\alpha = 2/5$ and $\beta = 1/5$, with cost 9/5. The costs of (102) and (320) are $2/5 + 2/5 + 6/5 = 2 > 9/5$. Therefore, my choices can be part of a Nash equilibrium. Suppose I choose (103), (213), and (310) with probabilities p, q and $1 - p - q$. If you use all three numbers, your payoffs are $[-p + 2, -2q + 3, p + q + 1]$. These are equal when $p = 1/5$ and $q = 3/5$, with payoff 9/5.

4.26 Target Selection

a. Suppose attacker uses mixed strategy $x = (x_1, \ldots, x_n)$ and defender uses strategy $y = (y_1, \ldots, y_n)$, and these form a Nash equilibrium. If $x_j = 0$, then the best response of defender must set $y_j = 0$. Suppose $x_i > 0$ for some $i > j$. Then, by switching x_i and x_j, attacker gains $a_j - pa_i y_i \geq a_j - a_i > 0$.

b. All payoffs to pure strategies used with positive probability in a best response must be equal when played against the mixed strategies of the other player(s).

4.27 A Reconnaissance Game

The normal form matrix is as follows:

	counter full defend	counter half defend	no counter full defend	no counter half defend
reconnoiter, full attack	$a_{11} - c + d$	$a_{12} - c + d$	$a_{11} - c$	$a_{22} - c$
reconnoiter, half attack	$a_{21} - c + d$	$a_{22} - c + d$	$a_{11} - c$	$a_{22} - c$
no reconnoiter, full attack	$a_{11} + d$	$a_{12} + d$	a_{11}	a_{12}
no reconnoiter, half attack	$a_{21} + d$	$a_{22} + d$	a_{21}	a_{22}

With the given payoffs and costs, the entries in the normal form game become

$$46,-46 \quad 22,-22 \quad 39,-39 \quad 27,-27$$
$$10,-10 \quad 34,-34 \quad 39,-39 \quad 27,-27$$
$$55,-55 \quad 31,-31 \quad 48,-48 \quad 24,-24$$
$$19,-19 \quad 43,-43 \quad 12,-12 \quad 36,-36.$$

Suppose defender doesn't counter and full defends with probability p. Then, attacker faces

$$39p + 27(1 - p) = 12p + 27$$
$$39p + 27(1 - p) = 12p + 27$$
$$48p + 24(1 - p) = 24p + 24$$
$$12p + 36(1 - p) = -24p + 36.$$

Check the third and fourth. We have $-24p + 36 = 24p + 24$, so $p = 1/4$. Suppose attacker doesn't reconnoiter and full attacks with probability q. Then, $-48q - 12(1 - q) = -24q - 36(1 - q)$, so $q = 1/2$. You must check that no other strategy has a higher payoff, and you will find this to be true. The payoffs are $(30, -30)$. If you are ambitious, you can check that there are many other Nash equilibria, all of which involve $(0,0,1/4,3/4)$ for Player 2. How do you interpret this fact?

4.28   Attack on Hidden Object

We have

	P	F
pp	$2\gamma - \gamma^2$	$\beta\gamma$
pF	γ	β
Fp	$\beta^2 - \beta\gamma + \gamma$	β
FF	β^2	$2\beta - \beta^2$

Note that the second row is weakly dominated by the third. Let p be the probability of defender using P. Then, attacker faces

$$p(2\gamma - \gamma^2) + (1 - p)\beta\gamma = p\gamma(2 - \gamma - \beta) + \beta\gamma$$

$$p(\beta^2 - \beta\gamma + \gamma) + (1 - p)\beta = p(\beta^2 - \gamma\beta - \beta + \gamma) + \beta$$

$$p\beta^2 + (1 - p)(2\beta - \beta^2) = -2p\beta(1 - \beta) + \beta(2 - \beta).$$

If attacker uses PP and PF, then

$$p = \frac{\beta(1 - \gamma)}{\gamma(1 - \gamma) + \beta(1 - \beta)}.$$

But if attacker uses PP with probability q and PF with probability $(1-q)$, then defender faces

$$[q(2\gamma - \gamma^2) + (1-q)\gamma q\beta\gamma + (1-q)\beta] = [q\gamma(1-\gamma) + \gamma - q\beta(1-\gamma) + \beta],$$

so

$$q = \frac{\beta - \gamma}{(\gamma + \beta)(1 - \gamma)}.$$

Try to find some other equilibria.

4.34   Robin Hood and Little John

a.   The payoff matrix is as follows:

	G	W
G	$-\delta - \tau_{lj}/2$ $-\delta - \tau_r/2$	0 $-\tau_r$
W	$-\tau_{lj}$ 0	$-\epsilon - \tau_{lj}/2$ $-\epsilon - \tau_r/2$

b. The pure Nash equilibria are:

$$GG: \quad \tau_r, \tau_{lj} \geq 2\delta$$
$$WG: \quad 2\delta \geq \tau_{lj}$$
$$GW: \quad 2\delta \geq \tau_r.$$

There is also a mixed strategy with α_r and α_{lj} being the probabilities of Robin Hood and Little John going

$$\alpha_{lj} = \frac{\epsilon + \tau_{lj}/2}{\epsilon + \delta}, \qquad \alpha_r = \frac{\epsilon + \tau_r/2}{\epsilon + \delta}$$

for $2\delta > \tau_r, \tau_{lj}$.

d. Suppose $\tau_r > \tau_{lj}$. Then, the socially optimal δ is any δ satisfying $\tau_r > 2\delta > \tau_{lj}$, since in this case it never pays to fight. The cost of crossing the bridge is τ_{lj} (or $\tau_r + 2\tau_{lj}$), including the crossing-time itself. Of course, this makes Robin Hood wait all the time. He might prefer to lower or raise the costs of fighting. Will he? The payoff to the game to the players when $\tau_r > 2\delta > \tau_{lj}$ is $(-\tau_{lj}, 0)$.

Suppose Robin Hood can shift to lower-cost confrontation: we lower δ so $\tau_r > \tau_{lj} > 2\delta$. Then, GG is dominant, and the gain to the two players is $(-\delta - \tau_{lj}/2, -\delta - \tau_r/2)$, which is better for Robin Hood if and only if $-\tau_{lj} < -\delta - \tau_{lj}/2$, or $2\delta < \tau_{lj}$, *which is true!* Therefore, *Robin Hood gains if he can shift to a lower-cost form of fighting.*

Suppose Robin Hood can shift to a higher-cost warfare. We raise δ so $2\delta > \tau_r > \tau_{lj}$. Now the mixed strategy solution obtains, and the payoff to Robin Hood is $(-\delta - \tau_{lj}/2)(\epsilon + \tau_{lj}/2)/(\epsilon + \delta)$, which it is easy to see is always less than $-\tau_{lj}$. Thus, *Robin Hood never wants to shift to a higher-cost form of fighting*, even though he would win some of the time.

4.35 The Motorist's Dilemma

Write $\sigma = \tau/2\delta < 1$, and let $u = (u_1, u_2)$ and $v = (v_1, v_2)$ represent George and Martha's mixed strategies, where (u_1, u_2) means play G with probability u_1, play W with probability u_2, and play C with probability $1 - u_1 - u_2$. Similarly for (v_1, v_2). Let $\delta = \{(x, y) | 0 \leq x, y, x + y \leq 1\}$, so δ is the strategy space for both players.[1] It is easy to check that the payoff

---

[1] As a notational convention, we write $\{x | p(x)\}$ to mean "the set of all x such that the assertion $p(x)$ is true."

to the pair of mixed strategies (u, v) for George is

$$f_1(u, v) = -(2\delta v_1 + (\delta + \tau/2)(v_2 - 1))u_1 - ((\delta - \tau/2)(v_1 - 1)$$
$$+ (\delta + \epsilon)v_2)u_2 + (\delta - \tau/2)v_1$$
$$+ (\delta + \tau/2)(v_2 - 1), \tag{A4.7}$$

and the payoff $f_2(u, v)$ to Martha is, by symmetry, $f_2(u, v) = f_1(v, u)$. The players reaction sets are given by

$$R_1 = \{(u, v) \in \delta \times \delta \,|\, f_1(u, v) = \max_\mu f_1(\mu, v)\}$$
$$R_2 = \{(u, v) \in \delta \times \delta \,|\, f_2(u, v) = \max_\mu f_2(\mu, v)\},$$

and the set of Nash equilibria is $R_1 \cap R_2$.

If the coefficients of u_1 and u_2 are negative in equation (A4.7), then $(0,0)$ is the only best response for George.

4.37   Frankie and Johnny

Let π be the payoff to Johnny, and write $\bar{x} = (x_f + x_j)/2$. If $x_f < x_j$, then $y < \bar{x}$ implies $\pi = x_f$, and otherwise $\pi = x_j$. If $x_f > x_j$, then $y < \bar{x}$ implies $\pi = x_j$, and otherwise $\pi = x_f$. Since $\Pr\{y < \bar{x}\} = F(\bar{x})$, we have $\pi = x_f F(\bar{x}) + x_j(1 - F(\bar{x}))$ for $x_f \le x_j$, and $\pi = x_j F(\bar{x}) + x_f(1 - F(\bar{x}))$ for $x_f > x_j$.

First, suppose $x_f < x_j$. The first-order conditions on x_f and x_j are then $\pi_{x_f} = F(\bar{x}) + f(\bar{x})(x_f - x_j)/2 = 0$, and $\pi_{x_j} = 1 - F(\bar{x}) + f(\bar{x})(x_f - x_j)/2 = 0$, from which it follows that $F(\bar{x}) = 1/2$. Substituting into the first order conditions gives $x_f = \bar{x} - 1/2f(\bar{x})$, $x_j = \bar{x} + 1/2f(\bar{x})$. Since π should be a minimum for Frankie, the second order condition must satisfy $\pi_{x_f x_f} = f(\bar{x}) + f'(\bar{x})(x_j - x_f)/4 > 0$. Since π should be a maximum for Johnny, the second order condition must satisfy $\pi_{x_j x_j} = -f(\bar{x}) + f'(\bar{x})(x_j - x_f)/4 < 0$.

For instance, if y is drawn from a uniform distribution then $\bar{x} = 1/2$ and $f(\bar{x}) = 1$, so $x_f = 0$ and $x_j = 1$. For another example, suppose $f(x)$ is quadratic, symmetric about $x = 1/2$, and $f(0) = f(1) = 0$. Then it is easy to check that $f(x) = 6x(1 - x)$. In this case $\bar{x} = 1/2$ and $f(\bar{x}) = 3/2$, so $x_f = 1/6$ and $x_j = 5/6$.

4.38   A Card Game

The only undominated strategy for each player is to choose a critical level x_i^* and to fold if $x_i < x_i^*$. Let (x_1^*, x_2^*) be Nash strategies. The payoff to player 1 is

$$-1 \cdot P[x_1 < x_1^*] + 1 \cdot P[x_1 > x_1^*, x_2 < x_2^*]$$
$$- 6 \cdot P[x_1 > x_1^*, x_2 > x_2^*, x_2 > x_1]$$
$$+ 6 \cdot P[x_1 > x_1^*, x_2 > x_2^*, x_2 < x_1].$$

Clearly, we have

$$P[x_1 < x_1^*] = x_1^*, \qquad P[x_1 > x_1^*, x_2 < x_2^*] = (1 - x_1^*)x_2^*.$$

We also know

$$P[x_1 > x_1^*, x_2 > x_2^*, x_2 > x_1] + P[x_1 > x_1^*, x_2 > x_2^*, x_2 < x_1]$$
$$= P[x_1 > x_1^*, x_2 > x_2^*]$$
$$= (1 - x_1^*)(1 - x_2^*).$$

To evaluate $P[x_1 > x_1^*, x_2 > x_2^*, x_2 > x_1]$, suppose $x_1^* > x_2^*$. Then,

$$P[x_1 > x_1^*, x_2 > x_2^*, x_2 > x_1] = P[x_1 > x_1^*, x_2 > x_1] = \frac{(1 - x_1^*)^2}{2}$$

To see this, consider the following diagram:

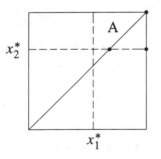

Since x_1 and x_2 are independently distributed, the pair (x_1, x_2) is uniformly distributed in the unit square depicted above. The case $P[x_1 > x_1^*, x_2 > x_1]$ is the little triangle labeled "A", which has area $(1 - x_1^*)^2/2$.

We thus have

$$P[x_1 > x_1^*, x_2 > x_2^*, x_2 < x_1] = (1 - x_1^*)(1 - x_2^*) - \frac{(1 - x_1^*)^2}{2}.$$

To evaluate $P[x_1 > x_1^*, x_2 > x_2^*, x_2 > x_1]$ when $x_1^* < x_2^*$, refer to the following diagram:

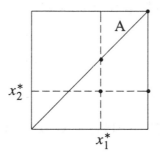

Calculating the area of trapezoid A representing the case $P[x_1 > x_1^*, x_2 > x_2^*, x_2 > x_1]$, we get

$$P[x_1 > x_1^*, x_2 > x_2^*, x_1 < x_2] = (1 - x_1^*)(1 - x_2^*) - \frac{(1 - x_2^*)^2}{2}.$$

Suppose $x_1^* > x_2^*$. The payoff to player 1 is then

$$\pi = -x_1^* + (1 - x_1^*)x_2^* - 6\frac{(1 - x_1^*)^2}{2}$$

$$+6\left[(1 - x_1^*)(1 - x_2^*) - \frac{(1 - x_1^*)^2}{2}\right]$$

$$= 5x_1^* - 5x_2^* - 6x_1^{*2} + 5x_1^*x_2^*.$$

The first-order condition on x_2^* is then $-5 + 5x_1^* = 0$, so $x_1^* = 1$. The first-order condition on x_1^* is $5 - 12x_1^* + 5x_2^* = 0$, so $x_2^* = 7/5$, which is impossible.

Thus, we must have $x_1^* < x_2^*$. The payoff to player 1 is then

$$-x_1^* + (1 - x_1^*)x_2^* - 6\left[(1 - x_1^*)(1 - x_2^*) - \frac{(1 - x_2^*)^2}{2}\right] + 6\frac{(1 - x_2^*)^2}{2},$$

which reduces to

$$5x_1^* - 5x_2^* - 7x_1^*x_2^* + 6x_2^{*2}.$$

The first-order condition on x_1^* gives $x_2^* = 5/7$, and the first-order condition on x_2^* then gives $x_1^* = 25/49$. Note that we indeed have $x_1^* < x_2^*$. The payoff of the game to player 1 is then

$$5\frac{25}{49} - 5\frac{5}{7} + 6\left(\frac{5}{7}\right)^2 - 7\left(\frac{25}{49}\right)\left(\frac{5}{7}\right) = -\frac{25}{49}.$$

4.39   Cheater-Inspector

Let α be the probability of trusting. If there is a mixed strategy equilibrium in the n-round game, the payoff to cheating in the first period is $\alpha n + (1 - \alpha)(-an) = \alpha n(1+a) - an$, and the payoff to being honest is $g_{n-1} + b(1-\alpha)$. Equating these, we find

$$\alpha = \frac{g_{n-1} + b + an}{n(1 + a) + b},$$

assuming $g_{n-1} < n$ (which is true for $n = 0$, and which we will show is true for larger n by induction). The payoff of the n-round game is then

$$g_n = g_{n-1} + b\frac{n - g_{n-1}}{n(1 + a) + b}.$$

It is easy to check that $g_1 = b/(1+a+b)$ and $g_2 = 2b/(1+a+b)$, which suggests that

$$g_n = \frac{nb}{1 + a + b}.$$

This can be checked directly by assuming it to be true for g_{n-1} and proving it true for g_n. This is called "proof by induction:" prove it for $n = 1$, then show that it is true for some integer n, it is true for $n + 1$. Then it is true for all integers n

$$g_n = g_{n-1} + b\frac{n - g_{n-1}}{n(1 + a) + b}$$

$$= \frac{b(n - 1)}{1 + a + b} + b\frac{n - \frac{b(n-1)}{1+a+b}}{n(1 + a) + b}$$

$$= \frac{b(n - 1)}{1 + a + b} + \frac{b}{1 + a + b}\frac{n + na + nb - b(n - 1)}{n(1 + a) + b}$$

$$= \frac{b(n-1)}{1+a+b} + \frac{b}{1+a+b}$$

$$= \frac{bn}{1+a+b}.$$

4.40   The Groucho Marx Game

a. Staying if you get the 3 is strictly dominated by raising, so there are four strategies left: rr, rs, sr, and ss (refer to the hint in the question for the meaning of these strategies). Here are the payoffs, where down the first column, 12 means (player 1 draws 1, player 2 draws 2), etc.

	rr/rr	rr/rs	rr/sr	rr/ss	rs/rs	rs/sr	rs/ss	sr/sr	sr/ss	ss/ss
12	$-a-b$	a	$-a-b$	a	a	$-a-b$	a	$-a$	0	0
13	$-a-b$	$-a-b$	$-a-b$	$-a-b$	$-a-b$	$-a-b$	$-a-b$	$-a$	$-a$	$-a$
21	$a+b$	$a+b$	a	a	$-a$	0	0	a	a	0
23	$-a-b$	$-a-b$	$-a-b$	$-a-b$	$-a$	$-a$	$-a$	$-a-b$	$-a-b$	$-a$
31	$a+b$	$a+b$	a	a	$a+b$	a	a	a	a	a
32	$a+b$	a	$a+b$	a	a	$a+b$	a	$a+b$	a	a
	0	$2a$	$-2b$	$2(a-b)$	0	$-a-b$	$a-b$	0	$a-b$	0

The answer follows directly from the resulting payoff matrix:

	rr	rs	sr	ss
rr	0	$a/3$	$-b/3$	$(a-b)/3$
rs	$-a/3$		$-(a+b)/3$	$(a-b)/3$
sr	$b/3$	$(a+b)/3$	0	$(a-b)/3$
ss	$-(a-b)/3$	$-(a-b)/3$	$-(a-b)/3$	0

b. Staying when you pick the 4 is strictly dominated by raising. This leaves us with eight strategies for each player. Note that staying with 2 and raising with 1 is weakly dominated by staying with 1 or 2 (explain). This generalizes to the conclusion that you only eliminate dominated strategies by staying unless the card you pick is greater than some number between zero and three. Thus, four strategies remain: {rrr, srr, ssr, sss}. The payoff of any strategy against itself is clearly zero. Thus, it remains to calculate the following:

	rrr/srr	rrr/ssr	rrr/sss	srr/ssr	srr/sss	ssr/sss
12	$-a-b$	a	a	0	0	0
13	$-a-b$	$-a-b$	a	$-a$	0	0
14	$-a-b$	$-a-b$	$-a-b$	$-a$	$-a$	$-a$
21	a	a	a	a	a	0
23	$-a-b$	$-a-b$	a	$-a-b$	a	0
24	$-a-b$	$-a-b$	$-a-b$	$-a-b$	$-a-b$	$-a$
31	a	a	a	a	a	a
32	$a+b$	a	a	a	a	a
34	$-a-b$	$-a-b$	$-a-b$	$-a-b$	$-a-b$	$-a-b$
41	a	a	a	a	a	a
42	$a+b$	a	a	a	a	a
43	$a+b$	$a+b$	a	$a+b$	a	$a+b$
	$-3b$	$2a-4b$	$6a-3b$	$a-2b$	$4a-2b$	$2a$

Here is twelve times the payoff matrix (only player 1's payoffs listed), from which the result follows:

	rrr	srr	ssr	sss
rrr	0	$-3b$	$2a-4b$	$6a-3b$
srr	$3b$	0	$a-2b$	$4a-2b$
ssr	$-2a+4b$	$-a+2b$	0	$2a$
sss	$6a-3b$	$-4a+2b$	$-2a$	0

c. We represent the strategy of raising if and only if the card chosen is greater than k by s_k. Thus, each player has n pure strategies (eliminating weakly dominated strategies). We must find the payoff to each pure strategy pair $\{(s_k, s_l)|k, l = 1, \ldots, n\}$. Suppose the pure strategies used are (s_k, s_l) and the cards picked from the hat by players 1 and 2 are $\tilde{k}$ and $\tilde{l}$, respectively.

First suppose $k \geq l$. The probability player 1 wins if both stay is

$$P\left[\tilde{k} > \tilde{l}|\tilde{k} \leq k, \tilde{l} \leq l\right] = P\left[\tilde{k} \leq l\right] P\left[\tilde{k} > \tilde{l}|\tilde{k}, \tilde{l} \leq l\right]$$

$$+P\left[\tilde{k} > l|\tilde{k} \leq k, \tilde{l} \leq l\right]$$

$$= \frac{l}{k}\frac{1}{2} + \frac{k-l}{k} = 1 - \frac{l}{2k}.$$

Since the probability that player 1 loses if both stay is one minus the above quantity, and player 1 stands to win or lose a in this case, we find that player 1's expected payoff in this case is

$$\pi_{k \geq l} \left[\tilde{k} > \tilde{l} | \tilde{k} \leq k, \tilde{l} \leq l \right] = a \left(1 - \frac{l}{k} \right).$$

By symmetry (interchange k and l and then negate—or you can calculate it out), we have

$$\pi_{k < l} \left[\tilde{k} > \tilde{l} | \tilde{k} \leq k, \tilde{l} \leq l \right] = -a \left(1 - \frac{k}{l} \right).$$

We also have the following easy payoffs:

$$\pi \left[\tilde{k} > k, \tilde{l} \leq l \right] = a$$

$$\pi \left[\tilde{k} \leq k, \tilde{l} > l \right] = -a$$

Finally, suppose both players raise. First assume $k \geq l$. Then,

$$\mathrm{P} \left[\tilde{k} > \tilde{l} | \tilde{k} > k, \tilde{l} > l \right] = \mathrm{P} \left[\tilde{k} > \tilde{l} | \tilde{k}, \tilde{l} > k \right] + \mathrm{P} \left[\tilde{l} \leq k | \tilde{l} > l \right]$$

$$= \frac{n-k}{n-l} \frac{1}{2} + \frac{k-l}{n-l}.$$

Since the probability that player 1 loses if both raise is one minus the above quantity, and player 1 stands to win or lose $a + b$ in this case, we find that player 1's expected payoff in this case is

$$\pi_{k \geq l} \left[\tilde{k} > \tilde{l} | \tilde{k} > k, \tilde{l} > l \right] = (a + b) \frac{k - l}{n - l}.$$

By symmetry (or you can calculate it out), we have

$$\pi_{k < l} \left[\tilde{k} > \tilde{l} | \tilde{k} > k, \tilde{l} > l \right] = (a + b) \frac{k - l}{n - k}.$$

Now we add everything up:

$$\pi_{k \geq l} = \mathrm{P} \left[\tilde{k} \leq k \right] \mathrm{P} \left[\tilde{l} \leq l \right] \pi_{k \geq l} \left[\tilde{k} > \tilde{l} | \tilde{k} \leq k, \tilde{l} \leq l \right]$$

$$+\text{P}\left[\tilde{k} \le k\right]\text{P}\left[\tilde{l} > l\right]\pi\left[\tilde{k} \le k, \tilde{l} > l\right]$$

$$+\text{P}\left[\tilde{k} > k\right]\text{P}\left[\tilde{l} \le l\right]\pi\left[\tilde{k} > k, \tilde{l} \le l\right]$$

$$+\text{P}\left[\tilde{k} > k\right]\text{P}\left[\tilde{l} > l\right]\pi_{k \ge l}\left[\tilde{k} > \tilde{l} | \tilde{k} > k, \tilde{l} > l\right]$$

$$= \frac{1}{n^2}(l - k)(a(k - l) - b(n - k)).$$

By symmetry (or calculation if you don't trust your answer—I did it by calculation and checked it by symmetry), we have

$$\pi_{k<l} = \frac{1}{n^2}(k - l)(a(k - l) + b(n - l)).$$

4.41 Real Men Don't Eat Quiche

Let B (drink beer) and Q (eat quiche) be the actions for Clem, and B (bully Clem) and D (defer to Clem) be the actions for the Dark Stranger. The strategies for Clem are BB (drink beer), BQ (drink beer if Tough, eat Quiche if Wimp), QB (eat quiche if Tough, drink beer if Wimp), and QQ (eat quiche), and those for the Dark Stranger are BB (bully), DB (defer if Clem drinks beer, bully if Clem eats quiche), BD (bully if Clem drinks beer, defer if Clem eats quiche), and DD (defer). The payoff matrices in the Tough and Wimp cases are given in the following diagram, where $a, b/c, d$ means "Clem's payoff is a if Tough and c if Wimp; Dark Stranger's payoff is b if Clem is Tough, and d if Clem is a Wimp":

	BB	BD	DB	DD
BB	1,0/0,1	1,0/0,1	3,1/2,0	3,1/2,0
BQ	1,0/1,1	1,0/3,0	3,1/1,1	3,1/3,0
QB	0,0/0,1	2,1/0,1	0,0/2,0	2,1/2,0
QQ	0,0/1,1	2,1/3,0	0,0/1,1	2,1/3,0

The expected return to the players is thus one-third times the first matrix plus two-thirds times the second matrix, since one-third is the probability that Clem is Tough. We get the payoff matrix (all payoffs multiplied by 3):

	BB	*BD*	*DB*	*DD*
BB	1,2	1,2	7,1	7,1
BQ	3,2	7,0	5,3	9,1
QB	0,2	2,3	4,0	6,1
QQ	2,2	8,1	2,2	8,1

Now QB is dominated by BQ, DD is dominated by BB, and BD is dominated by BB (since QB is out). But then QQ is dominated by BQ, so we have

	BB	*DB*
BB	1,2	7,1
BQ	3,2	5,3

This is sensible: Clem can bluff Tough or not, and the Dark Stranger can call the bluff or not. There is a mixed strategy equilibrium. Let α be the probability of BB. The payoff to BB and DB must then be equal for the Dark Stranger, so $2 = \alpha + 3(1 - \alpha)$, so $\alpha = 1/2$. If β is the probability of the Dark Stranger using BB, then $\beta + 7(1 - \beta) = 3\beta + 5(1 - \beta)$, or $\beta = 1/2$.

4.45   The Equivalence of Behavioral and Mixed Strategies

a. Suppose player i has information sets $v_1, \ldots, v_k$, so a pure strategy for i can be written as $a_1 a_2 \ldots a_k$, where $a_j \in v_j$ for $j = 1, \ldots, k$. Then,

$$\sum_{s \in S_i} \alpha_s^p = \sum_{a_1 \in v_1} \cdots \sum_{a_k \in v_k} p_i(a_1) \cdots p_i(a_k)$$

$$= \sum_{a_1 \in v_1} p_i(a_1) \ldots \sum_{a_k \in v_k} p_i(a_k) = 1.$$

b. Let σ be the mixed strategy representation of behavioral strategy p. We must show that for every player i and every information set $v \in \mathcal{N}_i$, if

$P[v|\sigma_i] > 0$, then for every $a \in \alpha^v$, we have $p(a) = P[a|\sigma_i]/p[v|\sigma_i]$. If $N \subseteq \mathcal{N}_i$, we denote by S_i/N the set of pure strategies over the nodes $\{v|v \in \mathcal{N}_i - N\}$, where for sets A and B, $A - B = \{a \in A|a \notin B\}$; i.e., $s \in S_i/N$ is a choice of a node in each of player i's information sets not in N. Similarly, we denote by $S_i/N[a]$ the pure strategies over $\mathcal{N}_i - N$ that lead to node a for some choice of pure strategies of the other players, and we denote by $S_i/N[v]$ the pure strategies over $\mathcal{N}_i - N$ that lead to information set v for choice of pure strategies of the other players. Finally, $n(\mu, a)$ is the statement "$\mu \in \mathcal{N}_i$ is not in the path from the root node r to node a." Then, for $\sigma_i = \sum_{s \in S_i} \alpha_s s$, $a \in v \in \mathcal{N}_i$, $\mu' \in N = \{\mu \in \mathcal{N}_i|n(\mu, a)\}$, we have

$$P[a|\sigma_i] = \sum_{s \in S_i[a]} \alpha_s$$

$$= \sum_{s \in S_i[a]} \prod_{\mu \in \mathcal{N}_i} p_i(s_i(\mu))$$

$$= \sum_{s \in S_i[a]} p_i(s_i(\mu')) \prod_{\substack{\mu \in \mathcal{N}_i \\ \mu \neq \mu'}} p_i(s_i(\mu))$$

$$= \sum_{s \in S_i/\{\mu'\}[a]} \prod_{\substack{\mu \in \mathcal{N}_i \\ \mu \neq \mu'}} p_i(s_i(\mu))$$

$$= \sum_{s \in S_i/N[a]} \prod_{\substack{\mu \in \mathcal{N}_i \\ \mu \notin N}} p_i(s_i(\mu))$$

$$= \prod_{\substack{\mu \in \mathcal{N}_i \\ \mu \notin N}} p_i(s_i^a(\mu)),$$

where s_i^a is the unique member of S_i/N that chooses at each information set on the path from r to a, the branch belonging to that path. But the last expression is the product of the probabilities assigned by p to i's choices along the path from r to a. A similar argument shows that $P[v|\sigma_i]$ is the sum of the product of the probabilities assigned by p to i's choices along all paths from r to nodes in v. But by the assumption of perfect recall, i must make the same choices to get to any node in v, so there is only one such path. It follows that, provided the denominator is not zero, the behavioral probability assigned to node a is just

$$\frac{P[a|\sigma_i]}{P[v|\sigma_i]} = p_i(a),$$

which proves that p is a behavioral representation of σ.

c. The payoff to player i given by behavioral strategy p is

$$\pi_i(p) = \sum_{t \in T} P[r, t|p]\pi_i(t),$$

and the payoff given by mixed strategy σ is

$$\pi_i(\sigma) = \sum_{t \in T} P[r, t|\sigma]\pi_i(t),$$

where $P[r, a|\sigma]$ is the probability of reaching a from the root node r if all players randomize their choice of pure strategies according to the weighting in σ. To complete the proof, we must show that $P[r, t|\sigma] = P[r, t|p]$.[2] We will show that for every node a, $P[r, a|\sigma] = P[r, a|p]$. This is clearly true for $a = r$, since then both sides of the equation are unity. Suppose it is true for node a, and a' is a child node of a. If Nature moves at a and chooses a' with probability q, then clearly $P[r, a'|p] = qP[r, a|p]$. Let $p_N(a)$ be the product of the probabilities of all the branches associated with Nature on the path from r to a. Then, if $\sigma_i = \sum_{s \in S_i} \alpha_s s$, we have

$$P[r, a'|\sigma] = p_N(a') \prod_{j=1}^{n} \sum_{s_j \in S_j[a']} \alpha_{s_j}$$

$$= p_N(a) \prod_{j=1}^{n} \sum_{s_j \in S_j[a']} \alpha_{s_j}$$

[2]The reader will note that to avoid a proliferation of new symbols, I have been using what is known as "functional overloading," by which is meant that two functions with the same function name but with different arguments represent two distinct functions. Thus, $P[a|\sigma_i]$, $P[v|\sigma_i]$, $P[r, a|\sigma]$, and $P[r, a|p]$ are notationally unambiguous but have distinct meanings, so long as a is a node, v is an information set, σ_i is a mixed strategy, and r is the root node of the game tree.

$$= p_N(a) \left(\prod_{\substack{j=1 \\ j \neq i}}^{n} \sum_{s_i \in S_i[a']} \right) \sum_{s_i \in S_i[a']} \alpha_{s_i}$$

$$= p_N(a) \left(\prod_{\substack{j=1 \\ j \neq i}}^{n} \sum_{s_i \in S_i[a']} \right) q \sum_{s_i \in S_i[a]} \alpha_{s_i}$$

$$= P[r, y|\sigma]q.$$

Note that we used perfect recall in the next-to-last step, where we used the equation

$$\sum_{s_i \in S_i[a']} \alpha_{s_i} = q \sum_{s_i \in S_i[a]} \alpha_{s_i}.$$

Under perfect recall, $S_i[a] = S_i[v]$, where $a \in v$, and with this substitution, the equation is the definition of $q = p(a')$.

d. If p_v is not a best response, then there is some q_v that gives i a higher payoff. Then, the mixed strategy representation of (q_v, p_{-v}) gives i a higher payoff than σ_i, which contradicts the fact that σ_i is a best response.

5

Moving through the Game Tree: Subgames, Incredible Threats, and Trembling Hands

5.4 The Subway Entry Deterrence Game

The game tree is as follows:

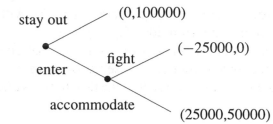

5.5 The Dr. Strangelove Game

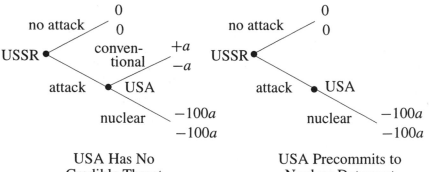

USA Has No
Credible Threat

USA Precommits to
Nuclear Deterrent

a. The figure on the left is the extensive form of the game without precommitment.
b. The figure on the right is the extensive form of the game with precommitment.

5.7   Huey, Dewey, and Louie Split a Dollar

Here is a game tree (written sideways), when the equilibrium shares are (h, d, l):

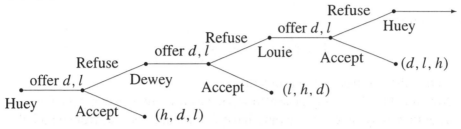

We work back the game tree (which is okay, since we are looking only for subgame perfect equilibria). At the second place where Huey gets to offer (at the right side of the game tree), the value of the game to Huey is h, since we assume a stationary equilibrium. Thus, Louie must offer Huey at least δh where Louie gets to offer, to get Huey to accept. Similarly, Louie must offer Dewey at least δd at this node. Thus, the value of the game where Louie gets to offer is $(1 - \delta h - \delta d)$.

When Dewey gets to offer, he must offer Louie at least δ times what Louie gets when it is Louie's turn to offer, to get Louie to accept. This amount is just $\delta(1 - \delta h - \delta d)$. Similarly, he must offer Huey $\delta^2 h$ to accept, since Huey gets δh when it is Louie's turn to offer. Thus, Dewey gets

$$1 - \delta(1 - \delta h - \delta d) - \delta^2 h = 1 - \delta(1 - \delta d)$$

when it is his turn to offer.

Now Huey, on his first turn to offer, must offer Dewey δ times what Dewey can get when it is Dewey's turn to offer, or $\delta(1 - \delta(1 - \delta d))$. But then we must have

$$d = \delta(1 - \delta(1 - \delta d)).$$

Solving this equation for d, we find

$$d = \frac{\delta}{1 + \delta + \delta^2}.$$

Moreover, Huey must offer Louie δ times what Dewey would offer Louie in the next period or $\delta^2(1 - \delta h - \delta d)$. Thus, Huey offers Dewey and Louie together

$$\delta(1 - \delta(1 - \delta d)) + \delta^2(1 - \delta h - \delta d) = \delta - \delta^3 h,$$

so Huey gets $1 - \delta + \delta^3 h$, and this must equal h. Solving, we get

$$h = \frac{1}{1 + \delta + \delta^2},$$

so we must have

$$l = 1 - d - h = \frac{\delta^2}{1 + \delta + \delta^2},$$

which is the solution to the problem.

Note that there is a simpler way to solve the problem, just using the fact that the solution is symmetric: we must have $d = \delta h$ and $l = \delta d$, from which the result follows. This does not make clear, however, where subgame perfection comes in.

5.10   Cooperation in an Overlapping-Generations Economy

Part (d): Let T^* be the age of veneration. Then for a member of age $t \leq T^*$, the gains from cooperating are $(T - t + 1)nT^* - (T^* - t + 1)\alpha$, and the gains from defecting are $nT^* - 1$. Thus, the net gains from cooperating are

$$f(t, T^*) = (T - t)nT^* - (T^* - t + 1)\alpha + 1.$$

Then T^* supports a Nash subgame perfect equilibrium of the desired form if and only if $f(t, T^*) \geq 0$ for all $t = 1, \ldots, T*$. In particular, we must have $f(T^*, T^*) \geq 0$. But $f(t, t) = (T - t)nt - (\alpha - 1)$ is a parabola with a maximum at $t = T/2$, and $f(T/2, T/2) = nT^2/4 - (\alpha - 1)$. Since this must be nonnegative, we see that

$$T^2 \geq \frac{4(\alpha - 1)}{n} \tag{A5.1}$$

is necessary.

Now suppose (5.1) holds, and choose T^* such that $f(T^*, T^*) \geq 0$. Since $f_t(t, T^*) = -nT^* + \alpha$, if $\alpha \leq nT^*$ then f is decreasing in t, so $f(t, T^*) \geq 0$ for all $t = 1, \ldots, T^*$. If $\alpha > nT^*$, $f(t, T^*)$ is increasing in t, so we must ensure that $f(1, T^*) \geq 0$. But $f(1, T^*) = T^*(n(T - 1) - \alpha) + 1$, which is strictly positive by assumption. Thus, (5.1) is sufficient.

Part (e): The total utility from the public good for a member is $T^*(nT - \alpha)$, which is an increasing function of T^*.

5.12   The Finitely Repeated Prisoner's Dilemma II

a. A string of k defections followed by a return to cooperation costs the player $k + 1 - (a - b)$, which is strictly positive for $k \geq 1$. To see this, we can clearly assume we are at round 1, since the argument is the same further down the line. Cooperating until the last round, then defecting, pays $n - 1 + a$, while defecting for k rounds and then cooperating returns $a - b + (n - k - 2) + a$. You get a on the first round; you get nothing for $k - 1$ rounds; you lose b when you return to cooperate, then you get 1 for $n - k - 2$ rounds; you defect on the last round and get a.

b. By preempting, player 1 is revealed to be a best responder (reciprocators never preempt). The statement is clearly true if player 2 is a reciprocator. If player 2 is a best responder, and if he does not defect, player 1 would know he is best responder. Since both players would now know they are not reciprocators, they would both defect forever. Meanwhile, player 2 would lose b on this round by cooperating. So player 2 should defect in response to preemption. Moreover, if later player 2 cooperated while player 1 continued to defect, player 1 would again know that player 2 is a best responder, and so both would defect forever. The assertion follows.

c. The best-case scenario is that when player 1 returns to C, player 2 does so as well. But in (a), we saw that player 1 can't gain from such a move.

d. We know that player 1 cannot gain by preempting at stage $k - 1$ and returning to C at some later stage. Thus, by preempting at $k - 1$, player 1 will defect thereafter in an optimal strategy. The payoff to this is a. But by waiting until next period to defect, he gets 1 now and ϵa next period. But by assumption $(1 - \epsilon)a < 1$, so $1 + \epsilon a > a$, so waiting dominates preempting.

e. We now know that a best responder should either cooperate until the last round, or preempt exactly when he expects his partner will preempt if his partner is a best responder. The total payoff to the latter strategy is $k - 1 + \epsilon a$ if he thinks a best responder will switch on round k, and the payoff to the former strategy is $(k - 1 - b)(1 - \epsilon) + (n - 1 + a)\epsilon$. The preempt strategy is thus superior precisely when $k > n - b(1 - \epsilon)/\epsilon$ and then only if the player believes a best responder will preempt on round k.

f. This follows from the fact that a best responder will never preempt.

5.15 Selten's Horse

If Walter's information set is not reached with positive probability, an equilibrium must have the form $(A, a, p_\lambda \lambda + (1 - p_\lambda)\rho)$. Franz's payoff to D is $4p_\lambda + (1 - p_\lambda)$, which must be at most 3, so $p_\lambda \leq 2/3$. Gustav's payoff to d is $5p_\lambda + 2(1 - p_\lambda)$, which must be at most 3, so $p_\lambda \leq 1/3$. This gives us the set M of equilibria.

Now assume Walter's information set is reached. If Walter chooses the pure strategy λ, either Gustav must not get to choose, or Gustav must choose d. If Gustav does not get to choose, Franz must choose D, with payoffs (4,4,4). If Gustav plays a with probability p_a, the payoff to A is $3p_a + 5(1 - p_a)$, which must be at most 4, so $p_a \geq 1/2$. This gives us the set N of equilibria. If Gustav does get to choose, Gustav chooses d, so Franz must randomize or else Walter would not choose λ. But the payoff to A for Walter is 5, and the payoff to D is 4, so Franz will not randomize. Thus, there are no Nash equilibria in this category.

If Walter's information set is reached and Walter chooses pure strategy ρ, either Gustav does not get to choose, or Gustav chooses a. If Gustav does not get to choose, Franz chooses D, which is clearly inferior to A, no matter what Gustav's strategy is. If Gustav does choose, Gustav chooses a, so $p_A = 1$, which contradicts the assumption that Walter's information set is reached with positive probability.

The remaining case is that Walter's information set is reached with positive probability, and Walter randomizes. The payoff to λ is $4p_{3l}$, where p_{3l} is the probability of being at $3l$, and the payoff to ρ is $p_{3l} + 2(1 - p_{3l})$, and since these must be equal, we have $p_{3l} = 2/5$. But clearly, $p_{3l} = (1 - p_A)/(1 - p_A + p_A(1 - p_a))$. This implies $p_A(5 - 2p_a) = 3$. Clearly, p_A cannot then be zero or one, so Franz randomizes, which implies

$$4p_\lambda + (1 - p_\lambda) = 3p_a + (1 - p_a)(5p_\lambda + 2(1 - p_\lambda)),$$

or $p_a(3p_\lambda - 1) = 1$. If Gustav randomizes, we must have $3 = 5p_\lambda + 2(1 - p_\lambda)$, so $p_\lambda = 1/3$, which is impossible. Thus, $p_a = 1$ and $p_\lambda = 1/3$, which is again impossible. So this case is impossible.

5.16 Trembling Hand Perfection

a. A straightforward calculation yields

$$p_{3l} = \frac{\epsilon_1^*}{\epsilon_1^* + \epsilon_2^*}$$

where $\epsilon_1^* = \epsilon_1 + (1 - 2\epsilon_1)(1 - p_A)$ and $\epsilon_2^* = \epsilon_1 + (1 - 2\epsilon_1)(1 - p_A) + (\epsilon_1 + (1 - 2\epsilon_1)p_A)(\epsilon_2 + (1 - 2\epsilon_2)(1 - p_a))$.

b. If $p_A < 1$, then p_{3l} approaches

$$p_{3l}^\infty = \frac{(1 - p_A)}{(1 - p_A) + p_A(1 - p_a)}$$

for small ϵ_1, ϵ_2. Suppose $p_A < 1$. Then $p_\lambda = 1$ for small ϵ_1, ϵ_2 if $p_{3l}^\infty \geq 2/5$, which reduces to $3 \geq p_A(5 - 2p_a)$. In this situation Gustav chooses d, so $p_a = 0$. The payoff of A to Walter is 5 and the payoff to D is 4, so $p_A = 1$, which is a contradiction. We next try $p_\lambda = 0$ for small ϵ_1, ϵ_2, can be true only if $3 \leq p_A(5 - 2p_a)$. Now $p_a = 1$, so $p_A = 1$, a contradiction. The only alternative if $p_A < 1$ is that Walter randomizes for small ϵ_1, ϵ_2, which means that $3 = p_A(5 - 2p_a)$. It follows that Franz randomizes as well, and the condition that the payoffs to A and D are equal for Franz reduces to $p_a(3p_\lambda - 1) = 1$. This implies $p_\lambda > 1/3$, so the payoff to d is greater than $5(1/3) + 2(2/3) = 3$, so $p_a = 0$, which is a contradiction.

We conclude that for sufficiently small ϵ_1, ϵ_2, $p_A = 1$, which implies

$$p_{3l} = \frac{\epsilon_1}{\epsilon_1 + (1 - \epsilon_1)(\epsilon_2 + (1 - 2\epsilon_2)(1 - p_a))}.$$

It is clear that in this case Walter cannot choose $p_\lambda = 1$ since then $p_a = 0 \to p_\lambda = 0$, a contradiction. If $p_\lambda = 0$ then $p_a = 1$, so

$$p_{3l} = \frac{\epsilon_1}{\epsilon_1 + (1 - \epsilon_1)\epsilon_2}.$$

This must be a local best response for Walter, which is the case so long as $p_{3l} \geq 2/5$, which is equivalent to $3\epsilon_1 \geq 2(1 - \epsilon_1)e_2$. If this inequality fails, then Walter must randomize, which means $p_{3l} = 2/5$, and given ϵ_1 and ϵ_2, this uniquely determines $p_a < 1$. In this case, as $\epsilon_1, \epsilon_2 \to 0$ while maintaining $3\epsilon_1 < (1 - \epsilon_1)e_2$, $p_a \to 1$, so in all cases for small ϵ_1, ϵ_2, the equilibrium is near the perfect equilibrium.

6

Repeated Games, Trigger Strategies, and Tacit Collusion

6.13   Reputational Equilibrium

If it is worthwhile for the firm to lie when it claims its product has quality $q > 0$, it might as well set its actual quality to 0, since the firm minimizes costs this way. Its profits are then

$$\pi_f = (4 + 6q_a - x - 2)x = (2 + 6q_a - x)x.$$

Profits are maximized when

$$\frac{d\pi_f}{dx} = 2 + 6q_a - 2x = 0,$$

so $x = 1 + 3q_a$, and $\pi_f = (1 + 3q_a)^2$.

Now suppose the firm tells the truth. Then, if π_t is per-period profits, we have

$$\pi_t = (2 + 6q_a - 6q_a^2 - x)x,$$
$$\frac{d\pi_t}{dx} = 2 + 6q_a - 6q_a^2 - 2x = 0,$$

so $x = 1 + 3q_a - 3q_a^2$, and $\pi_t = (1 + 3q_a - 3q_a^2)^2$. But total profits Π from truth-telling are π_t forever, discounted at rate $\delta = 0.9$, or

$$\Pi = \frac{\pi_t}{1 - \delta} = 10(1 + 3q_a - 3q_a^2)^2.$$

Truth-telling is profitable then when $\Pi \geq \pi_f$, or when

$$10(1 + 3q_a - 3q_a^2)^2 > (1 + 3q_a)^2. \tag{A6.1}$$

Note that equation (A6.1) is true for very small q_a (i.e., q_a near 0) and false for very large q_a (i.e., q_a near 1).

7

Biology Meets Economics: Evolutionary Stability and the Birth of Dynamic Game Theory

7.2 Properties of Evolutionarily Stable Strategies

a. Simple
b. The two conditions for an evolutionarily stable strategy imply that if σ is an evolutionarily stable strategy, then $\pi_{\tau\sigma} \leq \pi_{\sigma\sigma}$ for any other strategy τ. But this is just the Nash condition.
c. If σ is a strict Nash equilibrium, then $\pi_{\tau\sigma} < \pi_{\sigma\sigma}$ for any $\tau \neq \sigma$, so σ is an evolutionarily stable strategy.
d. Suppose $\pi_{11} > \pi_{21}$. Then pure strategy 1 is a strict Nash equilibrium, so it is an evolutionarily stable strategy. The same is true if $\pi_{22} > \pi_{12}$. So suppose $\pi_{11} < \pi_{21}$ and $\pi_{22} < \pi_{12}$. Then we can show that the game has a unique completely mixed symmetric equilibrium p, where each player uses strategy 1 with probability $\alpha_p \in (0, 1)$. The payoff to strategy 1 against the mixed strategy $(\alpha_p, 1-\alpha_p)$ is then $\alpha_p\pi_{11}+(1-\alpha_p)\pi_{12}$, and the payoff to strategy 2 against this mixed strategy is $\alpha_p\pi_{21}+(1-\alpha_p)\pi_{22}$. Since these must be equal, we find that $\alpha_p = (\pi_{22} - \pi_{12})/\Delta$, where $\Delta = \pi_{11} - \pi_{21} + \pi_{22} - \pi_{12} < 0$. Note that under our assumptions, $0 < \alpha_p < 1$, so there is a unique completely mixed Nash equilibrium $(\alpha_p, 1 - \alpha_p)$. Is this evolutionarily stable?

Let α_q be the probability a mutant player uses pure strategy 1. Since each pure strategy is a best response to α_p, α_q must also be a best response to α_p, so clearly, $\pi_{qp} = \pi_{pp}$. To show that p is evolutionarily stable, we must show that $\pi_{pq} > \pi_{qq}$. We have

$$\pi_{pq} = \alpha_p[a_{11}\alpha_q + \pi_{12}(1 - \alpha_q)] + (1 - \alpha_p)[\pi_{21}\alpha_q + \pi_{22}(1 - \alpha_q)]$$

and

$$\pi_{qq} = \alpha_q[\pi_{11}\alpha_q + \pi_{12}(1 - \alpha_q)] + (1 - \alpha_q)[\pi_{21}\alpha_q + \pi_{22}(1 - \alpha_q)].$$

Subtracting and simplifying, we get

$$\pi_{pq} - \pi_{qq} = -(\alpha_p - \alpha_q)^2 \Delta > 0,$$

which proves evolutionary stability.

e. It is easy to check that if there is a mixed strategy equilibrium, the frequency α of pure strategy 1 must satisfy

$$\alpha = \frac{\pi_{22} - \pi_{12}}{\Delta}, \qquad \text{where } \Delta = \pi_{11} - \pi_{21} + \pi_{22} - \pi_{12}.$$

Suppose $\Delta > 0$. Then $0 < \alpha < 1$ if and only if $0 < \pi_{22} - \pi_{12} < \pi_{11} - \pi_{21} + \pi_{22} - \pi_{12}$, which is true if and only if $\pi_{11} > \pi_{21}$ and $\pi_{22} > \pi_{12}$. If $\Delta < 0$, a similar argument shows that $0 < \alpha < 1$ if and only if the other pair of inequalities holds.

Suppose there is a "mutant" that uses pure strategy 1 with probability β. Thus, in general,

$$\pi_{\gamma\delta} = \gamma\delta\pi_{11} + \gamma(1 - \delta)\pi_{12} + (1 - \gamma)\delta\pi_{21} + (1 - \gamma)(1 - \delta)\pi_{22}$$
$$= \gamma\delta\Delta + \delta(\pi_{21} - \pi_{22}) + \gamma(\pi_{12} - \pi_{22}) + \pi_{22}.$$

It follows that

$$\pi_{\alpha\alpha} - \pi_{\beta\alpha} = (\alpha - \beta)[\alpha\Delta - (\pi_{22} - a_{12})] = 0,$$

so the equilibrium is evolutionarily stable if and only if $\pi_{\alpha\beta} > \pi_{\beta\beta}$. But

$$\pi_{\alpha\beta} - \pi_{\beta\beta} = \alpha\beta\Delta + \beta(a_{21} - a_{22}) + \alpha(a_{12} - a_{22}) + a_{22}$$
$$\qquad\qquad - \beta^2\Delta - \beta(a_{21} - a_{22}) - \beta(a_{12} - a_{22}) - a_{22}$$
$$= \beta(\alpha - \beta)\Delta + (\alpha - \beta)(a_{12} - a_{22})$$
$$= (\alpha - \beta)(\beta\Delta + a_{12} - a_{22})$$
$$= (\alpha - \beta)(\beta\Delta - \alpha\Delta)$$
$$= -(\alpha - \beta)^2\Delta.$$

Thus, the equilibrium is evolutionarily stable if and only if $\Delta < 0$, which is equivalent to $a_{11} < a_{21}$ and $a_{22} < a_{12}$. This proves the assertion.

f. Suppose there are an infinite number of distinct evolutionarily stable strategies. Then there must be two, say σ and τ, that use exactly the same pure strategies. Now τ is a best response to σ, so σ must do better against τ than τ does against itself. But σ does equally well against τ as τ does against τ. Thus, σ is not evolutionarily stable and similarly for τ.

g. First, suppose σ is evolutionarily stable, so for any $\tau \neq \sigma$, there is an $\tilde{\epsilon}(\tau)$ such that[1]

$$\pi_{\tau,(1-\epsilon)\sigma+\epsilon\tau} < \pi_{\sigma,(1-\epsilon)\sigma+\epsilon\tau} \quad \text{for all } \epsilon \in (0, \tilde{\epsilon}(\tau)). \tag{A7.1}$$

In fact, we can choose $\tilde{\epsilon}(\tau)$ as follows. If (A7.1) holds for all $\epsilon \in (0, 1)$, then let $\tilde{\epsilon}(\tau) = 1$. Otherwise, let $\tilde{\epsilon}$ be the smallest $\epsilon > 0$ such that (A7.1) is violated and define

$$\tilde{\epsilon}(\tau) = \frac{\pi_{\sigma\sigma} - \pi_{\tau\sigma}}{\pi_{\tau\tau} - \pi_{\tau\sigma} - \pi_{\sigma,\tau} + \pi_{\sigma\sigma}}.$$

It is easy to check that $\tilde{\epsilon}(\tau) \in (0, 1]$ and (A7.1) are satisfied. Let $T \subset S$ be the set of strategies such that if $\tau \in T$, then there is at least one pure strategy used in σ that is not used in τ. Clearly, T is closed and bounded, $\sigma \notin T$, $\tilde{\epsilon}(\tau)$ is continuous, and $\tilde{\epsilon}(\tau) > 0$ for all $\tau \in T$. Hence, $\tilde{\epsilon}(\tau)$ has a strictly positive minimum ϵ^* such that (A7.1) holds for all $\tau \in T$ and all $\epsilon \in (0, \epsilon^*)$.

If τ is a mixed strategy and s is a pure strategy, we define $s(\tau)$ to be the weight of s in τ (i.e., the probability that s will be played using τ). Now consider the neighborhood of s consisting of all strategies τ such that $|1 - s(\tau)| < \epsilon^*$ for all pure strategies s. If $\tau \neq s$, then $\epsilon^* > 1 - s(\tau) = \epsilon > 0$ for some pure strategy s. Then $\tau = (1-\epsilon)s + \epsilon r$, where $r \in T$. But then (A7.1) gives $\pi_{r\tau} < \pi_{s,\tau}$. If we multiply both sides of this inequality by ϵ and add $(1 - \epsilon)\pi_{s\tau}$ to both sides, we get $\pi_{\tau\tau} < \pi_{s,\tau}$, as required. The other direction is similar, which proves the assertion.

h. If σ is completely mixed, then for any $t \in S$, $\pi_{\sigma\sigma} = \pi_{t\sigma}$, simply because any pure strategy has the same payoff against σ as σ does against σ. Therefore, any mixed strategy has the same payoff against σ as σ has against σ. For similar reasons, $\pi_{\sigma\tau} = \pi_{\sigma\sigma}$. Thus, σ is evolutionarily stable and if τ is any other strategy, we must have $\pi_{\sigma\tau} > \pi_{\tau\tau}$.

---

[1]We write (a, b) to mean the set of numbers $\{x | a < x < b\}$ and we call this the *open interval* (a, b).

7.5   Cooperative Fishing

Here is the normal form game.

	Put Out	Free Ride
Put Out	$\frac{v}{2} - c_2, \frac{v}{2} - c_2$	$\frac{v}{2} - c_1, \frac{v}{2}$
Free Ride	$\frac{v}{2}, \frac{v}{2} - c_1$	0,0

It is easy to see there are no pure strategy symmetric equilibria, since $v/2 > c_1$. There are two pure strategy asymmetric equilibria, FP and PF. Consider a mixed strategy equilibrium where a fraction α of the population plays P. The payoff to P is then

$$\alpha \left(\frac{v}{2} - c_2 \right) + (1 - \alpha) \left(\frac{v}{2} - c_1 \right) = \frac{v}{2} - [\alpha c_2 + (1 - \alpha)c_1].$$

The payoff to F is simply $\alpha v/2$. Equating the two payoffs, we get

$$\alpha = \frac{\frac{v}{2} - c_1}{\frac{v}{2} + c_2 - c_1}.$$

Note that we have $0 < \alpha < 1$, so this is a strictly mixed Nash equilibrium. Is this mixed strategy, which we will call M, an evolutionarily stable strategy?

Let π_{AB} be the payoff to the agent playing A when the other agent plays B. Let $N \neq M$, so clearly $\pi_{NM} = \pi_{MM}$, since both pure strategies in N have equal payoffs against M (or else M would not be Nash, since M uses the same pure strategies as N). If this is *not* clear, consider the following argument: Suppose strategy N uses Put Out with probability β. Then $\pi_{NM} = \beta \pi_{PM} + (1 - \beta)\pi_{FM} = \beta \pi_{MM} + (1 - \beta)\pi_{MM} = \pi_{MM}$, the next-to-last step following from the fact that M is a mixed strategy Nash equilibrium, so both P and F have equal payoffs against M.

We thus must show that $\pi_{MN} > \pi_{NN}$ to prove that M is evolutionarily stable. Define $\pi_{\gamma\delta}$ as the payoff to player 1 when 1 uses Put Out with probability γ and 2 uses Put Out with probability δ. We have

$$\pi_{\gamma\delta} = \gamma \left[\delta \left(\frac{v}{2} - c_2 \right) + (1 - \delta) \left(\frac{v}{2} - c_1 \right) \right] + (1 - \gamma)\delta \frac{v}{2}$$

$$= \frac{v}{2}[\gamma + (1 - \gamma)\delta] + \gamma\delta(c_1 - c_2) - \gamma c_1.$$

But $\pi_{MN} = \pi_{\alpha\beta}$ and $\pi_{NN} = \pi_{\beta\beta}$, so

$$
\begin{aligned}
\pi_{MN} - \pi_{NN} &= \pi_{\alpha\beta} - \pi_{\beta\beta} \\
&= \frac{v}{2}[\alpha + (1-\alpha)\beta] + \alpha\beta(c_1 - c_2) - \alpha c_1 \\
&\quad - \frac{v}{2}[\beta + (1-\beta)\beta] - \beta^2(c_1 - c_2) + \beta c_1 \\
&= \frac{v}{2}[(\alpha - \beta) + (\beta - \alpha)\beta] \\
&\quad + (\alpha - b)\beta(c_1 - c_2) - (\alpha - \beta)c_1 \\
&= (\alpha - \beta)\left[\frac{v}{2}(1-\beta) + \beta(c_1 - c_2) - c_1\right] \\
&= (\alpha - \beta)\left[\frac{v}{2} - c_1 - \beta\left[\frac{v}{2} - c_1 + c_2\right]\right] \\
&= (\alpha - \beta)^2\left[\frac{v}{2} - c_1 + c_2\right] > 0.
\end{aligned}
$$

This completes the proof that the equilibrium is evolutionarily stable.

7.12   Hawks, Doves, and Bourgeois

c. The payoff to H is $\alpha(v - w)/2 + (1-\alpha)v = v - \alpha(v + w)/2$, and the
payoff to D is $(1-\alpha)(v/2 - t) = v/2 - t - \alpha(v/2 - t)$. These are
equated when $\alpha = (v + 2t)/(w + 2t)$, which is < 1 if $w > v$ and $t > 0$.

To show that this mixed strategy equilibrium is evolutionarily stable,
we can refer to the "Theorem" proved earlier, which says that evolutionary stability is equivalent to $a_{HH} < a_{HD}$, which is true. Or we can
do it out in full (it's going to look a lot like the proof of the "Theorem").
Here is the proof in full:

Suppose player 2 plays $\alpha H + (1-\alpha)D$ and player 1 uses $\beta H + (1-\beta)D$. Then

$$
\begin{aligned}
\pi_{\beta\alpha} &= \alpha\beta\frac{v-2}{2} + \beta(1-\alpha)v + (1-\alpha)(1-\beta)\left[\frac{v}{2} - t\right] \\
&= -\alpha\beta\left[\frac{w}{2} + t\right] - \alpha\left[\frac{v}{2} - t\right] + \beta\left[\frac{v}{2} + t\right] + \frac{v}{2} - t.
\end{aligned}
$$

Now, for evolutionary stability we must have either $\pi_{\alpha\alpha} > \pi_{\beta\alpha}$, or
$\pi_{\alpha\alpha} = \pi_{\beta\alpha}$ and $\pi_{\alpha\beta} > \pi_{\beta\beta}$. But

$$
\pi_{\alpha\alpha} - \pi_{\beta\alpha} = -\alpha^2\left[\frac{w}{2} + t\right] + 2\alpha t + \frac{v}{2} - t - \pi_{\beta\alpha}
$$

$$= -\alpha(\alpha - \beta)\left[\frac{w}{2} + t\right] + \alpha\left[\frac{v}{2} + t\right] - \beta\left[\frac{v}{2} + t\right]$$

$$= (\alpha - \beta)\left\{-\alpha\left[\frac{w}{2} + t\right] + \frac{v}{2} + t\right\} = 0.$$

Also,

$$\pi_{\alpha\beta} - \pi_{\beta\beta} = -(\beta - \alpha)\left\{-\beta\left[\frac{w}{2} + t\right] + \frac{v}{2} + t\right\}.$$

The term in brackets is positive if $\beta < \alpha$ and negative if $\beta > \alpha$, which proves evolutionary stability.

d. $\pi_{BB} > \pi_{HB}$ if and only if $v/2 > 3v/4 - w/4$, which is equivalent to $w > v$. $\pi_{BB} = \pi_{HB}$ and $\pi_{BH} > \pi_{HH}$ if and only if $v = w$ and $(v - w)/4 > (v - w)/2$, which is false. Thus, B can't be invaded by H if $w > v$. Meanwhile, $\pi_{BB} > \pi_{DB}$ if and only if $v/2 > v/4 - t/2$, which is true.

7.13   Trogs and Farfel

a. The payoff matrix to the game is as follows.

	Good	Bad
Good	$z - y, z - y$	$w - y, z - x$
Bad	$z - x, w - y$	$w - x, w - x$

By definition, a 2×2 prisoner's dilemma is given by

	C	D
C	r, r	s, t
D	t, s	p, p

where $t > r > p > s$ and $r > (s + t)/2$. This is true if and only if $z - w > y - x$, as can be seen from the following. In our case, $t > r > p > s$ becomes $z - x > z - y > w - x > w - y$. The first and third inequalities are always true, and the second is equivalent to $z - w > y - x$. Also, $r > (s + t)/2$ is equivalent to $2z - 2y > z - x + w - y$, which is equivalent to $z - y > w - x$.

b. Obvious, since "always give good farfel" leads to cooperation on every round, either against itself or against Tit-for-Tat.

c. First, we show that playing B forever is better than Tit-for-Tat if and only if $\delta < (y-x)/(z-w)$. Tit-for-Tat against Tit-for-Tat gives $z - y$ for all rounds, with present value $(z-y)/(1-\delta)$. The present value of defecting forever is $(z-x)+\delta(w-x)/(1-\delta)$. But $(z-y)/(1-\delta) > (z-x)+\delta(w-x)/(1-\delta)$ if and only if $z-y > (1-\delta)(z-x)+\delta(w-x) = z-x-\delta z+\delta w$ if and only if $y - x < \delta(z - w)$ if and only if $\delta > (y - x)/(z - w)$.

Next, we show that playing B for a certain number of periods, say $n \geq 1$, followed by a G is not a best response to Tit-for-Tat if and only if the above inequality holds. The history of play then looks like

$$GGG...BB.....BGxxxxx...$$
$$GGG...GB.....BBGxxxx...,$$

where we don't know what the x's are. Let us compare this to what happens if player 1 defects one fewer time, so we now have

$$GGG...BB.....GGxxxxx....$$
$$GGG...GB.....BGGxxxx....$$

The only changes in the payoff to player 1 are in periods $n - 1$ and n. Player 1 gains $(w - y) - (w - x) = x - y$ (which is negative) in period $n - 1$ and gains $(z - y) - (w - y) = z - w$ in period n. The total gain, discounted to period $n - 1$, is then $x - y + \delta(z - w)$, which is positive if and only if the above inequality holds.

7.14 Evolutionary Stability in Finite Populations

a. Let $r_{\mu\nu} = 0$, $r_{\nu\mu} = n$, $r_{\mu\mu} = n + 1$, and $r_{\nu\nu} = -1$. Then ν is not Nash, since $r_{\mu\nu} > r_{\nu\nu}$, μ is Nash since $r_{\mu\mu} > r_{\mu\nu}$ and $r_{\mu\mu} > r_{\nu\mu}$, but $r(\nu) - r(\mu) = 1/n > 0$ for any m.

b. This is trivial if there is an alternate best response to a Nash strategy.

c. Suppose ν is evolutionarily stable but is not Nash. Then there is some μ such that $r_{\nu\nu} < r_{\mu\nu}$. Let $m = 1$. Then for sufficiently large n we have $r(\nu) < r(\mu)$ in

$$r(\nu) - r(\mu) = \left(1 - \frac{m}{n}\right)(r_{\nu\nu} - r_{\mu\nu})$$

$$+ \frac{m}{n}(r_{\nu\mu} - r_{\mu\mu}) + \frac{1}{n}(r_{\mu\mu} - r_{\mu\nu}). \quad \text{(A7.2)}$$

Hence, ν must be Nash. Now suppose ν is evolutionarily stable and $r_{\nu\nu} = r_{\mu\nu}$ but $r_{\nu\mu} < r_{\mu\mu}$. Equation (A7.2) becomes

$$r(\nu) - r(\mu) = \frac{1}{n} \left\{ m[r_{\nu\mu} - r_{\mu\mu}] + [r_{\mu\mu} - r_{\mu\nu}] \right\}.$$

Given $\epsilon > 0$, choose $\overline{m}$ so that the term in brackets is negative, and then choose n so that $\overline{m}/n < \epsilon$. Then $r(\nu) < r(\mu)$ for all positive $m \le \overline{m}$, which is a contradiction. So suppose in addition to $r_{\nu\nu} = r_{\mu\nu}$ and $r_{\nu\mu} = r_{\mu\mu}$, we have $r_{\mu\mu} < r_{\mu\nu}$. Then clearly $r(\nu) - r(\mu) = [r_{\mu\mu} - r_{\mu\nu}]/n < 0$, again a contradiction. This proves that the stated conditions are necessary. We can reverse the argument to prove the conditions are sufficient as well.

d. In the limit we have

$$r(\nu) - r(\mu) = (1 - \epsilon)[r_{\nu\nu} - r_{\mu\nu}] + \epsilon[r_{\nu\mu} - r_{\mu\mu}].$$

The conclusion follows immediately from this equation. The limit argument cannot be used to conclude that $r(\nu) > r(\mu)$ in the "large finite" case if $r_{\nu\nu} = r_{\mu\nu}$ and $r_{\nu\mu} = r_{\mu\mu}$.

9

Evolutionary Dynamics

9.3 Properties of the Replicator System

Only the last part of the question might not be obvious. Let $p(t)$ be a trajectory of (9.5), and define

$$b(t) = \int_0^t \frac{dt}{a(p(t), t)},$$

which is possible since $a(p, t) > 0$. Clearly, $b(t)$ is positive and increasing. Let $q(t) = p(b(t))$. Then, by the Fundamental Theorem of the Calculus,

$$\dot{q}_i(t) = \dot{b}(t)\dot{p}_i(b(t)) = \frac{1}{a(t)}a(t)p_i(b(t))(\pi_i(p(b(t))) - \bar{\pi}(p(b(t))))$$
$$= q_i(t)(\pi_i(q(t)) - \bar{\pi}(q(t))). \text{ Q.E.D.}$$

9.13 The Dynamics of Rock-Paper-Scissors and Related Games

Let π_α, π_β, and π_γ be the payoffs to the three strategies. Then, we have

$$\pi_\alpha = \beta r + (1 - \alpha - \beta)s = \beta(r - s) - \alpha s + s,$$
$$\pi_\beta = \alpha s + (1 - \alpha - \beta)r = \alpha(s - r) - \beta r + r,$$
$$\pi_\gamma = \alpha r + \beta s.$$

It is easy to check that the average payoff is then

$$\bar{\pi} = \alpha\pi_\alpha + \beta\pi_\beta + (1 - \alpha - \beta)\pi_\gamma$$
$$= (r + s)(\alpha + \beta - \alpha^2 - \alpha\beta - \beta^2).$$

At any fixed point involving all three strategies with positive probability, we must have $\pi_\alpha = \pi_\beta = \pi_\gamma$. Solving these two equations, we find $\alpha = \beta = \gamma = 1/3$, which implies that $\bar{\pi} = (r + s)/3$.

In a replicator dynamic, we have

$$\dot{\alpha} = \alpha(\pi_\alpha - \bar{\pi}),$$
$$\dot{\beta} = \beta(\pi_\beta - \bar{\pi}).$$

Expanding these equations, we get

$$\dot{\alpha} = -2\alpha\beta s - (r + 2s)\alpha^2 + \alpha s + \alpha p(\alpha, \beta),$$
$$\dot{\beta} = -2\alpha\beta r - (2r + s)\beta^2 + \beta r + \beta p(\alpha, \beta),$$

where $p(\alpha, \beta) = (r + s)(\alpha^2 + \alpha\beta + \beta^2)$.

This is of course a nonlinear ordinary differential equation in two unknowns. It is easy to check that its unique fixed point for $\alpha, \beta > 0$ is $\alpha = \beta = 1/3$, the mixed strategy Nash equilibrium for this game.

For the dynamics, we linearize the pair of differential equations by evaluating the Jacobian matrix of the right-hand sides at the fixed point. The Jacobian is

$$J(\alpha, \beta) = \begin{pmatrix} a_{11} & a_{12} \\ a_{21} & a_{22} \end{pmatrix},$$

where

$$a_{11} = -2\beta s - 2\alpha(r + 2s) + s + p(\alpha, \beta) + \alpha(2\alpha + \beta)(r + s),$$
$$a_{12} = -2\alpha s + \alpha(\alpha + 2\beta)(r + s),$$
$$a_{21} = -2\beta r + \beta(2\alpha + \beta)(r + s),$$
$$a_{22} = r - 2\alpha r - 2\beta(2r + s) + p(\alpha, \beta) + \beta(\alpha + 2\beta)(r + s),$$

so

$$J(1/3, 1/3) = \frac{1}{3}\begin{pmatrix} -s & r - s \\ s - r & -r \end{pmatrix}.$$

The eigenvalues of the linearized system are thus

$$\frac{1}{6}\left[-(r + s) \pm i\sqrt{3}(r - s)\right].$$

We prove the assertions as follows:

a. The determinant of the Jacobian is $(r^2 - rs + s^2)/9$. This has a minimum where $2s - r = 0$, with the value $r^2/12 > 0$. This shows that the system is hyperbolic, and since the determinant is positive, it is a node or a focus.
b. The real parts of the eigenvalues are negative if and only if $r + s < 0$, and are positive if and only if $r + s > 0$.
c. The eigenvalues are complex for $r \neq s$.
d. If $r + s = 0$, the eigenvalues are purely imaginary, so origin is a center. We thus cannot tell how the nonlinear system behaves using the linearization.

However, we can show that the quantity $q(\alpha, \beta) = \alpha\beta(1 - \alpha - \beta)$ is constant along trajectories of the dynamical system. Assuming this (which we will prove in a moment), we argue as follows. Consider a ray R through the fixed point (1/3,1/3) pointing in the α-direction. Suppose $q(\alpha, \beta)$ is strictly decreasing along this ray (we will also prove this in a moment). Then, the trajectories of the dynamical system must be closed loops. To see this, note first that the fixed point cannot be a stable node, since if we start at a point on R near the fixed point, q decreases as we approach the fixed point, but q must be constant along trajectories, which is a contradiction. Thus, the trajectories of the system must be spirals or closed loops. But they cannot be spirals, because when they intersect R twice near the fixed point, the intersection points must be the same, since $q(\alpha, \beta)$ is constant on trajectories but decreasing on R near the fixed point.

To see that q is decreasing along R near (1/3,1/3), note that

$$q(1/3 + t, 1/3) = \frac{1}{3}\left(\frac{1}{3} - t\right)^2,$$

which has a derivative with respect to t that evaluates to $-2/9 < 0$ at $t = 0$.

To see that $q(\alpha, \beta)$ is constant along trajectories, note that the differential equations for the dynamical system, assuming $r = 1$, $s = -1$, can be written as

$$\dot{\alpha} = 2\alpha\beta + \alpha^2 - \alpha \tag{A9.1}$$
$$\dot{\beta} = -2\alpha\beta - \beta^2 + \beta. \tag{A9.2}$$

Then,

$$\frac{d}{dt}q(\alpha, \beta) = \frac{d}{dt}[\alpha\beta(1 - \alpha - \beta)]$$

$$= \beta(1 - \alpha - \beta)\dot{\alpha} + \alpha(1 - \alpha - \beta)\dot{\beta} + \alpha\beta(-\dot{\alpha} - \dot{\beta})$$
$$= 0,$$

where we get the last step by substituting the expressions for $\dot{\alpha}$ and $\dot{\beta}$ from (A9.1) and (A9.2).

9.14   The Lotka-Volterra Model and Biodiversity

a. This is simple algebra, though you should check that the restrictions on the signs of a, b, c, and d ensure that $p^* > 0$.

b. We have

$$\frac{\dot{p}}{p} = \frac{\dot{u}}{u} - \left[\frac{\dot{u}}{w} + \frac{\dot{v}}{w}\right]$$

$$= \frac{\dot{u}}{u} - \left[p\frac{\dot{u}}{u} + (1 - p)\frac{\dot{v}}{v}\right]$$

$$= ap + b(1 - p) - kw$$
$$\quad - [p[ap + b(1 - p) - kw] + (1 - p)[cp + d(1 - p) - kw]]$$

$$= ap + b(1 - p) - [p[ap + b(1 - p)] + (1 - p)[cp + d(1 - p)]]$$

$$= \pi_A - \bar{\pi}.$$

c. We have

$$\frac{\dot{p}_i}{p_i} = \frac{\dot{u}_i}{u_i} - \sum_{j=1}^{n}\frac{\dot{u}_j}{u}$$

$$= \frac{\dot{u}_i}{u_i} - \sum_{j=1}^{n}\frac{\dot{u}_j}{u_j}p_j$$

$$= \sum_{j=1}^{n}a_{ij}p_j - kw - \sum_{j=1}^{n}\left(\sum_{k=1}^{n}a_{jk}p_k - ku\right)p_j$$

$$= \sum_{j=1}^{n}a_{ij}p_j - ku - \sum_{j,k=1}^{n}a_{jk}p_k p_j + ku\sum_{k=1}^{n}p_j$$

$$= \sum_{j=1}^{n} a_{ij} p_j - \sum_{j,k=1}^{n} a_{jk} p_j p_k.$$

This proves the assertion, and the identification of the resulting equations as a replicator dynamic is clear from the derivation.

9.18   The Loraxes and Thoraxes

a. We have the following game tree, on which backward induction (pruning the game tree) gives the desired result.

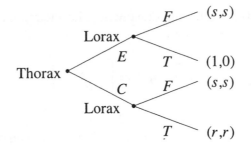

b. It is easy to show that there is no pure strategy Nash equilibrium other than FE, so we look for a mixed strategy Nash equilibrium. Let p be the fraction of Thoraxes who cooperate. Then, the payoff to T is $pr + (1 - p) \cdot 0 = pr$, and the payoff to F is s, so in mixed strategy equilibrium we must have $pr = s$. Let q be the fraction of trusters among the Lorax. The payoff to C is then $qr + (1 - q)s$, and the payoff to E is $q + (1 - q)s$. Thus, Thoraxes always eat, so $p = 1$, which contradicts $pr = s$.

c. The payoff to I is $pr + (1 - p)s - \delta$ for a Lorax, and the payoff to NI is $\max\{pr, s\}$, since if $pr > s$, the noninspector chooses T, and with $pr < s$, the noninspector chooses F. Clearly, some Loraxes must be NI types, since if all were I types, then all Thoraxes would cooperate, so a Lorax could gain from trusting rather than inspecting. If both I and NI are used, they must have equal payoffs, so $p^* = 1 - \delta/s$ if $pr > s$, and $p^* = \delta/(r - s)$ if $pr < s$. Suppose $s/r > \delta/(r - s)$. Then, $p^* = 1 - \delta/s > 1 - (r - s)/r = s/r$ is consistent with $pr > s$. If $s/r < \delta/(r - s)$, then we must have $p^* = \delta/(r - s) > s/r$, which implies $p^* = 1 - \delta/s$. This is only possible if $\delta/(r - s) = 1 - \delta/s$, or $s/r = \delta/(r - s)$, which is a contradiction. Hence, there is no mixed

strategy Nash equilibrium in this case. Assuming $pr > s$, the payoff
to C for a second-mover is r, and the payoff to E is $1 - q$, so a mixed
strategy equilibrium requires $q^* = 1 - r$.

d. Suppose $p > s/r$, so NI implies T for a Lorax. Then, (payoff to
    I)$-$(payoff to NI)$= (1 - p)s - \delta$. For a Thorax, (payoff to C)$-$(payoff
    to E)$= r - (1 - q)$. Then, the linear dynamic satisfies the equations

$$\dot{p} = b(q - (1 - r))$$
$$\dot{q} = -a\left[p - \left(1 - \frac{\delta}{s}\right)\right],$$

where $a, b > 0$ are rates of adjustment. The Jacobian at the fixed point
$p^* = 1 - \delta/s$, $q^* = 1 - r$ is

$$J(p^*, q^*) = \begin{bmatrix} 0 & b \\ -a & 0 \end{bmatrix}.$$

This gives $\alpha = \text{Trace}(J(p^*, q^*))/2 = 0$, $\beta = \det(J(p^*, q^*)) = ab >$
0, $\gamma = \alpha^2 - \beta = -ab < 0$. Thus, the fixed point is a center.

12

Learning Who Your Friends Are: Bayes' Rule and Private Information

12.3 Haggling at the Bazaar

c. Let $\mu = P(b_h|\text{refuse})$. Then by Bayes' Rule, with $x = P(\text{refuse}|b_h)$,

$$\mu = \frac{P(\text{refuse}|b_h)P(b_h)}{P(\text{refuse}|b_h)P(b_h) + P(\text{refuse}|b_l)P(b_l)}$$

$$= \frac{x\pi}{x\pi + 1 - \pi}$$

$$= \frac{\pi}{\pi + \frac{1-\pi}{x}}$$

$$\leq \pi.$$

f. All buyers accept $p_1 = b_l$, so $p_1 < b_l$ is dominated. Any player who accepts p_1 for $b_l < p_1 < p^*$ accepts $p_1 = p^*$. No buyer accepts $p_1 > p^*$, since both high and low types prefer to wait until the second round and get $p_2 = b_l$. At $p_1 = p^*$, the payoffs to "accept" and "reject" are equal for a high-value buyer, since then $b_h - p_1 = \delta_b(b_h - b_l)$, so such a buyer accepts on round one.

i. Suppose the seller chooses $p_2 = b_l$. Since the seller's posterior probability for $\{b = b_l\}$ cannot be less than π (for the same reason as in the last problem) and since he would charge b_h in the one-shot game, he must charge $p_2 = b_h$. So suppose the seller chooses $p_2 = b_h$. Then the only undominated strategies on the first round are $p_1 = \delta_b b_h$ and $p_1 = b_l$. But if a buyer rejects $p_1 = \delta_b b_h$, he must be a low-value buyer, so it is not subgame perfect to charge $p_2 = b_h$.

12.8   A Common Value Auction: The Winner's Curse

If $\tilde{v}$ is the measured value for any player, then

$$P[\tilde{v} \leq x | v] = \frac{x - v + a}{2a}.$$

Suppose your measured value, and hence bid, is x: The probability $F(x)$ that yours is the highest bid is just the probability that all $n - 1$ other measured values are less than x, which is given by

$$F(x) = \left(\frac{x - v + a}{2a} \right)^{n-1}.$$

Your expected profit π is given by

$$\pi = \frac{1}{2a} \int_{v-a}^{v+a} (v - x) F(x) dx$$

$$= \frac{1}{(2a)^n} \int_{v-a}^{v+a} (v - x)(x - v + a)^{n-1} dx$$

$$= -a \frac{n-1}{n(n+1)}.$$

12.9   A Common Value Auction: Quantum Spin Decoders

a.   If GE bids b, it wins if $b > (\alpha + \beta) y / 2\beta$, or $2b\beta / (\alpha + \beta) > y$. GE's expected profit is thus

$$\int_0^{\frac{2b\beta}{\alpha+\beta}} (x + y - b) \frac{1}{\beta} dy = \frac{2b}{(\alpha + \beta)^2} [(\alpha + \beta)x - b\alpha].$$

If we equate the derivative of this expression with respect to b to zero and solve for b, we get $b = x(\alpha + \beta)/2\alpha$. A similar reasoning holds with respect to Martin Marietta. GE's expected profit is then $x^2/2\alpha$, which can be found by substitution. GE then wins if $x/\alpha > y/\beta$, which clearly has probability 1/2.

b. Each firm bids 1/2 of its known value, plus 1/2 of a random guess of the value it does not know. Note that when α/β is very small, kramel inhibitors are worth little. In this case GE knows the value of $\tilde{x}$ but the knowledge is practically worthless, so GE's bid is roughly 1/2 of a random sample from the uniform distribution on $[0, \beta]$. GE's expected profit is thus close to zero, although its probability of winning remains 1/2. In this situation, Martin Marietta bids one half of the actual value of the beta-phase detector and can expect big profits.

c. If GE bids b having seen x, it wins if $b/\gamma > y$, so its expected profit is

$$\int_0^{\frac{b}{\gamma}} (x + y - b)\frac{1}{\beta}dy.$$

Evaluating this integral and setting its derivative to zero gives $b = \gamma x/(2\gamma - 1)$. A similar argument holds for Martin Marietta.

d. Suppose the value is $\tilde{x}+\tilde{y}+\tilde{z}$ where $\tilde{x}$, $\tilde{y}$, and $\tilde{z}$ are uniformly distributed on $[0, \alpha]$, $[0, \beta]$, and $[0, \gamma]$, respectively. Suppose the three bidders bid νx, ηy, and ζz, respectively. Bidder 1 then must determine ν given η and ζ. The expected profit of bidder 1 who sees x and bids b is given by

$$\int_0^{\frac{b}{\eta}} \int_0^{\frac{b}{\zeta}} (x + y + x - b)\frac{dy\,dz}{\eta\,\zeta}.$$

Evaluating this integral, setting its derivative with respect to b equal to zero and solving for b, we get

$$b = F(\eta, \zeta)x,$$

where

$$F(\lambda, \mu) = \frac{4\lambda\mu}{3(2\lambda\mu - \lambda - \mu)},$$

so

$$\nu = F(\eta, \zeta).$$

If we substitute $\eta = \zeta = 5/3$, we see that $\nu^* = 5/3$, which proves the existence part of the assertion. For uniqueness, let (ν^*, η^*, ζ^*) be any solution. Note that if we repeat the above analysis to find η and ζ, we will find

$$\nu^* = F(\eta^*, \zeta^*)j, \eta^* = F(\zeta^*, \nu^*), \zeta^* = F(\eta^*, \nu^*).$$

If we substitute the first equation into the second and solve for η^*, we get

$$\eta^* = \frac{7\zeta^*}{6\zeta^* - 3}.$$

Now, substituting ν^* and $\eta*$ in the equation for ζ^*, we find $\zeta^* = 5/3$, so $\eta^* = 5/3$ and finally $\nu^* = 5/3$.

12.10   Predatory Pricing: Pooling and Separating Equilibria

If the equilibrium is separating, then the sane incumbent accommodates and earns $d_1(1+\delta)$. If the incumbent preyed in the first period, his earning would be $-p_1 + \delta m$. Thus, a separating equilibrium requires (12.7). Clearly, this condition is also sufficient, when supplemented by the entrant's belief that the incumbent preys only if crazy, which is of course true if the equilibrium is separating.

   If there is a pooling equilibrium, clearly (12.7) must be violated, or else the sane incumbent would prefer to accommodate. In addition, the sane firm must induce exit, since otherwise it would not be profitable to prey in the first period. Thus, we must have $\pi_2 d_2 - (1 - \pi_2)p_2 \leq 0$, which becomes

$$\pi_2 \leq \frac{p_2}{d_2 + p_2},$$

where π_2 is the entrant's posterior on the incumbent being sane if he preys in the first period. Clearly, $\pi_1 = \pi_2$ in this case, since all firms prey in the first period and hence no information is gained by observing the behavior of the incumbent. Thus, the condition for a pooling equilibrium is (12.8). Note that if the frequency of sane firms is sufficiently high (i.e., if π_1 is sufficiently large), the pooling equilibrium cannot occur even if the incumbent gains from driving an entrant out of the market.

   Let us show that if equations (12.7) and (12.8) are both violated and if the entrant would enter the market if there were only one period, then we have a hybrid perfect Bayesian equilibrium, in which both parties randomize.

   Let α be the probability that a sane incumbent preys in the first period, and let β be the probability that the entrant stays in the second period if the incumbent preys in the first period. The payoff to "stay" in the second period if the incumbent preys in the first is

$$-(1 - \pi_2)p_2 + \pi_2 d_2,$$

and this must equal the payoff to "drop," which is zero. Thus, we must have

$$\pi_2 = \frac{p_2}{d_2 + p_2}.$$

This is prima facie possible, since (12.8) is violated and $\pi_2 \leq \pi_1$.

To find β, note that the payoff to "prey" is

$$\beta(-p_1 + \delta d_1) + (1 - \beta)(-p_1 + \delta m),$$

and the payoff to "accommodate" is $d_1(1 + \delta)$. These must be equal, which gives (12.10). Note that β is always positive, and $\beta < 1$ precisely when the separating equilibrium condition (12.7) is violated.

But how do we get α? Obviously we must use Bayes' Rule. We have

$$P[\text{sane}|\text{prey}] = \frac{P[\text{prey}|\text{sane}]P[\text{sane}]}{P[\text{prey}|\text{sane}]P[\text{sane}] + P[\text{prey}|\text{crazy}]P[\text{crazy}]},$$

which becomes

$$\pi_2 = \frac{\alpha\pi_1}{\alpha\pi_1 + (1 - \pi_1)}.$$

Solving for α, we get (12.9). This is clearly positive and because (12.8) is violated, it is easy to show that $\alpha < 1$. Thus, we have a mixed strategy perfect Bayesian equilibrium.

12.11 Limit Pricing

a. Let $q = d(p)$ be demand for the good, $d' < 0$, and let c be constant marginal cost. Then profits are given by $\pi = d(p)(p - c)$ and the first-order order condition for π maximization is

$$\pi_p(p_m) = (p_m - c)d'(p_m) + d(p_m) = 0.$$

We take the total derivative of this with respect to c, treating $p_m = p_m(c)$ as an implicit function of c. We get

$$\pi_{pp}\frac{dp_m}{dc} + \pi_{pc} = 0.$$

Now $\pi_{pp} < 0$ by the second-order condition for profit maximization and $\pi_{pc} = (\partial/\partial c)((p_m - c)d'(p_m) + d(p_m)) = -d'(p_m) > 0$. Thus, $dp_m/d_c > 0$.

b. In a separating equilibrium, the low-cost firm does not want to pick the high-cost firm's price and viceversa. Moreover, the entrant only enters if the incumbent charges the high price. Let p^l be the price charged by the low-cost firm and suppose that if $p^l = p^l_m$, then the high-cost firm would find it profitable to charge this price too, so we would not have a separating equilibrium. Knowing this, when $c = c_l$, the incumbent might be willing to charge $p^l < p^l_m$ (limit pricing) to make it too costly for the high-cost firm to mimic this behavior.

Thus, for $c = c_h$ in a separating equilibrium, if δ is the discount factor we must then have $m^h + \delta d^h \geq m^h(p^l) + \delta m^h$, since charging p^h_m must be better than charging p^l. Also, for $c = c_l$, $m^l(p^l) + \delta m^l \geq m^l + \delta d^l$ must hold, since the low-cost firm must prefer charging p^l and being a monopolist in the second period (charging p^l_m) to charging p^h in the first period and being a duopolist in the second. Finally, limit pricing requires $p^l < p^l_m$, so at $c = c_h$, the incumbent would prefer to charge p^l_m if that convinced the entrant not to enter. Thus, we must have $m^h(p^l_m) + \delta m^h > m^h + \delta d^h$. In sum, for limit pricing to obtain (i.e., a separating equilibrium with $p^l < p^l_m$), we must have the following three inequalities holding simultaneously:

$$m^h - m^h(p^l) \geq \delta(m^h - d^h)$$
$$\delta(m^h - d^h) \geq m^h - m^h(p^l_m)$$
$$\delta(m^l - d^l) \geq m^l - m^l(p^l).$$

c. Here is the beginning of an example. It's not complete. Suppose demand is given by $q = d(p) = 1 - p$, so monopoly profits are $m = (1-p)(p-c) - f$, where c is marginal cost and f is fixed cost. The first-order condition for monopoly profits gives $p_m = (1 + c)/2$, so $m(p_m) = (1 - c)^2/4 - f$. Note that, as expected, monopoly price is an increasing function of marginal cost.

In the duopoly case, we assume a Cournot duopoly. Let q_1 and q_2 be the quantities of the two firms, so $q = q_1 + q_2$, and the price is $p = 1 - q = 1 - q_1 - q_2$. Duopoly profits for firm 1 are $d_1(q_1) = (1 - q_1 - q_2 - c)q_1 - f$ and the first-order condition for profit maximization is $q_1 = (1 - q_2 - c)/2$. Let c_2 be the cost of the entrant, so $d_2(q_2) = (1 - q_1 - q_2 - c_2)q_2 - f$ and the first-order condition gives $q_2 = (1 - q_1 - c_2)/2$. Solving simultaneously (the intersection of the offer curves), we get $q_1 = (1 + c_2 - 2c)/3$, $q_2 = (1 + c - 2c_2)/3$, so $p = 1 - q_1 - q_2 = (1 + c + c_2)/3$. Then $d_1 = (1 + c_2 - 2c)^2/9 - f$,

$d_2 = (1 + c - 2c_2)^2/9 - f$. The condition $d_2^h > 0 > d_2^l$ becomes $c^h - 2c_2 > 3\sqrt{f} - 1 > c^l - 2c_2$, which will hold for some f as long as $c^h > c^l$ and $c^h > 2c_2 - 1$.

Suppose $\delta = 1$ for simplicity. In a separating equilibrium, the l and h types do different things, and the entrant uses the signal to decide whether or not to enter. In the simplest case, an l incumbent would charge $p^l = p_m^l$ and the h incumbent would not want to follow suit. This requires that $m^h + d^h \geq m^h(p_m^l) + m^h$, or $d^h \geq m^h(p_m^l)$, or $(1 + c_2 - 2c^h)^2/9 \geq (1 - c^l)(1 + c^l - 2c^h)/4$, or

$$c_2 \geq 3[(1 - c^l)(1 + c^l - 2c^h)]^{1/2}/2 - 1 + 2c^h.$$

For concreteness, let's take $c^l = 0.1$, $c^h = 0.3$. Then this inequality becomes $c_2 \geq 0.6062$. Note that $c^h = 0.3 > 2c_2 - 1 = 0.2124$, so the condition $c^h > 2c_2 - 1$ holds as long as $c_2 < 0.65$. We must also show that the l firm prefers choosing p_m^l over p_m^h, which is obvious, since choosing p_m^l gives higher profits in the first period and keeps the competitor out. Conclusion: we have a separating equilibrium without limit pricing when $c^l = 0.1$, $c^h = 0.3$, $0.6062 \leq c_2 < 0.65$ and f is chosen so that $c^h - 2c_2 > 3\sqrt{f} - 1 > c^l - 2c_2$ is satisfied.

But suppose $c_2 < 0.6062$, which is likely for a potentially profitable firm, since these marginal costs are twice as high as c^h. The l firm can still signal the fact that it has low costs by charging $p^l < p_m^l$, if this is a strategy that the h firm would not follow. The h incumbent will not charge p^l if $m^h + d^h > m^h(p^l) + m^h$ (i.e., charging the monopoly price in the first period and facing a duopoly in the second is better than imitating the l firm in the first and being a monopoly in the second), or $d^h > m^h(p^l)$, which is $(1 + c_2 - 2c^h)^2/9 > (1 - p^l)(p^l - c^h)$. Treating this as an equality to determine the highest possible p^l with this property, we get

$$p^{l2} - p^l(1 + c^h) + (1 + c_2^2 + 4c^{h2} + 2c_2 + 5c^h - 4c_2c^h)/9 = 0,$$

which is a quadratic equation. Using $c_2 = c^h = 0.3$, this becomes

$$p^{l2} - 1.3p^l(1 + c^h) + 0.354444 = 0,$$

whose relevant root is $p^l = 0.389125$. Note that $p_m^l = (1 + c^l)/2 = 0.55$, so this is a significant case of limit pricing. Is this the best strategy for the l firm? By doing so, it receives $m(p^l) + m^l - 2f$, since the entrant does not enter in the second period. By charging p^l, the high-cost firm would do the same thing, so say the entrant enters (this depends on the entrant's subjective prior concerning the probability that the incumbent is an h or an l). Then the l firm earns $m^l + d^l - 2f$. Thus, limit pricing is Nash if $m(p^l) + m^l > m^l + d^l$, or $m(p^l) > d^l$. But $m(p^l) = (p^l - c^l)(1 - p^l) = 0.176619$ and $d^l = 0.2025$, so this fails.

12.12   A Simple Limit-Pricing Model

If demand is $q = m - p$ and constant marginal cost is c, it is straightforward to check that the profit-maximizing price p^m, quantity q^m, and profit π^m for a monopolist are given by

$$q^m = \frac{m - c}{2}, \qquad p^m = \frac{m + c}{2}, \qquad \pi^m = \frac{(m - c)^2}{4}$$

provided $m \geq c$. Now suppose there are two firms in a Cournot duopoly, with costs c_1 and c_2, respectively. We assume c_1 and c_2 are common knowledge. It is straightforward to check that the optimal quantities q_i^d, prices p_i^d, and profits π_i^d for $i = 1, 2$ are given by

$$q_1^d = \frac{m + c_2 - 2c_1}{3}, \qquad q_2^d = \frac{m + c_1 - 2c_2}{3},$$

$$p^d = \frac{m + c_1 + c_2}{3}, \qquad \pi_1^d = \frac{(m + c_2 - 2c_1)^2}{9}, \qquad \pi_2^d = \frac{(m + c_1 - 2c_2)^2}{9}.$$

Also, the constraint that quantities be nonnegative requires $2c_1 \leq m + c_2$ and $2c_2 \leq m + c_1$. If one of the nonnegativity constraints is violated, it is easy to see that the higher-cost firm will not be in the market and the lower-cost firm will charge the monopoly price. For instance, suppose $c_1 > (m + c_2)/2$. If firm 2 produces the monopoly quantity, then $q_2 = (m - c_2)/2$, so

$$\frac{\partial \pi_1}{\partial q_1} = m - 2q_1 - q_2 - c_1 = m - 2q_1 - (m - c_2)/2 - c_1$$

$$< m - 2q_1 - (m - c_2)/2 - (m + c_2)/2 = -2q_1,$$

so the optimal response for firm 1 is to stay out of the market (i.e., to set $q_1 = 0$).

Suppose firm 1 is the incumbent (A) and firm 2 is the potential entrant (B), so by assumption $c_2 = c_h$. If firm 2 knew firm 1's costs, firm 2 would enter if and only if

$$\pi_2^d = (m + c_1 - 2c_h)^2/9 > f,$$

where f is the fixed entry cost. By assumption, this inequality must hold when $c_1 = c_h$ and fail when $c_1 = c_l$; i.e., we must have

$$(m + c_l - 2c_h)^2/9 \le f \le (m - c_h)^2/9.$$

In addition, it must not be profitable for A to pretend to be low-cost if A is in fact high-cost. We express this condition as follows. Let $(\pi_{mh}, \pi_{ml}, \pi_{dh}, \pi_{dl})$ be the monopoly profits of a high-cost firm, the monopoly profits of a low-cost firm, the duopoly profits of a high-cost firm facing a high-cost firm, and the duopoly profits of a low-cost firm facing a high-cost firm. Also, let π^* be the profits of a high-cost monopolist pretending to be a low-cost monopolist. For a separating equilibrium, a high-cost firm should not want to pretend to be low-cost. Assuming no discounting, this means we must have $\pi^* + \pi_{mh} < \pi_{mh} + \pi_{dh}$ and $(m + c_l - 2c_h)(m - c_l) < 4(m - c_h)^2/9$, or

$$\pi^* < \pi_{dh}.$$

This reduces to the condition

$$(m + c_l - 2c_h)(m - c_l) < \frac{4}{9}(m - c_h)^2.$$

Note that if c_l is close enough to c_h, this inequality fails.

13

When It Pays to Be Truthful: Signaling in Games with Friends, Adversaries, and Kin

13.3 Introductory Offers

If a high-quality firm sells to a consumer in the first period at some price p_1, then in the second period the consumer will be willing to pay $p_2 = h$, since he knows the product is of high quality. Knowing that it can make a profit $h - c_h$ from a customer in the second period, a high-quality firm might want to make a consumer an "introductory offer" at a price p_1 in the first period that would not be mimicked by the low-quality firm, in order to reap the second-period profit.

If $p_1 > c_l$, the low-quality firm could mimic the high-quality firm, so the best the high-quality firm can do is to charge $p_1 = c_l$, which the low-quality firm will not mimic, since the low-quality firm cannot profit by doing so (it cannot profit in the first period, and the consumer will not buy the low-quality product in the second period). In this case, the high-quality firm's profits are $(c_1 - c_h) + \delta(h - c_h)$. As long as these profits are positive, which reduces to $h > c_h + \delta(c_h - c_l)$, the high-quality firm will stay in business.

13.4 Web Sites (for Spiders)

a. In a truthful signaling equilibrium, strong spiders use saa and weak spiders use wwa. To see this, note that strong spiders say they're strong and weak spiders say they're weak, by definition of a truthful signaling equilibrium. Weak spiders withdraw against strong spiders because $d > 0$, and attack other weak spiders because $v - c_w > 0$. Strong spiders attack weak spiders if they do not withdraw, because $2v - b > 2v - c_s > v$.

b. If p is the fraction of strong spiders, then the expected payoff to a strong spider is $p(v - c_s) + 2(1 - p)v - e$, and the expected payoff to a weak spider is $(1 - p)(v - c_w)$. If these two are equal, then

$$p = \frac{v + c_w - e}{c_w + c_s}, \qquad (A13.1)$$

which is strictly between 0 and 1 if and only if $e - c_w < v < e + c_s$.

c. In a truthful signaling equilibrium, each spider has expected payoff

$$\pi = \frac{(v - c_w)(c_s + e - v)}{c_w + c_s}. \qquad (A13.2)$$

Suppose a weak spider signals that it is strong, and all other spiders play the truthful signaling equilibrium strategy. If the other spider is strong, it will attack and the weak spider will receive $-d$. If the other spider is weak it will withdraw, and the spider will gain $2v$. Thus, the payoff to the spider for a misleading communication is $-pd + 2(1 - p)v$, which cannot be greater than (13.2) if truth-telling is Nash. Solving for d, we get

$$d \geq \frac{(c_s + e - v)(v + c_w)}{c_w - e + v}.$$

Can a strong spider benefit from signaling that it is weak? To see that it cannot, suppose first that it faces a strong spider. If it attacks the strong spider after signaling that it is weak, it gets the same payoff as if it signalled strong (since its opponent always attacks). If it withdraws against its opponent, it gets 0, which is less than the $v - c$ it gets by attacking. Thus, signaling weak against a strong opponent can't lead to a gain. Suppose the opponent is weak. Then signaling weak means that the opponent will attack. Responding by withdrawing, it gets 0; responding by attacking, it gets $2v - b$, since it always defeats its weak opponent. But if it had signalled strong, it would have earned $2v > 2v - b$. Thus, it never pays a strong spider to signal that it is weak.

d. This result follows directly from equation (13.2). This result occurs because higher e entails a lower fraction of strong spiders, from (13.1). But weak spiders earn $(1 - p)(v - c_w)$, which is decreasing in p, and strong spiders earn the same as weak spiders in equilibrium.

e. We differentiate (13.2) with respect to v, getting

$$\pi_v = \frac{c_w + c_s + e - 2v}{c_w + c_s}.$$

When $v = e - c_w > 0$, its smallest value, $\pi_v = 3c_w + c_s - e$, has an indeterminate sign. If it is negative, lowering v would increase payoff, as asserted. So suppose $\pi_v > 0$ at $v = e - c_w$. When $v = e + c_s$, which is its largest value, $\pi_v = c_w - c_s - e$, which is negative. Thus, there is an interior optimum for v in general.

Note that this optimum is only local; if we increase v beyond $e + c_s$ only strong spiders remain, and their payoff is now strictly increasing in v. Here is a picture, showing the discontinuity in the payoffs, once there are no weak spiders left. At this point the strong spiders no longer signal or attack, since all know all are strong. They each get v in this case.

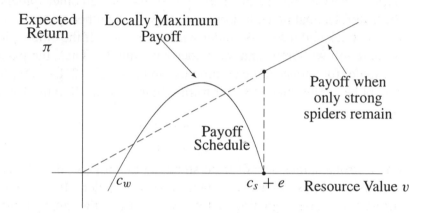

13.7   The Shepherds Who Never Cry Wolf

The following payoffs are easy to derive:

$$\pi_1(N, N) = p(1 - a) + (1 - p)(1 - b); \quad \pi_2(N, N) = 1;$$
$$\pi_1(N, H) = p(1 - a) + (1 - p)(1 - b); \quad \pi_2(N, H) = 1;$$
$$\pi_1(N, A) = 1; \quad \pi_2(N, A) = 1 - d;$$
$$\pi_1(H, N) = p(1 - a) + (1 - p)(1 - b) - pc; \quad \pi_2(H, N) = 1;$$
$$\pi_1(H, H) = p(1 - c) + (1 - p)(1 - b); \quad \pi_2(H, H) = p(1 - d) + 1 - p;$$
$$\pi_1(H, A) = 1 - pc; \quad \pi_2(H, A) = 1 - d;$$
$$\pi_1(A, N) = p(1 - a) + (1 - p)(1 - b) - c; \quad \pi_2(A, N) = 1;$$
$$\pi_1(A, H) = 1 - c; \quad \pi_2(A, H) = 1 - d;$$
$$\pi_1(A, A) = 1 - c; \quad \pi_2(A, A) = 1 - d.$$

Now the total payoff for shepherd 1 is $\pi_1' = \pi_1 + k\pi_2$, and the total payoff for shepherd 2 is $\pi_2' = \pi_1 + k\pi_1$. Substituting in numbers and forming the normal form matrix for the game, we get

	N	H	A
N	$\frac{19}{24}, \frac{37}{32}$	$\frac{19}{24}, \frac{37}{32}$	$\frac{21}{16}, \frac{7}{6}$
H	$\frac{95}{192}, \frac{793}{768}$	$\frac{47}{48}, \frac{829}{768}$	$\frac{65}{64}, \frac{267}{256}$
A	$\frac{19}{48}, \frac{571}{576}$	$\frac{11}{12}, \frac{577}{576}$	$\frac{11}{12}, \frac{577}{576}$

It is easy to see that (H, H) and (N, A) are Nash equilibria, and you can check that there is a mixed strategy equilibrium in which the threatened shepherd uses $\frac{1}{3}N + \frac{2}{3}H$ and the other shepherd uses $\frac{3}{5}H + \frac{2}{5}A$.

13.9 Honest Signaling among Partial Altruists

The payoff matrix for the encounter between a fisher observing a threatened fisher is as follows, where the first two lines are the payoffs to the individual players, and the third is the total payoff:

	Never Ask	Ask If Distressed	Always Ask
Never Help	$r(1-p)u$ $(1-p)u$ $(1+r)(1-p)u$	$r(1-p)u-rpt$ $(1-p)u-pt$ $(1+r)[(1-p)u-pt]$	$r(1-p)u-rt$ $(1-p)u-t$ $(1+r)[(1-p)u-t]$
Help If Asked	$r(1-p)u$ $(1-p)u$ $(1+r)(1-p)u$	$r[p(1-t)+(1-p)u]-pc$ $p(1-t)+(1-p)u$ $(1+r)[p(1-t)$ $+(1-p)u]-pc$	$r[p+(1-p)v-t]-c$ $p+(1-p)v-t$ $(1+r)[p+(1-p)v$ $-t]-c$
Always Help	$r[p+(1-p)v]-c$ $p+(1-p)v$ $(1+r)[p+(1-p)v]-c$	$r[p(1-t)+(1-p)v]-c$ $p(1-t)+(1-p)v$ $(1+r)[p(1-t)+$ $(1-p)v]-c$	$r[p+(1-p)v-t]-c$ $p+(1-p)v-t$ $(1+r)[p+(1-p)v$ $-t]-c$

The answers to the problem can be obtained in a straightforward manner from this matrix.

13.11   Education as a Screening Device

a. Given the probabilities (c), the wages (b) follow from

$$w_k = P[a_h|e_k]a_h + P[a_l|e_k]a_l, \qquad k = h, l. \qquad (A13.3)$$

Then, it is a best response for workers to choose low education whatever their ability type, so (a) follows. Since both types choose e_l, the conditional probability $P[a_l|e_l] = 1 - \alpha$ is consistent with the behavior of the agents, and since e_h is off the path of play, any conditional for $P[a_l|e_h]$ is acceptable, so long as it induces a Nash equilibrium.

b. Assume the above conditions hold, and suppose c satisfies $a_l(a_h - a_l) < c < a_h(a_h - a_l)$. The wage conditions (b) follow from (13.3) and (c). Also, $a_h - c/a_h > a_l$, so a high-ability worker prefers to choose $e = 1$ and signal his true type, rather than choose e_l and signal his type as low ability. Similarly, $a_l > a_h - c/a_l$, so a low-ability worker prefers to choose e_l and signal his true type, rather than choose e_h and signal his type as high ability.

c. The wage conditions (b) follow from (13.3) and (c). Suppose $c < a_l(a_h - a_l)$. Then both high- and low-ability workers prefer to get education and the higher wage w_h rather than signal that they are low quality.

d. Let $\bar{e} = \alpha a_l(a_h - a_l)/c$, and choose $e^* \in [0, \bar{e}]$. Given the employer's wage offer, if a worker does not choose $e = e^*$ he might as well choose $e = 0$, since his wage in any case must be $w = a_l$. A low-ability worker then prefers to get education e^* rather than any other educational level, since $a_l \le \alpha a_h + (1-\alpha)a_l - ce^*/a_l$. This is thus true for the high-ability worker, whose incentive compatibility constraint is not binding.

e. Consider the interval

$$\left[\frac{a_l(a_h - a_l)}{c}, \frac{a_h(a_h - a_l)}{c} \right].$$

If c is sufficiently large, this interval has a nonempty intersection with the unit interval $[0, 1]$. Suppose this intersection is $[e_{min}, e_{max}]$. Then, for $e^* \in [e_{min}, e_{max}]$, a high-ability worker prefers to acquire education e^* and receive the high wage $w = a_h$, while the low-ability worker prefers to receive $w = a_l$ with no education.

13.12 Capital as a Signaling Device

a. Given $p > 0$, choose k so that

$$1 > k(1 + \rho) > q + p(1 - q).$$

This is possible since $q + p(1 - q) < 1$. Then it is clear that the fraction q of good projects is socially productive. The interest rate r that a producer must offer then must satisfy

$$k(1 + \rho) = qk(1 + r) + (1 - q)kp(1 + r) = k(1 + r)[q + p(1 - q)],$$

so

$$r = \frac{1 + \rho}{q + p(1 - q)} - 1. \tag{A13.4}$$

The net profit of a producer with a good project is then

$$1 - k(1 + r) = \frac{q + p(1 - q) - k(1 + \rho)}{q + p(1 - q)} < 0,$$

so such producers will be unwilling to offer lenders an interest rate they are willing to accept. The same is clearly true of bad projects, so no projects get funded. Note that bad projects are not socially productive in this case, since $p - k(1 + \rho) < p - (q + p(1 - q)) = -q(1 - p) < 0$.

b. Choose k so that $p < k(1 + \rho) < q + p(1 - q)$, which is clearly always possible. Then the fraction $1 - q$ of bad projects are socially unproductive. The interest rate r must still satisfy equation (13.4), so the payoff to a successful project (good or bad) is

$$1 - k(1 + r) = \frac{q + p(1 - q) - k(1 + \rho)}{q + p(1 - q)} > 0,$$

so producers of both good and bad projects are willing to offer interest rate r, and lenders are willing to lend at this rate to all producers.

c. Let

$$k^p_{min} = \frac{p[1 - k(1 + \rho)]}{(1 - p)(1 + \rho)}.$$

Note that since good projects are socially productive, $k^p_{min} > 0$. Suppose all producers have wealth $k^p > k^p_{min}$, and lenders believe that only a producer with a good project will invest k^p in his project. Then lenders will be willing to lend at interest rate ρ. If a producer invests k^p in his project and borrows $k - k^p$, his return is 1 and his costs are foregone earnings $k^p(1 + \rho)$ and capital costs $(k - k^p)(1 + \rho)$. Thus, his profit is

$$1 - k^p(1 + \rho) - (k - k^p)(1 + \rho) = 1 - k(1 + \rho) > 0,$$

so such a producer is willing to undertake this transaction. If the producer with a bad project invests his capital k^p, his return is

$$p[1 - k(1 + \rho)] - (1 - p)k^p(1 + \rho) < 0,$$

so he will not put up the equity. This proves the theorem.

14

Bosses and Workers, Landlords and Peasants, and Other Principal-Agent Models

14.3 Labor as Gift Exchange

a. Choosing w and N to maximize profits gives the first-order conditions

$$\pi_w(w, N) = [f'(eN)e' - 1]N = 0 \qquad (A14.1)$$
$$\pi_N(w, N) = f'(eN)e - w = 0. \qquad (A14.2)$$

Solving these equations gives the Solow condition.

b. The second partials are

$$\pi_{ww} = [f''Ne'^2 + f'e'']N < 0, \qquad \pi_{NN} = f''e^2 < 0,$$
$$\pi_{wN} = f''Nee' + f'e' - 1 = f''Nee' < 0.$$

It is easy to check that the second-order conditions are satisfied: $\pi_{ww} < 0$, $\pi_{NN} < 0$, and $\pi_{ww}\pi_{NN} - \pi_{wN}^2 > 0$.

c. To show that $dw/dz > 1$, differentiate the first-order conditions (A14.2) totally with respect to w and N:

$$\pi_{ww}\frac{dw}{dz} + \pi_{wN}\frac{dN}{dz} + \pi_{wz} = 0$$

$$\pi_{Nw}\frac{dw}{dz} + \pi_{NN}\frac{dN}{dz} + \pi_{Nz} = 0. \qquad (A14.3)$$

Solving these two equations in the two unknowns dw/dz and dN/dz, we find

$$\frac{dw}{dz} = -\frac{\pi_{NN}\pi_{wz} - \pi_{Nw}\pi_{Nz}}{\pi_{NN}\pi_{wz} - \pi_{Nw}^2}. \qquad (A14.4)$$

But we also calculate directly that

$$\pi_{wz} = -[f''Ne'^2 + f'e'']N = -\pi_{ww},$$
$$\pi_{Nz} = -f'e' - f''Nee' = -f'e' - \pi_{Nw}.$$

Substituting these values in (14.4)', we get

$$\frac{dw}{dz} = 1 - \frac{\pi_{Nw}f'e'}{\pi_{NN}\pi_{wz} - \pi_{Nw}^2},$$

and the fraction in this expression is negative (the denominator is positive by the second-order conditions, while $\pi_{Nw} < 0$ and $f', e' > 0$).

Since $dw/dz > 1$, it follows from the chain rule that

$$\frac{de}{dz} = e'\left[\frac{dw}{dz} - 1\right] > 0,$$

$$\frac{dN}{dz} = \frac{-\pi_{wz} - \pi_{ww}\frac{dw}{dz}}{\pi_{wN}}$$

$$= \frac{\pi_{ww}}{\pi_{wN}}\left(1 - \frac{dw}{dz}\right) < 0 \qquad \text{[by (A14.3), (A14.4)]},$$

$$\frac{d\pi}{dz} = \frac{\partial\pi}{\partial w}\frac{dw}{dz} + \frac{\partial\pi}{\partial N}\frac{dN}{dz} + \frac{\partial\pi}{\partial z} = \frac{\partial\pi}{\partial z} = -f'e'N < 0.$$

14.4   Labor Discipline with Profit Signaling

b.   Treat w_H as a function of w_L, and differentiate the participation constraint, getting

$$p_h u'(w_H)\frac{dw_H}{dw_L} + (1 - p_h)u'(w_L) = 0.$$

Thus,

$$\frac{dw_H}{dw_L} = -\frac{1 - p_h}{p_h}\frac{u'(w_L)}{u'(w_H)} < -\frac{1 - p_h}{p_h} < 0. \qquad \text{(A14.5)}$$

The second inequality (which we use later) holds because $w_L < w_H$, so if the agent is strictly risk averse, u' is decreasing. The participation constraint is thus decreasing. Now take the derivative of equation (A14.5), getting

$$\frac{d^2 w_H}{dw_L^2} = -\frac{1 - p_h}{p_h} \left[\frac{u''(w_H)}{u'(w_H)} - \frac{u'(w_L)u''(w_H)}{u'(w_H)^2} \frac{dw_H}{dw_L} \right] > 0.$$

Thus, the participation constraint is convex.

c. We differentiate the incentive compatibility constraint $u(w_H) = u(w_L)$ + constant, getting

$$u'(w_H)\frac{dw_H}{dw_L} = u'(w_L),$$

so $dw_H/dw_L > 1 > 0$ and the incentive compatibility constraint is increasing. Differentiate again, getting

$$u''(w_H)\frac{dw_H}{dw_L} + u'(w_H)\frac{d^2 w_H}{dw_L^2} = u''(w_L).$$

Thus

$$u'(w_H)\frac{d^2 w_H}{dw_L^2} = u''(w_L) - u''(w_H)\frac{dw_H}{dw_L} < u''(w_L) - u''(w_H) < 0,$$

and the constraint is concave.

d. The slope of the iso-cost line is $|dw_H/dw_L| = (1 - p_h)/p_h$, which is less than the slope of the participation constraint, which is

$$|(1 - p_h)u'(w_L)/p_h u'(w_H)|,$$

by equation (A14.5).

14.5   Peasants and Landlords

a. First, w_H and w_L must satisfy a *participation constraint:* w_H and w_L must be sufficiently large that the peasant is willing to work at all. Suppose the peasant's next-best alternative gives utility z. Then the landowner must choose w_H and w_L so that the peasant's expected utility is at least z:

$$p_h u(w_H) + (1 - p_h)u(w_L) - d_h \geq z. \tag{PC}$$

Second, w_H and w_L must satisfy an *incentive compatibility constraint:* the payoff (i.e., the expected return) to the peasant for working hard must be at least as great as the payoff to not working hard. Thus, we must have

$$p_h u(w_H) + (1 - p_h)u(w_L) - d_h \geq p_l u(w_H) + (1 - p_l)u(w_L) - d_l.$$

We can rewrite this second condition as

$$[u(w_H) - u(w_L)](p_h - p_l) \geq d_h - d_l. \qquad \text{(ICC)}$$

b. The problem is to minimize $p_h w_H + (1 - p_h)w_L$ subject to PC and ICC. This is the same as maximizing $-p_h w_H - (1 - p_h)w_L$ subject to the same constraints, so we form the Lagrangian

$$\begin{aligned}
\mathcal{L}(w_H, w_L, \lambda, \mu) = &-p_h w_H - (1 - p_h)w_L \\
&+ \lambda[p_h u(w_H) + (1 - p_h)u(w_L) - d_h - z] \\
&+ \mu[(u(w_H) - u(w_L))(p_h - p_l) - (d_h - d_l)].
\end{aligned}$$

The first-order conditions can be written:

$$\mathcal{L}_H = 0, \mathcal{L}_L = 0, \qquad \lambda, \mu \geq 0;$$

if $\lambda > 0$ then the PC holds with equality;

if $\mu > 0$, then the ICC holds with equality.

But we have

$$\begin{aligned}
\mathcal{L}_H &= -p_h + \lambda p_h u'(w_H) + \mu u'(w_H)(p_h - p_l) = 0, \\
\mathcal{L}_L &= -1 + p_h + \lambda(1 - p_h)u'(w_L) - \mu u'(w_L)(p_h - p_l) = 0.
\end{aligned}$$

We show that $\lambda = 0$ is impossible. Assume the contrary, so $\lambda = 0$. Then, by adding the two first-order conditions, we get

$$\mu(u'(w_H) - u'(w_L))(p_h - p_l) = 1,$$

which implies $u'(w_H) > u'(w_L)$, so $w_H < w_L$ (by declining marginal utility of income). This is, of course, silly, since the peasant will not want to work hard if the wage given high profits is less than the wage given low profits! More formally, ICC implies $u(w_H) > u(w_L)$, so $w_H > w_L$. It follows that our assumption that $\lambda = 0$ was contradictory and hence $\lambda > 0$. So PC holds as an equality.

   We now show that $\mu = 0$ is impossible. Assume the contrary, so $\mu = 0$. Then the first-order conditions $\mathcal{L}_H = 0$ and $\mathcal{L}_L = 0$ imply $u'(w_H) = 1/\lambda$ and $u'(w_L) = 1/\lambda$. Since $u'(w_H) = u'(w_L) = 1/\lambda$, $w_H = w_L$ (because u' is strictly decreasing). This also is impossible by the ICC. Hence $\mu > 0$ and the ICC holds as an equality.

c. Now suppose the landlord has concave utility function v, with $v' > 0$ and $v'' < 0$. The peasant is risk neutral, so we can assume her utility function is $u(w, d) = w - d$, where w is income and d is effort. The assumption that high effort produces a surplus means that the following social optimality (SO) condition holds:

$$p_h H + (1 - p_h)L - d_h > p_l H + (1 - p_l)L - d_l,$$

or

$$(p_h - p_l)(H - L) > d_h - d_l. \tag{SO}$$

The landlord wants to maximize

$$p_h v(H - w_H) + (1 - p_h)v(L - w_L)$$

subject to the participation constraint

$$p_h w_H + (1 - p_h)w_L - d_h \geq z \tag{PC}$$

and the incentive compatibility constraint, which as before reduces to

$$(p_h - p_l)(w_h - w_L) \geq d_h - d_l. \tag{ICC}$$

We form the Lagrangian

$$\begin{aligned}
\mathcal{L} = &\; p_h v(H - w_H) + (1 - p_h)v(L - w_L) \\
&+ \lambda(p_h w_H + (1 - p_h)w_L - d_h - z) \\
&+ \mu((p_h - p_l)(w_h - w_L) - (d_h - d_l)),
\end{aligned}$$

so the first-order conditions are $\partial\mathcal{L}/\partial w_H = \partial\mathcal{L}/\partial w_L = 0$, $\lambda, \mu \geq 0$, $\lambda > 0$ or the PC holds as an equality, and $\mu > 0$ or the ICC holds as an equality. The conditions $\partial\mathcal{L}/\partial w_H = \partial\mathcal{L}/\partial w_L = 0$ can be written as

$$\frac{\partial\mathcal{L}}{\partial w_H} = -p_h v'(H - w_H) + \lambda p_h + \mu(p_h - p_l) = 0 \tag{FOC1}$$

$$\mu(p_h - p_l) = 0. \qquad\qquad \text{(FOC2)}$$

We first show that the PC holds as an equality by showing that $\lambda = 0$ is impossible. Suppose $\lambda = 0$. Then (FOC) gives

$$-p_h v'(H - w_H) + \mu(p_h - p_l) = 0$$
$$-(1 - p_h)v'(L - w_L) - \mu(p_h - p_l) = 0.$$

If $\mu > 0$, this says that $v'(L - w_L) < 0$, which is impossible. If $\mu = 0$, this says that $v'(L - w_L) = 0$, which is also impossible. Thus, $\lambda = 0$ is impossible, and the PC holds as an equality.

Now we can rewrite FOC1 and FOC2 as

$$v'(H - w_H) - \lambda = \mu(p_h - p_l)/p_h \qquad\qquad \text{(A14.6)}$$
$$v'(L - w_L) - \lambda = -\mu(p_h - p_l)/(1 - p_h). \qquad\qquad \text{(A14.7)}$$

If $\mu > 0$, then $v'(H - w_H) > v'(L - w_L)$, so $H - w_H < L - w_L$; or $H - L < w_H - w_L$. But $\mu > 0$ implies that the ICC holds as an equality, so $(p_h - p_l)(w_H - w_L) = d_h - d_l$, and $d_h - d_l < (p_h - p_l)(H - L)$ from SO, implying $H - L > w_H - w_L$. This is a contradiction and hence $\mu = 0$; i.e., there is no optimum in which the ICC holds as an equality!

What is an optimum? Well, if $\mu = 0$, equations (A14.6) and (A14.7) imply that $H - w_h = L - w_L$, since v' is strictly increasing (because the landlord is risk averse). This means the landlord gets a fixed rent, which proves the theorem.

14.6   Mr. Smith's Car Insurance

a. If he is careful, the value is $(1/2)\ln(1201) - \epsilon$, and if he is careless the value is $(1/4)\ln(1201)$. Being careful is worthwhile as long as $(1/2)\ln(1201) - \epsilon \geq (1/4)\ln(1201)$, or $\epsilon \leq \ln(1201)/4 = 1.77$.

b. If he buys the insurance, his utility is $\ln(1201 - x)$ if he is careless, and $\ln(1201 - x) - \epsilon$ if he is careful. Thus, he will not be careful. The probability of theft is then 75%, and since the insurance company must give a fair lottery to Mr. Smith, $x = (0.75)1200 = 900$.

c. The expected value of the car plus insurance is $\ln(1201 - 900) = \ln(301) = 5.707$.

d. This is preferable to being careless without insurance, which has value

$$(1/4)\ln(1201) = 1.77.$$

The value of being careful without insurance has value $(1/2)\ln(1201) - \epsilon < (1/2)\ln(1201) = 3.55$, so Mr. Smith should buy the insurance policy whether or not he would be careful without it.

e. Since Mr. Smith is careful without insurance, we know $\epsilon \leq 1.77$. Since the insurance company's lottery is fair, we have $x = (1200 - z)/2 = 600 - z/2$ if Mr. Smith is careful, and $x = 3(1200 - z)/4 = 900 - 3z/4$ if Mr. Smith is careless. If Mr. Smith is careless, the value of car plus insurance is

$$\frac{1}{4}\ln(1201 - x) + \frac{3}{4}\ln(1201 - z - x)$$

$$= \frac{1}{4}\ln\left(301 + \frac{3z}{4}\right) + \frac{3}{4}\ln\left(301 - \frac{z}{4}\right).$$

The derivative of this with respect to z is

$$(3/16)/(301 + 3z/4) - (3/16)/(301 - z/4) < 0,$$

so the optimal deductible is zero. Then $x = 900$, and the value of car plus insurance is $\ln(1201 - 900) = \ln(301)$. If Mr. Smith is careful, then the value of car plus insurance is

$$\frac{1}{2}\ln(1201 - x) + \frac{1}{2}\ln(1201 - z - x)$$

$$= \frac{1}{2}\ln\left(601 + \frac{z}{2}\right) + \frac{1}{2}\ln\left(601 - \frac{z}{2}\right).$$

The derivative of this with respect to z is $(1/8)/(601 + z/2) - (1/8)/(601 - z/2) < 0$, so again the optimal deductible is zero. But z must be sufficiently large that Mr. Smith wants to be careful, or the insurance company will not be willing to issue the insurance at the low rate $x = 600 - z/2$. To make taking care worthwhile, we must have

$$\frac{1}{2}\ln\left(601 - \frac{z}{2}\right) + \frac{1}{2}\ln\left(601 - \frac{z}{2}\right) - \epsilon$$

$$\geq \frac{1}{4}\ln\left(601 + \frac{z}{2}\right) + \frac{3}{4}\ln\left(601 - \frac{z}{2}\right),$$

$\ln(601 + z/2) - \ln(601 - z/2) \geq 4\epsilon$. The minimum z satisfying this is when the equality holds, and we have

$$z = \frac{4(e^{4\epsilon} - 1)}{e^{4\epsilon} + 1} > 0.$$

f. With insurance, the expected value of the lottery for Mr. Smith is unchanged, but the risk has decreased. Since he is risk averse, he is better off with the insurance than without.

14.7   A Generic One-Shot Principal-Agent Game

a. Intuitively, we argue as follows. Suppose the principal wants to induce the agent to choose action a_k. If the participation constraint is not binding, we can reduce all the payments $\{w_{kj}\}$ by a small amount without violating either the participation or the incentive compatibility constraints. Moreover, if all of the incentive compatibility constraints are nonbinding, then the payoff system $\{w_{kj}\}$ is excessively risky, in the sense that the various $\{w_{kj}\}$ can be "compressed" around their expected value without violating the incentive compatibility constraint.

Formally, we form the Lagrangian,

$$\mathcal{L} = \pi(a_k) - \mathbf{E}_k w_k + \lambda[\mathbf{E}_k u(w_k) - d(a_k) - u_o]$$
$$+ \sum_{\substack{i=1 \\ i \neq k}}^{n} \mu_i \{[\mathbf{E}_k u(w_k) - d(a_k)] - [\mathbf{E}_i u(w_k) - d(a_i)]\},$$

where $\mathbf{E}_i$ means take the expectation with respect to probabilities $\{p_{i1}, \ldots, p_{im}\}$, λ is the Lagrangian multiplier for the participation constraint, and μ_i is the Lagrangian multiplier for the ith incentive compatibility constraint. Writing the expectations out in full (in "real life" you wouldn't do this, but it's valuable for pedagogical purposes), we get

$$\mathcal{L} = \pi(a_k) - \sum_{j=1}^{m} p_{kj} w_{kj} + \lambda \left[\sum_{j=1}^{m} p_{kj} u(w_{kj}, a_k) - u_o \right]$$
$$+ \sum_{i=1}^{n} \mu_i \left[\sum_{j=1}^{m} p_{kj} u(w_{kj}, a_k) - \sum_{j=1}^{m} p_{ij} u(w_{kj}, a_i) \right].$$

The Kuhn-Tucker conditions for the problem assert that at a maximum,

1. $\frac{\partial \mathcal{L}}{\partial w_{kj}} = 0$ for $j = 1, \ldots, m$.

2. $\lambda, \mu_1, \ldots, \mu_n \geq 0$.

3. If $\lambda > 0$, then the participation constraint is binding (i.e., holds as an equality).

4. If $\mu_i > 0$ for some $i = 1, \ldots, n$, then the incentive compatibility constraint holds for action a_i.

In our case, we have

$$\frac{\partial \mathcal{L}}{w_{kj}} = -p_{kj} + \lambda p_{kj} u'(w_{kj}, a_k)$$

$$+ \sum_{i=1}^{n} \mu_i (p_{kj} - p_{ij}) u'(w_{kj}, a_k) = 0 \quad j = 1, \ldots, m.$$

Collecting terms, we have, for $j = 1, \ldots, m$,

$$\lambda p_{kj} + \sum_{i=1}^{n} \mu_i (p_{kj} - p_{ij}) = \frac{p_{kj}}{u'(w_{kj}, a_k)}. \tag{A14.8}$$

Now we sum this equation from $j = 1$ to m, noting that $\sum_j p_{ij} = 1$ for all i, getting

$$\lambda = \sum_{j=1}^{m} \frac{p_{kj}}{u'(w_{kj}, a_k)} > 0,$$

which proves that the participation constraint is binding.

1. To see that at least one incentive compatibility constraint is binding, suppose all the μ_i are zero. Then equation (A14.8) gives $\lambda = 1/u'(w_{kj}, a_k)$ for all j. If the agent is risk averse, this implies all the w_{kj} are equal (since risk aversion implies strictly concave preference, which implies strictly monotonic marginal utility), which means a_k must be the agent's most preferred action.

2. If the parties could write an enforceable contract, then only the participation constraint would be relevant. To induce the agent to perform a_i, the principal would pay w_i^*, where $u(w_i^*, a_i) = u_0$. The principal will then choose action a_l such that $\pi(a_l) - w_l^*$ is a

maximum.

Suppose the optimal action when no contract can be written is a_k, and the wage structure is $w_k(s)$. The participation constraint is binding, so $\mathbf{E}_k u(w_k) = d(a_k) + u_0$. Since a_k is not the agent's unconstrained preferred action (by assumption), $w_k(s)$ is not constant, and since the agent is strictly risk averse, we have

$$u(w_k^*, a_k) = u_0 = \mathbf{E}u(w_k, a_k) < u(\mathbf{E}_k w_k, a_k),$$

so $w_k^* < \mathbf{E}_k w_k$. Since $\pi(a_l) - w_l^* \geq \pi(a_k) - w_k^* > \pi(a_k) - \mathbf{E}_k w_k$, we are done.

b. Suppose again that a_l is the principal's optimal choice when an enforceable contract can be written. Then a_l maximizes $\pi(a_i) - w_i^*$ where $u(w_i^*, a_i) = u_0$. If the agent is risk neutral, suppose the agent receives $\pi(a)$ and pays the principal the fixed amount $\pi(a_l) - w_l^*$. We can assume $u(w, a) = w + d(a)$ (why?). The agent then maximizes

$$\pi(a_i) - d(a_i) = u(\pi(a_i)) - u(w_i^*) - u_0$$
$$= \pi(a_i) - w_i^* - u_0,$$

which of course occurs when $i = l$. This proves the theorem. Q.E.D.

15

Bargaining

15.2 The Nash Bargaining Model

Let $x = u(\pi_1^o)$ and $y = v(\pi_2^o)$. We maximize $(u(\pi_1) - x)(v(\pi_2) - y)$ subject to $g(\pi_1, \pi_2) = 0$. The solution turns out to depend directly on the second-order conditions for constrained maximization. We form the Lagrangian

$$\mathcal{L}(\pi_1, \pi_2, \lambda) = (u(\pi_1) - x)(v(\pi_2) - y) - \lambda g(\pi_1, \pi_2).$$

The first-order conditions for this constrained optimization problem are then

$$\mathcal{L}_{\pi_1} = u'(\pi_1)(v(\pi_2) - y) - \lambda g_{\pi_1} = 0$$
$$\mathcal{L}_{\pi_2} = v'(\pi_2)(u(\pi_1) - x) - \lambda g_{\pi_2} = 0.$$

Now let's differentiate the two first-order conditions and the constraint $g(\pi_1, \pi_2) = 0$ totally with respect to player 1's fallback x:

$$\mathcal{L}_{\pi_1\pi_1}\frac{d\pi_1}{dx} + \mathcal{L}_{\pi_1\pi_2}\frac{d\pi_2}{dx} + \mathcal{L}_{\pi_1\lambda}\frac{d\lambda}{dx} + \mathcal{L}_{\pi_1 x} = 0$$

$$\mathcal{L}_{\pi_2\pi_1}\frac{d\pi_1}{dx} + \mathcal{L}_{\pi_2\pi_2}\frac{d\pi_2}{dx} + \mathcal{L}_{\pi_2\lambda}\frac{d\lambda}{dx} + \mathcal{L}_{\pi_2 x} = 0$$

$$g_{\pi_1}\frac{d\pi_1}{dx} + g_{\pi_2}\frac{d\pi_2}{dx} = 0.$$

Now $\mathcal{L}_{\pi_1 x} = 0$, $\mathcal{L}_{\pi_2 x} = -v'(\pi_2)$, so we have

$$\begin{bmatrix} \mathcal{L}_{\pi_1\pi_1} & \mathcal{L}_{\pi_1\pi_2} & -g_{\pi_1} \\ \mathcal{L}_{\pi_2\pi_1} & \mathcal{L}_{\pi_2\pi_2} & -g_{\pi_2} \\ -g_{\pi_1} & -g_{\pi_2} & 0 \end{bmatrix} \begin{bmatrix} \dfrac{d\pi_1}{dx} \\ \dfrac{d\pi_2}{dx} \\ \dfrac{d\lambda}{dx} \end{bmatrix} = \begin{bmatrix} 0 \\ v'(\pi_2) \\ 0 \end{bmatrix}$$

Note that the matrix is the bordered Hessian of the problem, which has positive determinant D by the second-order conditions. If we solve for $d\pi_1/dx$ by using Cramer's rule, we get $d\pi_1/dx = g_{\pi_1}g_{\pi_2}v'/D$. The first-order conditions imply that g_{π_1} and g_{π_2} have the same sign, so $d\pi_1/dx > 0$.

15.3 Risk Aversion and the Nash Bargaining Solution

Suppose first that $v(x) = h(u(x))$, where h is concave. Then

$$v'(x) = h'(u(x))u'(x)$$

and

$$v''(x) = h''(u(x))u'^2(x) + h'(u(x))u''(x),$$

so

$$\lambda_v(x) = \lambda_u(x) - \frac{h''(u(x))u'(x)}{h'(u(x))} > \lambda_u(x).$$

Thus, $v(x)$ is uniformly more risk averse than $u(x)$.

Now assume $v(x)$ is uniformly more risk averse than $u(x)$. Since u is monotone increasing, u^{-1} exists, so we may define $h(y) = v(u^{-1}(y))$. Clearly, $h(0) = 0$. Also, $h(y)$ is increasing, since the identity $u(u^{-1}(y)) = y$ implies

$$\frac{d}{dy}u^{-1}(y) = \frac{1}{u'(u^{-1}(y))},$$

and hence,

$$\frac{dh}{dy} = \frac{d}{dy}v(u^{-1}(y)) = \frac{v'(u^{-1}(y))}{u'(u^{-1}(y))} > 0.$$

Differentiating again, we get

$$\frac{d^2h}{dy^2} = \frac{\lambda_u(u^{-1}(y)) - \lambda_v(u^{-1}(y))}{v'(u^{-1}(y))u'^2(u^{-1}(y))} < 0,$$

where the last inequality follows from the fact that $v(x)$ is more risk averse than $u(x)$.

15.4 Rubinstein Bargaining with Outside Options

a. Let π_s be the present value of not bargaining and simply waiting for the outside option to occur. Then we have the recursive equation $\pi_s = ps + (1 - p)\delta\pi_s$, which gives the desired result.

b. From the argument of §5.6, we know the proposed pair of strategies is a subgame perfect Nash equilibrium, as long as neither agent has an incentive to seek the outside option. Seeking the outside option for player i is a best response if and only if $ps_i + (1 - p)\delta\pi_1 \geq \delta\pi_1$, which reduces to $s_i \geq \delta/(1 + \delta)$, which is false by assumption.

c. Player 1's strategy as respondent is to reject an offer if and only if it is less than $\delta\pi_1$ and as proposer, to offer $1 - \pi_1$. Suppose player 2 seeks the outside option at A'. Then at B, player 2 must offer $\delta\pi_1$, and hence gets $1 - \delta\pi_1$. The value of this at A is $\delta(1 - \delta\pi_1)$. Thus, the expected payoff to player 2 at A' is $ps_2 + (1 - p)\delta(1 - \delta\pi_1)$. It is easy to check that this is just $1 - \pi_1$, so player 2 does no better by deviating in this manner. The only other possibility is that player 2 rejects at A'. This is better than seeking the outside option only if $s_2 > \delta(1 - \delta\pi_1)$. However, it is easy to check that this inequality is equivalent to $\delta > (1 + \delta)s_2$, which is false by assumption. This proves that player 2 cannot improve with a single deviation. Can player 1 improve by deviating? Clearly, he can gain by offering more at A only if he takes the outside option at B'. But the assumption $s_1 < \delta\pi_1$ means that this is not profitable.

d. The strategies and payoffs starting at B are the same as in the previous part, with subscripts 1 and 2 interchanged. Therefore, player 1 must offer $\delta\pi^*$ and hence receives $\pi_1 = 1 - \delta\pi^*$, where $\pi^* = (1 - (1 - p)\delta - ps_1)/(1 - (1 - p)\delta^2)$. This reduces to the desired expression.

e. Given the inequalities on s_1 and s_2, it is clear that seeking the outside option is better than rejecting. Can player 2 do better by seeking the outside offer? At C, player 1 gets π_1, so he must be offered $ps_1 + (1 - p)\delta\pi_1$ at B, so player 2 gets $1 - ps_1 - (1 - p)\delta\pi_1$ at B. The value of this at A' is thus $ps_2 + (1 - p)\delta(1 - ps_1 - (1 - p)\delta\pi_1)$, which must be greater than $1 - \pi_1$. But it is equal to π_1, as simple algebra shows, so player 2 cannot gain by deviating. This also shows that player 1 cannot offer less than $1 - \pi_1$, so neither player can gain by deviating.

15.6   Rubinstein Bargaining and Nash Bargaining

The game tree is as follows.

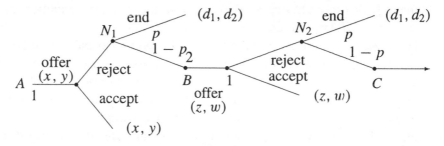

Let x be the maximum payoff to agent 1 at C. Then the maximum payoff to agent 1 at N_2 is $pd_1 + (1 - p)x$, so agent 2 must offer agent 1 at least $\delta(pd_1 + (1 - p)x)$ at B, so the minimum share of agent 2 at B is $g(\delta(pd_1 + (1 - p)x))$. Thus, the minimum share of agent 2 at N_1 is $(1 - p)g(\delta(pd_1 + (1 - p)x)) + pd_2$, so agent 1 must offer agent 2 at least

$$\delta(1 - p)g(\delta(pd_1 + (1 - p)x)) + \delta pd_2$$

at A'. Thus, the maximum agent 1 can get at A is

$$g^{-1}(\delta(1 - p)g(\delta(pd_1 + (1 - p)x)) + \delta pd_2).$$

This must equal x, so we have

$$\delta(1 - p)g(\delta(pd_1 + (1 - p)x)) + \delta pd_2 = g(x).$$

The solution to this equation is the Rubinstein bargaining equilibrium. If we let $\delta = 1$, this becomes

$$(1 - p)g(pd_1 + (1 - p)x) + pd_2 = g(x),$$

which we can rewrite as

$$(1 - p)\frac{g(x + p(d_1 - x)) - g(x)}{p(d_1 - x)} = \frac{g(x) - d_2}{d_1 - x}.$$

If we take the limit as $p \to 0$, this becomes

$$g(x) = d_2 - g'(x)(x - d_1).$$

But this is just the solution to the Nash bargaining problem

$$\max_x (x - d_1)(g(x) - d_2),$$

as can be seen by differentiating this function and setting it to zero.

15.7 Zeuthen Lotteries and the Nash Bargaining Solution

Suppose the theorem is false, and there are $s, s^* \in S$ such that s^* is a Zeuthen equilibrium, but

$$(u_1(s) - u_1(d))(u_2(s) - u_2(d)) > (u_1(s^*) - u_1(d))(u_2(s^*) - u_2(d)).$$

Then either $u_1(s) > u_1(s^*)$ or $u_2(s) > u_2(s^*)$; assume the former. Let $p^* = (u_1(s^*) - u_1(d))/(u_1(s) - u_1(d))$, so $0 \le p^* < 1$, and define $p_\epsilon = p^* + \epsilon$ for $0 < \epsilon < 1 - p^*$. Then $p_\epsilon(u_1(s) - u_1(d)) > u_1(s^*) - u_1(d)$ so $p_\epsilon u_1(s) + (1 - p_\epsilon)u_1(d) > u_1(s^*)$, which means that the expected utility from (p_ϵ, s) is greater than the (expected) utility from s; i.e., $(p_\epsilon, s) \succ_1 s$. By assumption, this means that $(p_\epsilon, s^*) \succeq_2 s$. In expected utility terms, this becomes $p_\epsilon u_2(s^*) + (1 - p_\epsilon)u_2(d) \ge u_2(s)$, or $p_\epsilon(u_2(s^*) - u_2(d)) \ge u_2(s) - u_2(d)$. Since this is true for arbitrarily small $\epsilon > 0$, it is true for $\epsilon = 0$, giving $p^*(u_2(s^*) - u_2(d)) \ge u_2(s) - u_2(d)$. But by the definition of p^*, we then have $((u_1(s^*) - u_1(d))/(u_1(s) - u_1(d)))(u_2(s^*) - u_2(d)) \ge u_2(s) - u_2(d)$, or $(u_1(s^*) - u_1(d))(u_2(s^*) - u_2(d)) \ge (u_1(s) - u_1(d))(u_2(s) - u_2(d))$, which contradicts our assumption.

15.8 Bargaining with Fixed Costs

a. Clearly, Mutt cannot do better by deviating. Suppose Jeff deviates on some round and then returns to his prescribed behavior. If any round other than the first is involved, Jeff cannot improve his payoff, because the game is already terminated! To deviate on the first round, Jeff must reject. This costs him c_2. He returns to his prescribed strategy by offering Mutt $1 - c_1$, which Mutt accepts. This leaves Jeff with $c_1 - c_2 < 0$, so Jeff is worse off.

b. Let l_2 be the least Jeff can get in any subgame perfect Nash equilibrium when he goes first. Since Mutt can get m_1 when it is his turn, Jeff must offer Mutt at most $m_1 - c_1$, which leaves Jeff with at least $l_1 = 1 - m_1 + c_1 \le 1$. Suppose $l_1 \ge c_2$. The most that Mutt can make is then $1 - (l_1 - c_2)$, so

$$m_1 = 1 - (l_1 - c_2) = m_1 - c_1 + c_2,$$

which implies $c_1 = c_2$, which is false. If $l_1 < c_2$, then Mutt offers Jeff 0, and $m_1 = 1$, which is also a contradiction.

c. In this case, $l_2 = 1$, since Jeff can offer Mutt zero when it is Jeff's turn. But then Mutt can offer Jeff $1 - c_2$, so Mutt earns at least $c_2 > c_1$, which is a contradiction.

15.9   Bargaining with Incomplete Information

a. The seller chooses p_2 to maximize

$$p\mathrm{P}\left[v > p\right] = p\mathrm{P}\left[\frac{v}{v_2} > \frac{p}{v_2}\right] = p\left(1 - \frac{p}{v_2}\right),$$

from which the result follows by setting the derivative to zero and solving for p_2.

b. If $v \geq p_2$, the buyer will accept the second-round offer, earning $v - p_2$, which is worth $\delta(v - p_2)$ in the first period. The buyer thus rejects the first offer if and only if $v - p_1 < \delta(v - p_2)$, which gives us the desired condition. If $v < p_2$, p_1 is accepted if and only if $v \geq p_1$.

c. Suppose $v \geq p_1$ or $v \geq p_2$. If p_1 is rejected, then $v < (p_1 - \delta p_2)/(1-\delta)$, and since $p_2 = v_2/2$, we can solve for v_2.

d. Suppose $v \geq p_1$ or $v \geq p_2$. The payoff to the seller from offering p in the first period is

$$p\mathrm{P}\left[v - p \geq \delta\left(v - \frac{p}{2 - \delta}\right)\right].$$

This evaluates directly to $p(1 - 2p/v_1(2 - \delta))$, which achieves its maximum when $p = v_1(2 - \delta)/4$. The rest follows by substitution.

16

Probability and Decision Theory

16.5   Probability as Frequency

16.6   Sampling

We do only part b. *A* die has six possible numbers. Throwing six dice is like sampling one die six times with replacement. Thus, there are $6^6 \times 6 = 46656$ ordered configurations of the 6 dice. There are 6 outcomes in which all the faces are the same. Thus, the probability is $6/46656 = 0.0001286$.

16.8   Social Isolation

There are n^r equiprobable arrangements of passengers in cars; i.e., the number of ordered samples with replacement. By assigning different passengers to different cars, we are looking at the subset of ordered samples without replacement (after one passenger enters a car, the car cannot be entered by another passenger). Thus, there are $n!/(n - r)!$ arrangements with no two passengers in the same car. The probability of the event $A = \{$no two passengers in the same car$\}$ is thus $P[A] = n!/(n - r)!n^r$.

16.9   Aces Up

There are 52 ways to choose the first card, and 51 ways to choose the second card. Since we don't care about the order of the choices, there are $52 \times 51/2 = 26 \times 51$ different ways to choose two cards from the deck. There are 4 ways to choose the first ace, and 3 ways to choose the second, and since we don't care about the order, there are $4 \times 3/2 = 6$ ways to choose a pair of aces. Thus, the probability of choosing a pair of aces is $6/(26 \times 51) = 1/(13 \times 17) = 1/221 = 0.0045248 = 0.45248\%$.

16.10   Mechanical Defection

This is sampling 2 times without replacement from a set of 7 objects. There are $7!/(7-2)! = 7 \times 6 = 42$ such samples. How many of these are two non-defective machines? How many samples of two are there from a population of 5 (the number of non-defectives)? The answer is $5!/(5-2)! = 5 \times 4 = 20$. Thus, the probability is $20/42 = 0.4762$.

16.11   Double Orders

There are n^r equiprobable assignments of customers to firms; i.e., the number of ordered samples with replacement. By assigning different customers to different firms, we are looking at the subset of ordered samples without replacement (after a customer places an order with a firm, the firm cannot receive another order). Thus, there are $n!/(n-r)!$ arrangements with no two customers using the same firm. The probability of the event $A = \{$no two customers use the same firm$\}$ is thus $P[A] = n!/(n-r)!n^r$.

16.13   Mass Defection

The number of ways of selecting 10 items from a batch of 100 items equals the number of combinations of 100 things taken 10 at a time, which is $100!/10!90!$. If the batch is accepted, all of the 10 items must have been chosen from the 90 non-defective items. The number of such combinations of ten items is $90!/10!80!$. Thus, the probability of accepting the batch is

$$\frac{(90!/10!80!)}{(100!/10!90!)} = 90!90!/80!100!$$

$$= \frac{90 \times 89 \times \ldots \times 81}{100 \times 99 \times \ldots 91},$$

which is approximately 36.8%.

16.14   An Unlucky Streak

There are $\binom{n}{b}$ ways of choosing b items from a lot of n items. There are $\binom{k}{a}$ ways of choosing a items from the k defective items, and $\binom{n-k}{b-a}$ ways of picking the other $b - a$ good items from the $n - k$ good items. Thus, there are $\binom{k}{a}\binom{n-k}{b-a}$ ways of choosing a sample with exactly a defective items. The probability of choosing exactly a defective items is thus

$$\frac{\binom{k}{a}\binom{n-k}{b-a}}{\binom{n}{k}}.$$

Note that the probability of getting *at least* c defective items is the sum of the above expression for $a = c, a = c + 1, \ldots$

16.15 House Rules

Here is an equivalent game: you *ante* $1000 and choose a number. The house rolls the three dice, and pays you $2000 for one match, $3000 for two matches, and $4000 for three matches. The probability of one match is

$$\binom{3}{1}\frac{1}{6} \times \frac{5}{6} \times \frac{5}{6} = \frac{75}{216},$$

the probability of two matches is

$$\binom{3}{2}\frac{1}{6} \times \frac{1}{6} \times \frac{5}{6} = \frac{15}{216},$$

and the probability of three matches is $1/216$. The expected payoff is thus

$$2\frac{75}{216} + 3\frac{15}{216} + 4\frac{1}{216} = \frac{199}{216} = 0.9213$$

times $1000, or $921.30. Thus, you can expect to lose $78.70 every time you play.

16.16 The Powerball Lottery

The number of ways to pick the five white balls and the one red Powerball is

$$\binom{49}{5} = \frac{49 \times 48 \times 47 \times 46 \times 45}{5 \times 4 \times 3 \times 2} \times 42 = 80089128.$$

Thus, the probability of winning is $p = 1/80089128$. The probability of no winner in $n = 138500000$ tries is then

$$\left(1 - \frac{1}{80089128}\right)^{138500000} \approx 0.1774.$$

If your calculator chokes on this calculation, try the formula

$$(1 - p)^n = e^{n \ln(1-p)}.$$

Thus, the probability of at least one winner is 82.26%.

The probability that the first bettor wins and nobody else wins is $p(1 - p)^{n-1}$, and the probability that exactly one bettor wins is n times this, or

$$n \times p \times (1 - p)^{n-1} \approx 30.68\%.$$

16.18   Die, Die!

Let A be the event "the two dice are the same" and let B be the event "the two dice add up to eight." There are six ways the dice can be the same, so $P[A] = 6/36 = 1/6$. There are 5 ways the dice can add up to eight (2 and 6, 3 and 5, 4 and 4, 5 and 3, 6 and 2), so $P[B] = 5/36$. There is one way the dice can be the same and add up to eight (4 and 4), so $P[A \cap B] = 1/36$. Thus, $P[A \cup B] = 1/6 + 5/36 - 1/36 = 15/54 = 5/18$.

16.20   A Guessing Game

Suppose the first guess is k. This is correct with probability $1/n$, high with probability $(k-1)/n$, and low with probability $(n-k)/n$. Thus, the expected number of guesses given that the first guess is k is given by

$$f(n|k) = \frac{1}{n} + \frac{(k-1)[1 + f(k-1)]}{n} + \frac{(n-k)[1 + f(n-k)]}{n},$$

where $f(0) = 0$. But we also know that

$$f(n) = f(n|1)/n + \ldots + f(n|n)/n.$$

Thus, we have

$$f(n) = \frac{1}{n} + \sum_{k=1}^{n}(k-1)[1 + f(k-1)]/n^2 + \sum_{k=1}^{n}(n-k)[1 + f(n-k)]/n^2$$

$$= \frac{1}{n} + \sum_{k=1}^{n}[n - 1 + (k-1)f(k-1) + (n-k)f(n-k)]/n^2$$

$$= 1 + \frac{2}{n^2}\sum_{k=1}^{n-1}kf(k).$$

Let us solve this recursive equation. Note that

$$f(n) = 1 + \frac{2}{n^2}[f(1) + 2f(2) + \dots + (n-1)f(n-1)]$$

$$= 1 + \frac{2(n-1)}{n^2}f(n-1)$$

$$+ \frac{(n-1)^2}{n^2}\frac{2}{(n-1)^2}$$
$$\times[f(1) + 2f(2) + \dots + (n-2)f(n-2)]$$

$$= 1 + \frac{2(n-1)}{n^2}f(n-1) + \frac{(n-1)^2}{n^2}[f(n-1) - 1].$$

Collecting terms and rearranging a bit, we have

$$\frac{nf(n) - 3}{n+1} = \frac{(n-1)f(n-1) - 3}{n} + \frac{2}{n}.$$

If we write $g(n) = [nf(n) - 3]/(n+1)$, the last equation becomes

$$g(n) = g(n-1) + \frac{2}{n},$$

with $g(1) = [f(1) - 3]/2 = -1$. Thus,

$$g(n) = -3 + 2\sum_{k=1}^{n}k^{-1}.$$

Finally,

$$f(n) = \frac{n+1}{n}\left[-3 + 2\sum_{k=1}^{n}k^{-1}\right] + \frac{3}{n}.$$

We can approximate $f(n)$ for large n by noting that

$$\sum_{k=1}^{n}k^{-1} = \frac{3}{2} \approx \frac{3}{2} + \int_{3}^{n}\frac{dk}{k} = \frac{3}{2} + \ln\left(\frac{n}{3}\right).$$

Thus,

$$f(n) \approx \frac{n+1}{n}\ln\left(\frac{n}{3}\right) + \frac{3}{n} \approx \ln\left(\frac{n}{3}\right) \approx \ln(n).$$

for large n.

16.23   Drug Testing

We have $P[A] = 1/20$ and $P[\text{Pos}|A] = P[\text{Neg}|A^c] = 19/20$. Thus,

$$
\begin{aligned}
P[A|\text{Pos}] &= \frac{P[\text{Pos}|A]\,P[A]}{P[\text{Pos}|A]\,P[A] + P[\text{Pos}|A^c]\,P[A^c]} \\
&= \frac{P[\text{Pos}|A]\,P[A]}{P[\text{Pos}|A]\,P[A] + (1 - P[\text{Neg}|A^c])P[A^c]} \\
&= \frac{(19/20)(1/20)}{(19/20)(1/20) + (19/20)(1/20)} = 1/2.
\end{aligned}
$$

16.30   The Greens and the Blacks

Let A be the event "A bridge hand contains at least two aces." Let B be the event "A bridge hand contains at least one ace." Let C be the event "A bridge hand contains the ace of spades."

Then $P[A|B]$ is the probability that a hand contains two aces if it contains one ace and hence is the first probability sought. Also $P[A|C]$ is the probability a hand contains two aces if it contains the ace of spades, which is the second probability sought. By Bayes' Rule,

$$
P[A|B] = \frac{P[AB]}{P[B]} = \frac{P[A]}{P[B]},
$$

and

$$
P[A|C] = \frac{P[AC]}{P[C]}.
$$

Clearly, $P[C] = 0.25$, since all four hands are equally likely to get the ace of spades.

To calculate $P[B]$, note that the total number of hands with no aces is the number of ways to take 13 objects from 48 (the 52 cards minus the four aces), which is $\binom{48}{13}$.

The probability of a hand having at least one ace is then

$$
P[B] = \frac{\binom{52}{13} - \binom{48}{13}}{\binom{52}{13}} = 1 - \frac{39 \times 38 \times 37 \times 36}{52 \times 51 \times 50 \times 49} = 0.6962.
$$

The probability of at least two aces is the probability of at least one ace minus the probability of exactly one ace. We know the former, so let's calculate the latter.

The number of hands with exactly one ace is four times $\binom{48}{12}$, since you can choose the ace in one of four ways, and then choose any combination of 12 cards from the 48 non-aces. But

$$\frac{4 \times \binom{48}{12}}{\binom{52}{13}} = \frac{39 \times 38 \times 37}{51 \times 50 \times 49} \approx 0.4388,$$

which is the probability of having exactly one ace. The probability of at least two aces is thus

$$P[A] = .6962 - .4388 = .2574$$

(to four decimal places).

Now $P[AC]$ is the probability of two aces including the ace of spades. The number of ways to get the ace of spades plus one other ace is calculated as follows: take the ace of spades out of the deck, and form hands of twelve cards. The number of ways of getting no aces from the remaining cards is $\binom{48}{12}$, so the number of hands with one other ace is $\binom{51}{12} - \binom{48}{12}$. The probability of two aces including the ace of spades is thus

$$\frac{\binom{51}{12} - \binom{48}{12}}{\binom{52}{13}} = .1402.$$

Thus, $P[AC] = .1402$. We now have

$$P[A|C] = \frac{P[AC]}{P[C]} = \frac{.1402}{.25} = .5608 > \frac{P[AB]}{P[B]} = \frac{.2574}{.6962} = .3697.$$

16.31   Laplace's Law of Succession

Suppose there are n balls in the urn, and assume the number of white balls is uniformly distributed between 0 and n. Let A_k be the event "there are k white balls," and let B_{rm} be the event "of m balls chosen with replacement, r are white." Then $P[A_k] = 1/(n+1)$, and by Bayes' Rule we have

$$P[A_k|B_{rm}] = \frac{P[B_{rm}|A_k]P[A_k]}{P[B_{rm}]}.$$

Now it is easy to check that

$$P[B_{rm}|A_k] = \binom{m}{r}\left(\frac{k}{n}\right)^r\left(1 - \frac{k}{n}\right)^{m-r}$$

and

$$P[B_{rm}] = \sum_{k=0}^{n} P[A_k]P[B_{rm}|A_k]. \qquad (A16.1)$$

The probability of choosing a white ball on the next draw is then

$$\sum_{k=0}^{n}\left(\frac{k}{n}\right)P[A_k|B_{rm}] = \sum_{k=0}^{n}\frac{kP[B_{rm}|A_k]}{n(n+1)P[B_{rm}]}$$

$$= \frac{1}{(n+1)P[B_{rm}]}\binom{m}{r}\sum_{k=0}^{n}\left(\frac{k}{n}\right)^{r+1}\left(1 - \frac{k}{n}\right)^{m-r}.$$

To approximate this expression, note that if n is large, equation (16.1) is a Riemann sum representing the integral

$$P[B_{rm}] \approx \frac{1}{n+1}\binom{m}{r}\int_0^1 x^r(1 - x)^{m-r}$$

$$= \frac{1}{(n+1)(m+1)},$$

where the integral is evaluated by integration by parts r times. Replacing m by $m+1$ and r by $r+1$ in the above expression, we see that equation (A16.2) is approximately

$$\frac{1}{(n+1)P[B_{rm}]}\frac{m!}{r!(m-r)!}\frac{(r+1)!(m-r)!}{(m+2)(m+1)!} = \frac{r+1}{m+2}.$$

16.32   The Brain and Kidney Problem

Let A be the event "the jar contains two brains" and let B be the event "the mad scientist pulls out a brain." Then $P[A] = P[A^c] = 1/2$, $P[B|A] = 1$, and $P[B|A^c] = 1/2$. Then from Bayes' Rule, the probability that the remaining blob is a brain is $P[A|B]$, which is given by

$$P[A|B] = \frac{P[B|A]P[A]}{P[B|A]P[A] + P[B|A^c]P[A^c]} = \frac{1/2}{1/2 + (1/2)(1/2)} = 2/3.$$

16.33   Sexual Harassment on the Job

If you are harassed in the first 10 years, you will quit. The probability that this does *not* happen is $p_0 = (0.95)^{10} \simeq 0.598737$, so with probability $1 - p_0$ you will be harassed exactly once. After 10 years you will not quit if harassed, and since you remain for 20 more years, the expected number of harassments is one. The conclusion is that you expect to be harassed on the job exactly once.

16.34   The Value of Eyewitness Testimony

Let G be the event "Cab that hit JD was green," let B be the event "cab that his JD was blue," let WB be the event "witness records seeing blue cab," and finally, let WG be the event "witness records seeing green cab." We have $P[G] = 85/100 = 17/20$, $P[B] = 15/100 = 3/20$, $P[WG|G] = P[WB|B] = 4/5$, $P[WB|G] = P[WG|B] = 1/5$. Then Bayes' Rule yields

$$P[B|WB] = \frac{P[WB|B]P[B]}{P[WB|B]P[B] + P[WB|G]P[G]},$$

which evaluates to 12/29.

16.36   Bill and Harry

Let $A =$ "Bill's statement is true" and let $B =$ "Harry says Bill's statement is true." Also let $A^c =$ "Bill's statement is false." Then $P[A] = P[B] = 1/3$, and $P[A^c] = 2/3$. From Bayes' Rule,

$$P[A|B] = \frac{P[B|A]P[A]}{P[B|A]P[A] + P[B|A^c]P[A^c]}$$

$$= \frac{(1/3)(1/3)}{(1/3)(1/3) + (2/3)(2/3)} = \frac{1}{5},$$

so the probability that Bill's statement is true given Harry's affirmation is 20%.

16.37   When Weakness Is Strength

a.   Clearly, if c aims at anybody, it should be a. If c hits a, then his payoff is $\pi_c(bc)$. But clearly $\pi_c(bc) = \pi_c(cb)/5$, since b misses c with probability 1/5, and if he misses, it is c's turn to shoot. But

$$\pi_c(cb) = \frac{1}{2} + \frac{1}{2} \times \frac{1}{5}\pi_c(cb),$$

since either c wins immediately (with probability 1/2), or if he misses (with probability 1/2) he gets another turn with probability 1/5. This gives $\pi_c(cb) = 5/9$, so $\pi_c(bc) = 1/9$. We conclude that if c hits a, he survives with probability 1/9. What if c shoots in the air? Clearly, a will shoot at b rather than c, and b will shoot at a rather than c. Thus, a and b will trade shots until one is gone, and then it is c's turn to shoot. Suppose it is a who remains. Then the probability that c survives is $\pi_c(ca)$, which is clearly 1/2 (c shoots at a and if he misses, he loses the game). If b remains, the probability c wins is $\pi_c(cb)$, which we have already calculated to be 5/9. Since both 5/9 and 1/2 are greater than 1/9, c does much better by shooting in the air.

b.   Suppose first that a goes before b, so the order is cab or acb. Since c fires in the air, a will take out b for sure, so $\pi_c(cab) = \pi_c(acb) = 1/2$, since then c has exactly one chance to shoot at a. Also, $\pi_a(cab) = \pi_a(acb) = 1/2$ and $\pi_b(cab) = \pi_b(acb) = 0$. Now suppose b goes before a. Then b gets one shot at a, and hits with probability 4/5. Thus,

$$\pi_c(cba) = \pi_c(bca) = \frac{4}{5}\pi_c(cb) + \frac{1}{5}\pi_c(ca)$$

$$= \frac{4}{5} \times \frac{5}{9} + \frac{1}{5} \times \frac{1}{2}$$

$$= \frac{49}{90}.$$

Moreover, $\pi_a(cba) = \pi_a(bca) = (1/5)(1/2) = 1/10$, and $\pi_b(cba) = \pi_b(bca) = (4/5)(4/9) = 16/45$. We then have $\pi_a = (1/2)(1/2 + 1/10) = 3/10$, $\pi_b = (1/2)(16/45) = 8/45$, and $\pi_c = (1/2)(1/2 + 49/90) = 23.5/45$. Notice that $\pi_c > \pi_a > \pi_b$.

c.   If the marksman who shoots next is randomly chosen, it is still true that a and b will shoot at each other until only one of them remains. However, clearly c now prefers to have a one-on-one against b rather than against a, so c will shoot at a if given the chance. Now

$$\pi_a(ab) = \frac{1}{2} + \frac{1}{2} \times \frac{1}{5}\pi_a(ab),$$

so $\pi_a(ab) = 5/9$ and $\pi_b(ab) = 4/9$. Similar reasoning gives $\pi_a(ac) = 2/3$ and $\pi_c(ac) = 1/3$. Finally,

$$\pi_b(bc) = \frac{1}{2}\left(\frac{4}{5} + \frac{1}{5}\pi_b(bc)\right) + \frac{1}{2} \times \frac{1}{2}\pi_b(bc),$$

from which we conclude $\pi_b(bc) = 8/13$ and $\pi_c(bc) = 5/13$. Now clearly $\pi_a[a] = \pi_a(ac) = 2/3, \pi_b[a] = 0$, and $\pi_c[a] = 1/3$. Similarly, it is easy to check that

$$\pi_b[b] = (4/5)\pi_b(bc) + (1/5)\pi_b$$
$$\pi_a[b] = (1/5)\pi_a$$
$$\pi_c[b] = (4/5)pi_c(bc) + (1/5)\pi_c$$
$$\pi_c[c] = (1/2)\pi_c(bc) + (1/2)\pi_c$$
$$\pi_b[c] = (1/2)\pi_b(bc) + (1/2)\pi_b$$
$$\pi_a[c] = (1/2)\pi_a.$$

Moving to the final calculations, we have

$$\pi_b = \frac{1}{3}\left[0 + \frac{4}{5}\pi_b(bc) + \frac{1}{5}\pi_b + \frac{1}{2}\pi_b(bc) + \frac{1}{2}\pi_b\right].$$

We can solve this for π_b, getting $\pi_b = 24/69$. The similar equation for marksman a is

$$\pi_a = \frac{1}{3}\left[\frac{2}{3} + \frac{1}{5}\pi_a + \frac{1}{2}\pi_a\right],$$

which gives $\pi_a = 20/69$. Finally,

$$\pi_c = \frac{1}{3}\left[\frac{1}{3} + \frac{4}{5}\pi_c(bc) + \frac{1}{5}\pi_c + \frac{1}{2}\pi_c(bc) + \frac{1}{2}\pi_c\right],$$

which gives $\pi_c = 25/69$. Clearly, $\pi_c > \pi_b > \pi_a$, so the meek inherit the earth.

Sources for Problems

1.2, 13.11 (Rasmusen 1989); 2.4, 2.15 (Morrow 1994); 2.7, 2.10, 4.24, 4.25, 4.27, 4.28 (Dresher 1961); 2.13, 2.14, 3.8, 4.18, 5.5, 6.9 (Dixit and Nalebuff 1991); 3.20, 6.3, 12.3, 12.11 (Tirole 1988); 3.21, 5.15, 6.13, 13.10, 14.7 (Kreps 1990); 4.9, 4.11 (Moulin 1986); 4.15 (Arthur 1995); 4.16 (Sinervo and Lively 1996); 4.19 (Shachat and Walker 1997); 4.20, 4.23 (Vorob'ev 1977); 4.22 (Shubik 1984); 4.30 (Olcina 1997); 4.31, 4.32 (Weissing and Ostrom 1991); 4.34, 4.35 (Mesterton-Gibbons 1991); 4.36, 7.2 (van Damme 1991); 4.41 (Cho and Kreps 1987); 4.45, 12.9 (Myerson 1991); 5.15 (Selten 1975); 6.3 (Rotemberg and Saloner 1991); 6.14 (Bowles and Gintis 1993b); 6.15 (Bowles and Gintis 1993a); 6.16 (Gintis 1989); 7.2, 8.11, 8.12, 9.3, 9.4, 9.6, 9.7 (Hofbauer and Sigmund 1998); 7.3 (Bendor and Swistak 1995); 7.10 (Bishop and Cannings 1975), 7.13 (Axelrod 1984); 7.14 (Riley 1979); 8.15 (Guckenheimer and Holmes 1986); 9.2.2 (Binmore 1993); 9.5 (Weibull 1995); 9.14 (Schuster and Sigmund 1983); 9.18 (Güth and Kliemt 1994); 10.3 (Young 1998); 11.3.1 and 11.3.3 (Rabin 1998); 13.4 (Hammerstein and Reichert 1988); 13.5 (Kirkpatrick 1982); 13.6 (Alcock 1993; Grafen 1990a); 13.7 (Bergstrom and Lachmann 1997); 13.8 (Lachmann and Bergstrom 1998); 13.10 (Gibbons 1992); 15.2, 15.3, 15.8 (Osborne and Rubinstein 1990); 15.4 (Shaked and Sutton 1984); 16.16 (Laurie Snell, Chance News 7.05, May 1998); 16.15 (vos Savant December 27, 1998); 16.23 (Casscells, Schoenberger, and Grayboys 1978); 16.30 (vos Savant 1991); 16.34 (Bar-Hillel 1980); 16.35 (Gott 1993; Leslie 1996); 16.37 (Shubik 1954).

References

AINSLIE, G. 1975. "Specious Reward: A Behavioral Theory of Impulsiveness and Impulse Control." *Psychological Bulletin* 82: 463–496.

AINSLIE, G., AND N. HASLAM 1992. "Hyperbolic Discounting." In *Choice Over Time*, ed. G. Loewenstein and J. Elster, 57–92. New York: Russell Sage.

AIYAGARI, S. R., AND N. WALLACE 1991. "Existence of Steady States with Positive Consumption in the Kiyotaki-Wright Model." *Review of Economic Studies* 58, no. 5: 901–916.

——— 1992. "Fiat Money in the Kiyotaki-Wright Model." *Economic Theory* 2, no. 4: 447–464.

AKERLOF, G. A. 1970. "The Market for 'Lemons': Quality Uncertainty and the Market Mechanism." *Quarterly Journal of Economics* 84: 488–500.

——— 1982. "Labor Contracts as Partial Gift Exchange." *Quarterly Journal of Economics* 97, no. 4: 543–569.

ALCOCK, J. 1993. *Animal Behavior: An Evolutionary Approach.* Sunderland, MA: Sinauer.

ALLAIS, M. 1953. "Le comportement de l'homme rationnel devant le risque, critique des postulats et axiomes de l'école Américaine." *Econometrica* 21: 503–546.

ALTONJI, J. G., F. HAYACHI, AND L. J. KOTLIKOFF 1992. "Is the Extended Family Altruistically Linked?" *American Economic Review* 82: 1177–1198.

——— 1997. "Parental Altruism and Inter Vivos Transfers: Theory and Evidence." *Journal of Political Economy* 105: 1121–1166.

ANDREONI, J. 1988. "Why Free Ride? Strategies and Learning in Public Good Experiments." *Journal of Public Economics* 37: 291–304.

——— 1995. "Cooperation in Public Goods Experiments: Kindness or Confusion." *American Economic Review* 85, no. 4: 891–904.

ANDREONI, J., AND J. H. MILLER 1993. "Rational Cooperation in the Finitely Repeated Prisoner's Dilemma: Experimental Evidence." *Economic Journal* 103: 570–585.

ANSCOMBE, F., AND R. AUMANN 1963. "A Definition of Subjective Probability." *Annals of Mathematical Statistics* 34: 199–205.

ARROW, K. J. 1951. "An Extension of the Basic Theorems of Classical Welfare Economics." In *Proceedings of the Second Berkeley Symposium on Mathematical*

Statistics and Probability, ed. J. Neyman, 507–532. Berkeley: University of California Press.

ARROW, K. J., AND F. HAHN 1971. *General Competitive Analysis*. San Francisco: Holden-Day.

ARTHUR, B. 1995. "Complexity in Economic and Financial Markets." Santa Fe, NM: Santa Fe Institute.

AUMANN, R., AND A. BRANDENBURGER 1995. "Epistemic Conditions for Nash Equilibrium." *Econometrica* 65, no. 5: 1161–80.

AUMANN, R. J. 1987a. "Correlated Equilibrium and an Expression of Bayesian Rationality." *Econometrica* 55: 1–18.

——— 1987b. "Game Theory." In *The New Palgrave: A Dictionary of Economics*, vol. 2, ed. J. Eatwell, M. Milgate, and P. Newman, 460–482. London: Macmillan.

AXELROD, R. 1984. *The Evolution of Cooperation*. New York: Basic Books.

AXELROD, R., AND W. D. HAMILTON 1981. "The Evolution of Cooperation." *Science* 211: 1390–1396.

BABCOCK, L., AND G. LOEWENSTEIN 1997. "Explaining Bargaining Impasse: The Role of Self-Serving Biases." *Journal of Economic Perspectives* 11: 109–126.

BABCOCK, L., G. LOEWENSTEIN, S. ISSACHAROFF, AND C. CAMERER 1995. "Biased Judgments of Fairness in Bargaining." *American Economic Review* 85: 1337–1342.

BABCOCK, L., G. LOEWENSTEIN, AND X. WANG 1995. "The Relationship between Uncertainty, the Contract Zone, and Efficiency in a Bargaining Experiment." *Journal of Economic Behavior and Organization* 27, no. 3: 475–485.

BALIKCI, A. 1970. *The Netsilik Eskimo*. New York: Natural History Press.

BANDURA, A. 1977. *Social Learning Theory*. Englewood Cliffs, NJ: Prentice Hall.

BANERJEE, A. V. 1992. "A Simple Model of Herd Behavior." *Quarterly Journal of Economics* 107: 797–817.

BAR-HILLEL, M. 1980. "The Base-rate Fallacy in Probability Judgments." *Acta Psychologica* 44: 211–233.

BARDHAN, P., S. BOWLES, AND H. GINTIS 2000. "Wealth Inequality, Credit Constraints, and Economic Performance." In *Handbook of Income Distribution*, ed. A. Atkinson and F. Bourguignon. Dortrecht: North-Holland.

BARONE, E. 1935. "The Ministry of Production in the Collectivist State." In *Collectivist Economic Planning*, ed. F. A. von Hayek, 245–290. London: Routledge.

BECKER, G. S. 1981. *A Treatise on the Family*. Cambridge, MA: Harvard University Press.

——— 1996. *Accounting for Tastes*. Cambridge, MA: Harvard University Press.

BECKER, G. S., AND C. B. MULLIGAN 1997. "The Endogenous Determination of Time Preference." *Quarterly Journal of Economics* 112, no. 3: 729–759.

BECKER, G. S., AND K. M. MURPHY 1988. "A Theory of Rational Addiction." *Journal of Political Economy* 96, no. 4: 675–700.

BENDOR, J., AND P. SWISTAK 1995. "Types of Evolutionary Stability and the Problem of Cooperation." *Proc. Natl. Acad. Sci. USA* 92: 3596–3600.

BENKMAN, C. W. 1988. "Flock Size, Food Dispersion, and the Feeding Behavior of Crossbills." *Behavioral Ecology and Sociobiology* 23: 167–175.

BERGSTROM, C. T., AND M. LACHMANN 1997. "Signalling among Relatives. I. Is Signalling *Too* Costly?" *Phil. Trans. R. Soc. Lond. B* 352: 609–617.

BIKHCHANDANI, S., D. HIRSHLEIFER, AND I. WELSH 1992. "A Theory of Fads, Fashion, Custom, and Cultural Change as Informational Cascades." *Journal of Political Economy* 100: 992–1026.

BINMORE, K. 1993. *Game Theory and the Social Contract: Playing Fair*. Cambridge, MA: MIT Press.

——— 1998. *Game Theory and the Social Contract: Just Playing*. Cambridge, MA: MIT Press.

——— 1999. "Why Experiment in Economics?" *Economic Journal* 109: F16–F24.

BISHOP, D. T., AND C. CANNINGS 1975. "A Generalized War of Attrition." *Journal of Theoretical Biology* 70: 85–124.

BLOUNT, S. 1995. "When Social Outcomes Aren't Fair: The Effect of Causal Attributions on Preferences." *Organizational Behavior & Human Decision Processes* 63, no. 2: 131–144.

BLURTON-JONES, N. G. 1987. "Tolerated Theft: Suggestions about the Ecology and Evolution of Sharing, Hoarding, and Scrounging." *Social Science Information* 26, no. 1: 31–54.

BOEHM, C. 1982. "The Evolutionary Development of Morality as an Effect of Dominance Behavior and Conflict Interference." *Journal of Social and Biological Structures* 5: 413–421.

——— 1993. "Egalitarian Behavior and Reverse Dominance Hierarchy." *Current Anthropology* 34, no. 3: 227–254.

BOWLES, S. 1985. "The Production Process in a Competitive Economy: Walrasian, Neo-Hobbesian, and Marxian Models." *American Economic Review* 75, no. 1: 16–36.

BOWLES, S., R. BOYD, E. FEHR, AND H. GINTIS 1997. "Homo Reciprocans: A Research Initiative on the Origins, Dimensions, and Policy Implications of Reciprocal Fairness." Research Proposal, University of Massachusetts.

BOWLES, S., AND H. GINTIS 1992. "Power and Wealth in a Competitive Capitalist Economy." *Philosophy and Public Affairs* 21, no. 4: 324–353.

——— 1993a. "The Democratic Firm: An Agency-Theoretic Evaluation." In *Democracy and Markets: Participation, Accountability, and Efficiency*, ed. S. Bowles, H. Gintis, and B. Gustafsson. Cambridge, UK: Cambridge University Press.

——— 1993b. "The Revenge of Homo Economicus: Contested Exchange and the Revival of Political Economy." *Journal of Economic Perspectives* 7, no. 1: 83–102.

BOYD, R. 1989. "Mistakes Allow Evolutionary Stability in the Repeated Prisoner's Dilemma Game." *Journal of Theoretical Biology* 136: 47–56.

BOYD, R., AND J. LORBERBAUM 1987. "No Pure Strategy Is Evolutionarily Stable in the Repeated Prisoner's Dilemma Game." *Nature* 327: 58–59.

BOYD, R., AND P. J. RICHERSON 1985. *Culture and the Evolutionary Process*. Chicago: University of Chicago Press.

——— 1990. "Group Selection among Alternative Evolutionarily Stable Strategies." *Journal of Theoretical Biology* 145: 331–342.

——— 1992. "Punishment Allows the Evolution of Cooperation (or Anything Else) in Sizeable Groups." *Ethology and Sociobiology* 113: 171–195.

BROWNING, E. K. 1997. "A Neglected Welfare Cost of Monopoly." *Journal of Public Economics* 66, no. 1: 127–144.

BUCHANAN, J. 1975. "The Samaritan's Dilemma." In *Altruism, Morality, and Economic Theory*, ed. E. S. Phelps. New York: Russell Sage.

BULMER, M. G. 1989. "Structural Stability in Models of Sexual Selection." *Theoretical Population Biology* 35: 195–206.

BYRNE, R., AND A. WHITEN 1988. *Machiavellian Intelligence: Social Expertise and the Evolution of Intellect in Monkeys, Apes, and Humans*. Oxford: Clarendon Press.

CAMERER, C., AND R. THALER 1995. "Ultimatums, Dictators, and Manners." *Journal of Economic Perspectives* 9, no. 2: 209–219.

CAMERON, L. 1995. "Raising the Stakes in the Ultimatum Game: Experimental Evidence from Indonesia." Discussion Paper no. 345, Department of Economics, Princeton University.

CASHDAN, E. A. 1980. "Egalitarianism among Hunters and Gatherers." *American Anthropologist* 82: 116–120.

CASSCELLS, W., A. SCHOENBERGER, AND T. GRAYBOYS 1978. "Interpretation by Physicians of Clinical Laboratory Results." *New England Journal of Medicine* 298: 999–1001.

CAVALLI-SFORZA, L. L., AND M. W. FELDMAN 1981. *Cultural Transmission and Evolution*. Princeton, NJ: Princeton University Press.

CHANG, W. W., D. HAMBERG, AND J. HIRATA 1983. "Liquidity Preference as Behavior toward Risk Is a Demand for Short-Term Securities—Not Money." *American Economic Review* 73, no. 3: 420–427.

CHICHILNISKY, G. 1997. "Market Arbitrage, Social Choice and the Core." *Social Choice and Welfare* 14, no. 2: 161–198.

CHO, I.-K., AND D. M. KREPS 1987. "Signalling Games and Stable Equilibria." *Quarterly Journal of Economics* 102, no. 2: 180–221.

CHUNG, S.-H., AND R. J. HERRNSTEIN 1967. "Choice and Delay of Reinforcement." *Journal of Experimental Analysis of Behavior* 10, no. 1: 67–74.

COLEMAN, J. S. 1988. "Free Riders and Zealots: The Role of Social Networks." *Sociological Theory* 6: 52–57.

COLMAN, A. M. 1995. *Game Theory and Its Applications in the Social and Biological Sciences*. Oxford: Butterworth-Heinemann Press.

COSMIDES, L., AND J. TOOBY 1992a. "Cognitive Adaptations for Social Exchange." In *The Adapted Mind: Evolutionary Psychology and the Generation of Culture*, ed. J. H. Barkow, L. Cosmides, and J. Tooby, 163–228. New York: Oxford University Press.

———— 1992b. "The Psychological Foundations of Culture." In *The Adapted Mind: Evolutionary Psychology and the Generation of Culture*, ed. J. H. Barkow, L. Cosmides, and J. Tooby, 19–136. New York: Oxford University Press.

COSMIDES, L., J. TOOBY, AND J. H. BARKOW 1992. "Introduction: Evolutionary Psychology and Conceptual Integration." In *The Adapted Mind: Evolutionary Psychology and the Generation of Culture*, ed. L. C. Jerome H. Barkow and J. Tooby, 3–15. New York: Oxford University Press.

COX, D. 1987. "Motives for Private Income Transfers." *Journal of Political Economy* 93: 508–546.

———— 1990. "Intergenerational Transfers and Liquidity Constraints." *Quarterly Journal of Economics* 105: 187–217.

COX, D., AND M. R. RANK 1992. "Inter-vivos Transfers and Intergenerational Exchange." *Review of Economics and Statistics* 74: 305–314.

DAHL, R. A. 1957. "The Concept of Power." *Behavioral Science* 2: 201–215.

DALY, M., AND M. WILSON 1983. *Sex, Evolution, and Behavior*. Boston, MA: Willard Grant Press.

DAMAS, D. 1972. "Central Eskimo Systems of Food Sharing." *Ethnology* 11, no. 3: 220–240.

DAMASIO, A. R. 1994. *Descartes' Error: Emotion, Reason, and the Human Brain*. New York: Avon Books.

DAVIS, D. D., AND C. A. HOLT 1993. *Experimental Economics*. Princeton, NJ: Princeton University Press.

DAWES, R. M., J. M. ORBELL, AND J. C. VAN DE KRAGT 1986. "Organizing Groups for Collective Action." *American Political Science Review* 80: 1171–1185.

DAWES, R. M., J. C. VAN DE KRAGT, AND J. M. ORBELL 1988. "Not Me or Thee, but We: The Importance of Group Identity in Eliciting Cooperation in Dilemma Situations: Experimental Manipulations." *Acta Psychologica* 68: 83–97.

DAWKINS, M. S., AND T. GUILFORD 1991. "The Corruption of Honest Signalling." *Animal Behaviour* 41: 865–873.

DEBREU, G. 1952. "A Social Equilibrium Existence Theorem." *Proceedings of the National Academy of Sciences* 38: 886–893.

DIXIT, A. 1993. *The Art of Smooth Pasting*. Chur, Switzerland: Harwood.

DIXIT, A. K., AND B. J. NALEBUFF 1991. *Thinking Strategically: The Competitive Edge in Business, Politics, and Everyday Life*. New York: Norton.

DRESHER, M. 1961. *The Mathematics of Games of Strategy: Theory and Applications*. New York: Dover.

DURRETT, R., AND S. LEVIN 1994. "The Importance of Being Discrete (and Spatial)." *Theoretical Population Biology* 46: 363–394.

EASTERLIN, R. A. 1974. "Does Economic Growth Improve the Human Lot? Some Empirical Evidence." In *Nations and Households in Economic Growth: Essays in Honor of Moses Abramovitz*. New York: Academic Press.

——— 1995. "Will Raising the Incomes of All Increase the Happiness of All?" *Journal of Economic Behavior and Organization* 27, no. 1: 35–47.

ELLSBERG, D. 1961. "Risk, Ambiguity, and the Savage Axioms." *Quarterly Journal of Economics* 75: 643–649.

ENDICOTT, K. 1988. "Property, Power and Conflict among the Batek of Malaysia." In *Hunters and Gatherers*, ed. T. Ingold, D. Riches, and J. Woodburn, 110–127. New York: St. Martin's Press.

EPSTEIN, J. M. 1997. *Nonlinear Dynamics, Mathematical Biology, and Social Science*. Reading, MA: Addison-Wesley.

FALK, A., AND U. FISCHBACHER 1998. "A Theory of Reciprocity." Unpublished Manuscript, Institute for Empirical Economic Research, University of Zurich.

FARRELL, J., AND R. WARE 1989. "Evolutionary Stability in the Repeated Prisoner's Dilemma Game." *Theoretical Population Biology* 36, no. 2: 161–166.

FEHR, E., AND S. GÄCHTER 1999. "Cooperation and Punishment." *American Economic Review* forthcoming.

FEHR, E., S. GÄCHTER, E. KIRCHLER, AND A. WEICHBOLD 1998. "When Social Norms Overpower Competition—Gift Exchange in Labor Markets." *Journal of Labor Economics* 16, no. 2: 324–351.

FEHR, E., S. GÄCHTER, AND G. KIRCHSTEIGER 1997. "Reciprocity as a Contract Enforcement Device: Experimental Evidence." *Econometrica* 65, no. 4: 833–860.

FEHR, E., G. KIRCHSTEIGER, AND A. RIEDL 1998. "Gift Exchange and Reciprocity in Competitive Experimental Markets." *European Economic Review* 42, no. 1: 1–34.

FEHR, E., AND K. M. SCHMIDT 1999. "A Theory of Fairness, Competition, and Cooperation." *Quarterly Journal of Economics* 114: 817–868.

FEHR, E., AND E. TOUGAREVA 1995. "Do Competitive Markets with High Stakes Remove Reciprocal Fairness? Experimental Evidence from Russia." Working Paper, Institute for Empirical Economic Research, University of Zurich.

FEHR, E., AND J.-R. TYRAN 1996. "Institutions and Reciprocal Fairness." *Nordic Journal of Political Economy*.

FEHR, E., AND P. ZYCH 1994. "The Power of Temptation: Irrationally Myopic Excess Consumption in an Addiction Experiment." Unpublished Manuscript, University of Zurich.

FELLER, W. 1950. *An Introduction to Probability Theory and Its Applications*, vol. 1. New York: Wiley.

FISHBURN, P. 1970. *Utility Theory for Decision Making*. New York: Wiley.

FISHER, F. M. 1983. *Disequilibrium Foundations of Equilibrium Economics*. Cambridge, UK: Cambridge University Press.

FISHER, R. A. 1915. "The Evolution of Sexual Preference." *Eugenics Review* 7: 184–192.

FOLEY, D. 1994. "A Statistical Equilibrium Theory of Markets." *Journal of Economic Theory* 62, no. 2: 321–345.

FORSYTHE, R., J. HOROWITZ, N. E. SAVIN, AND M. SEFTON 1994. "Replicability, Fairness and Pay in Experiments with Simple Bargaining Games." *Games and Economic Behavior* 6, no. 3: 347–369.

FOSTER, D., AND H. P. YOUNG 1990. "Stochastic Evolutionary Game Dynamics." *Theoretical Population Biology* 38: 219–232.

FREIDLIN, M. I., AND A. D. WENTZELL 1984. *Random Perturbations of Dynamical Systems*. New York: Springer-Verlag.

FRIEDMAN, D. 1991. "Evolutionary Games in Economics." *Econometrica* 59, no. 3: 637–666.

FRIEDMAN, M. 1953. *Essays in Positive Economics*. Chicago: University of Chicago Press.

FRIEDMAN, M., AND L. J. SAVAGE 1948. "The Utility Analysis of Choices Involving Risk." *Journal of Political Economy* 56: 279–304.

FUDENBERG, D., AND E. MASKIN 1986. "The Folk Theorem in Repeated Games with Discounting or with Incomplete Information." *Econometrica* 54, no. 3: 533–554.

FUDENBERG, D., AND J. TIROLE 1991. *Game Theory*. Cambridge, MA: MIT Press.

GEANAKOPLOS, J. 1996. "Promises, Promises." Yale Cowles Foundation Discussion Paper no. 1143.

GEANAKOPLOS, J., D. PEARCE, AND E. STACCHETTI 1989. "Psychological Games and Sequential Rationality." *Games and Economic Behavior* 1: 60–79.

GEANAKOPLOS, J., AND H. M. POLEMARCHAKIS 1996. "Existence, Regularity, and Constrained Suboptimality of Competitive Allocations When the Asset Market Is Incomplete." In *General Equilibrium Theory*, vol. 2, ed. G. Debreu, 67–97. Cheltenham, UK: Elgar.

GIBBONS, R. 1992. *Game Theory for Applied Economists*. Princeton, NJ: Princeton University Press.

GILBERT, D. T. 1991. "How Mental Systems Believe." *American Psychologist* 46, no. 2: 107–119.

GINTIS, H. 1972a. "Consumer Behavior and the Concept of Sovereignty." *American Economic Review* 42, no. 2: 267–278.

——— 1972b. "A Radical Analysis of Welfare Economics and Individual Development." *Quarterly Journal of Economics* 86, no. 4: 572–599.

——— 1974. "Welfare Criteria with Endogenous Preferences: The Economics of Education." *International Economic Review* 15, no. 2: 415–429.

——— 1975. "Welfare Economics and Individual Development: A Reply to Talcott Parsons." *Quarterly Journal of Economics* 89, no. 2: 291–302.

——— 1976. "The Nature of the Labor Exchange and the Theory of Capitalist Production." *Review of Radical Political Economics* 8, no. 2: 36–54.

——— 1989. "The Power to Switch: On the Political Economy of Consumer Sovereignty." In *Unconventional Wisdom: Essays in Honor of John Kenneth Galbraith*, ed. S. Bowles, R. C. Edwards, and W. G. Shepherd, 65–80. New York: Houghton-Mifflin.

——— 1997. "A Markov Model of Production, Trade, and Money: Theory and Artificial Life Simulation." *Computational and Mathematical Organization Theory* 3, no. 1: 19–41.

GLYNN, I. 1999. *An Anatomy of Thought: The Origin and Machinery of the Mind*. London: Weidenfeld & Nicolson.

GOTT, R. 1993. "Letter to the Editor." *Nature* 363: 315.

GRAFEN, A. 1984. "Natural Selection, Kin Selection, and Group Selection." In *Behavioural Ecology: An Evolutionary Approach*, ed. J. R. Krebs and N. B. Davies. Sunderland, MA: Sinauer.

———— 1990a. "Biological Signals as Handicaps." *Journal of Theoretical Biology* 144: 517–546.

———— 1990b. "Sexual Selection Unhandicapped by the Fisher Process." *Journal of Theoretical Biology* 144: 473–516.

GREENBERG, M. S., AND D. M. FRISCH 1972. "Effect of Intentionality on Willingness to Reciprocate a Favor." *Journal of Experimental Social Psychology* 8: 99–111.

GUCKENHEIMER, J., AND P. HOLMES 1986. *Nonlinear Oscillations, Dynamical Systems, and Bifurcations of Vector Fields*. New York: Springer-Verlag.

GUILFORD, T., AND M. S. DAWKINS 1991. "Receiver Psychology and the Evolution of Animal Signals." *Animal Behaviour* 42: 1–14.

———— 1993. "Receiver Psychology and the Design of Animal Signals." *Trends in Neuroscience* 16, no. 11: 420–436.

GÜTH, W., AND H. KLIEMT 1994. "Competition or Co-operation: On the Evolutionary Economics of Trust, Exploitation, and Moral Attitudes." *Metroeconomica* 45, no. 2: 155–187.

GÜTH, W., R. SCHMITTBERGER, AND B. SCHWARZ 1982. "An Experimental Analysis of Ultimatum Bargaining." *Journal of Economic Behavior and Organization* 3: 367–388.

GÜTH, W., AND R. TIETZ 1990. "Ultimatum Bargaining Behavior: A Survey and Comparison of Experimental Results." *Journal of Economic Psychology* 11: 417–449.

GUTTMAN, J. M. 1996. "Rational Actors, Tit-for-Tat Types, and the Evolution of Cooperation." *Journal of Economic Behavior and Organization* 29, no. 1: 27–56.

HACKETT, S., E. SCHLAGER, AND J. WALKER 1994. "The Role of Communication in Resolving Commons Dilemmas: Experimental Evidence with Heterogeneous Appropriators." *Journal of Environmental Economics and Management* 27, no. 2: 99–126.

HAIGH, J. 1975. "Game Theory and Evolution." *Advances in Applied Probability* 7, no. 1: 8–11.

HAMILTON, W. D. 1963. "The Evolution of Altruistic Behavior." *American Naturalist* 96: 354–356.

HAMMERSTEIN, P., AND S. REICHERT 1988. "Payoffs and Strategies in Spider Territorial Contests: ESS Analysis of Two Ecotypes." *Evolutionary Ecology* 2: 115–138.

HARDIN, G. 1968. "The Tragedy of the Commons." *Science* 162: 1243–1248.

HARDIN, R. 1982. *Collective Action*. Baltimore: Johns Hopkins University Press.

HARRINGTON, J. E. 1999. "Rigidity in Social Systems." *Journal of Political Economy* 107, no. 1: 40–64.

HARSANYI, J. C. 1962. "Measurement of Social Power, Opportunity Costs, and the Theory of Two-Person Bargaining Games." *Behavioral Science* 7: 67–81.

——— 1967. "Games with Incomplete Information Played by Bayesian Players, Parts I, II, and III." *Behavioral Science* 14: 159–182, 320–334, 486–502.

——— 1973. "Games with Randomly Distributed Payoffs: A New Rationale for Mixed–Strategy Equilibrium Points." *International Journal of Game Theory* 2: 1–23.

HARSANYI, J. C., AND R. SELTEN 1988. *A General Theory of Equilibrium Selection in Games*. Cambridge, MA: MIT Press.

HAWKES, K. 1992. "Sharing and Collective Action." In *Evolutionary Ecology and Human Behavior*, ed. E. Smith and B. Winterhalder, 269–300. New York: Aldine.

——— 1993. "Why Hunter-Gatherers Work: An Ancient Version of the Problem of Public Goods." *Current Anthropology* 34, no. 4: 341–361.

HAYEK, F. A. 1935. *Collectivist Economic Planning: Critical Studies on the Possibilities of Socialism*. London: George Routledge.

——— 1945. "The Use of Knowledge in Society." *American Economic Review* 35, no. 4: 519–530.

HEINER, R. A. 1983. "The Origin of Predictable Behavior." *American Economic Review* 73, no. 4: 560–595.

——— 1993. "Imperfect Choice and Rule-Governed Behavior." In *Markets and Democracy: Participation Accountability and Efficiency*, ed. S. Bowles, H. Gintis, and B. Gustafsson. Cambridge, UK: Cambridge University Press.

HELSON, H. 1964. *Adaptation Level Theory: An Experimental and Systematic Approach to Behavior*. New York: Harper and Row.

HENRICH, J. 2000. "Does Culture Matter in Economic Behavior? Ultimatum Game Bargaining among the Machiguenga." *American Economic Review*.

HERRNSTEIN, R. J., AND D. PRELEC 1992. "A Theory of Addiction." In *Choice over Time*, ed. G. Loewenstein and J. Elster, 331–360. New York: Russell Sage.

HIRSCH, M. W., AND S. SMALE 1974. *Differential Equations, Dynamical Systems, and Linear Systems*. San Diego: Academic Press.

HOFBAUER, J., AND K. SIGMUND 1998. *Evolutionary Games and Population Dynamics*. Cambridge, UK: Cambridge University Press.

HOFFMAN, E., K. MCCABE, K. SHACHAT, AND V. L. SMITH 1994. "Preferences, Property Rights, and Anonymity in Bargaining Games." *Games and Economic Behavior* 7: 346–380.

HOFFMAN, E., K. McCABE, AND V. L. SMITH 1996. "Social Distance and Other-Regarding Behavior in Dictator Games." *American Economic Review* 86, no. 3: 653–660.

——— 1998. "Behavioral Foundations of Reciprocity: Experimental Economics and Evolutionary Psychology." *Economic Inquiry* 36, no. 3: 335–352.

HÖLMSTROM, B. 1982. "Moral Hazard in Teams." *Bell Journal of Economics* 7: 324–340.

HORN, R. A., AND C. R. JOHNSON 1985. *Matrix Analysis*. Cambridge, UK: Cambridge University Press.

ISAAC, R. M., J. M. WALKER, AND A. W. WILLIAMS 1994. "Group Size and Voluntary Provision of Public Goods: Experimental Evidence Utilizing Large Groups." *Journal of Public Economics* 54: 1–36.

JOHNSTONE, R. A., AND A. GRAFEN 1992. "The Continuous Sir Philip Sidney Game: A Simple Model of Biological Signalling." *Journal of Theoretical Biology* 156: 215–234.

——— 1993. "Dishonesty and the Handicap Principle." *Animal Behavior* 46: 759–764.

KACHELMAIER, S. J., AND M. SHEHATA 1992. "Culture and Competition: A Laboratory Market Comparison between China and the West." *Journal of Economic Behavior and Organization* 19: 145–168.

KAGEL, J. H., AND A. E. ROTH 1995. *Handbook of Experimental Economics*. Princeton, NJ: Princeton University Press.

KAHN, L. M., AND J. K. MURNIGHAM 1993. "Conjecture, Uncertainty, and Cooperation in Prisoner's Dilemma Games: Some Experimental Evidence." *Journal of Economic Behavior and Organization* 22, no. 1: 91–117.

KAHNEMAN, D., J. L. KNETCH, AND R. H. THALER 1990. "Experimental Tests of the Endowment Effect and the Coase Theorem." *Journal of Political Economy* 98, no. 6: 1325–1348.

——— 1991. "The Endowment Effect, Loss Aversion, and Status Quo Bias." *Journal of Economic Perspectives* 5, no. 1: 193–206.

KAHNEMAN, D., P. SLOVIC, AND A. TVERSKY 1982. *Judgment under Uncertainty: Heuristics and Biases*. Cambridge, UK: Cambridge University Press.

KAPLAN, H., AND K. HILL 1985a. "Food Sharing among Ache Foragers: Tests of Explanatory Hypotheses." *Current Anthropology* 26, no. 2: 223–246.

——— 1985b. "Hunting Ability and Reproductive Success among Male Ache Foragers: Preliminary Results." *Current Anthropology* 26, no. 1: 131–133.

KAPLAN, H., K. HILL, K. HAWKES, AND A. HURTADO 1984. "Food Sharing among Ache Hunter-Gatherers of Eastern Paraguay." *Current Anthropology* 25, no. 1: 113–115.

KARLIN, S., AND H. M. TAYLOR 1975. *A First Course in Stochastic Processes.* Boston: Academic Press.

―――― 1981. *A Second Course in Stochastic Processes.* Boston: Academic Press.

KENNAN, J., AND R. WILSON 1990. "Theories of Bargaining Delays." *Science* 249: 1124–1128.

KENT, S. 1989. "And Justice for All: The Development of Political Centralization among Newly Sedentary Foragers." *American Anthropologist* 93, no. 1: 703–712.

KIRBY, K. N., AND R. J. HERRNSTEIN 1995. "Preference Reversals due to Myopic Discounting of Delayed Reward." *Psychological Science* 6, no. 2: 83–89.

KIRKPATRICK, M. 1982. "Sexual Selection and the Evolution of Female Choice." *Evolution* 36: 1–12.

KIYOTAKI, N., AND R. WRIGHT 1989. "On Money as a Medium of Exchange." *Journal of Political Economy* 94, no. 4: 927–954.

―――― 1991. "A Contribution to a Pure Theory of Money." *Journal of Economic Theory* 53, no. 2: 215–235.

―――― 1993. "A Search-Theoretic Approach to Monetary Economics." *American Economic Review* 83, no. 1: 63–77.

KLEIN, B., AND K. LEFFLER 1981. "The Role of Market Forces in Assuring Contractual Performance." *Journal of Political Economy* 89: 615–641.

KNAUFT, B. 1989. "Sociality versus Self-interest in Human Evolution." *Behavioral and Brain Sciences* 12, no. 4: 12–13.

―――― 1991. "Violence and Sociality in Human Evolution." *Current Anthropology* 32, no. 4: 391–428.

KOLLOCK, P. 1994. "The Emergence of Exchange Structures: An Experimental Study of Uncertainty, Commitment, and Trust." *American Journal of Sociology* 100, no. 2: 313–345.

KOOPMANS, T. 1957. "Allocation of Resources and the Price System." In *Three Essays on the State of Economic Science*, 4–95. New York: McGraw-Hill.

KREBS, J. R., AND N. B. DAVIES 1993. *An Introduction to Behavioral Ecology,.* Cambridge, UK: Cambridge University Press.

KREPS, D. M. 1988. *Notes on the Theory of Choice.* London: Westview.

―――― 1990. *A Course in Microeconomic Theory.* Princeton, NJ: Princeton University Press.

KREPS, D. M., P. MILGROM, J. ROBERTS, AND R. WILSON 1982. "Rational Cooperation in the Finitely Repeated Prisoner's Dilemma." *Journal of Economic Theory* 27: 245–252.

KREPS, D. M., AND R. WILSON 1982. "Sequential Equilibria." *Econometrica* 50, no. 4: 863–894.

KUHN, H. W. 1953. "Extensive Games and the Problem of Information." In *Contributions to the Theory of Games*, vol. 2 of *Annals of Mathematics Studies*, ed. H. W. Kuhn and A. W. Tucker, 193–216. Princeton, NJ: Princeton University Press.

KURZ, M. 1997. "Endogenous Economic Fluctuations and Rational Beliefs: A General Perspective." In *Endogenous Economic Fluctuations: Studies in the Theory of Rational Beliefs*, ed. M. Kurz, 1–37. Berlin: Springer-Verlag.

LACHMANN, M., AND C. T. BERGSTROM 1998. "Signalling among Relatives, II. Beyond the Tower of Babel." *Theoretical Population Biology* 54: 146–160.

LAIBSON, D. 1997. "Golden Eggs and Hyperbolic Discounting." *Quarterly Journal of Economics* 112, no. 2: 443–477.

LAIBSON, D., AND H. RACHLIN 1997. *The Matching Law: Papers on Psychology and Economics by Richard Herrnstein*. Cambridge, MA: Harvard University Press.

LANDE, R. 1981. "Models of Speciation by Sexual Selection of Polygenic Traits." *Proceedings of the National Academy of Sciences USA* 78: 3721–3725.

LANE, R. E. 1991. *The Market Experience*. Cambridge, UK: Cambridge University Press.

——— 1993. "Does Money Buy Happiness?" *The Public Interest* 113: 56–65.

LANGE, O., AND F. M. TAYLOR 1938. *On the Economic Theory of Socialism*. Minneapolis: University of Minnesota Press.

LEDYARD, J. O. 1995. "Public Goods: A Survey of Experimental Research." In *The Handbook of Experimental Economics*, ed. J. H. Kagel and A. E. Roth, 111–194. Princeton, NJ: Princeton University Press.

LEE, R. B. 1979. *The !Kung San: Men, Women and Work in a Foraging Society*. Cambridge, UK: Cambridge University Press.

LERNER, A. 1972. "The Economics and Politics of Consumer Sovereignty." *American Economic Review* 62, no. 2: 258–266.

LESLIE, J. 1996. *The End of the World: The Science and Ethics of Human Extinction*. London: Routledge.

LOEWENSTEIN, G. 1987. "Anticipation and the Valuation of Delayed Consumption." *Economic Journal* 97: 666–684.

——— 1999. "Experimental Economics from the Vantage Point of View of Behavioural Economics." *Economic Journal* 109: F25–F34.

LOEWENSTEIN, G., AND D. ADLER 1995. "A Bias in the Prediction of Tastes." *Economic Journal* 105 (431): 929–937.

LOEWENSTEIN, G., AND D. PRELEC 1992. "Anomalies in Intertemporal Choice: Evidence and an Interpretation." *Quarterly Journal of Economics* 57: 573–598.

LOEWENSTEIN, G., AND N. SICHERMAN 1991. "Do Workers Prefer Increasing Wage Profiles?" *Journal of Labor Economics* 91, no. 1: 67–84.

LOEWENSTEIN, G. F., S. ISSACHAROFF, C. CAMERER, AND L. BABCOCK 1992. "Self-serving Assessments of Fairness and Pretrial Bargaining." *Journal of Legal Studies* 22: 135–159.

LOEWENSTEIN, G. F., L. THOMPSON, AND M. H. BAZERMAN 1989. "Social Utility and Decision Making in Interpersonal Contexts." *Journal of Personality and Social Psychology* 57, no. 3: 426–441.

LOOMES, G. 1988. "When Actions Speak Louder than Prospects." *American Economic Review* 78, no. 3: 463–470.

LORBERBAUM, J. 1994. "No Strategy is Evolutionarily Stable in the Repeated Prisoner's Dilemma." *Journal of Theoretical Biology* 168, no. 2: 117–130.

LUMSDEN, C. J., AND E. O. WILSON 1981. *Genes, Mind, and Culture: The Coevolutionary Process*. Cambridge, MA: Harvard University Press.

MACHINA, M. J. 1987. "Choice under Uncertainty: Problems Solved and Unsolved." *Journal of Economic Perspectives* 1, no. 1: 121–154.

MAGILL, M., AND M. QUINZII 1996. *Theory of Incomplete Markets*. Cambridge, MA: MIT Press.

———— 1999. "Incentive Role of the Stock Market." University of Siena, Italy, Summer School. Unpublished Manuscript.

MAILATH, G. J. 1998. "Do People Play Nash Equilibrium? Lessons from Evolutionary Game Theory." *Journal of Economic Literature* 36: 1347–1374.

MANKIW, N. G., AND D. ROMER 1991. *New Keynesian Economics*. Cambridge, MA: MIT Press.

MAS-COLELL, A., M. D. WHINSTON, AND J. R. GREEN 1995. *Microeconomic Theory*. New York: Oxford University Press.

MAYNARD SMITH, J. 1982. *Evolution and the Theory of Games*. Cambridge, UK: Cambridge University Press.

———— 1991. "Honest Signalling: The Philip Sidney Game." *Animal Behavior* 42: 1034–1035.

MAYNARD SMITH, J., AND G. R. PRICE 1973. "The Logic of Animal Conflict." *Nature* 246: 15–18.

MCKELVEY, R. D., AND T. R. PALFREY 1992. "An Experimental Study of the Centipede Game." *Econometrica* 60: 803–836.

MERTENS, J.-F., AND S. ZAMIR 1985. "Formulations of Bayesian Analysis for Games with Incomplete Information." *International Journal of Game Theory* 14: 1–29.

MESTERTON-GIBBONS, M. 1991. *An Introduction to Game-Theoretic Modelling*. New York: Addison-Wesley.

MORROW, J. D. 1994. *Game Theory for Political Scientists*. Princeton, NJ: Princeton University Press.

MOTRO, U. 1991. "Co-operation and Defection: Playing the Field and the ESS." *Journal of Theoretical Biology* 151, no. 2: 145–154.

MOULIN, H. 1986. *Game Theory for the Social Sciences*. New York: New York University Press.

MYERSON, R. B. 1991. *Game Theory: Analysis of Conflict*. Cambridge, MA: Harvard University Press.

NASH, J. F. 1950. "Equilibrium Points in n-Person Games." *Proceedings of the National Academy of Sciences* 36: 48–49.

NEELIN, J., H. SONNENSCHEIN, AND M. SPIEGEL 1988. "A Further Test of Non-Cooperative Bargaining Theory." *American Economic Review* 78: 824–836.

NERLOVE, M., AND T. D. SOEDJIANA 1996. "Slamerans and Sheep: Savings and Small Ruminants in Semi-Subsistence Agriculture in Indonesia." Department of Agriculture and Resource Economics, University of Maryland.

NOWAK, M., AND K. SIGMUND 1992. "Tit-for-Tat in Heterogeneous Populations." *Nature* 355: 250–252.

——— 1993. "A Strategy of Win-Stay Lose-Shift that Outperforms Tit-for-Tat in the Prisoner's Dilemma Game." *Nature* 364: 56–58.

OLCINA, G. 1997. "Forward Induction in Games with an Outside Option." *Theory and Decision* 42: 177–192.

OLSON, V. A., AND I. OWENS 1998. "Costly Sexual Signals: Are Carotenoids Rare, Risky or Required?" *Trends in Evolution and Ecology* 13, no. 12: 510–514.

OSBORNE, M. J., AND A. RUBINSTEIN 1990. *Bargaining and Markets*. New York: Academic Press.

OSTROM, E. 1990. *Governing the Commons: The Evolution of Institutions for Collective Action*. Cambridge, UK: Cambridge University Press.

——— 1998. "A Behavioral Approach to the Rational Choice Theory of Collective Action." *American Political Science Review* 92, no. 1: 1–21.

OSTROM, E., R. GARDNER, AND J. WALKER 1994. *Rules, Games, and Common-Pool Resources*. Ann Arbor: University of Michigan Press.

OSTROM, E., J. WALKER, AND R. GARDNER 1992. "Covenants with and without a Sword: Self-Governance Is Possible." *American Political Science Review* 86, no. 2: 404–417.

OSWALD, A. J. 1997. "Happiness and Economic Performance." *Economic Journal* 107, no. 445: 1815–1831.

PARSONS, T. 1964. "Evolutionary Universals in Society." *American Sociological Review* 29, no. 3: 339–357.

PERKO, L. 1991. *Differential Equations and Dynamical Systems.* New York: Springer-Verlag.

PLOTT, C. R. 1979. "The Application of Laboratory Experimental Methods to Public Choice." In *Collective Decision Making: Applications from Public Choice Theory*, ed. C. S. Russell, 137–160. Baltimore, MD: Johns Hopkins University Press.

POMIANKOWSKI, A. N. 1987. "The Costs of Choice in Sexual Selection." *Journal of Theoretical Biology* 128: 195–218.

PONSATI, C., AND J. SÁKOVICS 1998. "Rubinstein Bargaining with Two-Sided Outside Options." *Economic Theory* 11: 667–672.

PRICE, G. R. 1970. "Selection and Covariance." *Nature* 227: 520–521.

PUSEY, A. E., AND C. PACKER 1997. "The Ecology of Relationships." In *Behavioral Ecology: An Evolutionary Approach,* 4th ed., ed. J. R. Krebs and N. B. Davies, 254–283. Oxford: Blackwell Science.

RABIN, M. 1993. "Incorporating Fairness into Game Theory and Economics." *American Economic Review* 83, no. 5: 1281–1302.

———— 1998. "Psychology and Economics." *Journal of Economic Literature* 36, no. 1: 11–46.

RASMUSEN, E. 1989. *Games and Information: An Introduction to Game Theory.* Cambridge, UK: Blackwell Scientific.

RILEY, J. G. 1979. "Evolutionary Equilibrium Strategies." *Journal of Theoretical Biology* 76: 109–123.

ROGERS, A. R. 1990. "Group Selection by Selective Emigration: The Effects of Migration and Kin Structure." *American Naturalist* 135, no. 3: 398–413.

ROSENZWEIG, M. R., AND K. I. WOLPIN 1993. "Credit Market Constraints, Consumption Smoothing, and the Accumulation of Durable Production Assets in Low-Income Countries: Investment in Bullocks in India." *Journal of Political Economy* 101, no. 2: 223–244.

ROTEMBERG, J., AND G. SALONER 1991. "A Supergame-Theoretic Model of Price Wars during Booms." In *New Keynesian Economics,* vol. 2, ed. G. N. Mankiw and D. Romer, 387–415. Cambridge, MA: MIT Press.

ROTH, A. E., V. PRASNIKAR, M. OKUNO-FUJIWARA, AND S. ZAMIR 1991. "Bargaining and Market Behavior in Jerusalem, Ljubljana, Pittsburgh, and Tokyo: An Experimental Study." *American Economic Review* 81, no. 5: 1068–1095.

RUBINSTEIN, A. 1982. "Perfect Equilibrium in a Bargaining Model." *Econometrica* 50: 97–109.

SAARI, D. 1995. "Mathematical Complexity of Simple Economics." *Notices of the American Mathematical Society* 42, no. 2: 222–230.

SAHA, A., R. C. SHUMWAY, AND H. TALPAZ 1994. "Joint Estimation of Risk Preference Structure and Technology Using Expo-Power Utility." *American Journal of Agricultural Economics* 76, no. 2: 173–184.

SALLY, D. 1995. "Conversation and Cooperation in Social Dilemmas." *Rationality and Society* 7, no. 1: 58–92.

SAMUELSON, L. 1997. *Evolutionary Games and Equilibrium Selection.* Cambridge, MA: MIT Press.

SAMUELSON, L., AND J. ZHANG 1992. "Evolutionary Stability in Asymmetric Games." *Journal of Economic Theory* 57, no. 2: 363–391.

SAMUELSON, P. 1957. "Wages and Interests: A Modern Dissection of Marxian Economics." *American Economic Review* 47: 884–921.

SATO, K. 1987. "Distribution and the Cost of Maintaining Common Property Resources." *Journal of Experimental Social Psychology* 23: 19–31.

SAVAGE, L. J. 1954. *The Foundations of Statistics.* New York: Wiley.

SCHUMPETER, J. 1934. *The Theory of Economic Development: An Inquiry into Profits, Capital, Credit, Interest and the Business Cycle.* Oxford: Oxford University Press.

——— 1942. *Capitalism, Socialism, and Democracy.* New York: Harper & Row.

SCHUSTER, P., AND K. SIGMUND 1983. "Replicator Dynamics." *Journal of Theoretical Biology* 100: 533–538.

SELTEN, R. 1975. "Re-examination of the Perfectness Concept for Equilibrium Points in Extensive Games." *International Journal of Game Theory* 4: 25–55.

——— 1978. "The Chain Store Paradox." *Theory and Decision* 9: 127–159.

——— 1980. "A Note on Evolutionarily Stable Strategies in Asymmetric Animal Conflicts." *Journal of Theoretical Biology* 84: 93–101.

——— 1993. "In Search of a Better Understanding of Economic Behavior." In *The Makers of Modern Economics,* vol. 1, ed. A. Heertje, 115–139. Harvester Wheatsheaf.

SETHI, R., AND E. SOMANATHAN 1999. "Preference Evolution and Reciprocity." Working Paper no. 99-06, Barnard College, New York.

SHACHAT, J., AND M. WALKER 1997. "Unobserved Heterogeneity and Equilibrium." University of California at San Diego. Unpublished Manuscript.

SHAFIR, E. 1994. "Uncertainty and the Difficulty of Thinking through Disjunctions." *Cognition* 50, no. 1–3: 403–430.

SHAFIR, E., AND A. TVERSKY 1992. "Thinking through Uncertainty: Nonconsequential Reasoning and Choice." *Cognitive Psychology* 24, no. 4: 449–474.

——— 1995. "Decision Making." In *Thinking: An Invitation to Cognitive Science,* vol. 3, 2nd ed., ed. E. E. Smith and D. N. Osherson, 77–100. Cambridge, MA: MIT Press.

SHAKED, A., AND J. SUTTON 1984. "Involuntary Unemployment as a Perfect Equilibrium in a Bargaining Model." *Econometrica* 52: 1351–1364.

SHAPIRO, C., AND J. STIGLITZ 1984. "Unemployment as a Worker Discipline Device." *American Economic Review* 74, no. 3: 433–444.

SHOGREN, J. F. 1989. "Fairness in Bargaining Requires a Context: An Experimental Examination of Loyalty." *Economic Letters* 31: 319–323.

SHUBIK, M. 1954. "Does the Fittest Necessarily Survive?" In *Readings in Game Theory and Political Behavior*, ed. M. Shubik, 43–46. New York: Doubleday.

——— 1971. "The Dollar Auction Game: A paradox in Noncooperative Behavior and Escalation." *Journal of Conflict Resolution* 15: 109–111.

——— 1984. *Game Theory in the Social Sciences*. Cambridge, MA: MIT Press.

SIMON, H. 1953. "Notes on the Observation and Measurement of Political Power." *Journal of Politics* 4: 500–516.

——— 1982. *Models of Bounded Rationality*. Cambridge, MA: MIT Press.

SINERVO, B., AND C. M. LIVELY 1996. "The Rock-Paper-Scissors Game and the Evolution of Alternative Male Strategies." *Nature* 380, no. 6571: 240–243.

SINN, H.-W. 1980. "A Rehabilitation of the Principle of Insufficient Reason." *Quarterly Journal of Economics* 94, no. 3: 493–506.

SMITH, V. 1982. "Microeconomic Systems as an Experimental Science." *American Economic Review* 72: 923–955.

SMITH, V., AND A. W. WILLIAMS 1992. "Experimental Market Economics." *Scientific American* 267, no. 6: 116–121.

SOLOW, R. 1979. "Another Possible Source of Wage Stickiness." *Journal of Macroeconomics* 1: 79–82.

STÅHL, I. 1971. *Bargaining Theory*. Stockholm: Stockholm School of Economics.

STIGLITZ, J. 1987. "The Causes and Consequences of the Dependence of Quality on Price." *Journal of Economic Literature* 25: 1–48.

STIGLITZ, J., AND A. WEISS 1981. "Credit Rationing in Markets with Imperfect Information." *American Economic Review* 71: 393–411.

STROTZ, R. H. 1955. "Myopia and Inconsistency in Dynamic Utility Maximization." *Review of Economic Studies* 23, no. 3: 165–180.

SUGDEN, R. 1993. "An Axiomatic Foundation for Regret Theory." *Journal of Economic Theory* 60, no. 1: 159–180.

SUTTON, J. 1997. "Gibrat's Legacy." *Journal of Economic Literature* 35, no. 1: 40–59.

TAN, T. C.-C., AND S. R. DA COSTA WERLANG 1988. "The Bayesian Foundations of Solution Concepts of Games." *Journal of Economic Theory* 45: 370–391.

TAYLOR, M. 1987. *The Possibility of Cooperation*. Cambridge, UK: Cambridge University Press.

TAYLOR, P., AND L. JONKER 1978. "Evolutionarily Stable Strategies and Game Dynamics." *Mathematical Biosciences* 40: 145–156.

TIROLE, J. 1988. *The Theory of Industrial Organization*. Cambridge, MA: MIT Press.

TRIVERS, R. L. 1971. "The Evolution of Reciprocal Altruism." *Quarterly Review of Biology* 46: 35–57.

———— 1985. *Social Evolution*. Menlo Park, CA: Benjamin Cummings.

TURNER, J. C. 1984. "Social Identification and Psychological Group Formation." In *The Social Dimension*, ed. H. Tajfel, 518–538. Cambridge, UK: Cambridge University Press.

TVERSKY, A., AND D. KAHNEMAN 1974. "Judgment under Uncertainty: Heuristics and Biases." *Science* 185: 1124–1131.

———— 1981a. "The Framing of Decisions and the Psychology of Choices." *Science* 211: 453–458.

———— 1981b. "Loss Aversion in Riskless Choice: A Reference-Dependent Model." *Quarterly Journal of Economics* 106, no. 4: 1039–1061.

TVERSKY, A., AND E. SHAFIR 1992. "The Disjunction Effect in Choice under Uncertainty." *Psychological Science* 3, no. 5: 305–309.

VAN DAMME, E. 1991. *Stability and Perfection of Nash Equilibria*. Berlin: Springer-Verlag.

VON NEUMANN, J., AND O. MORGENSTERN 1944. *Theory of Games and Economic Behavior*. Princeton, NJ: Princeton University Press.

VOROB'EV, N. N. 1977. *Game Theory: Lectures for Economists and Systems Scientists*. New York: Springer-Verlag.

VOS SAVANT, M. 1991. "Ask Marilyn." *Parade Magazine*.

———— December 27, 1998. "Ask Marilyn." *Parade Magazine*.

WALRAS, L. 1954 [1874]. *Elements of Pure Economics*. London: George Allen and Unwin.

WEDEKIND, C., AND M. MILINSKI 1993. "Human Cooperation in the Simultaneous and the Alternating Prisoner's Dilemma: Pavlov versus Generous Tit-for-Tat." *Proceedings of the National Academy of Sciences* 93: 2686–2689.

WEIBULL, J. W. 1995. *Evolutionary Game Theory*. Cambridge, MA: MIT Press.

WEISSING, F., AND E. OSTROM 1991. "Irrigation Institutions and the Games Irrigators Play: Rule Enforcement without Guards." In *Game Equilibrium Models II: Methods Morals and Markets*, ed. R. Selten, 188–262. Berlin: Springer-Verlag.

WENZEL, G. W. 1995. "Ningiqtuq: Resource Sharing and Generalized Reciprocity in Clyde River, Nunavut." *Arctic Anthropology* 32, no. 2: 43–60.

WILLIAMS, G. C. 1966. *Adaptation and Natural Selection: A Critique of Some Current Evolutionary Thought*. Princeton, NJ: Princeton University Press.

WILSON, E. O. 1975. *Sociobiology: The New Synthesis*. Cambridge, MA: Harvard University Press.

———— 1998. *Consilience: The Unity of Knowledge*. New York: Knopf.

WOODBURN, J. 1982. "Egalitarian Societies." *Man* 17, no. 3: 431–451.

WOODBURN, J., AND A. BARNARD 1988. "Property, Power and Ideology in Hunter-Gathering Societies: An Introduction." In *Hunters and Gatherers*, ed. T. Ingold, D. Riches, and J. Woodburn, 4–31. New York: St. Martin's Press.

WYNNE-EDWARDS, V. C. 1962. *Animal Dispersion in Relation to Social Behavior*. Edinburgh, UK: Oliver and Boyd.

YAMAGISHI, T. 1988a. "The Provision of a Sanctioning System in the United States and Japan." *Social Psychology Quarterly* 51, no. 3: 265–271.

———— 1988b. "Seriousness of Social Dilemmas and the Provision of a Sanctioning System." *Social Psychology Quarterly* 51, no. 1: 32–42.

———— 1992. "Group Size and the Provision of a Sanctioning System in a Social Dilemma." In *Social Dilemmas: Theoretical Issues and Research Findings*, ed. W. Liebrand, D. M. Messick, and H. Wilke, 267–287. Oxford: Pergamon Press.

YOUNG, H. P. 1998. *Individual Strategy and Social Structure: An Evolutionary Theory of Institutions*. Princeton, NJ: Princeton University Press.

ZAHAVI, A. 1975. "Mate Selection—A Selection for Handicap." *Journal of Theoretical Biology* 53: 205–214.

ZAHAVI, A., AND A. ZAHAVI 1997. *The Handicap Principle: A Missing Piece of Darwin's Puzzle*. New York: Oxford University Press.

ZAMBRANO, E. 1997. "The Revelation Principle of Bounded Rationality." Santa Fe Institute Working Paper no. 97-06-060.

ZERMELO, E. 1913. "Über eine Anwendung der Mengenlehrer auf der Theorie des Schachspiels." *Proceedings of the Fifth International Congress of Mathematicians*.

ZEUTHEN, F. 1930. *Problems of Monopoly and Economic Welfare*. London: George Routledge and Sons.

Index

(a, b), 445
$A \cap B$, $A \cup B$, A^c, 357
$[a, b]$, 112
$\mathbf{R}$, 10
$\mathbf{R}^n$, 165
ω-limit point, 185
$\{\cdot \mid \cdot\}$, 423
$\mathcal{N}_i$, 11

Aces Up, 361, 489
action, 5, 10
adaptive expectations, 230
Adaptive Learning, 229
   Conventions Not All Equal, 233
   with Errors, 234
Addition Rule for Probabilities, 362
Adverse Selection, 294
Advertising Game, 72, 417
affine transformation, 42
Agelenopsis aperta, 310
agent-based simulation, 40
agent-based simulation of
   Adaptive Learning with Errors, 235
   hawk-dove game, 155
   monetary economy, 225
   No-Draw High-Low Poker, 40, 405
   One-Card Two-Round Poker with Bluffing, 61, 162, 413
   perfect Bayesian Nash equilibrium, 290
   repeated Prisoner's Dilemma, 106

signaling model of conditional altruism, 322
Ah, Those Kids, 369
Ainslie, George, 246
Akerlof, George, 252, 295, 335
Allais, Maurice, 386
Allais paradox, 386
along the path of play, 309
altruism, 34
   and assortative interactions, 266
   in bird flocks, 79, 422
ancestor node, 10
Andrei Andreyevich's Two-Urn Problem, 380
Andreoni, James, 104, 255
Anscombe, F., 247
anticipatory pricing, 304
Are Evolutionarily Stable Strategies Unbeatable?, 152
Armaments Game, 20
Arrow, Kenneth, 43
Arthur, Brian, 500
artificial life, 61
assortative interaction, 211, 268
asymmetric binary relation, 382
Asymmetric Evolutionary Games, 210
   Reviewing the Troops, 214
asymptotically stable fixed point, 173
Attack on Hidden Object, 74, 422
Aumann, Robert, 247, 289
Axelrod, Robert, xxiii, 261, 500

backward induction, 17, 95
   Pruning the Game Tree, 16, 395
Baliksci, Asen, 258
Bandura, Albert, 189
Bardhan, Pranab, 258
Bargaining, 345, 483
   with Fixed Costs, 355, 487
   with Incomplete Information, 355, 488
   with Two-Sided Outside Options, 352
bargaining
   model, 345
   problem, 347
   solution, 347
basin of attraction, 173
Battle of the Sexes, 60, 410
Bayes' Rule, 364
Bayesian perfect equilibrium, 92
Bayesian Perfection and Stable Sets, 203
Bayesian updating, 113, 287
Becker, Gary, 34, 244
behavioral economics, 244
behavioral strategy, 63, 112, 286
   profile, 64, 286
     payoffs to, 286
   representation, 286
   representation of a mixed strategy, 88
Bergstrom, Carl, 500
Bertrand duopoly model, 30
Bertrand's Paradox, 122
best response, 6, 13
   local, 287
   schedule, 334
Big Fish and Little Fish, 119
Big Monkey and Little Monkey, 3
   Revisited, 59, 410
Bill and Harry, 371, 497
binary relation, 382
   asymmetric, 382
   complete, 382
   reflexive, 382
   symmetric, 382
   transitive, 382
Binmore, Ken, xxx, xxxiii, 500
Biological Signals as Handicaps, 317
Birth of Evolutionary Stability, 148

Blurton-Jones, Nicholas G., 258
Boehm, Christopher, 258
Bolt Factory, 365
bounded rationality, 243
Bowles, Samuel, 118, 137, 139, 254, 258
Boyd, Robert, xxiv, 133, 152, 189, 217,
   254
Brain and Kidney Problem, 370, 496
branches (of game tree), 4
Buchanan, James, 33
Bulmer, Michael, 313
Buying Fire Insurance, 42

Camerer, Colin, 253
Capital as a Signaling Device, 329, 471
Card Game, 82, 425
cardinal utility, 387
Cashdan, Elizabeth A., 258
Cavalli-Sforza, Luca, xxiv, 189, 217
center (property of a fixed point), 180
Centipede Game, 25
cheap talk, 256
Cheater-Inspector, 82, 427
Chess—The Trivial Pastime, 33, 401
Chichilnisky, Graciela, 43
child node (in a game tree), 10
Choice under Uncertainty, 247
choosing a frame, 242
Choosing an Exorcist, 296
Cinq Tiroirs, 363
cleaner fish, 216
closed interval, 112
closed orbit (of a dynamical system), 173
Coleman, James, xxiv
Colman, Andrew M., 33, 36
Colonel Blotto Game, 72, 419
Color Blindness, 365
combinations, 361
Combinations and Sampling, 361
common knowledge, 13, 53, 408
common pool resource, 257
   game, 256
common prior assumption, 289
Common Value Auction, 300, 458
   Quantum Spin Decoders, 300, 458

The Winner's Curse, 300, 458
Competition on Main Street, 28
   Revisited, 59, 410
complete binary relation, 382
complete information, 16
completely mixed Nash equilibrium, 56, 199
compound lotteries, 37
concave utility function, 388
conditional preference, 384
conditional probability, 363, 493
constant relative risk aversion, 390
Contingent Renewal, 134, 442
   Contracts, 134, 442
   Labor Markets, 140, 442
   Markets Do Not Clear, 136
conventions, 232
Cooperation in Overlapping-Generations
   Economy, 102, 438
Cooperative Fishing, 152, 446
Coordination Failure, 72, 417
Correlated Equilibria, 85
Cosmides, Leda, 246, 308
costless contract enforcement, 136
Cournot duopoly, 30
critical point, *see* fixed point
   degenerate, 181
cultural dynamics, 182
Cultural Transmission and Social Imita-
   tion, 217
curvature (of a utility function), 390

Dahl, Robert, 139
Daly, Martin, 239
Damas, David, 258
Damasio, Antonio R., 246
Darwin-Fisher Sexual Selection, 312
Davies, N. B., 239
Davis, Douglas D., xxiv
Dawes, Robyn M., xxiv, 256
Dawkins, Marian Stamp, 319
Death and Discount Rates, 131, 442
Debreu, Gérard, 43
Debtor and His Creditors, 22
decreasing function, 170

degenerate critical point, 181
degree of relatedness, 270
DeMorgan's Laws, 357
deMorgan's Laws, 358
denumerable Markov chain, 372
Die, Die, 363, 492
Direct Evaluation of Probabilities, 358
discount factor, 119
Dixit, Avenash, 229, 500
Do Dominated Strategies Survive under
   a Replicator Dynamic?, 199
Dominance Revisited, 59
dominant strategy, 16
dominant strategy equilibrium, 16
dominated strategies
   and dominant strategies, 15, 395
   elimination of, 18, 395
      ad absurdum, 23, 398
   iterated elimination of, 16
   strictly, 16
Double Orders, 361, 490
Dr. Strangelove Game, 96, 436
Dresher, Melvin, 500
Drug Testing, 365, 494
Dynamic Hawk/Dove Game, 193
dynamical systems, 165
   in one dimension, 175
   theory, 172
   in two dimensions, 178
Dynamics of Rock-Paper-Scissors, 207,
   451

Easterlin, Richard, 250
Economy Controlled by Wealthy, 140
Education as Screening Device, 328, 470
Educational Signaling I, 325
eigenvector, 233
   lcft, 375
Ellsberg, Daniel, 386
Ellsberg paradox, 386
End of the World, 371
Endicott, Kirk, 258
endowment effect, 250
epistatic genes, 197

Equilibrium and Stability with a Replicator Dynamic, 201
Equivalence of Behavioral and Mixed Strategies, 87, 432
ergodic, 212, 373, 379
    theorem for finite Markov chains, 223, 378, 379
events (in a probability space), 357
evolution, 271
    of Strong Reciprocity, 271
    of trust and honesty, 214, 455
evolutionarily stable strategy, 148, 150
    in asymmetric games, 161, 450
    in finite populations, 159, 449
    multiple, 154, 447
    not unbeatable, 152, 446
    properties of, 149, 443
    quasi, 161
    Rock, Paper and Scissors, 153
    sex ratios, 153, 447
evolutionary
    dynamic, 189
    equilibrium, 189
    focal point, 189
    game, 149
    stability, 148, 443
        in asymmetric games, 161, 450
        Birth of, 148, 443
        and evolutionary equilibrium, 202, 451
evolutionary equilibrium
    existence and uniqueness, 173
excess demand for copulations, 312
excess supply of labor, 294
Exercises in Two-Dimensional Linear Systems, 181
expected utility principle, 41, 247, 381, 405, 499
    Daniel Bernoulli, 389
    exceptions to, 385, 499
expected value, 36, 41
experimental game theory, xxiv, 240
    Interpreting the Results, 241
    The Laboratory Meets Strategic Interaction, 251

extensive form game, 4, 10
    Bayesian updating, 113, 287
    Behavioral Strategies in, 63, 413
    definition of, 10
    equivalent, 12
    Nature, as player in, 11
    notationally challenged:, 10
    subgame, 92

fair (of coin or die), 359
fair game, 362
Falk, Armin, 262
fallback position, 47
Family Politics, 81
Fathers and Sons, 53
Fehr, Ernst, 106, 246, 252, 256, 259, 335
Feldman, Marcus, xxiv, 189, 217
female choice, 313
fiat money, 225
finite game, 10, 33
finite Markov chain, 223
finitely repeated game, 103, 438
    Prisoner's Dilemma, 103, 109, 438, 439
first order ordinary differential equations, 165
First-Price Sealed-Bid Auction, 299
Fischbacher, Urs, 262
Fisher, Franklin, 45
Fisher, R. A., 196, 313
Fisher's runaway process, 313
fitness, 195
fixed point, 165
    asymptotically stable, 173
    center, 180
    degenerate, 181
    globally stable, 173
    stable focus, 180
    unstable, 173
    unstable focus, 180
    unstable node, 179
Foley, Duncan, 43
Folk theorem
    for repeated games, 126
Football Strategy, 22

forward induction, 76
  Introduction to, 76, 422
Foster, Dean, 193
framing effect, 250, 257
Frankie and Johnny, 81, 424
Freidlin, Mark I., 192
frequency dependent selection, 218
Friedman, Daniel, 190
Friedman, Milton, 247
Fudenberg, Drew, 129, 130
Fundamental Theorem
  of Bayesian updating, 113
Fundamental Theorem of
  Bayesian updating, 287
  game theory, 56, 410
  mixed strategy Nash equilibrium, 57
  natural selection, 196
  principal-agent model, 343
  Welfare Economics, 43, 136
fuzzy subgame, 110, 111, 439
  perfection, 110, 439

Gächeter, Simon, 256
game tree, 4, 10
games against Nature, 244
games against ourselves, 244
Gardner, Roy, 256
Geanakoplos, John, 43, 263
Generalization of Rock, Paper, and
  Scissors, 205, 451
Generic Principal-Agent Game, 342, 480
Generic Signaling Game, 308
genetic locus, 195
genotype, 226
Gibbons, Robert, 500
gift exchange, 335
globally stable fixed point, 173
Good Vibrations, 228
Grafen, Alan, 239, 307, 317, 324
Greens and Blacks, 369, 494
Groucho Marx Game, 82, 428
group selection, 155
Guessing Game, 363, 492
Guilford, Tim, 319
Güth, Werner, 252, 500

Guttman, Joel, 109

Hagar's Battles, 21, 395
Haggling at the Bazaar, 291, 457
Hamilton, William D., xxiii, 261, 268
Hamilton's Law, 268
handicap principle, 317
Hard Love, 71
Hardin, Garrett, xxiv, 32, 256
Hardin, Russell, xxiv
Harsanyi, John, xxxi, 77, 139
Hartman-Grobman Theorem, 184
Hawkes, Kristen, 258
Hawks, Doves, and Bourgeois, 157, 447
Hayek, Friedrich von, 44, 45
head node (of a game tree), 10
Heiner, Ronald, 117
Henrich, Joe, 254
Herrnstein, Richard, 246
Hill, Kim, 258
Hofbauer, Josef, 151, 500
Hoffman, Elizabeth, 242
Hölmstron, Bengt, 27
Holt, Charles A., xxiv
Homo
  economicus, 240
  egualis, 252, 258
  parochius, 252, 278
  reciprocans, 251
Honest Signaling among Partial Altruists,
  323, 469
horizontal transmission, 217
House Rules, 362, 491
How to Value Lotteries, 36, 404
Huey, Dewey, and Louie Split a Dollar,
  99, 437
hyperbolic discounting, 245, 246
hyperbolic fixed point, 175

I'd Rather Switch than Fight, 145
Illogic of Conflict Escalation, 35, 404
imitation, 249
incentive compatibility constraint, 47,
  337, 343
incentive contract, 336

incomplete information, 284
increasing function, 170
Increasing-Bid Auction, 21
incredible
    promise, 95
    threat, 7, 94, 398
independence from irrelevant alterna-
    tives, 247
information set, 8, 11
insiders, 252
Interocitors, 358
Introductory Offers, 310, 466
invadable, 160
invariant distribution, 375
invasion of pure strategy mutants, 154,
    204, 447, 451
invisible hand, 244

Jacobian, 174
Johnstone, Rufus A., 324
Jordan Curve Theorem, 185

Kagel, J. H., xxiv
Kahneman, Daniel, xxiv, 248
Kaplan, Hillard, 258
Karlin, Samuel, 220
Kent, Susan, 258
Keynes, John Maynard, 295
kin selection, 239
Kirkpatrick, M., 313
Klingons and the Snarks, 32, 400
Knauft, Bruce, 258
Kollock, Peter, xxiv
Koopmans, Tjalling, 43
Krebs, J. R., 239
Kreps, David, 91, 247, 289, 290, 500
Kuhn, Harold, 33, 89

Labor
    as Gift Exchange, 335, 473
    Discipline Model
        with Monitoring, 333, 473
        with Profit Signaling, 336, 474
        Properties of, 339
Laibson, David, 246
Lande, R., 313

Landlord and the Eviction Notice, 21
Lane, Robert, 250
Lange, Oskar, 44
Laplace's Law of Succession, 369, 495
leaf node (of a game tree), 5
Lee, Richard Borshay, 258
Liapunov function, 186
Liapunov's Theorem, 186
Limit Pricing, 304, 461
linear function, 42
linearization, 174
Linearization Theorem, 174
Lions and Antelope, 65
Little Miss Muffet Game, 99
local best response, 287
local interactions, 190
Loewenstein, George, 246, 250, 290
Logic
    of Animal Conflict, 155, 447
    of Murder and Abuse, 367, 494
Loomes, Graham, 247, 386
Loraxes and Thoraxes, 216, 455
loss aversion, 245, 386
    and status quo bias, 250
Lotka-Volterra
    with Limited Carrying Capacity, 183
    Predator-Prey Model, 168
lottery, 41, 383

Macbeth Effect, 36
Machina, Mark, 386
Magill, Michael, 43
Mailath, George J., 162
Manny and Moe, 132
Market for Lemons, 295
Markets as Disciplining Devices, 46, 405
Markov chain, 372
    Sisyphean, 379
    steady state, 232
Maskin, Eric, 129
Mass Defection, 362, 490
Mating Game, 70, 416
maximin solution, 75
Maynard Smith, John, xxiii, 148, 155
McCabe, Kevin, 242

McKelvey, Richard, 26
Mechanical Defection, 361, 490
meiotic drive, 219
Mertens, Jean-François, 290
Mesterson-Gibbons, Michael, 500
Microsoft-Netscape Game, 93
Milgrom, Paul, 91
Military Strategy Game, 22, 396
minimax point, 128
mixed strategy
    basic definitions, 55, 410
    Nash equilibrium, 9, 56
    profile, 56
    representation of a behavioral strategy,
        87, 286
    support of, 56
Modeling Insiders and Outsiders, 278
Modeling Strong Reciprocity, 261
Modeling the Human Actor, 239
money, 224
    Confers Short-Side Power, 139
    in a Markov economy, 221
Monty Hall Game, 365
Morgenstern, Oskar, 75, 247
Morrow, James D., 500
Motorist's Dilemma, 80, 423
Moulin, Hervé, 500
Mr. Smith's Car Insurance, 341, 478
Mulligan, Casey, 244
Multiple Evolutionarily Stable Strategies,
    154
Murphy, Kevin M., 244
Mutual Monitoring in a Partnership, 77
Mutual Monitoring in Teams, 78
My Brother's Keeper, 321
Myerson, Roger, xxxiii, 89, 500

Nalebuff, Barry, 500
Nash, John, 56
Nash Bargaining Model, 346, 483
Nash Bargaining Theorem, 348
Nash Equilibrium, 12
Nash equilibrium, 6
    of an asymmetric evolutionary game,
        210

in behavioral strategies, 89, 287
completely mixed, 56, 199
not evolutionarily stable, 153, 447
of evolutionary game, 150
existence, 56
mixed strategy, 9
pure strategy, 27
refinement, 76
simulating a perfect Bayesian, 290
subgame perfect, 7
Nature Abhors Low Probability Events,
    117
Nature in Action: No-Draw, High-Low
    Poker, 38
neighborhood, 172
Neoclassical economics
    and game theory, 43, 405
neoclassical economics, 43
neutrally stable fixed point, 173
nice guy principle, 355
Non-Hyperbolic Dynamical System, 185
nonclearing market for copulations, 313
noninvadable, 160
Normal Form Game, 12
notationally challenged, xxii
Nuisance Suits, 100
Number Guessing Game, 73, 420

oblique transmission, 217
Occam's razor of evolutionary game the-
    ory, xxx
off the path of play, 309
One-Card Two-Round Poker with Bluff-
    ing, 60, 412
one-shot game, 103
One-Stage Deviation Principle, 129, 351,
    355
open interval, 445
open set, 172
Orange-Throat, Blue-Throat, and Yellow-
    Striped Lizards, 67
ordinal utility, 387
Origins of Evolutionary Dynamics, 189
Osborne, Martin J., 348, 500
Ostrom, Elinor, xxiv, 256, 258

Oswald, Andrew, 250
outsiders, 252

Palfrey, Thomas R., 26
Panglossian fallacy, 197
parent node (in a game tree), 10
Pareto-dominates, 28
Pareto-efficient, 28
Pareto-inefficient, 28
Pareto-optimal, 28
Pareto-superior, 28
parochialism, 279
Parsons, Talcott, 189
participation constraint, 48, 337, 343
partition, 364
path in a game tree, 10
Payoffs in Games Where Nature Moves, 37
payoffs to a behavioral strategy profile, 64
Pearce, David, 263
Peasants and Landlords , 340, 475
perfect Bayesian Nash equilibrium, 114, 287
Perfect Behavioral Nash Equilibria, 112
perfect information, 33
perfect Nash equilibrium in behavioral strategies, 286
perfect recall, 11
perturbed game, 116
phase diagram, 169, 175
player type, in games with private information, 285
Plott, Charles R., 240
Poker with Bluffing, 24
    Revisited, 87, 432
Pomiankowski, A. N., 313
pooling equilibrium, 302, 303, 310, 324, 327, 460
population
    monomorphic, 150
    polymorphic, 150
Population Growth, 166
    with Limited Carrying Capacity, 166
Powerball Lottery, 362, 491

Predatory Pricing: Pooling and Separating Equilibria, 302, 460
preference relation, 382
Preservation of Ecology Game, 71, 416
Price, G. R., xxiii, 148, 155, 268
Price's equation, 239, 268
Price-Matching as Tacit Collusion, 31
principal, 332
principal-agent model, 47, 332
    agent, 135
    introduction to, 332, 473
    principal, 135
Principle of Insufficient Reason, 77, 369
Prisoner's Dilemma, 19
private information, 284, 295
probability, 359
Probability as Frequency, 358, 489
probability spaces, 357, 489
probability transition matrix, 230
Properties of the Labor Discipline Model, 339
pruning the game tree, 17
psychological game, 263
Public Goods
    Experiment, 133, 442
    Game, 254
Public Goods Game
    with Retaliation, 255
pure coordination games, 28, 29, 399
pure strategy, 5, 56

quasi-evolutionarily stable, 161
Quinzii, Martine, 43

Rabin, Matthew, 263, 500
random walk
    on a circle, 375
    with reflecting barriers, 376
Rasmusen, Eric, 500
rational actor model, 240
rational agent, 243
rational expectations equilibria, xxxiii
Real Men Don't Eat Quiche, 84, 431
reciprocal altruism, 238
reciprocity equilibrium, 263

Reconnaissance Game, 74, 421
recursion equations, 375
reflexive binary relation, 382
regret, 386
regret theory, 247
relative deprivation, 252
relative frequency, 359
repeated game, 119
replicator, 189
replicator dynamics, 190, 191, 211
    Characterizing the Two-Variable Case, 198
    Lotka-Volterra Model and Biodiversity, 208, 454
replicator system, 189
    properties of, 197, 451
Reputational Equilibrium, 134, 442
reservation wage, 47
restriction, of a strategy to a subgame, 93
restrictive character of the random pairing assumption, 190
Richerson, Peter, xxiv, 189, 217
risk aversion, 341, 389
    Arrow-Pratt coefficient, 390
    coefficient of relative, 390
    constant absolute, 390
    constant relative, 47
    decreasing absolute, 345, 390
    decreasing relative, 390
    increasing, 350
    more risk averse than, 389
    strictly, 338
    uniformly more risk averse, 350
    weakly decreasing, 338
Risk Aversion and the Nash Bargaining Solution, 349, 484
Risk Behavior and the Shape of the Utility Function, 387
risk dominance, 76
risk loving, 389
risk neutral, 52, 389
Roberts, John, 91
Robin Hood and Little John, 80, 422
Rogers, Alan, 277

Role of Beliefs in Games with Private Information, 289
root node (of a game tree), 4
Roth, Alvin, xxiv, 253
Rotten Kid Theorem, 34, 403
Rubinstein bargaining, 97, 437
    and Nash Bargaining, 353, 486
    with Outside Options, 350, 485
    solution, 353
Rubinstein, Ariel, 97, 348, 500

Saari, Donald, 45
saddle point, 179
Samaritan's Dilemma, 33, 401
sample space, 357
Sampling, 360, 489
sampling
    with replacement, 360
    without replacement, 360
Samuelson, Larry, 189, 193
Samuelson, Paul, 140
Santa Fé Bar, 66, 413
Savage, Leonard J., 247, 381
Schmidt, Klaus, 259
Schumpeter, Joseph, 45, 140
Second-Price Auction, 20, 395
self-fulfilling prophecy, 228
Self-Interest and Rationality, 243
Self-presentation, 360
self-regarding, 243
Selten, Reinhard, xxxiii, 77, 91, 96, 161
Selten's Horse, 114, 440
separating equilibrium, 302, 303, 324, 460
sequential equilibrium, 91, 289
sequential rationality, 289
Sethi, Rajiv, 279
Sex and Piety: The Darwin-Fisher Model of Sexual Selection, 312
Sex Ratios
    as Evolutionarily Stable Stratgies, 153, 447
    as Nash Equilibria, 68, 414
Sexual Harassment on the Job, 370, 497

Sexual Reproduction, Biological Fitness, and the Replicator Dynamic, 195
Shafir, Eldar, 247
Shapiro, Carl, 137
Shepherds Who Never Cry Wolf, 319, 468
Shopper and the Fish Merchant, 52, 407
short-side power, 139
Shubik, Martin, 35, 372, 500
Sigmund, Karl, 151, 500
signal, 307
signaling
    bilateral, 311
    as a Coevolutionary Process, 307, 466
    handicap principle, 317, 468
signaling game, 308, 466
    generic, 308, 466
Simon, Herbert, 139, 243
Simple Limit-Pricing Model, 305, 464
Sisyphean Markov Chain, 379
situational contexts, 92, 117, 242
Smith, Vernon, xxiv, 240, 242
Social Isolation, 361, 489
socialism debate, 44
Solow, Robert, 142, 336
Solow condition, 334, 336
Solving for Mixed Strategy Nash Equilibria, 57
Somanathan, E., 279
Special Features of Two-Dimensional Dynamical Systems, 185
St. Petersberg Paradox, 387
Ståhl, Ingolf, 97
stable focus, 180
stable manifold, 179
stable node, 179
stable set, 204
Stacchetti, Ennio, 263
Stackelberg duopoly model, 30, 332
Stackelberg Leadership, 95
stage game, 103, 119
states of nature, 383
stationary distribution, 375
stationary point, *see* fixed point
status quo bias, 251
Steady State of a Markov Chain, 232

Stiglitz, Joseph, 137, 295
Stochastic Stability, 235
strategic form, 6, 12
Strategic Voting, 23, 397
Strategies as Replicators, 190
strategy, 5
Strategy of an Oil Cartel, 132
strategy profile, 11, 12
strict Nash equilibrium, 58
strictly concave, 388
strictly decreasing function, 170
strictly dominated, 15
strictly increasing function, 170
strictly mixed, 56
strong reciprocity, 262
subgame perfection, 76, 93, 398
Subway Entry Deterrence Game, 96, 436
successor node, 10
Sugden, Robert, 247, 386
support (of a mixed strategy), 56
sure-thing principle, 247
symmetric binary relation, 382
symmetric equilibria, 78
symmetric in payoffs, 149
symmetric in strategies, 149
sympathy, 244

tacit collusion, 122
tail node (of a game tree), 10
Take No Prisoners, 183
Target Selection, 73, 420
Taylor, Howard M., 220
Taylor, Michael, xxiv
Tennis Strategy, 69
terminal node (of a game tree), 5
Thaler, Richard, xxiv, 253
Throwing Fingers, 60
time consistency, 245
Time Inconsistency and Hyperbolic Discounting, 245
Tirole, Jean, 130, 500
Tit-for-Tat, 132, 159
    contrite, 133
Tobacco Market, 31, 399
Tooby, John, 246, 308

topologically equivalent, 184
tragedy of the commons, 256
transition probability matrix, 372
transitive binary relation, 382
transitive preferences, 247
tree property, 10
trembling hand, 130
    Cooperative Equilibrium, 130, 442
    perfection, 92, 115, 116, 288, 441
trigger strategy
    in repeated game, 119, 132, 135
Trivers, Robert, 238, 261
Trogs and Farfel, 158, 448
Trust in Networks, 62
Trust in Networks II, 152
Trust in Networks III, 203
Truth Game, 51, 405
truthful signaling equilibrium, 310, 326
Tversky, Amos, xxiv, 247
Twin Sisters, 29
Two-Person Zero-Sum Games, 75

ultimatum game, 252
unbeatable strategy, 152
universal medium of exchange, 224
universe, 357
Unlucky Streak, 362, 490
unstable
    fixed point, 173
    focus, 180
    manifold, 179
    node, 179
Urns, 365
Uta stansburia in Motion, 206, 451
utility function, 382

Value of Eyewitness Testimony, 370, 497
van Damme, Eric, 16, 500

Variations on Duopoly, 30
Variations on the Folk Theorem, 127
vertical transmission, 217
Vindication of the Hawk, 84
von Neumann, John, 75, 247
Vorob'ev, N. N., 500

Walras, Léon, 45
Walrasian general equilibrium model, 43
weakly concave utility function, 388
weakly dominated strategy, 7
weakly evolutionarily stable, 159
Web Sites (for Spiders), 310, 466
Weber-Fechner Law, 250, 388
Weibull, Jörgen, 16, 500
Wentzell, Alexander D., 192
Wenzel, George W., 258
When Money Talks, People Listen, 139
When Weakness Is Strength, 371, 497
Where's Jack?, 37, 404
Williams, George C., 155
Wilson, E. O., 189, 217, 239
Wilson, Margo, 239
Wilson, Robert, 91, 289, 290
winner's curse, 300
Women of Sevitan, 53, 408
Woodburn, James, 258
Wynne-Edwards, V. C., 155

Yamagishi, Toshio, 256
Young, H. Peyton, 193, 220, 500

Zahavi, Amotz, 307, 317, 324
Zambrano, Eduardo, 243
Zamir, Shmuel, 290
zero-sum game, 75
Zeuthen, F., 354
Zeuthen Lotteries and the Nash Bargaining Solution, 354, 487